PHILIP'S

C000285829

STREET ATLAS
South Essex

Chelmsford, Harlow, Romford, Southend-on-Sea

www.philips-maps.co.uk

First published in 1999 by

Philip's, a division of
Octopus Publishing Group Ltd
www.octopusbooks.co.uk
2-4 Heron Quays, London E14 4JP
An Hachette Livre UK Company

Third edition 2008
Second impression 2010
SESCA

ISBN   978-0-540-09189-8 (spiral)

© Philip's 2008

 Ordnance Survey®

This product includes mapping data licensed from Ordnance Survey® with the permission of the Controller of Her Majesty's Stationery Office. © Crown copyright 2008. All rights reserved. Licence number 100011710.

Data for the speed cameras provided by PocketGPSWorld.com Ltd.

Ordnance Survey and the OS Symbol are registered trademarks of Ordnance Survey, the national mapping agency of Great Britain.

Printed by Toppan, China

Contents

II	**List of mobile speed cameras**
III	**Key to map symbols**
IV	**Key to map pages**
VI	**Route planning**
VIII	**Administrative and Postcode boundaries**
1	**Street maps** at 3½ inches to 1 mile
183	**Index** of towns, villages, streets, hospitals, industrial estates, railway stations, schools, shopping centres, universities and places of interest

Digital Data

The exceptionally high-quality mapping found in this atlas is available as digital data in TIFF format, which is easily convertible to other bitmapped (raster) image formats.

The index is also available in digital form as a standard database table. It contains all the details found in the printed index together with the National Grid reference for the map square in which each entry is named.

For further information, please contact victoria.dawbarn@philips-maps.co.uk

Mobile speed cameras

The vast majority of speed cameras used on Britain's roads are operated by safety camera partnerships. These comprise local authorities, the police, Her Majesty's Court Service (HMCS) and the Highways Agency.

This table lists the sites where each safety camera partnership may enforce speed limits through the use of mobile cameras or detectors. These are usually set up on the roadside or a bridge spanning the road and operated by a police or civilian enforcement officer. The speed limit at each site (if available) is shown in red type, followed by the approximate location in black type.

A12
- Braintree, Overbridge nr Kelvedon Interchange

A13
- 30 Castle Point, High St (Hadleigh twds London)
- 30 Leigh on Sea, London Rd
- Southend, Bournes Green Chase
- Southend, North Shoebury
- Southend, Southchurch Boulevard

A1016
- 30 Chelmsford, Waterhouse Lane

A1017
- 30 Sible Hedingham, Swan St
- 30 Witham / Braintree, Rickstone Rd

A1023
- 30 Brentwood, Chelmsford Rd
- 30 Brentwood, London Rd
- 30 Brentwood, Shenfield Rd

A1025
- 40 Harlow, Second Avenue
- 40 Harlow, Third Avenue

A1060
- Little Hallingbury, Lower Rd

A1090
- 30 Purfleet, London Rd
- 30 Purfleet, Tank Hill Rd

A1124
- 30 Colchester, Lexden Rd

A113
- 30 Epping, High Rd

A1158
- 30 Westcliff on Sea, Southbourne Grove

A1168
- 30 Loughton, Rectory Lane

A1169
- 40 Harlow, Southern Way

A120
- Little Bentley, Pellens Corner
- Wix, Harwich Rd nr Colchester Rd

A1205
- 40 Harlow, Second Avenue

A121
- 30 Epping, High Rd
- 30 Loughton, Goldings Hill (j/w Monkchester Close)
- Loughton, High Rd
- Waltham Abbey, Farm Hill Rd
- Waltham Abbey, Sewardstine Rd

A126
- 30 Grays, London Rd
- 30 Tilbury, Montreal Rd

A128
- Chipping Ongar, High St
- 30 Ingrave/Herongate, Brentwood Rd
- 40 Kelvedon Hatch, Ongar Rd

A129
- 30 Basildon, Crays Hill
- Billericay, Southend Rd
- Rayleigh, London Rd
- 30 Wickford, London Rd
- Wickford, Southend Rd

A130
- 30 Canvey Island, Long Rd
- South Benfleet, Canvey Way

A133
- 30 Elmstead Market, Clacton Rd
- Little Bentley, Colchester Rd

A134
- 40 Great Horkesley, Nayland Rd

A137
- 30 Lawford, Wignall St

B170
- Chigwell, Chigwell Rise
- Loughton, Roding Lane

B172
- Theydon Bois, Coppice Row

B173
- Chigwell, Lambourne Rd

B184
- 40 Great Easton, Snow Hill

B186
- 30 South Ockendon, South Rd

B1002
- 30 Ingatestone, High St

B1007
- 30 Billericay, Laindon Rd
- 30 Billericay, Stock Rd
- 40 Chelmsford, Stock Rd

B1008
- 30 Chelmsford, Broomfield Rd

B1013
- 30 Hawkwell, High Rd
- 30 Hawkwell, Main Rd
- 30 Hockley/Hawkwell, Southend Rd
- Rayleigh, High Rd

B1014
- 30 South Benfleet, Benfleet Rd

B1018
- 30 Latchingdon, The St
- 30 Maldon, The Causeway

B1019
- 30 Hatfield Peveral, Maldon Rd
- 30 Witham, Powers Hall End

B1021
- Burnham on Crouch, Church Rd

B1022
- 30 Colchester, Maldon Rd
- 30 Heckfordbridge, Maldon Rd
- 30 Maldon, Colchester Rd
- 30 Tiptree Heath, Maldon Rd

B1027
- 30 Clacton-on-Sea, Valley Rd/Old Rd
- 30 St Osyth, Pump Hill
- 40 Wivenhoe, Brightlingsea Rd

B1028
- 30 Wivenhoe, Colchester Rd
- 30 Wivenhoe, The Avenue

B1033
- 30 Kirby Cross, Frinton Rd

B1335
- 40 South Ockendon, Stifford Rd

B1352
- Harwich, Main Rd

B1383
- 30 Newport, London Rd Stansted Mountfitchet, Cambridge Rd

B1389
- 30 Witham, Colchester Rd
- 30 Witham, Hatfield Rd

B1393
- 30 Epping, Palmers Hill

B1441
- 30 Clacton-on-Sea, London Rd
- Tendring, Clacton Rd

B1442
- 30 Clacton-on-Sea, Thorpe Rd

B1464
- 30 Bowers Gifford, London Rd

UNCLASSIFIED
- 40 Alresford, St Osyth Rd
- 40 Aveley, Purfleet Rd
- Aveley, Romford Rd
- 30 Barstable, Sandon Rd
- 30 Basildon, Ashlyns
- Basildon, Clay Hill Rd
- 40 Basildon, Cranes Farm Rd (j/w Honywood Rd)
- 30 Basildon, Felmores
- Basildon, London Rd, Wickford
- 30 Basildon, Vange Hill Drive
- 30 Basildon, Whitmore Way
- 30 Basildon, Wickford Avenue
- 30 Billericay, Mountnessing Rd
- 30 Bowers Gifford, London Rd
- 30 Braintree, Coldnailhurst Avenue
- 30 Brentwood, Eagle Way (nr j/w Clive Rd twds Warley Rd)
- 30 Brentwood, Eagle Way
- 30 Buckhurst Hill, Buckhurst Way/Albert Rd
- 30 Canvey Island, Dovervelt Rd
- 30 Canvey Island, Link Rd
- 30 Canvey Island, Thorney Bay Rd
- Chadwell St Mary, Brentwood Rd
- 30 Chadwell St Mary, Linford Rd
- 30 Chadwell St Mary, Riverview
- 30 Chelmsford, Baddow Rd
- 30 Chelmsford, Chignall Rd
- 30 Chelmsford, Copperfield Rd
- Chelmsford, Galleywood Rd
- 30 Chelmsford, Longstomps Avenue
- 30 Clacton-on-Sea, St Johns Rd
- 30 Clacton, Kings Parade
- 30 Clacton, Marine Parade East
- 30 Colchester, Abbots Rd
- 30 Colchester, Avon Way
- 30 Colchester, Bromley Rd
- Colchester, Ipswich Rd
- 30 Colchester, Old Heath Rd
- 30 Colchester, Shrub End Rd
- 30 Corringham, Southend Rd
- 30 Corringham, Springhouse Rd
- Danbury, Maldon Rd
- 30 Daws Heath, Daws Heath Rd
- 30 Eastwood, Green Lane j/w Kendal Way
- 30 Eastwood, Western Approaches j/w Rockall
- 30 Grays, Blackshots Lane
- 30 Grays, Lodge Lane
- Grays, London Rd (nr Angel Rd)
- Grays, London Rd (nr Bransons Way)
- 30 Hainault, Fencepiece Rd
- 40 Harlow, Abercrombie Way, twds Southern Way
- 40 Harlow, Howard Way
- 30 Hawkwell, Rectory Rd
- 30 Hockley, High Rd
- 30 Hullbridge, Coventry Hill
- 30 Laindon, Durham Rd
- 30 Laindon, High Rd
- 30 Laindon, Nightingales
- 30 Laindon, Wash Rd
- Langdon Hills, High Rd
- 30 Leigh on Sea, Belton Way East
- 30 Leigh on Sea, Belton Way West
- 30 Leigh on Sea, Blenhelm Chase
- 30 Leigh on Sea, Grand Parade/Cliff Parade
- 30 Leigh on Sea, Hadleigh Rd
- 30 Leigh on Sea, Highlands Boulevard
- 30 Leigh on Sea, Manchester Drive
- 30 Leigh on Sea, Mountdale Gardens
- 30 Leigh on Sea, Western Rd
- 30 Loughton, Alderton Hill
- 30 Loughton, Loughton Way
- Loughton, Valley Hill
- 30 Maldon, Fambridge Rd
- 30 Maldon, Holloway Rd
- 30 Maldon, Mundon Rd
- 30 Pitsea, Rectory Rd
- 30 Prittlewell, Kenilworth Gardens
- 30 Prittlewell, Prittlewell Chase
- 30 Rayleigh, Bull Lane
- Rayleigh, Downhall Rd
- 30 Rayleigh, Trinity Rd, nr Church Rd
- 30 Rochford, Ashingdon Rd
- 30 Rochford, Rectory Rd
- Rush Green, St Osyth Rd
- 30 Shoeburyness, Ness Rd
- 30 South Woodham Ferrers, Hullbridge Rd
- 30 South Woodham Ferrers, Inchbonnie Rd
- 30 Southend on Sea, Lifstan Way
- Southend, Bournemouth Park Rd
- 30 Southend, Hamstel Rd
- Southend on Sea, Bournemouth Park Rd
- Southend, Western Esplanade/Westcliff on Sea
- 30 Springfield, New Bowers Way
- 30 Stanford le Hope, London Rd
- 30 Tendring, Burrs Rd, Clacton
- 30 Tendring, Frinton Rd, Frinton
- Tendring, Harwich Rd, Wix Arch Cottages to Cansey Lane
- 30 Tendring, Osyth Rd, Rush Green
- Theydon Bois, Piercing Hill
- 30 Thorpe Bay, Barnstaple Rd
- 30 Thorpe Bay, Thorpe Hall Avenue
- Waltham Abbey, Paternoster Hill
- Weeley Heath, Clacton Rd
- Weeley Heath, Clacton Rd
- 30 West Thurrock, London Rd
- 30 Westcliff on Sea, Chalkwell Avenue
- 30 Westcliff on Sea, Kings Rd
- 30 Wickford, London Rd
- 30 Wickford, Radwinter Avenue
- 30 Witham, Powers Hall End
- 30 Witham, Rickstones Rd

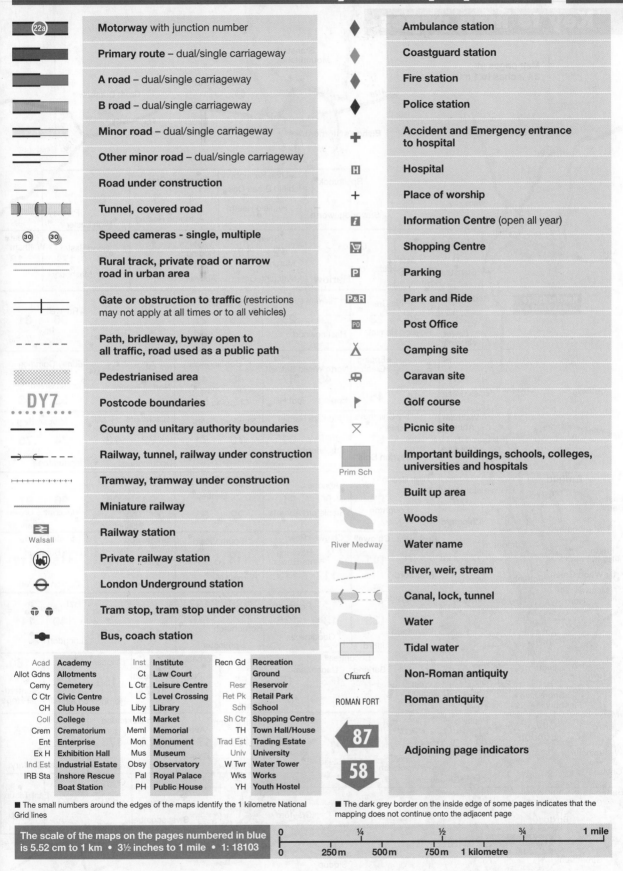

22a	**Motorway** with junction number
	Primary route – dual/single carriageway
	A road – dual/single carriageway
	B road – dual/single carriageway
	Minor road – dual/single carriageway
	Other minor road – dual/single carriageway
	Road under construction
	Tunnel, covered road
30 30	**Speed cameras - single, multiple**
	Rural track, private road or narrow road in urban area
	Gate or obstruction to traffic (restrictions may not apply at all times or to all vehicles)
	Path, bridleway, byway open to all traffic, road used as a public path
	Pedestrianised area
DY7	**Postcode boundaries**
	County and unitary authority boundaries
	Railway, tunnel, railway under construction
	Tramway, tramway under construction
	Miniature railway
Walsall	**Railway station**
	Private railway station
	London Underground station
	Tram stop, tram stop under construction
	Bus, coach station

◆	**Ambulance station**
◆	**Coastguard station**
◆	**Fire station**
◆	**Police station**
✚	**Accident and Emergency entrance to hospital**
H	**Hospital**
+	**Place of worship**
i	**Information Centre** (open all year)
🛒	**Shopping Centre**
P	**Parking**
P&R	**Park and Ride**
PO	**Post Office**
⋏	**Camping site**
🚐	**Caravan site**
▶	**Golf course**
✕	**Picnic site**
Prim Sch	**Important buildings, schools, colleges, universities and hospitals**
	Built up area
	Woods
River Medway	**Water name**
	River, weir, stream
	Canal, lock, tunnel
	Water
	Tidal water
Church	**Non-Roman antiquity**
ROMAN FORT	**Roman antiquity**
◀ 87 ▼ 58	**Adjoining page indicators**

Abbr	Full	Abbr	Full	Abbr	Full
Acad	**Academy**	Inst	**Institute**	Recn Gd	**Recreation Ground**
Allot Gdns	**Allotments**	Ct	**Law Court**		
Cemy	**Cemetery**	L Ctr	**Leisure Centre**	Resr	**Reservoir**
C Ctr	**Civic Centre**	LC	**Level Crossing**	Ret Pk	**Retail Park**
CH	**Club House**	Liby	**Library**	Sch	**School**
Coll	**College**	Mkt	**Market**	Sh Ctr	**Shopping Centre**
Crem	**Crematorium**	Meml	**Memorial**	TH	**Town Hall/House**
Ent	**Enterprise**	Mon	**Monument**	Trad Est	**Trading Estate**
Ex H	**Exhibition Hall**	Mus	**Museum**	Univ	**University**
Ind Est	**Industrial Estate**	Obsy	**Observatory**	W Twr	**Water Tower**
IRB Sta	**Inshore Rescue Boat Station**	Pal	**Royal Palace**	Wks	**Works**
		PH	**Public House**	YH	**Youth Hostel**

■ The small numbers around the edges of the maps identify the 1 kilometre National Grid lines

■ The dark grey border on the inside edge of some pages indicates that the mapping does not continue onto the adjacent page

The scale of the maps on the pages numbered in blue is 5.52 cm to 1 km • 3½ inches to 1 mile • 1: 18103

0	¼	½	¾	1 mile
0	250 m 500 m	750 m 1 kilometre		

Key to map pages

Buntingford

122 | Map pages at 3½ inches to 1 mile

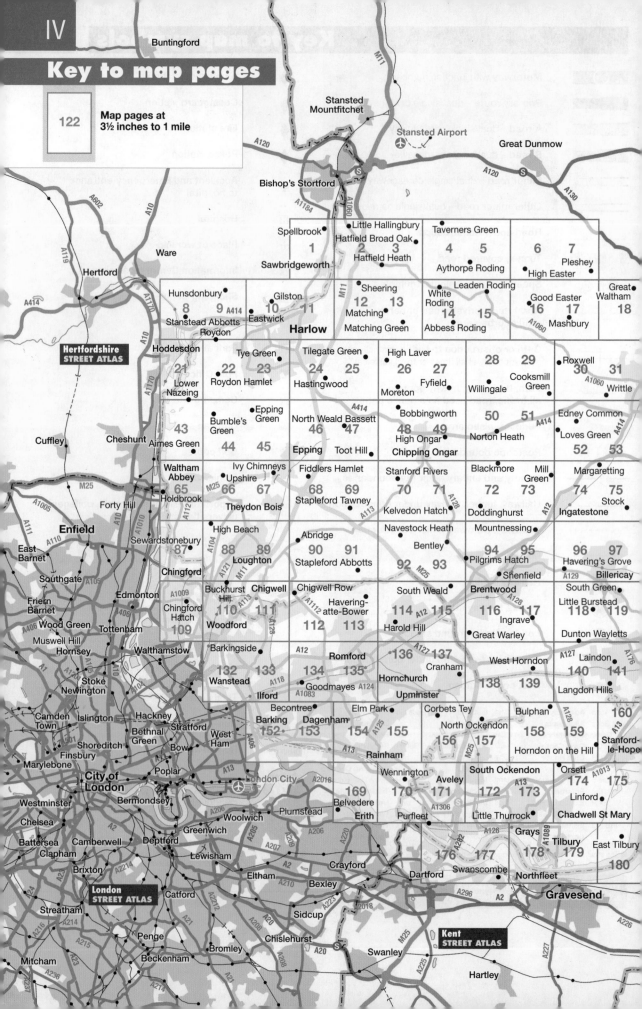

Stansted Mountfitchet

Stansted Airport

Great Dunmow

M11

A120

A120

A130

A1184

A1060

Bishop's Stortford

Ware

Hertford

A602

A10

A119

A414

A1170

A10

Spellbrook · 1

Little Hallingbury · 2
Hatfield Broad Oak · 3
Hatfield Heath

Taverners Green · 4 · 5
Aythorpe Roding

6 · 7 Pleshey
High Easter

Sawbridgeworth

Hunsdonbury · 8 · 9 A414 · 10 Gilston · 11
Stanstead Abbotts · Eastwick
Roydon

M11
Sheering · 12 · 13
Matching
Matching Green

White Roding · 14 · 15
Abbess Roding

Leaden Roding
Good Easter · 16 · 17
Mashbury
A1060

Great Waltham · 18

Harlow

Hoddesdon

Hertfordshire STREET ATLAS

A1170

A10

Tye Green · 22 · 23
Roydon Hamlet
21
Lower Nazeing

Tilegate Green · 24 · 25
Hastingwood

High Laver · 26 · 27
Moreton · Fyfield

28 · 29
Willingale · Cooksmill Green

Roxwell · 30 · 31
A1060 · Writtle

Cuffley

Cheshunt · Aimes Green

43 · 44 · 45
Bumble's Green · Epping Green
Epping

North Weald Bassett · 46 · 47
Toot Hill

Bobbingworth · 48 · 49
High Ongar · Chipping Ongar

50 · 51 A414
Norton Heath

Edney Common · Loves Green A414
52 · 53

Waltham Abbey · 65 · 66 · 67
Holdbrook · Upshire
Theydon Bois

Ivy Chimneys

M25

Fiddlers Hamlet · 68 · 69
Stapleford Tawney

Stanford Rivers · 70 · 71
Kelvedon Hatch

A128

Blackmore · Mill Green
72 · 73
Doddinghurst

A12

Margaretting · 74 · 75
Stock
Ingatestone

A1005

M25

Forty Hill

Enfield

East Barnet

Southgate

A110

A1010

A1170

A104

A121

M11

A1121

High Beach · 88 · 89
Loughton
Chingford

Abridge · 90 · 91
Stapleford Abbotts
92 · 93

Navestock Heath · Bentley
94 · 95
Pilgrims Hatch · Shenfield

Mountnessing

Havering's Grove · 96 · 97
A129 · Billericay

Sewardstonebury · 87

A111

A1005

A110

A105

Edmonton

Friern Barnet
A406
Wood Green
Muswell Hill
Hornsey

Tottenham

Walthamstow

A1009

Chingford Hatch · 109 · 110
Buckhurst Hill · Chigwell · 111
A113
Woodford
A123

Chigwell Row · 112 · 113
Havering-atte-Bower
A112

South Weald · 114 · 115
A12
Harold Hill

Brentwood · 116 · 117
Ingrave
Great Warley

South Green · Little Burstead
118 · 119
Dunton Wayletts

Stoke Newington

Camden Town
Islington

Hackney

Stratford
West Ham
Bow
Poplar

A12

Barkingside · 132 · 133
Wanstead · A118
Ilford

Romford · 134 · 135
Goodmayes · A124

136 A127 · 137
Cranham
Hornchurch
Upminster

A127
West Horndon · 138 · 139

Laindon · 140 · 141 A176
Langdon Hills

Shoreditch
Finsbury
Bethnal Green

Marylebone

City of London

Westminster

Bermondsey

A206

Becontree · 152 · 153
Barking
Dagenham

Elm Park · 154 · 155
A125
Rainham

Corbets Tey · 156 · 157
North Ockendon
M25

Bulphan · 158 · 159 A128
Horndon on the Hill

160
Stanford-le-Hope
A13

Chelsea
Battersea
Clapham
Brixton

Camberwell

Deptford
Greenwich
Lewisham

A2016 London City
A206
Plumstead
Woolwich

A2
A207

169 · 170 · 171
Belvedere · Aveley
Erith · Purfleet

South Ockendon · 172 · 173
A1306
Little Thurrock

Orsett · 174 · 175 A1013
Linford
Chadwell St Mary

London STREET ATLAS

Catford

Eltham
Crayford
Bexley

A210

176 · 177
Swanscombe
Dartford

Grays · 178 · 179
Northfleet · Tilbury
East Tilbury
180

Streatham
Penge
Mitcham

Beckenham
Bromley

Sidcup
Chislehurst

Kent STREET ATLAS

Swanley
A225 S

Gravesend
A296
A2
A227

Hartley

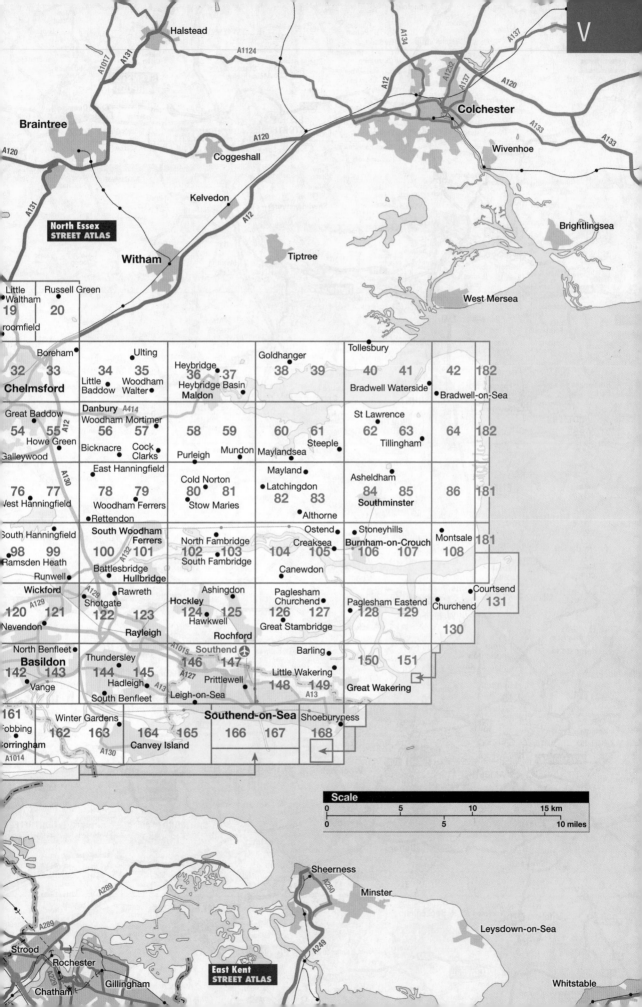

Halstead

A1124

A134

A137

A12

A137

A120

A1017

A131

Colchester

A1232

A120

A133

A133

Braintree

A120

Coggeshall

Wivenhoe

A131

Kelvedon

A12

Brightlingsea

North Essex
STREET ATLAS

Witham

Tiptree

Little
Waltham
19

Russell Green
20

West Mersea

roomfield

Boreham
32   **33**
Chelmsford

Ulting
34   **35**
Little   Woodham
Baddow   Walter

Heybridge
36   **37**
Heybridge Basin
Maldon

Goldhanger
38   **39**

Tollesbury
40   **41**
Bradwell Waterside

42   **182**

Bradwell-on-Sea

Great Baddow
54   **55**
Howe Green
Galleywood

Danbury A414
Woodham Mortimer
56   **57**
Bicknacre   Cock
Clarks

58   **59**

Purleigh   Mundon

60   **61**
Steeple
Maylandsea

St Lawrence
62   **63**
Tillingham

64   **182**

West Hanningfield
76   **77**
West Hanningfield

East Hanningfield
78   **79**
Woodham Ferrers
Rettendon

Cold Norton
80   **81**
Stow Maries

Mayland
Latchingdon
82   **83**
Althorne

Asheldham
84   **85**
Southminster

86   **181**

South Hanningfield
98   **99**
Ramsden Heath
Runwell

South Woodham
Ferrers
100   **101**
Battlesbridge
Hullbridge

North Fambridge
102   **103**
South Fambridge

Ostend
Creaksea
104   **105**
Canewdon

Stoneyhills
Burnham-on-Crouch
106   **107**

Montsale
108   **181**

Wickford
120   **121**
Nevendon

A129
Rawreth
Shotgate
122   **123**
Rayleigh

Ashingdon
Hockley
124   **125**
Hawkwell
Rochford

Paglesham
Churchend
126   **127**
Great Stambridge

Paglesham Eastend
128   **129**
Churchend

Courtsend
131

130

North Benfleet
Basildon
142   **143**
Vange

Thundersley
144   **145**
Hadleigh
South Benfleet

A1015
Southend
146   **147**
A127
Prittlewell
Leigh-on-Sea

Barling
Little Wakering
148   **149**
A13

150   **151**

Great Wakering

161
Fobbing
orringham

Winter Gardens
162   **163**

A130

164   **165**
Canvey Island

166   **167**

Southend-on-Sea
Shoeburyness
168

A1014

Scale

0   5   10   15 km

0   5   10 miles

Sheerness

A289

A250
Minster

Leysdown-on-Sea

A289

Strood

Rochester

A249
East Kent
STREET ATLAS

Gillingham

Whitstable

Chatham

Route planning

Scale

0		5			10 km
0	1	2	3	4	5	6 miles

Major administrative and Postcode boundaries

County and unitary authority boundaries
District boundaries
Postcode boundaries
Area covered by this atlas

Scale

0   5   10   15 km
0   5   10 miles

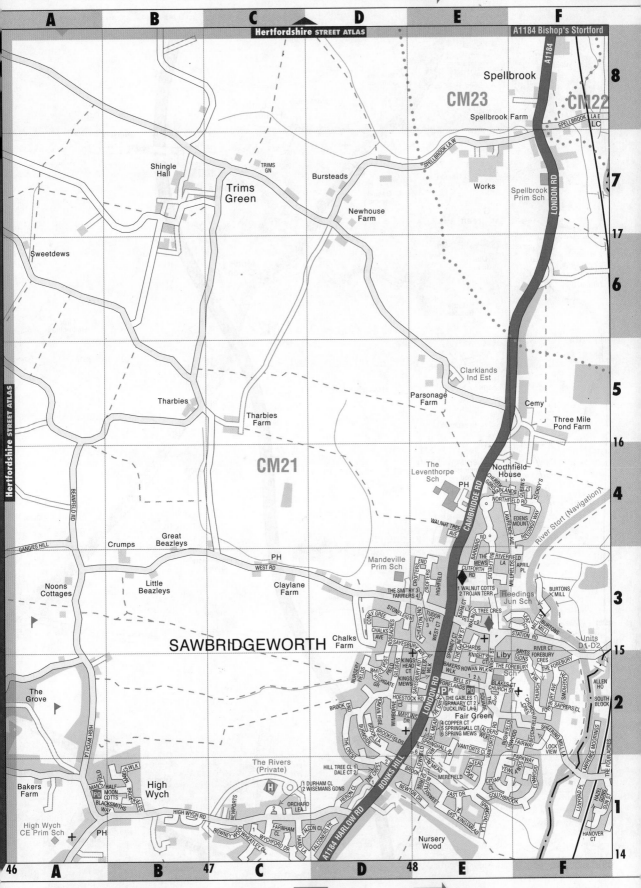

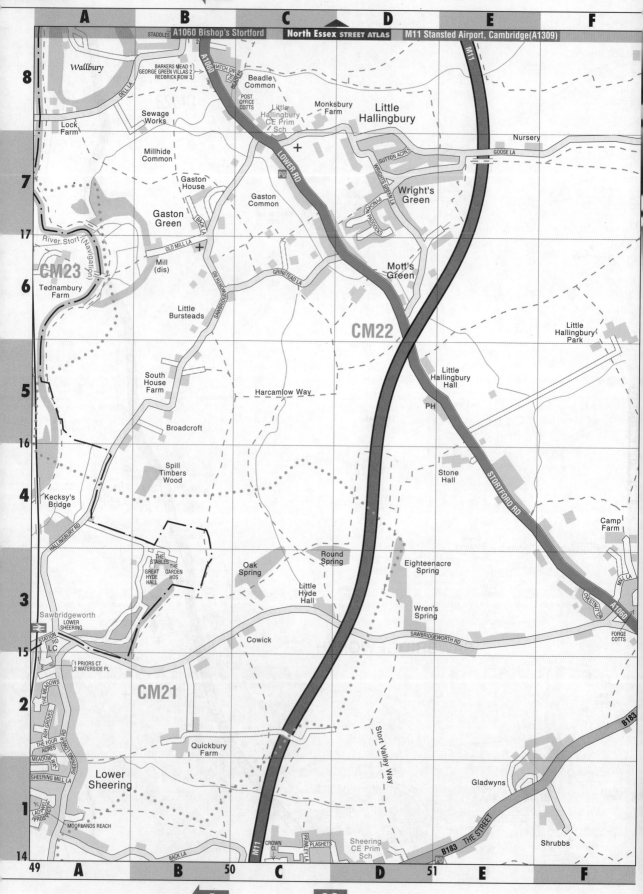

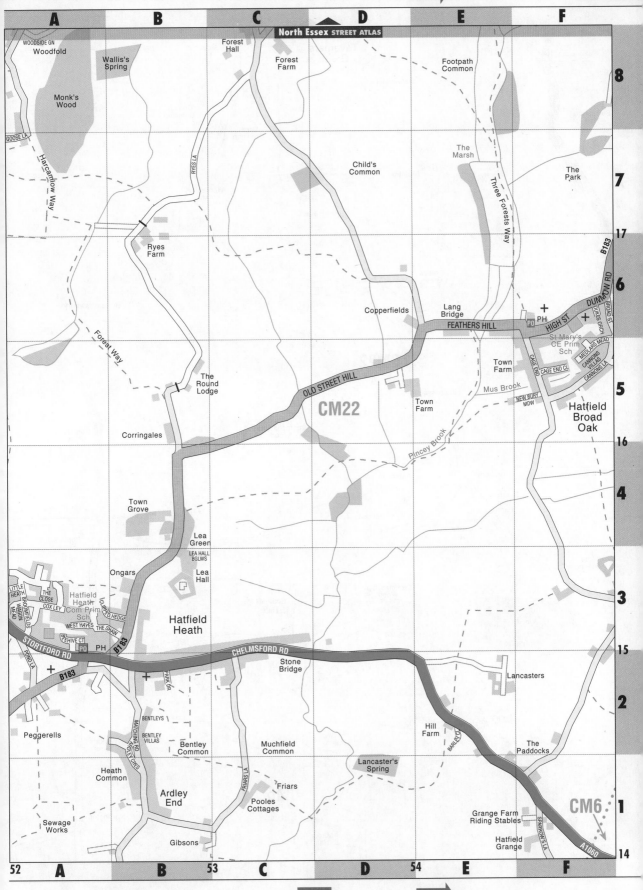

A   B   C   D   E   F

WOODSIDE GN
Woodfold

Wallis's
Spring

Forest
Hall

Forest
Farm

Footpath
Common

8

Monk's
Wood

The
Marsh

The
Park

7

GOOSE LA

Harcamlow Way

RYES LA

Child's
Common

Three Forests Way

17

Ryes
Farm

B183

DUNMOW RD

6

Forest Way

Copperfields

Lang
Bridge

FEATHERS HILL

HIGH ST

BROAD ST

JUKES ORCH

PO PH

St Mary's
CE Prim
Sch

MEDLARS MEAD

CANNONS
VILLAS

CANNONS LA

The
Round
Lodge

OLD STREET HILL

CM22

Town
Farm

Town
Farm

CAGE END

CAGE END CL

NEW BURY
MDW

5

Mus Brook

Corringales

Pincey Brook

Hatfield
Broad
Oak

16

4

Town
Grove

Lea
Green

LEA HALL
BGLWS

3

LITTLE
HEATH

THE
CLOSE

BROOMFIELDS

WAGGON
MEAD

COX LEY

Ongars

ICKLETON HEDGE

Lea
Hall

Hatfield
Heath
Com Prim
Sch

WEST HAYES

THE SHAW

Hatfield
Heath

Lancasters

15

STORTFORD RD

PONDLA

BEEHIVE CT

PO

PH

B183

CHELMSFORD RD

Stone
Bridge

B183

PARK DR

Hill
Farm

BARLEY CL

The
Paddocks

2

Peggerells

MATCHING RD

ARDLEY CRES

BENTLEYS

Bentley
Villas

Bentley
Common

Muchfield
Common

Lancaster's
Spring

CM6

1

Heath
Common

FRIARS LA

Friars

Grange Farm
Riding Stables

SPARROWS LA

A1060

Sewage
Works

Ardley
End

Pooles
Cottages

Hatfield
Grange

14

Gibsons

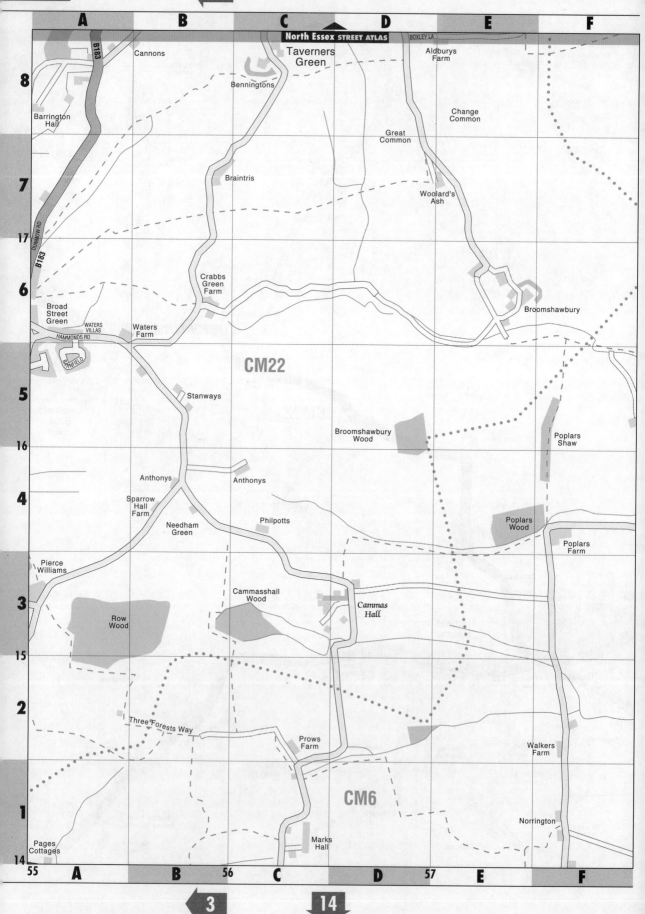

North Essex STREET ATLAS

A B C D E F

BOXLEY LA

8

B183

Cannons

Taverners
Green

Benningtons

Aldburys
Farm

Barrington
Hall

Change
Common

7

Braintris

Great
Common

DUNMOW RD

17

Woolard's
Ash

B183

6

Crabbs
Green
Farm

Broad
Street
Green

WATERS
VILLAS

Waters
Farm

Broomshawbury

HAMMONDS RD

BANFIELD

CM22

5

Stanways

16

Broomshawbury
Wood

Poplars
Shaw

4

Anthonys

Anthonys

Sparrow
Hall
Farm

Poplars
Wood

Needham
Green

Philpotts

Poplars
Farm

Pierce
Williams

3

Cammasshall
Wood

Cammas
Hall

Row
Wood

15

2

Three Forests Way

Prows
Farm

Walkers
Farm

CM6

1

Norrington

Pages
Cottages

Marks
Hall

14

55 A B 56 C D 57 E F

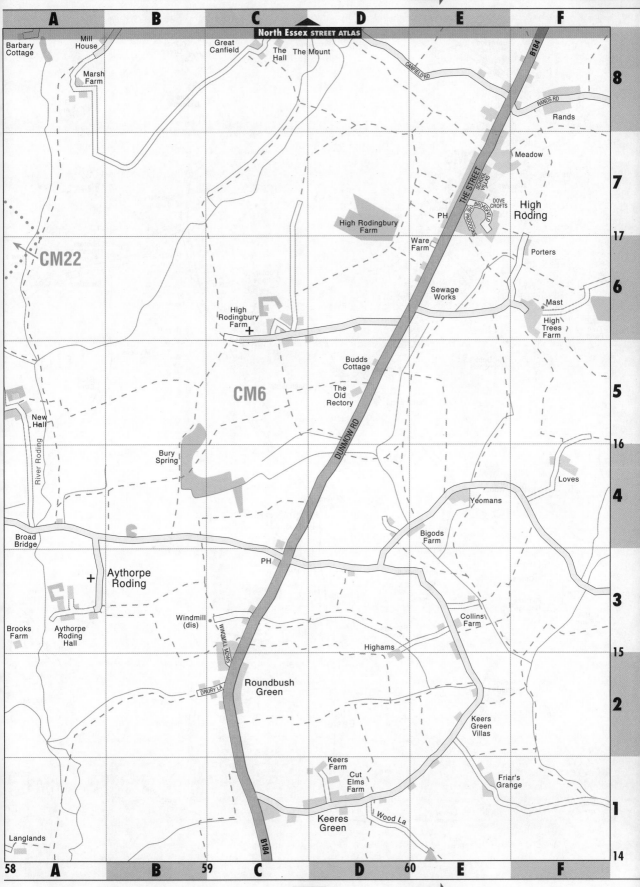

Barbary Cottage

Mill House

Great Canfield

The Hall

The Mount

CANFIELD RD

B184

8

RANDS RD

Rands

Marsh Farm

Meadow

7

THE STREET

SCHOOL VILLAS

BROADFIELD

DOVE CROFTS

High Roding

PH

THE PADDOCKS

CM22

High Rodingbury Farm

17

Ware Farm

Porters

6

High Rodingbury Farm

Sewage Works

Mast

High Trees Farm

Budds Cottage

CM6

The Old Rectory

DUNMOW RD

5

New Hall

River Roding

Bury Spring

16

Loves

Yeomans

4

Broad Bridge

Bigods Farm

PH

Aythorpe Roding

Brooks Farm

Aythorpe Roding Hall

Windmill (dis)

WINDMILL MDWS

PH

Highams

Collins Farm

3

15

DRURY LA

Roundbush Green

Keers Green Villas

2

Keers Farm

Cut Elms Farm

Friar's Grange

Langlands

B184

Keeres Green

Wood La

1

14

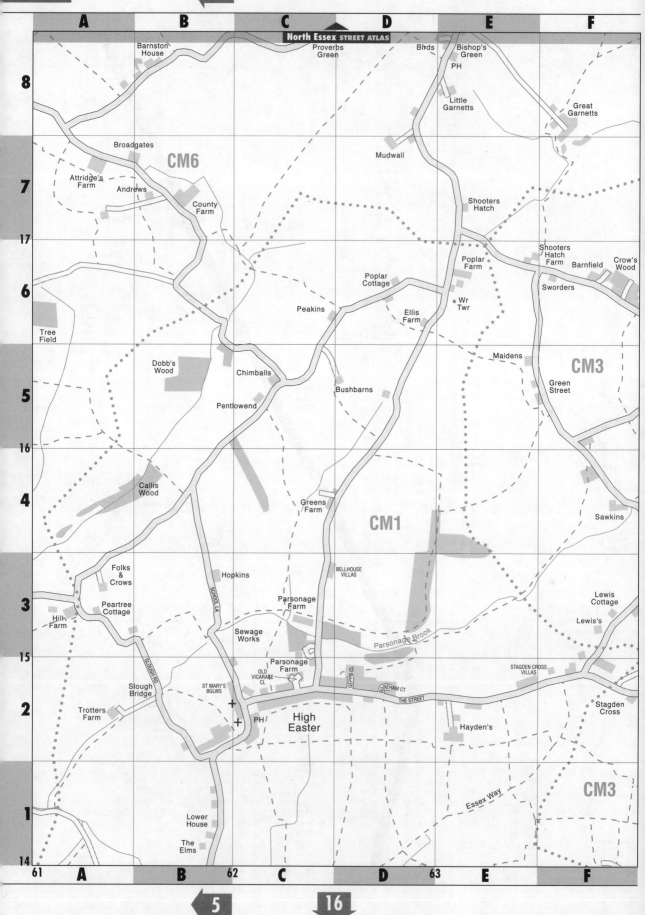

A   B   C   D   E   F

Barnston House

Proverbs Green

Birds

Bishop's Green

PH

8

Little Garnetts

Great Garnetts

Broadgates

CM6

Mudwall

Attridge's Farm

Andrews

7

County Farm

Shooters Hatch

17

Shooters Hatch Farm

Barnfield

Crow's Wood

Poplar Cottage

Poplar Farm

Peakins

6

Ellis Farm

Wr Twr

Sworders

Tree Field

Maidens

CM3

Dobb's Wood

Chimballs

Green Street

5

Pentlowend

Bushbarns

16

Callis Wood

4

Greens Farm

CM1

Sawkins

Folks & Crows

Hopkins

Bellhouse Villas

Lewis Cottage

Peartree Cottage

Parsonage Farm

3

Hilh Farm

Lewis's

SCHOOL LA

Sewage Works

Parsonage Brook

Stagden Cross Villas

15

Old Vicarage Cl

Parsonage Farm

GEPP'S CL

SLOUGH RD

Slough Bridge

St Mary's Bglws

High Easter

THE STREET

BREHAM CT

Stagden Cross

2

Trotters Farm

PH

Hayden's

Essex Way

CM3

Lower House

1

The Elms

14

61   A   B   62   C   D   63   E   F

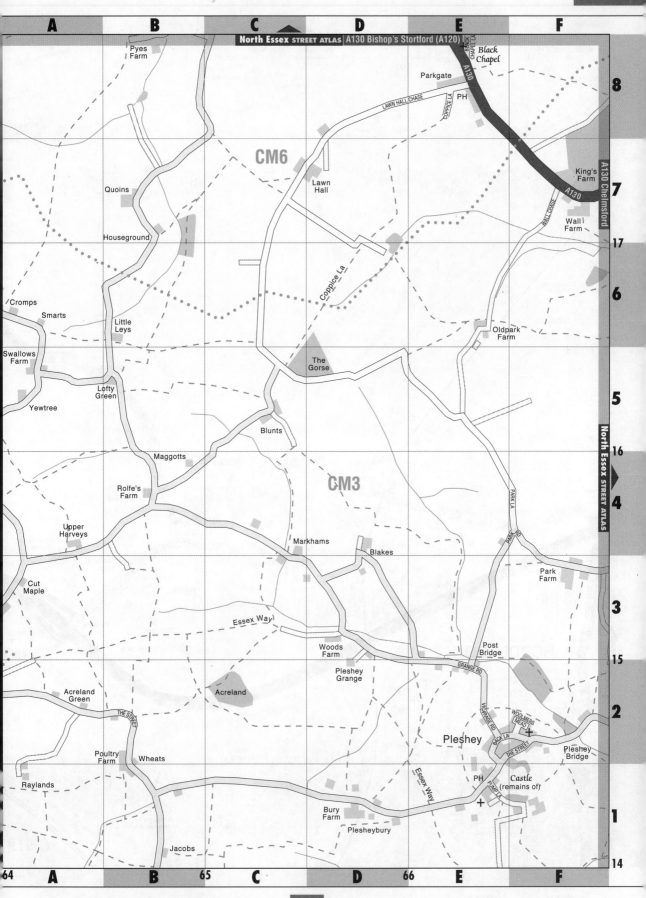

A · B · C · D · E · F

8

Pyes Farm

Black Chapel

Parkgate

A130

LAWN HALL CHASE

CM6

Quoins

Lawn Hall

COPPICE LA

BACK CHAPEL LA

PH

A130

King's Farm

A130 Chelmsford

7

17

Houseground

Coppice La

WALL CHASE

Wall Farm

6

Cromps

Smarts

Little Leys

Oldpark Farm

Swallows Farm

The Gorse

Yewtree

Lofty Green

5

Blunts

16

Maggotts

CM3

PARK LA

4

Rolfe's Farm

Upper Harveys

Markhams

Blakes

PARK RD

Park Farm

Cut Maple

Essex Way

Post Bridge

3

Woods Farm

GRANGE RD

15

Pleshey Grange

Acreland Green

Acreland

VICARAGE RD

WOOLMERS MEAD

2

THE STREET

Pleshey

BACK LA

THE STREET

Pleshey Bridge

Poultry Farm

Wheats

PH

Castle (remains of)

PUMP LA

Raylands

Essex Way

Bury Farm

1

Plesheybury

Jacobs

14

North Essex STREET ATLAS

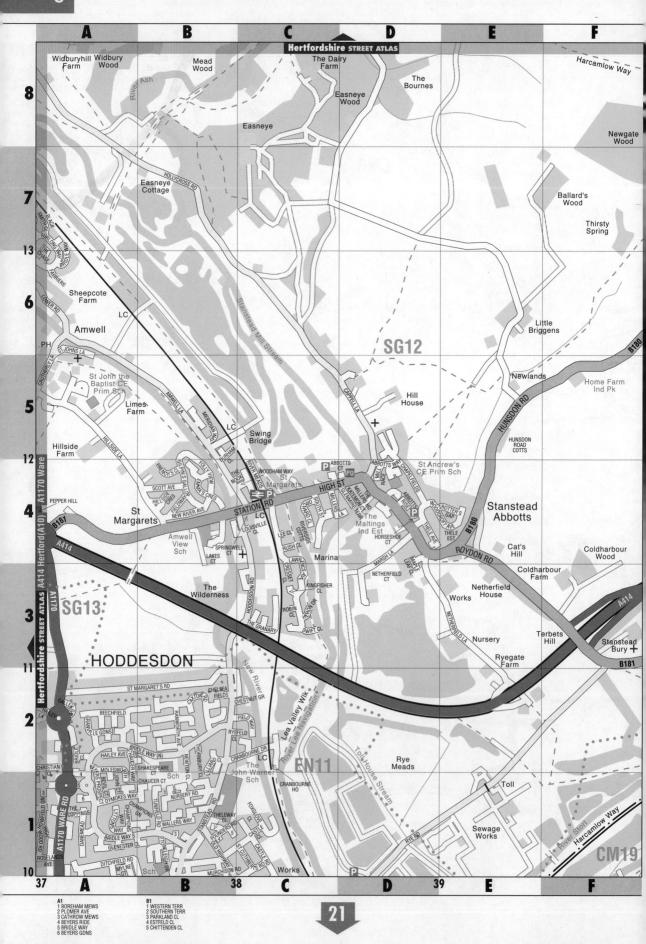

21

A1
1 BOREHAM MEWS
2 PLOMER AVE
3 CATHROW MEWS
4 BEYERS RIDE
5 BRIDLE WAY
6 BEYERS GDNS

B1
1 WESTERN TERR
2 SOUTHERN TERR
3 PARKLAND CL
4 ESTFELD CL
5 CHITTENDEN CL

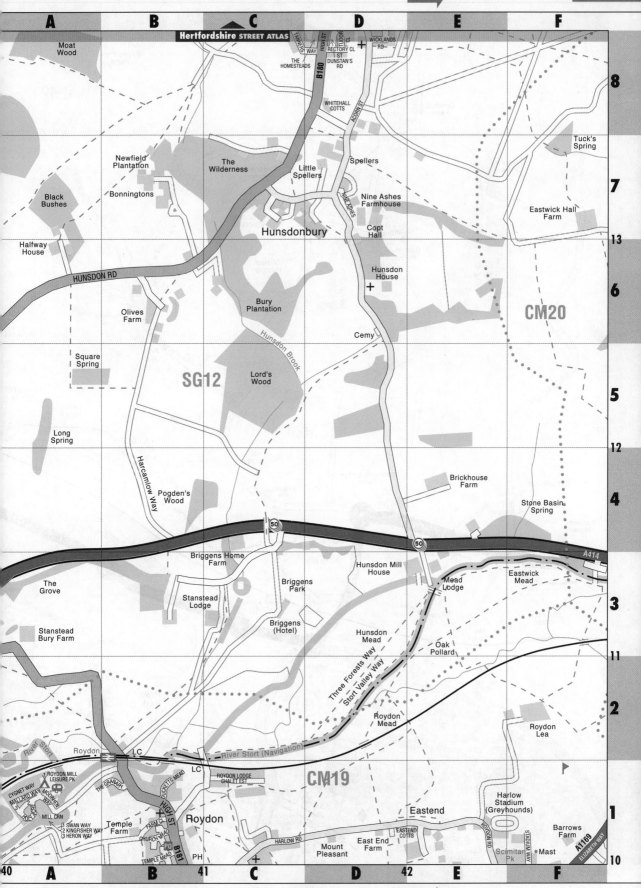

HERTFORDSHIRE STREET ATLAS

Moat
Wood

Newfield
Plantation

The Wilderness

Little
Spellers

Spellers

Tuck's
Spring

Black
Bushes

Bonningtons

Nine Ashes
Farmhouse

Eastwick Hall
Farm

Halfway
House

Hunsdonbury

Copt
Hall

HUNSDON RD

Olives
Farm

Hunsdon
House

CM20

Bury
Plantation

Cemy

Square
Spring

SG12

Lord's
Wood

Hunsdon Brook

Long
Spring

Harcamlow Way

Pogden's
Wood

Brickhouse
Farm

Stone Basin
Spring

Briggens Home
Farm

Hunsdon Mill
House

Mead
Lodge

Eastwick
Mead

A414

The
Grove

Stanstead
Lodge

Briggens
Park

Stanstead
Bury Farm

Briggens
(Hotel)

Hunsdon
Mead

Oak
Pollard

Three Forests Way
Stort Valley Way

Roydon
Mead

Roydon
Lea

River Stort

Roydon

LC

River Stort (Navigation)

CM19

Roydon Lodge
Chalet Est

ROYDON MILL
LEISURE PK

LC

Harlow
Stadium
(Greyhounds)

CYGNET WAY
MALLARD WAY
MOORHEN
WAY

THE GRANARY

DUCKETTS MEAD

Barrows
Farm

MILL CRN

HIGH ST

Temple
Farm

Roydon

Eastend

Scimitar
Pk

Mast

A1169
ELIZABETH WAY

1 SWAN WAY
2 KINGFISHER WAY
3 HERON WAY

CHURCH MEAD
FARM CL

TEMPLE MEAD

B181

PH

HARLOW RD

Mount
Pleasant

East End
Farm

EASTEND
COTTS

STADIUM WAY
ROYDON RD

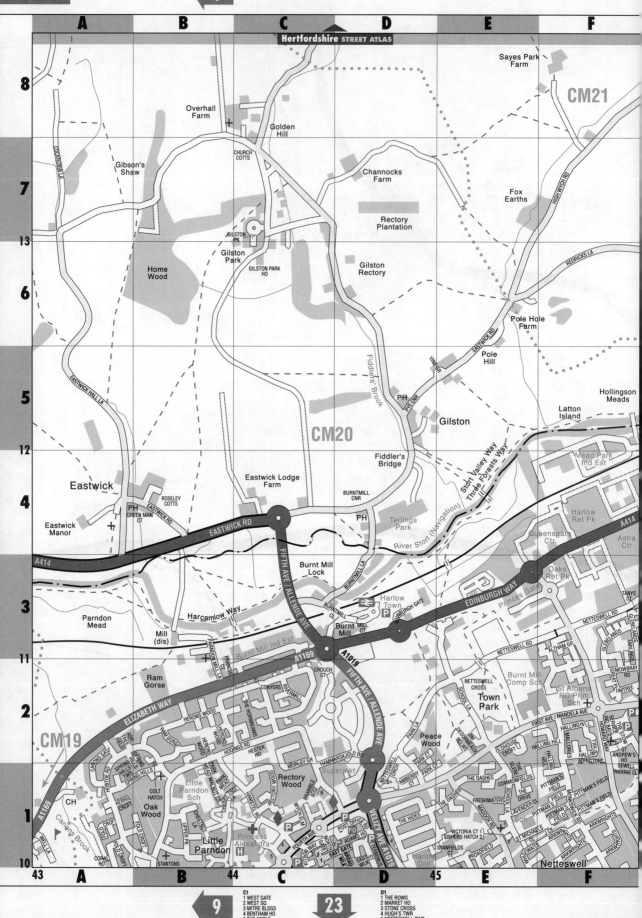

Hertfordshire STREET ATLAS

CM21

CM20

CM19

Sayes Park
Farm

Overhall
Farm

Golden
Hill

Gibson's
Shaw

CHURCH
COTTS

Channocks
Farm

Fox
Earths

Rectory
Plantation

GILSTON
PK

Gilston
Park

GILSTON PARK
HO

Gilston
Rectory

REDRICKS LA

Home
Wood

Pole Hole
Farm

COCKROBIN LA

HIGH WYCH RD

EASTWICK RD

Pole
Hill

PH
PYE CNR

Gilston

VINE GR

Hollingson
Meads

Latton
Island

EASTWICK HALL LA

Fiddlers' Brook

Fiddler's
Bridge

Stort Valley Way

Three Forests Way

Mead Park
Ind Est

Eastwick

Eastwick Lodge
Farm

BURNTMILL
CNR

Terlings
Park

Harlow
Ret Pk

A414

PH
GREEN MAN
CT

ROSELEY
COTTS

EASTWICK RD

PH

River Stort (Navigation)

Queensgate
Ctr

Astra
Ctr

Eastwick
Manor

A414

BURNTMILL LA

Princes Gate

Oaks
Ret Pk

Parndon
Mead

Harcamlow Way

Burnt Mill
Lock

Harlow
Town

EDINBURGH WAY

NETTESWELL RD

Mill
(dis)

BURNTMILL
CL

EDINBURGH GATE

BURNT MILL
CT

Burnt
Mill

NETTESWELL RD

GLEBELANDS

TANYS
CT

ALTHAM GR

Burnt Mill Ind Est

A1169

A1019

NETTESWELL
CROSS

Burnt Mill
Comp Sch

MOWBRAY
RD

St Albans
RC Prim
Sch

ELIZABETH WAY

Ram
Gorse

CROUCH
CT

FIFTH AVE / ALLENDE AVE

PARNDON MILL LA

FRANCIS
CT

CONYERS

RIVERMILL

THE HORNBEAMS

HERONS WOOD

HODDINGS RD

HESTER
HO

MORLEY GR

HAMMARSKJOLD RD

Supermkt

NETTESWELL
ORCH

SCHOOL LA

PARK LA

Town
Park

DESMOND AVE

PARK CT
PARK CT

Peace
Wood

AMBERLY
CT

MANDELA AVE

FIRST AVE

HALLING HILL

OLDHOUSE
CROFT

THE
DRIVE

MALLORIES

HALLING HILL

HALLING HILL

St Andrew's
Ho

SEWELL
HARRIS CL

RAM GORSE

SPRING HILLS

PARK MEAD

WALNUT TREE RD

BRAMBLE
RISE

WYCH ELM

THE DASHES

FRESHWATERS

COMMONFIELDS

THE
GLEBE

LAVENDER CL

TILTH

PITTMAN'S
FIELD

THE DASHES

PITTMAN'S FIELD

MOONSHINE
CL

HAMLET
RD

RECTORY RD

Rectory
Wood

Little
Parndon
Sch

KINGSMOOR
RD

HALLING HILL

CANONS GATE

KIBBLE RD

SPRING HILLS

Little
Parndon

Oak
Wood

COLT
HATCH

KERRIL
CROFT

CHESTNUT
LA

UPPER PK

FOLD CROFT

Princess
Alexandra
H

POST OFFICE
RD

ADAMS HO

FOURTH AVE

EAST GATE
WLK

EASTWICK
WLK

VELIZY AVE A1019

THE
TERMINUS

The HIDES

VICTORIA CT
TEISHERS HATCH

STANFIELDS
CT

A1169

WELL LA

Canons Brook

CH

CORAL
HO

CROFT

OLD CROFT

STANTONS

MADDOX RD

BROADFIELD

Harlow
Coll

ST MICHAEL'S

J

ARKWRIGHTS

Netteswell

9

23

C1
1 WEST GATE
2 WEST SQ
3 MITRE BLDGS
4 BENTHAM HO
5 THE ANGLE
6 AMHERST LO

D1
1 THE ROWS
2 MARKET HO
3 STONE CROSS
4 HUGH'S TWR
5 NETTESWELL TWR

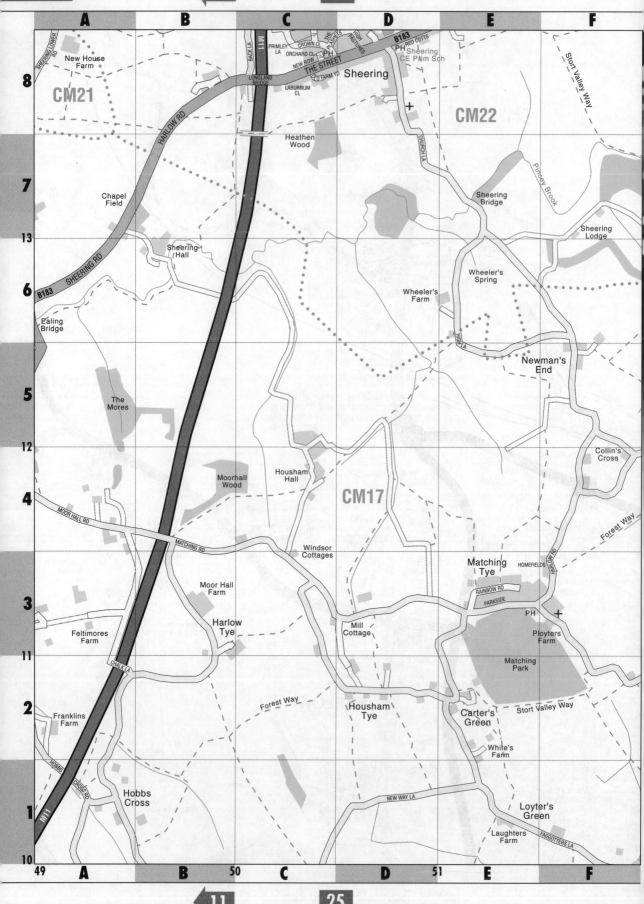

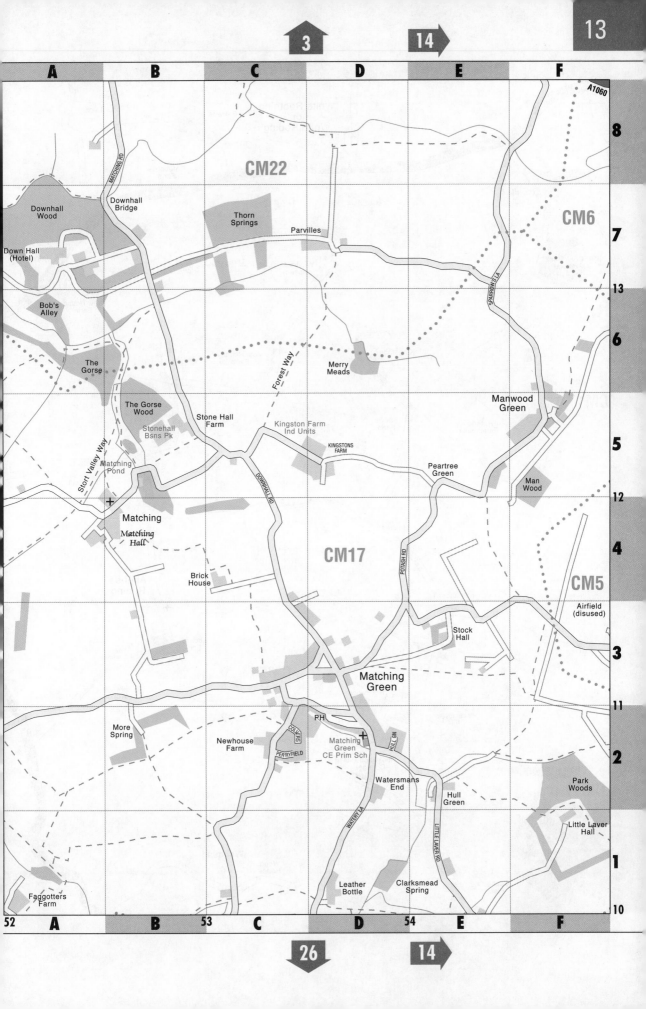

A1060

A **B** **C** **D** **E** **F**

White Roothing
or
White Roding

Sewage
Works

Lucas
Farm

8

BRETTS
VILAS

PH

Gatehouse
Farm

The
Elms

Colville
Hall

St MARTINS CL

CM6

7

CHURCH LA

STORTFORD RD

Uptrees

A1060

Colvillehall
Wood

Windmill
(disused)

Three Forests Way

13

New House
Farm

6

Kingstons

Mascallsbury
Farm

CM17

MATCHING LA

Three Forests Way

Waterloo
Farmhouse

Snows
Farm

Berwick
Hall

5

12

ANCHOR LA

The
Rectory

Anchor
House

Green Hill
Farm

4

Abbess Hall
Farm

Abbess
Roding

Fairlands

Abbess
End

THE
BUNGALOWS

3

SCHOOL LA

B184

Sewage
Works

Longbarns

Rookwood
Hall

11

WATER TOWER
SITE

HORSECROFT

CM5

DUNMOW RD

Rookwoodhall
Wood

Rookwood Hall
Cottages

2

CM17

Brickles
Wood

Woodend

1

Wood
House

SCHOOL LA

Cobbler's
Pieces

B184

10

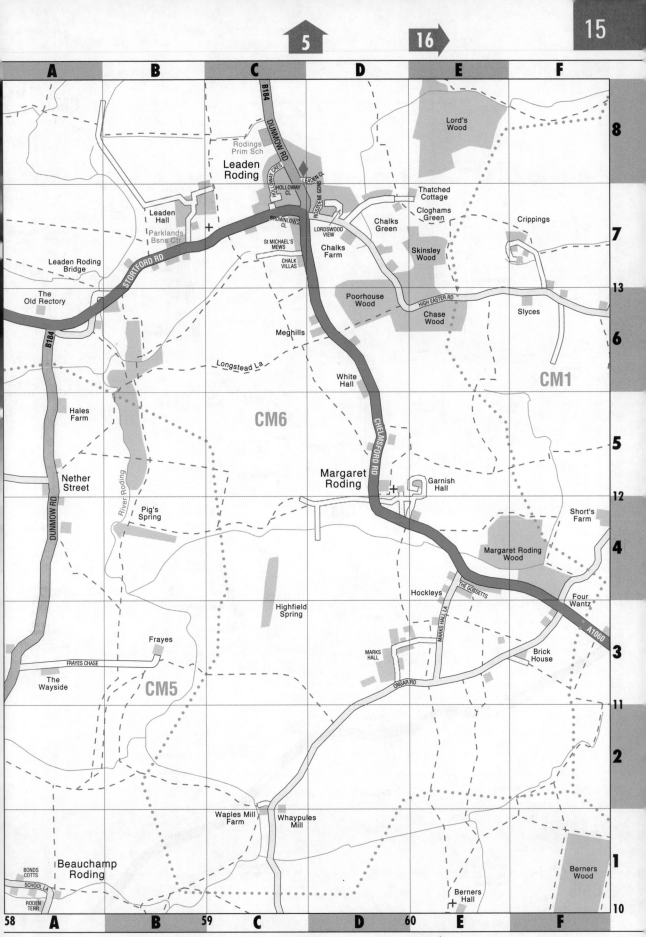

A B C D E F

8

7

13

6

5

12

4

3

11

2

1

10

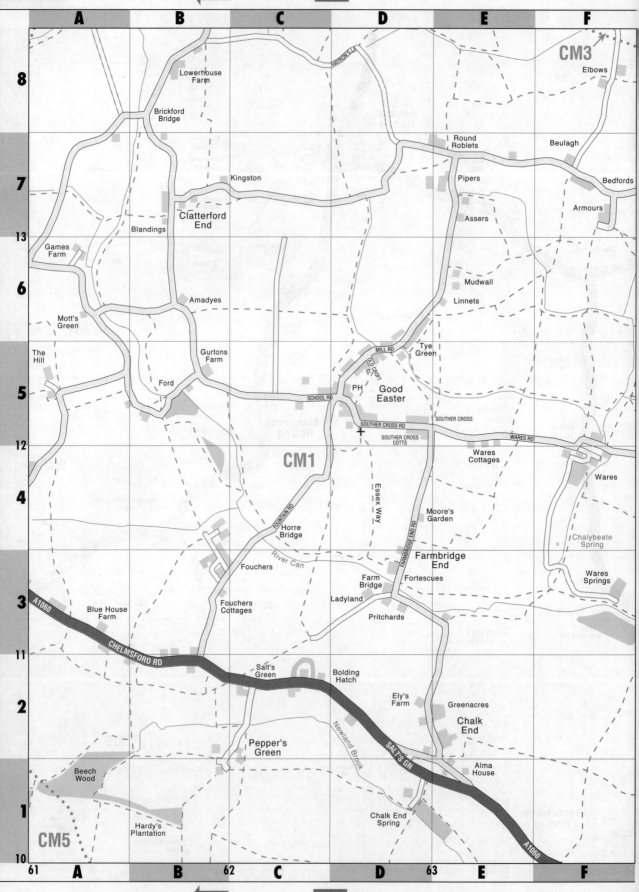

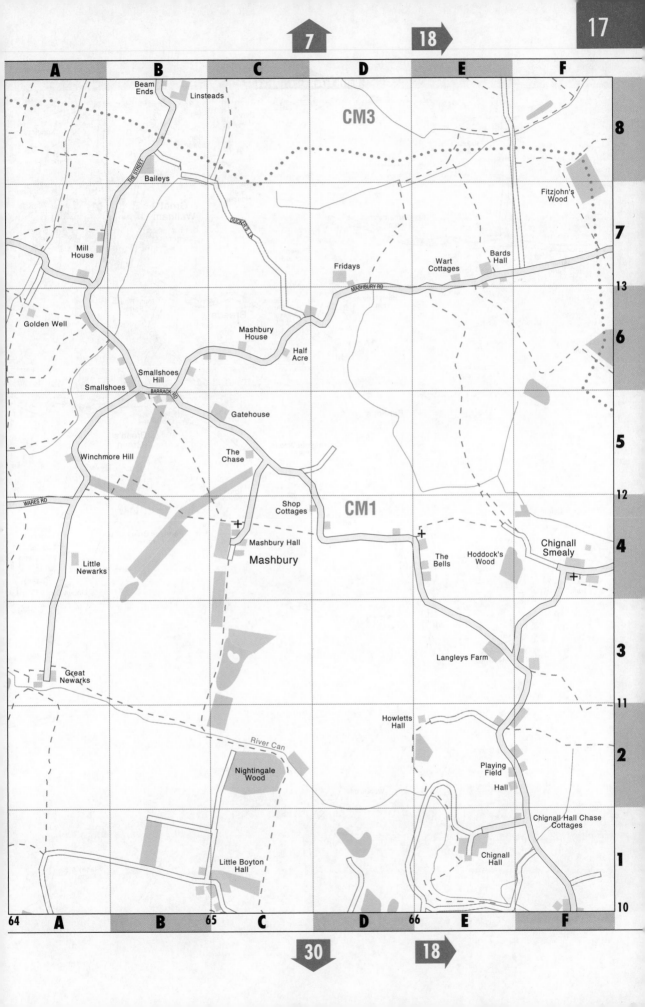

7 18

A B C D E F

8

Beam Ends
Linsteads

CM3

Fitzjohn's Wood

THE STREET

Baileys

7

DUCKER'S LA

Mill House

Bards Hall

Wart Cottages

Fridays

13

MASHBURY RD

Golden Well

Mashbury House

Half Acre

6

Smallshoes Hill

Smallshoes

BARRACK RD

Gatehouse

5

Winchmore Hill

The Chase

Shop Cottages

CM1

12

WARES RD

Mashbury Hall

Mashbury

The Bells

Hoddock's Wood

Chignall Smealy

4

Little Newarks

Langleys Farm

3

Great Newarks

11

Howletts Hall

River Can

Nightingale Wood

Playing Field

Hall

2

Chignall Hall Chase Cottages

Little Boyton Hall

Chignall Hall

1

10

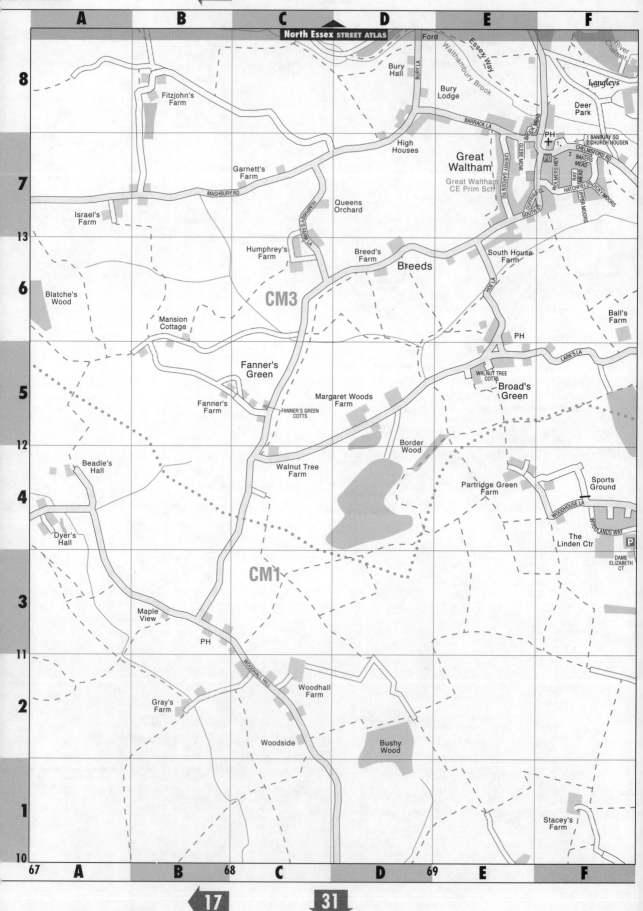

North Essex STREET ATLAS

A **B** **C** **D** **E** **F**

8

Fitzjohn's Farm

Bury Hall

Ford

Bury Lodge

Essex Way

Walthambury Brook

River Chelmer

Langleys

Deer Park

BARRACK LA

BURY LA

High Houses

CHELMSFORD RD

Great Waltham

1 BANBURY SQ
2 CHURCH HOUSEN

PH

PO

BAKERS MEAD

7

Garnett's Farm

MASHBURY RD

Great Waltham CE Prim Sch

CHERRY GARDEN RD

GLEBE MDW

WOLMERS HEY

DUFFIES CL

SOUTH ST

RAY MEAD

HATCHFIELDS

DUCKY MOORS

UPPER MOORS

Queens Orchard

13

Israel's Farm

HUMPHREY'S FARM LA

Humphrey's Farm

Breed's Farm

Breeds

South House Farm

6

Blatche's Wood

CM3

HOPE LA

Ball's Farm

Mansion Cottage

PH

Fanner's Green

LARK'S LA

5

Fanner's Farm

FANNER'S GREEN COTTS

Margaret Woods Farm

WALNUT TREE COTTS

Broad's Green

12

Border Wood

Partridge Green Farm

Sports Ground

4

Beadle's Hall

Walnut Tree Farm

WOODHOUSE LA

WOODLANDS WAY

The Linden Ctr

Dyer's Hall

DAME ELIZABETH CT

3

CM1

Maple View

PH

11

Woodhall Farm

WOODHALL HILL

2

Gray's Farm

Woodside

Bushy Wood

1

Stacey's Farm

10

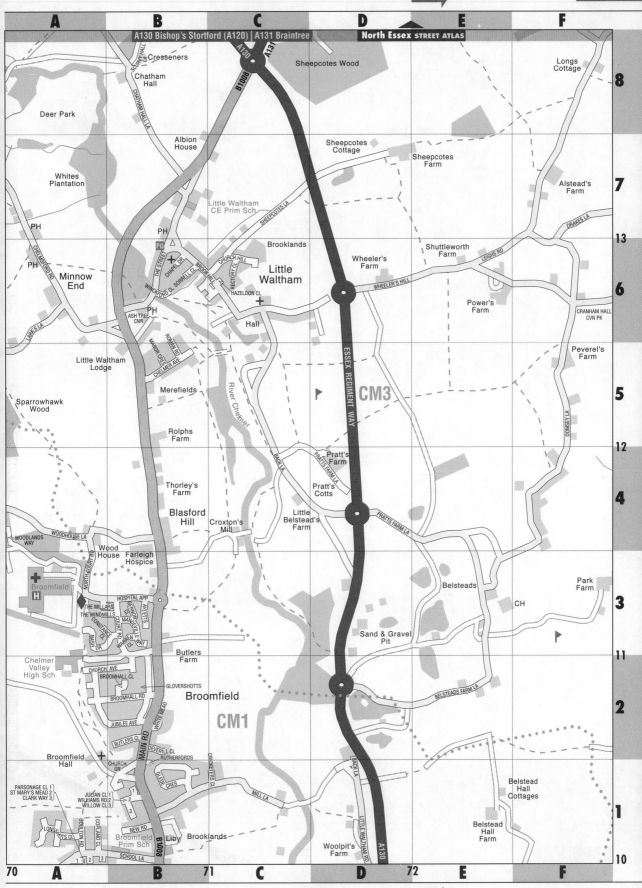

North Essex STREET ATLAS

A130 Bishop's Stortford (A120) | A131 Braintree

Cresseners

Chatham Hall

Sheepcotes Wood

Longs Cottage

Deer Park

Albion House

Sheepcotes Cottage

Sheepcotes Farm

Whites Plantation

Little Waltham CE Prim Sch

Alstead's Farm

PH

PH

PH

Brooklands

Wheeler's Farm

Shuttleworth Farm

Minnow End

Little Waltham

PH

PO

Hazeldon Cl

Wheeler's Hill

Power's Farm

Cranham Hall CVN PK

Hall

Ash Tree Cnr

Peverel's Farm

Little Waltham Lodge

Merefields

River Chelmer

Essex Regiment Way

CM3

Sparrowhawk Wood

Rolphs Farm

Pratt's Farm

Pratt's Cotts

Thorley's Farm

Blasford Hill

Croxton's Mill

Little Belstead's Farm

Park Farm

Woodlands Way

Woodhouse La

Wood House

Farleigh Hospice

Belsteads

CH

Broomfield H

The Millars
The Windmills

Sand & Gravel Pit

Hospital App

Chelmer Valley High Sch

Butlers Farm

Broomhall Cl

Glovershotts

Broomfield

Belsteads Farm La

Broomhall Rd

CM1

Jubilee Ave

Butlers Cl

Broomfield Hall

Church Gn

Deverill Cl
Rutherfords

Cricketers Cl

Belstead Hall Cottages

Parsonage Cl 1
St Mary's Mead 2
Clark Way 3

Julian Cl 1
Williams Rd 2
Willow Cl 3

Mill La

New Rd

Belstead Hall Farm

Longs Cots Cl

School La

Broomfield Prim Sch

Liby

Brooklands

Woolpit's Farm

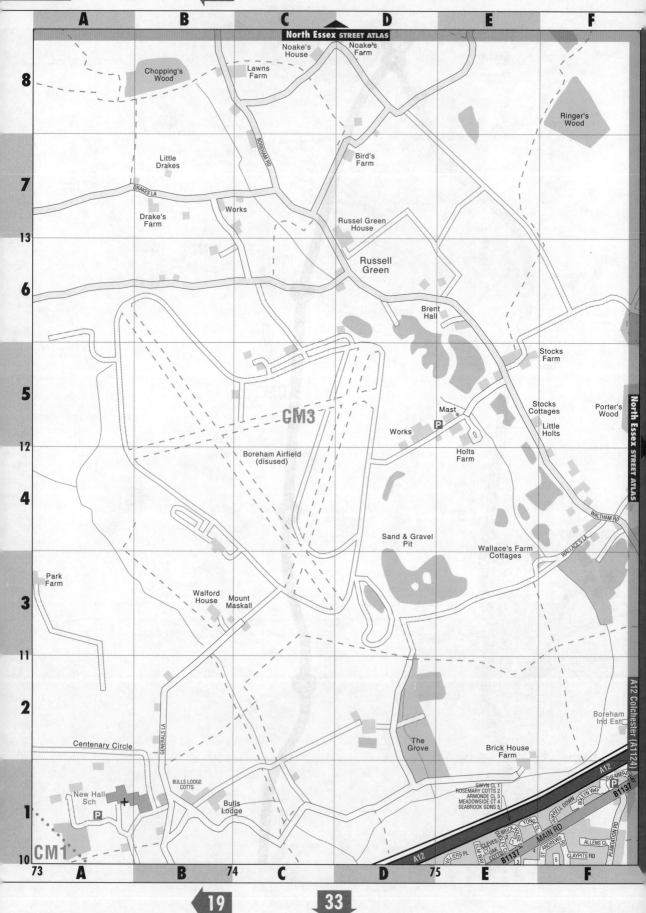

A   B   C   D   E   F

8

Chopping's Wood

Noake's House

Noake's Farm

Lawns Farm

Ringer's Wood

Little Drakes

BOREHAM RD

Bird's Farm

7

DRAKES LA

Drake's Farm

Works

Russel Green House

13

Russell Green

6

Brent Hall

Stocks Farm

5

Mast

Stocks Cottages

Porter's Wood

CM3

Works

P

Little Holts

12

Holts Farm

Boreham Airfield (disused)

4

WALTHAM RD

Sand & Gravel Pit

Wallace's Farm Cottages

WALLACE'S LA

Park Farm

3

Walford House

Mount Maskall

11

2

The Grove

Boreham Ind Est

Centenary Circle

GENERALS LA

Brick House Farm

A12 Colchester (A1124)

GWYN CL 1
ROSEMARY COTTS 2
ARMONDE CL 3
MEADOWSIDE CT 4
SEABROOK GDNS 5

A12

SHEARERS WAY

P

B1137

BULLS LODGE COTTS

New Hall Sch

P

1

Bulls Lodge

HURRELL DOWN

SQ LYN WAY

MAIN RD

ALLENS CL

CM1

10

A12

B1137

VILLIERS PL

ST ANDREWS RD

PLANTATION RD

CLAYPITS RD

A6
1 Tower Ctr
2 Highbourne Ct
3 The Old Maltings Ct
4 Hopps Ho
5 Christies Ct
6 Buckingham Lodge

7 Sandringham Lodge
8 Clarence Lodge
9 Bensted Ct
10 Pearl Ct
11 Eversley Lodge
12 Acacias Ct
13 Comroston

14 Lowfield Ct
15 Brocket Ct
16 Hogges Cl
17 Limes Ct

A7
1 Fourways Ct
2 Cumberland Ct
3 Westfield Rd
4 Norris Rise
5 Winterscroft Rd
6 Belcher Rd

7 Roman Mews
8 Roman St
9 Burford Mews
10 Tower Hts
11 Burford Pl

D8
1 Nectar Ct
2 Barley Ct
3 Mead Lodge
4 Pepys Ct
5 Teale Ho
6 Leaside Lodge

D8
7 Plotters Ct
8 Charles Ho
9 Malsters Lodge

8

22

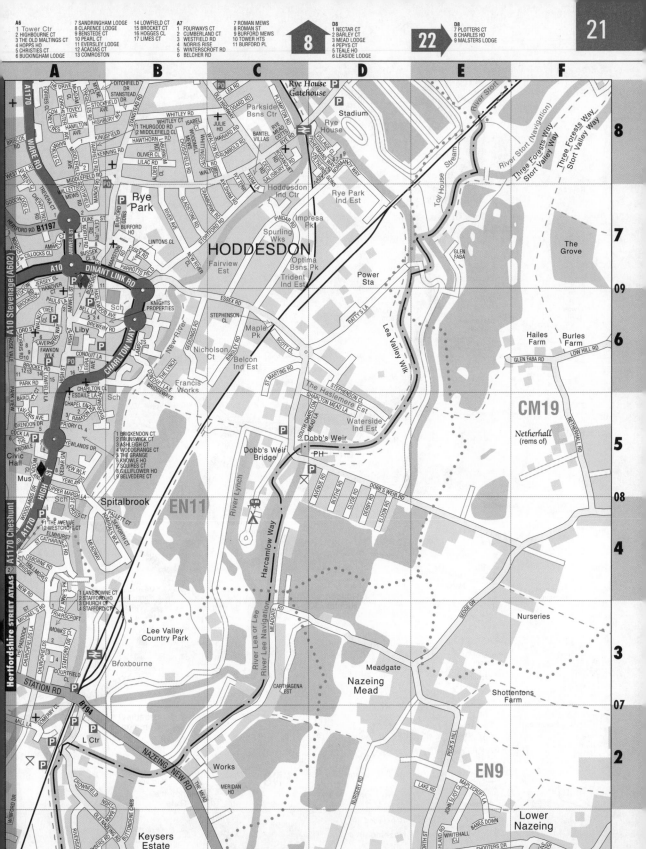

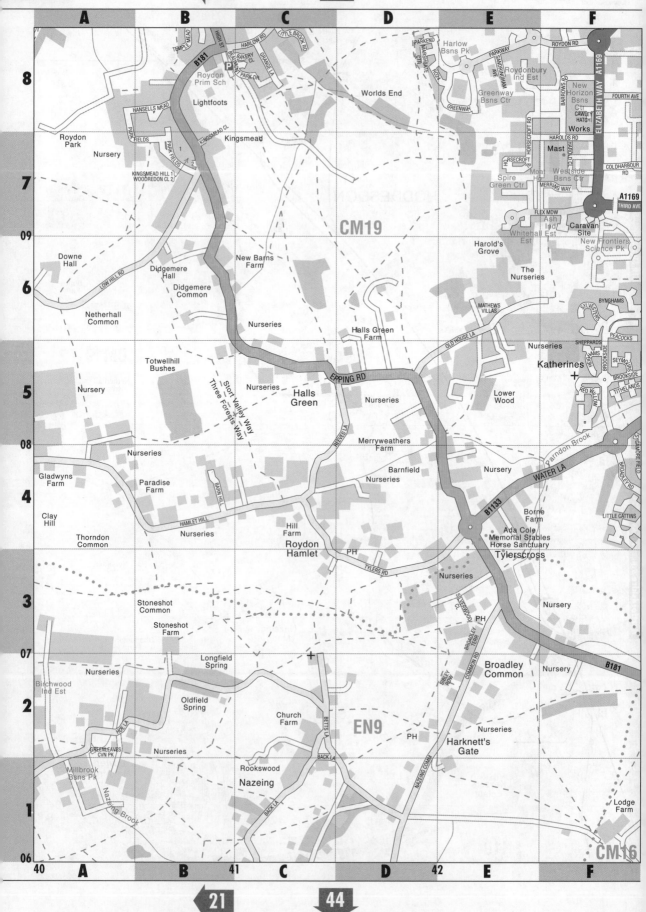

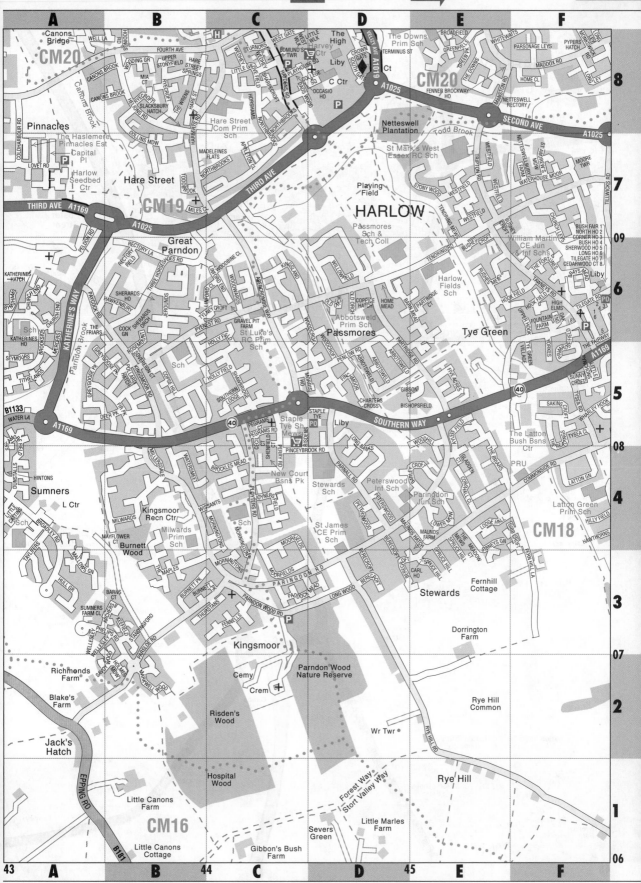

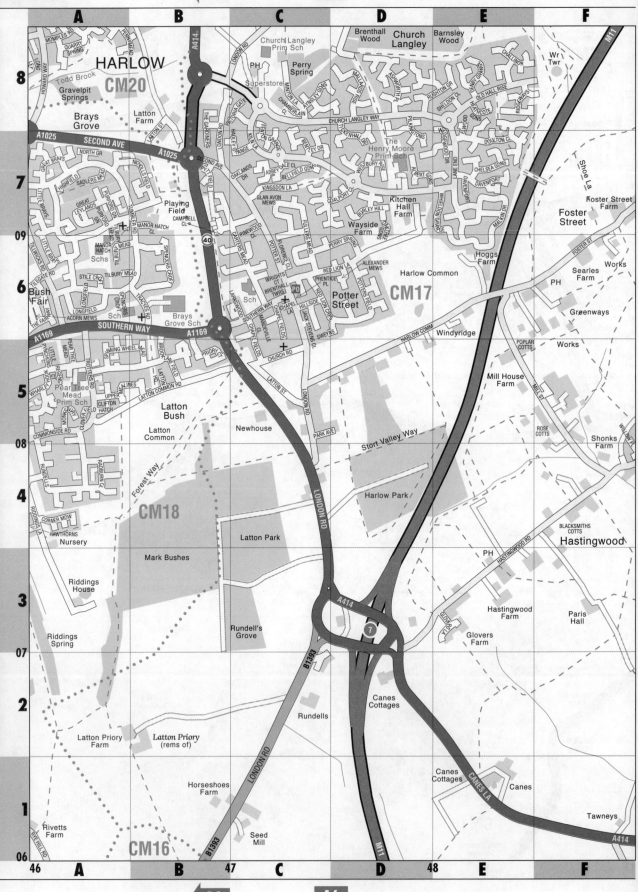

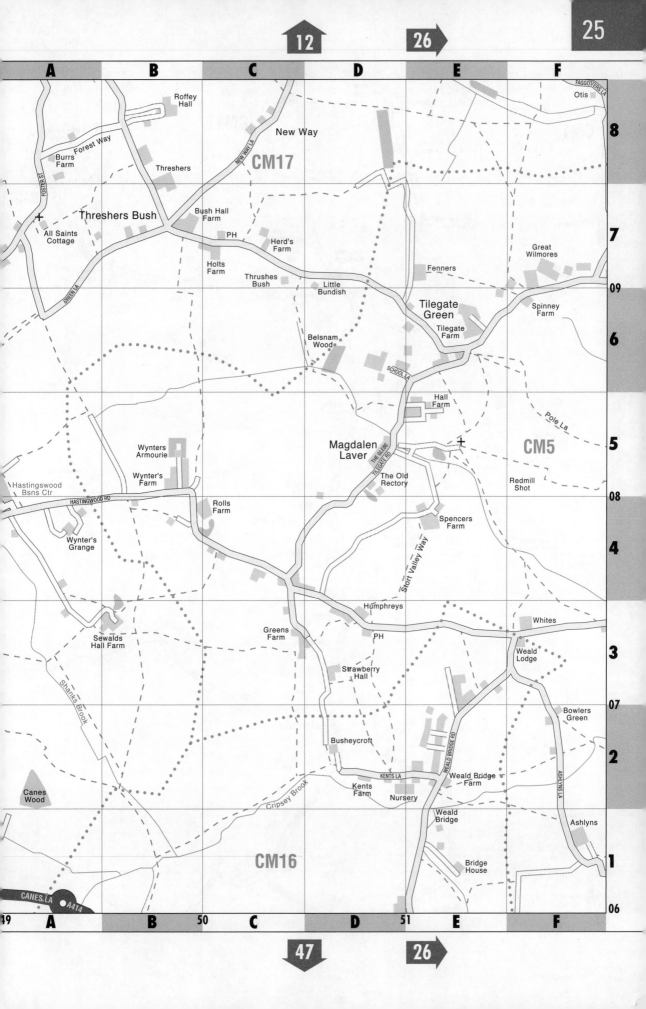

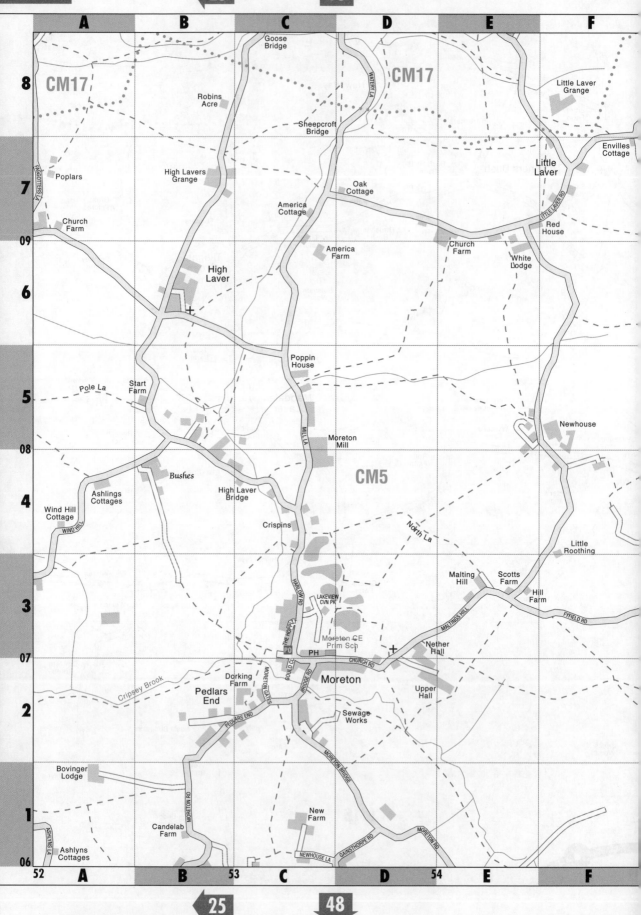

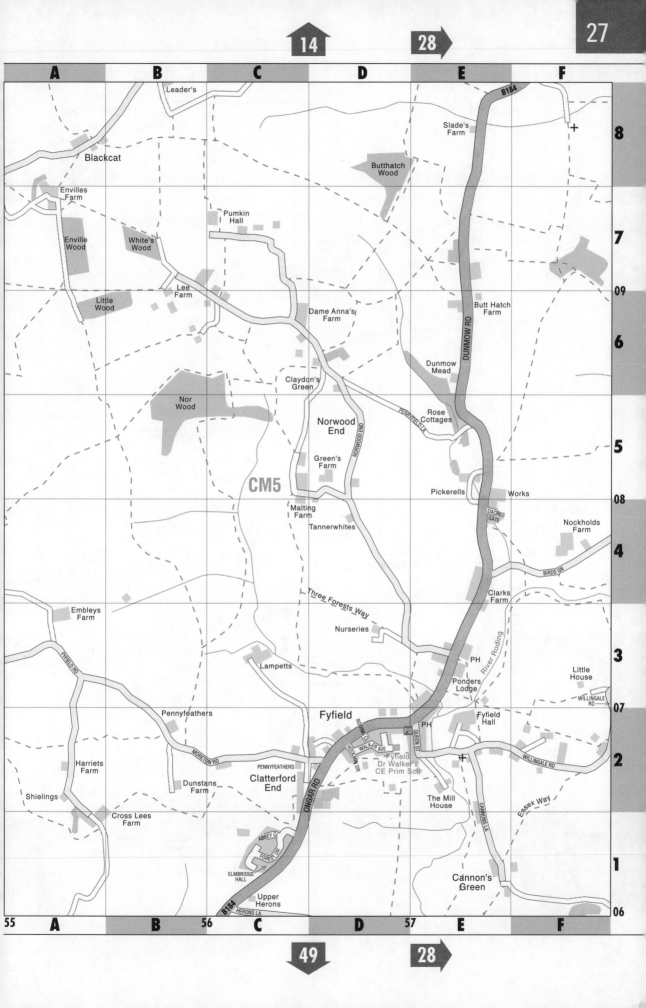

A   **B**   **C**   **D**   **E**   **F**

Leader's

8

Slade's Farm

B184

+

Blackcat

Butthatch Wood

Envilles Farm

7

Pumkin Hall

White's Wood

Enville Wood

09

Little Wood

Lee Farm

Butt Hatch Farm

Dame Anna's Farm

DUNMOW RD

6

Claydon's Green

Dunmow Mead

Nor Wood

Norwood End

PERRYFIELD LA

Rose Cottages

5

Green's Farm

CM5

Pickerells   Works

08

Malting Farm

DACRES GATE

Nockholds Farm

Tannerwhites

4

BIRDS GN

NORWOOD END

Clarks Farm

Three Forests Way

Embleys Farm

River Roding

Nurseries

Little House

3

FYFIELD RD

Lampetts

PH

WILLINGALE RD

07

Ponders Lodge

Pennyfeathers

Fyfield

PH   Fyfield Hall

MORETON RD

RODING CL

WALKER AVE

PO

HOUCHIN DR

QUEEN ST

WILLINGALE RD

2

PENNYFEATHERS

Harriets Farm

Fyfield Dr Walker's CE Prim Sch

+

Dunstans Farm

ONGAR RD

CANNONS LA

Essex Way

Shielings

Clatterford End

The Mill House

Cross Lees Farm

ABBEY CL

FOREST DR

1

ELMBRIDGE HALL

Cannon's Green

Upper Herons

06

B184

HERONS LA

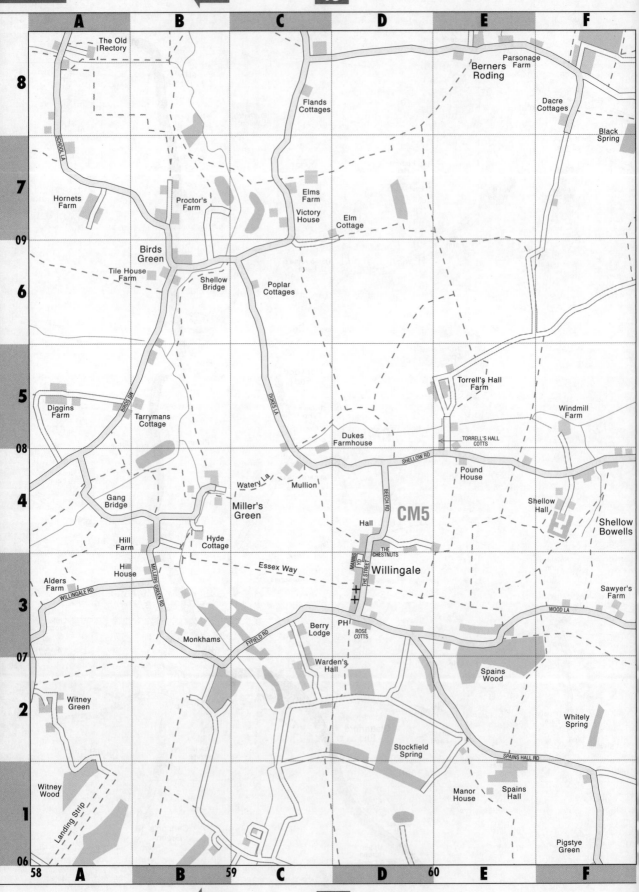

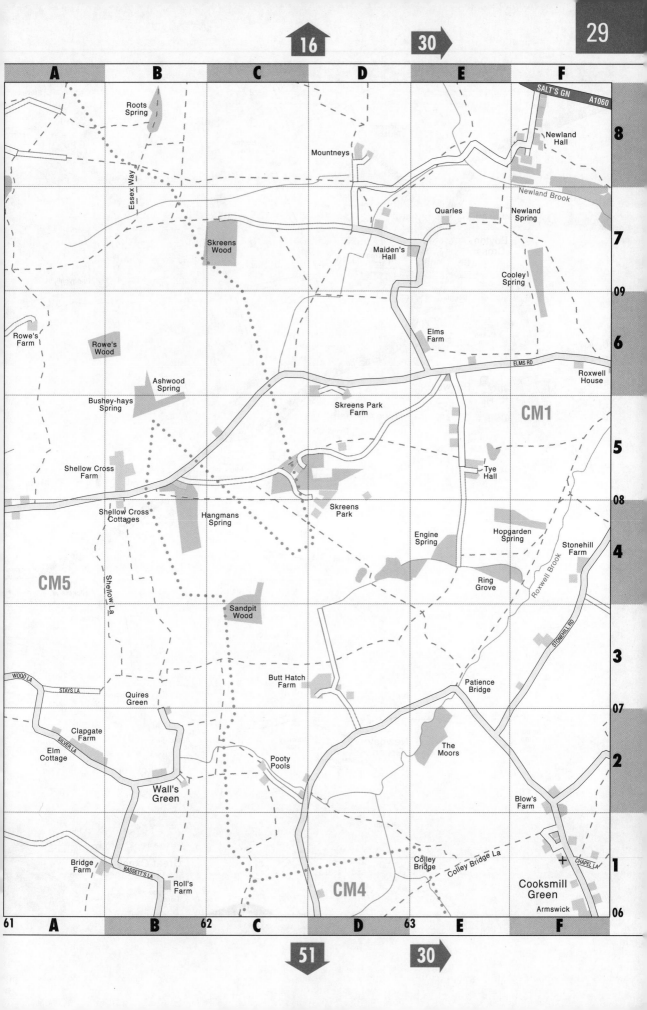

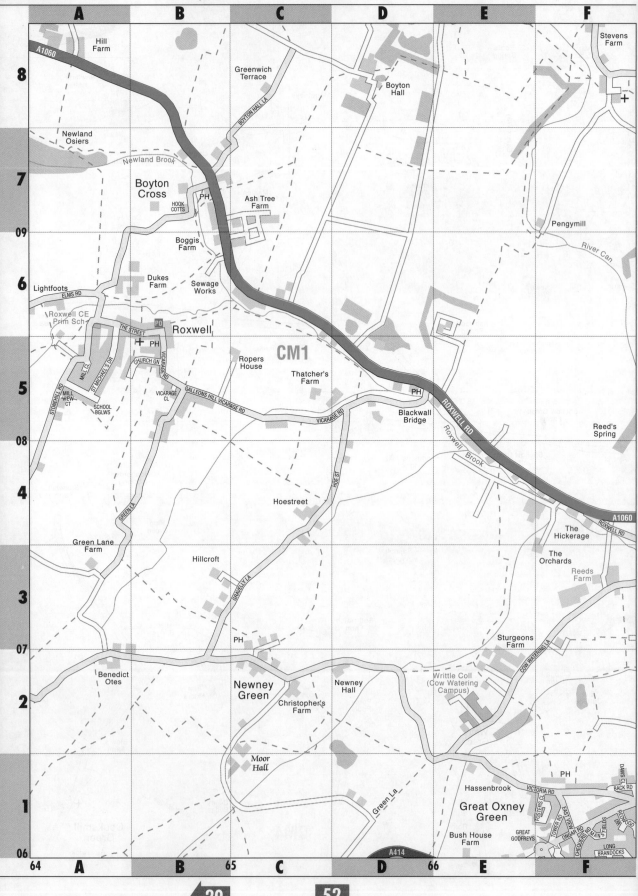

A B C D E F

8

A1060

Hill
Farm

Stevens
Farm

Greenwich
Terrace

Boyton
Hall

Newland
Osiers

Newland Brook

7

Boyton
Cross

Pengymill

River Can

PH

HOOK
COTTS

Ash Tree
Farm

09

Boggis
Farm

6

Dukes
Farm

Sewage
Works

Lightfoots

ELMS RD

Roxwell CE
Prim Sch

PO

Roxwell

CM1

Ropers
House

Thatcher's
Farm

Reed's
Spring

PH

THE STREET

PH

CHURCH GN

5

MILL CL

ST MICHAEL'S DR

VICARAGE RD

VICARAGE
CL

GALLEONS HILL VICARAGE RD

Blackwall
Bridge

ROXWELL RD

Roxwell Brook

MILL
VIEW
CT

SCHOOL
BGLWS

STONEHILL RD

08

VICARAGE RD

HOE ST

4

GREEN LA

Hoestreet

A1060

ROXWELL RD

Green Lane
Farm

Hillcroft

The
Hickerage

The
Orchards

Reeds
Farm

3

GRAVELLY LA

07

PH

Sturgeons
Farm

COW WATERING LA

Benedict
Otes

Newney
Green

Newney
Hall

Writtle Coll
(Cow Watering
Campus)

2

Christopher's
Farm

Moor
Hall

Hassenbrook

VICTORIA RD

PH

BACK RD

DAVIS CL

1

Green La

Great Oxney
Green

FOSTERS CL

EAST VIEW

TOWER RD

ONGAR RD

CHEQUERS RD

MANS FIELDS

REDWOOD DR

GREAT
GODFREYS

Bush House
Farm

LONG
BRANDOCKS

06

A414

64 A B 65 C D 66 E F

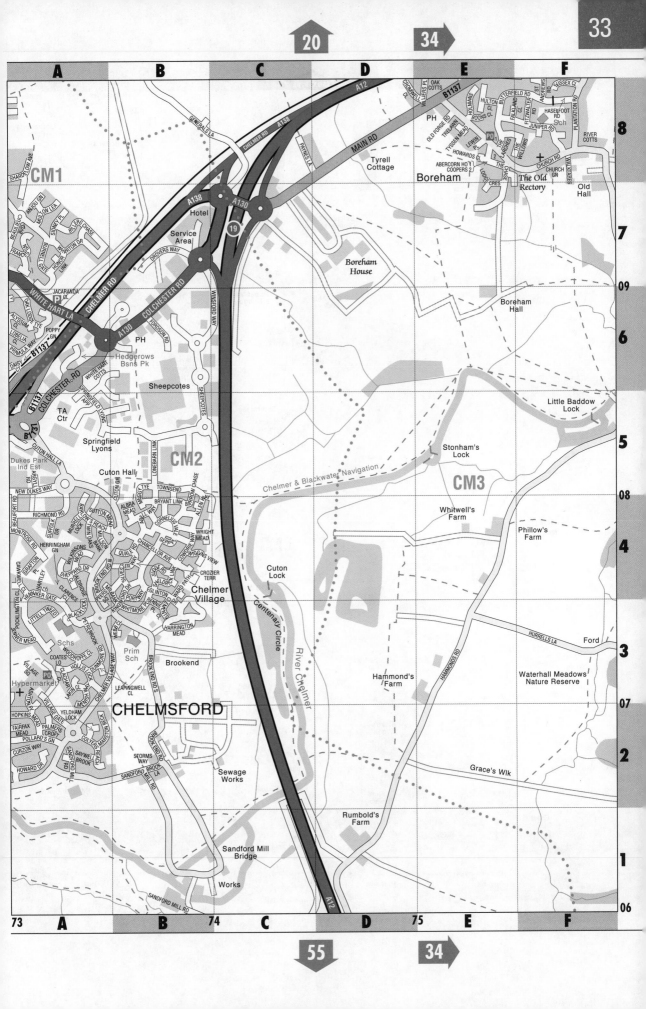

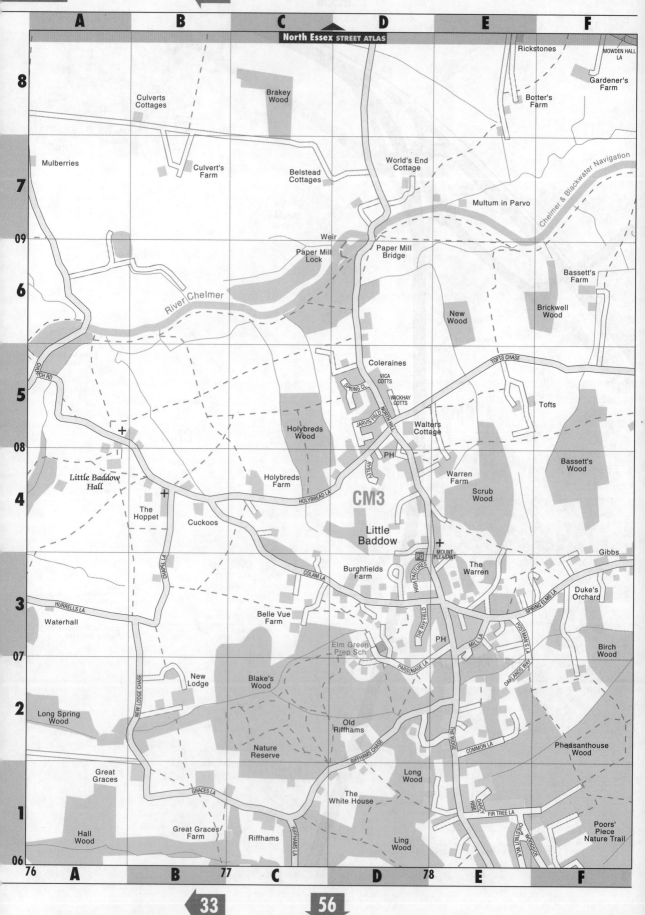

A   B   C   D   E   F

8

Culverts
Cottages

Brakey
Wood

Rickstones

MOWDEN HALL
LA

Gardener's
Farm

Botter's
Farm

Mulberries

Culvert's
Farm

Belstead
Cottages

World's End
Cottage

7

Multum in Parvo

Chelmer & Blackwater Navigation

09

Weir

Paper Mill
Lock

Paper Mill
Bridge

Bassett's
Farm

6

River Chelmer

New
Wood

Brickwell
Wood

CH PCH RD

Coleraines

Tofts Chase

5

VICA
COTTS

WICKHAY
COTTS

Tofts

SPRING CL

Holybreds
Wood

JARVIS FIELD

NORTH HILL

Walters
Cottage

Bassett's
Wood

08

Little Baddow
Hall

Holybreds
Farm

RYSLEY

PH

Warren
Farm

Scrub
Wood

4

The
Hoppet

Cuckoos

HOLYBREAD LA

CM3

Little
Baddow

Gibbs

CHAPEL LA

Colam La

Burghfields
Farm

PO

MOUNT
PLEASANT

The
Warren

Duke's
Orchard

SPRING ELMS LA

3

HURRELLS LA

Waterhall

Belle Vue
Farm

HIGH PASTURES

THE RYE FIELD

PH

MILL LA

POSTMAN'S LA

Birch
Wood

07

Elm Green
Prep Sch

PARSONAGE LA

OAKLANDS WAY

New Lodge Chase

New
Lodge

Blake's
Wood

Long Spring
Wood

2

Nature
Reserve

Old
Riffhams

THE RIDGE

COMMON LA

Pheasanthouse
Wood

Great
Graces

RIFFHAMS CHASE

Long
Wood

DARCY RISE

FIR TREE LA

1

GRACES LA

The
White House

RIFFHAMS LA

CHESTNUT WLK

WOODSIDE

Poors'
Piece
Nature Trail

Hall
Wood

Great Graces
Farm

Riffhams

Ling
Wood

06

76   A   B   77   C   D   78   E   F

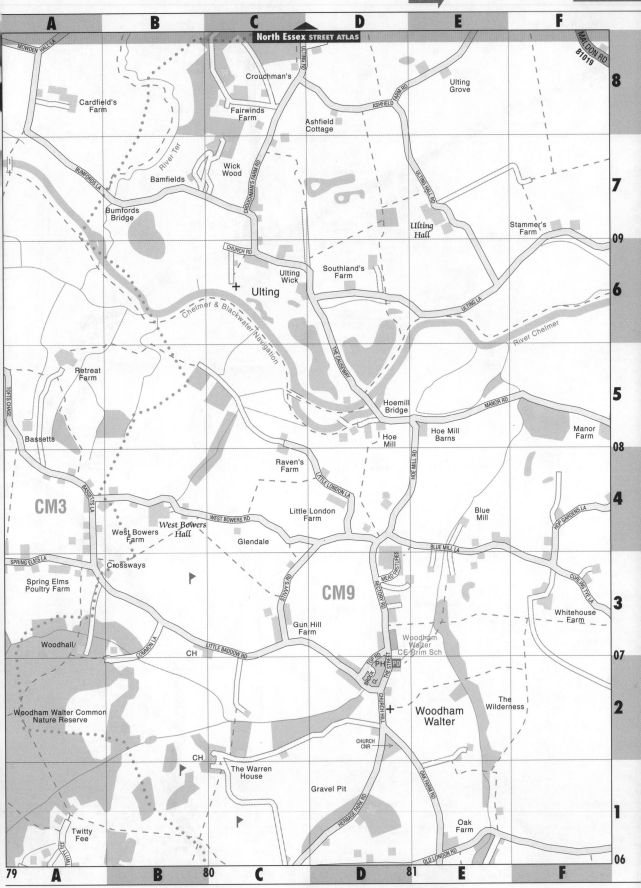

North Essex STREET ATLAS

MALDON RD B1019

Mowden Hall La

Cardfield's Farm

Crouchman's

Fairwinds Farm

Ashfield Cottage

Ulting Grove

ASHFIELD FARM RD

River Ter

Bumfords La

Bamfields

Wick Wood

CROUCHMAN'S FARM RD

ULTING HALL RD

Bumfords Bridge

Stammer's Farm

CHURCH RD

Ulting Wick

Southland's Farm

Ulting Hall

Ulting Wick

+ Ulting

Chelmer & Blackwater Navigation

ULTING LA

River Chelmer

Retreat Farm

THE CAUSEWAY

Hoemill Bridge

MANOR RD

Bassetts

Raven's Farm

Hoe Mill

Hoe Mill Barns

Manor Farm

TOFTS CHASE

LITTLE LONDON LA

HOE MILL RD

CM3

BASSETTS LA

WEST BOWERS RD

Little London Farm

Blue Mill

HOP GARDENS LA

West Bowers Farm

West Bowers Hall

Glendale

BLUE MILL LA

CURLING TYE LA

SPRING ELMS LA

Crossways

MEAD PASTURES

Whitehouse Farm

Spring Elms Poultry Farm

COMMON LA

ST IVES RD

CM9

RECTORY RD

Gun Hill Farm

Woodham Walter CE Prim Sch

Woodhall

CH

LITTLE BADDOW RD

TOP RD

PH

THE STREET

PO

The Wilderness

Woodham Walter Common Nature Reserve

BROOK CL

CHURCH HILL

+ Woodham Walter

CH

CHURCH CNR

The Warren House

Gravel Pit

HERBAGE PARK RD

OAK FARM RD

Oak Farm

Twitty Fee

TWITTY FEE

OLD LONDON RD

09
8
7
09
6
5
08
4
3
07
2
1
06

79   A   B   80   C   D   81   E   F

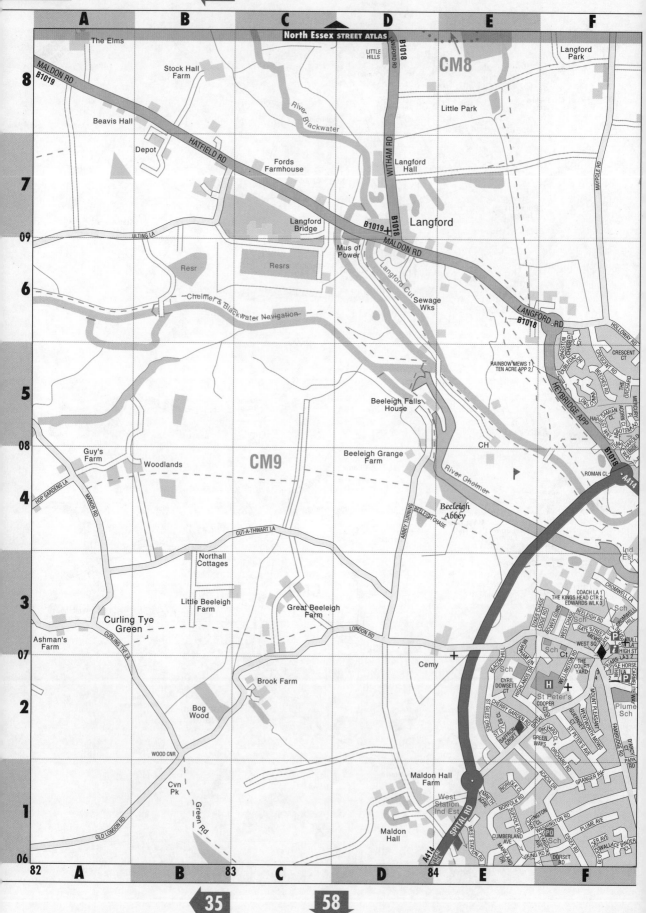

North Essex STREET ATLAS

CM8

A B C D E F

8

MALDON RD
B1019

The Elms

Stock Hall
Farm

Beavis Hall

Depot

HATFIELD RD

Fords
Farmhouse

River Blackwater

LITTLE
HILLS

LANGFORD RD
B1018

WITHAM RD

Little Park

Langford
Hall

Langford Park

7

09

Langford
Bridge

ULTING LA

B1019

B1018

MALDON RD

Langford

Mus of
Power

6

Resr

Resrs

Chelmer & Blackwater Navigation

Langford Cut

Sewage
Wks

LANGFORD RD
B1018

HOLLOWAY RD

CRESCENT
CT

5

Beeleigh Falls
House

RAINBOW MEWS 1
TEN ACRE APP 2

HETHBRIDGE APP

08

Guy's
Farm

Woodlands

CM9

Beeleigh Grange
Farm

CH

River Chelmer

B1018

A414

ROMAN CL

4

HOP GARDENS LA

MANOR RD

CUT-A-THWART LA

ABBEY TURNING

BEELEIGH CHASE

Beeleigh
Abbey

Ind
Est

3

Northall
Cottages

Little Beeleigh
Farm

Great Beeleigh
Farm

LONDON RD

CROMWELL LA

COACH LA 1
THE KINGS HEAD CTR 2
EDWARDS WLK 3

Curling Tye
Green

CURLING TYE LA

Ashman's
Farm

Cemy

07

Brook Farm

Bog
Wood

WOOD CNR

Cvn
Pk

Green Rd

Cyril
Dowsett
Ct

St Peter's
Cooper
Ct

H

Plume
Sch

2

Maldon Hall
Farm

West
Station
Ind Est

SPITAL RD

A414

Maldon
Hall

OLD LONDON RD

1

06

82 A B 83 C D 84 E F

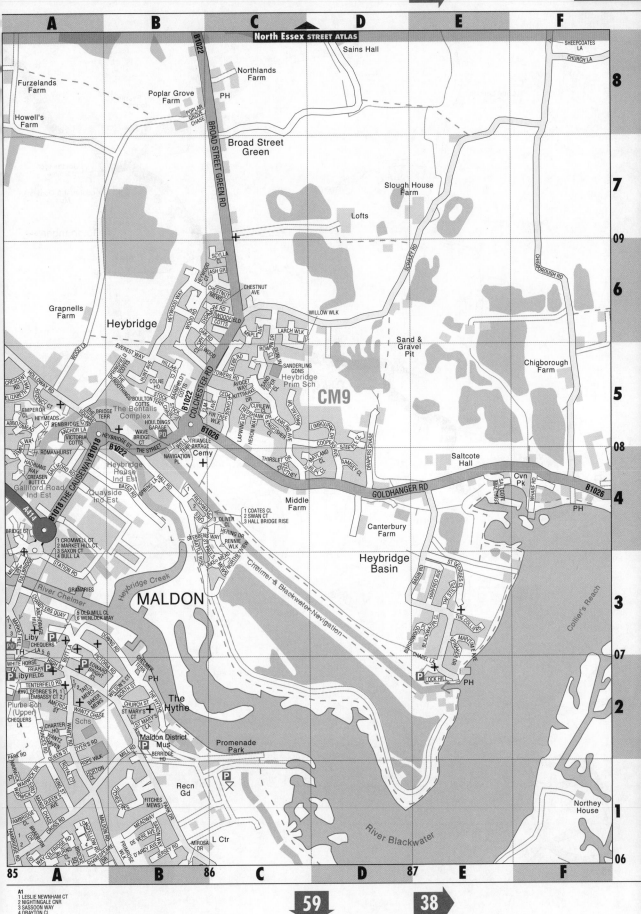

North Essex STREET ATLAS

A B C D E F

8
7
09
6
5
08
4
3
07
2
1
06

Furzelands Farm
Howell's Farm
Poplar Grove Farm
POPLAR GROVE CHASE
PH
Northlands Farm
Sains Hall
Broad Street Green
Slough House Farm
Lofts
BROAD STREET GREEN RD
B1022
SCRALEY RD
CHIGBOROUGH RD
SHEEPCOATES LA
CHURCH LA

Grapnells Farm
Heybridge
SCYLLA CL
ASH GR
CHESTNUT MEWS
CHESTNUT AVE
HEYWOOD WAY
WOODFIELD COTTS
WILLOW WLK
Sand & Gravel Pit
Chigborough Farm

Heybridge Prim Sch
CM9
Saltcote Hall
Cvn Pk
SALTCOTE MALTINGS
WHARF RD
B1026
PH

Everest Way
COLNE RD
TOWERS RD
GLEBE RD
Sanderling Gdns
COLCHESTER RD
B1022
B1026
The Bentalls Complex
HOULDINGS GARAGE
PO
WAVE BRIDGE CT
Cemy
NAVIGATION PL
Heybridge House Ind Est
Quayside Ind Est
B1022
B1018 THE CAUSEWAY
Galliford Road Ind Est
A414
1 CROMWELL CT
2 MARKET HILL CT
3 SAXON CT
4 BULL LA
STATION RD
GRANARIES
River Chelmer
Heybridge Creek
MALDON
1 COATES CL
2 SWAN CT
3 HALL BRIDGE RISE
OLIVER CL
HERING DR
RENNIE WLK
NORTHEY VIEW
Chelmer & Blackwater Navigation
Middle Farm
Canterbury Farm
GOLDHANGER RD
Heybridge Basin
Colliers Reach
St GEORGES CL
THE STILES
MARITIME AVE
HARTFIELD AVE
BASIN RD
BURNSWOOD PL
BLACKWATER CL
CHAPEL LA
THE COLLIERS
P
LOCK HILL
PH

1 OLD MILL CL
6 WENLOCK WAY
CHANDLERS QUAY
ANCHORAGE HILL
Liby
P
CHEQUERS
TH
PO
WHITE HORSE LA
P Liby FIELDS
FRIARY ST
TENTERFIELD RD
EDWARD BRIGHT CL
PH
DOWNS RD
VICTORIA RD
WILSON'S CT
NORTH ST
BAKER MEWS
KING GEORGE'S PL 1
EMBASSY CT 2
AMERICA ST
CHURCH ST
St MARY'S CT
St MARY'S
The Hythe
Plume Sch (Upper)
CHEQUERS LA
CHARTER HO
PRINCES RD
DYER'S RD
Maldon District Mus
BERRIDGE HO
Promenade Park
PARK RD
WARWICK DR
WARWICK CL
QUEEN'S AVE
MANSE CHASE
KING'S AVE
FAMBRIDGE RD
BROADGREEN
CROSS RD
LANGFORD RD
BURNS RD
BROOKE RD
OLDERIDGE RD
FAMBRIDGE CL
MALDON RD
CHESTER CRES
MEADOW
DE VERE AVE
SAXON WAY
PRIMROSE WLK
MIROSA DR
SHAKESPEARE
D'ARCY AVE
JERSEY RD
L Ctr
Recn Gd
FITCHES MEWS
River Blackwater
Northey House

A1
1 LESLIE NEWNHAM CT
2 NIGHTINGALE CNR
3 SASSOON WAY
4 DRAYTON CL

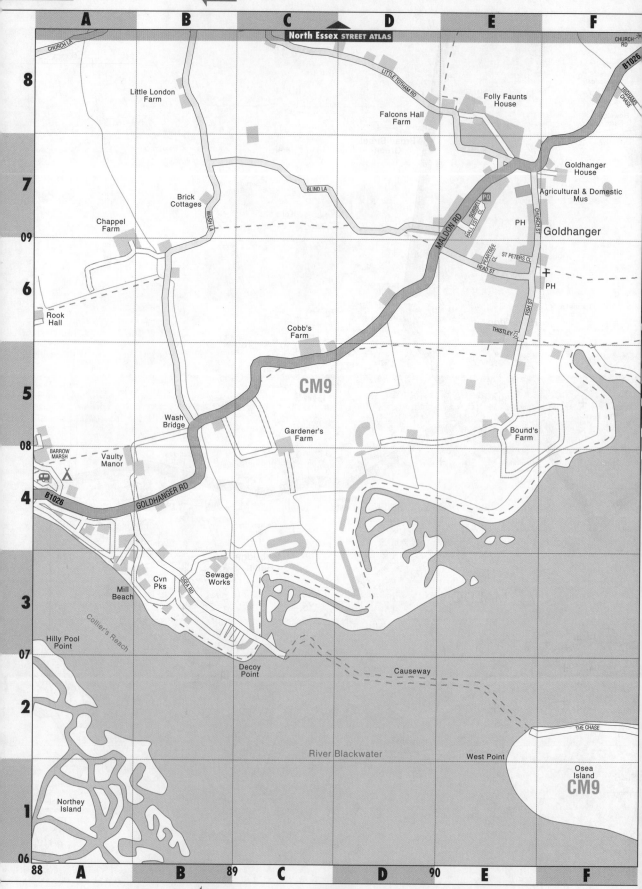

North Essex STREET ATLAS

CHURCH LA

Little London
Farm

LITTLE TOTHAM RD

Falcons Hall
Farm

Folly Faunts
House

CHURCH
RD

B1026

HIGHAMS CHASE

Goldhanger
House

Brick
Cottages

BLIND LA

Agricultural & Domestic
Mus

Chappel
Farm

WASH LA

MALDON RD

HALL EST
SORREL CL

PO

PH

CHURCH ST

Goldhanger

PEARTREE CL

ST PETERS CL

HEAD ST

+

FISH ST

PH

Rook
Hall

THISTLEY CL

Cobb's
Farm

CM9

Wash
Bridge

Gardener's
Farm

Bound's
Farm

BARROW
MARSH

Vaulty
Manor

B1026

GOLDHANGER RD

OSEA RD

Mill
Beach

Cvn
Pks

Sewage
Works

Collier's Reach

Hilly Pool
Point

Decoy
Point

Causeway

THE CHASE

Northey
Island

River Blackwater

West Point

Osea
Island
CM9

North Essex STREET ATLAS

B1026

MALDON RD

A   B   C   D   E   F

8

New
Barn

HIGHAMS CHASE

JOYCE'S CHASE

Lower
Grove

PARdS LA

Wycke
Farm

Highams
Farm

Longwick
Farm

7

Bowstead Brook

09

JOYCE'S CHASE

Lauriston
Farm

6

Joyce's
Farm

LAURISTON
BGLWS

Gore
Saltings

CM9

5

08

4

River Blackwater

3

07

2

Osea
Island

Works

East
Point

1

Osea
Farm

THE CHASE

Wr
Twr

06

North Essex STREET ATLAS

North Essex STREET ATLAS

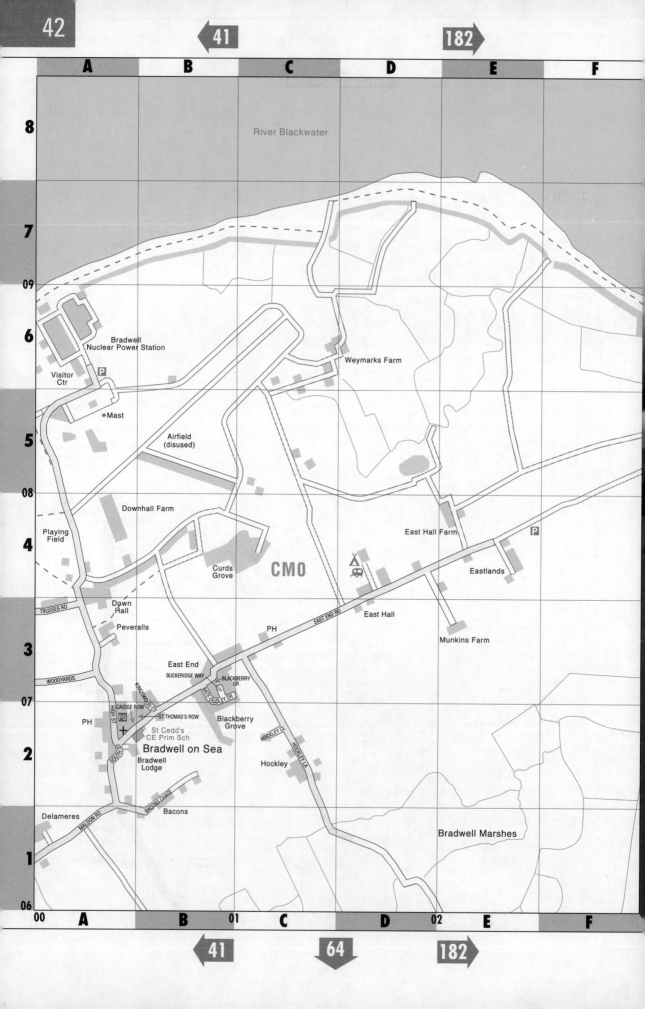

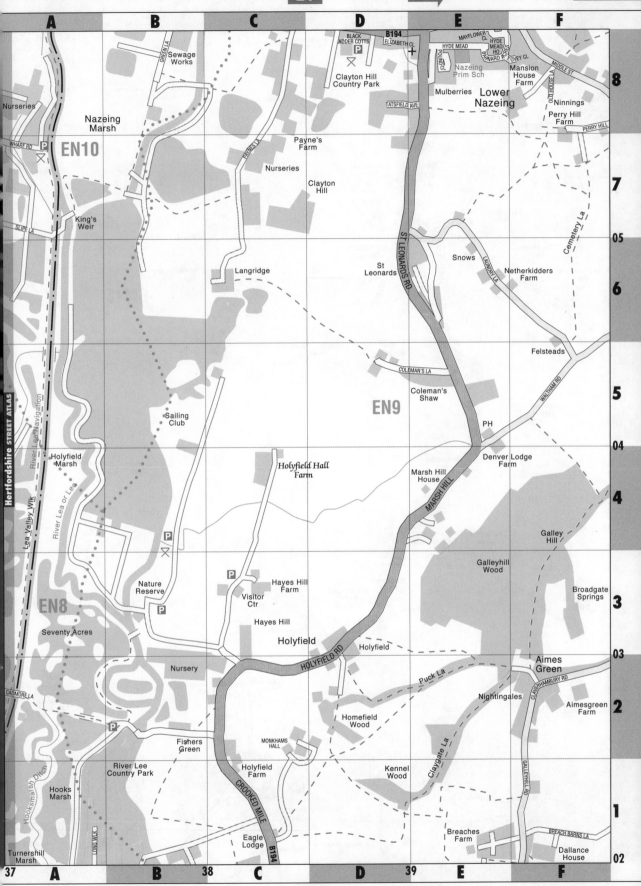

8
7
05
6
5
04
4
3
03
2
1
02

A   B   C   D   E   F

EN10
EN9
EN8

Hertfordshire STREET ATLAS

Nurseries
Nazeing Marsh
Wharf Rd
Slipe La
King's Weir
Green La
Sewage Works
Paynes La
Nurseries
Payne's Farm
Clayton Hill
Langridge
Sailing Club
Holyfield Marsh
River Lea or Lee
Lea Valley Wlk
River Lea Navigation
Nature Reserve
Seventy Acres
Hooksmarsh Ditch
Cadmore La
Long Wlk
Hooks Marsh
River Lee Country Park
Turnershill Marsh
Fishers Green
Nursery
Hayes Hill Farm
Visitor Ctr
Hayes Hill
Holyfield
Monkhams Hall
Holyfield Farm
Eagle Lodge
Crooked Mile
B194
Holyfield Rd
Holyfield Hall Farm
Homefield Wood
Kennel Wood
Marsh Hill House
Marsh Hill
Black Adder Cotts
Elizabeth Cl
B194
Clayton Hill Country Park
Tatsfield Ave
St Leonards Rd
St Leonards
Coleman's La
Coleman's Shaw
EN9
PH
Denver Lodge Farm
Holyfield
Puck La
Claygate La
Nightingales
Breaches Farm
Mayflower Cl
Hyde Mead
Hyde Mead Ho
Pound Cl
Byward Rd
Ovey Cl
Middle St
Oldhouse La
Nazeing Prim Sch
Mulberries
Lower Nazeing
Mansion House Farm
Ninnings
Perry Hill Farm
Perry Hill
Cemetery La
Snows
Netherkidders Farm
Felsteads
Waltham Rd
Laundry La
Galley Hill
Galleyhill Wood
Broadgate Springs
Aimes Green
Clenchambury Rd
Aimesgreen Farm
Galleyhill Rd
Breach Barns La
Dallance House

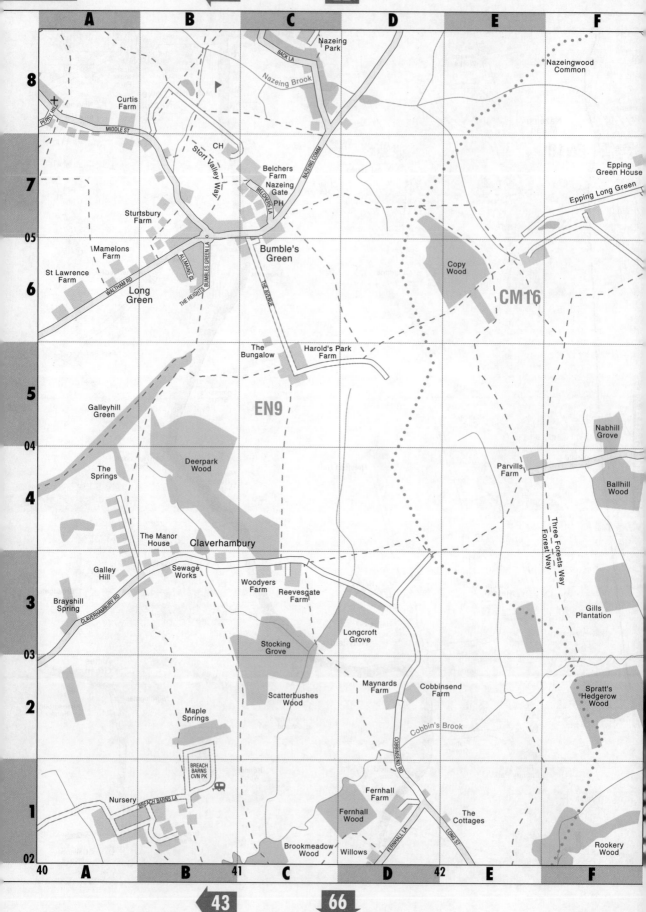

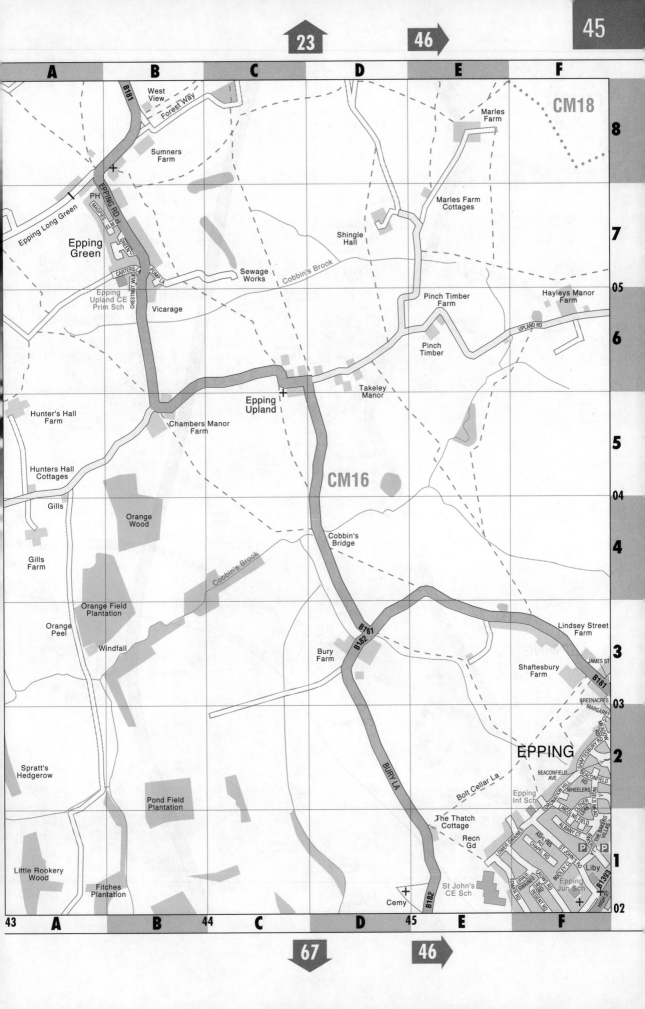

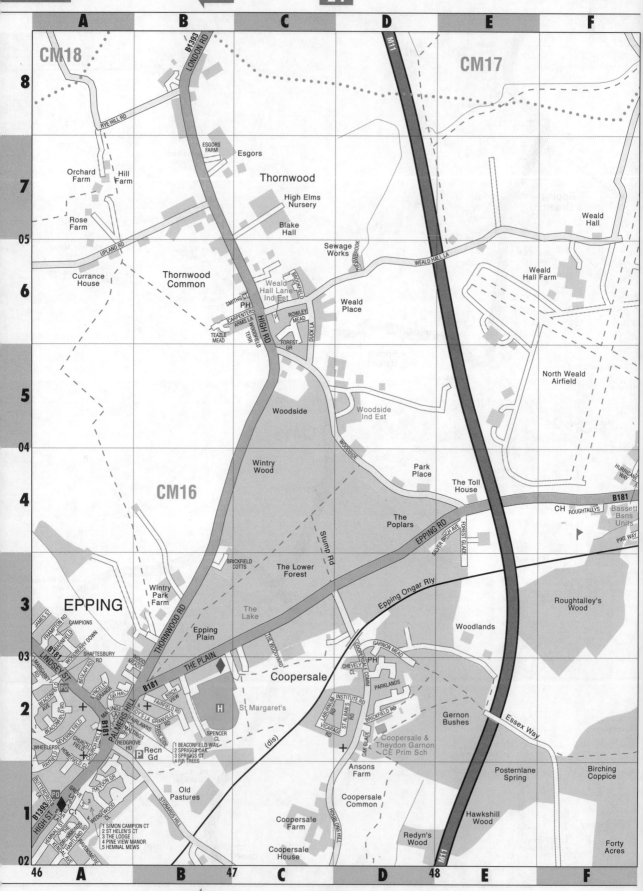

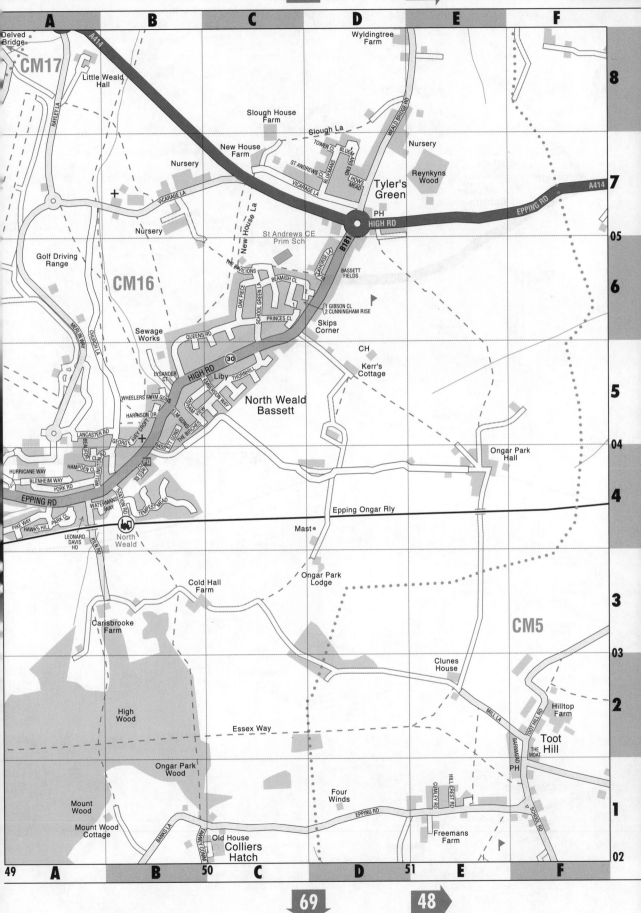

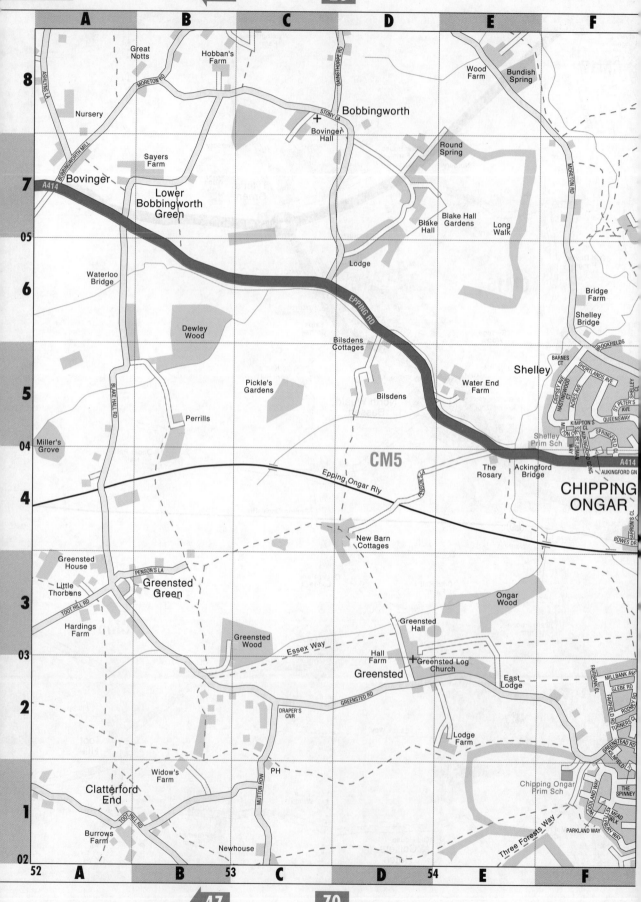

	A	B	C	D	E	F

8

Great Notts

Hobban's Farm

Wood Farm

Bundish Spring

Nursery

STONY LA

Bobbingworth

Bovinger Hall

Round Spring

7

Bovinger

A414

Sayers Farm

Lower Bobbingworth Green

BOBBINGWORTH MILL LA

MORETON RD

GAINSTHORPE RD

Blake Hall

Blake Hall Gardens

Long Walk

MORETON RD

05

6

Waterloo Bridge

Lodge

EPPING RD

Bridge Farm

Shelley Bridge

Dewley Wood

BLAKE HALL RD

Bilsdens Cottages

BROOKFIELDS

Shelley

BARNES CT

SHORTLANDS AVE

5

Pickle's Gardens

Bilsdens

Water End Farm

COPPSEL AVE

HASTINGWOOD CT

ACRES AVE

QUEENSWAY

ST PETER'S AVE

SHELLEY CL

Perrills

04

Miller's Grove

Shelley Prim Sch

SPRINGFIELD

AUKINGFORD GDNS

BETJEMAN WAY

KIMPTON'S CL

CM5

The Rosary

Ackingford Bridge

A414

AUKINGFORD GN

4

Epping Ongar Rly

CHIPPING ONGAR

BARROWS CL

BOWES DR

New Barn Cottages

Greensted House

Ongar Wood

FAIRBANK CL

MILLBANK AVE

GLEBE AVE

3

Little Thorbens

PENSON'S LA

Greensted Green

Greensted Hall

Greensted Log Church

FAIRBANK CL

FAIRFIELD CL

ROOSEY RD

TOOT HILL RD

Hardings Farm

Greensted Wood

Essex Way

Hall Farm

East Lodge

TURNERS CL

GREENSTEAD RD

03

Greensted

KILIMRO

2

DRAPER'S CNR

GREENSTED RD

Lodge Farm

GREENSTEAD RD

SPINNEY

Widow's Farm

PH

Chipping Ongar Prim Sch

THE SPINNEY

MUTTON ROW

1

Clatterford End

MOON HALL WAY

MEAD WALK

KETLEBURY WAY

TOOT HILL RD

Three Forests Way

PARKLAND WAY

Burrows Farm

Newhouse

Parkland Way

02

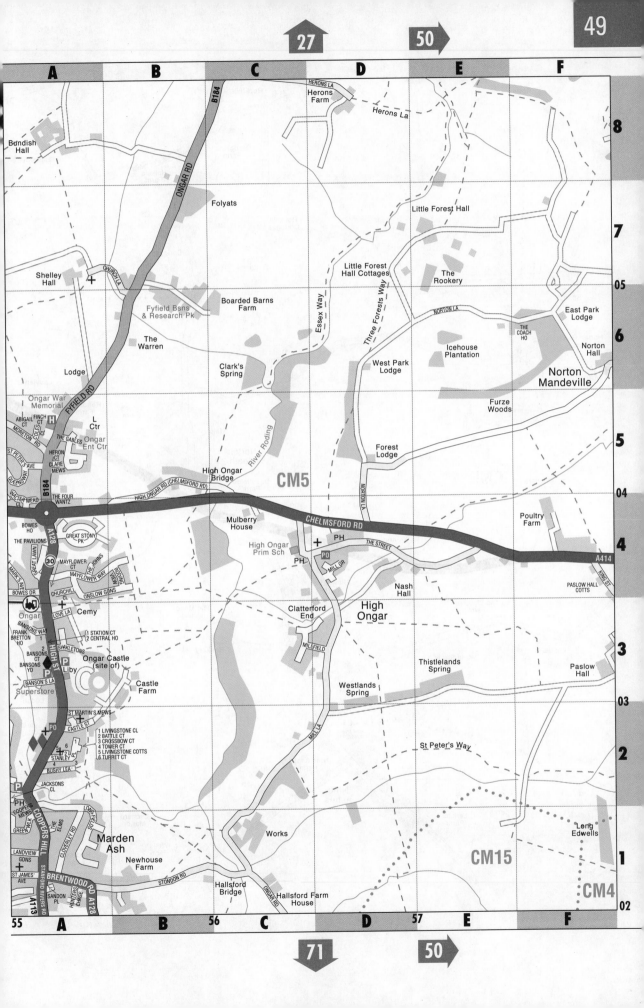

A B C D E F

8

Hedge Rows

Rockhills

Hodgkins Farm

NORTON HEATH RD

Hulke's Farm

Bonsgrove

7

Rockhill Cottages

Spriggs

05

Long Spring

Offin's Cottages

WILLINGALE RD

6

Norton Glebe House

NORTON LA

Dodd's Farm

Ladylands

+ Norton Mandeville

Norton Manor

Tyler's Farm

Readings Farm

A414

5

Norton Heath

PH

CM5

Chevers Hall

Dovefields Farm

FINGRITH HALL LA

CM4

04

Spurriers

The Orchard

4

A414

Cozen's Farm

CHELMSFORD RD

A414

Blewgates Farm

Old Wythers Farm

The Manor House

3

KING ST

ROOKERY RD

Lodge

King Street Farm

Rookery Farm

FINGRITH HALL COTTS

FINGRITH HALL LA

SPRIGGS LA

Saybridge Lodge

03

PH

Saybridge Cottage

2

NINE ASHES FARM COTTS

Nine Ashes Farm

Nine Ashes

Orchard Manor

1

Sparks Farm

Larkins Farm

NINE ASHES RD

NINE ASHES RD

Wells Farm

Redrose Farm

St Peter's Way

REDROSE LA

ELM COURT PK

02

Blackmore Prim Sch

WOOLARD WAY

WOOLARD WAY

FINGRITH RD

ORCHARD PIECE

CHELMSFORD RD

58 A 59 B C 60 D E F

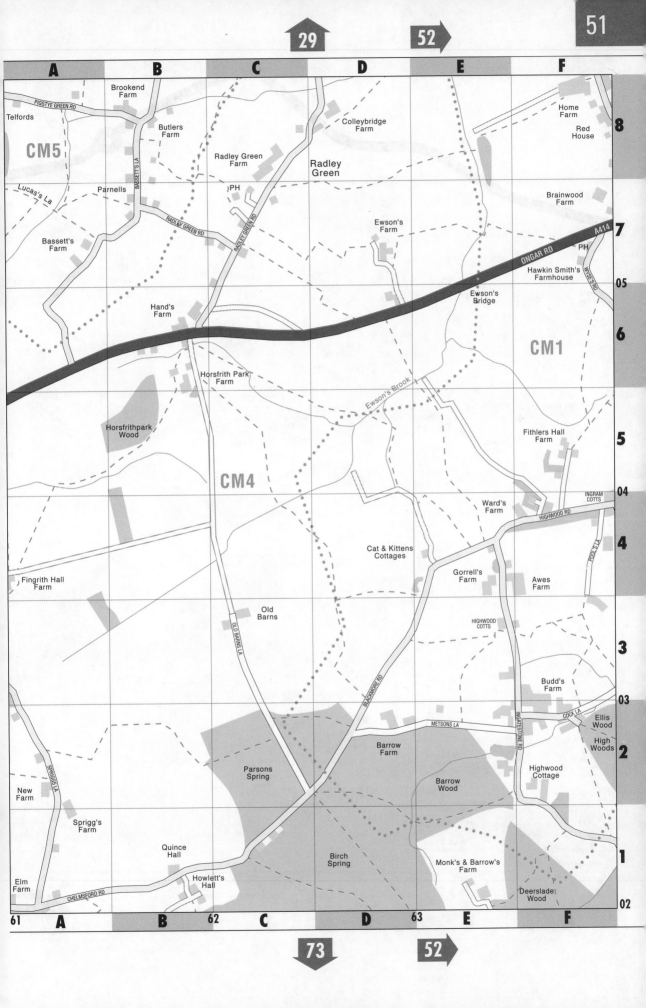

A **B** **C** **D** **E** **F**

Wellington House

Cooksmill Nursery

8

Landview House

Four Gables

7

A414

05

Wyse's Cottage

Wyse's Rd

6

Montague Farm

Sparrows Cl

Loves Green

5

PH

Highwood Prim Sch

Bucknells Mead

Highwood

04

4

Writtle Park Cotts

Writtle Park Farm

Writtle Park

Chalk Hill

Cock La

3

03

High Woods

2

Parkponds Wood

Redindyke Farm

CM4

1

Whitegates

Ingatestone Rd

02

Wells & Sheds

Dawes Farm

Little Moor Hall

ONGAR RD

Lady Grove

Range Cottage

A414

A414

ONGAR RD

Little Oxney Green

BULMERS WAY

CHEQUERS RD

OXNEY MEAD

LODGE RD

ROLLESTONS

THE SHRUBBERIES

HIGHWOOD RD

CAUSEWAY COTTS

Halfway House

Roper's Farm

A414

Lee Cottages

THE CAUSEWAY

Montpelier's Farm

Bramwood Farm

Southridge Farm

Nursery

HIGHWOOD RD

Lee Wood

Lee Farm

Edney Common

WOODSIDE COTTS

Sewage Works

Jordan's Farm

CM1

NATHAN'S LA

ENDEY WOOD

Little Edney Wood

Great Edney Wood

Mast

Baker's Wood

King Wood

Writtlepark Wood

Coptfold Hall

WHITTLE RD

Furness Wood

Coptfoldhall Farm

Park Lodge

Hockley Shaw

Coptfold Farm Cottages

Furness Farm

Chatterbox Wood

Bearman's Farm

IVY BARNS LA

Handley Green Farm

Furze Hill

Hotel

A12

MAIN RD

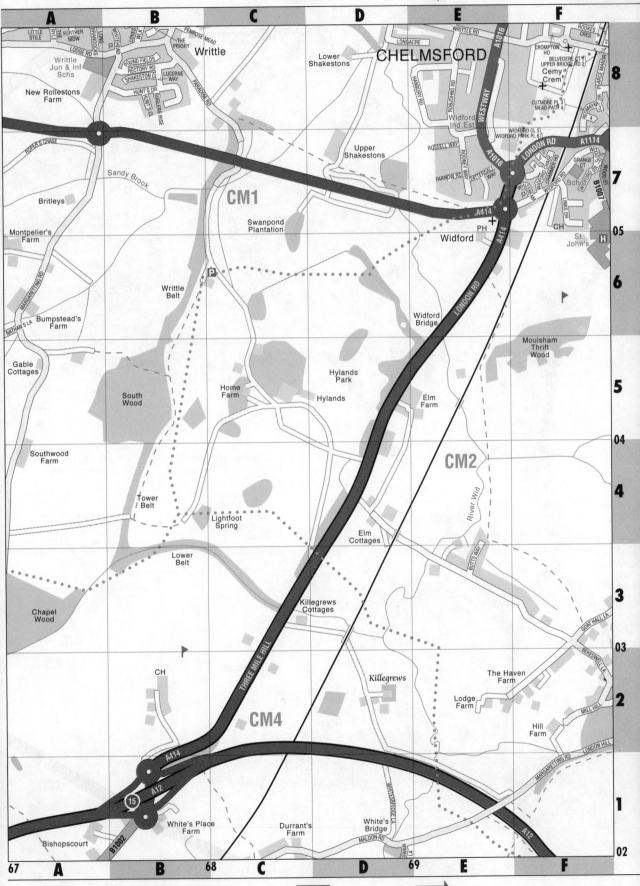

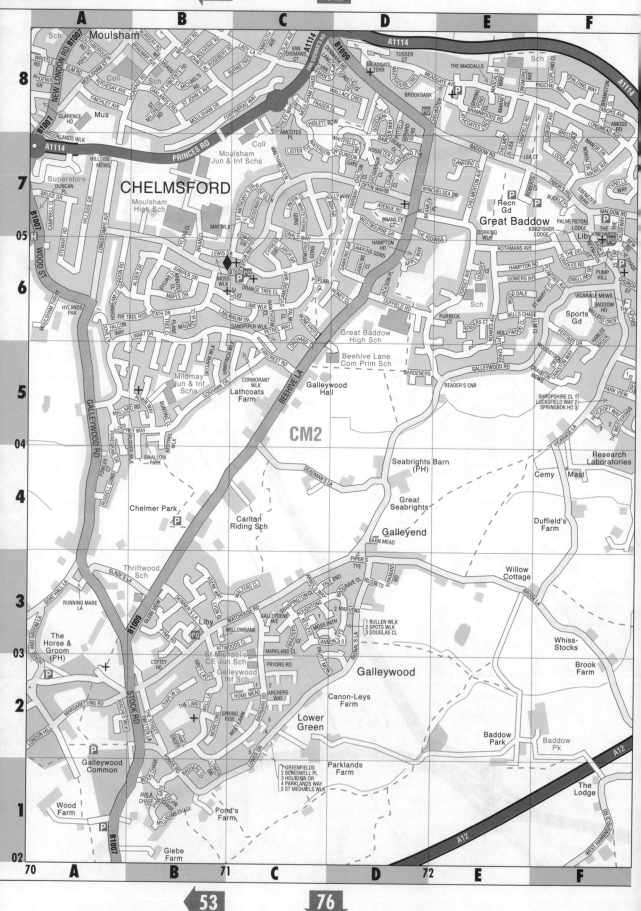

33
56

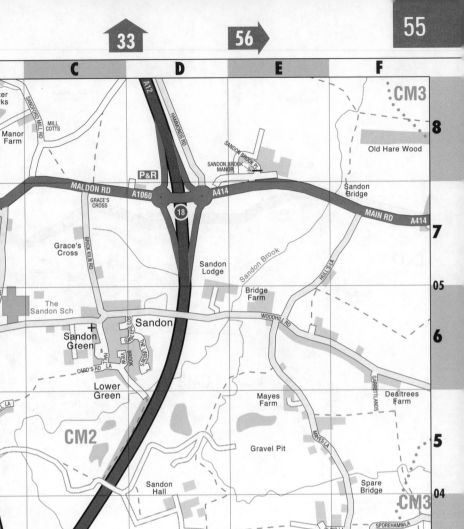

A B C D E F

CM3

8

Water Works

MILL COTTS

Manor Farm

Old Hare Wood

Sandon Brook Pl

Sandon Brook Manor

SANDFORD MILL RD

BADDOW HALL AVE

A1060

P&R

MALDON RD   A1060

GRACE'S CROSS

18

Sandon Bridge

MAIN RD   A414

A414

7

05

BIFFANS

LYSTER AVE
LONGMEAD AVE
MALDON

JEFFERY RD

CRESCENT RD

BARCLAY RD

NEW RD

HALL

BADDOW

HEREFORD CT

HALE RD

BALFN POWELL CL

PAWLE CL

BADDOW HALL CRES

STUART CL

LEACH CL

MARION WAY

NEWPORT CL

GILMORE WAY

ISAAC CS

BARRINGTON CL

HOLLYCROFT

MOLRAMS LA

Grace's Cross

BRICK KILN RD

Sandon Lodge

Sandon Brook

Bridge Farm

WOODHILL RD

HULL SCA

The Sandon Sch

Sandon

Sandon Green

GREBES

GREBES

BROOK

THE LION'S

CARD'S RD

HALL LA

VIEW

6

JACKSONS CT

SEABROOK PLACE AVE

THE BRINGEY

CHURCH'S RD

SMITHERS CL

JOHNSON RD

Baddow Hall Jun & Inf Schs

Lower Green

CM2

Mayes Farm

GARRETTLANDS

Dealtrees Farm

5

WORCESTER CT
MERCIA CL
EASTWOOD

SYDNEY

PK

MALTINGS RD

Brewery Fields

LADYWELL LA

Gravel Pit

MAYES LA

04

Hotel

Pontlands Farm

The Grove

Sandon Hall

Spare Bridge

CM3

BLIND LA

SPOREHAMS LA

Hillview

4

SOUTHEND RD

A1114

WEST HANNINGFIELD RD

17

SANDON HALL BRIDLEWAY

BUTT'S GREEN RD

Gingerbreadhall Bridge

White Lodge Farm

Butt's Green

3

A130

ST SWITHINS COTTS

Howe Farm

Howe Green

CHALKLANDS

ALEXANDER MEWS

EAST HANNINGFIELD RD

03

Great Mascalls

Sandon Brook

THE TYCHINGS

OLD ORCHARD

THE OLD ORCHARD

SOUTHLANDS CHASE

2

BROOK LA

LITTLE AND GREAT SIR HUGHES LA

Little Sir Hughes

Three Oaks

OLD SOUTHEND RD

Southlands Farm

Grove Farm

Little Mascalls

1

Great Sir Hughes

A130

Rowlands

CM3

02

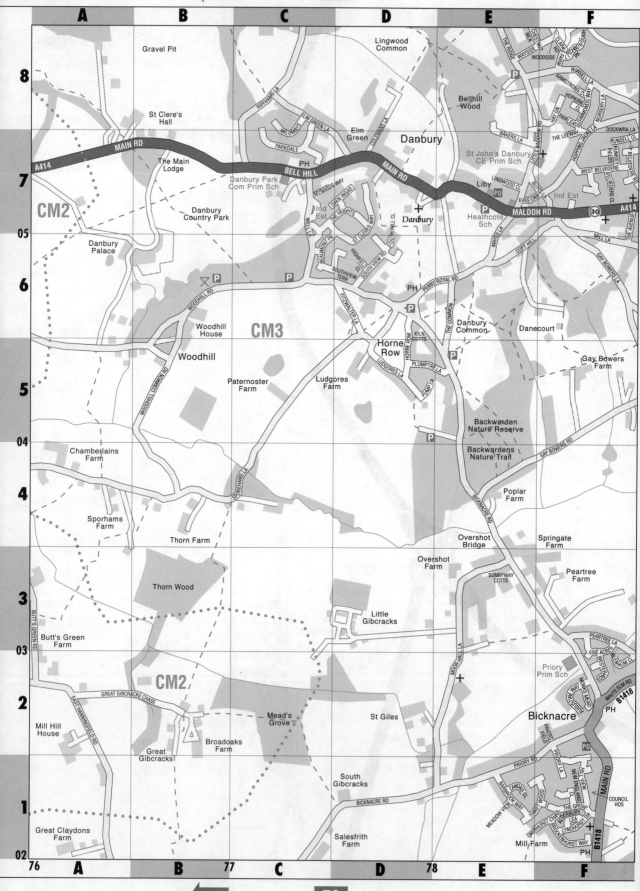

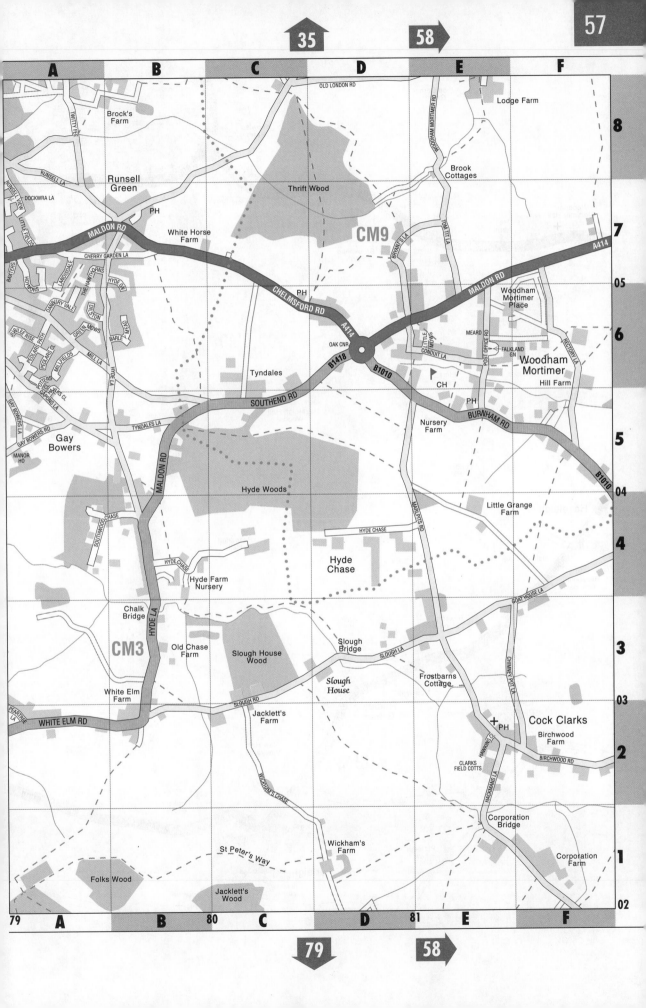

A B C D E F

8

7

05

6

5

04

4

3

03

2

1

02

TWITTY FEE
Brock's Farm
Runsell Green
RUNSELL LA
DOCKWRA LA
RUNSELL VIEW
LITTLE FIELDS
MALDON RD
PH
White Horse Farm
CHERRY GARDEN LA
BAXTERS
HONORS
LANSDODALE
THE HAWTHORNS
HYDE GN
DITTON
DANBURY VALE
GREEN MEWS
BARLE
M MEAD
JUBILEE RISE
PEDLARS PATH
PEDLARS CL
MILLFIELDS
FOLKS CL
DUPONS CL
MILL LA
HYDE LA
Gay Bowers
GAY BOWERS LA
GAY BOWERS RD
MANOR HO
TYNDALES LA
Tyndales
SOUTHEND RD
CHELMSFORD RD
A414
OAK CNR
B1418
B1010
OLD LONDON RD
Thrift Wood
CM9
WOODHAM MORTIMER RD
Lodge Farm
Brook Cottages
TOM TIT LA
A414
BRYANT'S LA
MALDON RD
Woodham Mortimer Place
MEARD
POST OFFICE RD
FALKLAND GN
RECTORY LA
Woodham Mortimer
Hill Farm
LITTLE MEWS
CONDUIT LA
CH
PH
Nursery Farm
BURNHAM RD
B1010
Little Grange Farm
Hyde Woods
HYDE CHASE
MARLPITS RD
Hyde Chase
GOAT HOUSE LA
SOUTHWOOD CHASE
MALDON RD
HYDE LA
Chalk Bridge
HYDE CHASE
Hyde Farm Nursery
CM3
Old Chase Farm
Slough House Wood
Slough Bridge
Slough House
SLOUGH LA
Frostbarns Cottage
CHIMNEY POT LA
+ PH
Cock Clarks
Birchwood Farm
White Elm Farm
SLOUGH RD
Jacklett's Farm
CLARKS FIELD COTTS
HAWKINS CL
BIRCHWOOD RD
PEARTREE LA
WHITE ELM RD
WICKHAM'S CHASE
St Peter's Way
Wickham's Farm
HACKMANS LA
Corporation Bridge
Corporation Farm
Folks Wood
Jacklett's Wood

79 A B 80 C D 81 E F

A B C D E F

8

Wood Corner Grove

Knowles Farm

West Station Ind Est
Wycke Hill Bsns Pk
Superstore
WEST STATION YD

1 Lindisfarne Ct
2 Bergen Ct

VOLWYCKE AVE

LAMBOURNE GR

WYCKE HILL A414
B1018
SPITAL RD

LIMEBROOK WAY

Woodham Mortimer Hall

Hall Farm

Riding Sch

Limebrook Farm

Lime Brook

MALDON

7

A414
MALDON RD

Brookhead Farm

GLOUCESTER AVE 1
COURTLAND PL 2
COURTLAND MEWS 3
NORDIC LODGE 4
ODIN LODGE 5
CONYER CL 6
RANDOLPH CL 7.

FAMBRIDGE RD

05

6

Parsonage Wood

Woodham Mortimer Brook

CM9

BURY FARM COTTS

PH

B1018

Elms Farm

Lodge

Hazeleigh Hall Wood

5

LODGE RD

Loddart's Hill

HAZELEIGH HALL LA

Bury Farm

04

B1010

Hazeleigh

Lodge Farm

Cemy

Hazeleigh Hall

4

GOAT HOUSE LA

BURNHAM RD

Hatch House Farm

Hazeleigh Grange

Boxiron Wood

Spar Hill

3

CHELMSFORD RD

SPAR LA

PH

03

Kent Wood

Mosklyns

Rudley Green

New Hall Vineyards

2

BIRCHWOOD RD

Scotts Farm

CM3

LODGE LA

Sewage Works

Rookery Grove

B1010

BARON'S LA

1

St Peter's Way

Purleigh Com Prim Sch

WALTON HALL LA

Purleigh Law

HAWTHORNES

TUMP LA

WESTERINGS

PO

02

MILL HILL

MILL LA

Purleigh

THORNHILL
CALLOWOOD CROFT

THE GLEBE

FAIRFIELDS

PH

CHURCH HILL

THE STREET

82 A 83 B C 83 D 84 E F

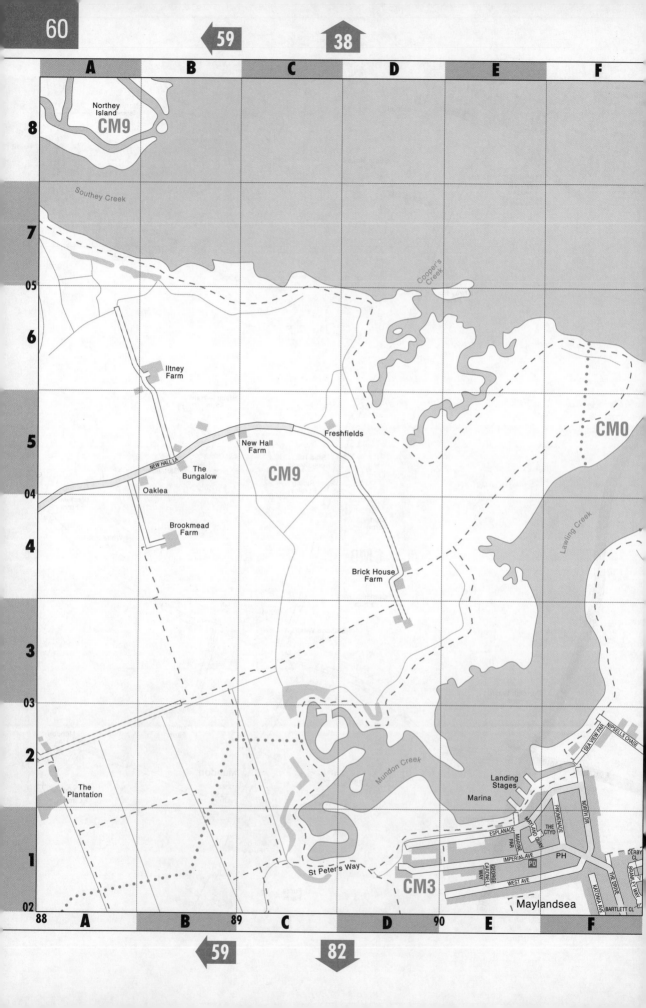

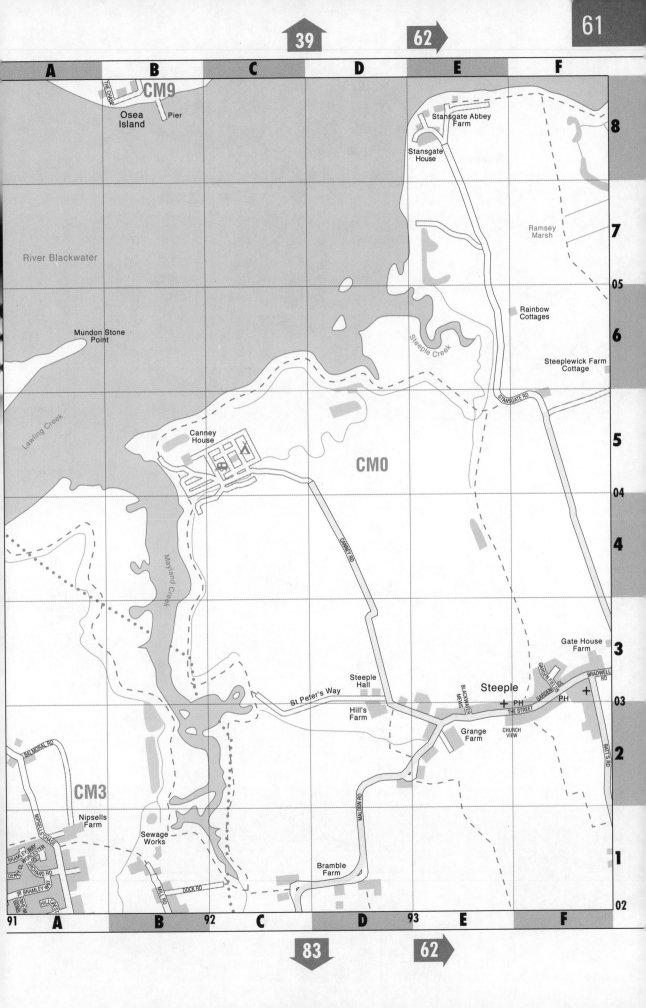

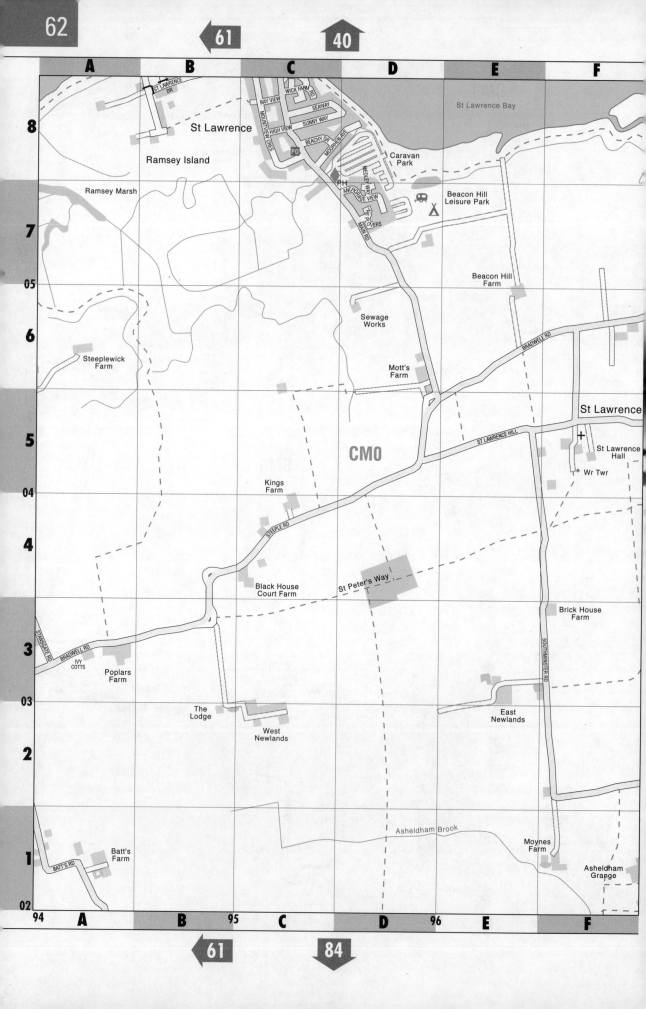

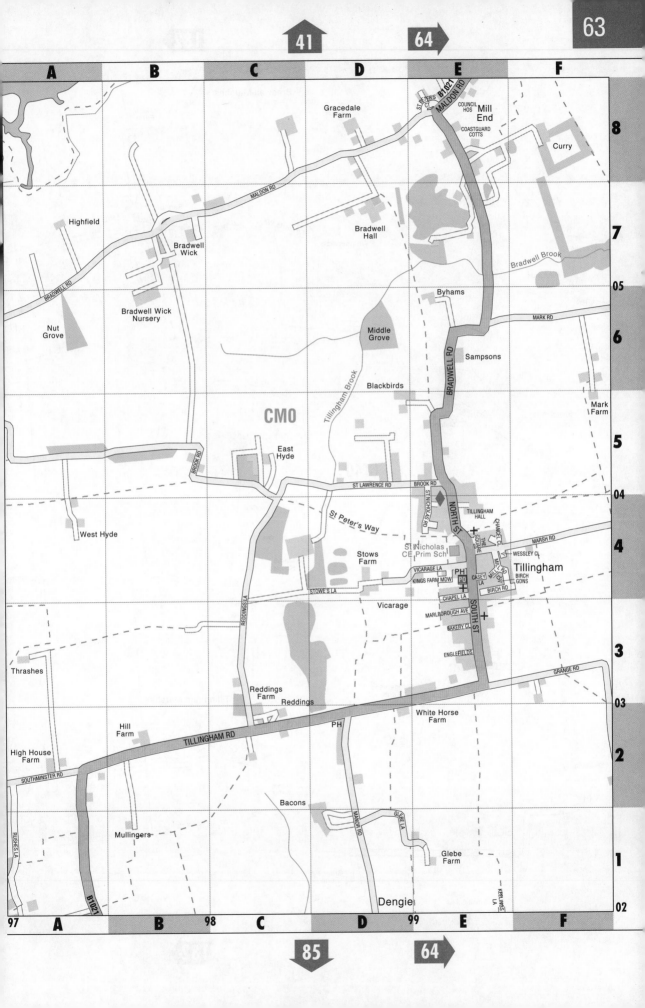

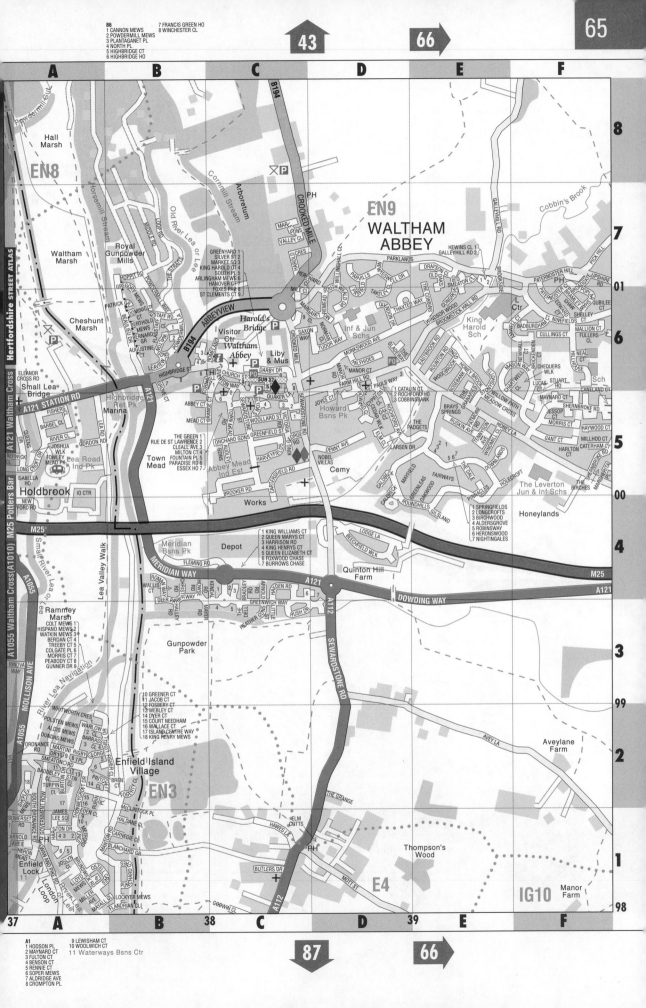

B6
1 CANNON MEWS
2 POWDERMILL MEWS
3 PLANTAGANET PL
4 NORTH PL
5 HIGHBRIDGE CT
6 HIGHBRIDGE HO

7 FRANCIS GREEN HO
8 WINCHESTER CL

EN8

Hall Marsh

Waltham Marsh

Royal Gunpowder Mills

Cheshunt Marsh

Small Lea Bridge

Marina

Holdbrook

EN9

WALTHAM ABBEY

Cobbin's Brook

King Harold Sch

Harold's Bridge
Visitor Ctr Waltham Abbey
Liby & Mus

GREENYARD 1
SILVER ST 2
MARKET SQ 3
KING HAROLD CT 4
SOUTH PL 5
ARLINGHAM MEWS 6
HANOVER CT 7
FOXES PAR 8
ST CLEMENTS CT 9

Inf & Jun Schs

Howard Bsns Pk

Abbey Mead Ind Est

Cemy

THE GREEN 1
RUE DE ST LAWRENCE 2
CLEALL AVE 3
MILTON CT 4
FOUNTAIN PL 5
PARADISE RD 6
ESSEX HO 7

Town Mead

Works

1 CATALIN CT
2 ROCHFORD HO
3 COBBINSBANK

The Padgets

Brays Springs

The Leverton Jun & Inf Schs

The Birches

Honeylands

1 SPRINGFIELDS
2 LONGCROFTS
3 BIRCHWOOD
4 ALDERSGROVE
5 ROBINSWAY
6 HERONSWOOD
7 NIGHTINGALES

M25

Meridian Bsns Pk

Depot

1 KING WILLIAMS CT
2 QUEEN MARYS CT
3 HARRISON RD
4 KING HENRYS CT
5 QUEEN ELIZABETH CT
6 FOXWOOD CHASE
7 BURROWS CHASE

Quinton Hill Farm

Aveylane Farm

Rammey Marsh

COLT MEWS 1
HISPANO MEWS 2
WATKIN MEWS 3
BERDAN CT 4
TREEBY CT 5
COLGATE PL 6
MORRIS CT 7
PEABODY CT 8
GUNNER DR 9

Gunpowder Park

10 GREENER CT
11 JACOB CT
12 FOSBERY CT
13 WEBLEY CT
14 DYER CT
15 COURT NEEDHAM
16 WALLACE CT
17 ISLAND CENTRE WAY
18 KING HENRY MEWS

Enfield Island Village

EN3

The Grange

Thompson's Wood

Manor Farm

IG10

Enfield Lock

E4

A1
1 HODSON PL
2 MAYNARD CT
3 FULTON CT
4 BENSON CT
5 RENNIE CT
6 SOPER MEWS
7 ALDRIDGE AVE
8 CROMPTON PL

9 LEWISHAM CT
10 WOOLWICH CT
11 WATERWAYS BSNS CTR

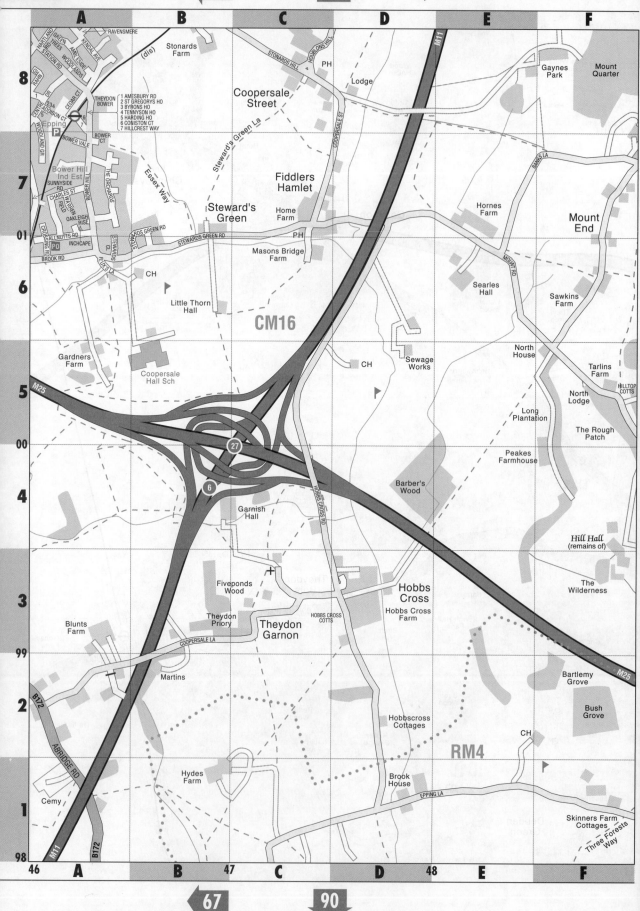

A B C D E F

8
7
01
6
5
00
4
3
99
2
1
98

Ravensmere

Stonards
Farm

(dis)

Coopersale
Street

STONARDS HILL

PH

Lodge

Gaynes
Park

Mount
Quarter

THEYDON
BOWER

1 AMESBURY RD
2 ST GREGORYS HO
3 BYRONS HO
4 TENNYSON HO
5 HARDING HO
6 CONISTON CT
7 HILLCREST WAY

BOWER
CT

Epping

BOWER VALE

Bower Hill
Ind Est

SUNNYSIDE
RD

THE ORCHARDS

CHARLES ST

OAKLEIGH
RISE

Essex Way

Fiddlers
Hamlet

BANKS LA

Hornes
Farm

Mount
End

Steward's
Green

Home
Farm

STEWARDS CL

ALLNUTTS RD

STEWARDS GREEN RD

STEWARDS GREEN RD

PH

Masons Bridge
Farm

MOUNT RD

Searles
Hall

Sawkins
Farm

BROOK RD

FULLER LA

CH

Little Thorn
Hall

CM16

CH

Sewage
Works

North
House

Tarlins
Farm

HILLTOP
COTTS

Gardners
Farm

Coopersale
Hall Sch

M25

27

6

CH

Barber's
Wood

North
Lodge

Long
Plantation

Peakes
Farmhouse

The Rough
Patch

Garnish
Hall

HOBBS CROSS RD

Hill Hall
(remains of)

The
Wilderness

Fiveponds
Wood

Theydon
Priory

Theydon
Garnon

Hobbs
Cross

HOBBS CROSS
COTTS

Hobbs Cross
Farm

M25

Blunts
Farm

COOPERSALE LA

Martins

Bartlemy
Grove

Bush
Grove

B172

ABRIDGE RD

Hydes
Farm

Hobbscross
Cottages

Brook
House

RM4

CH

Cemy

M11

B172

EPPING LA

Skinners Farm
Cottages

Three Forests
Way

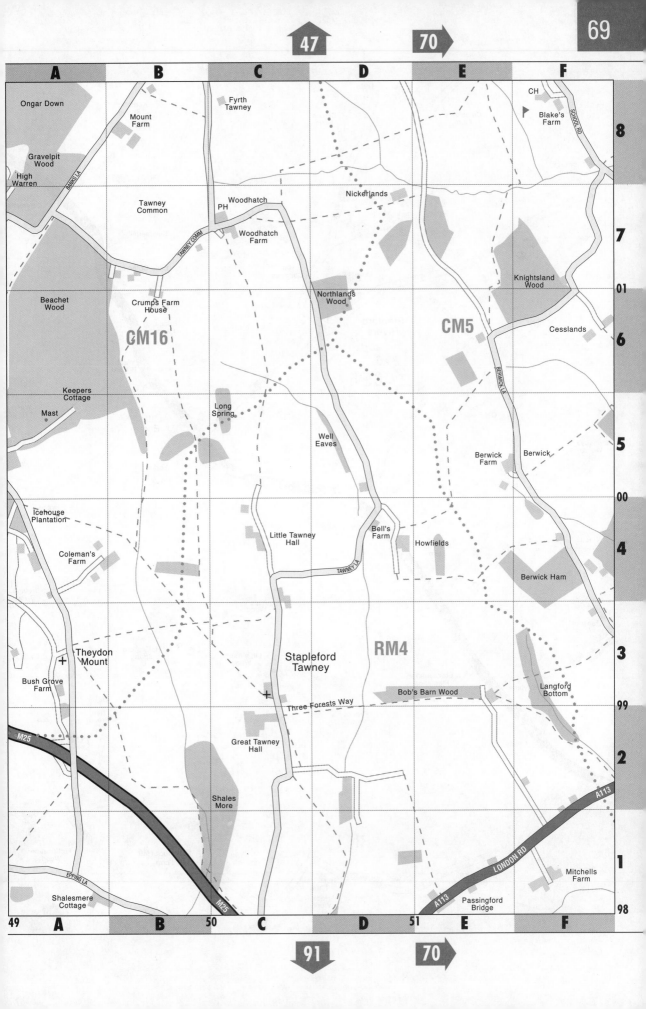

A B C D E F

8

Coleman's Farm

Clark's Farm

Kettlebury Spring

Stewart's Farm

A113

Great Colemans

7

HOP GDNS

SCHOOL RD

MUTTON ROW

Three Forests Way

Summerhill

ROMFORD RD

01

CHURCH COTTS

Hall Cottages

Little Colemans

THE HALL BARNS

Three Forests Way

Stanford Rivers

6

CM5

Bridge Farm

Wash Bridge

CHURCH RD

The Old Rectory

RECTORY RD

Little End

Park Wood

5

Icehouse Wood

GARDENS FIELDS

HARE ST

Works

00

Twentyacre Wood

LONDON RD

White Bear (PH)

Sewage Works

4

Murrells Farm

River Roding

Traceys Farm

Ireland Grove

Aspen Wood

3

Tenacre Wood

BERWICK LA

Little Aspen Wood

Hollingford Spring

Wayletts

Stoneyrocks Plantation

Red Wood

CM14

99

Broom Wood

Lawns

Lady's Pond

Church Wood

2

A113

RM4

Navestock Hall Farm

Fortification Wood

1

Shank's Mill Bridge

MILL LA

SHONKS MILL RD

Rose Hall Farm

Hook Wood

CHURCH RD

LADY'S HILL

PRINCE'S RD

DUDBROOK ROAD

98

52 A B 53 C D 54 E F

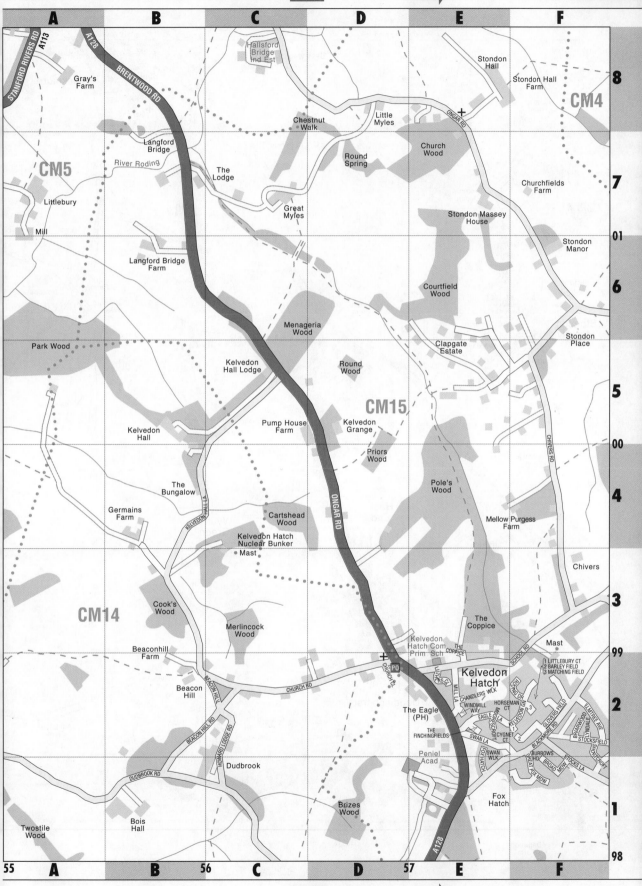

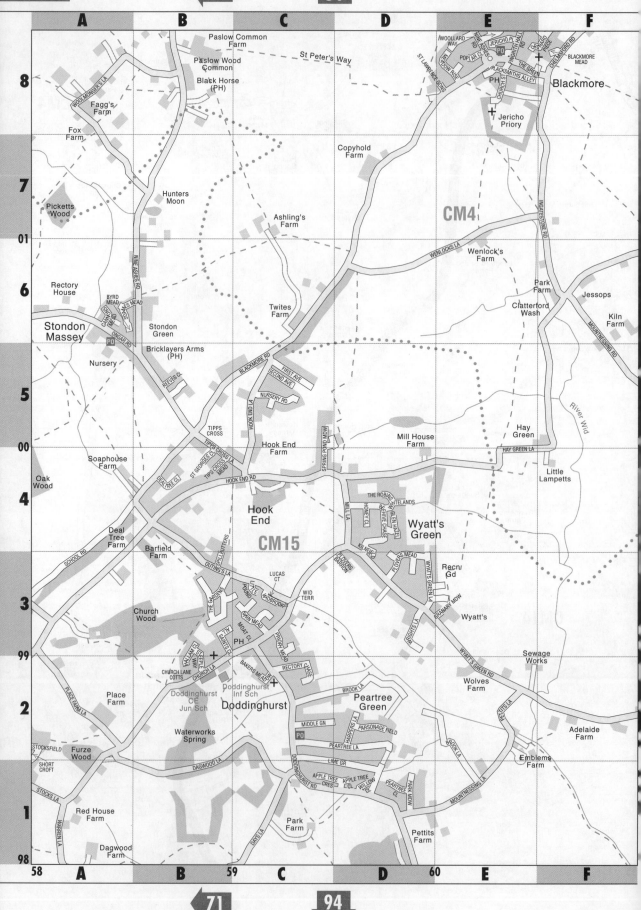

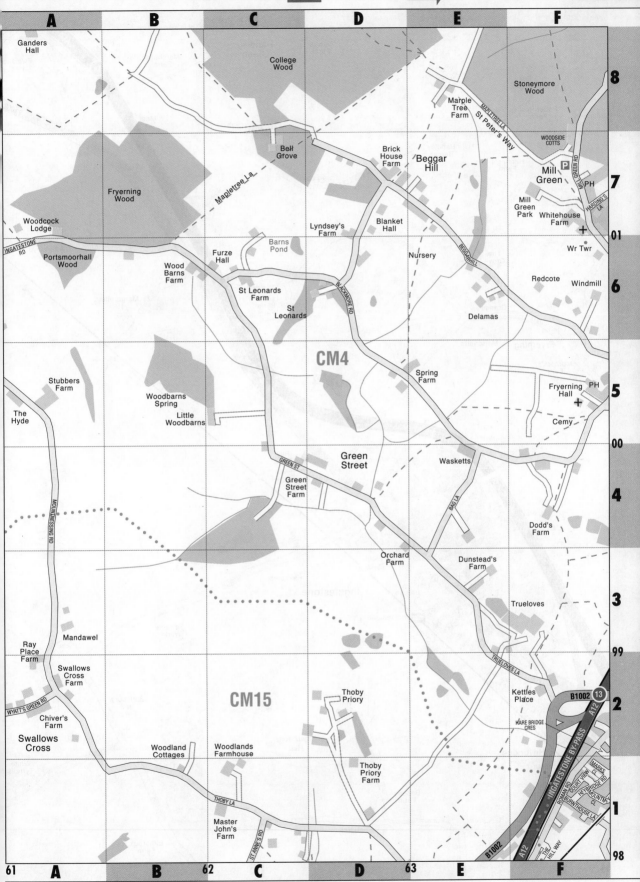

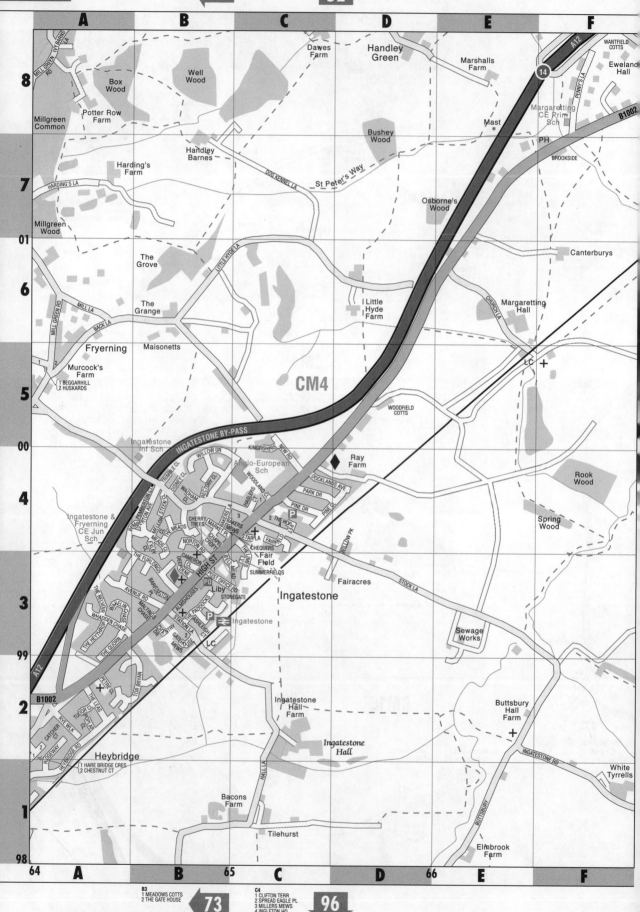

B3
1 MEADOWS COTTS
2 THE GATE HOUSE

73

C4
1 CLIFTON TERR
2 SPREAD EAGLE PL
3 MILLERS MEWS
4 INGLETON HO

96

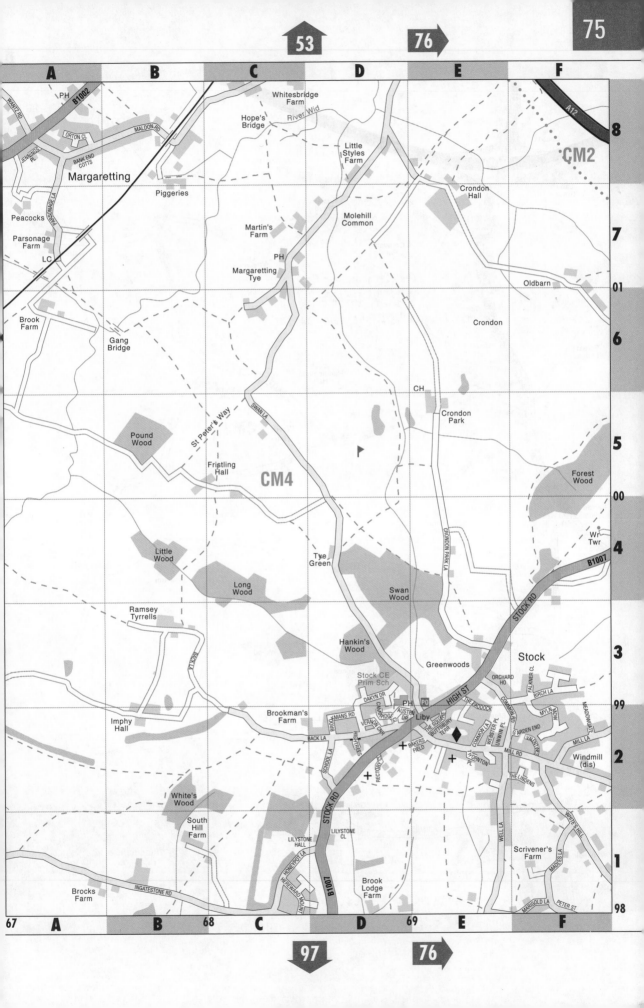

75
54

A B C D E F

A12

The Chase

A12

16

Lady Grove

Works

Gay Bowers Farm

Peveril Hall

Temple Grove

Tanfield Tye

8

BAKERS LA

Caravan Park

Little Peverels

TANFIELD TYE COTTS

WEST HANNINGFIELD RD

7

01

STOCK RD

Temple Wood

Temple Farm Trad Est

Forest Lodge

Temple Farm Ind Est

Temple Farm

6

Temple Wood

SHIP EST COTTS

West Hanningfield Hall

Mast

HALL LA

Elm's Farm

Motel

Clovile Hall

CM2

PH

Foxburrow Wood

SHIP RD

WANTZ CNR

BLIND LA

5

FOXBOROUGH CHASE

Daylands Farm

00

Farrow's Farm

Foxborough Farm

KENT'S FARM LA

Kent's Farm

Hicks Farm

St Peters CE Prim Sch

B1007

HOLIDAY HILL

CROWSFIELD COTTS

CHURCH RD

MIDDLE MEAD

4

DOWNHAM RD

LOWER STOCK RD

Slough House Farm

PH

MIDDLE MEAD

Keelings

Holes Place Farm

St Peter's Way

Blythhedges Spring Wood

3

Blythhedges Wood

99

MILL LA

Steel's Farm

CM4

SEAMANS LA

2

LEATHERBOTTLE HILL

App's Farm

MILL RD

DOWNHAM RD

Great Prestons

Outlet Twr

CM3

Albards

Whiteholme

Hanningfield Reservoir

CM11

1

RUB LA

WHITE'S HILL

98

70 A B 71 C D 72 E F

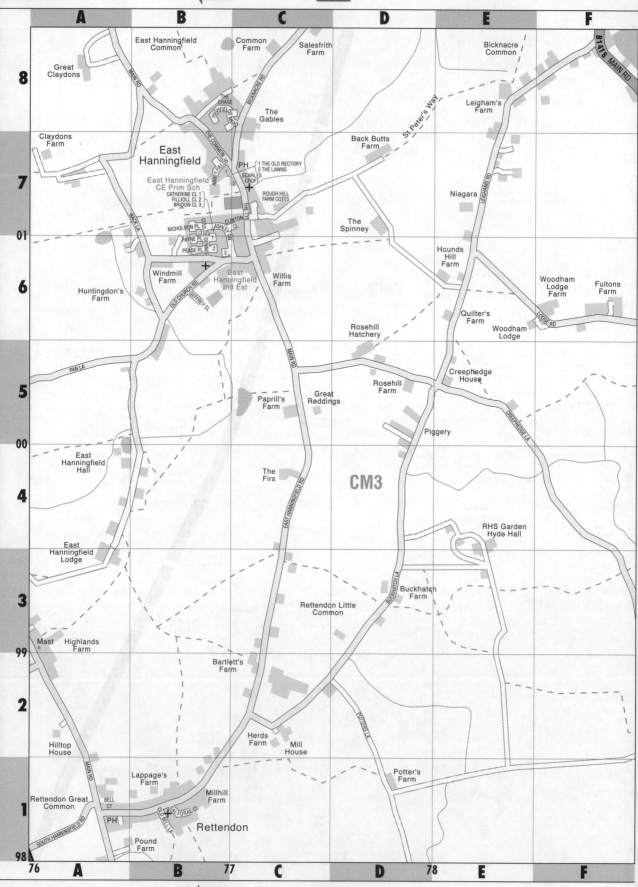

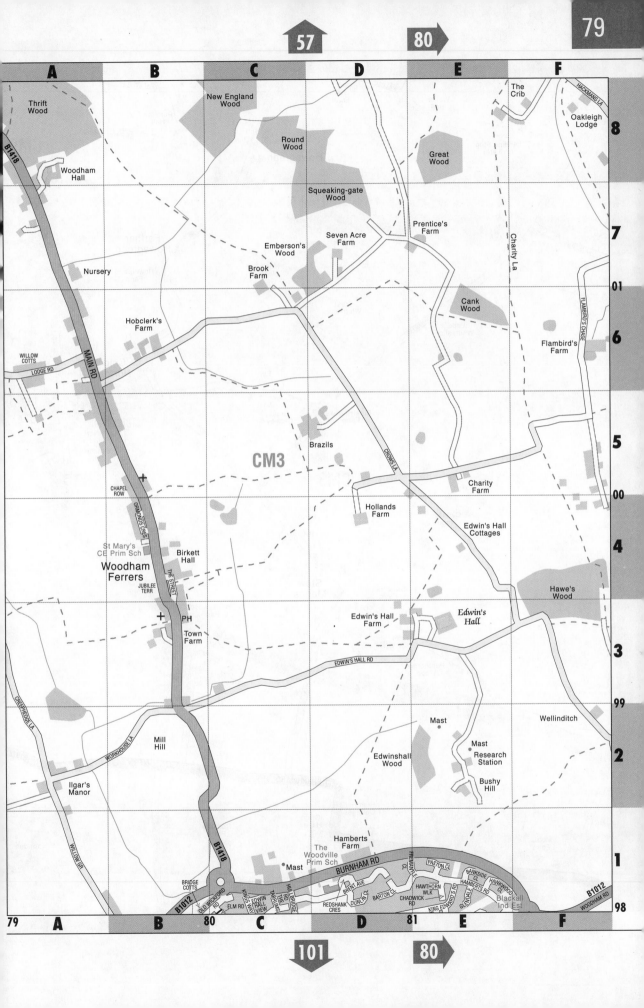

A B C D E F

8

7

01

6

5

00

4

3

99

2

1

98

82 A B 83 C D 84 E F

Walton Hall

MILL HILL

Hill Farm

THE GLEBE

THE STREET

Purleigh Hall

St Peter's Way

CM9

Landing Strip (Private)

Howegreen

CHAPEL LA

Farther Howegreen

HOWE GREEN RD

Howegreen Farm

FLAMBIRD'S CHASE

Howe Wood

HACKMANS LA

Great Whitmans

Little Whitmans

Wr Twr

Cold Norton

CHERRY BLOSSOM LA

CROWN RD

BRENNAN CL

VICTORIA RD

LATCHINGDON RD

CLARKE RISE

GREEN TREES

TO KELVEDON

Blue House Farm

Great Canney

HAGG HILL

STOW RD

CHARTERHOUSE COTTS 1
EAST CANNEY COTTS 2

Cold Norton Prim Sch

PH

FERRIS AVE

STATION CRES

CH

Beacon Hill

ST STEPHENS RD

THE FAIRWANS

CM3

Canney Wood

New Farm

PH

Wright's Ley Wood

PH

THE STREET

1 SMYTHE ROW
2 STOW VILLAS

Stow Maries

Honeywood Farm

Stow Hall Farm

HONEY POT LA

PH

RIDLEY COTTS

Poorhouse Wood

WOODHAM RD

Pantile Wood

Brookmead Grove

BAUBGH LA

99

B1012

Lower Burnham Rd

LOWER BURNHAM RD

High Hall Cottages

Great Hayes

Rookery Farm

ROOKERY LA

Yondah

FRENCH RD

Morris Farm

HIGWELL CHASE

Slate Hall Cottages

LITTLE HAYES CHASE

Skinner's Wick

B1012

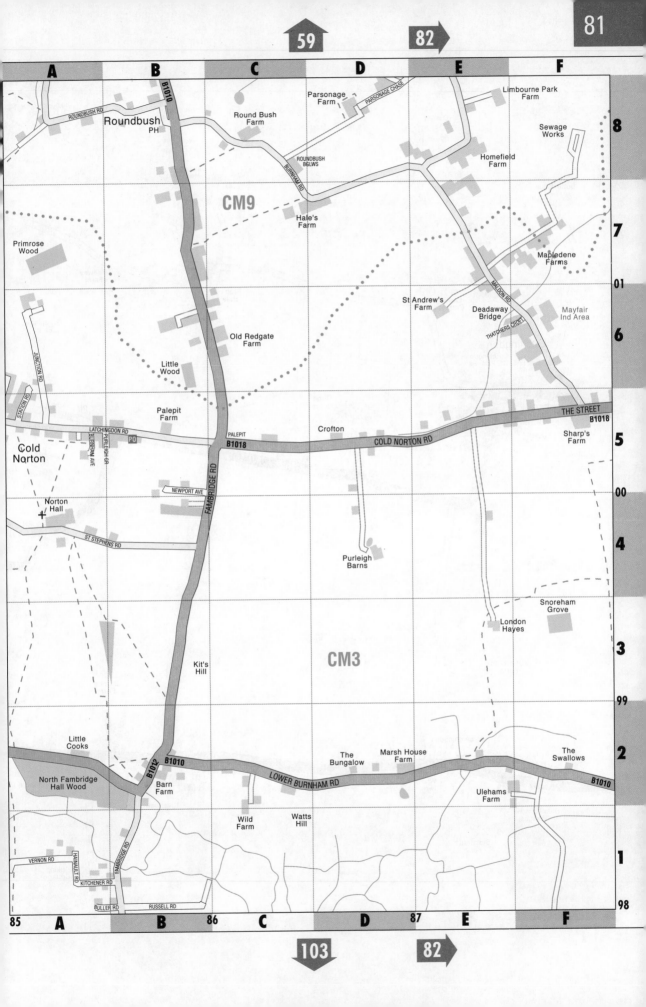

81
60

A B C D E F

8

7

01

6

Butterfields

Lawling Hall

Maylandsea Prim Sch

KATONIA AVE
THE DRIVE
BAKERSFIELD

STEEPLE RD

Lawling Cottages

Brook Hall

Tideway Farm

Latchingdon

Latchingdon CE Prim Sch

Greenlane Farm

5

BIRCHMANS SCH
CHASE
ELSINGS
LUDGROVE
MEADOW WAY
GRANARY CL
BUCKNHAM WAY
THE STREET
CLEAR CT
LAWLING RD

B1018
PO PH
St Michaels Cl
SNOREHAM GDNS
HERITAGE WAY

Good Hares

PH
GREEN LA
Warden's Farm

Arley Grange

BURNHAM RD

00

Red Lyons Farm

PH
GARDEN CL
PO
HAMILTON CT

4

Snoreham Hall

The Beeches

CM3

B1018

Nursery
LOWER CHASE
BURNHAM RD

3

RECTORY LA

Surridges

Rosedale Farm

Scatterbrook Farm

Barnes Farm

UPPER CHASE

99

CHESTNUT FARM DR
BARNES FARM DR
SUNNINGDALE RD

2

Latchingdon Hall

Cemy

Tyle Hall

Grange Farm

FAMBRIDGE RD
B1010

EAST AVE
CENTRAL AVE
WEST AVE
RIVER VIEW TERR

Althorne Hall

B1010
LOWER BURNHAM RD
Wr Twr

Riverview Park

STATION RD

Stamfords Hill Cottages

1

Stamfords Farm

Viking Cottage

98

88 A B 89 C D 90 E F

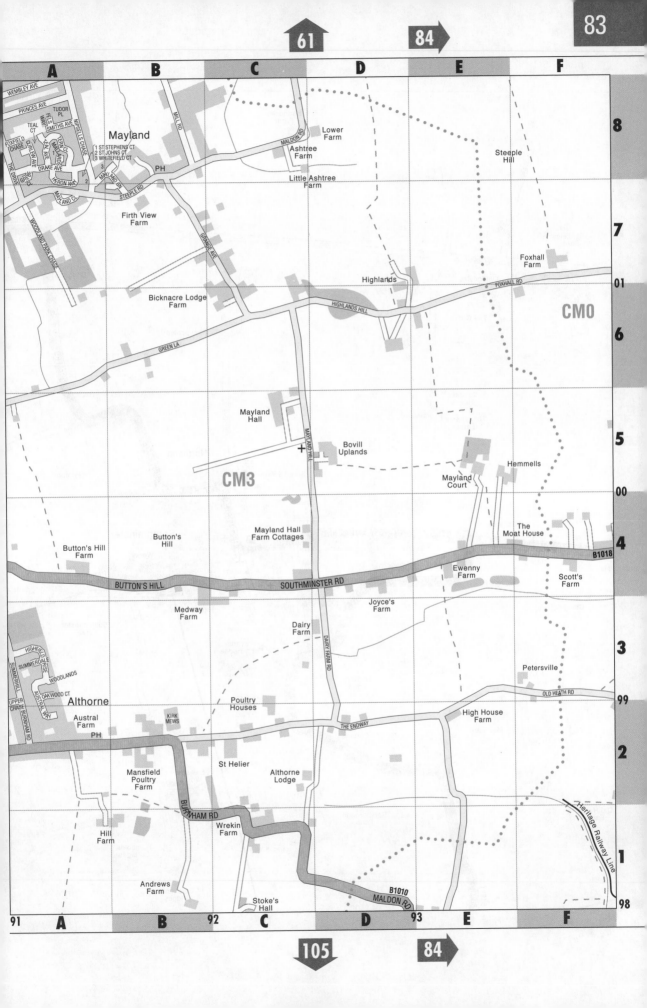

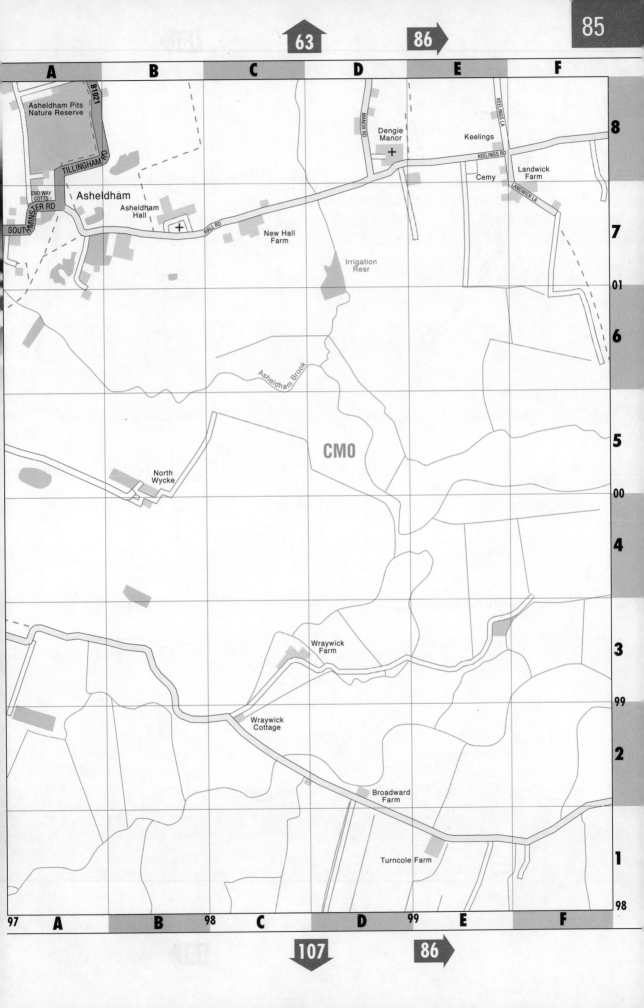

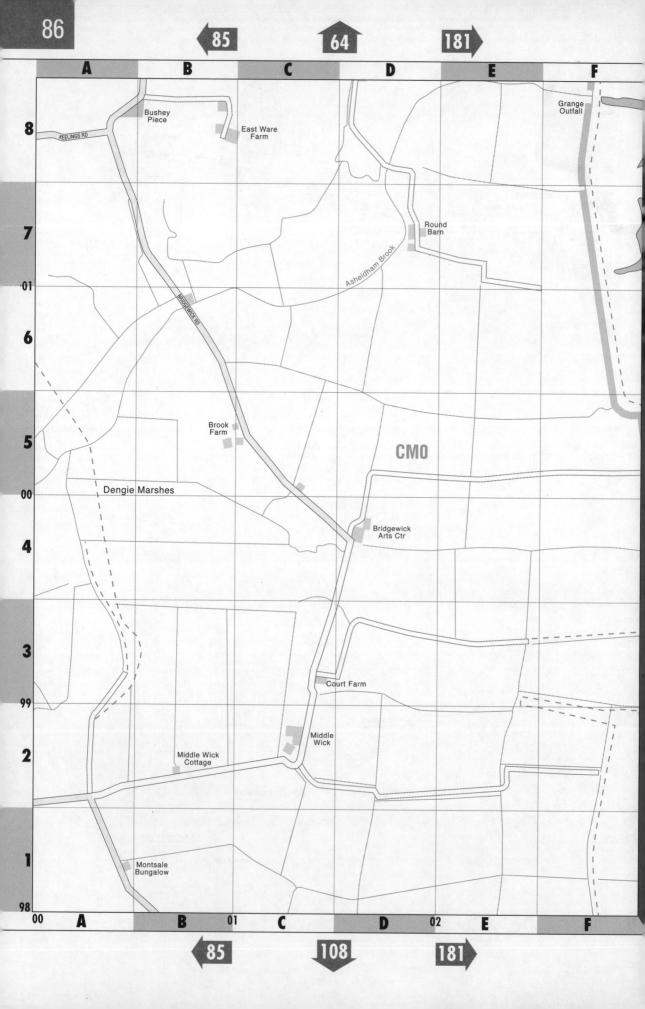

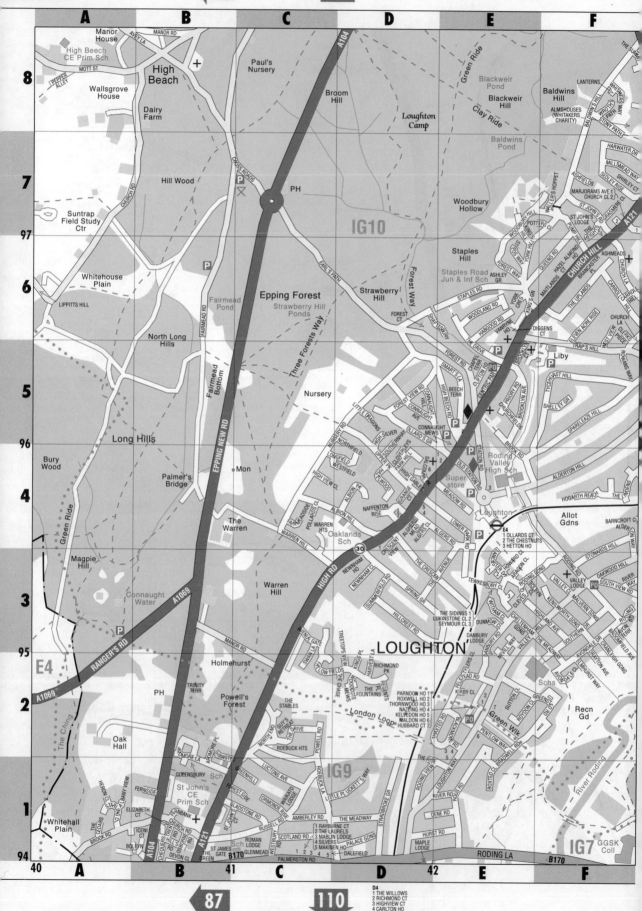

D4
1 THE WILLOWS
2 RICHMOND CT
3 HIGHVIEW CT
4 CARLTON HO
5 COLLINS CT
6 HOMECHERRY HO

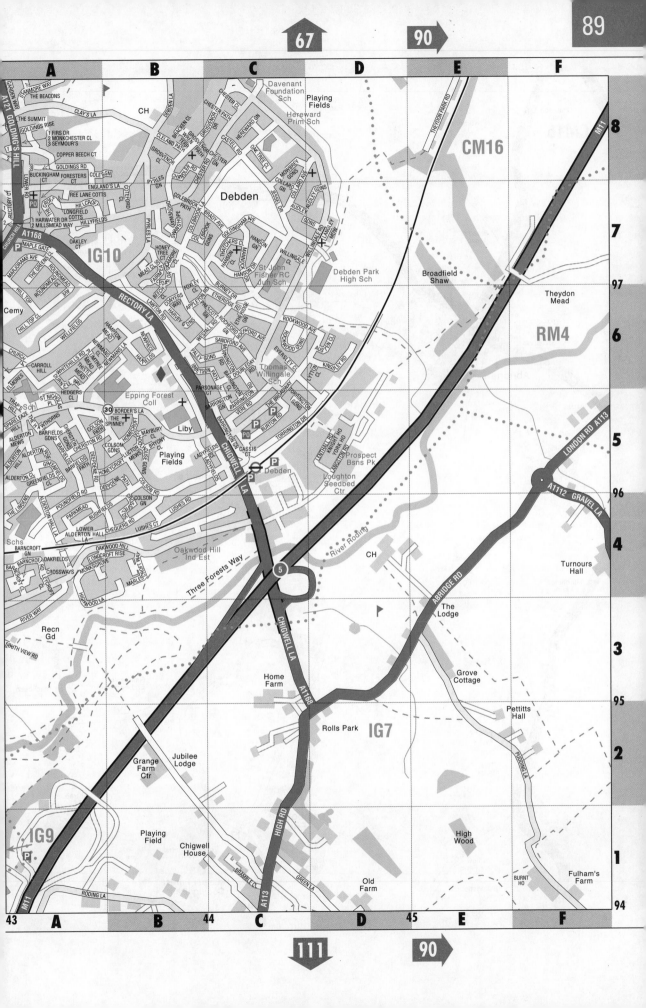

A B C D E F

8

CM16

Theydon Hall

Nurseries

Hill Farm

Sewage Works

River Roding

A113

ONGAR RD

M11

B172

ABRIDGE RD

Piggotts Farm

7

Bloody Mead

EPPING LA

Pryors Farm

Lambourne Place

Lower Wood

97

TURNERS CT

Ape's Grove

Patch Park

RODING HALL

SAWYER'S CHASE

NEW PAINT DR

B172

SILVER ST

MARKET PL

WILLOW TREES

6

GOULDS COTTS 1
AUCTION PL 2
WHITE HALL 3
ABRIDGE MEWS 4
THE CHESTNUTS 5

PH

PO

THE POPLARS

FIR TREES

PANGS

KNIGHT'S WLK

MIDDLE BOY

ORCHID CL

ALDERWOOD CL

FIELD

ALDERWOOD

SPUR CL

New Farm

Alder Wood

CHURCH LA

LONDON RD

A113

Abridge

Lambourne Prim Sch

RM4

ABRIDGE PK

Lambourne Hall

Great Wood

5

Great Downs Farm

Soapley's Wood

Lambourne

Three Forests Way

96

A1112

Halfmoon Wood

Bishop's Moat

4

GRAVEL LA

Marchings Farm

Clark's Wood

HOE LA

Bishop's Hall

Dews Hall Farm

3

Taylors Farm

St John's Farm

NEW RD

PARK SQ

Mast

Gallman's End Farm

HOOK LA

Blackbush Farm

95

TAYLORS

IG7

TUTTLEBY COTTS

BOURNEBRIDGE LA

2

The Manor House

MANOR RD

Playing Fields

The Blue House

Mansfield Outdoor Ctr

Brownings Farm

Hop Pole Farm

PH

Lambourne End

Crabtree Hill

1

MILLER'S LA

Willow Park Farm

P

Three Cornered Plain

Billingsbourne

A1112

Harmes Farm

LAMBOURNE SQ

Hainault Forest Country Park

94

Banks Farm

Taylor's Plain

Spurgate Plain

46

A B 47 C D 48 E F

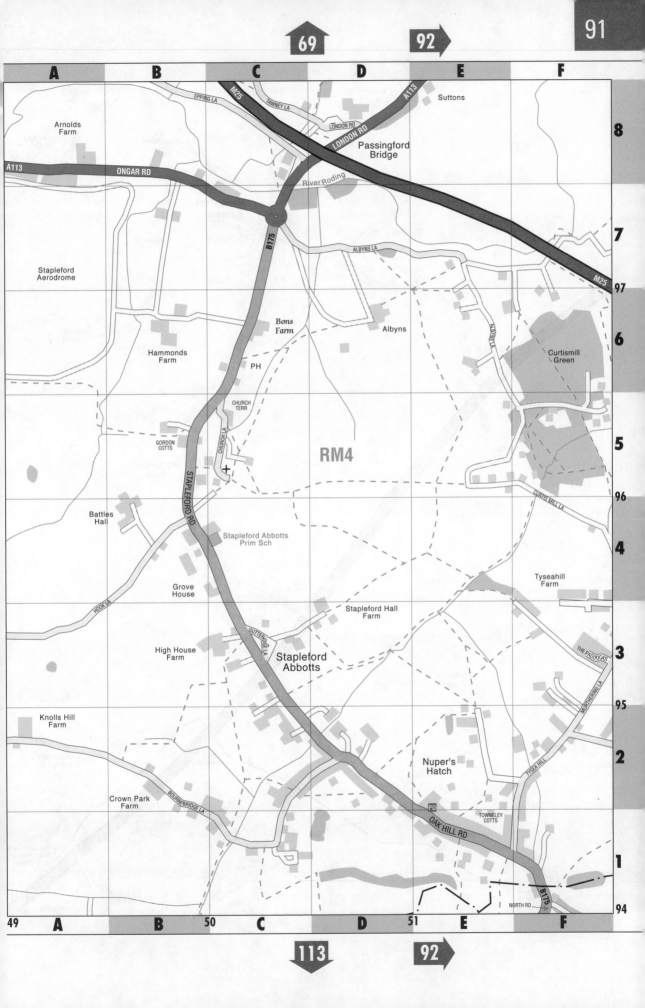

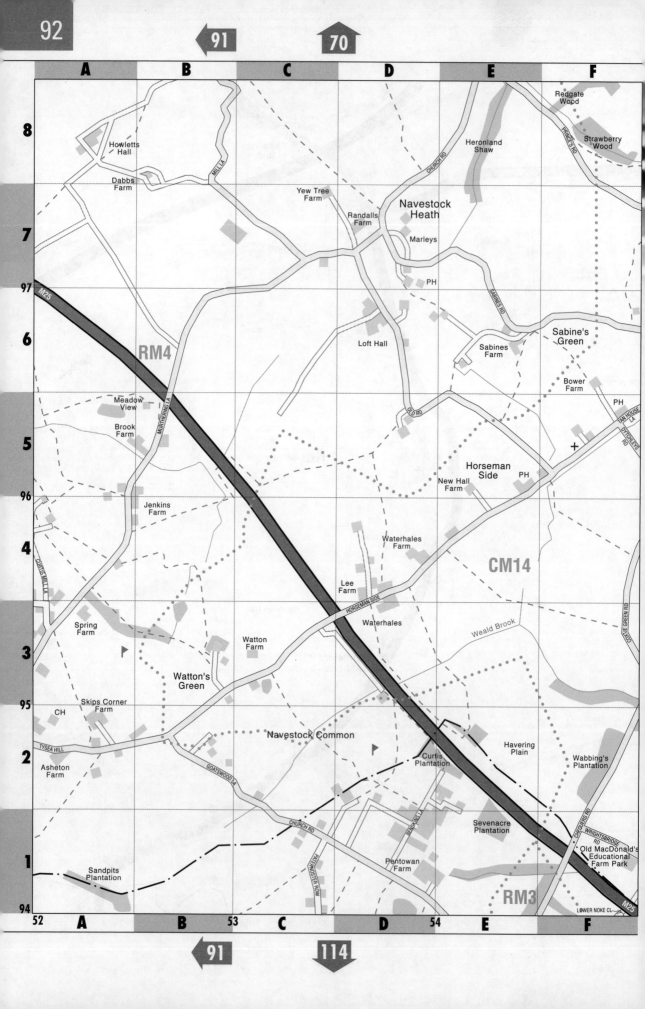

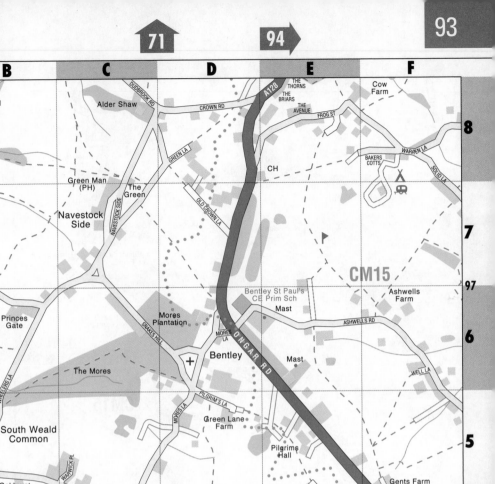

A B C D E F

8

Cowes Farm
Park Wood
America Farm

Heard's Farm

7

Wishfields Farm
Sumner's Farm
Rosecroft

97

Palmers Farm
Bennett's Farm
HALL LA

6

Days Farm
Howe's Farm
Brickhouse Farm
CM15

5

Crow Green
Brickhouse Wood
Canterbury Tye Hall
DODDINGHURST RD
A12

96

Palmers
ORCHARD LA
CATHERINE CL
CROW GREEN LA
HATCH RD
ALDERTON CL
BEADS HALL LA
ASCELLES CL

4

Pilgrims Hatch
Larchwood Prim Sch
HONEYSUCKLE CL
MIMOSA CL
TULIP CL
POPPY CL
HEATHER CL
MAGNOLIA WAY
WISTERIA GDNS
LILAC CL
MARCONI GDNS
Bishop's Hall Park
1 PEONY CL
2 ELIZABETH HO
3 MEADOW VIEW
4 WEALDEN HO
Shenfield Hall Farm

THE FIRS
A128
LARCHWOOD GDNS
BALMORAL RD
IVER RD
HAREWOOD RD
CLARENCE RD
CARISBROOK RD
ALBANY RD
PO
The Brentwood Ctr
Hall Wood
Shenfield Hall

3

DOUNSELL CT
DARLINGTON CT
ONGAR RD
BROOMWOOD GDNS
MARLBOROUGH RD
KING GEORGE'S RD
OSBORNE RD
KENSINGTON RD
BISHOP'S HILL
HIGHGROVE
ELIZABETH RD
CROSSWAYS
TUDOR CL
MARGARET AVE
St Mary's CE Prm Sch
SAWYERS CT
CHELMSFORD RD
A1023

95

High Wood
WINDSOR RD
VIKING WAY
HURSTWOOD AVE
WARESCOT CL
RUSSELL RD
ST KILDA'S RD
KAREN CL
RUSHDENE RD
RUSHDENE CT
LEWIS
HUTTON RD
A129

2

Calcott Hall Farm
ONGAR RD
ST GEORGE'S CL
HIGHWOOD CL
ROBIN HOOD RD
KIMPTON AVE
1 DRUMMOND CT
2 GEARY CT
Sawyers Hall Coll
St Helens RC Jun Sch
Convent of Mercy
St Thomas of Canterbury CE Jun & Inf Schs
PO
Shenfield
SHENFIELD PL
HALLWOOD CRES
GLENDALE
YORK HILL
PRIEST'S LA

1

CM14
PORTERS CL
GREENSHAW
THORNRIDGE
UPPER PYLE
CLEVES WAY
COSTEAD MANOR RD
THE COURTYARD
MONTBAZON
High Wood
MELFORD PL
DODDINGHURST RD
FARROW HO
TREE TOPS
SPRINGFIELD
HIGHLAND AVE
SAWYERS HALL LA
3 DUKE'S PL
4 INVERMAY CT
5 LAVENHAM CT
6 BURGESS CT
7 HIGHMEAD CT
8 ARGYLL CT
9 RAVENSCOURT
MERRYMEADE CHASE
The Essex Nuffield
SHEN PLACE
TROTWOOD CL
MILL HILL
CLIVEDEN CL
COOMBE RISE
PARK WAY

94

WEALD RD
A12
ST CHARLES RD
CHAFFORD
CAPON CL
BLACK WATER RODING
PARK RD
VINE WAY
PARK VALE CT
WESTERN AVE
THE VALE
WATERLOO
WHELLER RD
NORTH RD
A128
BURLAND RD
YATE'S WAY
BRENTWOOD
ENDWAYS
HOLLY HO
HOMEHURST HO
LIMES CT
A1023
SHENFIELD RD
MOORTON HALL
Brentwood Sch
WORRIN CL
PRIEST'S LA

58 A B 59 C D 60 E F

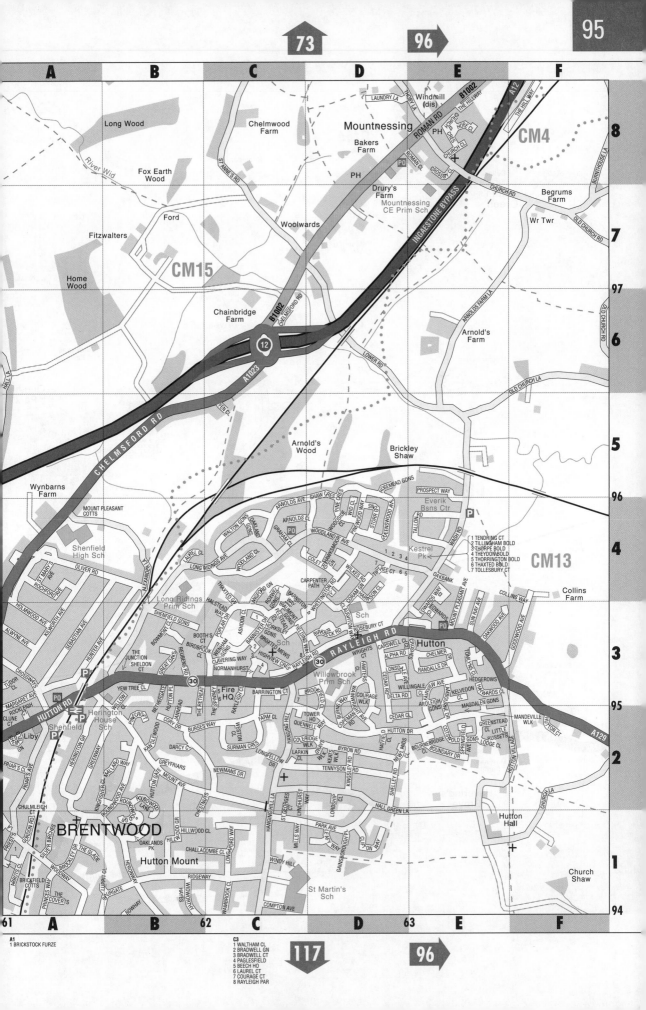

95
74

A　　B　　C　　D　　E　　F

8

BURNT HOUSE LA

Lodge Wood

Kitchen Wood

CM4

HALL LA

Little Farm

BUTTSBURY

Shoulder Hall

CHURCH RD

Bellman's Farm

Westlands Farm

PADHAM'S GREEN RD

MARSH LA

Padham's Green

7

North Nook

97

Harespring Wood

BUCKWYNS CHASE

6

Wardroper's

Buckwyns Farm

Mountnessing Hall

OLD CHURCH LA

OLD CHURCH LA

Queens Park

MUNSTER CT

Lawness

COLVILLE MEWS 1
BERESFORD CT 2
GRANVILLE CL 3
LORRIMORE CL 4
DOLPHIN GDNS 5
OAKLEY DR 6
QUEEN'S GATE MEWS 7
QUEENS PARK CT 8
TAVISTOCK DR 9
SLOANE MEWS 10
EDWARD CL 11

BETONY CRES
MALLOW
GDNS
MILNER CL
SPENCER

ARLINGTON WAY

ROSEBAY AVE

Recn Gd

5

River Wid

Brightside Prim Sch

96

CM13

Cock Wood

Clapgate Wood

Sewage Works

Brightside CL

CORNFLOWER GDNS

UPLAND RD

4

THE LINGS

LINDA GDNS

CHERRY GDNS

THE WARREN

Little Cowbridge Grange Farm

BLUEBELL WOOD

MOUNTNESSING RD

BRIGHTSIDE

MARK'S CL

PAULINE GDNS

ST HELENS WALK

IAN RD

ORCHARD CL

RAVEN CL

THE FOXGLOVES 1
BUCKWYNS CT 2
HALLAM CT 3
UPLAND DR 4
COOMBES CL 5
PAVILLION PL 6
EARL MOUNTBATTEN DR 7
CRESCENT GDNS 8
CRESCENT CL 9

CRESCENT RD

MAGENTA

INVICTA

PLEASANT DR

CARPENTER CL

GORDON CL

RICKETTS DR

Radford Bsns Ctr

3

Great Cowbridge Grange Farm

CM12

LEIGHS RIFLEMAN 1
BRIDGE PAR 2
Lake Meadows Office Village 3
BRATHERTONS CT 4
FORESTER CT 5
TRUMPETER CT 6
LEVELLER ROW 7
WARRINGTON SQ 8

RUMBULLION DR

WHITESMITH DR

WHIM

THE MULLIONS

WOODBROOK CRES

CHARITY FARM CHASE

Bushwood Farm

95

BURNTWOOD CL

GROVE RD

BELLEVUE RD

ROBERT CL

STATION RD

Ellices Farm

NORTH DR

PH

BEAUFORT RD

ROSSLYN

A129

RAYLEIGH RD

Martines Farm

HUNTERS CHASE

FOXES GR

Shipmans House

KENILWORTH CL

COURTLANDS

LONDON RD

WESTERN RD

EVEREST RISE

HILLARY MOUNT

CHURCH LA

2

Humes Farm

Havering's Grove

TALLY-HO DR

Shipmans Shaw

Greenleas Farm

WESTERN VIEW

A129

GILMOUR RISE

1

HEATH CL

TYE COMMON RD

ABBEY RD

ROMNEY RD

BOOTHAM

RUSHDENE RD

Blunts Wall Farm

Billericay Com

H

BLUNTS WALL RD

94

64　A　　B　65　C　　D　66　E　　F

95
118

A B C D E F

8

White's Hill
Bishop's Farm
FURZE LA
Kiln Common
Whitelilies Farm
GOATSMOOR LA
BRITTONS LA
Great Bishop's Wood
BROOMWOOD LA
CM4
Broom Wood
7
DOWNHAM RD
Fremnells
Hanningfield Resr
Visitor Ctr
97
Crowsheath Farm
HAWKSWOOD RD
Common Farm
Hilltop Nursery
Little Abbott's
CROWSHEATH LA
6
DOWSETTS LA
Ramsden Back Common
Cock Wood
Thrift Wood
MILL LA
PH
5
TIPLERS BRIDGE
NORTON RD
ALLENS RD
STONEY HILLS
BIRDS CL
RECREATION WLK
Nursery
DOWNHAM RD
SCHOOL RD
WILLOWMEADE
1 2
96
MILL LA
PH
POST OFFICE ST JOHNS PL
LINDHURST DR
PH
DOVEDALE CL
DOWNHAM RD
1 BAKERS CT
2 FARRIER SQ
WINDSOR RD
OAK RD
Downham
HEATH RD
ORCHARD CL
Windsor Trad Est
Greenacres Farm
Hunt's Farm
HOMELANDS GR
CM11
4
Ramsden Heath
Chitham's Farm
BRABNER GDNS
Downham CE Prim Sch
Rectory Wood
SHORT LA
MANOR CL
Cox Green
The Orchard Farm
De Beauvoir House
CASTLEDON RD
3
Meepshole Wood
PARK LA
DE BEAUVOIR CHASE
95
2
Crays Wood
Kent Hill
Pump Hill
CHURCH RD
PH
Barrenleys Wood
Claypitshills Wood
Ramsden Park Farm
RAMSDEN PARK RD
ORCHARD AVE
1
Ramsden Bellhouse
GLEBE RD
94

70 A B 71 C D 72 E F

77 100

A B C D E F

8

South
Hanningfield

Romans
Farm

BROAD MEAD

BEARMANS

MIDDLEMEAD

CHURCH VW

South
Hanningfield
Tye

Works

SOUTH HANNINGFIELD RD

Marks
Farm

MARKS LA

Landing
Stage

Hanningfield
Nature Trail

CH

PH

Claydons
Farm

Coalhill

7

Nature
Reserve

CM3

Scrub
Wood

Stacey's
Farm

CHALK ST

Well
Wood

WARREN RD

Millhill
Farm

97

Foxearth
Wood

HAWKSWOOD RD

Runningwell

HOE LA

6

Poplars
Lodge

Poplar's
Farm

Runwell Hall
Farm

Harrow
Farm

Flemings
Farm

Laylands
Farm

SUDBURY RD

Brock
Hill

Pitfield
Shaw

5

Sudbury's
Farm

The
Elms

H

96

CASTLEDON RD

The
Grange

Moorgarden
Wood

Runwell

4

CM11

Brock Hill
Farm

BROCK HILL

LYNFORDS DR

LYNFORDS AVE

+

Downham
Hall

THE GREENWAY

BROCK HILL DR

SS11

MEADOW LA

3

Downham Hall
Farm

WAVERLEY CRES

LINDON RD

DOWNHAM RD

95

GRANGE RD

DELMAR GDNS

CARLTON RD

HOMEHOLLY
HO

SOUTH HANNINGFIELD WAY

CHURCH END LA

LYNFORDS DR

A132

BROWNS AVE

BARNET PARK RD

Quart Pot
(PH)

2

CASTLEDON RD

VERA RD

CUMMING RD

STATION RD

SWALLOW

RICHM'D

HASLEMERE RD

ALDERNEY GDNS

LAPWING RD

MORELAND RD

SWAN LA

GUERNSEY GDNS

CLARE AVE

RUNWELL

RUNWELL
GDNS

DAVID
AVE

CANEWDON
CL

CANEWDON
GDNS

VIKING WAY

REGENCY CL

TIDWORTH
AVE

CHURCH END AVE

WINDSOR

CLEARING AVE

RUNWELL RD

Runwell

PARK VIEW
CT

ARUN

KEITH AVE

BIRS CL

EGBERT GDNS

SAXON

+

1

Runwell
Prim Sch

PEARMAIN CL

MERLIN WAY

ETHELRED GDNS

RETTENDON GDNS

30

Recn Gd

P

CARRUTHERS CL

CARRUTHERS

ATHELSTAN GDNS

ALFRED
GDNS

HENGIST

WHITELANDS
CL

HAROLD GDNS

ILGARS
RD

A132

P

WHIST AVE

94

SS12

STATION AVE

THE HASTINGS

HEREWARD GDNS

BERENS CL

121 100

A | B | C | D | E | F

A130

RAWLINGS FARM

The Wheatsheaf (PH)

Workhouse La

CM3

HOE LA

White House Farm

HALL COTTS

MAIN RD

Rettendon Hall

Gorse Wood

Old Rettendon Hall

Rettendon Shaw

Rettendon Prim Sch

New Hall Fruit Farm

SONTERS DOWN

PO

MEESON BGLWS

PLACE COTTS

CHURCH CHASE

CROUCH VIEW COTTS

SOUTH VIEW COTTS

MEADOW RD

Curry Hill

H

Runwell

Rettendon Place

Mark's Farm

RECTORY LA

Rettendon Grange Farm

Woods Lodge

Smithfield Nursery

The Lodge Hotel

A132

Oakwood Nurseries

FARM CRES

WOODHAM RD

HAYES CHASE

HAYES CHASE

LYNFORDS DR

LYNFORDS AVE

RUNWELL CHASE

Hotel

RETTENDON TURNPIKE

A1245

High House Farm

BURNHAM RD

Woods Farm

Gosse's Farm

RUNWELL RD

A132

Battlesbridge

Muggeridge Farm

MALTINGS RD

Battles Bridge Motorcycle Mus

The Hawk (PH)

HAWK HILL

HAWK LA

PH

Battlesbridge Antiques Ctr

TIMBER WHARF COTTS

BEECHES RD

River Crouch

Telfords

Battlesbridge

SS11

A130

A1245

Southlands Farm

GOOSE COTTS

CHELMSFORD RD

RAWRETH GDNS

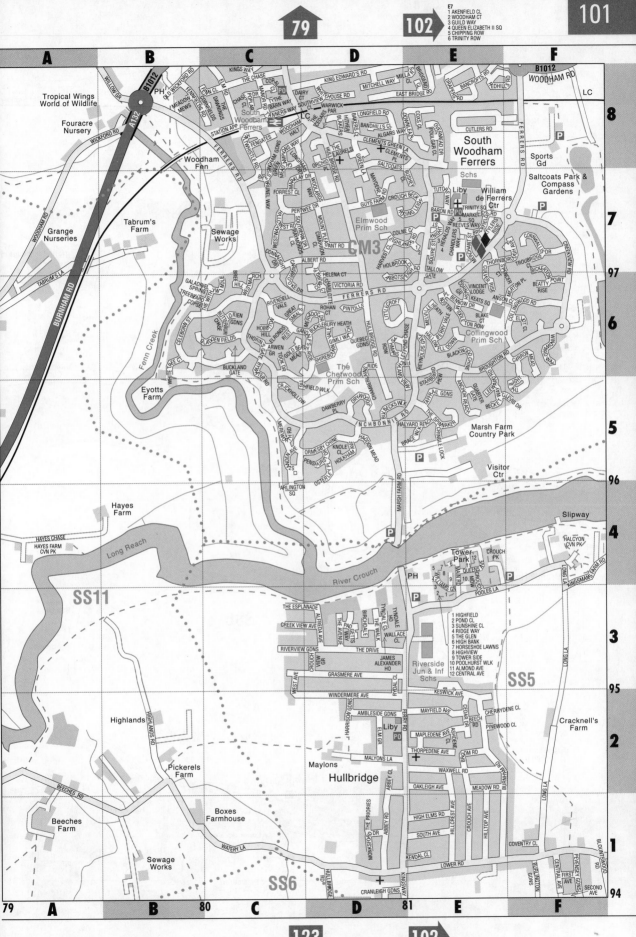

E7
1 AKENFIELD CL
2 WOODHAM CT
3 GUILD WAY
4 QUEEN ELIZABETH II SQ
5 CHIPPING ROW
6 TRINITY ROW

South Woodham Ferrers

CM3

Tropical Wings World of Wildlife

Fouracre Nursery

Grange Nurseries

Tabrum's Farm

Woodham Fen

Sewage Works

Eyotts Farm

Hayes Farm

SS11

Hayes Chase
HAYES FARM CVN PK

Long Reach

River Crouch

Highlands

Pickerels Farm

Beeches Farm

Boxes Farmhouse

Sewage Works

SS6

Saltcoats Park & Compass Gardens

Sports Gd

Elmwood Prim Sch

Liby

William de Ferrers Ctr

Collingwood Prim Sch

The Chetwood Prim Sch

Marsh Farm Country Park

Visitor Ctr

Slipway

Halcyon CVN PK

Tower Park

PH

SS5

1 HIGHFIELD
2 POND CL
3 SUNSHINE CL
4 RIDGE WAY
5 THE GLEN
6 HIGH BANK
7 HORSESHOE LAWNS
8 HIGHVIEW
9 TOWER SIDE
10 POOLHURST WLK
11 ALMOND AVE
12 CENTRAL AVE

Riverside Jun & Inf Schs

James Alexander Ho

Liby PO

Maylons

Hullbridge

Cracknell's Farm

101
80

A | **B** | **C** | **D** | **E** | **F**

ROOKERY RD

The Old Rectory

8

Hogwell Farm

Hogwell Chase

LC

Little Hayes Farm

Little Hayes Chase

LC

LC

Groom's Farm

CM3

7

Stow Creek

North Fambridge Hall

97

6

Clementsgreen Creek

Port Moor Cottage

Hawbush Creek

River Crouch

5

Brandyhole Reach

96

4

KINGSMANS FARM RD

Brandy Hole

Beckney Farm

New Bungalow

SS5

Uguess

3

95

Lovedown

2

Sheepcotes Farm

DOME CVN PK

The Dome Country Club

PO

New Hockley Hall Farm

ROSLAN DR

LOWER RD

PLUMBEROW AVE

GRANVILLE RD

CLARENDON RD

WELLINGTON RD

Barton's Farm

Lower Hockley Hall

1

WADHAM PARK AVE

CHURCH RD

WOODSIDE RD

Plumberow Wood

BECKNEY AVE

94

82 | **A** | **B** | **83** | **C** | **D** | **84** | **E** | **F**

101
124

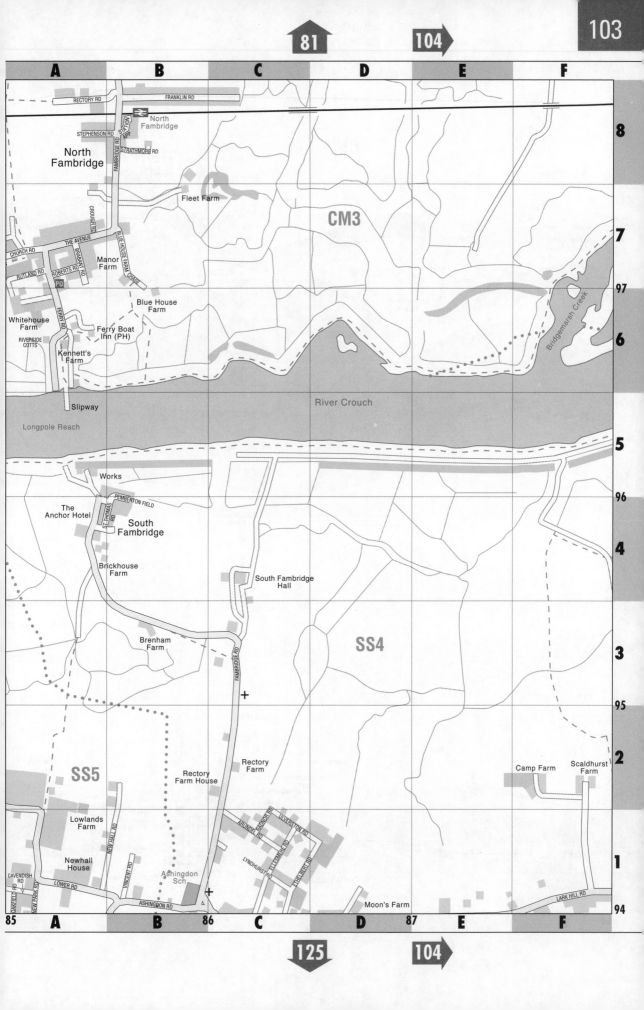

103
82

A   B   C   D   E   F

8

CM3

STATION RD

Althorne   LC

Bridgemarsh LA

Marina

7   Bridgemarsh Creek

Althorne Creek

97

Bridgemarsh
Island

6

Shortpole   Reach

Raypits Reach

Landsend
Point

5   River Crouch   Easter Reach

96

Upper Raypits
Farm

4

Old Fleet

3   SS4

Pudsey Hall

Market
Hill

95

Butts Hill

2   Bolt Hall

Beacon Hill   New Hall
Farm

Canewdon Hall
Farm   GAYS LA

BUTTS PADDOCK

DUCKETTS MEAD

AUGUSTINE WAY

CANUTE CL

Canewdon Hall   CROUCH VIEW
VILLAS

PUDSEY HALL LA   HIGH ST

LAMBOURNE HALL RD

LARKHILL AVE   CHESTNUT PATH   CHURCH LA   PO   REST COTTS

VILLAGE   SYCAMORE WAY   BIRCH CL   ORCHARD
GN   Canewdon   BGLWS

ASH GN   WILLOW WLK   ROWAN WAY   CE Prim Sch

CEDAR   ANCHOR
WLK   PAR

1   LARK HILL RD   ANCHOR LA   GARDENERS LA

ANCHOR LANE
COTTS

White House   SCOTTS HALL RD   Canewdon   Gardeners
Farm

94

88   A   B   89   C   D   90   E   F

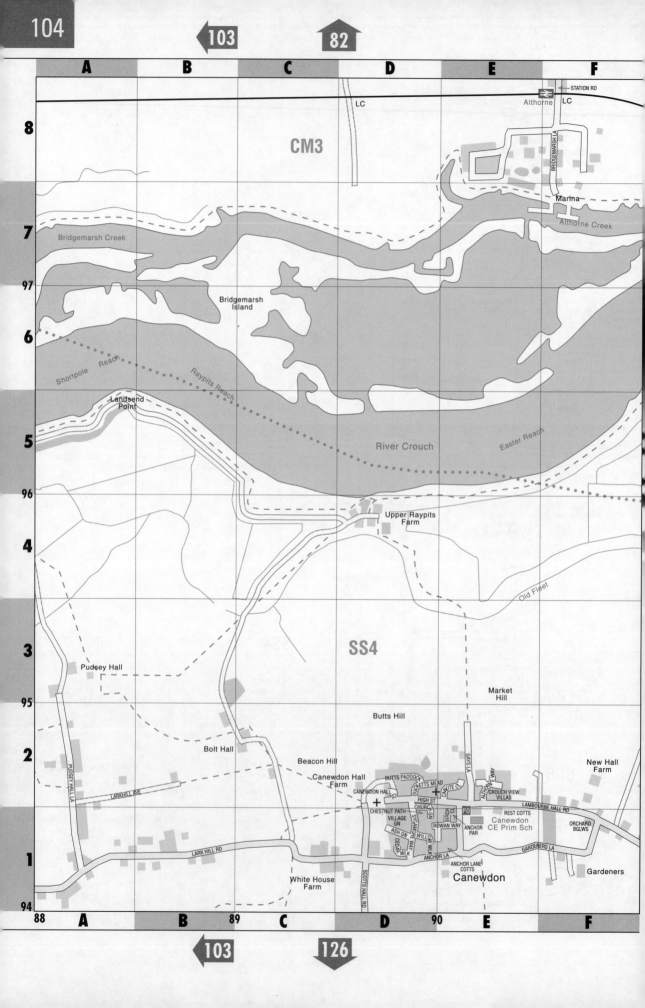

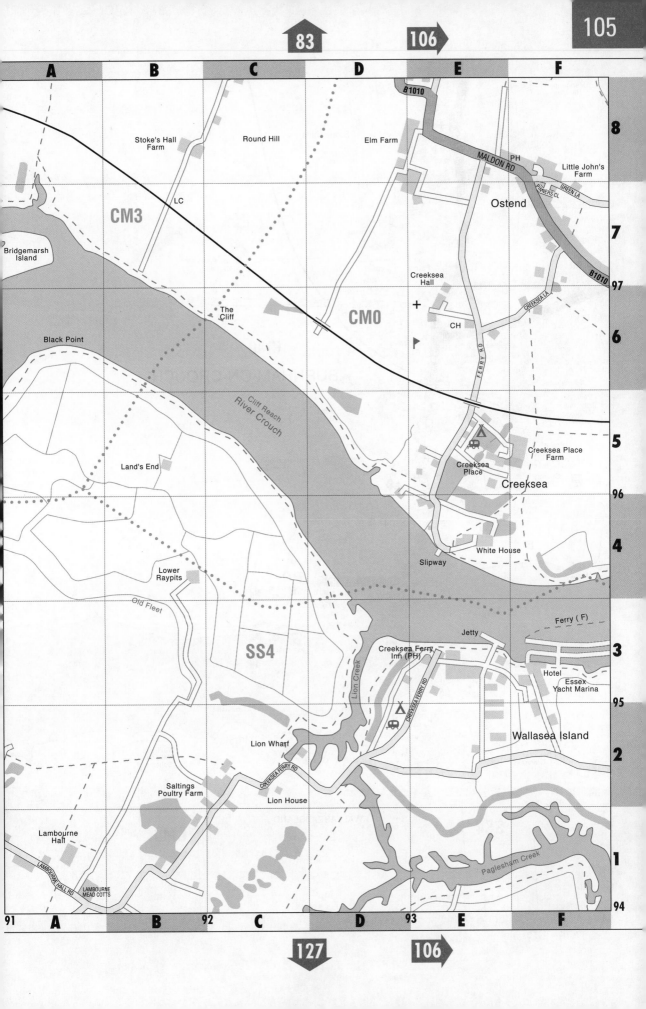

A B C D E F

8

7

97

6

CM3

Bridgemarsh
Island

Stoke's Hall
Farm

Round Hill

Elm Farm

LC

The Cliff

CM0

Black Point

Clift Reach
River Crouch

Creeksea
Hall

CH

Ostend

Little John's
Farm

MALDON RD

PH

GREEN LA

PINERS CL

B1010

CREEKSEA LA

FERRY RD

5

96

4

Land's End

Creeksea
Place

Creeksea Place
Farm

Creeksea

White House

Slipway

Lower
Raypits

Old Fleet

SS4

Lion Creek

Creeksea Ferry
Inn (PH)

Jetty

Ferry (F)

Hotel

Essex
Yacht Marina

3

95

2

Lion Wharf

Lion House

Saltings
Poultry Farm

CREEKSEA FERRY RD

Wallasea Island

Lambourne
Hall

LAMBOURNE HALL RD

LAMBOURNE
MEAD COTTS

Paglesham Creek

1

94

91 A B 92 C D 93 E F 94

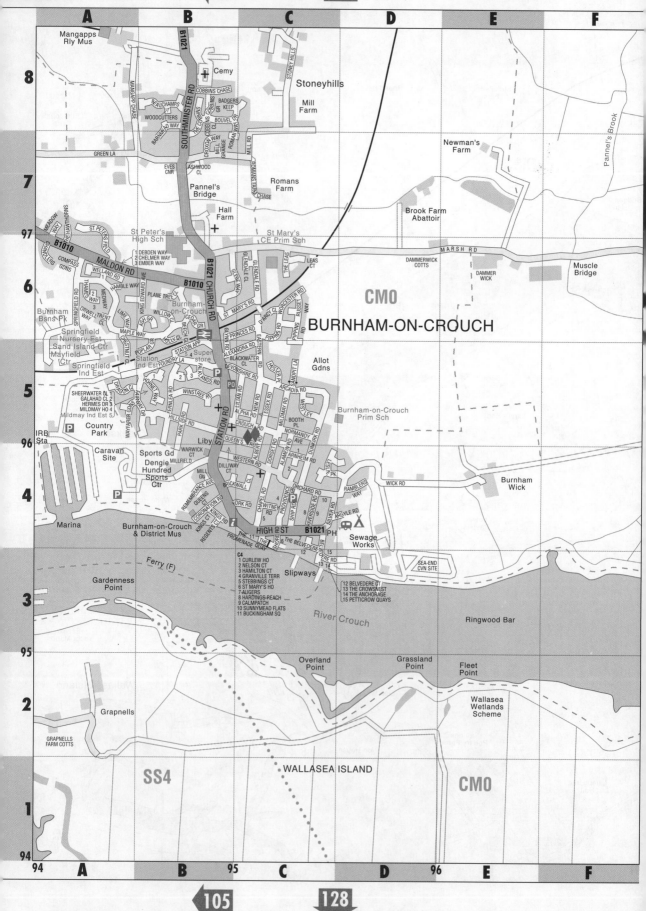

A B C D E F

8

7

97

6

5

96

4

3

95

2

1

94

Mangapps
Rly Mus

Cemy

COBBINS CHASE

Stoneyhills

Mill
Farm

SOUTHMINSTER RD

B1021

BEAUCHAMPS

WOODCUTTERS

BARNHEAD WAY

MANGAPP CHASE

THE COBBINS

CROXONS CL

CROXON WAY

GRANGE

MILL RD

ROMAN WAY

BADGERS
KEEP

BOUVEL

GREEN LA

EVES
CNR

ASHWOOD
CL

ROMANS FARN

ROMANS CHASE

Pannel's
Bridge

Romans
Farm

Newman's
Farm

Pannel's Brook

ST PETERS FIELD

THE HAWTHORNS

MEADOW
WAY

St Peter's
High Sch

Hall
Farm

St Mary's
CE Prim Sch

Brook Farm
Abattoir

B1010

CHANDLERS

COMPASS
GDNS

MALDON RD

1 DEBDEN WAY
2 CHELMER WAY
3 EMBER WAY

CHURCH RD

B1010

LEAS
CT

DAMMERWICK
COTTS

MARSH RD

DAMMER
WICK

Muscle
Bridge

Burnham
Bsns Pk

SPRINGFIELD RD

THAMES RD

ORWELL
WAY

MEDWAY

TRENT
CL

WELLAND RD

HAMBLE WAY

KING EDWARD AVE

PLANE TREE

WILLOW CL

ASH GR

BEECH

GLENDALE CL

GLENDALE RD

ST MARY'S RD

D'ARCY RD

WORCESTER RD

PIPPINS

RUSSET

Burnham-
on-Crouch

CMO

BURNHAM-ON-CROUCH

Springfield
Nursery Est
Sand Island Ctr
Mayfield
Ctr

Springfield
Ind Est

LIME
WAY

MAPLE WAY

CHESTNUT CL

POPLAR DR

OLLY CL

CEDAR

Station
Ind Est

STATION APP

FOUNDRY LA

Super
store

PRINCES RD

ALEXANDRA
CL

EASTERN RD

CHESTER RD

SANDPIT LA

Allot
Gdns

SHEERWATER CL
GALAHAD CL 2
HERMES DR 3
MILDMAY HO 4
Mildmay Ind Est 5

Country
Park

DRAGON CL

GARNALT DR

FERNLEA RD

HORNET

HILLSIDE RD

PARK RD

Station
Rd

WINSTREE RD

DEVONSHIRE RD

ALPHA RD

NEW RD

ESSEX RD

MILLWAY RD

BOOTH
PL

NORMANDY
AVE

ARCADIA RD

WESLEY

Burnham-on-Crouch
Prim Sch

IRB
Sta

Caravan
Site

Sports Gd
Dengie
Hundred
Sports
Ctr

WARWICK
CL

MILLFIELD

STATION RD

THE CROUCH

QUEEN'S

ALBERT RD

WESTERN RD

ALAMEDA RD

DORSET RD

ARNHEIM RD

DUNWICK RD

PK

RAMBLERS
WAY

WICK RD

Burnham
Wick

Marina

WAYFARER GDNS

REMEMBRANCE AVE

QUEENS

CORONATION RD

MILL
GN

DILLIWAY
CT

BRICKWALL

CHAPEL RD

WITNEY
RD

PROVIDENCE

ORCHARD RD

RIVERSIDE RD

SILVER RD

ARGYLE RD

Sewage
Works

PH

Burnham-on-Crouch
& District Mus

KINGS RD

REGENTS CL

YORK RD

SHIP RD

THE BELVEDERE

BELVEDERE RD

SEA-END
CVN SITE

THE SHORE

HIGH ST

B1021

PROMENADE QUAY

Slipways

C4
1 CURLEW HO
2 NELSON CT
3 HAMILTON CT
4 GRANVILLE TERR
5 STEBBINGS CT
6 ST MARY'S HO
7 AUGERS
8 HARDINGS-REACH
9 CALMPATCH
10 SUNNYMEAD FLATS
11 BUCKINGHAM SQ

12 BELVEDERE CT
13 THE CROWSNEST
14 THE ANCHORAGE
15 PETTICROW QUAYS

Ferry (F)

Gardenness
Point

River Crouch

Ringwood Bar

Overland
Point

Grassland
Point

Fleet
Point

Grapnells

Wallasea
Wetlands
Scheme

GRAPNELLS
FARM COTTS

SS4

WALLASEA ISLAND

CMO

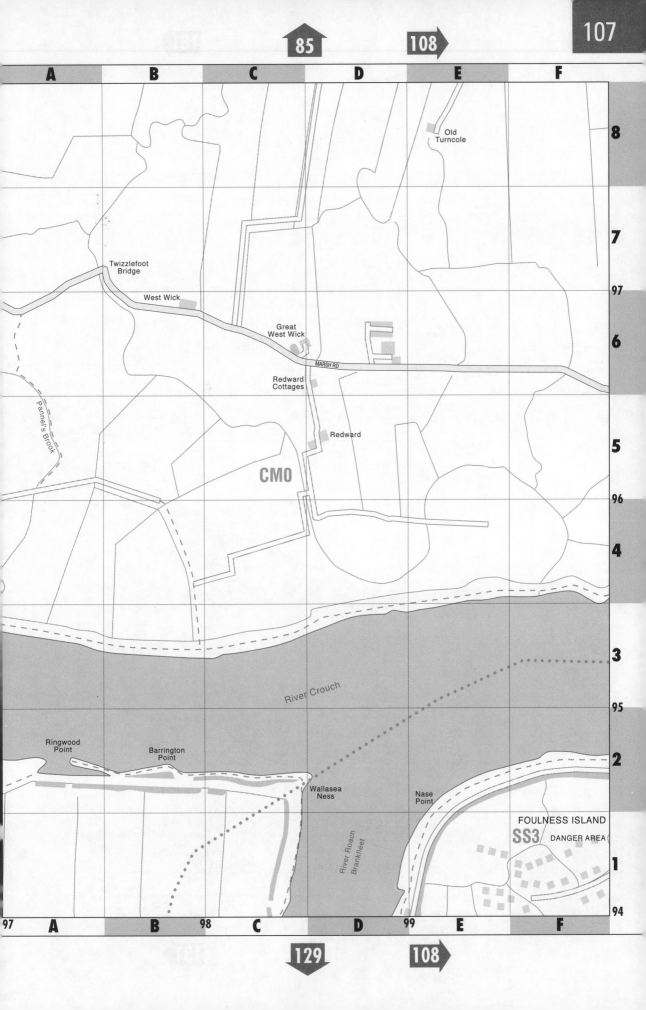

A B C D E F

8
7
97
6
5
96
4
3
95
2
1
94

Old
Turncole

Twizzlefoot
Bridge

West Wick

Great
West Wick

MARSH RD

Redward
Cottages

Redward

Pannel's Brook

CMO

River Crouch

Ringwood
Point

Barrington
Point

Wallasea
Ness

Nase
Point

River Roach
Brankfleet

FOULNESS ISLAND

SS3

DANGER AREA (

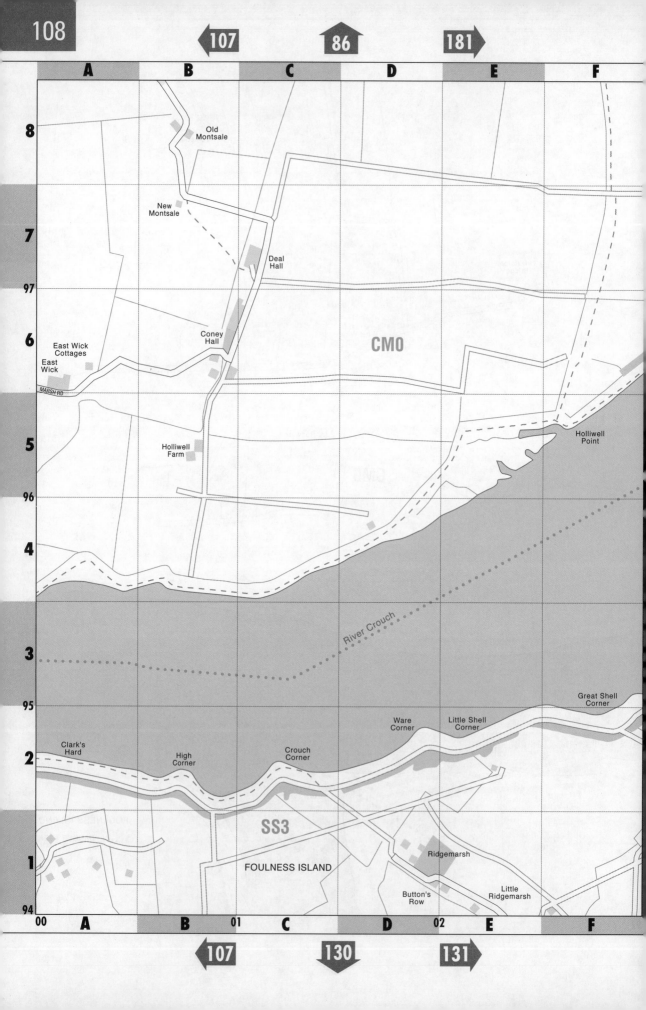

A B C D E F

8

Old
Montsale

New
Montsale

7

Deal
Hall

97

Coney
Hall

CMO

6

East Wick
Cottages

East
Wick

MARSH RD

5

Holliwell
Point

Holliwell
Farm

96

CMO

4

River Crouch

3

95

Great Shell
Corner

Ware
Corner

Little Shell
Corner

Clark's
Hard

2

High
Corner

Crouch
Corner

SS3

FOULNESS ISLAND

Ridgemarsh

1

Button's
Row

Little
Ridgemarsh

94

00 A B 01 C D 02 E F

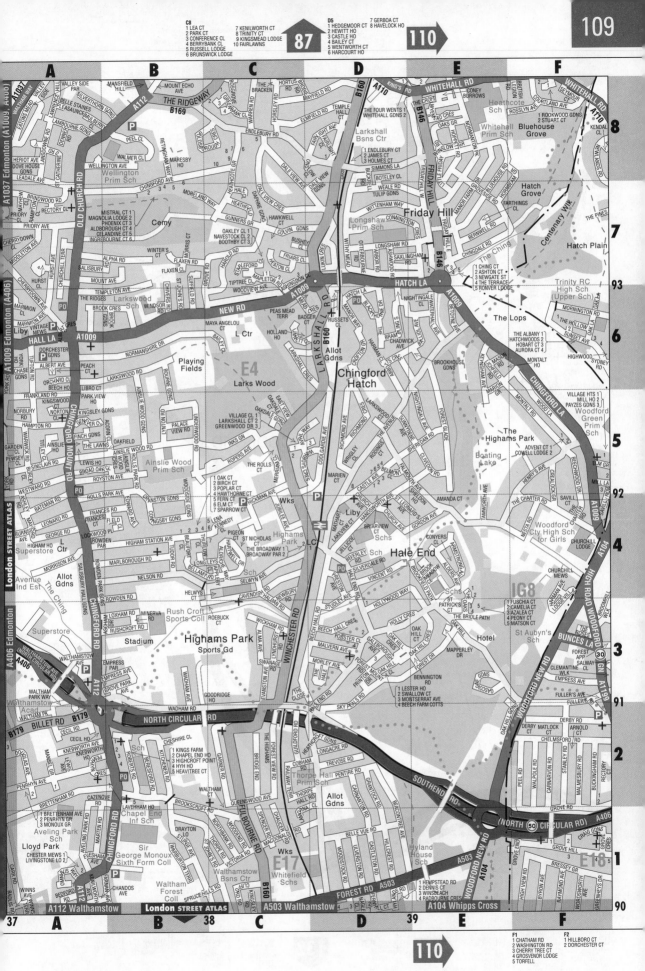

← **109**

C8
1 WESTBURY CT
2 WESTBURY RD
3 PALMERSTON CT
4 IBROX CT
5 RICHARD BURTON CT
6 QUEENS MEWS

88 ↑

C8
7 MIRRAVALE CT
8 GUNNELS CT & HASTINGWOOD CT
9 SOMERSET CT
10 MARLBOROUGH CT
11 THE AVENUE
12 TORA CT

D8
1 REGENCY LODGE
2 BUCKHURST CT
3 KINGS CT
4 SALISBURY GDNS
5 PEGASUS CT
6 BEECH CT

7 SYCAMORE HO
8 GEORGE CT
9 ATRIUM

(map of Woodford, Buckhurst Hill, Woodford Green, Woodford Bridge, Clayhall — grid A–F, 90–8)

A1
1 ESTON CT
2 REGENCY CT
3 COWLEY CT
4 THE CHILTONS
5 HIGH OAKS LODGE
6 MILLBROOK
7 LANSDOWNE RD
8 WOBURN CT
9 ULLSWATER CT

10 CLEVELAND RD
11 LEIGH CT
12 ALVESTON SQ
13 MARLBOROUGH RD
A2
1 LINDAL CT
2 HOCKLEY CT
3 WOODLEIGH
4 MILNE CT
5 CEDAR CT

6 ELIZABETH CT
7 SILVERMEAD
8 LAUREL MEAD CT
9 MITRE CT
10 PEVENSEY CT
11 LYNDHURST CT
12 RECTORY CT
13 MANOR COURT LODGE
14 QUEEN MARY VILLAS

A3
1 NEW JUBILEE CT
2 CHARTWELL CT
3 GREENWOOD
4 CLEMENTINE WLK
A4
1 THE TERRACE
2 BROOMHILL CT
3 CLIFTON CT
4 FAIRSTEAD LODGE

A4
5 HADLEIGH LODGE
6 BROADMEAD CT
7 WILTON CT
8 FAIRFIELD CT
9 HIGHAM CT
10 ASTON CT
A6
1 TREE TOPS
2 CRANFIELD CT

3 PERCIVAL HO
4 RAINE GDNS
B1
1 STATION EST
2 STATION APP
3 JAMES CT

C3
1 LISTON WAY
2 ELIZABETH CT
3 COOPERSALE CL
4 SUNSET CT
5 LAMBOURNE CT
C4
1 COWAN LODGE
2 HOPE CL
3 REX PAR

4 SHALFORD
5 THE RODINGS
6 LAWRENCE CT

A3
1 TAVISTOCK HO
2 ROSEBURY SQ
3 THE BOULEVARD
4 BRANDESBURY SQ
5 SUTHERLAND HO
6 WENTWORTH HO
7 KENSINGTON HO
8 HAMPSTEAD AVE
9 RICHMOND DR
10 OSBORNE HO
11 NORTHUMBERLAND HO
12 MARLOWE HO
13 MONTAGUE HO
14 ARLINGTON HO
15 ALEXANDRA HO
16 BARTHOLOMEW HO
17 CADOGAN HO

A   B   C   D   E   F

8

A1112
PUDDING LA
GRAVEL LA
GRAVEL CL

Chigwell Row

MILLERS STA
COOPERS CL
MILLERS CL
MANOR RD
P

RM4

Cabin Hill

7

MARDEN CL
Chigwell Row Inf Sch
FAVERSHAM CL
LAMBOURNE CRES
ANYMEDE
PO
LAMBOURNE RD
PEREA WAY
LAMMOND GDNS
MAXWELL CT
Weddrell's Plain

Hainault Forest (Country Park)

Three Forests Way

Fox Burrows Farm

WILLOWMEAD
CHASE LA
CROSBY CT
MAYPOLE CL
WHITEHALL CL
ORCHARD WAY
ALL SAINTS GR
IGONS
NGLEBY
GLEBE GDNS
DAVLOW
WOOLHAMPTON
SYLVAN WAY
B173 LAMBOURNE RD
B173

93

LODGE CL
IG7

Fox Burrows
P

Fox Burrows RD

6

CROSSBOW RD
BROCKET WAY
BEARING WAY
MANFORD CL
GREENWOOD
LATCHFORD PL
BACHELORS
LAKELAND
TERCEL
TELLGROVE PATH
FELLOWSHIP WAY
P0
KESTREL CL
MERLIN CL
50

The Lake

IG7

Dog Kennel Hill

5

VERDERERS RD
NORTH BURROW RD
LOWE CL
REDWOODS
AGISTER RD
MANFORD WAY
REGAR NEWTON RD
COPPICE PATH
HAWKINS WAY
BRANCH RD
HARBOURER RD
HUNTSMAN RD
HARBOURER CL
TALCONER
MARLYN RD
STUGHTER GDNS
BEANS B
PEREGRINE RD
FOWLER RD
Coppice Prim Sch
Manford Cross
Hainault Forest High Sch
CROMWELL CTR
Burnside Ind Est
Works
50
ROMFORD RD
30
50

FIVE OAKS LA

CH Hainault Cottages

92

PO
BURSLEM AVE
STOKE AVE
LONGPORT RD
TUNSTALL RD
NEWCASTLE AVE
LEINSTER CT
ARROWSMITH RD
POLLARD CL
FERNIE CL
BOAR CL
HURSLEY RD
The Acorn Ctr
Roebuck Trad Est
ROEBUCK RD
IG6
Works
ELMBRIDGE RD
FOREST RD
John Bramston Prim Sch
IG2

Hog Hill

4

NORTH VIEW CARAVAN SITE
KENNYLANDS RD
Forest Farm

B174 ROMFORD RD
Cold Blow Farm
FRINTON RD
BROWNING CL
WALTON RD

3

HOG HILL RD
Crown Cotts

91

RM5

Works
HAINAULT RD
WHALEBONE LA N
COLLIER ROW RD
PROVIDER
Northgate Ind Pk

2

P

Hainault Farm
RM6
Marks Gate
Furze House Farm
FURZE FARM CL
Whites Farm

1

Fairlop Plain
Seven Kingswater
BILLET RD
KINGSTON HILL AVE
A1112

90

46   A   B   47   C   D   48   E   F

91
114

A B C D E F

8

Sandhills

Hilly Park

Witch Hill Plantation

LIBERTY COTTS

B175

Horseshoe Farm

Bower Farm

Dame Tipping CE Prim Sch

NORTH RD

RM4

7

Lower Sandhills

Foreberry Wood North

BOWER FARM RD

Pheasant Wood

THE PARADE

Havering-atte-Bower

SAMANTHA MEWS

Park Farm

Avenue Wood

FAIRLIGHT VILLAS

PH

ROWLAND WLK

Round House Farm

Wr Twr

ELDAN HO

WELLINGTON AVE

BROXHILL RD

93

Foreberry Wood South

Havering Country Park

St Francis Hospice

6

Pine Wood

PINEWOOD RD

ORANGE TREE HILL

Bower House

Bower Wood

Lower Park Farm

P

RM5

Willoughby's Hill

THISTLEDENE AVE

Pinewood Prim Sch

ST JOHNS RD

KILN WOOD LA

Immanuel Sch

Bedfords Park Nature Trails

5

CRAVEN GDNS

PATMORE WAY

RAY RD

FIRBANK RD

LULWORTH DR

WARDEN AVE

Larch Wood

Deer Park

SHERBORNE GDNS

MORANT GDNS

CORNELL WAY

RAVENSWOOD CL

CLITHEROE RD

TRESODE

PRESTON

HIGHFIELDS TWRS

WENSLEY CL

OATES RD

HUNTER'S GR

HENDON GDNS

BARRY CT

CROMWELLS MERE

92

PORTMORE GDNS

FOX CL

BROWNE CL

SILVERMERE AVE

HARLOW GDNS

MAYFIELD LINK

HURST

ASHVALE GDNS

CHIGWELL VIEW

PENNINGTON CL

GRIMSTONE CL

VICTORIA AVE

BRADNICK

HILLCREST

VERNON RD

MERLIN RD

Bower Park Sch

4

ABRIDGE GDNS

BEREHAM

CHARLOTTE CL

LARCHWOOD AVE

HIGHFIELD RD

MOUNT PLEASANT RD

MERLIN GDNS

STAPLEFORD GDNS

ARAGON CL

DOMINION DR

LARCHWOOD GDNS

SUNSET MEWS

AVELON RD

Chase Cross

LOWER BEDFORDS RD

LODGE

UDALL GDNS

LYNWOOD CL

HIGHFIELD CL

BELL VIEW RD

PACEHEATH RD

PHILAN WAY

B1459

CHASE CROSS

CAMPBELL CT

NEVIS CL

Sunnyside Farm

DEFOE WAY

TURPIN AVE

BACON LINK

JUDITH AVE

Clockhouse Jun & Inf Sch

BURLAND RD

FELSTEAD RD

GABRIEL RD

CHELMSFORD AVE

BROOMFIELD RD

GOBIONS AVE

PO

GALLOWS CROSS

GLENDON RD

GREENOCK WAY

GLENTON WAY

HELMSDALE CL

ISBELL GDNS

SEAFORTH CL

RISEBRIDGE CHASE

CH

3

FERN CT

QUAR CL

CARTER CL

SHEILA RD

WOOD DR

SUNNY MEWS

IRONS WAY

RIVERSDALE RD

HAMPDEN RD

FULLER CL

BERKELEY AVE

WILTON DR

FAIRCHILD DRIVE

ROBIN CL

BOWER CL

TWEED GLEN

HAVERING RD

MORAY WAY

ESK WAY

SPEYSIDE

GARRY WAY

AYR GN

CREE WAY

RM1

FRINTON RD

TAYLOR CL

PENN GDNS

DOWNHAM CL

MILLER CL

RAMSDEN DR

GELSTHORP

COLLIER ROW RD

B1459

PO

EATON DR

BURCHWALL CL

FULLERS CL

VIRGINIA CL

BROCKLEY CRES

LAWNS WAY

THE MEWS

1 TWEED GN

2 TWEED GLEN

AYR GN

Rise Park

TAY WAY

91

B174 HOG HILL RD

HAMLET RD

HAMLET CL

RIDLEY GDNS

P

COLLIER ROW RD Liby

B174

HAZELL CRES

LOWSHOE LA

PLAYFIELD AVE

SELSDON RD

EARLS CRES

BARTLOW GDNS

WALLACE WAY

Schs

ANNAN WAY

PETTITS LAN

DEVERON WAY

GLYDON WAY

BEAULY WAY

A12

RISE PARK BVD

50

2

COLLIER ROW RD

RENOWN CL

RAIDER CL

Sch

HULSE AVE

ELIZABETH CL

GORING AVE

HILLFOOT AVE

HORNDON GN

COOK'S CL

HILLCREST CT

SMITHERS HILL

ROMFORD

HEATHER GDNS

PETTITS LAN

HEATHER WAY

PETTITS BVD

BROOK RD

HEATON WAY

HEATON GRANGE RD

RISEBRIDGE RD

RM2

SUFFOLK HO

NORFOLK HO

SUSSEX HO

SURREY HO

KENT HO

DURHAM HO

DEVON HO

CUMBERLAND HO

RUTLAND HO

River Rom

Collier Row

CLOVELLY GDNS

LYNTON AVE

HOWE CL

ROONEY WAY

NELSON CL

ARGYLE WAY

DOWN WLK

ORCHARD RD

ELM CL

CHERRY

COLLIER ROW LA

HENHAM CL

MOWBRAYS RD

WILLIAM CL

HILLFOOT AVE

LONGVIEW

TAKE LE

DELDERFIELD HO

HEATHER DR

HEATHER AVE

HEATHER GLEN

LINTON CL

TOTOM

PETTITS CT

GREAT PETTITS CT

THE ELKINS

PETTITS CL

NETHERPARK DR

ROSLYN GDNS

Marshalls Park Sch

Raphael Park

1

RM7

VANGUARD CL

BARHAM CL

MAVIS

CROSS RD

WALMER CL

DUNSTER CL

DOVER

LARKSHALL

REDRIFF RD

KENWAY

NORMAN RD

MAIDSTONE AVE

PROSPECT

FERNDALE RD

SAFFRON RD

THAMESHILL AVE

ROSEDALE

HAYDEN

WAINFLEET

PO

B174

B175

Parklands Jun & Inf Sch

HAMILTON

OAKS AVE

PRIESTS AVE

ASHMOUR GDNS

A12

50

EASTERN AVE E

MILLBROOK GDNS

LEADOAK AVE

FONTAYNE AVE

PARKSIDE AVE

MASHITERS WLK

MARSHALLS DR

PARKLAND AVE

LAKE RISE

REED POND WLK

PARKWAY

MEADWAY

90

Crownfield Inf & Jun Schs

49 A B 50 C D 51 E F

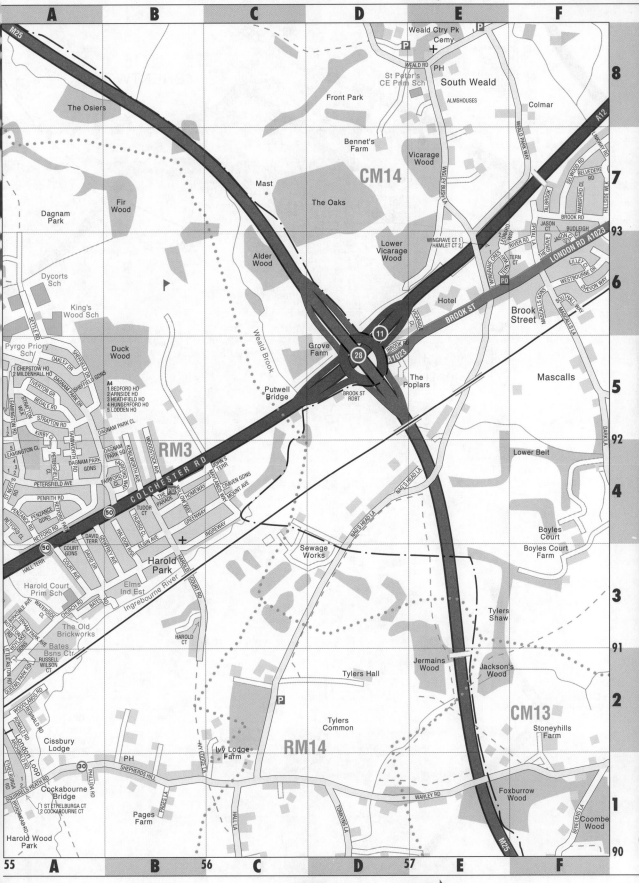

A B C D E F

8 7 6 5 4 3 2 1

CM14

South Weald

Colmar

The Osiers

Front Park

Bennet's Farm

Vicarage Wood

Mast

The Oaks

Lower Vicarage Wood

Fir Wood

Dagnam Park

Alder Wood

Dycorts Sch

King's Wood Sch

Duck Wood

Weald Brook

Grove Farm

Hotel

Brook Street

Mascalls

Pyrgo Priory Sch

RM3

Putwell Bridge

The Poplars

Lower Belt

Sewage Works

Boyles Court

Boyles Court Farm

COLCHESTER RD

Harold Park

Tylers Shaw

CM13

Harold Court Prim Sch

Elms Ind Est

Ingrebourne River

The Old Brickworks

Tylers Hall

Jermains Wood

Jackson's Wood

Bates Bsns Ctr

Tylers Common

Stoneyhills Farm

RM14

Cissbury Lodge

Ivy Lodge Farm

Cockabourne Bridge

Shepherds Hill

Pages Farm

Warley Rd

Foxburrow Wood

Coombe Wood

Harold Wood Park

←115   94

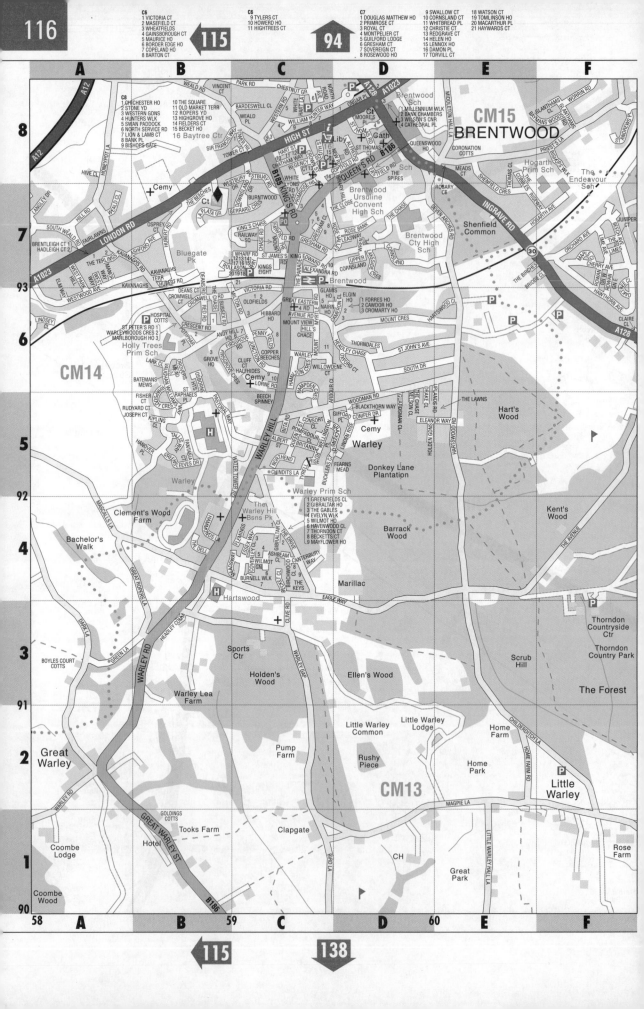

←115   138

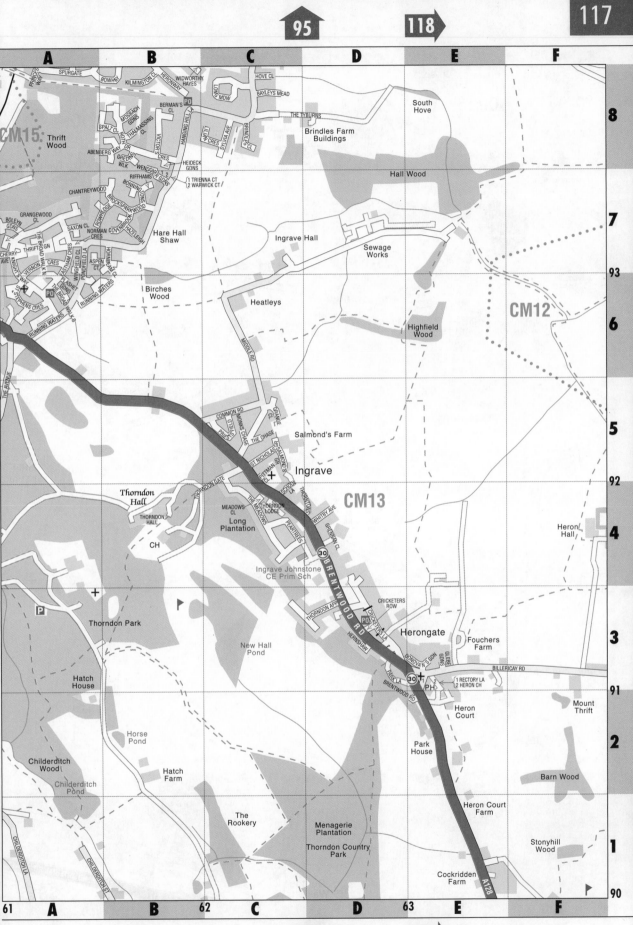

95
118

A B C D E F

8
7
93
6
5
92
4
3
91
2
1
90

CM15 · Thrift Wood

SPURGATE
PRINCES WAY
BOWRH
KILMINGTON CL
HERONWAY
WIDWORTHY HAYES
HOVE CL
BAYLEYS MEAD
THE TYBURNS
South Hove

MOSBACH GDNS
THALMASSING CL
SPALT CL
BERMAN'S CL
PO
HANGING HILL
LONG MDW
CRES
SYLVIA AVE
BRINDLES CL
Brindles Farm Buildings

ABENBERG WAY
GREDW DR
WENDOVER GDNS
VICTOR'S CRES
HEIDECK GDNS
1 TRIENNA CT
2 WARWICK CT
Hall Wood

RIFFHAMS
BONNYGINS
CHANTREYWOOD
BROCKSPARKWOOD
HAZELEIGH
Hare Hall Shaw
Ingrave Hall
Sewage Works

GRANGEWOOD CL
BOLEYN GDNS
ROWHEDGE
COVENDALE
SAXON CL
NORMAN CRES
ASPEN
Birches Wood
Heatleys
Highfield Wood
CM12

THE BROAD WALK
CHERRY AVE
THRIFTWOOD
KNIGHTS WAY
STEPHENS CRES
VERNOR CRES
EASTHAM CRES
WINGFIELD CL
PONDFIELD LA
SALMON'S DR
Running Waters
PO
MIDDLE RD

THE AVENUE

COMMON RD
MONKS CHASE
PRIORY
THE CHASE
ST NICHOLAS DR
SALMON'S DR
GITTMAN DR
SCHOOL LA
THORNTON'S
GRANGE CL
WHITBY AVE
Salmond's Farm
Ingrave
CM13

Thorndon Hall
THORNDON GATE
MEADOWS CL
THE MEADOWS
THORNDON LODGE
PEARTREES
THORNDON HALL
Long Plantation
CH
Ingrave Johnstone CE Prim Sch
GRENVAN CL
30
BRENTWOOD RD
Heron Hall

P
Thorndon Park
New Hall Pond
THORNDON APP
HERNSHAW
CRICKETERS ROW
PO
CRICKETERS LA
Herongate
Fouchers Farm
GLEBE GDNS
DONOVAN'S GDN
BILLERICAY RD

Hatch House
30
PH
1 RECTORY LA
2 HERON CH
PARK LA
BRENTWOOD RD
Heron Court
Mount Thrift

Horse Pond
Park House
Barn Wood

Childerditch Wood
Childerditch Pond
Hatch Farm
Heron Court Farm
Stonyhill Wood

The Rookery
Menagerie Plantation
Thorndon Country Park
Cockridden Farm
A128

CHILDERDITCH LA
CHILDERDITCH ST

61 A B 62 C D 63 E F

A **B** **C** **D** **E** **F**

8

Creaseys Farm

James's Wood

CM13

Bluntswall Wood

Bluntswall Shaws

Curd Farm

FAIRFIELD RISE

CHERRYTREES

TYELANDS

Kingsmans Farm

SCRUB RISE

Tye Common

Primstock

Elmshaws Farm

7

Little Bladen's Wood

TYE COMMON RD

CM12

WIGGIN'S LA

FRITHWOOD CL

TREVOR LA

FIRST AVE

SECOND AVE

Frith Wood

93

Bladen's Wood

Ninges Corner

Sudbury's Farm

Salmon's Farm

SUDBURYS FARM RD

6

Long Shaw

Babshole Farm

Avalon Cottage

WIGGINS LA

Stockwell Hall

CH

Round Wood

BLIND LA

5

HATCHES FARM RD

Hatches Farm

CLOCK HOUSE RD

LANGDON COMMON RD

Little Bursted

92

Buller's Farm

BOTNEY HILL RD

4

Botney Hill Farm

St Margaret's Farm

Chase Farm

RECTORY RD

BILLERICAY RD

Parkhill Wood

3

Green Lane

91

Spearshill Wood

PH

2

Dog Wood

DUNTON RD

Park Farm

CM13

Lady Spring Wood

Carvers Farm

Poles Wood

DUNTON RD

1

SOUTHFIELD CHASE

A127

SOUTHEND ARTERIAL RD

A127

90

Dunton Wayletts

SS15

64 **A** **B** 65 **C** **D** 66 **E** **F**

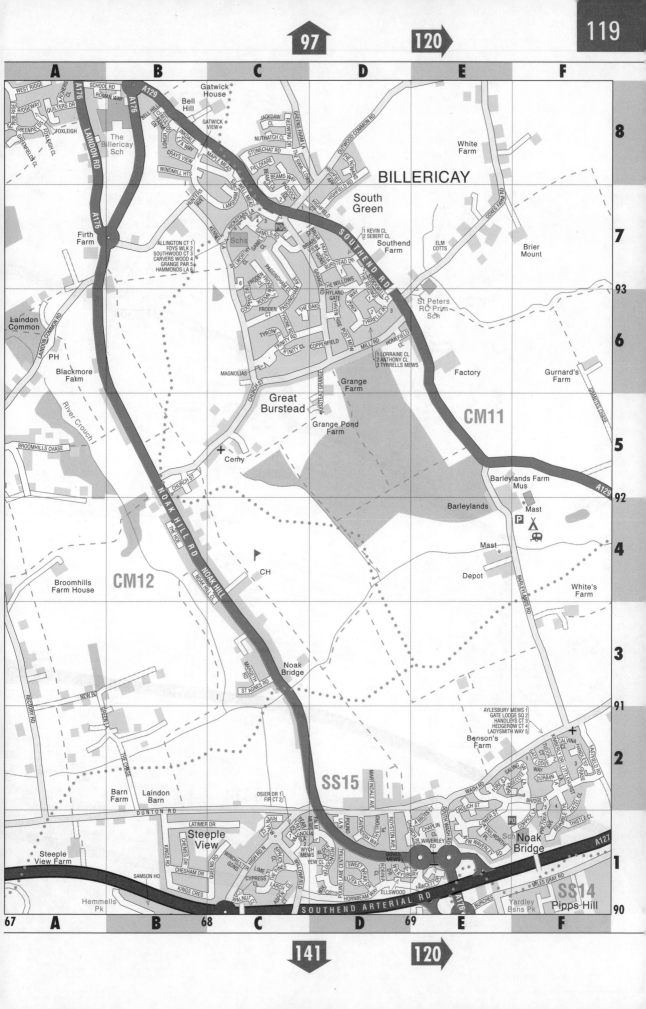

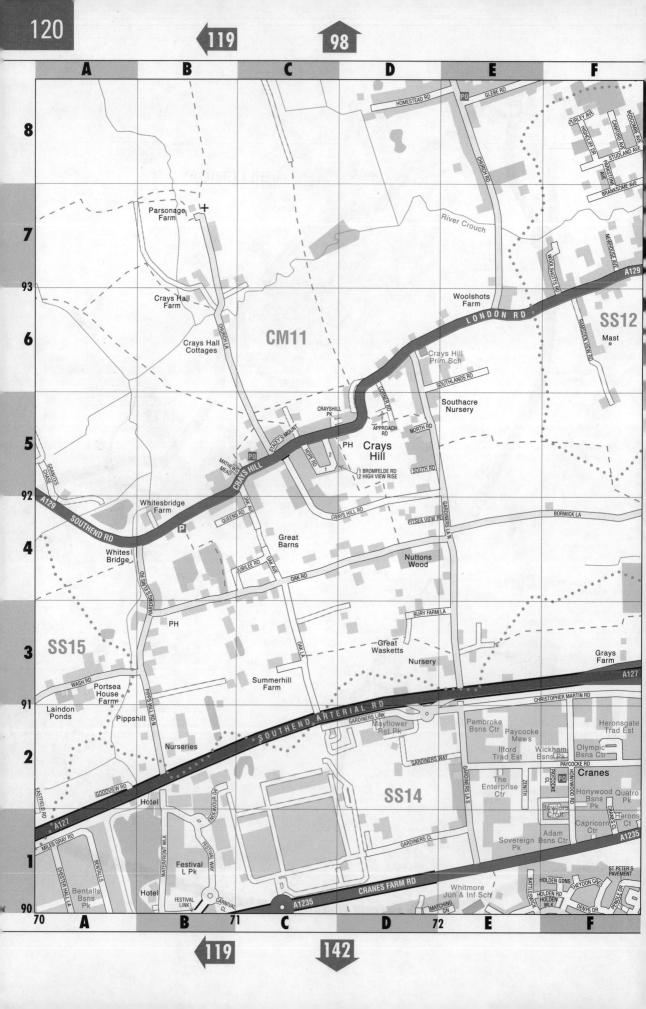

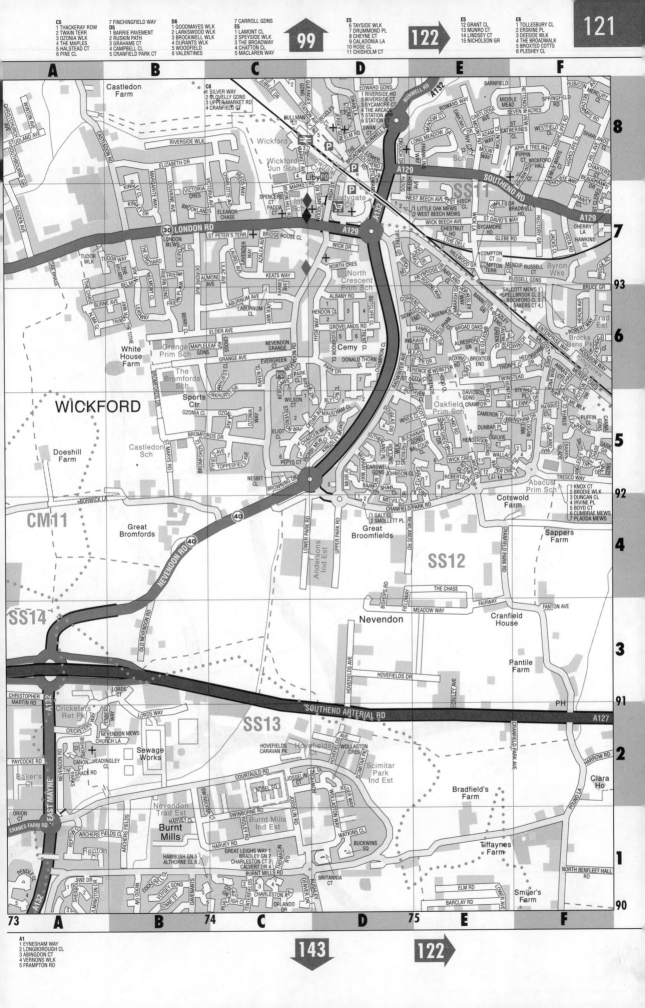

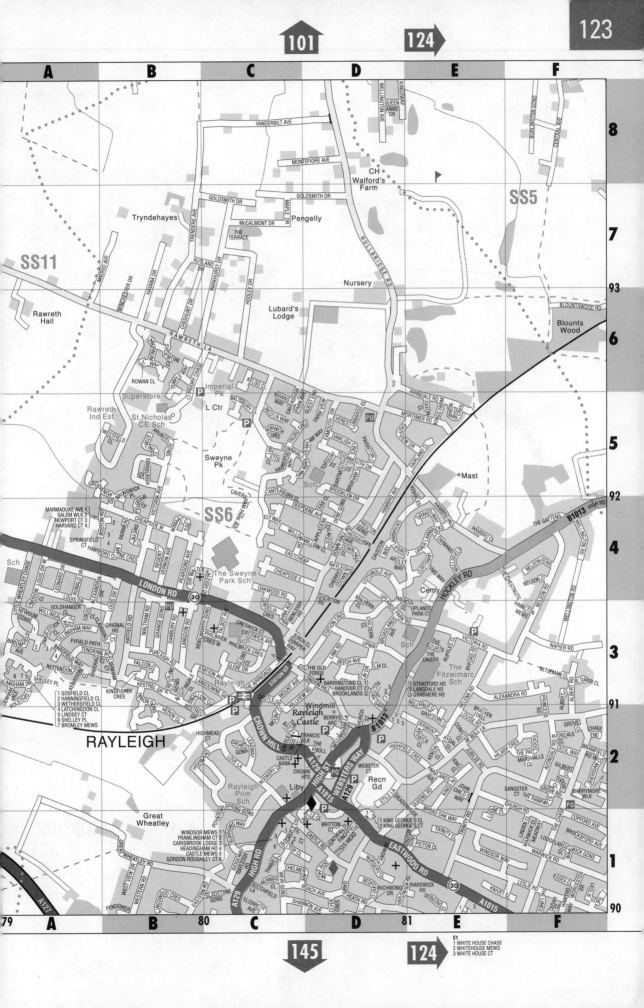

125
104

A B C D E F

8

7

93

6

Scotts Hall
Cotts

Scott's
Hall

Ballards
Gore

Apton Hall
Farm

CH PH

GORE RD PAGLESHAM RD

Old
Rectory

APTON HALL RD

Breade
House

Gore Farm

Wood
Sloppy

Stewards Elm
Farm

Moat & Springs

5

92

Doggetts

Little Stambridge
Hall

STEWARDS ELM FARM LA

FIELDS
ST
PO
CAGEFIELD RD

SS4

Great
Stambridge

PH

CAGE FIELD
COTTS

4

ASH TREE CT

Ragstone
Lodge

Brick
House

Stambridge
Fisheries

Hampton
Barns

LITTLE STAMBRIDGE HALL RD

3

91

DOGGETTS CHASE

STILLWELL'S
CL

LINGFIELD DR

RUSSEL CTR

COOMBES GR

Winters

PH

Bartonhall
Creek

MORNINGTON AVE

Allott
Gdns

Coombes
Farm

STAMBRIDGE RD

Stambridge
Prim Sch

2

ROCHEWAY

MILL LA

Great Stambridge
Hall

Waldens

Stambridge
Mills

Broomhills

River Roach

1

90

TINKER'S LA

BRICKFIELDS WAY

FEATHERBY WAY

... TON WAY

MALTHEAD WAY

Roach View
Bsns Pk

88 A B 89 C D 90 E F

125
148

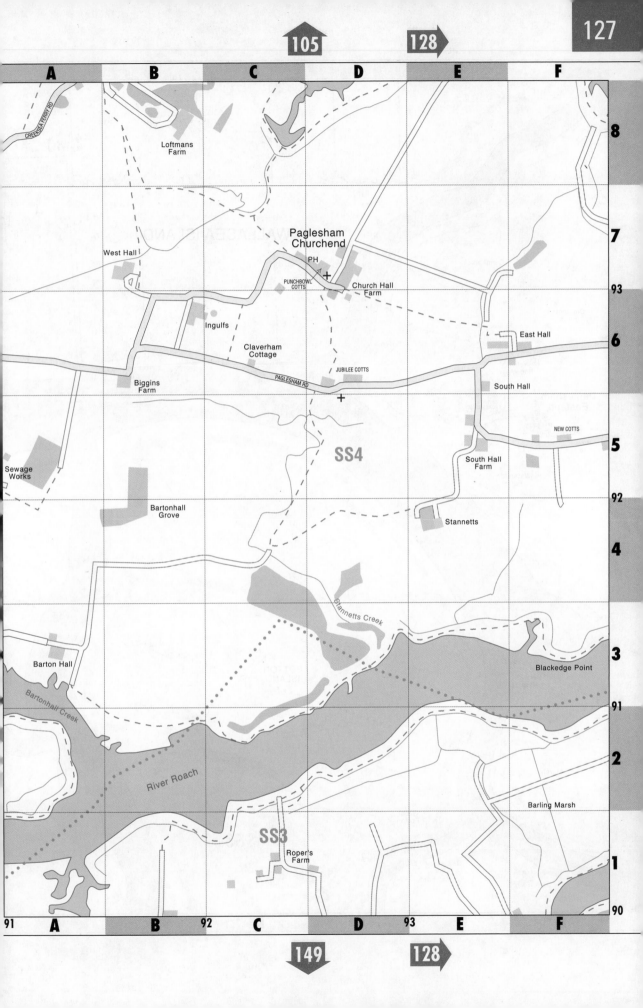

105
128

A B C D E F

8

7

93

6

92

5

4

91

3

2

1

90

CREEKSEA FERRY RD

Loftmans Farm

West Hall

Paglesham Churchend

PH

PUNCHBOWL COTTS

Church Hall Farm

Ingulfs

Claverham Cottage

East Hall

JUBILEE COTTS

PAGLESHAM RD

South Hall

Biggins Farm

NEW COTTS

SS4

South Hall Farm

Sewage Works

Bartonhall Grove

Stannetts

Stannetts Creek

Barton Hall

Blackedge Point

Bartonhall Creek

River Roach

Barling Marsh

SS3

Roper's Farm

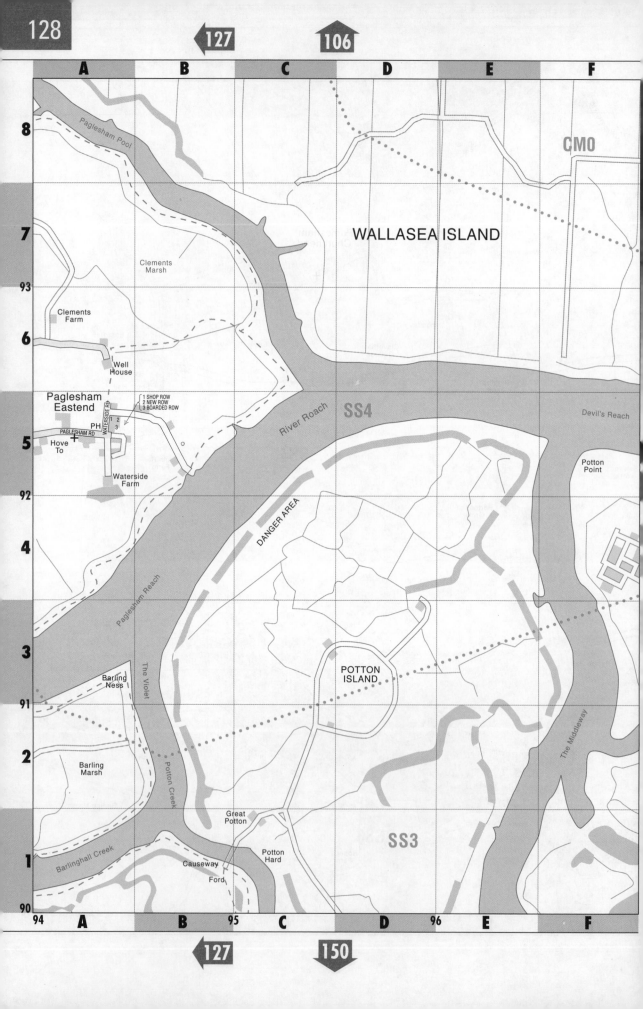

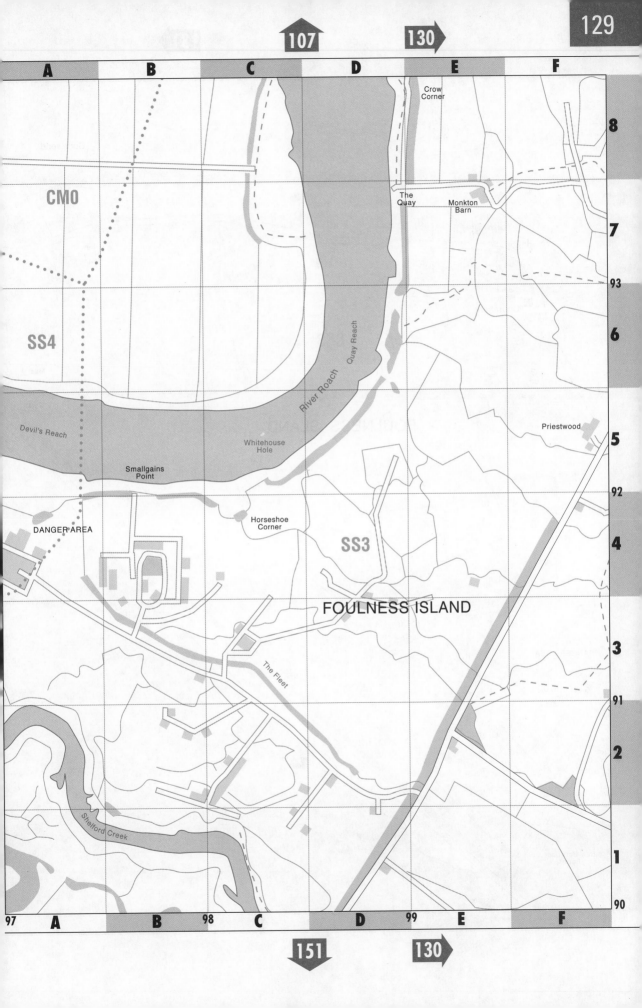

A   B   C   D   E   F

8

CM0

7

93

SS4

6

92

Crow
Corner

The
Quay

Monkton
Barn

Priestwood

River Roach

Quay Reach

Devil's Reach

Whitehouse
Hole

5

Smallgains
Point

Horseshoe
Corner

SS3

4

DANGER AREA

FOULNESS ISLAND

3

The Fleet

91

2

Shelford Creek

1

90

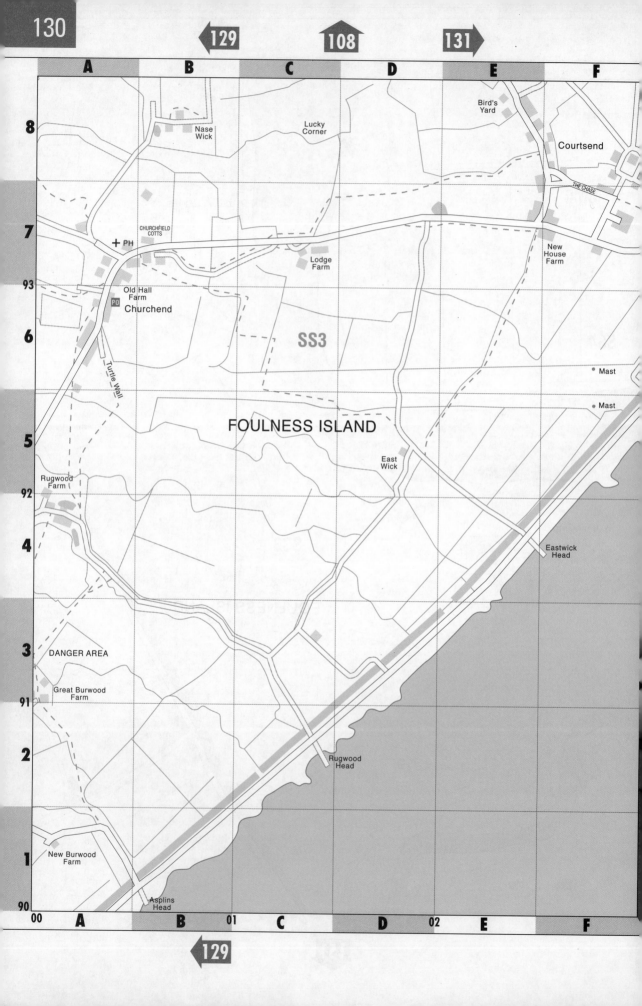

A B C D E F

8

Nase
Wick

Lucky
Corner

Bird's
Yard

Courtsend

THE CHASE

7

CHURCHFIELD
COTTS

+ PH

Lodge
Farm

New
House
Farm

93

Old Hall
Farm

PO

Churchend

SS3

6

Turtle Wall

• Mast

FOULNESS ISLAND

• Mast

5

East
Wick

Rugwood
Farm

92

4

Eastwick
Head

3

DANGER AREA

Great Burwood
Farm

91

2

Rugwood
Head

1

New Burwood
Farm

90

00 A B 01 C D 02 E F

Asplins
Head

108

River Crouch

Foulness Point

East
Newlands

The Drift
(dis)

SS3

DANGER AREA

Masts

Mast

Northern
Corner

Fisherman's
Head

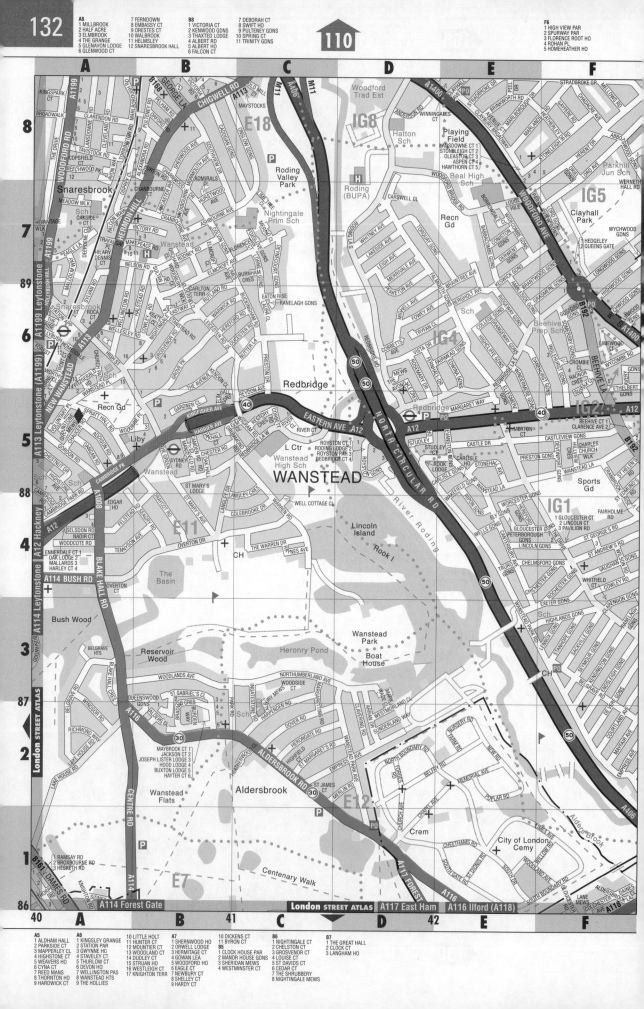

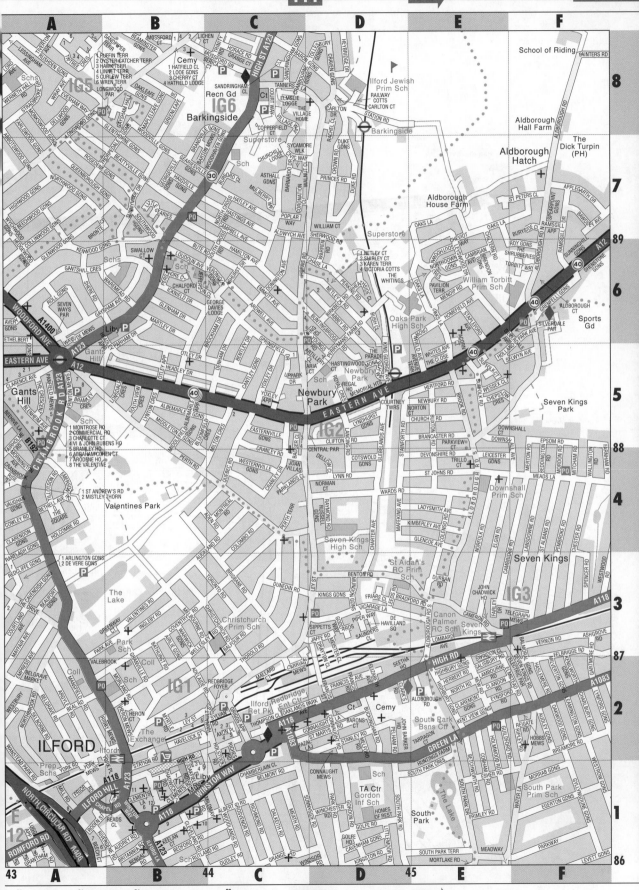

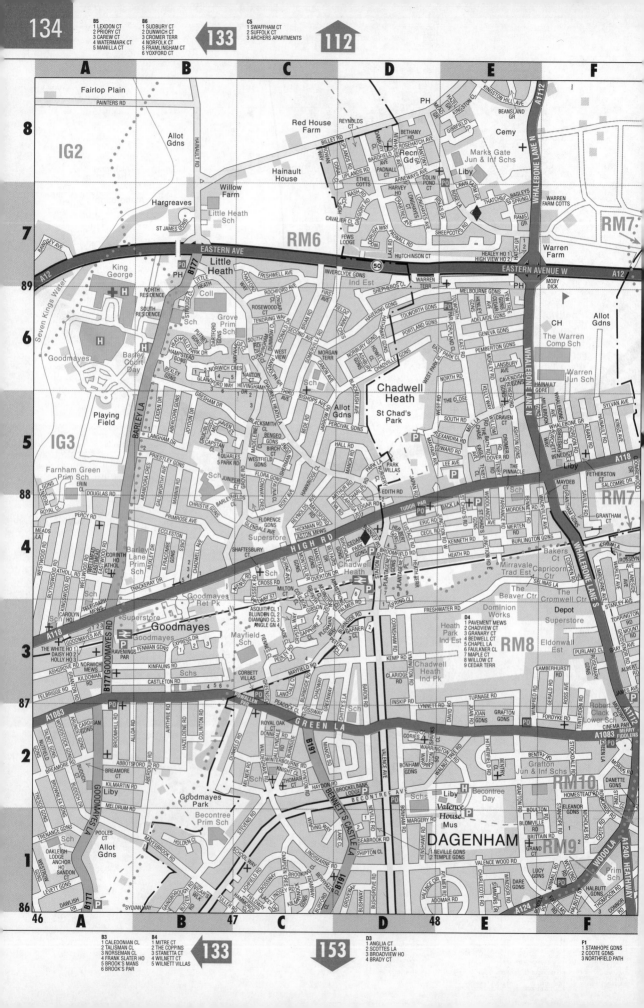

113 136

154 136

B6
1 ACADEMY SQ
2 SCHOLARS CT
3 MASTERS CT
4 SCHOLARS WAY
5 COLLEGE CT
6 HAVERSTOCK PL

← 135

C7
1 EDINBURGH HO
2 VICTORIA HO
3 ELIZABETH HO
4 MOUNTBATTEN HO
5 SNOWDON CT

↑ 114

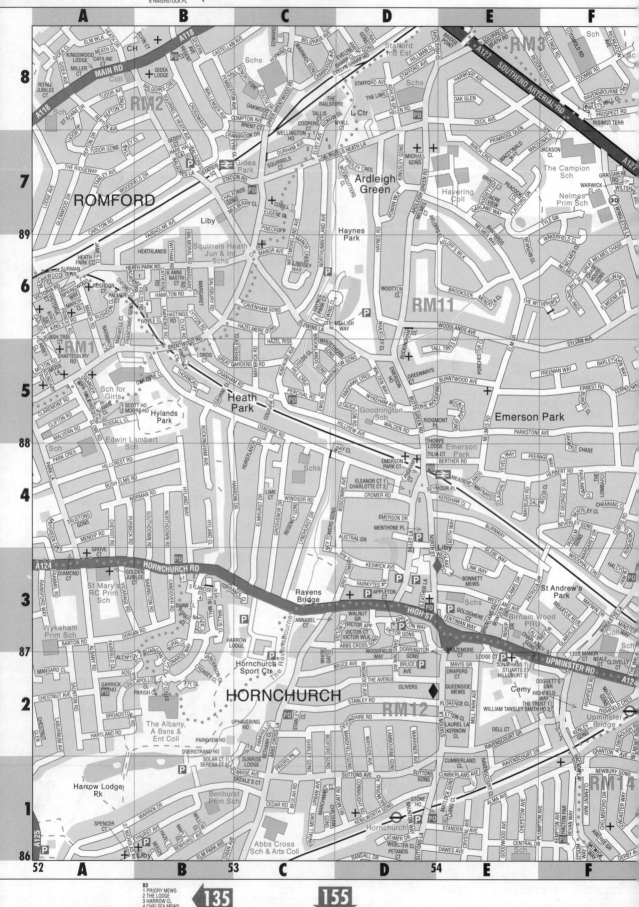

B3
1 PRIORY MEWS
2 THE LODGE
3 HARROW CL
4 CHELSEA MEWS
5 THE CHAPEL

← 135

↓ 155

A B C D E F

8 Harold Wood Prim Sch

RM3

Greathouse

Sutton's Farm

CM13

Prospect Farm

Ingrebourne Farm

London Loop

Great Tomkyns

Howard's Farm

Emery Farm

GRAYS COTTS

7 Hotel
1 Pembroke Cl
2 Hampshire Rd

Mount Pleasant Farm

Upminster Lodge Farm

FOLKES LA

89

The Rosary

SOUTHEND ARTERIAL RD

6 The Strawberry Farm

BIRD LA

PANTILE COTTS

BROOKMANS PARK DR

Little Tabrams Farm

A127

Nursery

RM11

Lillyputts Equestrian Ctr

Engayne Prim Sch

FAIRHOLME

5

THE COBBLES

London Loop

Ingrebourne River

RIVER DR

88

Emerson Park Sch

Playing Fields

Brunswick Ct

ACACIA GDNS

SUNNYCROFT GDNS

4 CH

Tithe Barn Mus

Cranham

LIMERICK GDNS

THE FAIRWAY

Hall Mead Sch

INGREBOURNE GDNS

3 WILLOW PAR

ASHBURNHAM GDNS

HURSTWOOD CT

WALDEGRAVE GDNS

ABINGTON CT

DEYNCOURT GDNS

87

St Kathryns Pl

2 UPMINSTER RD

Upminster Mill

St Kathryns Pl
Upminster

UPMINSTER

STATION APP

ST MARY'S LA

B187

PH TAMA COTTS

The James Oglethorpe Prim Sch

Hornchurch Sports Stad

Sacred Heart of Mary Girls' Sch

A124 B187

Upminster Pk

THE CLOCKHOUSE

The Coopers' Company & Coborn Sch

RM14

1 Branfil Inf Sch

London Loop

STEWART AVE

SPRINGFIELD GDNS

Cranham Hall

86

A B C D E F

8

Dunton Wayletts

CM12

Eastlands Spring

Friern Manor Wood

SOUTHEND ARTERIAL RD

A127

B148

Automobile Research Ctr

Green Meadows Nurseries

7

Brookman's Farm

Friern Manor

MERRYLANDS CHASE

SS15

COMMERCIAL WAY

CHRISTY CT

CHRISTY WAY

HORNSBY SQ

SEAX CT

SEAX WAY

SABLE WAY

ARGENT CT

SYLVAN CT

FENTON WAY

Southfields

1 BROADWATER GN
2 WOODSTOCK CRES
3 WOODSTOCK GDNS
4 PRESIDENTS CT
5 HELMORE CT

89

BRAMSTON LINK

BRAMSTON WAY

B148

6

Dunton Hills Farm

CM13

The Old Rectory

WEST MAYNE

SAFFRON CT

BUTTON LINK

Westmayne Ind Pk

SUMPNERS LINK

B1036

DURHAM RD

FRASER

BLACKMORES

PALATINE

PAYFORDS

KENN

DR

5

+

Dunton Hall

CHURCH RD

ORCHARD VIEW

MAIN DR

DUNTON VIEW

BULPHAN VIEW

Dunton Park CVN PK

MANDEVILLE

WAY

B1036

KENTON

WORCESTER CL 1
SHREWSBURY CL 2
OSTERLEY DR 3
AMERSHAM AVE 4
MAHONIA DR 5
IPSWICH MEWS 6
ALNWICK CL 7
OXFORD CL 8
CAMBRIDGE CL 9
MONMOUTH MEWS 10

NOTTINGHAM WAY

READING

CHORLEY

MARLE TREE WAY

NIGHTINGALES

APPLE TOR DR

HOLLY AV

88

BURR

FERN WLK

AYLESBURY DR

OAKHAM CL

NORTHAMPTON DR

Great Berry

MIMOSA CL

+

JASMINE

4

WOODVIEW

WEST AVE

OAKENHURST GDNS

GLENWOOD GDNS

MILTON AVE

MEADROW

STAFFORD GN

FOREST GLADE

SUNNYSIDE

HILLTOP RISE

TORNEY CL

Great Berry Prim Sch

LAKE VIEW

FIRST AVE

CENTRAL AVE

HIGH BANK 1
REEVES CL 2

KILOWAN CL

SECOND AVE

Plotlands Mus

THIRD AVE

P

3

Poultry Farm

Langdon Conservation Ctr

FOURTH AVE

SS16

Dunton Poultry Farm

87

Lower Dunton Hall

2

A128

RM14

Balgownie Farm

BRENTWOOD RD

Motel Garlesters

BULPHAN BY-PASS

BRENTWOOD RD

Noke Hall Farm

Doesgate Farm

Bentley Farm

1

DOESGATE LA

OLD CHURCH HILL

Little Malgraves Ind Est

86

A128

Manor House

Little Malgraves

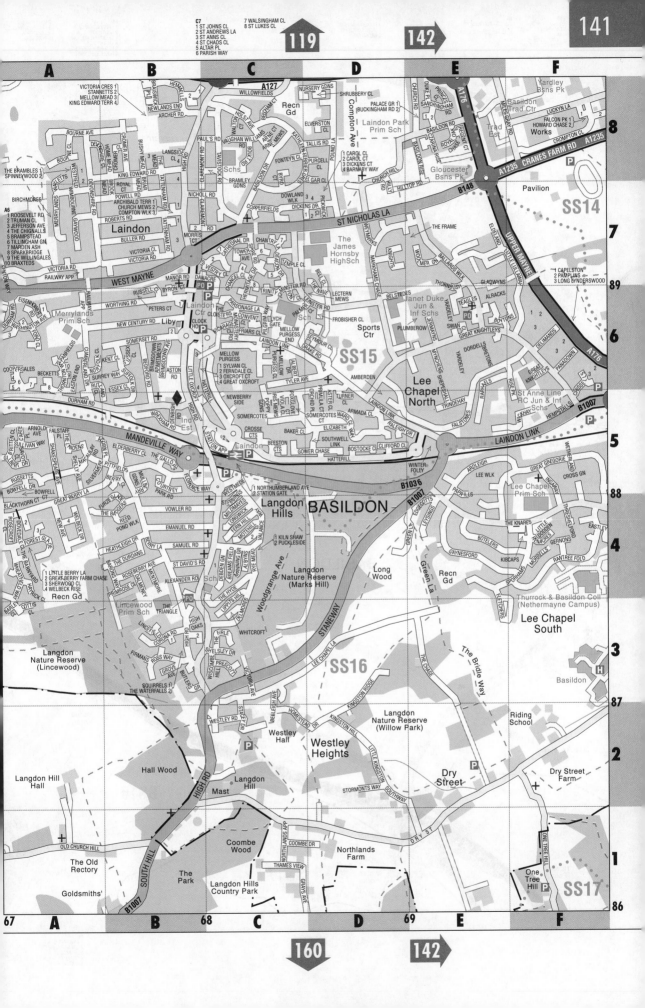

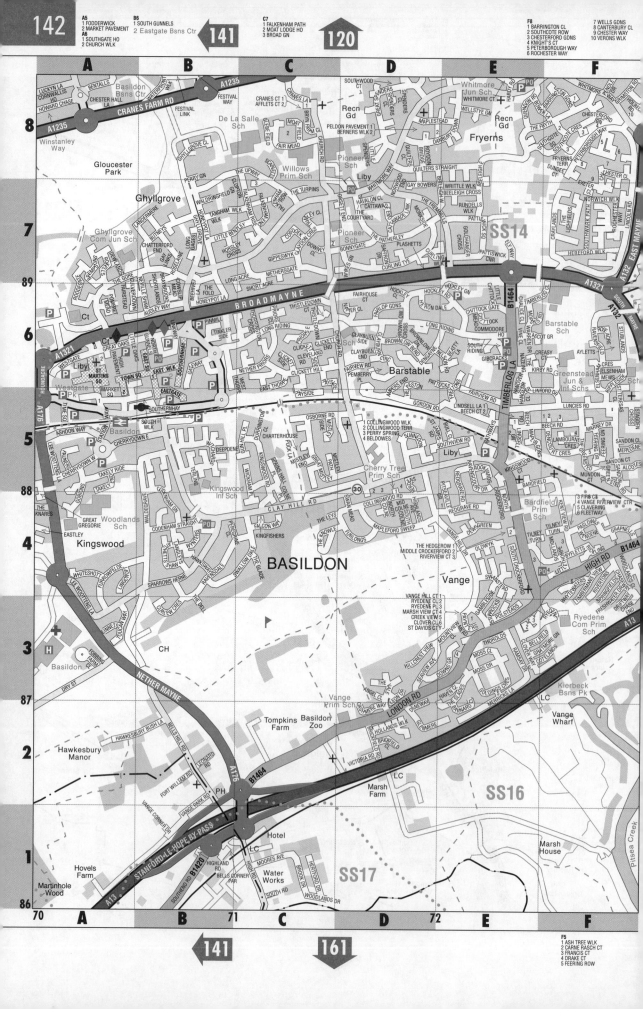

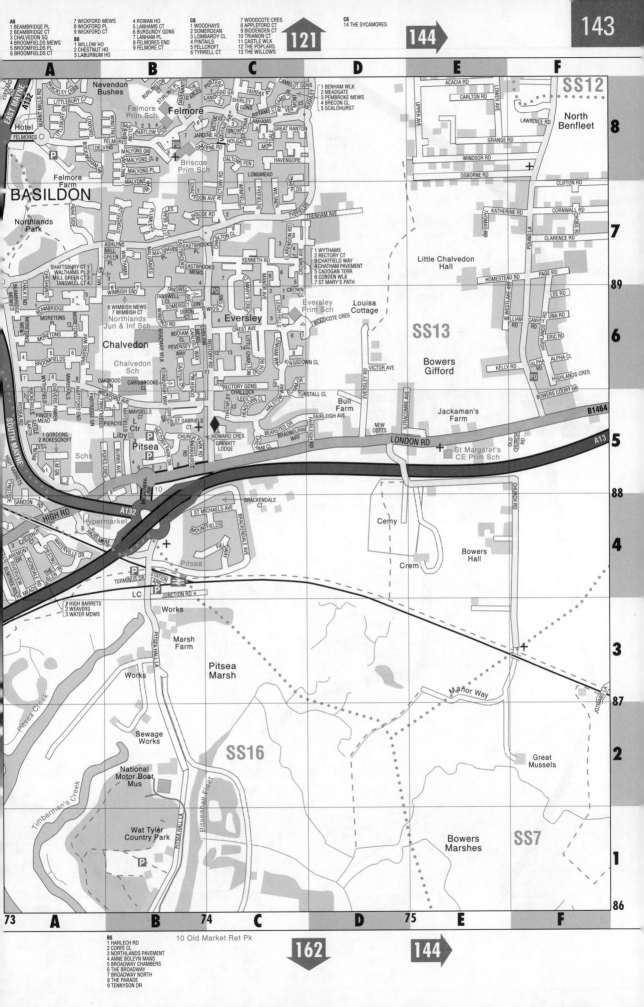

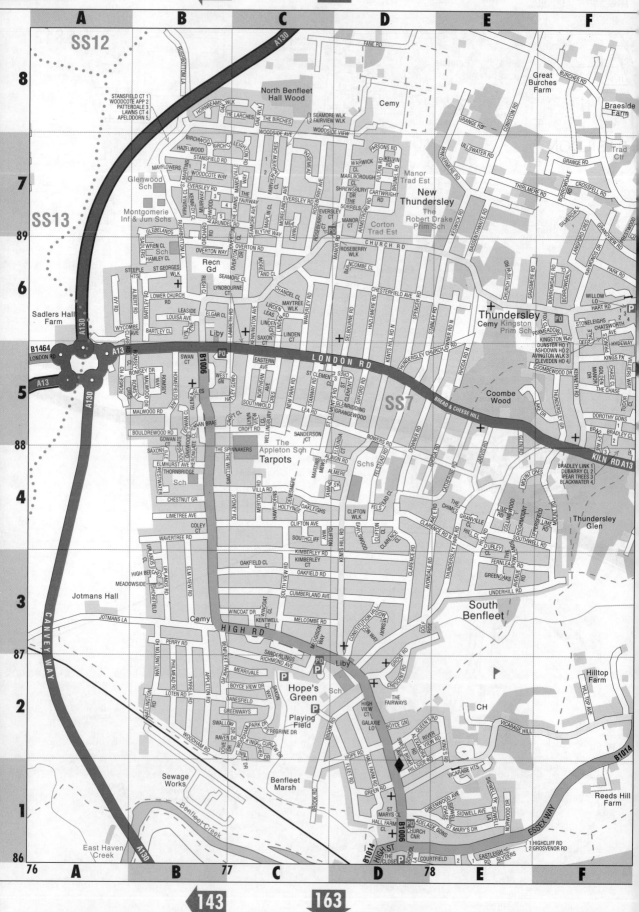

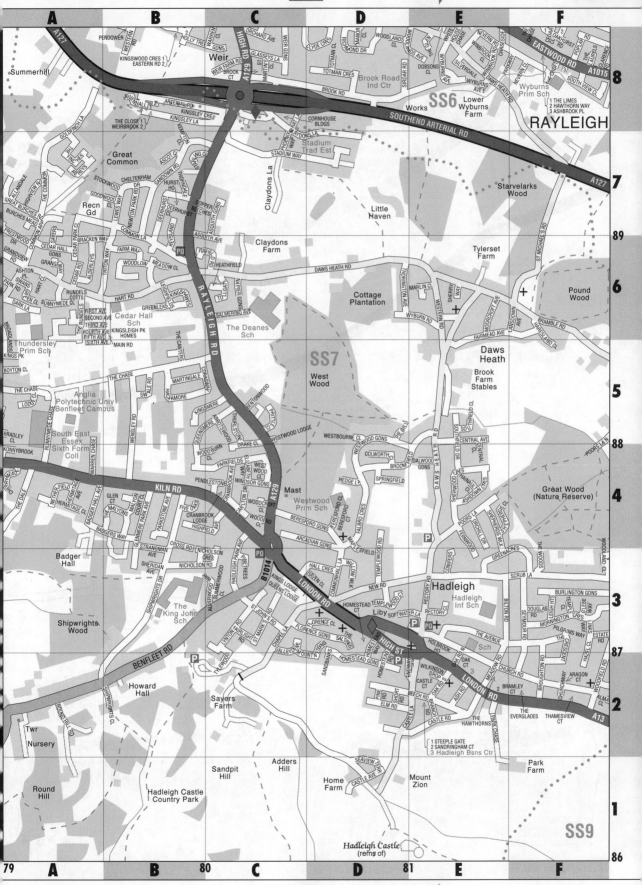

125 148 166 148

8
7
89
6
5
88
4
3
87
2
1
86

A B C D E F

85 86 87

SOUTHEND-ON-SEA

SS9
SS4
SS2
SS0

Roach Valley Way
Works
Cherry Orchard
CHERRY ORCHARD LA
CHERRY ORCHARD WAY
B1013
Aviation Way
Lancaster Bsns Pk
London Southend Airport
Hotel
Britannia Bsns Pk
Laurence Ind Est
Eastwoodbury La
SUTTON RD
ROCHEFORT DR
LEICESTER AVE
QUEEN ELIZABETH CHASE
KING HENRY'S DR
ANN BOLEYN DR
QUEENSLAND CHASE
RAVENSWOOD CHASE
Prittle Brook
WARNERS BRIDGE CHASE
Airport Ret Pk
A1159 WARNERS
SHERBOURNE RD
FARRIERS WAY
SUMPTERS WAY
Brookside Ct Ctr
Baron
Parkside Ctr
Robert Leonard Ind Est
Cemy
Prittlebrook Ind Est

Neil Armstrong Way
Fastnet
Scott Cl
Meakins
Whitehouse Mews
L Ctr
Kingsdown Sch
Sports Gd
NESTUDA WAY B1013
Comet Way
Lympstone Cl
Brendon Way
Snakes La

North Cres
Feeches Rd
South Cres
Purley Way
Denton Cl
Hornby Cl
Hornby Ave

Willmott Rd
Bristol Rd
Vickers Rd
Wells Ave
Nightingale Cl
Smallholdings
Eastwoodbury
Rochford Rd
Alton Gdns
Audleys Cl
Oaken Grange Dr
Keith Way
Farlawn Gdns
Byrne Dr
Marlow Gdns
Beverley Gdns
Beechmont Gdns
Aragon Cl
Princes
Marina Cl
Hampton Ct

PRINCE AVE
A1158
A40
Prince Avenue Prim Sch
Earls Hall Jun & Inf Schs
Midhurst Ave
Parkstone Dr
Beeleigh Cl
Mayfield Ave
POST HALL LA
CUCKOO CNR
A1159 PRIORY CRES
Prittlewell Priory Mus
Priory Park
A1159

St Thomas More High Sch for Boys
Westcliff High Schs
SOUTHBOURNE GR
WESTBOURNE GR
Holmsdale Cl
Cardigan Ave
General H
Carlingford Dr
Lavender Mews
Hillborough Rd
Chase Gdns
Southend High Sch for Boys
Cecil Ct
Hardwick Ct
Burr Hill Ch

The Prittlewell Sch
Lancaster Sch
Prittlewell
Grove Ct
Prittlewell Chase
Balmoral Terr 1
Avocoa Terr 2
Springleigh Pl 3
Fielding Way 4
Brook Ct 5
Spring Ct 6
Fairings Ct 7
Highfield Way
Shakespeare Ave
Phoenix
Southend United FC
The Westborough Prim Sch
Station App
Priory Cres
Regency Gn
EAST ST B1015

SS0
VICTORIA AVE
Fairfax Dr
St George's Park Ave
Westminster Dr
Fairmead Ave
Hildaville Dr
Fleetwood Ave
Southview Dr
Electric Ave
Northview Dr
Westcliff Park Dr
Beedell Ave
Ramuz Dr
Brightwell Ave
Glenwood Ave
Silverdale Ave
Wenham Dr
Macdonald Ave
Gainsborough Dr
St George's Dr
Berkley Rd
WEST ST
WEST RD
St Mary's Prittlewell CE Prim Sch
1 REYNOLDS HO
2 STABLE MEWS
Colchester Rd
Harcourt Ave
C Coll
P C Ctr
A127

Our Lady of Lourdes RC Prim Sch
Manchester Dr
Cavendish Gdns
Greenbanks
Eastwood La S
Southborough La S
Kingsway Mews
Silversea Dr
Wellington Ave
A1158
Liby
Tintern Mews
Westborough Rd
Rochford Ave
Rayleigh Ave
Hamlet Court Mews
Salisbury Ave
Albany Ave
The Westborough Prim Sch
St Mary's Rd
Sweyne Ave
Boston Ave
St Helen's RC Prim Sch

Spencer Ho
Birchwood Gr
Woodfield
Leigh Rd
Brayburn
Chalkwell Ave
LONDON RD
Chalkwell Lodge/Churchgate
Osbourne Ho
Imperial Lodge
Winton Lodge
Imperial Lodge
St Hildas Sch
Crowstone Rd
Chalkwell Ave
Cranley Ave
Cotswold Rd
Valkyrie
Argyll Rd
B1015
Claremont Rd
Albion Rd
Osborne Rd
Grampian
Windsor Rd
Brecon
Blackdown
A13
Carnarvon Rd
Cumberland
A127

King's Rd
Park Side
The Drive
Leigh Rd
Savannah Hts

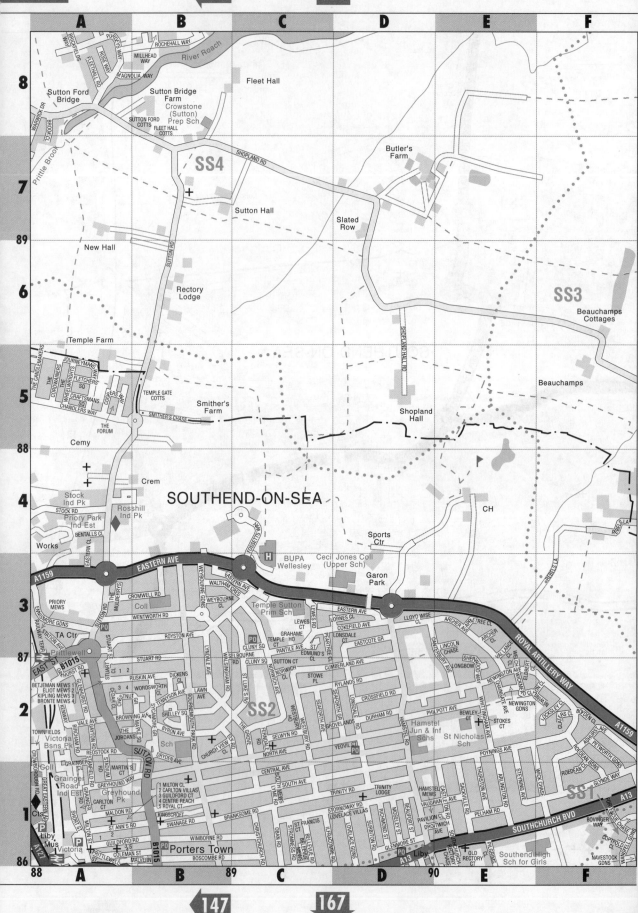

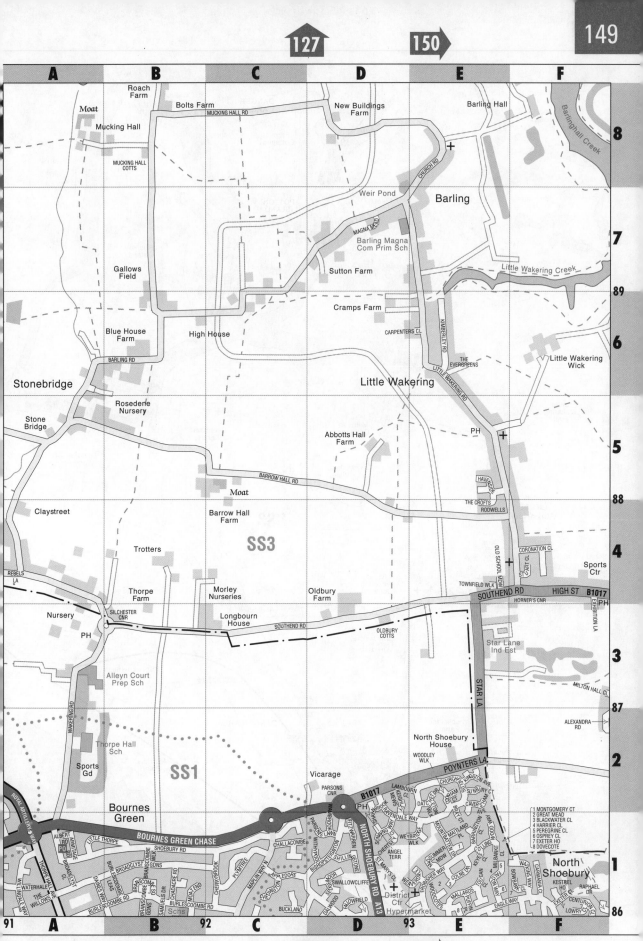

149
128

A B C D E F

8

DANGER AREA

Farm Cottages

The Middleway

Narrow Guls

Fleethead Creek

7

Brimstone Hill

Swing Bridge

Fleet Head

POTTON ISLAND

Rushley Island

Wakering Creek

89

Halfway House Farm

Mill Head

6

Rushley Farm

Ford

Havengore Creek

Little Wakering Hall

Millhead Cottages

Oxenham Farm

Sewage Works

5

Millhead Villas

88

Great Wakering

SS3

Bridge Rd

4

LITTLE WAKERING HALL LA

THE MALLARDS
BROUGHAM CL
RUSHLEY CL
MORELAND CL
LEE LOTTS
TWYFORD AVE
MERCER AVE
CRES
NORTHFIELD CRES
OLIVERS CL
ORCHARD CL
NORTH ST
CHAPEL LA
ANSTEAD
LINDSEY RD
HAVERING RD
WHITE HALL RD
HOME FARM CL
WEDDS WAY
COMMON

Landwick Cotts

Stairs Rd

B1017
HIGH ST
B1017
Liby
Great Wakering Common
NEW RD

PO
GOODMANS
CONWAY AVE
BELL HO
ALP CT
FAIRFIELD
ST JOHN'S RD
GLEBE CL
MORRINS CL
SAMUEL'S CNR

Great Wakering Prim Sch

1 LION FIELDS
2 SOUTHGATE MEWS
3 ST JOHN'S CL
4 THE ANCHORAGE
5 RODING CL
6 THE CEDARS

3

ALEXANDRA RD

OLD HALL CT 7
CROUCHMANS AVE 8

LC
Morrin's Chase
Shoeburyness New Ranges

MILTON HALL CL

SHOEBURY RD

87

Crouchmans Farm

MARINERS CT
BEACH CT
GOODMANS
HAVENGORE CL
SEAVIEW DR

DANGER AREA

BROOKSIDE AVE
ESTUARY GDNS
GOLDSWORTHY DR
NEW ENGLAND CRES

Morrin's Point

Crouchmans Cottage

The Lansdowne

VICTORIA DR
CUPIDS CHASE

2

POYNTERS LA

CUPID'S CNR

SEETONS RD
CHERRYTREE CHASE

1

PICASSO WAY

Poynter's Point

86

RAPHAEL DR
BRODIE RD
BUTTS RD

94 A B 95 C D 96 E F

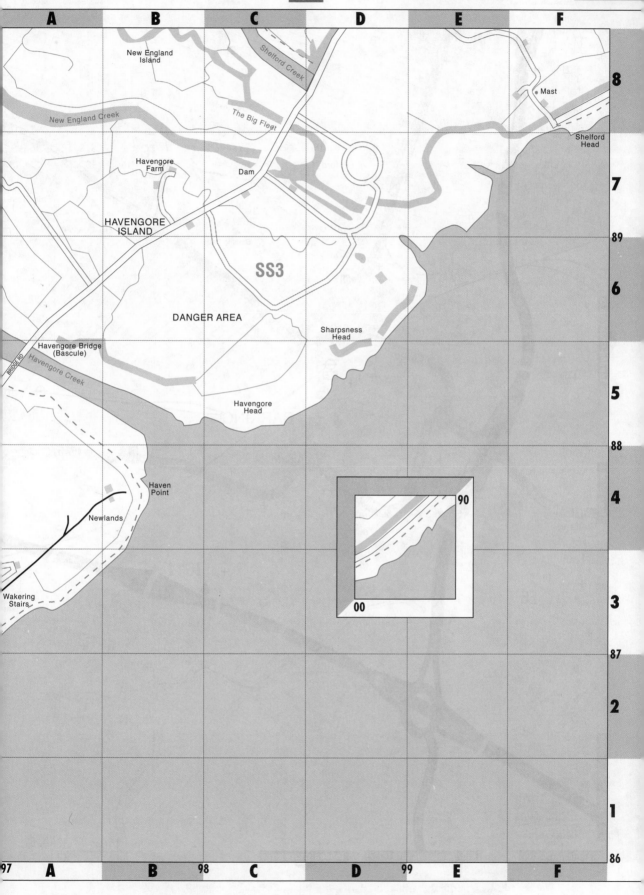

A B C D E F

New England
Island

Shelford Creek

8

New England Creek

The Big Fleet

Mast

Shelford
Head

Havengore
Farm

Dam

7

HAVENGORE
ISLAND

89

SS3

6

DANGER AREA

Sharpsness
Head

Havengore Bridge
(Bascule)

BRIDGE RD

Havengore Creek

Havengore
Head

5

88

Haven
Point

4

90

Newlands

00

Wakering
Stairs

3

87

2

1

97 A   B   98   C   D   99   E   F

86

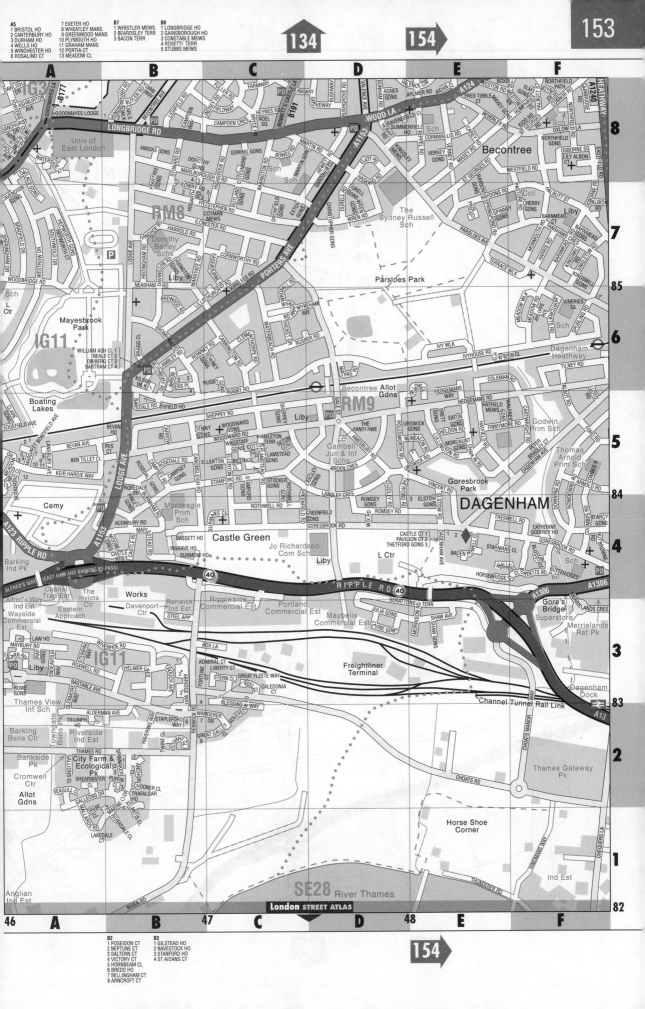

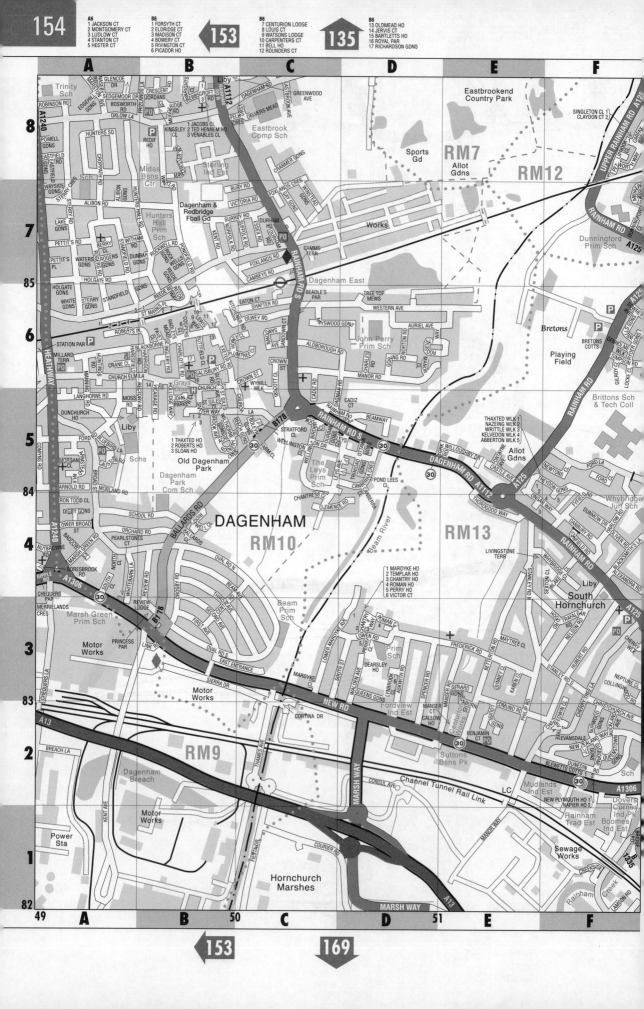

155
137

A **B** **C** **D** **E** **F**

Sch

Aspen Gr
Lime Ave
Hornbeam Ave
Cedar Ave
Acacia Dr
Sycamore Ave
Maple Ave
Oak Ave
Beech Ave
Elm Ave
B1421
Meadow Way
Leasway
Fairfield Ave
Rushmere Ave
Roxburgh Ave
Ashleigh Gdns
Argyle Gdns

Park Dr

8

Alder Ave
Little Gaynes La
Grove Ct
Pine Ct
Gaynes Park Rd
Gaynes Ct
Little Gaynes Gdns
Melstock Ave
Coniston Ave
Bracendale Gdns
Cranston Park Ave

Murfitt Way

Cranham Marsh
Nature Reserve

Spring Wood

Corbets Tey Rd

Tawny Ave
Tadlows Cl
Freshfields Ave
Longwood Ct
Longwood Cl
Hall Park Rd
Gaynes Sch

The Grove
Clayton Ave
Corbets Ave
Parkland Ave

Foxhall Rd
Meadowside Rd
Huntsmans Dr
The Glade

Middle
Wood

Bonus
Wood

7

Corbets Tey

Crem
Cemy

Redcrofts
Farm

PO

Pire La

Lowdons Cl

85

Corbets
Tey Sch

B1421

Park Farm Rd

P

Harwood Hall La
Bearblock
Cotts

Harwood
Hall

Ockendon Rd

Manor Farm

Lodge
Farm

6

Derham
House

Sullens
Farm

Russell's
Lake

Stubbers
Outdoor Pursuits
Ctr

Central
Farm

RM14

Sunnings La

Stubbers La

5

Bush
Farm

84

Little Gerpins Rd
Mast

Gerpins La

Gerpins
Farm

Aveley Rd

Bramble
Farm

Dennises La

Dennises
Cottages

4

Bramble La

Freeman's
Shaw

3

Hunts Hill
Cotts

Hunts Hill
Farm

Baldwins
Farm

83

Warwick La

Cockhide

RM13

Warwick
Wood

White Post
Wood

2

Belhus Woods
Country Park

Whitehall
Wood

Romford Rd

P

1

Running Water
Wood

RM15

Brickkiln
Wood

Running Water Brook

M25

82

55 **A** **B** 56 **C** **D** 57 **E** **F**

157
139

A B C D E F

8

Bullens & Herds

Blankets Farm

Bulphan CE Prim Sch

CHINA LA

Hatch Farm

Brandon Hall

CHURCH RD

P O

ALBERT RD

STANLEY RD

Bulphan

VICTORIA RD

FEN CL

Home Farm

DUNNINGS LA

Caylock's Farm

7

Corner Farm

FEN LA

HARROW RD

Stone Hall

PH

RM14

CHURCH LA

Martin's Farm

85

Fen Farm

HARROW LA

The Elms Farm

Greystead

6

Bulphan Fen

Judds Farm

The Downes

5

Stringcock Fen

PARKER'S FARM RD

84

Mar Dyke

Castle's Gorse

4

RM15

Fen Covert

3

Orsett Fen

83

Hobletts

RM16

2

FEN LA

The Decoy

1

MEDEBRIDGE RD

Poplars Farm

FEN LA

Orsett House

GREEN LA

Works

82

61 A B 62 C D 63 E F

A B C D E F

8

RM14

CH

7

85

B1007
SOUTH HILL

6

Great
Malgraves

NORTH HILL

5

84

B1007

Brooklyn
Farm

North Hill
Farm

SS17

North Hill
Bens Pk

Rose
Valley

Maplecroft
Farm

4

Golden
Bridge

B188

BRENTWOOD RD

Lorkins
Farm

Gore-Ox
Farm

Aquatic
Lodge

Black
Bushes

ROBINSON RD

OXFORD RD

YORK RD

FLORENCE
TERR

ELM
BANK PL

HILLCREST RD

HILLCREST RD

Sch

VINCENT
AVE

Parker's
Farm

RM16

Conway's
Farm

PARKER'S FARM RD

CONWAY'S RD

Gorwyn's
Plantation

Snake
Spinney

New
Covert

Sticking
Hill

Sticking Hill
Covert

BLACK BUSH LA

Avondale

Horndon
on the Hill

Recn
Gd

VICEROY
CT

VICTORIA RD

GORDON RD

HOLMES
CT

HOBBS CRES

MILL LA

ROMAGNE
CL

HIGH RD

CHURCH CL

THE
SQUARE

3

83

Blackbush
Farm

ORSETT RD

Cranfield

2

Home
Farm

Cherry
Orchard
Farm

Well
Wood

Fox
Holes

Orsett Hall
(Hotel)

Lyndfield

Linsteads
Farm

Cholley's
Farm

1

Old Hall
Farm

Orsett Park

Orsett Park
Farm

CHURCH ROW

MALTING LA

HIGWELL LA

POUND LA

THE
SPINNEY

PENN CL

PRINCE CHARLES AVE

RECTORY RD **B188**

Orsett
Fruit Farm

A128

Saffron
Gardens

SAFFRON GDNS

82

A128 BULPHAN BY-PASS
BRENTWOOD RD
CHURCH RD
MANOR
COTTS
CHURCH RD

Wick
Place

Mast

Wick Place
Farm

Barrow
Cottages

Burrows
Farm

Landing Strip

PH

Kings
Farm

Ongar Hall
Farm

Wyfields
Farm

KIRKHAM RD
KIRKHAM
SHAW
KIRKHAM
AVE
LOWER DUNTON RD
MALVINA
CL

A B C D E F

8

GRAYS AVE
BLACKHEATH CHASE
Larkspur
Green Trees Farm
Old Hill
Great Sutton Wood
Northlands Wood
Langdon Hills Country Park
The Briars
Milo

B1007
SOUTH HILL
OLD HILL AVE
MEADOW DR
SOUTH AVE

ONE TREE HILL
A13
Cawder Hall

7

Gary Owen Poultry Farm
Tyelands Farm
Sutton Hall Farm

SS16

85

B1007

6

The Chase

STRUAN AVE

5

Wrens Park Farm

84

Greenacres Farm

Arden Hall

4

B1007
NORTH HILL
STANFORD-LE-HOPE BY-PASS

SS17

FARNABY WAY 1
BYRD WAY 2
DOWLAND CL 3
DELIUS WAY 4
PURCELL WAY 5

1 MORLEY LINK
2 BENTON GDNS
3 ASHDOWN CL
4 BRACELET CL

Balstonia

Liby
Arthur Bugler Jun & Inf Schs

3

PH
Saffron Cl
SOUTH HILL CRES
HIGH RD
SOUTH HILL
BY-PASS RD

B1007

83

PUMP ST

Horndon House
The Gables

A1014
A1013
O'DONOGHUE HO
THE MANORWAY

A1014

2

Saffron Garden Cottages

Hassenbrook Sch

1 HASKINS
2 SEMPLES
3 CORRINGHAM RD

F3
1 STANFORD HALL
2 PEARSONS
3 PALMERS
4 GOLDSMITHS AVE
5 JEFFERIES WAY
6 CROSSWAY

KINGS PAR 1
RUNNYMEDE CT 2
RECTORY TERR 3

St Joseph's RC Prim Sch

Hassenbrook Ct

Ivy Wall House

Sports Gd

1

Old Jenkins Cl 1
Romsey Cl 2

STANFORD RD
HORNDON RD

LC

Liby

Stanford-le-Hope Prim Sch

1 THE PRECINCT
2 WENDOVER CT
3 THE GREEN
4 WALKERS SQ

Recn Gd

Stanford-le-Hope

PH

82

A13
A1013

ST MARGARET'S AVE

67   A   B   68   C   D   69   E   F

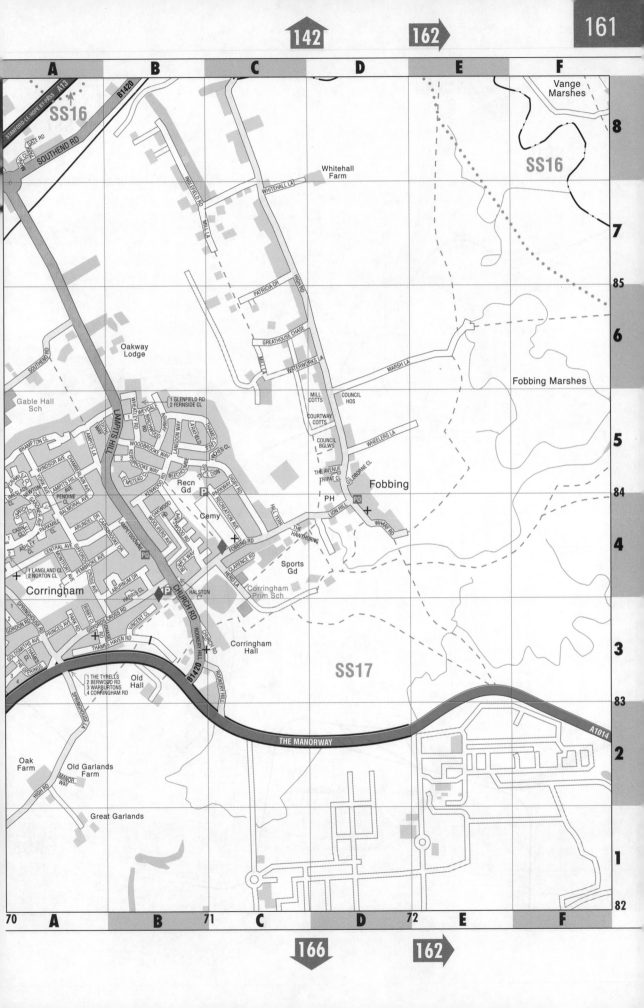

SS16

Vange Marshes

SS16

Whitehall Farm

WHITEHALL LA

INGLEFIELD RD

MILL LA

PATRICIA DR

HIGH RD

GREATHOUSE CHASE

MILL LA

WATERWORKS LA

MARSH LA

Fobbing Marshes

Oakway Lodge

1 GLENFIELD RD
2 FERNSIDE CL

MILL COTTS

COUNCIL HOS

COURTWAY COTTS

Gable Hall Sch

WHEATLEY RD

WEYDALE

BIRCHWOOD RD

ASHWAY

LANGDON WAY

THAMES RD

TARGFIELD

INCHES CL

COUNCIL BGLWS

WHEELERS LA

BRAMPTON CL

WINDSOR AVE

CHAMBERLAIN AVE

LAMPITS LA

WOODBROOKE WAY

KERRSBROOKE WAY

BEECHCOMBE

DON

THE AVENUE

TRIPAT CL

GILBORNE CL

Fobbing

PRAWLE

UMFS SLADE

NEWTON

YORK AVE

PENDINE

LAMPITS HILL AVE

KENWOOD

OAKWOOD

WOOLFERS AVE

THAMES RD

PARKWAY

DIGBY RD

RECREATION AVE

PH

LION HILL

PO

84

CASNE CL

CROMER AVE

BALMORAL AVE

ARUNDEL DR

CARISBROOKE DR

Recn Gd

P

Cemy

HILL TERR

WHARF RD

ASHLEY CL

CENTRAL AVE

MONTFORT AVE

PEMBROKE AVE

GIFFORDS CROSS AVE

LABURNUM DR

BRIS WAY

CLARENCE RD

HERD LA

FOBBING RD

THE HAWTHORNS

1 LANGLAND CL
2 NORTON CL

PO

Sports Gd

Corringham

HARRIS CL

P

CHURCH RD

HALSTON CT

Corringham Prim Sch

SPRINGHOUSE RD

GORDON RD

PRINCES AVE

PARK RD

BIBBY CL

CHASE

GIFFORDS CROSS RD

VINCENT CL

ROOKERY HILL

CHURCH RD

Corringham Hall

GOLDSMITHS AVE

THAMES CL

THE PERINGS

THAMES HAVEN RD

B1420

SS17

1 THE TYRELLS
2 BERWOOD RD
3 WARBURTONS
4 CORRINGHAM RD

Old Hall

ROOKERY HILL

83

A1014

THE MANORWAY

Oak Farm

Old Garlands Farm

MANOR WAY

Great Garlands

HIGH RD

SPRINGHOUSE LA

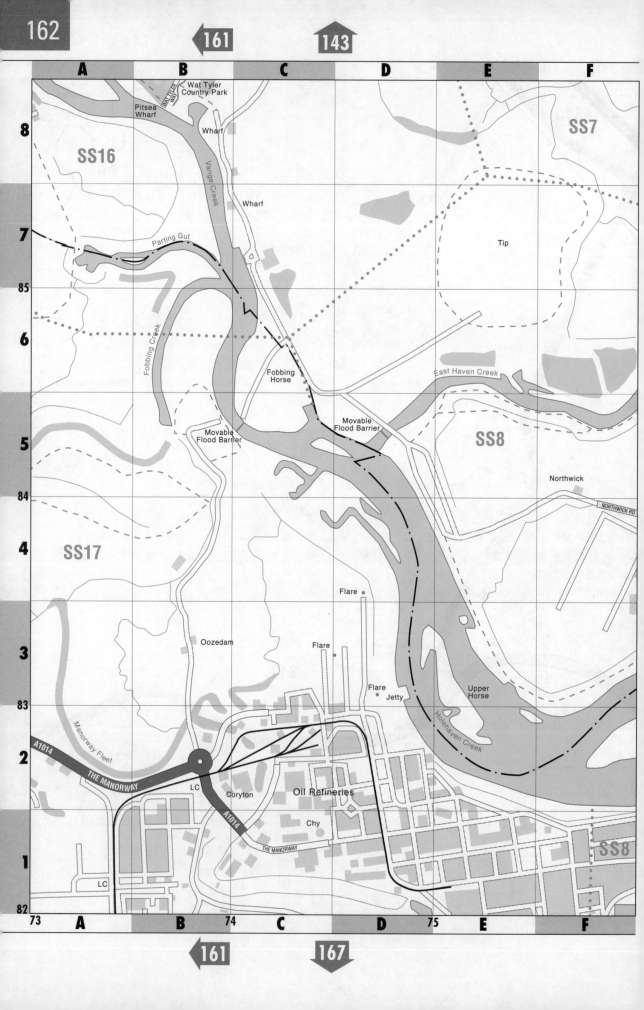

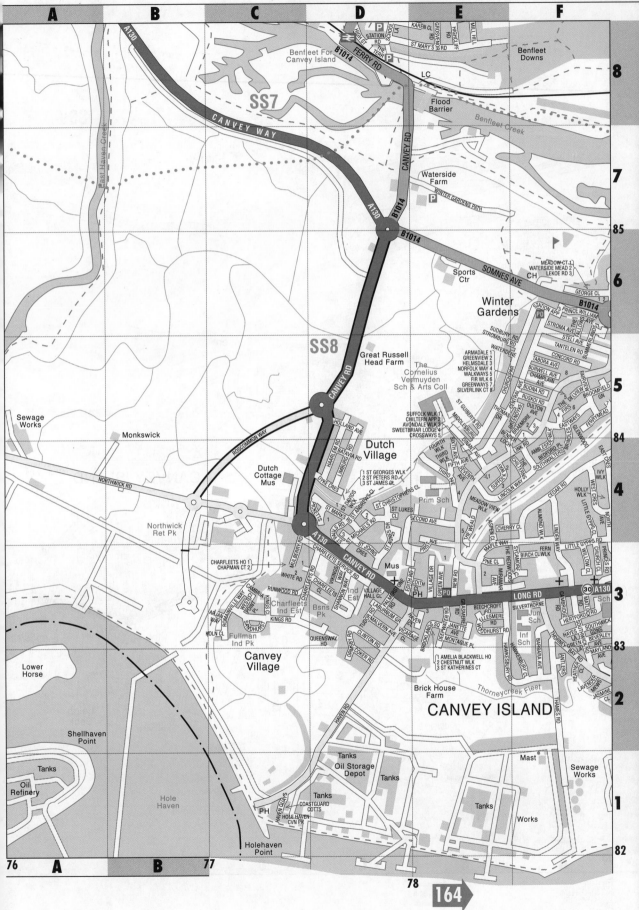

A B C D E F

8

7

85

6

5

84

4

3

83

2

1

82

SS7

CANVEY WAY

Benfleet For
Canvey Island

FERRY RD

Benfleet
Downs

Benfleet Creek

Flood
Barrier

Waterside
Farm

WINTER GARDENS PATH

B1014

SOMNES AVE

Sports
Ctr

Winter
Gardens

MEADOW CT 1
WATERSIDE MEAD 2
LEKOE RD 3

GEORGE CL

B1014

SS8

Great Russell
Head Farm

The
Cornelius
Vermuyden
Sch & Arts Coll

CANVEY RD

Sewage
Works

Monkswick

NORTHWICK RD

ROSCOMMON WAY

Dutch
Village

Dutch Cottage
Mus

HOLLAND AVE

1 ST GEORGES WLK
2 ST PETERS RD
3 ST JAMES PL

ARMADALE 1
GREENVIEW 2
HELMSDALE 3
NORFOLK WAY 4
WALKWAYS 5
FIR WLK 6
GREENWAYS 7
SILVERLINK CT 8

SUFFOLK WLK 1
CHILTERN APP 2
AVONDALE WLK 3
SWEETBRIAR LODGE 4
CROSSWAYS 5

Prim Sch

MEADOW VIEW
WLK

Northwick
Ret Pk

CHARFLEETS HO 1
CHAPMAN CT 2

WHITE RD

A130

CANVEY SERVICE RD

CANVEY RD

Mus

PH
PO

LONG RD

A130

30

Jun
Sch

Inf
Sch

1 AMELIA BLACKWELL HO
2 CHESTNUT WLK
3 ST KATHERINES CT

Sch

Charfleets Ind Est

Bsns
Pk

Ind Est

Village
Hall Cl

Canvey
Village

Fullman
Ind Pk

Queensway
Ho

CANVEY ISLAND

Brick House
Farm

Thorneycreek Fleet

Lower
Horse

Shellhaven
Point

Tanks

Oil
Refinery

Hole
Haven

PH

HOLE HAVEN
CVN PK

COASTGUARD
COTTS

Tanks

Tanks
Oil Storage
Depot

Tanks

Mast

Sewage
Works

Tanks

Works

Holehaven
Point

76 A 77 B 78

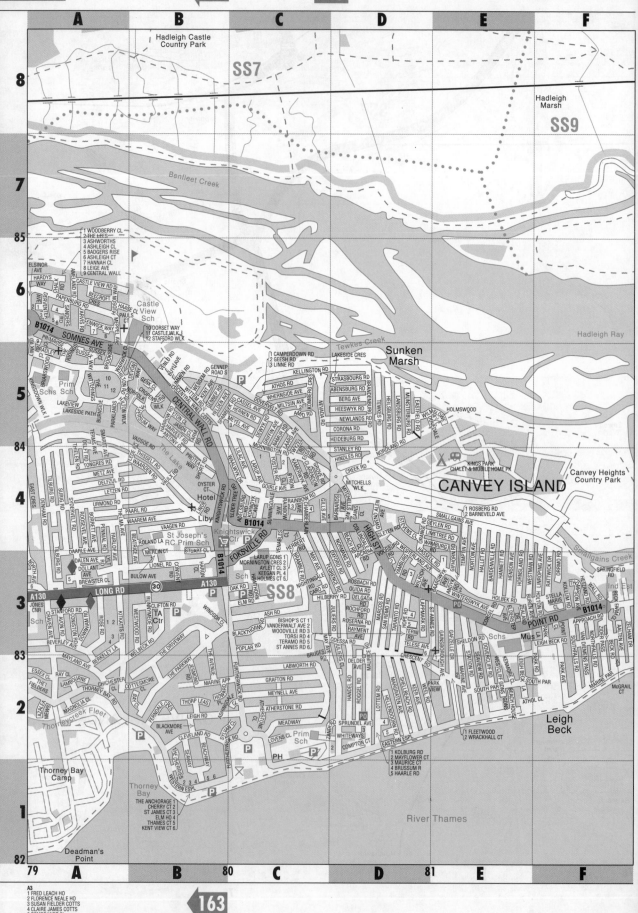

A B C D E F

8 · Hadleigh Castle Country Park

SS7

Hadleigh Marsh

SS9

7 · Benfleet Creek

85

1 WOODBERRY CL
2 THE LEES
3 ASHWORTHS
4 ASHLEIGH CL
5 BADGERS RISE
6 ASHLEIGH CT
7 HANNAH CL
8 LEIGE AVE
9 CENTRAL WALL

Hadleigh Ray

ELSINOR AVE

6 · HARDYS WAY

CASTLE VIEW RD

Castle View Sch

10 DORSET WAY
11 CASTLE WLK
12 STAFORD WLK

Sunken Marsh

B1014 SOMNES AVE

1 CAMPERDOWN RD
2 GEESH RD
3 LINNE RD

Tewkes Creek

5 · Prim Schs

CENTRAL WALL RD

STRASBOURG RD
ABENSBURG RD
BERG AVE
HEESWYK RD

84 · The Lake

Hotel

CANVEY ISLAND

Canvey Heights Country Park

4 · East Cres

St Joseph's RC Prim Sch

Knightswick Ctr

B1014

Kings Park CHALET & MOBILE HOME PK

1 ROSBERG RD
2 BARNEVELD AVE

HIGH ST

POINT RD

Sprallgains Creek

B1014

3 · A130 JONES CNR Sch

LONG RD 30 A130

FOKSVILLE RD SS8

1 LARUP GDNS
2 MORNINGTON CRES 2
3 AYLETT CL 3
4 KEEGAN PL 4
5 HOLMES CT 5

Schs Mus

Ind Est

TA Ctr

CLIFTON RD WINDSOR CL

BISHOP'S CT 1
1 VANDERWALT AVE 2
2 WOODVILLE CT 3
3 TORSI RD 4
4 TERAMO RD 5
5 ST ANNES RD 6

83

LABWORTH RD

GRAFTON RD

2 · Thorneycreek Fleet

MEYNELL AVE

ATHERSTONE RD

MEADWAY

Leigh Beck

Thorney Bay Camp

LOVENS CL Prim Sch

WHITEWAYS

COMPTON ST

Eastern Espl

1 FLEETWOOD
2 WRACKHALL CT

PH

1 KOLBURG RD
2 MAYFLOWER CT
3 MAURICE CT
4 BRUSSUM R
5 HAARLE RD

Thorney Bay

THE ANCHORAGE 1
CHERRY CT 2
ST JAMES CT 3
ELM HO 4
THAMES CT 5
KENT VIEW CT 6

1 · River Thames

82 · Deadman's Point

79 A 80 B C 80 C D 81 D E 81 F

163

A3
1 FRED LEACH HO
2 FLORENCE NEALE HO
3 SUSAN FIELDER COTTS
4 CLAIRE JAMES COTTS
5 REMBRANDT CL
6 THAMESIDE CRES

A B C D E F

SS9

Belton Hills

Belton Gardens

BELTON WAY W

CASTLE DR

BELTON WAY E

BELTON GDNS

Playing Field

Leigh-on-Sea

MARINE PAR

RECTORY GR   PO

SANS SOUCI

LEIGH PARK CT 2

ST CLEMENT'S CT

BROADWAY

Schs

Liby

Leigh

HALL END RD

LEIGH RD

NEW RD

LAURE

UTTONS

LEIGH HO.

CHURCH HILL

CHURCH

ELM RD

WEST ST

NORTH ST

EAST ST

ALEXANDRA RD

VICTORIA RD

SEAVIEW RD

BROADWAY W

SEA REACH

CLIFF PAR

4   MAPLE AVE

VICTOR DR

ASHLEIGH DR

REDCLIFF DR

GRAND DR

HAMPTON CT

HIGH CLIFF DR

CLIFF RD

SOMERVILLE GDNS

WOODSFIELD GDNS

COCKLE SHEDS

BELTON BRIDGE

HIGH ST

ALLEY DOCK

Leigh Heritage Ctr

LEIGH

THE GARDENS

Leigh Cliffs

QUEENS RD

QUEENS CT

AVENUE RD

GRAND PAR

REGATTA CT

UNDERCLIFF GDNS

8

Leigh Creek

1 BARYTA CT
2 THE TERRACE
3 PLEASANT TERR
4 NORMAN PL
5 NORMAN TERR
6 HILLSIDE RD

ESTUARY CT 1
RICHMOND CT 2
GRAND COURT W 3
SOUTHDOWN CT 4

SOUTHEND-ON-SEA

7

Sewage Works

Leigh Marsh

85

Two Tree Island / Nature Reserve

6

Slipway

Hadleigh Ray

5

84

Oyster Creek

4

SS8

Canvey Point

Smallgains Creek

Leighbeck Point

3

SILVERPOINT MARINE

POINT RD

CHAPMAN RD

BOMMEL AVE

BEVELAND RD

MARINE PAR

83

2

1

82

A   83   B   C   83   D   84   E   F

82

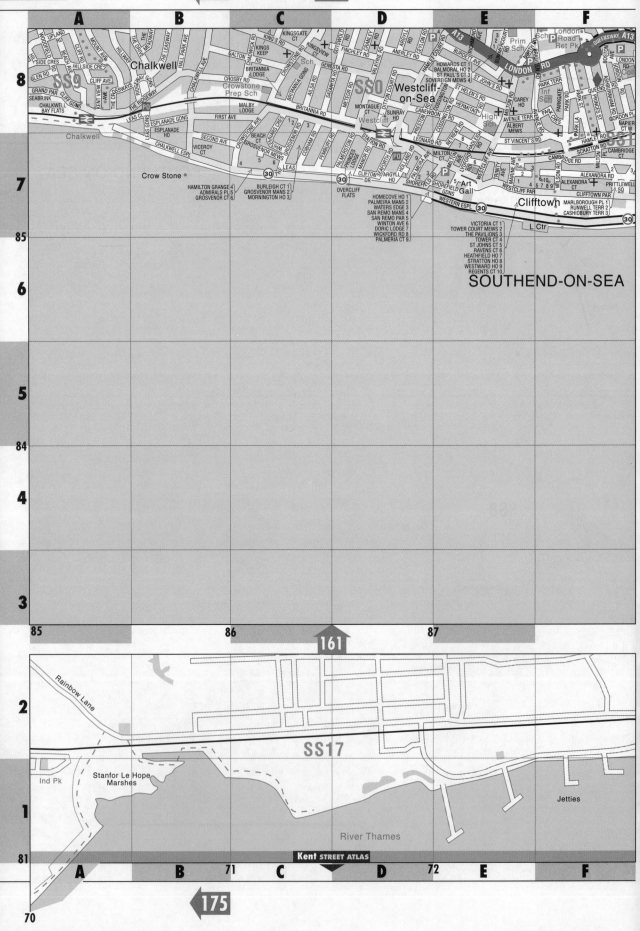

161

SS17

Rainbow Lane

Stanfor Le Hope Marshes

Ind Pk

Jetties

River Thames

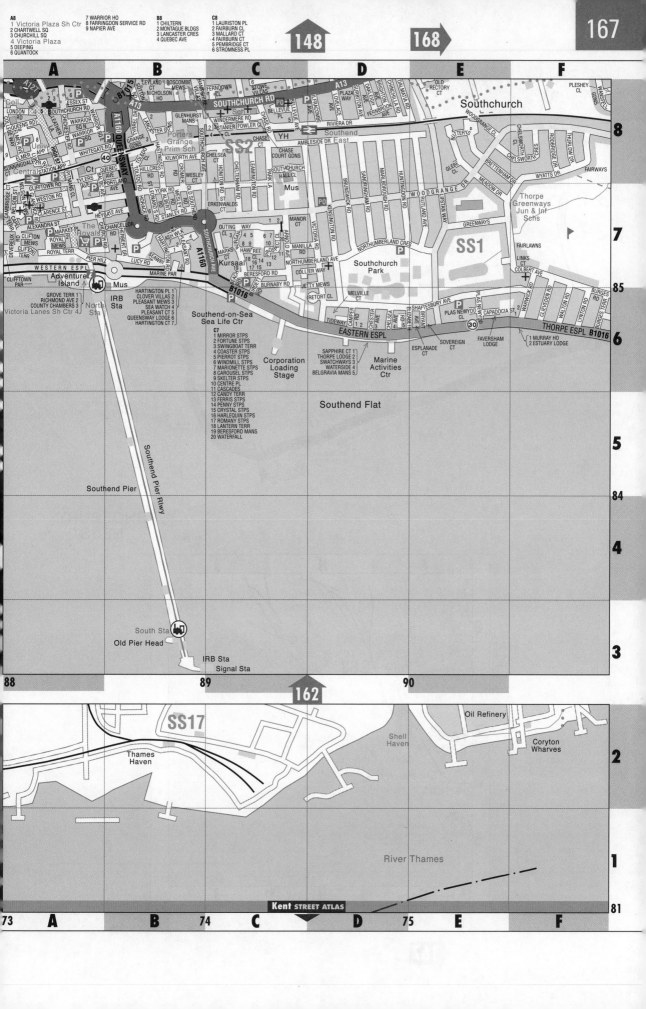

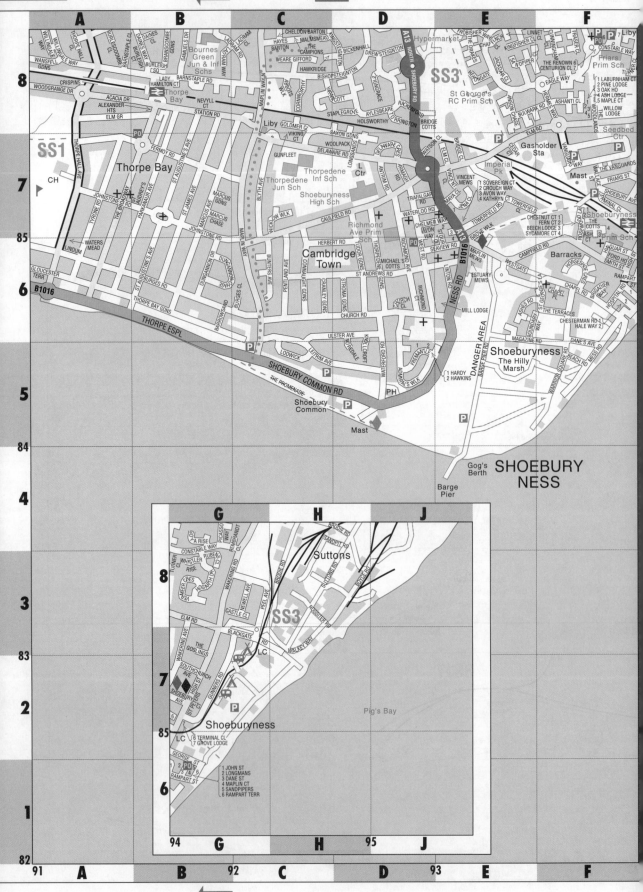

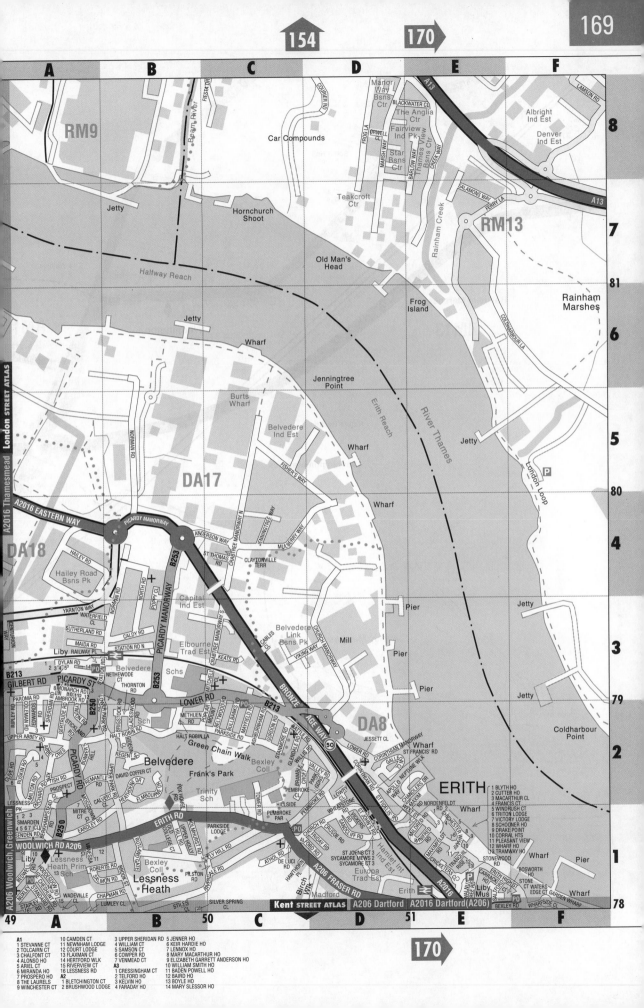

A   B   C   D   E   F

RM9

Beam River

Fiesta Dr

Coiper Rd

A13

Manor Way Bsns Ctr

BLACKWATER CL

The Anglia Ctr

Fairview Ind Pk

Orwell Cl

Frog La

Marsh Way

Star Bsns Ctr

Barlow Way

Thames View Bsns Ctr

Creek Way

Albright Ind Est

Denver Ind Est

LAMSON RD

8

Car Compounds

Teakcroft Ctr

SALAMONS WAY

FERRY LA

RM13

7

Jetty

Hornchurch Shoot

Halfway Reach

Old Man's Head

Frog Island

Rainham Creek

COLDHARBOUR LA

Rainham Marshes

81

Jetty

Wharf

Jenningtree Point

Burts Wharf

Erith Reach

River Thames

Jetty

London Loop

P

6

5

80

DA17

Belvedere Ind Est

Wharf

Fisher's Way

Wharf

DA18

A2016 EASTERN WAY

PICARDY MANORWAY

NORMAN RD

ANDERSON WAY

St THOMAS RD

CRABTREE MANORWAY N

JENNINGTREE RD

MULBERRY WAY

CLAYTONVILLE TERR

Pier

4

Hailey Rd

Hailey Road Bsns Pk

B253

Capital Ind Est

Belvedere Link Bsns Pk

CABLES CL

VIKING WAY

CHURCH MANORWAY

Pier

Mill

Pier

Jetty

YARNTON WAY

WATERFIELD CL

SUTHERLAND RD

CALDY RD

NORTH RD

POPPY CL

STATION RD N

Elbourne Trad Est

CRABTREE MANORWAY S

KEATS RD

Pier

3

MAIDA RD

Liby RAILWAY PL

DYLAN RD

PO

14

Belvedere NETHEWODE CT

THORNTON RD

Schs

B253

MITCHELL

LOWER RD

PO

B213

BRONZE AGE WAY

50

DA8

Jetty

79

Coldharbour Point

B213

GILBERT RD   PICARDY ST

PAROMA RD

COLEMAN RD

RIPLEY RD

B250

STICKLAND RD

LYNTON RD

GERTRUDE RD

HALT ROBIN LA

METHUEN RD

ASHBURNHAM RD

MAYFIELD RD

GORDON RD

BULLBANKS RD

BRIGSTOCK RD

POS

BATTLE RD

GLENDALE RD

WILLIS RD

STAMFORD RD

LOWER RD

CORINTHIAN MANORWAY

St FRANCIS' RD

Jessett Cl

Wharf

ERITH

1 BLYTH HO

2 CUTTER HO

3 MACARTHUR CL

4 FRANCIS' CT

5 WINDRUSH CT

6 TRITON LODGE

7 VICTORY LODGE

8 SCHOONER HO

9 DRAKE POINT

10 CORRAL HTS

11 PLEASANT VIEW

12 WHARF HO

13 TRAMWAY HO

2

UPPER ABBEY RD

ABBEY RD

HALT ROBIN LA

Green Chain Walk

Bexley Coll

Belvedere

Frank's Park

FOX HOUSE LA

Trinity Sch

TOWER RD

PEMBROKE RD

PEMBROKE PAR

WHEATSTONE

St FIELDS' RD

APOLLO

NEPTUNE WLK

CHANDLERS DR

NORDENFELDT RD

MAXIM RD

STONEWOOD RD

Wharf

Pier

1

Liby

Lessness Heath Prim Sch

CLIVE RD

RUSKIN RD

MINTON RD

PICARDY RD

UPPER ABBEY RD

MITRE CT

EARDLEY RD

KOLMURST RD

UPPER HOLLY HILL RD

COLLEGE RD

Parkside Lodge

Bexley Coll

HOLLY HILL RD

DE LUCI RD

CRESSING

St JOHN'S RD

CRUSOE RD

SADCLIFF RD

LOWRY

RIGGERS

St JOHN'S CT 3

SYCAMORE MEWS 2

SYCAMORE CT 3

Hamlet Int Ind Est

CRICKETERS' CT

BOSWORTH HO

Wharf

WOOLWICH RD A206

ERITH RD

PARKSIDE RD

ALFORD RD

A206 FRASER RD

Birch Wlk

Madford

Europa Trad Est

A206

Erith ≠

A2016

Liby Mus

P

BEXLEY RD

WHARFSIDE CL

CARRACK HO

STONE CT

GARDEN WHARF

Wharf

78

Lessness Heath

SILVER SPRING CL

Kent STREET ATLAS   A206 Dartford   A2016 Dartford(A206)

London STREET ATLAS

A206 Thames mead London STREET ATLAS

A206 Woolwich: Greenwich

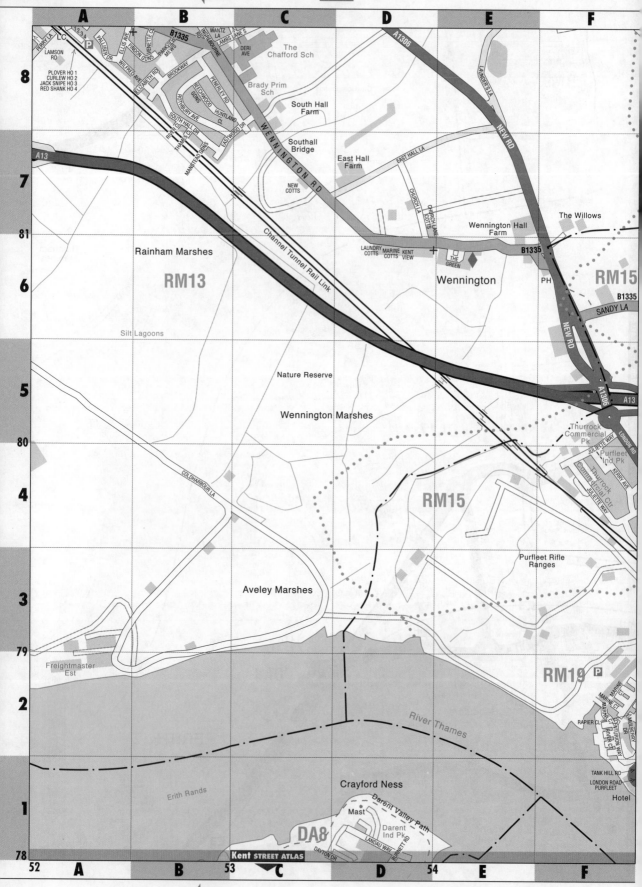

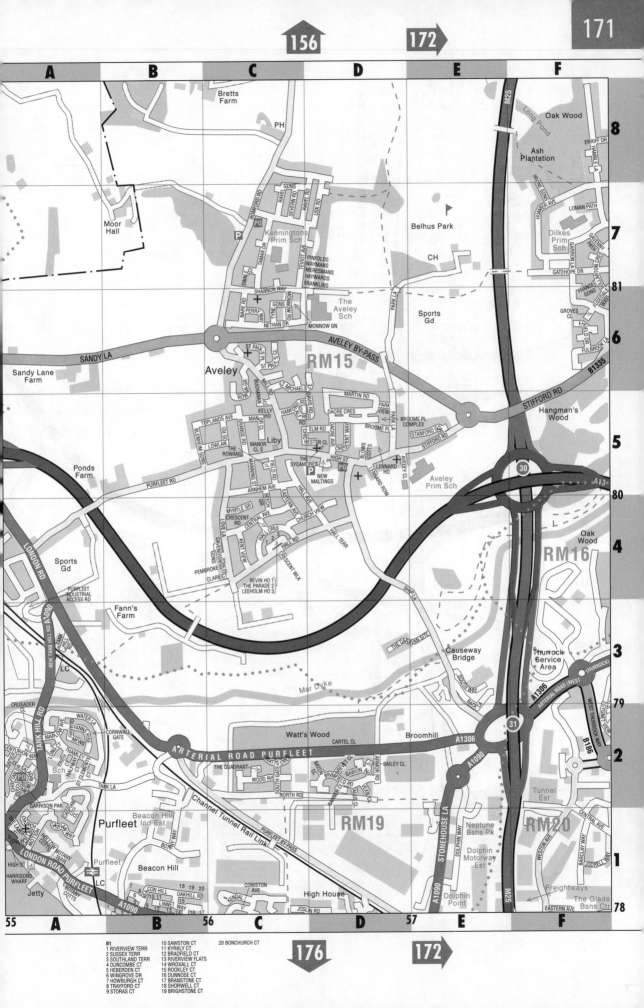

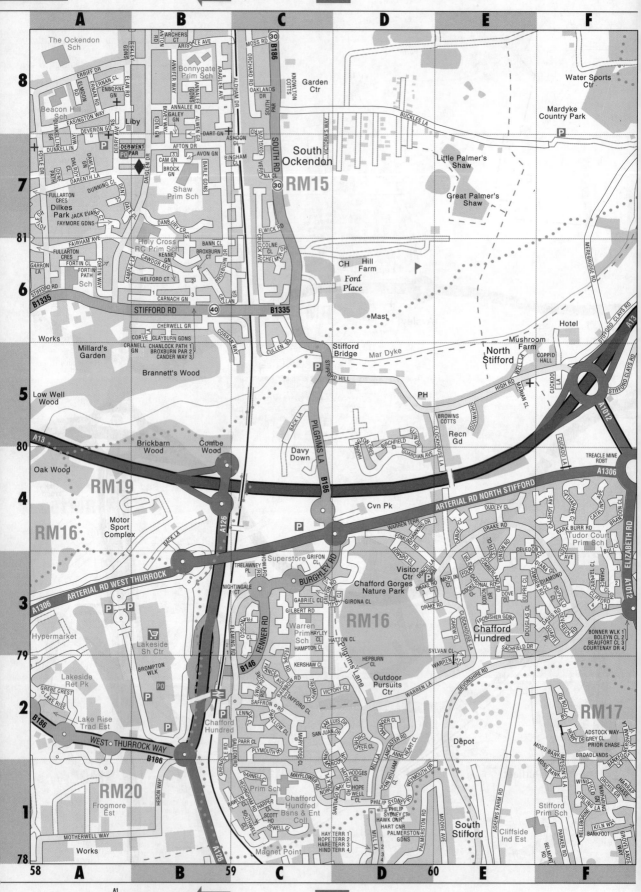

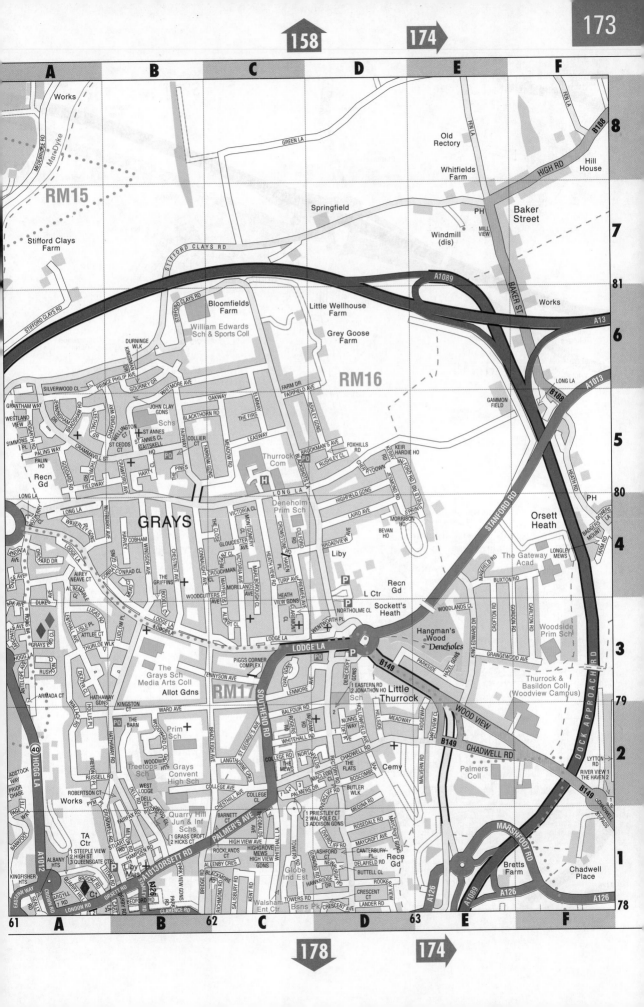

A13 STANFORD RD A1013

CH St Cleres Hall
Singlewell
LUUVICK CL
BROCKENHURST DR
PROSPECT AVE
WILSON CL
St Clere's Sch
ST MARGARET'S AVE
RIDE LA
FAIRVIEW CHASE
CARABINERS CT
GROVE
KING EDWARD'S RD
WHITWELL CT
THE GROVE
BROADHOPE AVE
NITON CT
CHALE CT

Mayland

BUTTS LA

BUCKINGHAM HILL RD

Cemy

Sewage Works

The Warren

Ind Pk

Thames Haven Junction

WADER RD

LC
Mucking
MUCKING WHARF RD
Bluehouse Farm

Stanford Marshes Nature Reserve

SS17

Sluice

Mucking Creek

Golden Cottages

WALTON'S HALL RD

Mucking Marshes

Travelling Crane
Jetty

Walton Hall Farm Mus
Walton's Hall
Turner's Farm
Sutton's Farm

BUCKINGHAM HILL RD

Linford
NORTHUMBERLAND RD
ESSEX GDNS
DORSET GDNS
EAST TILBURY RD
DEVONSHIRE GDNS
HAMPSHIRE GDNS
SOMERSET RD
STAFFORD CL
LOWER CRES
SIDDONS CL
REDBROOK CT
WATER MDWS
MEADOW CL
PH

RM18

Sewage Works

MUCKINGFORD RD
HIGH ASH
HAZELWOOD
HALT DR
TRINDLES CL
BEECROFT AVE
PINEFORD CL
STENNING AVE
LC

East Tilbury

ALEXANDRA WAY
QUEEN ELIZABETH AVE
KING GEORGE V AVE
THOMAS BATA AVE
PRINCESS MARGARET RD
SOLWAY
SEVERN
DEBEN
BLYE
HAYLE
COLNE
TORRIDGE
ROMAN
CORONATION AVE
COLNE CT
ASHLANDS CT
WELLAND
TYNE
CALDER
ROACH
CLYDE
STRATHMORE
TWEED
FROME
LAMBOURNE CROFT
ORWELL
ARUN
QUEEN MARY AVE
CORONATION CT
KENSINGTON GDNS
Liby
PRINCESS AVE
STANFORD HO
BATA AVE
GLOUCESTER AVE
FARM RD

River Thames

Thames Ind Pk

East Tilbury Inf Sch
East Tilbury Jun Sch

East Tilbury

East Tilbury Marshes

Sand & Gravel Pit

Kent STREET ATLAS

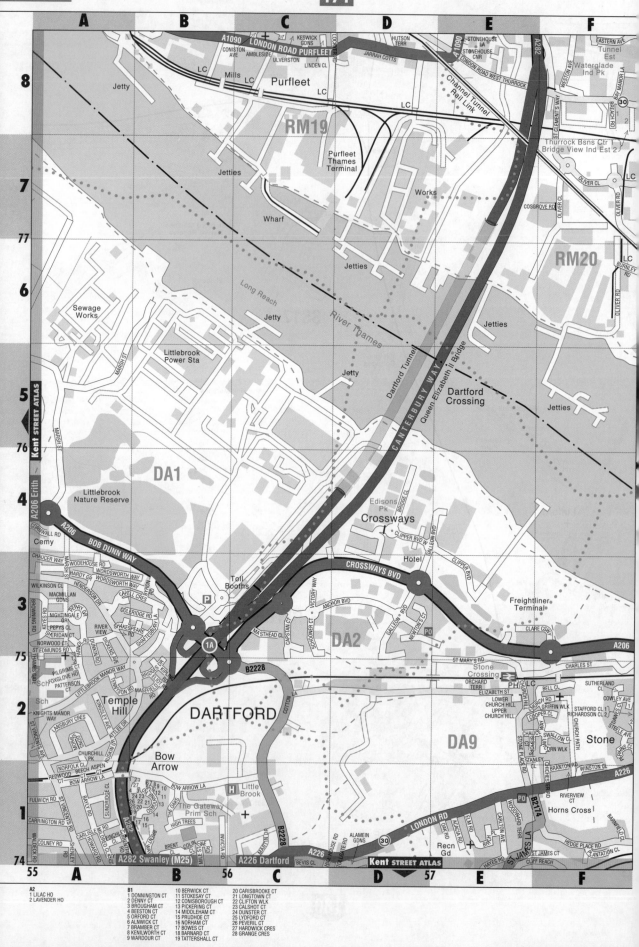

171

A2
1 LILAC HO
2 LAVENDER HO

B1
1 DONNINGTON CT
2 DENNY CT
3 BROUGHAM CT
4 BEESTON CT
5 ORFORD CT
6 ALNWICK CT
7 BRAMBER CT
8 KENILWORTH CT
9 WARDOUR CT

10 BERWICK CT
11 STOKESAY CT
12 CONISBOROUGH CT
13 PICKERING CT
14 MIDDLEHAM CT
15 PRUDHOE CT
16 NORHAM CT
17 BOWES CT
18 BARNARD CT
19 TATTERSHALL CT

20 CARISBROOKE CT
21 LONGTOWN CT
22 CLIFTON WLK
23 CALSHOT CT
24 DUNSTER CT
25 LYDFORD CT
26 PEVERIL CT
27 HARDWICK CRES
28 GRANGE CRES

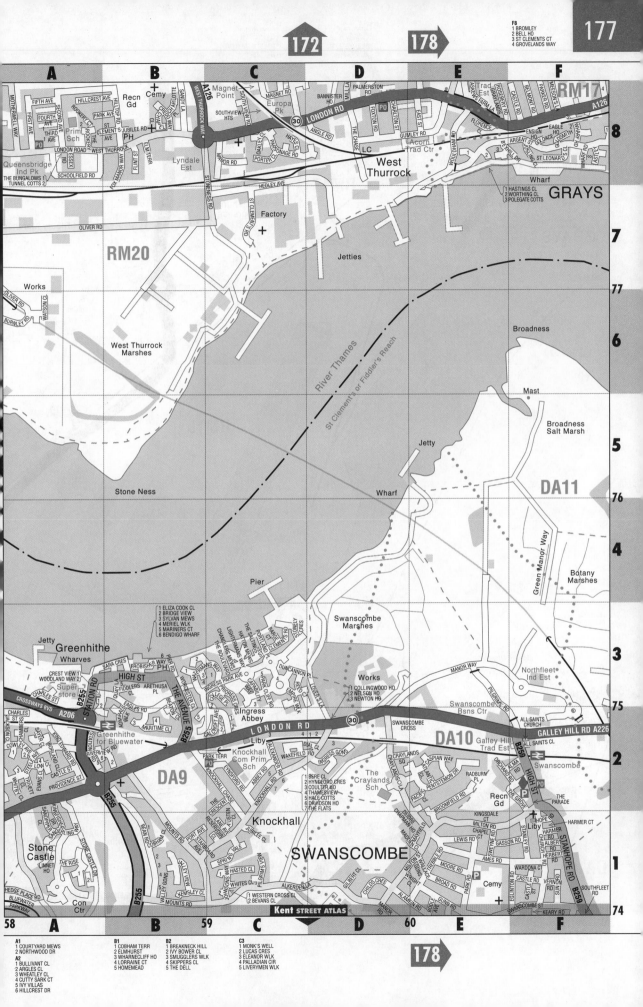

178

← 177   173

C8
1 ALFRED ST
2 PERCY ST
3 HENRY ST
4 ST THOMAS'S PL
5 RICHMOND RD
6 SALISBURY RD

C8
7 HARWOOD CT
8 KENSINGTON CT
9 TRASA CT
10 CEMENT BLOCK COTTS
11 SPURGEON CL
12 ARTHUR CT

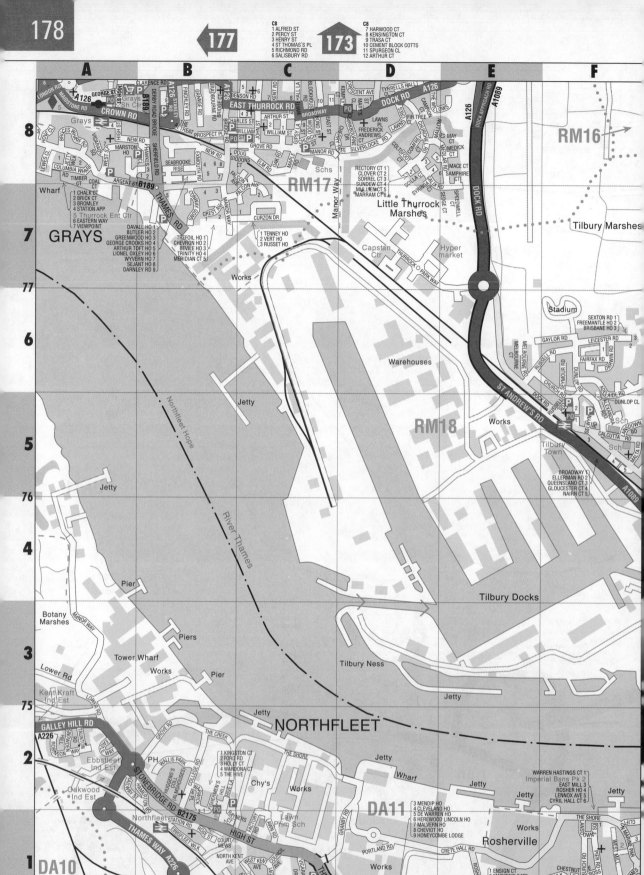

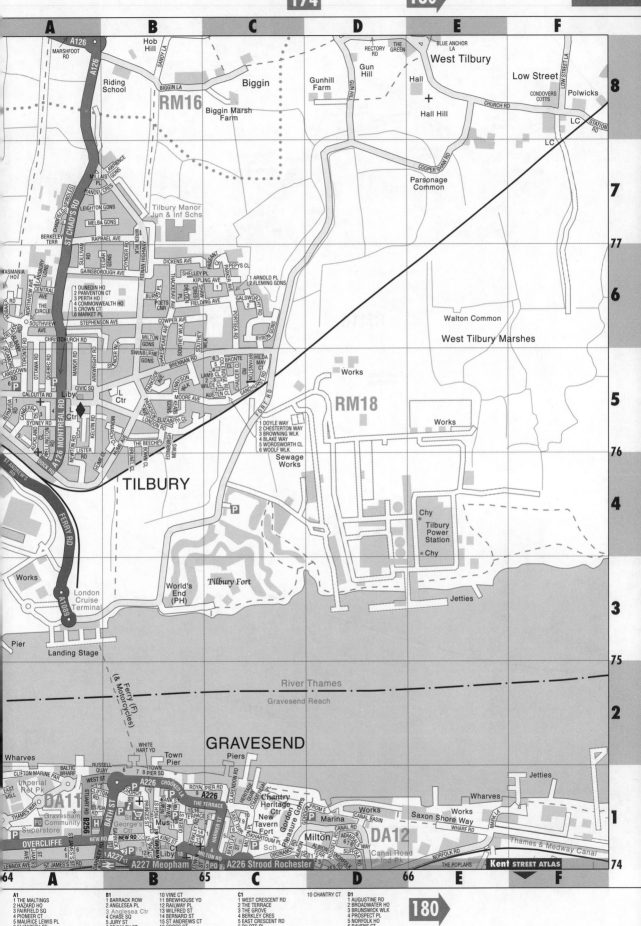

A126
MARSHFOOT RD
Hob Hill
Riding School
Biggin
SANDY LA
BIGGIN LA
RM16
Biggin Marsh Farm
Gunhill Farm
Gun Hill
RECTORY RD
THE GREEN
BLUE ANCHOR LA
West Tilbury
Low Street
Polwicks
CONDOVERS COTTS
8
Hall
+
Hall Hill
CHURCH RD
STATION RD
LC
LC

7

77

Tilbury Manor Jun & Inf Schs

West Tilbury Marshes

6

1 DUNEDIN HO
2 PANVENTON CT
3 PERTH HO
4 COMMONWEALTH HO
5 CROWN CT
6 MARKET PL

1 ARNOLD PL
2 FLEMING GDNS

Walton Common

5

Works

RM18

Works

76

1 DOYLE WAY
2 CHESTERTON WAY
3 BROWNING WLK
4 BLAKE WAY
5 WORDSWORTH CL
6 WOOLF WLK

Sewage Works

TILBURY

4

P

Chy
Tilbury Power Station
• Chy

Works
Ferry Rd
A1089

London Cruise Terminal

World's End (PH)
Tilbury Fort

Jetties

3

Pier

Landing Stage

75

Ferry (F) (& Motorcycles)

River Thames
Gravesend Reach

2

Wharves
BALTIC WHARF
CLIFTON MARINE PAR
Imperial Ret Pk
EAST ST
Thames Way

WHITE HART YD
RUSSELL QUAY
Town Pier

GRAVESEND

Piers

Jetties
Wharves

1

DA11
Gravesham Community Superstore
PO
B256
BATH ST
STUART RD
A226
George's Ctr
Mus
A226
THE TERRACE
New Tavern Fort
Heritage Gdns
Gordon Gdns
Pleasure Gdns
Marina
CANAL BASIN
Saxon Shore Way
WHARF RD
Works
Works
MARK LA
DA12
Canal Road Ind Pk
THE POPLARS
Thames & Medway Canal

OVERCLIFFE
NEW RD
A227 Meopham
A226 Strood Rochester
Milton
Liby
Sch
NORFOLK RD
Kent STREET ATLAS

74

A1
1 THE MALTINGS
2 HAZARD HO
3 FAIRFIELD SQ
4 PIONEER CT
5 MAURICE LEWIS PL
6 ELIZABETH CT

B1
1 BARRACK ROW
2 ANGLESEA PL
3 Anglesea Ctr
4 CHASE SQ
5 JURY ST
6 CRAWLEY CT
7 REGENTS CT
8 MELBOURNE QUAY
9 ROYAL PIER MEWS

10 VINE CT
11 BREWHOUSE YD
12 RAILWAY PL
13 WILFRED ST
14 BERNARD ST
15 ST ANDREWS CT
16 CROSS ST
17 CLIVE RD
18 PARROCK ST
19 Thamesgate Sh Ctr

C1
1 WEST CRESCENT RD
2 THE TERRACE
3 THE GROVE
4 BERKLEY CRES
5 EAST CRESCENT RD
6 PILOTS PL
7 PEACOCK ST
8 Bentley Street Ind Est
9 GORDON PL

10 CHANTRY CT

D1
1 AUGUSTINE RD
2 BROADWATER HO
3 BRUNSWICK WLK
4 PROSPECT PL
5 NORFOLK HO
6 RAVENS CT
7 MEDUZA CT
8 AMAZON CT
9 FISGARD CT

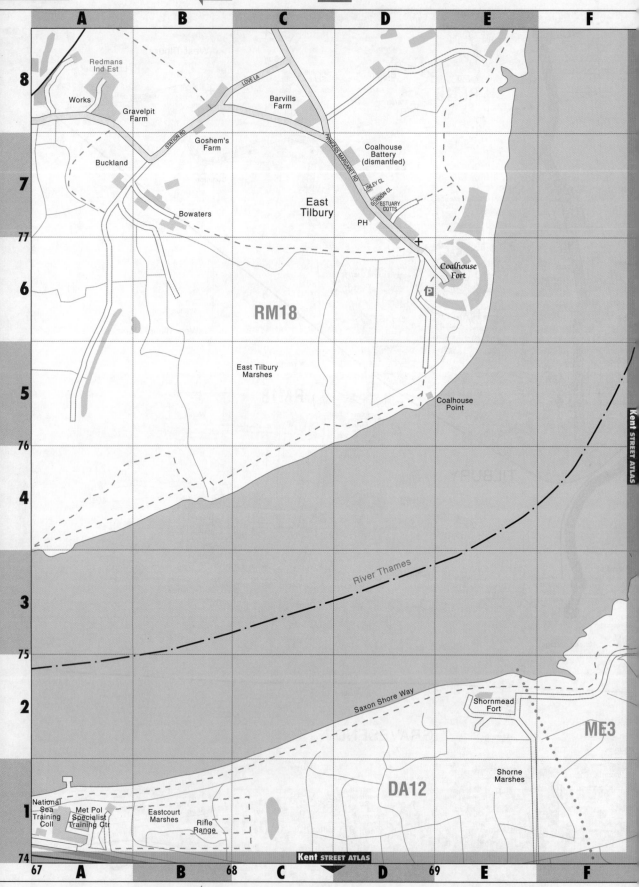

A B C D E F

8

Redmans
Ind Est

Works

LOVE LA

Gravelpit
Farm

Barvills
Farm

STATION RD

Goshem's
Farm

PRINCESS MARGARET RD

Coalhouse
Battery
(dismantled)

7

Buckland

LINLEY CL

GORDON CL

Bowaters

ESTUARY
COTTS

East
Tilbury

PH

77

+

Coalhouse
Fort

6

P

RM18

East Tilbury
Marshes

Coalhouse
Point

5

76

4

River Thames

Kent STREET ATLAS

3

75

Saxon Shore Way

Shornmead
Fort

2

ME3

Shorne
Marshes

DA12

National
Sea
Training
Coll

Met Pol
Specialist
Training Ctr

Eastcourt
Marshes

Rifle
Range

1

74

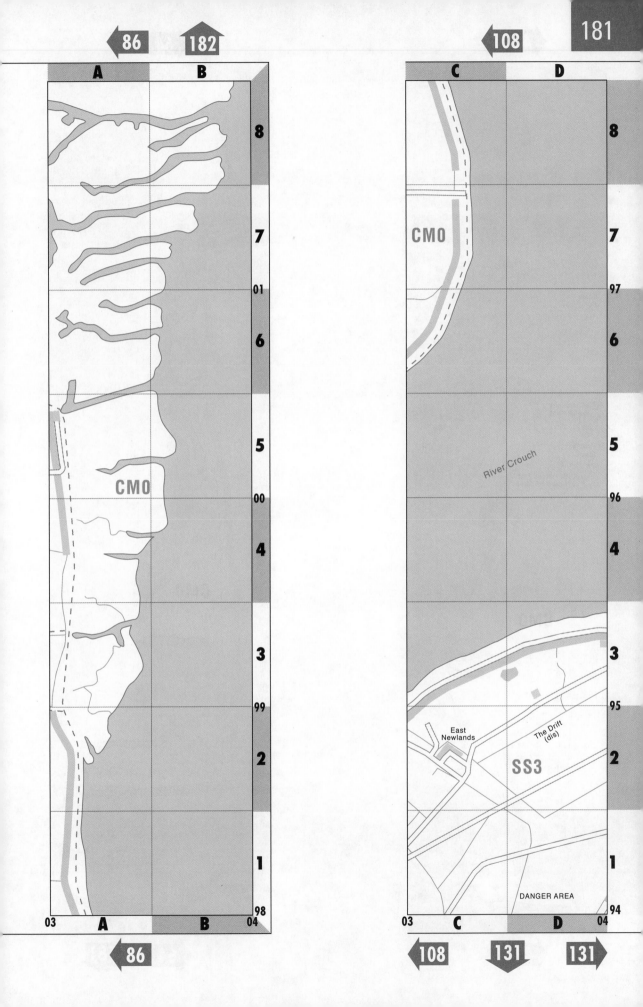

A   B   C   D

8

7

01

6

5

00

4

CMO

3

99

2

1

98

CMO

River Crouch

East
Newlands

The Drift
(dis)

SS3

DANGER AREA

8

7

97

6

5

96

4

3

95

2

1

94

03   A   B   04   03   C   D   04

42

64

A　　　　B

C　　　　D

8

7

09
Sales
Point

6

Tip
Head

Community
Settlement

5
St Peter's
Chapel
✝

St Peter's Flat
Nature Reserve

08

4

Gunner's Creek

CMO

3

07

St Peter's Way

2

1

06
03　　A　　B　　04

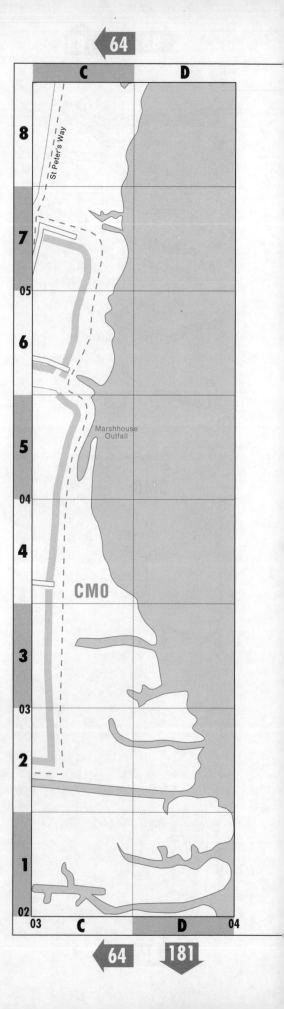

8
St Peter's Way

7

05

6

Marshhouse
Outfall

5

04

4

CMO

3

03

2

1

02
03　　C　　D　　04

42

64

181

Index

Place name May be abbreviated on the map

Location number Present when a number indicates the place's position in a crowded area of mapping

Locality, town or village Shown when more than one place has the same name

Postcode district District for the indexed place

Page and grid square Page number and grid reference for the standard mapping

Church Rd 6 Beckenham BR2.........**53** C6

Cities, towns and villages are listed in CAPITAL LETTERS

Public and commercial buildings are highlighted in magenta   **Places of interest** are highlighted in blue with a star★

Abbreviations used in the index

Acad	Academy	Comm	Common	Gd	Ground	L	Leisure	Prom	Promenade
App	Approach	Cott	Cottage	Gdn	Garden	La	Lane	Rd	Road
Arc	Arcade	Cres	Crescent	Gn	Green	Liby	Library	Recn	Recreation
Ave	Avenue	Cswy	Causeway	Gr	Grove	Mdw	Meadow	Ret	Retail
Bglw	Bungalow	Ct	Court	H	Hall	Meml	Memorial	Sh	Shopping
Bldg	Building	Ctr	Centre	Ho	House	Mkt	Market	Sq	Square
Bsns, Bus	Business	Ctry	Country	Hospl	Hospital	Mus	Museum	St	Street
Bvd	Boulevard	Cty	County	HQ	Headquarters	Orch	Orchard	Sta	Station
Cath	Cathedral	Dr	Drive	Hts	Heights	Pal	Palace	Terr	Terrace
Cir	Circus	Dro	Drove	Ind	Industrial	Par	Parade	TH	Town Hall
Cl	Close	Ed	Education	Inst	Institute	Pas	Passage	Univ	University
Cnr	Corner	Emb	Embankment	Int	International	Pk	Park	Wk, Wlk	Walk
Coll	College	Est	Estate	Intc	Interchange	Pl	Place	Wr	Water
Com	Community	Ex	Exhibition	Junc	Junction	Prec	Precinct	Yd	Yard

Index of towns, villages, streets, hospitals, industrial estates, railway stations, schools, shopping centres, universities and places of interest

A

Aalten Ave SS8 . . . . 164 F3
Abacus Prim Sch
SS12 . . . . 121 F5
Abberton IG8 . . . . 110 C5
Abberton Wlk RM13 . . . . 154 F4
Abbess Cl CM1 . . . . 31 E2
ABBESS RODING 14 E4
Abbey Cl
Fyfield CM5 . . . . 27 C1
Hullbridge SS5 . . . . 101 D2
Romford RM1 . . . . 136 A5
Abbey Cres DA17 . . . . . 169 A2
Abbey Ct EN9 . . . . 65 B5
Abbey Dale Cl CM17 . . . 24 C7
Abbey Fields CM3 . . . . . 78 B7
Abbey Ho EN9 . . . . 66 A5
Abbey Mead Ind Est
EN9 . . . . 65 C5
Abbey Park Ind Est
IG11 . . . . 152 C4
Abbey Rd
Barking IG11 . . . . 152 B4
Barking IG11 . . . . 152 C3
Billericay CM12 . . . . 96 F1
Greenhithe DA9 . . . . . . 177 C2
Hullbridge SS5 . . . . 101 D1
Ilford IG2 . . . . 133 D6
Abbey Turning CM9 . . . . 36 D4
Abbeyview EN9 . . . . 65 C6
Abbey Wood La
RM13 . . . . 155 D3
Abbots Cl
Brentwood CM15 . . . . . . 95 A1
Rainham RM13 . . . . 155 C3
Abbots Ct SS15 . . . . 119 E1
Abbotsford Gdns IG8 . . . 110 A3
Abbotsford Rd IG3 . . . . . 134 B2
Abbots Hall Prim Sch
SS17 . . . . 160 E3
Abbotsleigh Rd CM3 . . . 101 E7
Abbotsmead CM9 . . . . . 36 F5
Abbots Ride CM11 . . . . . 97 C2
Abbotsweld CM18 . . . . . 23 D5
Abbotsweld Prim Sch
CM18 . . . . 23 D6
Abbots Wlk SS3 . . . . . . 168 C8
Abbotswood SS7 . . . . . . 145 C5
Abbotswood Gdns
Ilford IG5 . . . . 133 A7
Redbridge IG5 . . . . 132 F8

Abbotts Cl
Romford RM7 . . . . 135 B8
Southend-on-S SS9 . . . . 146 E5
Abbotts Cres E4 . . . . . . 109 D6
Abbotts Ct
Romford RM3 . . . . 114 F2
Stanstead Abbotts SG12 . . 8 D4
Abbotts Dr
Stanford-le-H SS17 . . . . 160 D2
Waltham Abbey EN9 . . . . 66 A6
Abbotts Hall Chase
SS17 . . . . 160 E2
Abbotts Pl CM2 . . . . 32 D3
Abbotts Rise SG12 . . . . . 8 D4
Abbotts Way SG12 . . . . . 8 D4
Abbs Cross Gdns
RM12 . . . . 136 D3
Abbs Cross La RM12 . . . 136 C2
Abbs Cross Sch & Arts
Coll RM12 . . . . 136 C1
Abell Way CM2 . . . . 33 B4
Abenberg Way CM13 . . . 117 B8
Abensburg Rd SS8 . . . . 164 D5
Abercorn Gdns RM6 . . . 134 B5
Abercorn Ho CM3 . . . . . 33 E8
Abercrombie Ho 17
RM3 . . . . 114 D5
Abercrombie Way CM18,
CM19 . . . . 23 C6
Aberdeen Gdns SS9 . . . 146 A2
Aberdour Rd IG3 . . . . . . 134 B2
Abigail Ct CM5 . . . . 49 A5
Abigail Mews RM3 . . . . . 114 F1
Abingdon Ct 3 SS13 . . . 121 A1
Abinger Cl IG11 . . . . 153 A8
Abington Ct RM14 . . . . . 137 C3
Abraham Cohen Ct
IG1 . . . . 133 A5
Abraham Ct RM14 . . . . . 137 A2
Abraham Fisher Ho
E12 . . . . 152 A7
Abreys SS7 . . . . 145 A7
ABRIDGE 90 A6
Abridge Gdns RM5 . . . . 113 A4
Abridge Mews RM4 . . . . 90 B6
Abridge Pk RM4 . . . . . . 90 A5
Abridge Rd
Chigwell IG7 . . . . 89 E4
Theydon Bois RM4 . . . . . 68 A1
Abridge Way IG11 . . . . . 153 B1
Acacia Ave RM12 . . . . . 135 F2
Acacia Ct EN9 . . . . 66 A5

Acacia Dr
Maldon CM9 . . . . 36 F1
Southend-on-S SS1 . . . . 168 A8
Upminster RM14 . . . . . . 156 A8
Acacia Gdns RM14 . . . . 137 F4
Acacia Rd
Basildon SS13 . . . . 143 E8
Greenhithe DA9 . . . . . . 176 E1
Acacias Ct 12 EN11 . . . . 21 A6
Academy Fields Rd
RM2 . . . . 136 B6
Academy Sq 1 RM2 . . . 136 B6
Accrington Ho 10
RM3 . . . . 114 D5
Acer Ave RM13 . . . . 155 D2
Acer Gr CM1 . . . . 32 D4
Acle Cl IG6 . . . . 111 B3
Aconbury Rd RM9 . . . . . 153 B4
Acorn Cl E4 . . . . 109 B5
Acorn Ct IG2 . . . . 133 E6
Acorn Ctr The IG6 . . . . 112 B4
Acorn Mews CM18 . . . . 24 A6
Acorn Pl
Basildon SS16 . . . . 141 B5
Maldon CM9 . . . . 36 F5
Acorn St SG12 . . . . 9 D8
Acorns The
Chigwell IG7 . . . . 111 E6
Hockley SS5 . . . . 124 E7
Acorn Trad Ctr RM20 . . 177 E8
Acre Rd RM10 . . . . 154 B5
Acres Ave CM5 . . . . 48 F5
Acres End CM1 . . . . 31 E4
Acres The SS17 . . . . 160 F3
Acre View RM11 . . . . . . 136 F4
Ada Cole Meml Stables
Horse Sanctuary★
CM19 . . . . 22 E4
Adalia Cres SS9 . . . . . . 146 B3
Adalia Way SS9 . . . . . . 146 B2
Adam Bsns Ctr SS14 . . 120 F1
Adam's Elm Ho SS9 . . . 146 E2
Adams Glade SS4 . . . . . 125 D6
Adams Ho CM20 . . . . . . 10 D1
Adams Rd SS17 . . . . . . 160 E1
Adam Way SS11 . . . . . . 121 E8
Addison Ct CM16 . . . . . 68 A8
Addison Gdns RM17 . . . 173 C2
Addison Rd
Redbridge IG6 . . . . 111 C2
Wanstead E11 . . . . 132 A5
Adelaide Gdns
Dagenham RM6 . . . . 134 E6

Adelaide Gdns continued
South Benfleet SS7 . . . . 144 D1
Adelaide Rd
Ilford IG1 . . . . 133 B2
Tilbury RM18 . . . . 178 F6
Adeliza Cl IG11 . . . . 152 C5
Adelphi Cres RM12 . . . . 136 B2
Adelsburg Rd SS8 . . . . . 164 C8
Aden Rd IG1 . . . . 133 C4
Adingtons CM20 . . . . . . 10 F2
Admiral Ct IG11 . . . . 153 C3
Admirals Cl E18 . . . . 132 B7
Admirals Lo RM1 . . . . . . 135 F6
Admirals Pl SS0 . . . . . . 166 C7
Admirals Way DA12 . . . . 179 D1
Admirals Wlk
Chelmsford CM1 . . . . . . 31 F3
Greenhithe DA9 . . . . . . 177 B2
Hoddesdon EN11 . . . . . . 21 B4
Southend-on-S SS3 . . . . 168 D5
Adnams Wlk RM12 . . . . 155 A7
Adomar Rd RM8 . . . . . . 134 E1
Adstock Way RM17 . . . . 172 F2
Adult Coll of Barking &
Dagenham RM9 . . . . . 153 F7
Advent Ct IG8 . . . . 109 F5
Adventure Island★
SS1 . . . . 167 A2
Advice Ave RM16 . . . . . 173 A4
Afflets Ct SS14 . . . . 142 C8
Afton Dr RM15 . . . . 172 B7
Agister Rd IG7 . . . . 112 A5
Agnes Ave
Ilford IG1 . . . . 152 B8
Southend-on-S SS9 . . . . 146 B2
Agnes Gdns RM8 . . . . . 153 D8
Agricultural/Domestic
Mus★ CM9 . . . . 38 E7
Aidan Cl RM8 . . . . 153 E8
Ailsa Rd SS0 . . . . 166 C8
AIMES GREEN 43 F2
Ainsley Ave RM7 . . . . . . 135 C5
Ainslie Ho E4 . . . . 109 A5
Ainslie Wood Cres E4 . . 109 B5
Ainslie Wood Gdns
E4 . . . . 109 B5
Ainslie Wood Prim Sch
E4 . . . . 109 B5
Ainslie Wood Rd E4 . . . . 109 B5
Aintree Cres IG6 . . . . . . 111 C1
Aintree Gr CM14 . . . . . . 116 F1
Airborne Cl SS9 . . . . . . 146 E5
Airborne Ind Est SS9 . . 146 E5

Aal – Alb 183

Aire Dr RM15 . . . . 157 B1
Airey Neave Ct RM16 . . 173 A4
Airfield Way RM12 . . . . . 155 C6
Airlie Gdns IG1 . . . . 133 B3
Airthrie Rd IG3 . . . . 134 B2
Akenfield Cl 1 CM3 . . . . 101 E7
Alamein Gdns DA2 . . . . 176 D1
Alamein Rd
Burnham-on-C CM0 . . . . 106 C4
Chelmsford CM1 . . . . . . 31 F6
Swanscombe DA10 . . . . 177 D1
Alan Cl SS9 . . . . 146 E6
Alan Gdns RM7 . . . . 135 A4
Alan Gr SS9 . . . . 146 E6
Albany Ave SS0 . . . . . . 147 E1
Albany Cl CM1 . . . . 31 E5
Albany Ct
Chingford E4 . . . . 87 B3
Epping CM16 . . . . 45 F1
Albany Hts RM17 . . . . . . 173 A1
Albany Rd
Dagenham RM6 . . . . 134 F5
Hornchurch RM12 . . . . . 136 A2
Pilgrims Hatch CM15 . . . 94 B3
Rayleigh SS6 . . . . 124 C4
Tilbury RM18 . . . . 179 A6
Wickford SS12 . . . . 121 C6
Albany The IG8 . . . . . . 109 F6
Albany The, A Bsns & Ent
Coll RM12 . . . . 136 B2
Albany View IG9 . . . . . . 88 A1
Alba Rd CM17 . . . . 11 C1
Albemarle App IG1 . . . . 133 B5
Albemarle Cl RM17 . . . . 173 A4
Albemarle Gdns IG2 . . . 133 B5
Albemarle Link CM2 . . . 32 F8
Albert Ave E4 . . . . 109 A6
Albert Cl
Grays RM16 . . . . 173 C3
Rayleigh SS6 . . . . 123 F3
Rochford SS4 . . . . 125 C6
Albert Cres E4 . . . . 109 A6
Albert Dr SS15 . . . . 141 C6
Albert Gdns CM17 . . . . . 24 D7
Albert Ho 5 E18 . . . . . . 132 B8
Albert Mews
Romford RM1 . . . . 135 F5
Southend-on-S SS0 . . . . 166 E8

Albert Rd
Buckhurst Hill IG9 110 D8
Bulphan RM14 158 F8
Burnham-on-C CM0 106 C2
Dagenham RM8 135 A3
Ilford IG1 133 C1
Rayleigh SS6 123 F3
Rochford SS4 125 C7
Romford RM1 135 F5
South Benfleet SS7 144 B6
Southend-on-S, Bournes Green SS1 149 A1
Southend-on-S SS1 167 B7
South Woodham Ferrers CM3 101 D7
Swanscombe DA10 177 F1
4 Wanstead E18 132 B8
Albert St CM14 116 C5
Albert Terr IG9 110 E8
Albion Cl RM7 135 D5
Albion Ct
Billericay CM12 97 A1
Chelmsford CM2 32 B1
Albion Hill IG10 88 D4
Albion Pk IG10 88 D4
Albion Rd
Dagenham RM10 153 F7
Gravesend DA12 179 D1
South Benfleet SS7 144 D4
Southend-on-S SS0 147 E1
Albion Terr
Gravesend DA12 179 D1
Sewardstone E4 87 B5
Albra Mead CM2 33 B4
Albright Ind Est RM13 169 F8
Albury Mews E12 132 C2
Albyns SS16 141 C4
Albyns Cl RM13 155 A5
Albyns La RM4 91 D7
Alcester Ho 14 RM3 114 D5
Alcotes SS14 142 F5
Aldborough Ct
Chingford E4 109 B7
Ilford IG2 133 F6
ALDBOROUGH HATCH 133 F7
Aldborough Rd
Dagenham RM10 154 C6
Ilford, Aldborough Hatch IG2 133 F8
Ilford IG1 133 E2
Upminster RM14 137 A2
Aldborough Rd N IG2 133 F6
Aldborough Rd S IG3 133 E4
Aldeburgh Pl IG8 110 A6
Aldeburgh Way CM1 32 D5
Alder Ave RM14 155 F8
Alderbury Lea CM3 56 F1
Alder Cl
Basildon SS15 119 D1
Hoddesdon EN11 21 B8
Alder Dr
Chelmsford CM2 54 B6
South Ockendon RM15 157 C1
Aldergrove Wlk RM12 155 C6
Alderleys SS7 145 A6
Alderman Ave IG11 153 A2
Aldermans Hill SS5 124 C5
Alderman Wlk SS17 160 E5
Alderney Gdns SS11 99 C2
Alders Ave IG8 109 E4
ALDERSBROOK 132 C2
Aldersbrook La E12 132 F1
Aldersbrook Prim Sch E12 132 C2
Aldersbrook Rd E12 132 C2
Alders Cl E11 132 B2
Aldersey Gdns IG11 152 D6
Aldersgrove EN9 65 E5
Alders Wlk CM21 1 E2
Alderton Cl
Loughton IG10 89 A5
Pilgrims Hatch CM15 94 B4
Alderton Hall La IG10 89 A5
Alderton Hill IG10 88 F4
Alderton Jun & Inf Schs The IG10 89 A4
Alderton Mews IG10 89 A5
Alderton Rd RM16 174 E7
Alderton Rise IG10 89 A5
Alderton Way IG10 88 F4
Alder Wlk IG1 152 D7
Alderwood Cl RM4 90 B6
Alderwood Dr RM4 90 B6
Alderwood Way SS7 145 C3
Aldham Dr RM15 172 C8
Aldham Gdns SS6 122 F3
Aldham Hall 1 E11 132 A5
Aldingham Ct RM12 155 B7
Aldingham Gdns RM12 155 A7
Aldington Cl RM8 134 C3
Aldis Mews EN3 65 A2
Aldria Rd SS17 160 E5
Aldriche Way E4 109 C4
Aldridge Ave 7 EN3 65 A1
Aldridge Cl CM2 33 A4
Aldrin Cl SS17 160 E2
Aldrin Way SS9 147 A6
Aldwych Ave IG6 133 C7
Aldwych Cl RM12 136 B2
Alexander Ct
1 Chelmsford CM1 32 E7
Epping CM16 67 F8
Romford RM7 135 D3
Alexander Hts SS1 168 B8
Alexander La CM15 95 B4
Alexander Mews
Billericay CM12 97 B2
Harlow CM17 24 D6
Howe Green CM2 55 D2
Alexander Rd
Basildon SS16 141 B4
Greenhithe DA9 177 C2
Alexandra Cl RM16 174 C4
Alexandra Ct
Southend-on-S, Clifftown SS1 166 F7
7 Southend-on-S SS2 147 F1
Alexandra Ho 15 IG8 111 A3
Alexandra Pl 3 RM1 135 F5
Alexandra Rd
Brentwood CM14 116 C7
Burnham-on-C CM0 106 C5
Dagenham RM6 134 E5
Great Wakering SS3 150 A3
Rainham RM13 154 F4
Rayleigh SS6 123 F3
Rochford SS4 125 C7
Romford RM1 135 F5
South Benfleet SS7 144 D2
Southend-on-S, Clifftown SS1 166 F7
Southend-on-S, Leigh Cliffs SS9 165 E8
Tilbury RM18 178 F5
Wallend E6 152 A2
Wanstead E18 132 B8
Alexandra St SS1 167 A7
Alexandra Way RM18 175 B3
Alexandria Dr SS6 123 A4
Alf Lowne Ct RM16 174 A3
Alford Rd DA8 169 C1
Alfreda Ave SS5 101 D3
Alfred Gdns SS11 99 D1
Alfred Prior Ho 7 E12 152 A8
Alfred Rd
Aveley RM15 171 C5
Brentwood CM14 116 D8
Buckhurst Hill IG9 110 D8
Alfred's Gdns IG11 152 E3
Alfred St 1 RM17 178 C8
Alfred's Way (East Ham & Barking By-Pass) IG11 152 D3
Alfred's Way Ind Est IG11 153 A4
Algars Way CM3 101 D8
Algers Cl IG10 88 D4
Algers Rd IG10 88 E4
Alghers Mead IG10 88 D4
Alibon Gdns RM10 154 A7
Alibon Rd RM10 154 A7
Alicia Ave SS11 122 A7
Alicia Cl SS11 122 A7
Alicia Way SS11 122 A7
Alicia Wlk SS11 122 A7
Alkerden La DA9, DA10 177 C1
Allandale SS7 145 A7
Allandale Rd RM11 135 F4
Allenby Cres RM17 173 C1
Allenby Dr RM11 136 F3
Allender Ct 2 RM1 135 D7
Allen Ho CM21 1 F2
Allen Rd RM13 155 C2
Allens Cl CM3 20 F1
Allens Rd CM11 98 C5
Allensway SS17 160 F3
Allen Way CM2 33 B4
Allerton Cl SS4 125 C6
Alley Dock SS9 165 D8
Alleyn Court Prep Sch SS3 149 A3
Alleyn Court Sch SS0 147 C1
Alleyndale Rd RM8 134 C2
Alleyn Pl SS0 147 C1
Allington Ct CM11 119 C7
Allis Mews 5 CM17 11 C1
Allison Cl EN9 66 A7
Allistonway SS17 160 F3
Allmains Cl EN9 44 B6
Allnutts Rd CM16 68 A6
Alloa Rd IG3 134 A2
All Saints Church DA10 177 F2
All Saints Cl
Chelmsford CM1 32 E4
Chigwell IG7 112 A7
Doddinghurst CM15 72 B3
Swanscombe DA10 177 F2
All Saints Maldon CE Prim Sch CM9 36 E2
All Saints RC Sch & Tech Coll RM8 135 A3
Allysum Wlk CM12 96 F5
Alma Ave
Chingford E4 109 C3
Hornchurch RM12 136 E1
Alma Cl
South Benfleet SS7 146 A2
Wickford SS12 121 A6
Alma Dr CM1 32 A2
Alma Link CM12 97 A1
Alma Rd
South Benfleet SS7 146 A2
Swanscombe DA10 177 F2
Almere SS7 144 D4
Almond Ave
Hullbridge SS5 101 E4
Wickford SS12 121 C7
Almond Cl RM16 174 A3
Almond Ho IG10 88 F6
Almonds Ave IG9 110 A8
Almond Wlk SS8 163 F4
Almshouses CM14 115 E8
Almshouses The 3 IG11 152 C6
Almshouses (Whitakers Charity) IG10 88 F8
Al-Noor Muslim Prim Sch IG3 134 B3
Alnwick Cl SS16 140 F5
Alnwick Ct 6 DA2 176 B1
Alonso Ho 4 DA17 169 A1
Alp Ct SS3 150 A3
Alpha Cl SS13 143 F6
Alpha Rd
Basildon SS13 143 F6
Brentwood CM13 95 D3
Burnham-on-C CM0 106 C5
Chingford E4 109 B7
Alracks SS15 141 E6
Alresford Gn SS12 121 E6
Alston Ct SS0 147 C1
Altar Pl 5 SS15 141 C7
Altham Gr CM20 10 F3
ALTHORNE 83 A3
Althorne Cl SS13 121 B1
Althorne Sta CM3 104 F8
Althorne Way
Canewdon SS4 104 E2
Dagenham RM10 135 A2
Althorpe Cl SS5 124 D6
Alton Gdns SS2 147 E5
Aluric Cl RM16 174 B2
Alverstoke Rd RM3 114 E3
Alverstone Rd E12 152 A8
Alveston Sq 12 E18 110 A1
Alwen Gr RM15 172 B8
Alwyne Ave CM15 95 A3
Alyssum Cl CM1 33 A6
Amanda Cl IG7 111 D4
Amanda Ct E4 109 E4
Amanda Mews RM7 135 C6
Amazon Ct 8 DA12 179 D1
Amber Ct 5 RM1 135 E6
Amberden SS15 141 D5
Amber La IG6 111 B3
Amberley Rd IG9 88 C1
Amberley Way RM7 135 B7
Amberry Ct CM20 10 D1
Ambleside
Epping CM16 68 A8
Purfleet RM19 176 C8
Ambleside Ave RM12 155 B7
Ambleside Dr SS1 167 D8
Ambleside Gdns
Hullbridge SS5 101 D2
Redbridge IG4 132 E6
Ambleside Wlk SS8 163 F5
Ambrook Rd DA17 169 A3
Amcotes Pl CM2 54 C8
Ameland Rd SS8 164 A6
Amelia Blackwell Ho SS8 163 E3
America St CM9 37 A2
Amersham Ave SS16 140 F5
Amersham Cl RM3 114 F4
Amersham Dr RM3 114 F4
Amersham Rd RM3 114 F4
Amersham Wlk RM3 114 F4
Amery Gdns RM2 136 D8
Amesbury EN9 66 A7
Amesbury Cl CM16 67 F8
Amesbury Dr E4 87 B3
Amesbury Rd
Dagenham RM9 153 D5
Epping CM16 67 F8
Ames Rd DA10 177 E1
Amherst Lo 6 CM20 10 C1
Amidas Gdns RM8 153 B8
Amid Rd SS8 164 C5
Amoss Rd CM2 54 F8
Ampers End SS14 142 D6
Ampthill Ho 2 RM3 114 D5
AMWELL 8 A6
Amwell Ct
Hoddesdon EN11 21 A7
Waltham Abbey EN9 65 E6
Amwell La SG12 8 B5
Amwell St EN11 21 A7
Amwell View Sch SG12 8 B4
Anchorage Hill CM9 37 A3
Anchorage The
Burnham-on-C CM0 106 C3
Canvey Island SS8 164 B1
Great Wakering SS3 150 B4
Anchorage View CM0 62 D7
Anchor Bvd DA2 176 D3
Anchor Cl IG11 153 B2
Anchor Dr RM13 155 B2
Anchor Ho IG3 134 A1
Anchor La
Abbess Roding CM5 14 C4
Canewdon SS4 104 E1
Heybridge CM9 37 A5
Anchor Lane Cotts SS4 104 E1
Anchor Par SS4 104 E1
Anchor Reach CM3 101 E5
Anchor St CM2 32 B1
Anders Fall SS9 147 A6
Anderson Ave CM1 31 F5
Anderson Ho 1 IG11 152 D3
Anderson Rd IG8 132 D8
Andersons SS17 160 F3
Andersons Ind Est SS12 121 D4
Anderson Way DA17 169 C4
Andrea Ave RM16 173 A4
Andrew Cl
Redbridge IG6 111 D3
Stanford-le-H SS17 160 D4
Andrews Cl IG9 110 C8
Andrews Pl CM1 31 F3
Andromeda Ct RM3 114 C4
Andy Hill Ho CM14 116 B6
Andyk Rd SS8 164 E3
Anerley Rd SS0 166 D8
Angel Cl SS16 142 D3
Angel Terr SS3 149 D1
Angel Way RM1 135 E6
Angle Gn RM8 134 C3
Angle Rd RM20 177 D8
Anglesea Ctr 3 DA11 179 B1
Anglesea Pl 2 DA11 179 B1
Anglesey Dr RM13 155 A1
Anglesey Gdns SS12 121 F5
Angle The 5 CM20 10 C1
Anglia Ct 1 RM8 134 D3
Anglia Ctr The RM13 169 E8
Anglian Ind Est IG11 153 A1
Anglia Polytechnic Univ Benfleet Campus SS7 145 A5
Anglia Poly Univ
Chelmsford CM1 32 B2
Chelmsford CM1 32 B4
Anglia Wlk E6 152 A4
Anglo-European Sch CM4 74 C4
Angmering Ho 1 RM3 114 D5
Anjou Gn CM1 33 A7
Annabel Ct RM12 136 C3
Annabell Ave RM16 174 D7
Annalee Gdns RM15 172 B8
Annalee Rd RM15 172 B8
Annan Way RM1 113 E2
Ann Boleyn Dr SS4 147 F7
Anne Boleyn Mans 4 SS13 143 B5
Anne Heart Cl RM16 172 D2
Anne Nastri Ct RM2 136 B6
Annett Cl 7 SS12 122 A5
Anne Way IG6 111 C4
Annie Taylor Ho 2 E12 152 A8
Annifer Way RM15 172 B8
Annonay Wlk 7 CM2 32 C2
Annwood Lodge Bsns Pk SS6 122 D2
Anson Chase SS3 168 E8
Anson Cl
Romford RM7 113 B1
South Woodham Ferrers CM3 101 F6
Anstead Dr RM13 155 A3
Anstey Cl SS9 146 D7
Antelope Ave RM16 173 A3
Anthony Cl CM11 119 D6
Anthony Dr SS17 160 E4
Antlers SS8 163 F2
Antlers Hill E4 87 B4
Anton Rd RM15 157 B1
Antony Cl SS8 164 B5
Antrim Rd SS3 168 D7
Anvil Way
Billericay CM12 97 B5
Chelmsford CM1 32 E8
Anworth Cl IG8 110 B4
Apeldoorn SS7 144 B7
Apex Ct SS5 124 E7
Apollo Cl RM12 136 B2
Apollo Way DA8 169 D2
Appleby Cl E4 109 C4
Appleby Dr
Basildon SS16 140 F5
Romford RM3 114 C5
Appleby Gn RM3 114 C5
Appledene Cl SS6 123 D4
Appledore SS3 149 C1
Appledore Cl RM3 114 C2
Appleford Ct 8 SS13 143 C6
Applegarth Dr IG2 133 F7
Apple Gate CM14 93 F4
Applerow SS9 146 F6
Appleton Cl CM19 23 C7
Appleton Ct RM12 136 D3
Appleton Rd
Loughton IG10 89 B6
South Benfleet SS7 144 B2
Appleton Sch The SS7 144 C5
Appleton Way RM11 136 D3
Appletree Cl SS2 148 E3
Apple Tree Cl CM15 72 D1
Apple Tree Cres CM15 72 C1
Apple Tree Way SS11 121 F8
Apple Way CM2 54 D6
Appleyard Ave SS5 124 E8
Approach Rd
Canvey Island SS8 164 F3
Crays Hill CM11 120 D5
Approach The
Rayleigh SS6 123 C3
Upminster RM14 137 B1
April Pl CM21 1 F3
Apton Hall Rd SS4 126 C6
Arabia Cl E4 87 D2
Araglen Ave RM15 172 B8
Aragon Cl
Loughton IG10 88 E3
Romford RM5 113 B4
Southend-on-S SS2 147 E4
Aragon Ct
Hadleigh SS7 145 F2
Aragon Ct *continued*
Redbridge IG6 111 C4
Aragon Dr IG6 111 C3
Arandora Cres RM6 134 B5
Arbor Rd E4 109 D7
Arbour Cl CM14 116 C5
Arbour La CM1 32 D4
Arbour Way RM12 155 B7
Arbutus Cl CM2 54 B6
Arcade Pl 8 RM1 135 E6
Arcade The
18 Romford RM3 114 D5
Wickford SS11 121 D8
Arcadian Gdns SS7 145 D4
Arcadia Rd
Burnham-on-C CM0 106 C5
Canvey Island SS8 164 D3
Arcany Rd RM15 157 B1
Archates Ave RM16 173 A3
Archer Ave SS2 148 E3
Archer Cl SS2 148 E3
Archer Ho CM12 97 A1
Archer Rd SS15 141 B8
Archers CM19 23 B3
Archers Apartments 3 RM6 134 C5
Archers Cl CM12 119 A8
Archers Ct RM15 172 B8
Archers Fields SS13 121 B1
Archers Fields Cl SS13 121 A1
Archers Way CM2 54 C2
Archibald Rd RM3 115 A1
Archibald Terr SS15 141 B7
Archway RM3 114 B4
Arden Cres RM9 153 D5
Ardleigh SS16 141 E5
Ardleigh Cl RM11 136 D8
Ardleigh Ct CM15 94 F2
Ardleigh Gdns CM13 95 E3
ARDLEIGH GREEN 136 D7
Ardleigh Green Inf Sch RM11 136 D8
Ardleigh Green Jun Sch RM11 136 D8
Ardleigh Green Rd RM11 136 D7
Ardleigh Ho 5 IG11 152 C4
Ardley Cres CM22 3 B2
ARDLEY END 3 B1
Ardley Way SS6 123 D4
Ardmore La IG9 88 B2
Ardmore Pl IG9 88 B2
Ardmore Rd RM15 157 B1
Ardwell Ave IG6 133 C6
Arethusa Pl DA9 177 B3
Argent Ct SS15 140 F7
Argent St RM17 178 A8
Argles Cl DA9 177 A2
Argus Cl RM7 113 B2
Argyle Gdns RM14 137 D1
Argyle Rd
Burnham-on-C CM0 106 D4
Ilford IG1 133 A2
Argyll Ct CM15 94 D1
Argyll Ho SS0 166 D7
Argyll Rd
Chelmsford CM2 33 A5
Grays RM17 173 A1
Southend-on-S SS0 147 D1
Aria Ct IG2 133 D5
Ariel Ct 5 DA17 169 A1
Arisdale Ave RM15 157 B1
Arjan Way SS8 163 C3
Ark Ave RM16 173 A4
Ark La SS4 125 A1
Arkwright Rd RM18 179 B5
Arkwrights CM20 10 F1
Arlingham Mews EN9 65 C6
Arlington Gdns
Ilford IG1 133 A3
Romford RM3 114 E2
Arlington Ho 14 IG8 111 A3
Arlington Rd
Southend-on-S SS2 148 E1
Woodford IG8 110 B3
Arlington Sq CM3 101 C4
Arlington Way CM12 96 F5
Armada Cl SS15 141 D5
Armada Ct RM16 173 A3
Armadale SS8 163 F5
Armagh Rd SS3 168 D7
Armath Pl SS16 140 F4
Armitage Rd SS1 149 A1
Armonde Cl CM3 20 E1
Armor Rd RM19 171 D2
Armstead Wlk RM10 154 A5
Armstrong Ave IG8 109 E4
Armstrong Cl
Dagenham RM8 134 D4
Danbury CM3 56 F8
Stanford-le-H SS17 160 E2
Armstrong Rd SS7 144 D7
Arncroft Ct 8 IG11 153 B2
Arne Cl SS17 160 D3
Arne Ct SS15 141 C8
Arne Mews SS15 141 C8
Arneways Ave RM6 134 D8
Arnheim Rd CM0 106 C4
Arnhem Ave RM15 171 C5
Arnhem Rd CM1 31 E6
Arnold Ave
Basildon SS16 141 A5
Southend-on-S SS1 167 C7
Arnold Ave E EN3 65 A1
Arnold Ct E18 109 F2
Arnold Ho CM2 32 A1
Arnold Pl RM18 179 C6

Arnold Rd
Dagenham RM9 . . . . **153** F5
Dagenham RM10 . . . . **154** A5
Waltham Abbey EN9 . . . . . . **65** C4
Arnolds Ave CM13 . . . . . . **95** C4
Arnolds Cl CM13 . . . . **95** C4
Arnolds Farm La CM13 . . **95** E6
Arnolds Way SS4 . . . . . . **125** D7
Arnold Way CM2 . . . . **54** C3
Arnside Ho ☑ RM3 . . . . **115** A4
Arodene Ho IG2 . . . . **133** A5
Arran Ct SS12 . . . . **121** F6
Arran Dr E12 . . . . **132** D2
Arrowsmith Cl IG7 . . . . . **111** F5
Arrowsmith Path IG7 . . **111** F5
Arrowsmith Rd IG7 . . . . **111** F5
Arterial Ave RM13 . . . . . **155** C1
Arterial Rd
Southend-on-S SS6,
SS9 . . . . **146** C6
Thundersley SS6 . . . . **145** B8
Arterial Rd North Stifford
RM16 . . . . **172** E4
Arterial Rd West Thurrock
RM20 . . . . **172** A3
Arterial Road Purfleet
RM19 . . . . **171** C2
Artesian Dr RM11 . . . . . **135** F4
Arthur Barnes Ct
RM16 . . . . **174** C3
Arthur Bugler Inf Sch
SS17 . . . . **160** E3
Arthur Bugler Jun Sch
SS17 . . . . **160** E3
Arthur Ct
Chelmsford CM1 . . . . **31** F5
☑ Grays RM17 . . . . **178** C8
Arthur Rd RM6 . . . . **134** D5
Arthur St RM17 . . . . **178** C8
Arthur Toft Ho RM17 . . **178** B8
Arthur Walls Ho ☑
E12 . . . . **133** A1
Artillery Cl IG2 . . . . **133** C5
Arun RM18 . . . . **175** C2
Arun Cl CM1 . . . . **32** C5
Arundel Cl CM12 . . . . **97** C6
Arundel Dr
Corringham SS17 . . . . **161** A3
Woodford IG8 . . . . **110** A3
Arundel Gdns
Ilford IG3 . . . . **134** A2
Rayleigh SS6 . . . . **123** B5
Southend-on-S SS0 . . . . . **147** A3
Arundel Mews CM12 . . . **97** C6
Arundel Rd
Rochford SS4 . . . . **103** C1
Romford RM3 . . . . **114** F2
South Benfleet SS7 . . . . . **144** B7
Wickford SS11 . . . . **99** C1
Arundel Way CM12 . . . . . **97** C6
Arwen Gr CM3 . . . . **101** C4
Ascension Bsns Pk ☑
RM16 . . . . **172** B3
Ascension Rd RM5 . . . . **113** C4
Ascent Pk CM20 . . . . **11** B5
Ascham Dr E4 . . . . **109** A3
Ascot Cl
Redbridge IG6 . . . . **111** E4
Thundersley SS7 . . . . **145** B7
Ascot Gdns RM12 . . . . . **155** E8
Ascot Gr SS14 . . . . **142** E6
Ascot Mews CM0 . . . . . . **84** E4
Ashanti Cl SS3 . . . . **168** F8
Ashbeam Cl CM13 . . . . . **116** C4
Ashbourne Ave E18 . . . . **132** B7
Ashbourne Rd RM3 . . . . **114** D6
Ashbrook Pl SS6 . . . . . . **145** F8
Ashbrook Rd RM10 . . . . **135** B1
Ashburnham Gdns
RM14 . . . . **137** C3
Ashburnham Rd
Belvedere DA17 . . . . **169** C2
Southend-on-S SS1 . . . . . **166** F8
Ashburton Ave IG3 . . . . **152** F8
Ashbury Gdns RM6 . . . . **134** D6
Ashby Cl
Hornchurch RM11 . . . . . . **137** A3
Orsett RM16 . . . . **174** E7
Ash Cl
Pilgrims Hatch CM15 . . . . **93** F4
Romford RM5 . . . . **113** B3
Ashcombe SS4 . . . . **125** D4
Ashcombe Cl SS9 . . . . . **146** B6
Ash Ct
Chingford E4 . . . . **87** D2
Romford RM7 . . . . **135** B5
Southend-on-S SS3 . . . . . **168** F7
Woodford E18 . . . . **110** C2
Ashdene Cl SS5 . . . . **101** E2
Ashdon Cl
Brentwood CM13 . . . . **95** C3
South Ockendon RM15 . . **172** C7
Woodford IG8 . . . . **110** B4
Ashdon Way SS16 . . . . . **142** A5
Ashdown Cl SS7 . . . . . . **160** F5
Ashdown Cres SS7 . . . . **145** E4
Ashdown Ct IG11 . . . . . . **152** B6
Ashdown Ho SS7 . . . . . . **144** F6
Ashdown Wlk RM7 . . . . **113** B2
ASHELDHAM **85** A7
**Asheldham Pits Nature
Reserve★** CM0 . . . . **85** A8
Ashes Rd SS3 . . . . **168** E6
Ashfields SS6 . . . . **122** F3
Ashfield Farm Rd CM9 . . **35** D8
Ashfields
Basildon SS13 . . . . **143** C8
Loughton IG10 . . . . **88** F7

Ashford Ave CM14 . . . . . **116** B7
Ashford Ct RM17 . . . . . . **173** D1
Ashford Rd
Chelmsford CM1 . . . . **31** E2
Wallend E6 . . . . **152** A5
Woodford E18 . . . . **110** B1
Ash Gn
Billericay CM11 . . . . **97** E2
Canewdon SS4 . . . . **104** D1
Ash Gr
Burnham-on-C CM0 . . . . . **106** B6
Chelmsford CM2 . . . . **54** D7
Heybridge CM9 . . . . **37** C6
Ashgrove Rd IG3 . . . . . . **134** A3
Ash Groves CM21 . . . . **2** A2
Ash Ind Est CM19 . . . . . . **22** F7
Ashingdon Cl E4 . . . . . . **109** C7
Ashingdon Hts SS4 . . . . **125** B7
Ashingdon Rd SS4 . . . . **125** D6
Ashingdon Sch SS4 . . . **103** B1
Ashlands Ct RM18 . . . . . **175** C2
Ashleigh Cl SS8 . . . . **164** A6
Ashleigh Ct
Canvey Island SS8 . . . . . **164** A6
Hoddesdon EN11 . . . . **21** A5
Ingatestone CM4 . . . . **74** B3
Waltham Abbey EN9 . . . . . **66** A5
Ashleigh Dr SS9 . . . . . . **165** F8
Ashleigh Gdns RM14 . . **137** D1
Ashley Ave IG6 . . . . **111** B1
Ashley Gdns RM16 . . . . **173** D5
Ashley Gn CM3 . . . . **78** B7
Ashley Gr IG10 . . . . **88** C6
Ashley Rd E4 . . . . **109** A4
Ashley Gdns SS17 . . . . . **161** A3
Ash Lo SS3 . . . . **168** F8
Ashlyn Gr RM11 . . . . **136** D8
Ashlyns SS13 . . . . **143** B7
Ashlyns La CM5 . . . . **25** F2
Ashlyns Rd CM5 . . . . **45** F1
Ashmans Row CM3 . . . . **101** D6
Ashmeads IG10 . . . . **88** F6
Ashmour Gdns RM1 . . . **113** D3
Ash Rd
Canvey Island SS8 . . . . . **164** C3
Hadleigh SS7 . . . . **145** E3
Ashton Ct E4 . . . . **109** E7
Ashton Gdns RM6 . . . . . **134** E5
Ashton Pl
Chelmsford CM2 . . . . **33** A3
Thundersley SS7 . . . . **145** A6
Ashton Rd RM3 . . . . **114** D2
Ash Tree Cl CM1 . . . . **31** F2
Ash Tree Cnr CM3 . . . . . . **19** B6
Ash Tree Cres CM1 . . . . . **31** F2
Ashtree Ct EN9 . . . . **66** A5
Ash Tree Ct
Rochford SS4 . . . . **126** D4
Romford RM1 . . . . **136** A6
Ash Tree Fld CM20 . . . . . **10** A2
Ash Tree Wlk ☑ SS14 . . **142** F6
Ashurst Ave SS2 . . . . . . **148** F2
Ashurst Dr
Chelmsford CM1 . . . . **32** D7
Ilford IG6 . . . . **133** C6
Ashvale Dr RM14 . . . . . . **137** E2
Ashvale Gdns
Romford RM5 . . . . **113** D5
Upminster RM14 . . . . **137** F2
Ashway SS17 . . . . **161** B4
Ash Way SS5 . . . . **124** F8
Ashwells Rd CM15 . . . . . . **93** E6
Ash Wlk
Southend-on-S SS1 . . . . . **167** B7
South Ockendon RM15 . . **157** D2
Ashwood SS7 . . . . **144** B7
Ashwood Ave RM13 . . . . **155** B1
Ashwood Cl CM0 . . . . . . **106** B7
Ashwood Rd E4 . . . . **109** D7
Ashworth Pl CM17 . . . . . **24** D8
Ashworths
Canvey Island SS8 . . . . . **164** A6
Rochford SS4 . . . . **125** C6
Askews Farm Rd
RM17 . . . . **172** E1
Askwith Rd RM13 . . . . . **154** D3
Aspen Cl SS8 . . . . **163** E4
Aspen Ct
Basildon SS15 . . . . **119** C1
Brentwood CM13 . . . . **117** A4
Dartford DA1 . . . . **176** A1
Redbridge IG5 . . . . **132** E8
Aspen Gn SS4 . . . . **125** C7
Aspen Gr RM14 . . . . **156** A8
Aspens EN9 . . . . **66** C4
Aspen Way RM15 . . . . . **157** D2
Asquith Ave SS7 . . . . . . **145** B7
Asquith Cl RM8 . . . . **134** C3
Asquith Gdns SS4 . . . . . **145** C7
Assandune Cl SS4 . . . . . **125** D7
Aster Cl
Basildon SS15 . . . . **141** D5
☑ Chelmsford CM1 . . . . . **32** F6
Asthall Gdns IG6 . . . . . . **133** C7
Astley RM17 . . . . **177** F8
Aston Ct ☑ IG8 . . . . **110** A4
Aston Mews RM6 . . . . . **134** C4
Aston Rd SS15 . . . . **141** B6
Astor Ave RM7 . . . . **135** C5
Astra Cl RM12 . . . . **155** B6
Astra Ct E ☑ RM12 . . . . **155** B6
Astra Ctr CM20 . . . . **10** F4
Astra Ct W ☑ RM12 . . . **155** B6
Athelstan Cl RM3 . . . . . **114** F1
Athelstan Ct E6 . . . . **152** A3

Athelstan Gdns SS11 . . . **99** D1
Athelstan Rd CM14 . . . . **114** F1
Athena Est CM20 . . . . **11** B4
Atherstone Cl SS8 . . . . . **164** C2
Atherstone Rd SS8 . . . . **164** C2
Atherton End CM21 . . . . . . **1** E3
Atherton Gdns RM16 . . **174** C2
Atherton Ho ☑
Romford RM3 . . . . **114** A3
Woodford IG5 . . . . **110** E1
Atherton Rd IG5 . . . . **110** F1
Athol Cl SS8 . . . . **164** C2
Athol Ct IG3 . . . . **134** A4
Atholl Rd
Chelmsford CM2 . . . . **32** F5
Ilford IG3 . . . . **134** A4
Athol Rd DA17 . . . . **169** C1
Athos Rd SS8 . . . . **164** C5
Atlanta Bvd RM1 . . . . . . **135** E5
Atlantic Cl DA10 . . . . **177** E2
Atlantis Cl IG11 . . . . **153** B2
Atridge Chase CM12 . . . . **97** A4
Atrium ☑ IG9 . . . . **110** D8
Attlee Ct RM17 . . . . **173** A3
Attlee Dr DA1 . . . . **176** A2
Attwoods Cl CM2 . . . . **54** C3
Aubrey Cl CM1 . . . . **32** B7
Aubrietia Cl RM3 . . . . . . **114** E2
Auckland Ave RM13 . . . **154** F2
Auckland Cl
Chelmsford CM1 . . . . **31** E5
Tilbury RM18 . . . . **179** A5
Auckland Rd IG1 . . . . **133** C4
Auction Pl RM4 . . . . **90** B6
Audleigh Pl IG7 . . . . **111** A4
Audley Gdns
Ilford IG3 . . . . **133** F2
Loughton IG10 . . . . **89** D7
Waltham Abbey EN9 . . . . . **65** C5
Audleys Cl SS2 . . . . **147** E5
Audley Way SS14 . . . . . . **142** B6
Audrey Rd IG1 . . . . **133** B1
Augers ☑ CM0 . . . . **106** C4
Augustine Ct EN9 . . . . . . **65** B6
Augustine Rd ☑
DA12 . . . . **179** D1
Augustine Way CM3 . . . . **56** F2
Aukingford Gdns CM5 . . **48** F5
Aukingford Gn CM5 . . . . . **48** F4
Aundle Ho IG8 . . . . **111** A4
Auriel Ave RM10 . . . . . . **154** D6
Aurora Ct IG8 . . . . **109** F6
Austen Cl
Greenhithe DA9 . . . . **177** C1
Loughton IG10 . . . . **89** D6
Tilbury RM18 . . . . **179** C5
Austen Dr CM4 . . . . **75** D2
Austral Dr RM11 . . . . . . **136** D4
Austral Way CM3 . . . . **83** A3
Avcoca Terr SS4 . . . . **147** D2
Avebury Rd SS0 . . . . **147** E2
AVELEY **171** C6
Aveley By-Pass RM15 . . **171** C6
Aveley Cl RM15 . . . . **171** D5
Aveley Mans ☑ IG11 . . . **152** B5
Aveley Prim Sch
RM15 . . . . **171** E5
Aveley Rd
Romford RM1 . . . . **135** E7
Upminster RM15 . . . . **156** C4
Aveley Sch The RM15. . . **171** D6
Aveling Park Rd E17 . . . **109** A1
Aveling Park Sch E17 . . **109** A1
Avelon Rd
Rainham RM13 . . . . **155** A4
Romford RM5 . . . . **113** D4
Avenue Cl RM3 . . . . **114** F3
Avenue Ct IG5 . . . . **132** E8
Avenue Gate IG10 . . . . . . **88** C3
Avenue Ind Est
Chingford E4 . . . . **109** A4
Romford RM3 . . . . **114** D2
Avenue Rd
Brentwood CM14 . . . . **116** C6
Chelmsford CM2 . . . . **54** D7
Hoddesdon EN11 . . . . **21** D5
Ilford IG1 . . . . **134** C4
Ingatestone CM4 . . . . **74** B3
Romford RM3 . . . . **114** F3
South Benfleet SS7 . . . . . **144** E3
Southend-on-S, Clifftown
SS0 . . . . **166** F8
Southend-on-S, Leigh Cliffs
SS9 . . . . **165** E8
Theydon Bois CM16 . . . . . **67** D3
Woodford IG8 . . . . **110** C4
Avenue Terr
Ilford IG2 . . . . **133** E5
Southend-on-S SS0 . . . . . **166** E8
Avenue The
Billericay CM12 . . . . **97** A2
Brentwood CM13 . . . . **116** F4
☑ Buckhurst Hill IG9 . . . **110** C8
Canvey Island SS8 . . . . . **164** B2
Chingford E4 . . . . **109** D5
Danbury CM3 . . . . **56** F7
Fobbing SS17 . . . . **161** D4
Greenhithe DA9 . . . . **177** B2
Hadleigh SS7 . . . . **145** E3
Hoddesdon EN11 . . . . **21** A4
Hornchurch RM12 . . . . . . **136** D2
Hullbridge SS5 . . . . **101** D3
Kelvedon Hatch CM15 . . . **93** E8
Loughton IG10 . . . . **88** E3
Lower Nazeing EN9 . . . . . **44** A7
North Fambridge CM3 . . . **103** A7
Romford RM1 . . . . **135** D7

Avenue The continued
Wanstead E11 . . . . **132** B6
Avery Gdns
Ilford IG2 . . . . **133** A6
Redbridge IG2 . . . . **132** F6
Avey La
High Beach IG10 . . . . **88** A8
Waltham Abbey EN9 . . . . . **65** E2
Aviation Way SS2 . . . . . **147** B7
Avila Chase CM2 . . . . **54** B1
Avington Wlk SS7. . . . . . **144** F6
Avocet Way CM9 . . . . **37** C5
Avon Cl SS4 . . . . **125** C5
Avon Ct
☑ Chingford E4 . . . . **87** C1
Upminster RM14 . . . . **137** E4
Avondale Cl
Loughton IG10 . . . . **88** F2
Rayleigh SS6 . . . . **123** F2
Avondale Cres IG4 . . . . . **132** D6
Avondale Ct
Southend-on-S SS9 . . . . . **146** D1
Woodford E18 . . . . **110** B2
Avondale Dr
Loughton IG10 . . . . **88** F3
Southend-on-S SS9 . . . . . **146** F4
Avondale Gdns SS17 . . . **160** E5
Avondale Rd
Basildon SS16 . . . . **143** A4
Rayleigh SS6 . . . . **123** F2
South Benfleet SS7 . . . . . **144** D3
Avondale Wlk SS8 . . . . . **163** E4
Avon Gn RM15 . . . . **172** B7
Avon Ho RM14 . . . . **137** E4
Avon House Sch IG8. . . . **110** A6
Avon Rd
Canvey Island SS8 . . . . . **164** A3
Chelmsford CM1 . . . . **31** C5
Upminster RM14 . . . . **137** D5
Avontar Rd RM15 . . . . . . **157** B1
Avon Terr IG10 . . . . **88** F3
Avon Way
Southend-on-S SS3 . . . . . **168** E7
Wanstead E18 . . . . **132** A8
Avril Way E4 . . . . **109** C5
Avro Rd SS2 . . . . **147** D6
Axe St IG11 . . . . **152** C4
Axon Pl IG1 . . . . **133** C2
Aylesbeare SS3 . . . . **168** D8
Aylesbury Dr SS16 . . . . . **140** F5
Aylesbury Mews SS15 . . **119** F2
Aylets Field CM18 . . . . . . **23** C5
Aylett Cl SS8 . . . . **164** C4
Aylett Rd RM14 . . . . **137** C2
Ayletts
Basildon SS14 . . . . **142** F6
Broomfield CM1 . . . . **19** B3
Aylmer Rd RM8 . . . . **134** E1
Ayloffe Rd RM9 . . . . **153** F6
Ayloff Prim Sch RM12 . . **155** B8
Ayloffs Wlk RM11 . . . . . **136** E6
Ayloff's Wlk RM11 . . . . . **136** E6
Aylsham La RM3 . . . . . . **114** D6
Aylsham Rd EN11 . . . . . . **21** C8
Aynsley Gdns CM17 . . . . **24** C8
Ayr Gn RM1 . . . . **113** E2
Ayron Rd RM15 . . . . **157** B1
Ayrton Ho SS9 . . . . **146** A2
Ayr Way RM1 . . . . **113** E2
AYTHORPE RODING **5** B3
Azalea Ave SS12 . . . . . . **121** C7
Azalea Cl IG1 . . . . **152** B7
Azalea Ct
☑ Chelmsford CM1 . . . . . **32** F6
Chingford IG8 . . . . **109** E3
Azalea Mews SS8 . . . . . **164** A2

B

Baardwyk Ave SS8 . . . . . **164** E3
Babbacombe Gdns
IG4 . . . . **132** E7
Babington Rd
Dagenham RM8 . . . . **153** C8
Hornchurch RM12 . . . . . . **136** B3
Back La
Broomfield CM1 . . . . **19** D1
Buckhurst Hill IG9 . . . . . . **110** D8
Dagenham RM6 . . . . **134** E4
East Hanningfield CM3 . . . **78** B7
Grays RM20 . . . . **172** B4
Ingatestone CM4 . . . . **74** A6
Little Hallingbury CM22 . . . **2** B7
Little Waltham CM3 . . . . . **19** C4
Lower Nazeing EN9 . . . . . **22** C1
Pleshey CM3 . . . . **7** E2
Purfleet RM19 . . . . **171** E3
Rochford SS4 . . . . **125** F1
Sheering CM22 . . . . **2** B1
South Ockendon RM16 . . **172** C5
Stock CM4 . . . . **75** D2
Backnang Sq ☑ CM2 . . . **32** C2
Back Rd CM1 . . . . **31** A1
**Backwarden Nature
Reserve★** CM3 . . . . **56** E5
**Backwardens Nature
Trail★** CM3 . . . . **56** E4
Bacon Link RM5 . . . . **113** B4
Bacons Chase CM0 . . . . . **42** B2
Bacon Terr ☑ RM8 . . . . **153** B7
Badburgham Ct EN9 . . . . **65** F6
Baddeley Cl EN3 . . . . **65** A2
Baddow Cl
Dagenham RM10 . . . . **154** A4
Woodford IG8 . . . . **110** D4
Baddow Ct CM2 . . . . **55** A6
Baddow Hall Ave CM2 . . **55** A7

Baddow Hall Cres CM2 . . **55** B7
Baddow Hall Jun & Inf Sch
CM2 . . . . **55** A6
Baddow Place Ave
CM2 . . . . **55** A6
Baddow Rd
Chelmsford CM2 . . . . **32** C1
Great Baddow CM2 . . . . . . **54** E7
Baden Powell Cl RM9 . . **153** E4
Baden Powell Ho ☑
DA17 . . . . **169** A3
Baden Rd IG1 . . . . **152** B7
Bader Way RM13 . . . . . . **155** B6
Badger Cl IG2 . . . . **133** C4
Badger Ct E4 . . . . **109** D6
Badger Hall Ave SS7 . . . **145** A4
Badgers Cl
Galleywood CM2 . . . . **54** B1
Southend-on-S SS0 . . . . . **147** B4
Badgers Keep CM0 . . . . **106** B8
Badgers Mount
Chadwell St M RM16 . . . . **173** F4
Hockley SS5 . . . . **124** C5
Badgers Rise SS8 . . . . . . **164** A6
Badgers The SS16 . . . . . **141** B4
Badgers Way SS7 . . . . . . **145** A4
Badlis Rd E17 . . . . **109** A1
Bag La CM4 . . . . **73** A2
Bagleys Spring RM6 . . . **134** E7
Bailey Cl
Chingford E4 . . . . **109** C6
Purfleet RM19 . . . . **171** D2
Bailey Ct ☑ E4 . . . . **109** D5
Bailey Rd SS9 . . . . **146** B2
Bailey The SS6 . . . . **123** C4
Baillie Cl RM13 . . . . **155** B1
Bainbridge Rd RM9 . . . . **153** F8
Baird Ho ☑ DA17 . . . . . . **169** A3
Bairny Wood App IG8 . . **110** B4
Baker Cl SS15 . . . . **141** B6
Baker Mews CM9 . . . . **37** A2
Bakers Cl CM3 . . . . **101** D8
Bakers Cotts CM15 . . . . . **93** F8
Bakers Ct RM8 . . . . **134** F4
Bakers Ct
Ramsden Heath CM11 . . . . **98** C4
Wickford SS11 . . . . **121** F6
Baker's Ct SS14 . . . . **121** A2
Bakers Farm Cl SS11 . . . **122** A7
Bakersfield CM3 . . . . **82** F8
Bakers Field CM4 . . . . **75** E2
Bakers La
Danbury CM3 . . . . **56** E7
Epping CM16 . . . . **45** F1
Ingatestone CM4 . . . . **74** B4
West Hanningfield CM2 . . . **76** B7
Bakers Mdw CM15 . . . . . **72** C2
Bakers Mead CM3 . . . . . . **18** F7
Bakers Mews CM4 . . . . . **74** B4
Baker St
Chelmsford CM2 . . . . **32** A1
Orsett RM16 . . . . **173** F6
BAKER STREET **173** F7
Bakers Villas The
CM16 . . . . **45** F1
Bakers Wlk CM21 . . . . **1** E2
Bakery Cl
Roydon CM19 . . . . **22** C8
Tillingham CM0 . . . . **63** E3
Baldocks Rd CM16 . . . . . **67** E4
Baldwin Ho E6 . . . . **152** A5
Baldwin's Hill IG10 . . . . . **88** F8
Balfour Cl SS12 . . . . **121** E5
Balfour Dr
Grays RM17 . . . . **173** C2
Ilford IG3 . . . . **133** C3
Balgonie Rd E4 . . . . **87** D3
Balgores Cres RM2 . . . . **136** B8
Balgores La RM2 . . . . . . **136** B7
Balgores Sq RM2 . . . . . . **136** B7
Ballards Cl RM10 . . . . . . **154** B4
BALLARDS GORE **126** F6
Ballards Rd RM10 . . . . . **154** B3
Ballards Wlk SS15 . . . . . **141** E7
Balliol Ave E4 . . . . **109** E6
Balmerino Ave SS7 . . . . **145** C6
Balmoral Ave
Corringham SS17 . . . . **161** A3
Stanford-le-H SS17 . . . . . **160** E3
Balmoral Cl CM11 . . . . . . **97** E1
Balmoral Ct CM2 . . . . **32** C2
Balmoral Gdns
Hockley SS5 . . . . **124** C6
Ilford IG3 . . . . **133** F3
Balmoral Ho SS0 . . . . . . **166** E8
Balmoral Rd
Hornchurch RM12 . . . . . . **136** D1
Mayland CM3 . . . . **61** A2
Pilgrims Hatch CM15 . . . . **94** B4
Romford RM2 . . . . **136** B6
Southend-on-S SS0 . . . . . **147** L1
Balmoral Terr SS0 . . . . . **147** D2
Balstonia Dr SS17 . . . . . **160** F5
Baltic Ave SS1 . . . . **167** A8
Baltic Wharf DA11 . . . . . **179** A1
Bamber Ho ☑ IG11 . . . . **152** C4
Bamford Rd IG11 . . . . . . **152** C6
Bamford Way RM5 . . . . . **113** B5
Bampton Rd RM3 . . . . . . **114** E2
Bancroft Ave IG9 . . . . . . **110** A8
Bancroft Chase RM12 . . **135** F2
Bancrofts Rd CM3 . . . . . **101** E8
Bancroft's Sch IG8 . . . . **110** A7
Bandhills Cl CM3 . . . . . . **101** D8
Banes Down EN9 . . . . . . **21** E1

Bankart La CM2 . . . . 32 F4
Bank Chambers
  CM15 . . . . 116 D8
Bank End Cotts CM4 . . . . 75 A8
Bankfoot RM17 . . . . 173 A1
Bank Pl 8 CM14 . . . . . . 116 C8
Bankside DA11 . . . . 178 C1
Bankside CM3. . . . . 79 E1
Bankside Pk IG11 . . . . . . 153 E4
Bankside Rd IG1 . . . . . . 152 D7
Banks La
  Epping CM16 . . . . 68 F7
  Stapleford Tawney CM16 . . 69 A8
Bank St DA11, DA12 . . . . 179 B1
Banks Way E12 . . . . 152 A8
Bann Cl RM15 . . . . 172 B6
Banner Cl RM19 . . . . . . 171 D2
Bannister Dr CM13 . . . . . 95 C3
Bannister Gn SS12 . . . . . 121 E6
Bannister Ho RM20 . . . . 177 D8
Bansons Ct CM5 . . . . 49 A3
Banson's La CM5 . . . . . . 49 A3
Bansons Way CM5 . . . . . 49 A3
Bansons Yd CM5. . . . . . . 49 A3
Bantel Villas EN11 . . . . . 21 C8
Banyards RM11 . . . . 136 E7
Banyard Way SS4 . . . . . 125 C4
Barbara Ave SS8 . . . . . . 163 F2
Barbara Cl SS4 . . . . 125 E2
Barbary Lo CM2 . . . . 32 A2
Barbel Cl EN8 . . . . 65 A5
Barberry Cl RM13 . . . . . 114 C3
Barbour Gn SS12 . . . . . 121 D5
Barbrook Way CM3 . . . . . 56 E1
Barclay Ct EN11 . . . . 21 A5
Barclay Oval IG8 . . . . . . 110 A6
Barclay Rd SS13 . . . . . . 121 E1
Barclay Way RM20 . . . . 171 F1
Bardell Cl CM1 . . . . 31 F6
Bardenville Rd SS8 . . . . 164 E3
Bardeswell Cl CM14 . . . . 116 C8
Bardfield SS16 . . . . 142 E5
Bardfield Ave RM6 . . . . . 134 D8
Bardfield Prim Sch
  SS16 . . . . 142 E4
Bardfield Way SS6 . . . . . 123 A3
Bards Ct RM3 . . . . 114 B3
Barfields IG10 . . . . 89 A5
Barfields Gdns IG10 . . . . 89 A5
Barfields Path IG10 . . . . . 89 A5
Barge Ct DA9 . . . . 177 C3
Barge Pier Rd SS3 . . . . . 168 E5
Barham Cl RM7 . . . . 113 B1
Bark Burr Rd RM16 . . . . 172 F4
Barkers Mead CM22. . . . . . 2 B8
BARKING 152 D5
Barking Abbey Comp Sch
  (Lower Sch) IG11 . . . . 152 E7
Barking Abbey Sch
  IG11 . . . . 152 F6
Barking Bsns Ctr
  IG11 . . . . 153 A2
Barking Coll RM7 . . . . . 135 D2
Barking Hospl IG11 . . . . 152 F5
Barking Ind Pk IG11 . . . . 153 A4
Barking Rd E6 . . . . 152 A4
BARKINGSIDE 133 C8
Barkingside Sta IG6 . . . . 133 D8
Barking Sta IG11 . . . . . . 152 C5
Barkis Cl CM1 . . . . 31 D7
Barkwood RM7. . . . . . . 135 C6
Barle Gdns RM15 . . . . . 172 B7
Barley Cl
  Basildon SS16 . . . . . . 141 A3
  Hatfield Heath CM22. . . . . 3 E2
Barleycorn Way RM11. . . 136 F5
Barley Court Day Hospl
  IG3 . . . . 134 B6
Barley Croft CM18 . . . . . 23 E4
Barley Ct 2 EN11 . . . . . 21 D8
Barley Field CM15 . . . . . 71 F2
Barleyfields Cl RM4 . . . . 134 C4
Barley La IG3, RM6 . . . . 134 B5
Barleylands Farm Mus★
  CM11 . . . . 119 F5
Barleylands Rd CM11,
  SS15 . . . . 119 D6
Barley Lane Prim Sch
  RM6 . . . . 134 B4
Barley Mead CM3 . . . . . . 57 B6
BARLING 149 E7
Barling Magna Com Prim
  Sch SS3 . . . . 149 D7
Barling Rd SS3 . . . . 149 B6
Barlow Way E18 . . . . . . 169 E8
Barlow Way RM13 . . . . . 135 B3
Barnaby Rudge CM1 . . . . 31 F7
Barnaby Way
  Basildon SS15 . . . . . . 141 D7
  Chigwell IG7 . . . . 111 B7
Barnard Acres EN9. . . . . 43 E8
Barnard Cl SS16 . . . . . . 142 E2
Barnard Ct 18 DA2 . . . . 176 B1
Barnard Ho RM3 . . . . . . 114 E1
Barnardo Dr IG6. . . . . . 133 C7
Barnard Rd
  Galleywood CM2 . . . . . . 54 C2
  Sawbridgeworth CM21 . . . . 1 E4
  Southend-on-S SS9 . . . . 146 C2
Barnards Ave SS8 . . . . . 164 D4
Barncombe Cl SS7 . . . . 144 D6
Barncroft Cl IG10 . . . . . . 89 A4
Barncroft Gn IG10 . . . . . 89 A4
Barncroft Rd IG10 . . . . . 89 A4

Barn Ct CM21. . . . . 1 E3
Barnes Ct
  Chipping Ongar CM5 . . . 48 F5
  Woodford IG8 . . . . 110 D5
Barnes Farm Dr CM3 . . . 82 F7
Barnes Farm Jun & Inf
  Schs CM3 . . . . 33 A3
Barnes Ho 8 IG11 . . . . 152 D4
Barnes Mill Rd CM2 . . . . 32 F2
Barnes Rd IG1 . . . . 152 C7
Barnet Park Rd SS11 . . . 99 F2
Barnett Ct RM17 . . . . . . 173 C1
Barneveld Ave SS8 . . . . 164 E3
Barnfield
  Epping CM16 . . . . 46 A3
  Hatfield Broad Oak CM22 . . 4 A5
  Wickford SS11 . . . . . . 121 E8
Barnfield Cl
  Greenhithe DA9 . . . . . 176 F1
  Hoddesdon EN11 . . . . . 21 A8
  Lower Nazeing EN9 . . . . 21 F1
Barnfield Cotts CM9 . . . . 37 B5
Barnfield Mews CM1 . . . . 32 A6
Barn Gn CM1 . . . . 32 E8
Barn Hill CM19 . . . . 22 B4
Barnmead CM5 . . . . 47 F2
Barn Mead
  Doddinghurst CM15. . . . 72 C3
  Harlow CM18. . . . . 23 E6
  Theydon Bois CM16 . . . . 67 E3
Barnmead Ct RM9 . . . . . 153 F7
Barnmead Gdns RM9 . . . 153 F7
Barnmead Rd RM9 . . . . 153 F7
Barnmead Way CM0 . . . 106 B8
Barns Ct CM19 . . . . 23 B3
Barnsley Rd RM3 . . . . . 114 F3
Barnstaple Cl SS1. . . . . 168 A8
Barnstaple Path 7
  RM3 . . . . 114 D5
Barnstaple Rd
  Romford RM3 . . . . 114 C5
  Southend-on-S SS1 . . . 168 B8
Barnston Way CM13. . . . 95 C4
Barn The RM17 . . . . 173 B2
Barnwell Dr SS5 . . . . . . 124 D6
Barnyard The SS16. . . . . 141 A4
Baron Ct RM3 . . . . 114 F2
Baron Ct SS2 . . . . 147 F8
Baron Gdns IG6 . . . . . . 133 C8
Baron Rd
  Dagenham RM8 . . . . . 134 D3
  South Woodham Ferrers
  CM3 . . . . 101 E7
Barons Court Inf Sch
  SS0 . . . . 166 F8
Barons Ct IG1 . . . . 133 D2
Baron's La CM3, CM9 . . . 58 L1
Barons Way SS16 . . . . . 141 B4
Barrack La CM3. . . . . . . 18 E8
Barrack Rd CM1 . . . . . . 17 B5
Barrack Row 1 DA11 . . . 179 B1
Barrack Sq 10 CM2 . . . . 32 B2
Barra Glade SS12 . . . . . 121 F5
Barrass Cl EN3 . . . . 65 A2
Barrett Cl RM3. . . . . . . 114 B3
Barrie Pavement 1
  SS12 . . . . 121 D5
Barrington Cl
  1 Basildon SS14 . . . . 142 F8
  Great Baddow CM2 . . . . 55 A6
  Loughton IG10 . . . . . . 89 C5
  Southend-on-S SS3 . . . 149 L1
  Woodford IG5 . . . . 110 F2
Barrington Ct CM13 . . . . 95 C3
Barrington Gdns
  SS14 . . . . 142 F8
Barrington Pl CM4 . . . . . 74 B3
Barrington Rd
  Little Ilford E12. . . . . . 152 A6
  Loughton IG10. . . . . . . 89 C5
Barringtons Cl SS6. . . . . 123 D3
Barron's Cl CM5 . . . . . . 48 F4
Barrow Chase CM2. . . . . 33 B4
Barrow Hall Rd SS3 . . . . 149 C5
Barrow Marsh CM9 . . . . 38 A4
Barrowsand SS1 . . . . . . 168 B4
Barrows Rd CM19 . . . . . 22 F8
Barry Cl RM16 . . . . 174 A3
Barry Ct RM5 . . . . 113 D5
Barrymore Wlk SS6 . . . . 124 A2
BARSTABLE 142 D6
Barstable Rd SS17 . . . . 160 D1
Barstable Sch SS14 . . . . 142 F6
Bartholomew Dr RM3 . . 114 D1
Bartholomew Ho 16
  IG8. . . . . 111 A3
Bartlett Cl CM3 . . . . 60 F1
Bartletts SS6 . . . . 146 A8
Bartletts Ho 15 RM10. . . 154 B6
Bartley Cl SS7 . . . . 144 B6
Bartley Rd SS7 . . . . 144 B6
Bartlow End SS13. . . . . 143 B8
Bartlow Gdns RM5 . . . . 113 D2
Bartlow Side SS13 . . . . 143 B8
Barton Ave RM7 . . . . . . 135 B3
Barton Cl
  Chigwell IG7 . . . . 111 C8
  South Woodham Ferrers
  CM3 . . . . 79 D1
Barton Ct 8 CM14 . . . . 116 C6
Barton Friars IG7. . . . . . 111 C8
Barton Mdws IG6. . . . . 133 B7
Barton Rd RM12 . . . . . . 136 A3
Bartram Ct RM8 . . . . . . 153 B6
Baryta Cl SS17 . . . . . . 160 C1
Baryta Cl SS9. . . . . 165 E8
Basedale Rd RM9 . . . . . 153 B5

BASILDON 142 C4
Basildon Ave IG5 . . . . . 111 A2
Basildon Bsns Ctr
  SS14 . . . . 142 A8
Basildon Dr SS15 . . . . . 141 C8
Basildon Hospl SS16 . . . 142 A3
Basildon Rd SS15 . . . . . 141 E8
Basildon Rise SS15 . . . . 141 E8
Basildon Sta SS14 . . . . . 142 A5
Basildon Trad Ctr
  SS14 . . . . 141 F8
Basildon Zoo★ SS16 . . . 142 C2
Basilica Ho SS11. . . . . . 122 B7
Basil Mews 1 CM11 . . . 11 C1
Basin Ho 7 IG11 . . . . . 152 D4
Basin Rd IG11 . . . . 37 E3
Bassenthwaite Rd
  SS7 . . . . 144 E7
Bassett Bsns Units
  CM16 . . . . 46 F4
Bassett Fields CM16 . . . 47 D6
Bassett Gdns CM16 . . . . 47 B5
Bassett Ho RM9. . . . . . 153 B4
Bassetts La CM3, CM9. . . 35 A4
Bassett's Ct CM5 . . . . . 51 B8
Bastable Ave IG11 . . . . . 153 A4
Bata Ave RM18 . . . . . . 175 B1
Batavia Rd SS8 . . . . . . 163 D4
Bate-Dudley Dr CM0 . . . 42 B3
Bateman Cl 2 IG11 . . . . 152 C6
Bateman Rd E4 . . . . . . 109 A4
Batemans Mews
  CM14 . . . . 116 B6
Bates Bsns Ctr RM3 . . . 115 A3
Bates Rd
  Maldon CM9 . . . . 37 B4
  Romford RM3 . . . . 115 A3
Bath Rd RM6 . . . . 134 E5
Bath St DA11 . . . . 179 B1
Bathurst Rd IG1 . . . . . . 133 B3
Baton Cl RM19 . . . . 171 D2
Battis The 1 RM1. . . . . 135 E5
Battle Cl CM5. . . . . 49 A2
Battle Rd DA17 . . . . . . 169 C2
BATTLESBRIDGE 100 D1
Battlesbridge Antiques
  Ctr★ SS11. . . . . 100 E2
Battles Bridge Motorcycle
  Mus★ SS11. . . . . . . 100 D2
Battlesbridge Sta
  SS11 . . . . 100 D2
Battleswick SS14 . . . . . 120 E1
Batt's Rd CM19 . . . . . . 84 A8
Bawden Way CM2. . . . . 54 D8
Bawdsey Ave IG2. . . . . 133 F4
Baxter Ave SS2 . . . . . . 147 F1
Baxter Gdns RM3 . . . . . 114 C8
Baxter Rd IG1 . . . . 152 B7
Baxters CM3. . . . . 57 A7
Bay Cl SS8 . . . . 164 B2
Bayleys Mead CM13. . . . 117 C8
Bayly Rd DA1 . . . . 176 A1
Bay Manor La RM20 . . . 176 F8
Baymans Woods
  CM15 . . . . 116 F8
Bay Tree Cl IG6. . . . . . . 111 B3
Baytree Ct 16 CM14 . . . 116 C8
Baytree Ho E4 . . . . 87 B2
Bay View CM0 . . . . 62 C8
Baywood Sq IG4 . . . . . 112 B6
Beach Ave SS9 . . . . . . 166 A8
Beach Ct
  Great Wakering SS3 . . . 150 C4
  Southend-on-S SS0 . . . 166 C7
Beaches Cl SS5 . . . . . . 125 A6
Beach House Gdns
  SS8 . . . . 164 C2
Beach Rd
  Canvey Island SS8. . . . 164 D4
  Southend-on-S, Shoeburyness
  SS1 . . . . 168 F5
  Southend-on-S SS1 . . . 167 F5
Beach's Dr CM1 . . . . . . 31 D3
Beachway SS8 . . . . 164 B2
Beachy Dr CM0 . . . . . . 62 C8
Beaconfield Ave CM16 . . 46 A2
Beaconfield Rd CM16 . . . 46 A2
Beaconfield Way CM16. . 46 A2
Beacon Hill
  Kelvedon Hatch CM14 . . 71 C2
  Maldon CM9 . . . . 36 E2
  Purfleet RM19 . . . . . . 171 B1
Beacon Hill Ind Est
  RM19 . . . . 171 B1
Beacon Hill Rd CM14. . . 71 B2
Beacon Hill Sch
  RM15 . . . . 172 A8
Beacons The IG10 . . . . . 67 A1
Beacontree Ave E17 . . . 109 D1
Beadle's Par RM10 . . . . 154 C6
Beadles The CM22. . . . . . 2 B8
Beads Hall La CM15 . . . 94 B4
Beal High Sch IG4 . . . . 132 E7
Beal Rd IG1 . . . . 133 A2
Beam Ave RM10 . . . . . 154 B4
Beambridge SS13. . . . . 143 A6
Beambridge Ct 2
  SS13 . . . . 143 A6
Beambridge Mews
  SS13 . . . . 143 A6
Beambridge Pl 1
  SS13 . . . . 143 A6
Beaminster Gdns
  Ilford IG6 . . . . 133 B8
  Redbridge IG6 . . . . . . 111 B1
Beamish Cl CM16 . . . . . 47 C8
Beam Prim Sch RM10. . . 154 C3
Beams Cl CM11 . . . . . . 119 C8

Beams Way CM11 . . . . . 119 C8
Beamway RM10. . . . . . 154 D5
Beanfield Rd CM21 . . . . . 1 A4
Bean Rd DA9 . . . . 177 B1
Beansland Gr RM6 . . . . 134 E8
Bearblock Cotts
  RM14 . . . . 156 C6
Bear Cl RM7 . . . . 135 B5
Beardsley Dr CM1. . . . . 32 F7
Beardsley Terr 2
  RM8 . . . . 153 B7
Bearing Cl IG7 . . . . 112 A6
Bearing Way IG7 . . . . . 112 A6
Bearsted Dr SS13 . . . . 143 C5
Beaton Cl DA9 . . . . 177 B2
Beatrice Ave SS8 . . . . . 164 B4
Beatrice Cl SS5 . . . . . . 124 D6
Beatrice Ct IG9 . . . . . . 110 D8
Beatty La SS14 . . . . . . 142 E6
Beatty Rise CM3 . . . . . 101 F6
Beattyville Gdns IG6 . . . 133 D7
BEAUCHAMP RODING
  . . . . 15 A1
Beauchamps CM0 . . . . . 106 B8
Beauchamps Dr SS11 . . 122 A8
Beauchamps Sch
  SS11 . . . . 122 A8
Beaufort Cl
  Chingford E4 . . . . 109 B4
  Grays RM16 . . . . 172 F3
  North Weald Bassett
  CM16 . . . . 47 A4
  Romford RM7 . . . . 135 C7
Beaufort Gdns IG1. . . . . 133 A3
Beaufort Rd
  Billericay CM12 . . . . . . 96 F2
  Chelmsford CM2 . . . . . 33 A4
Beaufort St SS2 . . . . . 148 D1
Beaulieu Bvd CM1 . . . . 33 A7
Beaulieu Dr EN9 . . . . . . 65 B6
Beauly Ct RM1 . . . . . . 113 E2
Beauly Way RM1 . . . . . 113 E2
Beaumaris Dr IG8 . . . . . 110 D3
Beaumont Cl RM2. . . . . 114 C1
Beaumont Cres RM13 . . 155 A6
Beaumont Gdns CM13. . . 95 C3
Beaumont Park Dr
  CM19 . . . . 22 B8
Beaumont Pk CM3 . . . . 56 C6
Beaumont Way CM9 . . . 59 B8
Beaumont Wlk CM1. . . . 31 D5
Beaver Ctr The RM8. . . . 134 E4
Beaver Rd IG6. . . . . . . 112 C5
Beaver Twr SS9. . . . . . 146 E6
Beazley End SS12 . . . . 121 E6
Bebington Cl CM12 . . . . 97 A3
Beccles Cl SS11 . . . . . . 121 D8
Beccles Dr IG11 . . . . . . 152 F6
Becket Ave E6 . . . . 152 A2
Becket Cl
  Brentwood CM13 . . . . . 116 C4
  Rochford SS4. . . . . . . 125 D5
Becket Ho 15 CM14 . . . 116 C8
Beckett Dr SS17 . . . . . 160 D4
Becketts SS15 . . . . 141 A6
Becketts Ct
  Brentwood CM13 . . . . . 116 C4
  Chelmsford CM1 . . . . . 32 A3
Becket Way CM3. . . . . . 101 E5
Beck Farm Cl SS8 . . . . 164 F3
Beckney Ave SS5 . . . . . 102 E1
Beck Rd SS8 . . . . 164 F3
Beckton Alps Ski Ctr★
  E6. . . . . 152 A1
Beckton Triangle Ret Pk
  E6. . . . . 152 B1
BECONTREE 153 E8
Becontree Ave RM8 . . . 134 D2
Becontree Day Hospl
  RM8 . . . . 134 E2
Becontree Prim Sch
  RM8 . . . . 134 B1
Becontree Sta RM9 . . . . 153 D6
Bedale Rd RM3 . . . . . . 115 A5
Beddington Rd IG3 . . . . 133 F4
Bede Rd RM6 . . . . 134 C5
Bedford Cl SS6. . . . . . . 123 D1
Bedford Gdns RM12 . . . 136 C2
Bedford Ho 1 RM3 . . . . 115 A4
Bedford Pl SS8 . . . . . . 163 F4
Bedford Rd
  Basildon SS15 . . . . . . 141 B6
  Chingford E17 . . . . . . 109 A1
  Grays RM17. . . . . 173 B1
  Ilford IG1 . . . . 133 B1
  Wallend E6. . . . . 152 A4
  Woodford E18 . . . . . . 110 A1
Bedfords Pk Nature
  Trails★ RM4. . . . . . . 113 F5
Bedloes Ave SS11 . . . . 122 E7
Bedloes Cnr SS11 . . . . 122 F7
Bedwell Ct 4 RM6 . . . . 134 D4
Bedwell Rd DA17 . . . . . 169 A1
Beecham Ct SS15 . . . . 141 C8
Beech Ave
  Brentwood CM13 . . . . . 116 C4
  Rayleigh SS6 . . . . 123 D3
  Upminster RM14 . . . . . 156 B8
  Woodford IG9 . . . . 110 B8
Beech Cl
  Burnham-on-C CM0 . . . 106 B6
  Hornchurch RM12 . . . . 136 B1
  Loughton IG10. . . . . . . 89 B6
Beechcombe SS17 . . . . 161 B4
Beechcroft Ave SS17. . . 175 A2

Beechcroft Rd
  Canvey Island SS8. . . . 163 E3
  Woodford E18 . . . . . . 110 B1
Beech Ct
  Basildon SS14 . . . . . . 142 E5
  6 Buckhurst Hill IG9 . . . 110 D8
  Dartford DA1. . . . . . . 176 A1
  Ilford E12 . . . . 133 A1
Beech Dr CM21 . . . . . . 11 C8
Beeches EN9 . . . . 66 C4
Beeches Cl CM1 . . . . . . 31 E2
Beeches Rd
  Chelmsford CM1 . . . . . 31 E2
  Heybridge CM9 . . . . . . 36 F5
  Rawreth SS11. . . . . . . 101 A2
Beeches The
  Brentwood CM14 . . . . . 116 B7
  Tilbury RM18. . . . . . . 179 B5
Beech Farm Cotts
  IG8. . . . . 109 D3
Beechfield
  Hoddesdon EN11 . . . . . 8 A3
  Sawbridgeworth CM21 . . . 1 F2
Beechfield Gdns RM7 . . . 135 C4
Beechfield Wlk EN9 . . . . 65 D4
Beech Gdns RM10 . . . . 154 C5
Beech Gr
  Aveley RM15 . . . . 171 C4
  Redbridge IG6 . . . . . . 111 E4
Beech Hall Cres E4 . . . . 109 D3
Beech Hall Rd E4 . . . . . 109 D3
Beech Hill Gdns EN9 . . . 66 B2
Beech Ho
  5 Brentwood CM13 . . . 95 C3
  Chingford E4 . . . . 109 A6
Beech La IG9 . . . . 110 B8
Beech Lo SS3. . . . . 168 F7
Beechmont Gdns SS2 . . 147 E4
Beech Pl CM16 . . . . 67 F8
Beech Rd
  Basildon SS14 . . . . . . 142 E5
  Hadleigh SS7 . . . . 145 E2
  Hullbridge SS5. . . . . . 101 E2
  Willingale CM5 . . . . . . 28 D4
Beech Spinney CM14 . . . 116 C5
Beech St RM7 . . . . 135 C7
Beech Terr IG10 . . . . . . 88 E5
Beech Tree Glade E4 . . . 87 F1
Beechwood Dr IG8 . . . . 109 F5
Beechwood Gdns
  Ilford IG5 . . . . 133 A7
  Rainham RM13 . . . . . . 170 B8
  Redbridge IG5 . . . . . . 132 F5
Beechwood Pk E18 . . . . 132 A8
Beecroft Cres SS8 . . . . 164 A6
Beedell Ave
  Southend-on-S SS0 . . . 147 C4
  Wickford SS11. . . . . . 122 A6
Beehive Chase CM15. . . 72 D4
Beehive Ct
  Hatfield Heath CM22. . . . 3 A3
  Redbridge IG1 . . . . . . 132 F5
  Romford RM3 . . . . 114 F3
Beehive La
  Basildon SS14 . . . . . . 142 B6
  Chelmsford CM2 . . . . . 54 C5
  Ilford IG1 . . . . 133 A5
  Redbridge IG1 . . . . . . 132 F6
Beehive Lane Prim Sch
  CM2 . . . . 54 D5
Beehive Prep Sch
  IG4 . . . . 132 F6
Beeleigh Ave SS16 . . . . 141 C3
Beeleigh Chase CM9 . . . 36 D4
Beeleigh Cl SS2 . . . . . . 147 E3
Beeleigh Cross SS14 . . . 142 E7
Beeleigh E SS14 . . . . . 142 E8
Beeleigh Link CM2 . . . . 32 F3
Beeleigh Rd CM9 . . . . . 36 F3
Beeleigh W SS14 . . . . . 142 E7
Beeston Ct 4 DA2 . . . . 176 B1
Beeston Cts SS15 . . . . 141 C5
Beggarhill CM4 . . . . . . 73 C6
BEGGAR HILL 73 E7
Begonia Cl CM1 . . . . . . 32 F6
Beke Hall Chase N
  SS6 . . . . 122 C4
Beke Hall Chase S
  SS6 . . . . 122 C4
Bekeswell La CM2 . . . . 53 F2
Bekeswell Pl CM2. . . . . 54 C2
Belchamps Rd SS11 . . . 121 F8
Belchamps Way SS5 . . . 124 E5
Belcher Rd 6 EN11 . . . . 21 D7
Belchers La EN9 . . . . . . 44 C7
Belcon Ind Est EN11 . . . 21 C6
Beldowes SS16 . . . . . . 142 E5
Belfairs Cl SS9 . . . . . . 146 D2
Belfairs Ct SS9 . . . . . . 146 B6
Belfairs Dr
  Dagenham RM6. . . . . . 134 C4
  Southend-on-S SS9 . . . 146 D2
Belfairs High Sch
  SS9 . . . . 146 C2
Belfairs Park Cl SS9 . . . 146 C5
Belfairs Park Dr SS9 . . . 146 B5
Belfry Rd E12 . . . . 132 D2
Belgrave Ave RM2 . . . . 114 D1
Belgrave Cl
  Chelmsford CM2 . . . . . 54 D7
  Rayleigh SS6 . . . . 123 B4
  Southend-on-S SS9 . . . 146 B7
Belgrave Hts E11 . . . . . 132 A3
Belgrave Market IG1. . . 133 A2
Belgrave Rd
  Billericay CM12 . . . . . . 97 A4
  Ilford IG1 . . . . 133 A2
  Redbridge IG1 . . . . . . 132 F3

Belgrave Rd continued
Southend-on-S SS9 . . . . **146** B7
Wanstead E11 . . . . **132** A3
Belgrave Terr IG8 . . . . **110** A7
Belgravia Mans SS1 . . . **167** D6
Belhus Woods Ctry Pk★
RM15 . . . . **156** D2
Bellamy Rd E4 . . . . **109** B4
Bell Ave RM3 . . . . **114** B2
Bell Cl
Basildon SS15 . . . . **141** D7
Greenhithe DA9 . . . . . . **176** F2
Bell Cnr RM14 . . . . **137** C2
Bell Comm CM16 . . . . . . **67** E7
BELL COMMON **67** C7
Bell Ct CM3. . . . . **78** A1
Belle Staines Pleasaunce
E4. . . . . **109** A8
Belle Vue CM2. . . . . **32** A1
Bellevue Ave SS1 . . . . . **167** E4
Bellevue Mews SS2 . . . . **148** C1
Bellevue Pl SS1 . . . . . . **167** C8
Bellevue Rd
Billericay CM12 . . . . **96** F2
Hornchurch RM11 . . . . . **136** F3
Southend-on-S SS2 . . . . **148** C1
Belle Vue Rd
Chingford E17 . . . . **109** D1
Romford RM5 . . . . **113** C4
Bell Farm Ave RM10 . . . **135** C1
Bell Farm Gn CM12 . . . . **119** B8
Bellfield SS16 . . . . **142** E3
Bellfield Gdns **24** C7
Bellflower Path RM3 . . . **114** C3
Bell Hill CM3 . . . . **56** C7
Bell Hill Cl CM12 . . . . . **119** B8
Bell Ho
1 Dagenham RM10 . . . **154** B6
2 Grays RM17 . . . . . . **177** E3
Great Wakering SS3 . . . . **150** A3
Bellhouse Cres SS9 . . . **146** D5
Bellhouse La
Pilgrims Hatch CM14 . . . . **93** E4
Southend-on-S SS9 . . . . **146** D5
Bellhouse Rd SS9 . . . . . **146** D6
Bell House Rd RM7 . . . . **135** C3
Bellhouse Villas CM1. . . . **6** D3
Bellingham Ct **7**
IG11 . . . . **153** B2
Bellingham La SS6 . . . . **123** D2
Bell La EN11 . . . . **21** A6
Bellmaine Ave SS17 . . . **160** F4
Bellman Ho **3** IG7 . . . . **112** A5
Bellmead CM1 . . . . **32** B2
Bell Mead
Ingatestone CM4. . . . . . **74** B3
Sawbridgeworth CM21 . . . . **1** E2
Bell-Reeves Cl SS17 . . . **160** C2
Bells Chase CM2 . . . . . . **54** E6
Bells Corner Par
SS17 . . . . **142** B1
Bells Hill Rd SS16 . . . . . **142** B2
Bell St
Great Baddow CM2 . . . . . **54** F6
Sawbridgeworth CM21 . . . . **1** E2
Bells Wlk CM21 . . . . **1** E2
Bell Wlk SS2 . . . . **147** D4
Belmonde Dr CM1 . . . . . **32** E7
Belmont Ave
Upminster RM14 . . . . . . **136** F2
Wickford SS12 . . . . **121** B7
Belmont Cl
Chelmsford CM1 . . . . **32** E7
Chingford E4 . . . . **109** D5
Wickford SS12 . . . . **121** B7
Woodford IG8 . . . . **110** B6
Belmont Rd
Grays RM17 . . . . **177** F8
Hornchurch RM12 . . . . . **136** D1
Ilford IG1 . . . . **133** C1
Belsteads Farm La
CM3 . . . . **19** E2
Belstedes SS15 . . . . . . **141** D6
Beltinge Rd RM3 . . . . . **136** F8
Belton Bridge SS9 . . . . **165** D8
Belton Gdns SS9 . . . . . **165** C8
Belton Way E SS9 . . . . . **165** C8
Belton Way W SS9 . . . . **165** B8
Beltwood Rd DA17 . . . . **169** C2
Belvawney CM1 . . . . **31** E6
BELVEDERE **169** B2
Belvedere Ave
Hockley SS5 . . . . **124** C6
Redbridge IG5 . . . . **111** B1
Belvedere Cl CM3 . . . . . . **56** F7
Belvedere Ct
Burnham-on-C CM0 . . . . **106** C3
Chelmsford CM2 . . . . . . **53** F8
Hoddesdon EN11 . . . . . . **21** A5
Maldon CM9. . . . . **58** F8
Belvedere Ind Est
DA17 . . . . **169** C5
Belvedere Inf Sch
DA17 . . . . **169** B3
Belvedere Jun Sch
DA17 . . . . **169** B3
Belvedere Link Bsns Pk
DA8. . . . . **169** C3
Belvedere Pl CM9. . . . . . **58** F8
Belvedere Rd
Brentwood CM14 . . . . . **115** F7
Burnham-on-C CM0 . . . . **106** C3
Danbury CM3. . . . . **56** F7
Belvedere Sta DA17 . . . **169** B3
Belvedere The CM0 . . . . **106** C4
Belvoir The CM4 . . . . . . **74** A3
Benbow Dr CM3 . . . . . . **101** E6
Benderloch SS8 . . . . . . **163** E4

Bendigo Wharf DA9 . . . . **177** B3
Benedict Ct RM6. . . . . . **134** F5
Benedict Dr CM1 . . . . . . **31** E2
Benets Rd RM11 . . . . . . **137** A3
Benfleet For Canvey
Island Sta SS7. . . . . . **163** D8
Benfleet Park Rd SS7 . . **144** B2
Benfleet Rd SS7 . . . . . . **145** B2
Bengal Rd IG1. . . . . **133** B1
Bengeo Gdns RM6 . . . . **134** C5
Benham Wlk SS13 . . . . **143** C8
Benhurst Ave RM11 . . . **136** B1
Benhurst Prim Sch
RM12 . . . . **136** B1
Benjamin Cl RM11 . . . . **136** A5
Benjamin Ct RM13 . . . . **154** E2
Bennett Rd RM6 . . . . . . **134** E6
Bennett's Ave CM3. . . . . **77** F3
Bennett's Castle La
RM8 . . . . **134** D1
Bennington Rd IG8 . . . . **109** E3
Bennions Cl RM12 . . . . **155** D6
Bennison Dr RM3 . . . . . **114** E1
Benrek Cl IG6 . . . . **111** C2
Benskins La RM4 . . . . . . **92** D1
Benson Cl **4** EN3 . . . . . . **65** A1
Benson Rd RM17 . . . . . **178** C8
Bensted Ct **9** EN11 . . . . **21** A6
Bentalls SS14. . . . . **120** A1
Bentalls Bsns Pk
SS14 . . . . **120** A1
Bentalls Cl SS2 . . . . . . **148** A4
Bentalls Complex The
CM9 . . . . **37** B5
Bentham Ho **4** CM20 . . . **10** C1
Ben Tillet Cl IG11 . . . . . **153** A5
BENTLEY **93** D6
Bentley Dr
Harlow CM17. . . . . **24** C7
Ilford IG2 . . . . **133** C3
Bentleys CM22. . . . . **3** B2
Bentley St Paul's CE Prim
Sch CM15 . . . . **93** D6
Bentley St DA12 . . . . . **179** C1
Bentleys The SS2 . . . . . **147** A7
Bentley Street Ind Est **4**
DA12. . . . . **179** C1
Bentley Villas CM22 . . . . **3** B2
Bentley Way IG8. . . . . . **110** A7
Benton Gdns SS17 . . . . **160** F5
Benton Rd IG1. . . . . **133** D3
Bentonwood SS7 . . . . . **145** C5
Bentry Cl RM8 . . . . **134** E2
Bentry Rd RM8 . . . . **134** F2
Benvenue Ave SS9 . . . . **146** F6
Benyon Ct RM15 . . . . . **157** C3
Benyon Path RM15 . . . . **157** C3
Benyon Prim Sch
RM15 . . . . **157** C3
Berberis Cl SS16 . . . . . **140** F4
Berberis Ct **2** IG11 . . . . **152** B6
Berdan Ct EN3. . . . . **65** A2
Berdens SS16. . . . . **142** D5
Bere Cl DA9 . . . . **177** C2
Berecroft CM18 . . . . **23** D3
Beredens La CM13 . . . . **115** F1
Berengers Pl RM9 . . . . **153** B6
Berens Cl SS11 . . . . **99** F1
Beresford Cl SS7 . . . . . **145** D4
Beresford Ct
Billericay CM12 . . . . **96** F5
Hadleigh SS7 . . . . **145** D4
Beresford Dr IG8 . . . . . **110** C6
Beresford Gdns
Dagenham RM6 . . . . . . **134** E6
Hadleigh SS7 . . . . **145** D4
Beresford Mans **19**
SS1 . . . . **167** C7
Beresford Rd
Chingford, Chingford Green
E4 . . . . **87** E1
Chingford, Highams Park
E17. . . . . **109** B2
Gravesend DA11 . . . . . . **178** E1
Southend-on-S SS1 . . . . **167** C7
Berg Ave SS8 . . . . **164** D5
Bergen Ct CM9 . . . . **58** D8
Bergholt Ave IG4 . . . . . **132** E6
Berica Ct IG6. . . . . **133** C8
Berkeley Ave
Redbridge IG5 . . . . **111** B1
Romford RM5 . . . . **113** C3
Berkeley Ct RM11 . . . . . **137** B2
Berkeley Ct SS4 . . . . . . **147** F7
Berkeley Dr
Billericay CM12 . . . . **97** A5
Hornchurch RM11 . . . . . **137** A2
Berkeley Gdns SS9 . . . . **146** A1
Berkeley La SS8 . . . . . . **164** A3
Berkeley Terr RM18 . . . **179** A7
Berkely Dr CM2 . . . . **32** F2
Berkhampstead Rd
DA17. . . . . **169** A1
Berkley Cres **5** DA12 . . **179** C1
Berkley Ct SS0. . . . . . . **147** E2
Berkley Hill SS17 . . . . . **160** E4
Berkley Rd DA12. . . . . . **179** B1
Berkshire Cl SS9. . . . . . **146** C5
Berkshire Way RM11 . . **137** A7
Berman's Cl CM13 . . . . **117** B8
Bermuda Rd RM18 . . . . **179** A5
Bernard Gr EN9. . . . . . . **65** B6
Bernard Rd RM7 . . . . . . **135** C4
Bernards Cl IG6 . . . . . . **111** D3
Bernard St **14** DA12 . . . **179** B1
BERNERS RODING **28** E8
Berners St SS14. . . . . . **142** D8

Bernice Cl RM13 . . . . . **155** C1
Bernwell Rd E4. . . . . . . **109** E7
Berrybank Cl **4** E4 . . . . **109** C8
Berry Cl
Basildon SS16 . . . . **141** B5
Dagenham RM10 . . . . . **154** A7
Hornchurch RM12 . . . . . **155** D7
Wickford SS12 . . . . **121** B6
Berry La SS16 . . . . **141** B4
Berryman CI RM8 . . . . . **134** C1
Berrymore Wlk SS6 . . . **123** F2
Berrys Arc SS6 . . . . **123** D2
Berry Vale CM3 . . . . . . **101** E6
Bersham RM17 . . . . **172** F2
Berther Rd RM11 . . . . . **136** E4
Berwick Ave CM1 . . . . . **32** B7
Berwick Cl **10** DA2 . . . . **176** B1
Berwick La CM5 . . . . . . **69** E6
Berwick Pond Cl
RM13 . . . . **155** D3
Berwick Pond Rd
RM13 . . . . **155** F5
Berwick Rd RM13 . . . . . **155** D3
Berwood Rd SS17 . . . . . **160** F3
Betchworth Rd IG3 . . . . **133** E1
Bethany Cl RM12. . . . . . **136** C2
Bethany Ho RM6 . . . . . **134** D8
Bethell Ave IG1. . . . . . . **133** A4
Betjeman Cl SS6 . . . . . . **123** F3
Betjeman Mews SS2 . . . **148** A2
Betjeman Way CM5 . . . . **48** F5
Betony Cres CM12 . . . . . **96** F5
Betony Rd RM3 . . . . **114** D4
Betoyne Ave E4. . . . . . . **109** E6
Betoyne Cl CM11. . . . . . . **97** D2
Betterton Rd RM13. . . . **154** E3
Betts La EN9. . . . . **22** C2
Bett's La SS5 . . . . **124** D6
Betula Wlk RM13 . . . . . **155** D2
Beulah Rd
Epping CM16 . . . . **46** A2
Hornchurch RM12 . . . . . **136** C1
Bevan Ave IG11. . . . . . . **153** A5
Bevan Ho
Barking IG11 . . . . **153** B5
Grays RM16. . . . . **173** D4
Bevans Cl DA9. . . . . **177** C1
Bevan Way RM12 . . . . . **136** F1
Beveland Rd SS8 . . . . . **165** A3
Beverley Ave SS8 . . . . . **164** A3
Beverley Cl
Hornchurch RM11 . . . . . **136** F4
Orsett RM16 . . . . **174** D7
Beverley Cres IG8 . . . . **110** B3
Beverley Gdns
Hornchurch RM11 . . . . . **136** F4
Southend-on-S SS9 . . . . **147** E4
Beverley Rd
Chingford E4 . . . . **109** C4
Dagenham RM9 . . . . . . **153** E8
Beverley Rise CM11 . . . . **97** C1
Bevil Ct EN11 . . . . **8** A1
Bevile Ho RM17 . . . . . . **178** B7
Bevin Ho RM15 . . . . . . **171** C4
Bevin Wlk SS17 . . . . . . **160** D2
Bevis Cl DA2. . . . . **176** C1
Bewley Ct SS2 . . . . **148** E2
Bexhill Dr RM17 . . . . . . **177** F8
Bibby Cl SS17 . . . . **161** A2
Bickenhall SS3 . . . . **168** D8
Bickerton Point CM3. . . **101** F6
BICKNACRE **56** F2
Bicknacre Rd
Danbury CM3. . . . . **56** F4
East Hanningfield CM3 . . **78** C8
Biddenden Ct **9**
SS13 . . . . **143** C6
Bideford Cl
Romford RM3 . . . . **114** C2
Southend-on-S SS0 . . . . **147** A5
BIGGIN **179** C8
Biggin La RM16. . . . . . . **179** B8
Bight The CM3 . . . . **101** F5
BILLERICAY **97** B1
Billericay Com Hospl
CM12 . . . . **96** F1
Billericay Rd
Ingrave CM13 . . . . **117** F3
Little Burstead CM12,
CM13 . . . . **118** B3
Billericay Sch The
CM12 . . . . **119** B8
Billericay Sta CM12 . . . . **97** A3
Billers Chase CM1 . . . . . **33** A7
Billet La
Hornchurch RM11 . . . . . **136** D4
Stanford-le-H SS17 . . . . **160** E1
Billet Rd
Chingford E17 . . . . **109** A2
Ilford RM6. . . . . **134** C8
Billings Pl RM9 . . . . **153** C5
Bilton Rd
Chelmsford CM1 . . . . . . **31** F1
Hadleigh SS7 . . . . **145** E4
Bingham St RM15. . . . . **172** B7
Bingley Rd EN11 . . . . . . **21** C6
Binley Rd RM3 . . . . **32** F2
Bircham Rd SS2 . . . . . . **148** A2

Birch Cl
Buckhurst Hill IG9 . . . . . **110** D7
Canewdon SS4. . . . . . . **104** E1
Canvey Island SS8. . . . . **163** F3
Rayleigh SS6 . . . . **123** C3
Romford RM7 . . . . **135** B8
South Benfleet SS7 . . . . **144** B7
South Ockendon RM15 . . **157** D1
Birch Cres
Hornchurch RM11 . . . . . **136** E7
South Ockendon RM15 . . **157** D2
Birch Ct
Chingford E4 . . . . **109** B4
Dagenham RM6 . . . . . . **134** C5
Birchdale SS5 . . . . **101** D3
Birchdale Gdns RM6 . . . **134** D4
Birche Cl SS9 . . . . **146** E4
Birches The
Brentwood CM13. . . . . . **116** E7
North Weald Bassett
CM16 . . . . **47** B5
South Benfleet SS7 . . . . **144** C8
Waltham Abbey EN9 . . . . **65** F5
Birches Wlk CM2 . . . . . . **54** A2
Birchfield RM16 . . . . . . **172** D5
Birch Gdns
Dagenham RM10 . . . . . **135** C1
Tillingham CM0 . . . . **63** E4
Birch Gn SS12 . . . . **121** D7
Birch La CM4 . . . . **75** F3
Birchmores SS15 . . . . . **141** A7
Birch Pl DA9. . . . . **176** E1
Birch Rd
Romford RM7 . . . . **135** B8
Tillingham CM0 . . . . **63** E4
Birch View CM16. . . . . . **46** B2
Birchwood
South Benfleet SS7 . . . . **144** B7
Waltham Abbey EN9 . . . . **65** E5
Birchwood Cl CM3. . . . . **116** C4
Birchwood Dr SS9 . . . . . **147** A2
Birchwood Ind Est
EN9. . . . . **22** C2
Birchwood Rd
Cock Clarks CM3 . . . . . . **57** F2
Corringham SS17. . . . . . **161** B4
Birdbrook Cl
Brentwood CM13. . . . . . **95** B3
Dagenham RM10 . . . . . **154** C5
Bird La
Great Warley CM13 . . . . **138** D8
Little Warley CM13 . . . . **116** C1
Upminster RM14 . . . . . . **137** D6
Birds Cl CM11 . . . . **98** C5
Birds Farm Ave RM5 . . . **113** B2
Birds Gn CM5. . . . . **28** A5
BIRDS GREEN **28** B6
Birk Beck CM1 . . . . **32** C5
Birkbeck Gdns IG8. . . . . **110** A8
Birkbeck Rd
Brentwood CM13. . . . . . **95** D3
Ilford IG2 . . . . **133** D6
Romford RM7 . . . . **135** D3
Birkdale Ave RM3 . . . . . **115** A3
Birnam Wood Pru
RM11 . . . . **136** E3
Birs Cl SS11 . . . . **99** D1
Biscay SS17 . . . . **147** A2
Bishop Hall La CM1 . . . . **32** B4
Bishop Rd CM1 . . . . **32** B3
Bishops Ave RM6 . . . . . **134** C5
Bishops' CE & RC Prim
Sch CM1 . . . . **32** F6
Bishops Cl SS13 . . . . . . **121** A2
Bishops Court Gdns
CM2 . . . . **32** E4
Bishops Ct
Greenhithe DA9 . . . . . . **176** F2
Romford RM7 . . . . **135** B7
Bishop's Ct CM3 . . . . . . **164** D3
Bishopsfield CM18 . . . . . **23** E5
Bishops Gate **9**
CM14 . . . . **116** C8
Bishop's Hall Rd CM15 . . **94** B3
Bishops Rd
Stanford-le-H SS17 . . . . **160** F3
Wickford SS12 . . . . **121** D3
Bishopsteignton SS3 . . **149** D1
Bishops Wlk CM15 . . . . **116** F8
Bittern Ct E4 . . . . **87** D2
Blackacre Rd CM16 . . . . **67** E2
Black Adder Cotts EN9 . . **43** D8
Blackberry Gr CM0. . . . . **42** B3
Blackborne Rd RM10. . . **154** B6
Blackbush Ave RM6 . . . **134** D6
Blackbush Spring
CM20 . . . . **11** A1
BLACKCAT **27** A8
Black Chapel La CM6. . . . **7** E8
Blackdown SS0. . . . . . . **147** E1
Blackgate Rd SS3 . . . . . **168** G7
Blackheath Chase
SS16 . . . . **160** D8
Blackhorse La CM16 . . . . **47** D6
Black Lion Ct CM17 . . . . **11** C4
Blacklock CM2. . . . . **33** A3
BLACKMORE **72** C8
Blackmore Ave SS8 . . . . **164** B2
Blackmore Ct EN9 . . . . . **66** A6
Blackmore Mead CM4 . . **72** F8
Blackmore Prim Sch
CM4 . . . . **50** E1
Blackmore Rd
Blackmore CM1. . . . . . . **51** D3
Buckhurst Hill IG9 . . . . . **88** E2
Grays RM17. . . . . **173** C5

Bel–Blu **187**

Blackmore Rd continued
Hook End CM15 . . . . **72** C5
Ingatestone CM4 . . . . . . **73** D6
Kelvedon Hatch CM15 . . . **71** F2
Blackmores SS15 . . . . . **140** F6
Blackmore Wlk SS6 . . . **124** A2
Blackshots La RM16. . . . **173** C5
Blacksmith Cl
Billericay CM12 . . . . **97** B5
Chelmsford CM1 . . . . . . **32** E8
Dagenham RM6 . . . . . . **134** C5
Blacksmiths Alley CM4 . . **72** E8
Black Smiths Cl SG12 . . . . **8** A7
Blacksmiths Cotts
CM17. . . . . **24** F4
Blacksmith's La RM13 . . **154** F4
Blacksmiths Cotts
CM17. . . . . **24** F4
Blacksmiths Way CM21 . . .**1** B1
Blackthorn Cl CM1 . . . . . **31** A1
Blackthorn Ct SS16 . . . . **141** A4
Blackthorn Dr E4 . . . . . **109** D6
Blackthorne Rd SS8. . . . **164** C3
Blackthorn Rd
Barking IG1 . . . . **152** D7
Grays RM16. . . . . **173** B5
Hockley SS5. . . . . **124** F8
Blackthorn Way
CM14 . . . . **116** D5
Blackwater SS7. . . . . . . **144** F4
Black Water CM14 . . . . . **94** B1
Blackwater Ct
Burnham-on-C CM0 . . . . **106** C5
Chelmsford CM1 . . . . . . **32** C6
Heybridge Basin CM9 . . . **37** E3
Rainham RM13 . . . . **169** E8
Southend-on-S SS3 . . . . **149** E1
Blackwater Mews CM0 . . **61** C2
Blackwood Chine
CM3 . . . . **101** E6
Blake Ave IG11 . . . . **152** F4
Blakeborough Dr
RM3 . . . . **114** E1
Blake Cl RM13 . . . . **154** F4
Blake Ct CM3. . . . . **101** E6
Blake Hall Cres E11. . . . **132** A3
Blake Hall Dr SS11 . . . . **122** A6
Blake Hall Gdns★ CM5 . . **48** E7
Blake Hall Rd
Chipping Ongar CM5. . . . **48** A5
Wanstead E11 . . . . **132** A4
Blakes Ct CM21 . . . . **1** E2
Blakesley Ho **4** E12 . . . **133** A1
Blake Way E18 . . . . **179** C3
Blanchard Gr EN3. . . . . . **65** B1
Blanchard Mews RM3 . . **114** F3
Blandford Cl RM7 . . . . . **135** B7
Blandford Cres E4 . . . . . **87** C2
Blaney Cres E6 . . . . **152** B2
Blatches Chase
Rayleigh SS2 . . . . **146** F7
Southend-on-S SS2 . . . . **147** A8
Blatchford Ho **8**
RM10 . . . . **135** A1
Blenheim Ave IG2 . . . . . **133** A5
Blenheim Chase SS9 . . . **146** E3
Blenheim Cl
Bicknacre CM3. . . . . **56** F2
Hockley SS5. . . . . **124** E8
Romford RM7 . . . . **135** C7
Sawbridgeworth CM21 . . . **11** C8
Upminster RM14 . . . . . . **137** E3
Blenheim Cres SS9 . . . . **146** E3
Blenheim Ct
Hornchurch RM12 . . . . . **155** C7
4 Wickford SS11 . . . . **122** A5
Woodford IG8 . . . . **110** B3
Woodford IG8 . . . . **110** C2
Blenheim Gdns
Aveley RM15 . . . . **171** B5
Mayland CM3 . . . . **61** A1
Blenheim Mews SS9 . . . **146** E3
Blenheim Park Cl
SS9 . . . . **146** F4
Blenheim Prim Sch
SS9 . . . . **146** F4
Blenheim Rd CM15. . . . . **94** A3
Blenheim Way SS16 . . . . **47** A4
Blessing Way IG11. . . . . **153** C3
Bletchington Ct **1**
DA17. . . . . **169** A2
Blewetts Cotts RM13 . . . **154** F2
Bligh Rd DA11 . . . . **179** A1
Blind La
Goldhanger CM9 . . . . . . **38** C7
Howe Green CM2 . . . . . . **55** F4
Little Burstead CM12. . . . **118** B5
Mundon CM9. . . . . **59** C2
West Hanningfield CM2. . . **76** F5
Blithbury Rd RM9 . . . . . **153** B6
Blockhouse Rd RM17. . . **178** C8
Blomville Rd RM8 . . . . . **134** E1
Bloomfield Cres IG2 . . . **133** B5
Bloomsbury Ho IG8 . . . . **110** E4
Bloomsbury Mews
IG8. . . . . **110** E4
Blossom Cl RM9 . . . . . . **153** F4
Blountswood Rd
Hockley SS5. . . . . **124** A8
Hullbridge SS5 . . . . **123** F6
Blower Cl SS6 . . . . **123** F3
Blows Cotts RM15. . . . . **171** D5
Blue Anchor La RM18 . . . **174** E1
Bluebell Cl RM7 . . . . . . **135** C2
Bluebell Gn **5** CM1 . . . . **32** E7
Bluebell Way IG1 . . . . . **152** B6
Bluebell Wood CM12 . . . . **96** E4

Blueberry Cl IG8 . . . . 110 A4
Bluebird La RM10 . . . . . . 154 A5
Bluegate Pk CM14 . . . . . . 116 B7
Blue House Farm Chase
  CM3 . . . . 103 B7
Bluehouse Rd E4 . . . . 109 C7
Bluemans CM16 . . . . 47 D7
Bluemans End CM16 . . . . . 47 D7
Blue Mill La RM9 . . . . 35 E4
Blunden Cl RM8 . . . . 134 C3
Blunts Wall Rd CM12 . . . . 96 E1
Blyth Ave SS3 . . . . 168 C7
Blythe Rd
  Hoddesdon EN11 . . . . 21 D5
  Stanford-le-H SS17 . . . . . 160 E4
Blythe Way
  Maldon CM9 . . . . 59 A8
  South Benfleet SS7 . . . . . 144 C7
Blyth Ho DA8 . . . . 169 E1
Blythswood Rd IG3 . . . . . 134 A4
Blyth Wlk RM12 . . . . 137 E5
Blyton Cl SS12 . . . . 121 D5
Boar Cl IG7 . . . . 112 A5
Boarded Row SS4 . . . . . . 128 A5
Boardman Ave E4 . . . . 87 B4
Bobbing Cl RM12 . . . . . . 125 F2
BOBBINGWORTH 48 D8
Bobbingworth Mill
  CM5 . . . . 48 A7
Bob Dunn Way DA1 . . . . . 176 A4
Bockingham Gn SS13 . . . 143 A8
Bodell Cl RM16 . . . . 173 B3
Bodle Ave DA10 . . . . 177 C1
Bodiam Cl SS13 . . . . 143 B6
Bodley Cl CM16 . . . . 45 F1
Bodmin Rd CM1 . . . . 32 D5
Bohemia Chase SS9 . . . . 146 D5
Boiler Ho The SS4 . . . . . . 125 E2
Boleyn Cl
  Billericay CM12 . . . . 97 A5
  Grays RM16 . . . . 172 F3
  Loughton IG8 . . . . 88 E3
  Southend-on-S SS9 . . . . 146 C7
Boleyn Ct IG9 . . . . 88 B1
Boleyn Gdns
  Brentwood CM13 . . . . . . 117 A7
  Dagenham RM10 . . . . . . 154 C5
Boleyn Ho **1** SS4 . . . . . . 125 F2
Boleyn Way
  Boreham CM3 . . . . 20 F1
  Redbridge IG6 . . . . 111 C4
Bolney Dr SS9 . . . . 146 C7
Boltons The IG8 . . . . 110 A6
Bommel Ave SS8 . . . . . . 165 A3
Bonchurch Ave SS9 . . . . 146 D2
Bonchurch Ct **20**
  RM19 . . . . 171 B1
Bonds Cotts CM5 . . . . 15 A1
Bond St
  Chelmsford CM2 . . . . 32 C2
  Grays RM17 . . . . 178 C8
Bonham Ho RM16 . . . . . . 174 A8
Bonham Gdns RM8 . . . . . 134 D2
Bonham Rd RM8 . . . . 134 D1
Bonington Chase CM1 . . . 32 E6
Bonington Rd RM12 . . . . 155 D7
Bonks Hill CM21 . . . . 1 D1
Bonner Wlk RM16 . . . . . . 172 F3
Bonnett Mews RM11 . . . . 136 E3
Bonningtons CM13 . . . . . 117 B7
Bonnygate SS14 . . . . 142 D7
Bonnygate Prim Sch
  RM15 . . . . 172 B8
Boomes Ind Est RM13 . . . 154 F1
Boons Cl CM3 . . . . 33 E8
Bootham Cl CM12 . . . . . . 96 F1
Bootham Rd CM12 . . . . . . 96 F1
Boothby Ct E4 . . . . 109 C7
Booth Pl CM0 . . . . 106 C5
Booth's Ct CM13 . . . . 95 B3
Borda Cl CM1 . . . . 32 A5
Border Edge Ho **6**
  CM14 . . . . 116 C6
Border's La IG10 . . . . 89 B5
BOREHAM 33 E8
Boreham Ct SS11 . . . . . . 122 B5
Boreham Ct 6 D2
Boreham Ind Est CM3 . . . 20 F2
Boreham Mews **1** EN11 . . 8 A1
Boreham Prim Sch
  CM3 . . . . 33 F8
Borland Cl DA9 . . . . 177 A2
Borley Ct RM16 . . . . 174 D7
Borman Cl SS9 . . . . 147 A6
Borrett Ave SS8 . . . . 164 A4
Borrowdale Cl
  Redbridge IG4 . . . . 132 E7
  Thundersley SS7 . . . . . . 144 F6
Borrowdale Rd
  Thundersley SS7 . . . . . . 144 F6
  Thundersley SS7 . . . . . . 144 F7
Borwick La
  Crays Hill CM11 . . . . 120 F4
  Wickford CM11, SS12 . . . 121 A4
Bosanquet Rd EN11 . . . . . 21 C8
Boscombe Ave
  Grays RM17 . . . . 173 D2
  Hornchurch RM11 . . . . . 136 D4
  Wickford SS12 . . . . 120 F8
Boscombe Mews SS2 . . . 167 B8
Boscombe Rd SS2 . . . . . 148 B3
Bosgrove E4 . . . . 109 C8
Bostocke Cl SS15 . . . . . . 141 D5
Boston Ave
  Rayleigh SS6 . . . . 123 B4

Boston Ave continued
  Southend-on-S SS2 . . . . 147 F1
Boston Lofts **2** SS2 . . . . . 147 F1
Boswell Ave SS4 . . . . 125 D5
Boswells Dr CM2 . . . . 32 C2
Boswells Sch The CM1 . . . 32 D6
Bosworth Cl SS5 . . . . 124 F4
Bosworth Cres RM3 . . . . . 114 C4
Bosworth Ho DA8 . . . . . . 169 E1
Bosworth Rd
  Dagenham RM10 . . . . . . 135 A1
  Southend-on-S SS9 . . . . 146 C7
Botany Cotts RM19 . . . . . 171 A1
Botany Terr RM19 . . . . . . 171 A1
Botany Way RM19 . . . . . . 171 B1
Botelers SS16 . . . . 141 E4
Boteley Cl E4 . . . . 109 D8
Botney Hill Rd CM12 . . . . 118 D4
Bouchers Mead CM1 . . . . 32 F7
Bouchier Wlk **2**
  RM13 . . . . 155 A6
Boudicca Mews **5**
  CM2 . . . . 32 B1
Bouldrewood Rd SS7 . . . . 144 B5
Boulevard The
  Greenhithe DA9 . . . . 177 C3
  3 Redbridge IG8 . . . . . 111 A3
  Rochford SS4 . . . . 125 F3
Boulter Gdns RM13 . . . . . 155 A7
Boulton Cotts CM9 . . . . . . 37 B5
Boulton Rd RM8 . . . . 134 F2
Boult Rd SS15 . . . . 141 C8
Boundary Cl IG3 . . . . 152 E8
Boundary Ct CM16 . . . . . . 67 D7
Boundary Dr CM13 . . . . . . 95 E2
Boundary Rd
  Barking IG11 . . . . 152 C3
  Barking IG11 . . . . 152 D4
  Romford RM1 . . . . 136 A5
  Southend-on-S SS9 . . . . 146 B8
  Upminster RM14 . . . . . . 137 B2
Boundary Way SS3 . . . . . 168 E6
Bounderby Gr CM1 . . . . . . 31 E7
Bourne Ave SS15 . . . . . . 141 A8
Bournebridge Cl **1** 95 E2
Bournebridge La RM4 . . . . 91 B2
Bourne Ct SS15 . . . . 141 A8
Bourne Ct
  Wanstead E11 . . . . 132 A6
  Woodford IG8 . . . . 110 D1
Bourne End RM11 . . . . . . 137 A4
Bourne Gdns E4 . . . . 109 B6
Bourne Ho IG9 . . . . 110 D7
Bournemouth Park Prim
  Sch SS2 . . . . 148 B2
Bournemouth Park Rd
  SS2 . . . . 148 B2
BOURNES GREEN 149 B1
Bournes Green Chase
  SS3 . . . . 149 B1
Bournes Green Inf Sch
  SS1 . . . . 168 B8
Bournes Green Jun Sch
  SS1 . . . . 168 B8
Bouvel Dr CM0 . . . . 106 B8
Bouverie Rd CM2 . . . . 54 B8
Bovey Way RM15 . . . . . . 172 B8
BOVINGER 48 A7
Bovinger Way SS1 . . . . . . 148 F1
BOW ARROW 176 B1
Bow Arrow La
  Dartford DA1 . . . . 176 A1
  Dartford DA2 . . . . 176 B1
Bowbank Cl SS3 . . . . 149 F1
Bowden Dr RM11 . . . . . . 136 E3
Bower Cl RM5 . . . . 113 D3
Bower Ct CM16 . . . . 68 A7
Bower Farm Rd RM4 . . . . 113 C4
Bower Gdns CM9 . . . . 36 F3
Bower Hill CM16 . . . . 68 A7
Bower Hill Ind Est
  CM16 . . . . 68 A7
Bower La SS14 . . . . 142 E8
Bowerman Rd RM16 . . . . 174 A2
Bower Park Sch RM1 . . . . 113 E4
Bowers Court Dr
  SS13 . . . . 143 F5
BOWERS GIFFORD 143 E6
Bowers Ho **5** IG11 . . . . . 152 B5
Bowers Rd SS7 . . . . 144 D5
Bower Vale CM16 . . . . 68 A7
Bowery Ct **4** RM10 . . . . 154 B6
Bowes Ct **17** DA2 . . . . . . 176 B1
Bowes Dr CM5 . . . . 49 A4
Bowes Ho CM5 . . . . 49 A4
Bowes Rd RM8 . . . . 153 C8
Bowfell Ct SS16 . . . . 141 A5
Bowfell Dr SS16 . . . . 141 A5
Bowhay CM13 . . . . 117 B8
Bowland Rd IG8 . . . . 110 C4
Bowlers Croft SS14 . . . . . 120 F2
Bowls The IG7 . . . . 111 F7
Bowman Ave SS9 . . . . . . 146 B6
Bowmont Ct CM13 . . . . . . 95 B3
Bown Cl RM18 . . . . 179 B5
Bowness Way RM12 . . . . 155 A7
Bowyer Ct **4** E4 . . . . 87 C1
Box Cl SS15 . . . . 119 D1
Boxford Cl SS6 . . . . 122 F3
Box La IG11 . . . . 153 C3
Boxley La CM22 . . . . 4 D8
Boxmoor Rd RM5 . . . . . . 113 C5
Boxoll Rd RM9 . . . . 134 F1
Boxted Cl IG9 . . . . 88 E1
Boyce Gn SS7 . . . . 144 D2
Boyce Hill Cl SS9 . . . . . . 146 B5
Boyce Rd
  Southend-on-S SS3 . . . . 168 H8

Boyce Rd continued
  Stanford-le-H SS17 . . . . 160 C3
Boyce View Dr SS7 . . . . . 144 C2
Boyd Ct SS12 . . . . 121 F5
Boyden Cl SS2 . . . . 148 F2
Boyle Ho **13** DA17 . . . . . 169 A3
Boyles Court Cotts
  CM14 . . . . 116 A3
Boyne Dr CM1 . . . . 32 D6
Boyne Rd RM10 . . . . 135 A1
Boyton Cl SS7 . . . . 145 A5
BOYTON CROSS 30 B7
Boyton Hall La CM1 . . . . . 30 C8
Boytons SS15 . . . . 141 E6
Brabant Rd CM3 . . . . 103 A3
Brabner Gdns CM11 . . . . . 98 C4
Bracelet Cl SS17 . . . . 160 F5
Brace Wlk CM3 . . . . 101 C5
Bracken Cl IG10 . . . . 89 B8
Bracken Ct **1** IG6 . . . . . 111 F4
Brackendale Ave
  SS13 . . . . 143 C4
Brackendale Cl SS5 . . . . . 124 E7
Brackendale Ct SS13 . . . . 143 C4
Brackendale Gdns
  RM14 . . . . 156 C8
Bracken Dell SS6 . . . . . . 123 E2
Brackendene Dr CM1 . . . . 32 D7
Bracken Dr IG7 . . . . 111 C4
Bracken Ind Est IG6 . . . . 111 F2
Bracken Mews
  Chingford E4 . . . . 87 C1
  Romford RM7 . . . . 135 B5
Brackens Dr CM14 . . . . . 116 D5
Bracken The E4 . . . . 109 C8
Bracken Way SS7 . . . . . . 145 A6
Brackley Cres SS13 . . . . 143 A8
Brackley Ho **4** RM3 . . . . 114 C4
Brackley Sq IG8 . . . . 110 D3
Bracknell Ho **3** RM3 . . . 114 F4
Bradbourne Rd RM17 . . . 178 B8
Bradbourne Way
  SS13 . . . . 143 C5
Bradd Cl RM15 . . . . 157 C2
Braddock Cl RM5 . . . . . . 113 C4
Bradfield Ct **12** RM19 . . . 171 B1
Bradfield Dr IG11 . . . . . . 153 A4
Bradfield Ho IG8 . . . . 111 A4
Bradford Bury SS9 . . . . . 146 C6
Bradford Rd IG1 . . . . 133 D3
Bradford St CM2 . . . . 32 A1
Brading Cres E11 . . . . . . 132 B2
Bradleigh Ave RM17 . . . . 173 C2
Bradley Ave SS7 . . . . 144 F5
Bradley Cl
  Canvey Island SS8 . . . . . 164 A5
  Thundersley SS7 . . . . . . 144 F5
Bradley Gn SS13 . . . . 121 C1
Bradley Ho IG8 . . . . 110 A3
Bradley Link SS7 . . . . . . 144 F5
Bradley Rd EN9 . . . . 65 C4
Bradley Way SS4 . . . . . . 125 F1
Bradshaw Rd RM16 . . . . 173 A5
Bradwell Ave RM10 . . . . . 135 A2
Bradwell Cl RM12 . . . . . . 155 B6
Bradwell Ct **3** CM13 . . . . 95 C3
Bradwell Gn **2** CM13 . . . . 95 C3
Bradwell Ho SS11 . . . . . . 121 F7
BRADWELL-ON-SEA 42 B2
Bradwell Power Sta
  Visitor Ctr★ CM0 . . . . . . 42 A6
Bradwell Rd
  Buckhurst Hill IG9 . . . . . . 88 E2
  Steeple CM0 . . . . 62 A3
  St Lawrence CM0 . . . . . . 62 C6
  Tillingham CM0 . . . . 63 E6
BRADWELL WATERSIDE
  . . . . 41 F4
Brady Ave IG10 . . . . 89 C7
Brady Ct **4** RM8 . . . . . . 134 D3
Brady Prim Sch RM13 . . . 170 C8
Braemar Ave CM2 . . . . . . 54 B8
Braemar Cres SS9 . . . . . 146 A2
Braemar Gdns RM11 . . . . 137 A5
Braemar Wlk SS13 . . . . . 143 B6
Braemore SS8 . . . . 163 F5
Braeside Sch
  Buckhurst Hill IG9 . . . . . . 88 B1
  Buckhurst Hill IG9 . . . . . 110 B1
Bragg Cl RM8 . . . . 153 B6
Braintree Ave IG4 . . . . . . 132 E7
Braintree Rd RM10 . . . . . 135 A1
Brairwood Cl SS9 . . . . . . 146 D5
Braiswick Pl SS15 . . . . . . 141 B8
Braithwaite Ave RM7 . . . . 135 A4
Bramber Ct **7** DA2 . . . . . 176 B1
Bramble Cl
  Chigwell IG7 . . . . 89 C1
  Southend-on-S SS9 . . . . 146 B7
Bramble Cres SS7 . . . . . 146 A5
Bramble Croft DA8 . . . . . 169 C2
Bramble Ct **2** IG6 . . . . . 111 F4
Bramble La RM14 . . . . . . 156 D4
Bramble Rd
  Canvey Island SS8 . . . . . 164 C3
  Hadleigh SS7 . . . . 145 F6
  Southend-on-S SS9 . . . . 146 B7
Bramble Rise CM20 . . . . . 10 C1
Brambles The
  Basildon SS15 . . . . 141 A8
  Chigwell IG7 . . . . 111 C4
  Southminster CM0 . . . . . . 84 D3
  Steeple CM0 . . . . 84 A3
Bramble Tye SS15 . . . . . 119 F1
Bramblings The E4 . . . . . 109 D6
Bramerton Rd SS5 . . . . . 124 D6
Bramfield Rd E SS6 . . . . 124 A2

Bramfield Rd W SS6 . . . . 123 F2
Bramley Cl IG8 . . . . 110 C3
Bramley Cres IG2 . . . . . . 133 A5
Bramley Ct
  7 Chingford E4 . . . . . . 87 C1
  Hadleigh SS7 . . . . 145 E2
Bramley Gdns SS15 . . . . 141 C8
Bramley Ho IG2 . . . . 133 A5
Bramley Pl CM2 . . . . 54 D7
Bramleys SS17 . . . . 160 D3
Bramleys The SS4 . . . . . 125 D5
Bramley Shaw EN9 . . . . . 65 F6
Bramley The SS4 . . . . . . 125 D5
Bramley Way CM3 . . . . . . 61 A1
Brampstead **1** SS15 . . . . 141 A6
Brampton Cl
  Corringham SS17 . . . . . . 161 A4
  Southend-on-S SS9 . . . . 147 A4
Bramshill Cl IG7 . . . . 111 E5
Bramston Cl
  Great Baddow CM2 . . . . . 54 F8
  Redbridge IG6 . . . . 111 F4
Bramston Link SS15 . . . . 140 E7
Bramston Way SS15 . . . . 140 E6
Bramwoods Rd CM2 . . . . . 54 E8
Brancaster Pl IG10 . . . . . . 88 F6
Brancaster Rd IG2 . . . . . 133 E5
Brancepeth Gdns IG9 . . . 110 A8
Branch Rd
  Hadleigh SS7 . . . . 145 E2
  Redbridge IG6 . . . . 112 B5
Brandenburg Rd SS8 . . . . 164 D5
Brandesbury Sq **4**
  IG8 . . . . 111 A3
Brandon Cl
  Billericay CM12 . . . . 97 A5
  Grays RM16 . . . . 172 F4
Brandon Groves Ave
  RM15 . . . . 157 D2
Brandville Gdns IG6 . . . . 133 B8
BRANDY HOLE 102 A4
Branfil Inf Sch RM14 . . . . 137 A1
Branfil Jun Sch RM14 . . . 156 A8
Branfill Rd RM14 . . . . 137 B2
Branksome Ave
  Hockley SS5 . . . . 124 E8
  Stanford-le-H SS17 . . . . 160 E4
  Wickford SS12 . . . . 120 F7
Branksome Cl SS17 . . . . 160 D3
Branksome Rd SS2 . . . . . 148 C1
Branscombe Gdns
  SS1 . . . . 149 B1
Branscombe Sq SS1 . . . . 149 B1
Branscombe Wlk SS1 . . . 149 B1
Branstone Ct **17**
  RM19 . . . . 171 B1
Brant Ct **3** RM1 . . . . 135 D7
Branton Rd DA9 . . . . 176 F1
Brantwood Gdns IG4 . . . . 132 E7
Brathertons Ct CM12 . . . . 96 F3
Braxted Cl SS4 . . . . 125 C4
Braxteds **10** SS15 . . . . . 141 A6
Braybrooke SS14 . . . . . . 142 B6
Brayburn Ct SS0 . . . . 147 A1
Bray Ct SS3 . . . . 149 E2
Brayers Mews SS4 . . . . . 125 F1
Brayfield Ct SS9 . . . . 146 E4
BRAYS GROVE 24 A8
Brays Grove Sch CM18 . . . 24 B6
Brays La CM18 . . . . 125 C8
Brays Mead CM18 . . . . . . 23 F6
Brays Springs EN9 . . . . . 65 E5
Brazemore Ct RM12 . . . . 136 D3
Braziers Ct CM2 . . . . 54 C3
Breach Barns Cvn Pk
  EN9 . . . . 44 B1
Breach Barns La EN9 . . . . 43 F1
Breach La RM9 . . . . 154 A2
Breach Rd RM20 . . . . 176 F8
Bread & Cheese Hill
  SS7 . . . . 144 E5
Break Egg Hill CM11 . . . . 97 D3
Breakneck Hill **1**
  DA9 . . . . 177 B2
Bream Gdns E6 . . . . 152 A2
Breamore Ct IG3 . . . . 134 A2
Breamore Rd IG3 . . . . . . 133 F2
Breams Field SS16 . . . . . 141 C4
Brecon Cl SS13 . . . . 143 C8
Brede Cl E6 . . . . 152 A2
Bredo Ho **6** IG11 . . . . . . 153 B2
Bree Hill CM3 . . . . 101 C6
Brempsons SS14 . . . . 142 A7
Bren Ct EN3 . . . . 65 A2
Brendans Cl RM11 . . . . . 136 E3
Brendon Gdns IG2 . . . . . 133 E6
Brendon Pl CM1 . . . . 31 E1
Brendon Rd RM8 . . . . 135 A3
Brendon Way SS0 . . . . . . 147 A5
Brennan Cl CM3 . . . . 80 F6
Brennan Rd RM18 . . . . . . 179 B5
Brent Ave CM3 . . . . 79 D1
Brent Cl DA2 . . . . 176 B1
Brent Ct RM2 . . . . 136 C8
Brentfield Rd DA1 . . . . . . 176 A1
Brenthall Twrs CM17 . . . . 24 C6
Brentleigh Ct CM14 . . . . . 116 A7
Brent Way DA2 . . . . 176 A2
BRENTWOOD★ 116 E8
Brentwood Cathedral★
  CM14 . . . . 116 D8
Brentwood Ctr The★
  CM15 . . . . 94 C3
Brentwood Cty High Sch
  CM14 . . . . 116 D7
Brentwood Pl CM15 . . . . . 94 D1
Brentwood Rd
  Bulphan CM14 . . . . 139 F3

Brentwood Rd continued
  Chipping Ongar CM5,
  CM15 . . . . 71 B8
  Grays RM16 . . . . 174 C8
  Ingrave CM13 . . . . 117 D3
  Orsett RM16, RM14 . . . . 159 B4
  Romford RM1, RM2 . . . . 136 B5
  West Horndon CM13 . . . 139 E8
Brentwood Sch
  Brentwood CM15 . . . . . . 116 D8
  Shenfield CM15 . . . . 94 E1
Brentwood Sta CM14 . . . 116 C7
Brentwood Ursuline
  Convent High Sch
  CM14 . . . . 116 D8
Bressey Gr E18 . . . . 109 F1
Bressingham Gdns
  CM3 . . . . 101 C7
Bretons SS15 . . . . 141 E6
Bretons Cotts RM13 . . . . 154 E6
Brettenham Ave E17 . . . . 109 A2
Brettenham Dr SS1 . . . . . 167 E8
Brettenham Rd E17 . . . . . 109 A2
Brett Gdns RM9 . . . . 153 E5
Bretts Villas CM6 . . . . 14 C8
Brevet Cl RM19 . . . . 171 D2
Brewers Yd CM0 . . . . 84 D4
Brewery Fields CM2 . . . . . 55 A5
Brewery Rd EN11 . . . . 21 B6
Brewery The RM1 . . . . . . 135 D6
Brewery Wlk **7** RM1 . . . . 135 E6
Brewhouse Yd **11**
  DA11 . . . . 179 B1
Brewood Rd RM8 . . . . . . 153 B6
Brewster Cl SS8 . . . . 164 A3
Brian Cl
  Chelmsford CM2 . . . . 54 B6
  Hornchurch RM12 . . . . . 155 B8
Brian Rd RM6 . . . . 134 C6
Briar Cl
  Billericay CM11 . . . . 119 D3
  Buckhurst Hill IG9 . . . . . 110 D8
  Hockley SS5 . . . . 124 F4
Briarleas Gdns RM14 . . . 137 E4
Briar Lo E18 . . . . 110 C2
Briar Mead SS15 . . . . . . 141 B8
Briar Rd RM3 . . . . 114 D3
Briars The
  Harlow CM18 . . . . 23 E4
  Kelvedon Hatch CM15 . . . 93 E8
Briars Wlk RM3 . . . . 114 F1
Briarswood
  Canvey Island SS8 . . . . . 164 A5
  Chelmsford CM1 . . . . 32 D7
Briar View CM11 . . . . 119 D3
Briarview Ct E4 . . . . 109 D4
Briarwood CM15 . . . . 71 F2
Briarwood Dr SS9 . . . . . . 146 E5
Briary The SS12 . . . . 121 B7
Briceway SS17 . . . . 160 F4
Brick Ct RM17 . . . . 178 A8
Brickenden Ct EN9 . . . . . . 65 F6
Brickenden Ct EN11 . . . . . 21 A5
Brickfield Cl SS16 . . . . . . 142 D2
Brickfield Cotts
  Brentwood CM15 . . . . . . 95 A1
  Epping CM16 . . . . 46 B3
Brickfield Rd
  Basildon SS16 . . . . 142 D2
  Coopersale CM16 . . . . . . 46 D2
Brickfields Rd CM3 . . . . . 101 E7
Brickfields Way SS4 . . . . 148 A8
Brick House La CM3 . . . . . 20 E1
Brick Kiln Rd CM2 . . . . . . 55 C7
Brickstock Furze **1**
  CM15 . . . . 95 A1
Brickwall Cl CM0 . . . . . . 106 C4
Bridge Ave RM14 . . . . . . 137 A1
Bridge Cl
  Brentwood CM13 . . . . . . 116 F7
  Dartford DA2 . . . . 176 B1
  Romford RM7 . . . . 135 E5
  Southend-on-S SS3 . . . . 168 E7
Bridgecote La SS15 . . . . 119 F2
Bridge Cotts
  Southend-on-S SS3 . . . . 168 D3
  South Woodham Ferrers
  CM3 . . . . 79 B1
Bridge Ct
  Grays RM17 . . . . 178 B8
  Maldon CM9 . . . . 37 A3
Bridge End E17 . . . . 109 C2
Bridge Hill CM16 . . . . 67 F6
Bridge House Cl
  SS12 . . . . 121 C7
Bridgemans Gn CM3 . . . . 82 A6
Bridgemarsh La CM3 . . . 104 F8
Bridgend Cl CM3 . . . . . . 101 E8
Bridge Par CM12 . . . . 96 F3
Bridge Point RM11 . . . . . 136 E8
Bridge Rd
  Grays RM17 . . . . 178 B8
  Great Wakering SS3 . . . . 150 F4
  Moreton CM5 . . . . 26 C2
  Rainham RM13 . . . . 155 A1
  Wickford SS11 . . . . 122 A4
Bridges Dr DA1 . . . . 176 B2
Bridge St
  Basildon SS15 . . . . 119 F2
  Writtle CM1 . . . . 31 C1
Bridge View DA9 . . . . 177 B3
Bridgeview Ct IG6 . . . . . . 111 D4
Bridge View Ind Est
  RM20 . . . . 176 F8
Bridgeway IG11 . . . . 152 F5
Bridgeways EN11 . . . . 21 B6
Bridgewick Rd CM0 . . . . . 86 B6
Bridgwater Cl RM3 . . . . . 114 D5

Bridgwater Dr SS0 . . . . . . **147** A4
Bridgwater Rd RM3 . . . . . . **114** D5
Bridgwater Wlk RM3 . . . . . . **114** D5
Bridle Cl EN11 . . . . 8 A2
Bridle Path The IG8 . . . **109** E3
Bridleway CM11 . . . . **97** D6
Bridle Way
　Great Amwell SG12 . . . . 8 A6
　5 Hoddesdon EN11 . . . . 8 A1
Bridle Way (N) EN11 . . . .8 B2
Bridle Way (S) EN11 . . . . 8 A1
Bridon Cl CM3 . . . . **78** B6
Bridport Ave RM7 . . . . **135** B5
Bridport Rd CM1 . . . . . . **32** D5
Brierley Cl RM11 . . . . . . **136** C5
Brigadier Way SS3 . . . . **168** F6
Brighstone Ct **19**
　RM19 . . . . **171** B1
Brighten Rd SS1 . . . . . . **166** F8
Brighton Ave SS1 . . . . . . **167** D8
Brighton Rd E6 . . . . **152** A2
Brights Ave RM13 . . . . . **155** B1
Brightside CM12 . . . . . . **96** E4
Brightside Cl CM12 . . . . **96** F4
Brightside Prim Sch
　CM12 . . . . **96** F5
Brightwell Ave SS0 . . . . **147** D2
Brigstock Rd DA17 . . . . **169** B2
Brimfield Rd RM19 . . . . **171** D2
Brimsdown Apartments
　SS15 . . . . **141** B6
Brimsdown Ave SS15. . . **141** B6
Brindles
　Canvey Island SS8. . . **163** F5
　Hornchurch RM11 . . . **136** E7
Brindles Cl
　Brentwood CM13 . . . . **117** C8
　Linford SS17 . . . . **175** A2
Brindwood Rd E4 . . . . . **109** A7
Bringey The CM2 . . . . . . **55** A6
Brinkworth Cl SS5 . . . . **124** F6
Brinkworth Rd IG5. . . . **132** E8
Brinsmead Rd RM3 . . . . **115** A1
Brisbane Ho RM18 . . . . **178** F6
Brisbane Rd IG1 . . . . . . **133** C3
Briscoe Prim Sch
　SS13 . . . . **143** B8
Briscoe Rd
　Basildon SS13 . . . . . . **143** B7
　Hoddesdon EN11 . . . . **21** A8
　Rainham RM13 . . . . . **155** D3
Bristol Cl SS6 . . . . **123** C5
Bristol Ho **1** IG11 . . . . **153** A5
Bristol Rd SS2 . . . . **147** D6
Bristowe Ave CM2 . . . . . **55** A6
Bristowe Dr RM16 . . . . **174** D7
Britannia Bsns Pk
　SS2 . . . . **147** B7
Britannia Cl CM11 . . . . . **97** B2
Britannia Ct SS13 . . . . **121** D1
Britannia Gdns SS0 . . . **166** C8
Britannia Lo SS0. . . . . **166** C8
Britannia Rd
　Brentwood CM14 . . . **116** C5
　Ilford IG1 . . . . **133** B1
　Southend-on-S SS0 . **166** C8
British Legion Rd E4 . . **109** F8
Brittain Rd RM8 . . . . . . **134** F1
Britten Cl SS16 . . . . . . **141** A5
Britten Cres CM2 . . . . . **54** F8
Britton Ct SS6 . . . . **123** D1
Brittons La CM4 . . . . . . **97** F8
Brittons Sch & Tech Coll
　RM13 . . . . **154** F5
Brixham Cl SS6 . . . . . . **123** D5
Brixham Gdns IG3 . . . . **152** E7
Broad Cl SS5 . . . . **124** E6
Broadclyst Ave SS9 . . . **146** D5
Broadclyst Cl SS1 . . . . **149** A1
Broadclyst Gdns SS1 . . **149** B1
Broadfield
　Harlow CM20 . . . . **10** E1
　High Roding CM6. . . . 5 E7
Broadfield Cl RM1 . . . . **135** F6
Broadfields CM21 . . . . . .1 B1
Broadfields Prim Sch
　CM20 . . . . **10** E1
Broadfield Way CM20 . . **110** C7
Broadford Prim Sch
　RM3 . . . . **114** D4
Broadgate EN9 . . . . **65** F7
Broad Gn **3** SS14 . . . . **142** C7
Broadhope Ave SS17 . . **175** C8
Broadhurst Ave IG3 . . . **152** F8
Broadhurst Gdns IG7 . . **111** C6
Broadhurst Wlk **3**
　RM13 . . . . **155** A6
Broadlands
　Grays RM17 . . . . **172** F1
　Thundersley SS7 . . . . **145** A6
Broadlands Ave
　Hockley SS5. . . . . . . **124** F6
　Rayleigh SS6 . . . . . . **123** D3
Broadlands Rd SS5 . . . **124** F6
Broadlawn SS9 . . . . . . **146** C4
BROADLEY COMMON **22** E2
Broadley Rd EN19 . . . . **23** A4
Broadley Terr EN9 . . . . **22** E3
Broadmayne SS14,
　SS15 . . . . **142** C6
Broad Mdw CM15 . . . . . **71** F1
Broad Mead CM3 . . . . . **99** C8
Broadmead Ct **6** IG8 . . **110** A4
Broadmead
　Woodford IG8 . . . . . . **110** B3
　Woodford IG8 . . . . . . **110** D3
Broad Oak IG8 . . . . . . **110** B5
Broad Oak Cl E4 . . . . . **109** A5

Broadoaks CM16. . . . . . . **67** F8
Broad Oaks SS12 . . . . . **121** E6
Broad Oak Way SS6 . . . **123** E1
Broad Par SS5 . . . . **124** F6
Broad Rd DA10 . . . . . . **177** E1
BROAD'S GREEN **18** E5
Broad St
　Dagenham RM10 . . . . **154** A5
　Hatfield Broad Oak CM22 . . .3 C6
BROAD STREET GREEN **37** C7
Broad Street Green Rd
　CM9 . . . . **37** C7
Broadstrood IG10 . . . . . **67** A1
Broadview Are RM16 . . . **173** D4
Broadview Ho **3**
　RM8 . . . . **134** D3
Broadwalk E18 . . . . . . **132** A8
Broadwalk The **4**
　SS12 . . . . **121** E6
Broadwater Gn SS15 . . **140** F6
Broadwater Ho **2**
　DA12 . . . . **179** D1
Broadway
　Barking IG11 . . . . . . **152** C4
　Grays RM17 . . . . **178** C8
　Rainham RM13 . . . . . **155** A1
　Romford RM2 . . . . . . **114** A1
　Southend-on-S SS9 . **165** E8
　Tilbury RM18 . . . . . . **178** F5
Broad Way SS5 . . . . . . **124** F6
Broadway Ave CM17 . . . 11 B4
Broadway Chambers 5
　SS13 . . . . **143** B5
Broadway Cl IG8 . . . . . **110** B5
Broadway Gdns SS13 . . **110** B4
Broadway Link SS13 . . **143** B5
Broadway Mkt IG6. . . . **111** D1
Broadway N **7** SS13 . . **143** B5
Broadway Par
　Chingford E4 . . . . . . **109** C4
　Hornchurch RM12 . . . **155** B8
Broadway The
　6 Basildon SS13 . . . . **143** B5
　Chingford E4 . . . . . . **109** D4
　Dagenham RM8 . . . . **135** A4
　Hornchurch RM12 . . . **155** B8
　Loughton IG10. . . . . . **89** C5
　Southend-on-S SS1 . **168** A7
　3 Wickford, Nevendon
　　SS12 . . . . **121** E5
　Wickford SS11 . . . . . **121** D8
　Woodford IG8 . . . . . . **110** B4
Broadway W SS9 . . . . . **165** E8
Broad Wk N The
　CM13 . . . . **117** A7
Broad Wk S The
　CM13 . . . . **117** A6
Broad Wlk
　Harlow CM20 . . . . . . **10** D1
　Hockley SS5. . . . . . . **124** F6
Brockdish Rd IG11 . . . . **152** F7
Brockenhurst Dr
　SS17 . . . . **175** C8
Brockenhurst Gdns
　IG1 . . . . **152** C7
Brockenhurst Way
　CM3 . . . . **56** F1
Brocket Cl IG7 . . . . . . **111** F6
Brocket **15** EN11 . . . . . . **21** A6
Brocket Rd EN11. . . . . **21** A6
Brockett Rd RM16 . . . . **174** B3
Brocket Way IG7 . . . . . **111** F5
Brock Gn RM15 . . . . . . **172** B7
Brockham Dr IG2 . . . . **133** C4
BROCK HILL **99** B5
Brock Hill SS11 . . . . . **99** C4
Brock Hill Dr SS11 . . . **99** C3
Brockles Mead CM19. . **23** C4
Brockley Cres RM5. . . **113** C3
Brockley Gr CM13 . . . . **95** A1
Brockley Rd CM2 . . . . **32** D2
Brocksford Ave SS6. . . **123** F1
Brocksparkwood
　CM13 . . . . **117** B7
Brockton Cl RM1. . . . . **135** F7
Brockwell Wlk **3**
　SS12 . . . . **121** D6
Brodie Rd
　Chingford E4 . . . . . . **109** C8
　Southend-on-S SS3 . **168** H8
Brodie Wlk SS12 . . . . . **121** F5
Brograve Cl CM2. . . . . **54** D7
Bromefield Ct EN9 . . . . **66** A6
Bromfelde Rd RM11 . . **120** C5
Bromfords Cl SS12. . . . **121** B5
Bromfords Dr SS12 . . . **121** B5
Bromfords Sch The
　SS12 . . . . **121** B6
Bromhall Rd RM8 . . . . **153** B6
Bromley **1** RM17 . . . . **177** F8
Bromley Cl CM20 . . . . **11** B4
Bromley Mews SS6 . . . **123** A3
Brompton Cl CM12. . . . **97** A5
Brompton Gdns CM9 . . **58** E8
Brompton Wlk RM20 . . **172** B2
Bronte Cl
　Ilford IG2 . . . . **133** B7
　Tilbury RM18 . . . . . . **179** C5
Bronte Mews SS2 . . . . **148** A2
Bronze Age Way
　DA17 . . . . **169** C2
Brook Ave RM10 . . . . . **154** B5
Brookbank CM2 . . . . . **54** E8

Brook Cl
　Rochford SS4. . . . . . **148** A8
　Romford RM2 . . . . . . **113** F2
　Woodham Walter CM9. . **35** D2
Brook Cres E4 . . . . . . **109** B6
Brook Ct
　6 Barking IG11 . . . . **152** C3
　Barking IG11 . . . . . . **152** F4
　Rayleigh SS6 . . . . . . **145** C8
　Southend-on-S SS0 . **147** D2
Brookdale CM14 . . . . . **137** B1
Brookdale Ave RM14 . . **137** B1
Brook Dr
　Basildon SS17 . . . . . **142** C1
　Wickford, SS12 . . . . **121** C6
Brook End CM21 . . . . . . 1 D2
Brook End Rd N CM2. . **33** A4
Brook End Rd S CM2 . . **33** B3
Brooke Rd RM17 . . . . **173** B5
Brooker Rd EN9 . . . . . **65** C5
Brooke Sq CM9 . . . . . **37** A1
Brooke Trad Est RM1 . . **135** F4
Brookfield CM16. . . . . **46** C6
Brookfield Cl RM13 . . . . **95** D3
Brookfield House Sch
　IG8 . . . . **109** E4
Brookfield Path IG8 . . **109** E4
Brookfields
　Chipping Ongar CM5 . . **48** F6
　Sawbridgeworth CM21 . . . 1 D2
　Southend-on-S SS9 . **146** D5
Brookfields Cl SS9 . . . **146** D5
Brook Gdns E4 . . . . . . **109** B6
Brook Hill CM3 . . . . . **19** B6
Brookhouse Gdns E4. . **109** E6
Brookhurst Cl CM2. . . **32** D3
Brooking Ct RM8. . . . . **134** C1
Brook La
　Chelmsford CM2 . . . . **33** B2
　Doddinghurst CM15. . **72** C2
　Doddinghurst CM15. . **72** E2
　Galleywood CM2 . . . . **54** E3
　Sawbridgeworth CM21 . . . 1 D2
Brooklands
　Rayleigh SS6 . . . . . . **123** D3
　Wickford SS12 . . . . . **121** B6
Brooklands App 7
　RM1 . . . . **135** D7
Brooklands Ave SS9 . . **146** F6
Brooklands Cl 5
　RM7 . . . . **135** D7
Brooklands Gdns
　RM11 . . . . **136** C5
Brooklands La RM7 . . . **135** D7
Brooklands Pk SS5 . . . **140** F6
Brooklands Rd RM7. . . **135** D7
Brooklands Sq SS8 . . . **163** E3
Brooklands Wlk CM3 . . **121** B9
Brooklane Field CM18. . **24** B5
Brook Lo
　Romford RM7 . . . . . . **135** D7
　Southend-on-S SS9 . **146** B7
Brooklyn Ave IG10 . . . . **88** E5
Brooklyn Ct IG10 . . . . . **88** E5
Brooklyn Ho SS6 . . . . **123** D5
Brook Mead
　Basildon SS15 . . . . . **141** B7
　Great Waltham CM3 . . **18** E8
Brook Meadow Cl
　IG8 . . . . **109** E4
Brook Par IG7 . . . . . . **111** B7
Brook Rd
　Brentwood, Brook Street
　　CM14 . . . . **115** F7
　Brentwood CM14. . . . **115** D5
　Buckhurst Hill IG9 . . **88** A1
　Epping CM16 . . . . . . **68** A6
　Ilford IG2 . . . . **133** C5
　Loughton IG10. . . . . . **88** E4
　Rayleigh SS6 . . . . . . **145** D8
　Romford RM2 . . . . . . **113** F2
　Sawbridgeworth CM21 . . . 1 E1
　South Benfleet SS7 . **144** C2
　St Lawrence CM0 . . . **63** B5
　Tillingham CM0 . . . . **63** C5
Brook Rise IG7 . . . . . **111** A7
Brook Road Ind Ctr
　SS6 . . . . **145** D8
Brook St Rdbt CM14. . . **115** D5
Brookscroft Rd E17 . . **109** B2
Brookside
　Billericay CM11 . . . . **97** C6
　Canvey Island SS8. . **164** A5
　Harlow CM19 . . . . . . **23** A5
　Hockley SS5. . . . . . . **124** F4
　Hoddesdon EN11 . . . . **21** A6
　Hornchurch RM11 . . . **136** E6
　Margaretting CM4 . . . **74** F7
　Redbridge IG6 . . . . . **111** C4
　Waltham Abbey EN9 . . **65** E7
Brookside Ave SS3. . . **150** C2
Brookside Cl CM11. . . . **97** C6
Brookside Ctr SS2 . . . **147** F5
Brookside Jun & Inf Schs
　RM3 . . . . **114** C5
Brook's Mans 5 IG3 . . **134** B3
Brook's Par 6 IG3 . . . **134** B3
Brook St
　Belvedere DA17 . . . . **169** B1
　Brentwood CM14 . . . . **115** E6
　Chelmsford CM1 . . . . **32** B3
BROOK STREET **115** F6
Brook View CM2 . . . . **55** C6
Brookway RM13 . . . . **170** B8

Brook Way IG7 . . . . . . **111** B7
Broome Cl CM11 . . . . . **97** D5
Broome Pl RM15. . . . . **171** D5
Broome Pl Complex
　RM15 . . . . **171** D5
Broome Rd CM11 . . . . **97** D5
BROOMFIELD **19** B2
Broomfield
　Hadleigh SS7 . . . . . . **145** D4
　Harlow CM20 . . . . . . **11** B3
Broomfield Ave
　Loughton IG10 . . . . . **88** F3
　Rayleigh SS6 . . . . . . **123** A3
　Southend-on-S SS9 . **146** F5
Broomfield Cl RM5. . . . **113** D3
Broomfield Gn SS8 . . . **163** F5
Broomfield Prim Sch
　CM1 . . . . **19** B1
Broomfield Rd
　Chelmsford CM1 . . . . **32** A5
　Dagenham RM6 . . . . **134** D4
　Swanscombe DA10 . . **177** E2
Broomfields
　Basildon SS13 . . . . . **143** A6
　Hatfield Heath CM22 . . .3 A3
Broomfields Ct 6
　SS13 . . . . **143** A6
Broomfields Mews 4
　SS13 . . . . **143** A6
Broomfields Pl 5
　SS13 . . . . **143** A6
Broomhall Cl CM1 . . . . **19** B2
Broomhall Rd CM1 . . . . **19** B2
Broomhill Ct **2** IG8. . . **110** A4
Broomhill Rd
　Ilford IG3 . . . . **134** A2
　Woodford IG8 . . . . . . **110** A4
Broomhills Chase
　CM12 . . . . **119** A5
Broomhill Wlk IG8. . . . **109** F3
Broom Rd SS5 . . . . . . **101** E2
Broomstick Hall Rd
　EN9 . . . . **65** E6
Broomways SS3 . . . . . **150** C3
Broomwood Gdns
　CM15 . . . . **94** A3
Broomwood La CM11 . . **98** B8
Broughton Rd
　Hadleigh SS7 . . . . . . **145** F2
　South Woodham Ferrers
　　CM3 . . . . **101** E6
Browne Cl
　Brentwood CM14. . . . **94** B1
　Romford RM5 . . . . . . **113** C3
Browning Ave SS2 . . . **148** B2
Browning Cl RM5 . . . . **112** F3
Browning Dr SS12 . . . **121** C5
Browning Rd
　Dartford DA1 . . . . . . **176** A3
　Maldon CM9. . . . . . . **59** A8
Brownings Ave CM1. . . **32** A5
Browning Wlk RM18 . . **179** C5
Brownlea Gdns IG3 . . . **134** A2
Brownlow Bend SS14 . . **142** D6
Brownlow Cross
　SS14 . . . . **142** D6
Brownlow Gn SS14 . . . **142** D6
Brownlows Cl IG6. . . . . **15** C7
Browns Ave SS11 . . . . **99** F2
Browns Cotts RM16 . . . **172** E5
Brownsea Dr SS12 . . . **122** A5
Broxbourne Ave E18 . . **132** B7
Broxbourne Rd E7 . . . **132** A1
Broxbourne Sta EN10 . . **21** A3
Broxburn Ct RM15 . . . **172** B6
Broxburn Dr RM15 . . . **172** B6
Broxburn Par RM15 . . **172** B6
Broxhill Rd
　Havering-atte-B RM4. . **114** B7
　Romford RM4 . . . . . . **113** F7
Broxted Cotts 5
　SS12 . . . . **121** E6
Broxted Dr SS12 . . . . **121** E6
Broxted End SS12 . . . **121** E6
Broxted Mews CM13 . . **95** C3
Bruce Ave RM12 . . . . **136** D2
Bruce Gr
　Chelmsford CM2 . . . . **54** A7
　Wickford SS11 . . . . . **122** A7
Bruce Rd CM1 . . . . . . **31** B1
Bruces Wharf Rd
　RM17 . . . . **178** A8
Bruges Rd SS8 . . . . . **164** C5
Brummell Pl CM17 . . . **11** C3
Brundish SS13 . . . . . . **143** A5
Brunel Cl
　Romford RM1 . . . . . . **135** E7
　Tilbury RM18 . . . . . . **179** B5
Brunel Rd
　Chigwell IG8 . . . . . . **110** F3
　South Benfleet SS7 . **144** D7
　Southend-on-S SS9 . **146** C4
Brunel Way CM3 . . . . **101** C7
Brunswick Ave RM14 . . **137** E4
Brunswick Ct
　Hoddesdon EN11 . . . . **21** A5
　Upminster RM14 . . . . **137** E4
Brunswick Gdns IG6 . . **111** C3
Brunswick Lo E6 . . . . **109** C8
Brunswick Pl SS6 . . . **123** C5
Brunswick Rd
　Holdbrook EN3. . . . . **65** A1
　Southend-on-S SS1 . **167** D7

Bri–Bun 189

Brunswick Wlk **3**
　DA12 . . . . **179** D1
Brunwins Cl SS11 . . . . **121** F8
Brushwood Lo **2**
　DA17 . . . . **169** A2
Brussum Rd SS8 . . . . . **164** D2
Bruton Ave SS0 . . . . . **147** A5
Bryanston Rd RM18 . . **179** C5
Bryant Ave
　Romford RM3 . . . . . . **114** D1
　Southend-on-S SS1 . **167** E6
Bryant Link CM2 . . . . . **33** B4
Bryant Row RM3 . . . . **114** C8
Bryant's La CM9 . . . . . **57** D7
Bryce Rd RM8 . . . . . . **153** C8
Bryn Farm Cl SS14 . . . **142** C8
Bryony Cl IG10 . . . . . . **89** B5
Buchanan Cl RM15 . . . **171** C5
Buchanan Gdns SS12 . . **121** E5
Buchanan Way SS2. . . **82** B5
Buckbean Path RM3 . . **114** C3
Buckeridge Way CM0 . . **42** B3
Buckerills SS13 . . . . . . **143** A6
Buckhatch La CM3 . . . **78** D3
Buckhurst Ct **2** IG9 . . **110** C8
BUCKHURST HILL **110** C8
Buckhurst Hill Com Prim
　Sch IG9 . . . . **110** E8
Buckhurst Hill Ho
　IG9. . . . . **110** B8
Buckhurst Hill Sta
　IG9 . . . . **110** D8
Buckhurst Way IG9 . . . **110** D7
Buckingham Cl RM11 . . **136** D6
Buckingham Ct
　2 Chelmsford CM2 . . **32** F4
　Loughton IG10. . . . . . **89** A7
　3 Romford RM1 . . . . **135** F6
Buckingham Hill Rd
　Linford SS17, RM16. . **174** F5
　Stanford-le-H SS17 . . **175** A7
Buckingham Lo **6**
　EN11 . . . . **21** A6
Buckingham Rd
　Basildon SS15 . . . . . **141** E8
　Hockley SS5. . . . . . . **124** D6
　Ilford IG1 . . . . **133** D2
　Wanstead E11 . . . . . . **132** C6
　Woodford E18 . . . . . . **109** F2
Buckinghamshire Sq
　SS11 . . . . **122** A5
Buckingham Sq **11**
　CM0 . . . . **106** C4
Buckland SS3 . . . . **149** C1
Buckland Gate CM3 . . **101** C6
Bucklebury Heath
　CM3 . . . . **101** D6
Bucklers Ct CM14 . . . . **116** C5
Buckles La RM15 . . . . **172** D8
Buckley Cl SS17 . . . . . **160** F5
Bucknells Mead CM1 . . **52** A4
Buckrell Rd E4 . . . . . . **109** D8
Buckthorne Ho 4
　IG7. . . . . **112** B6
Buckwins Sq SS13 . . . **121** D1
Buckwyns Chase CM12 . . **96** F5
Buckwyns Ct CM12. . . . **96** F4
Budleigh Cl CM14. . . . **116** C5
Budna Rd SS8 . . . . . . **163** F5
Budoch Ct IG3. . . . . . . **134** A2
Budoch Dr IG3 . . . . . . **134** A2
Buglers Rise CM1 . . . . **53** B8
Bulbecks Wlk CM3 . . . **101** C5
Bull Cl
　Basildon SS16 . . . . . **142** E5
　Grays RM16 . . . . **172** F4
Bullen Cl IG6 . . . . **111** E4
Bullen Wlk CM2 . . . . . **54** C3
Buller Rd
　Barking IG11 . . . . . . **152** E5
　Basildon SS15 . . . . . **141** B7
　North Fambridge CM3 . . **81** A1
Bullfields CM21 . . . . .1 E3
Bullivant Cl DA9 . . . . **177** A2
Bull La
　Dagenham RM10. . . . **135** B1
　Hockley SS5. . . . . . . **124** C6
　Maldon CM9. . . . . . . **37** A3
　Rayleigh SS6 . . . . . . **123** E2
Bulls Lodge Cotts CM3 . . **20** B1
Bullwood App SS5 . . . **124** B5
Bullwood Hall La SS5 . . **124** A4
Bullwood Rd SS5 . . . . **124** D5
Bulmers Wlk RM13 . . . **155** C3
Bulow Ave SS8 . . . . . **164** B3
BULPHAN **158** F8
Bulphan By-Pass
　RM14 . . . . **140** A1
Bulphan CE Prim Sch
　RM14 . . . . **158** F8
Bulphan Cl SS12 . . . . **121** E6
Bulphan View CM13. . . **140** E5
Bulwark Rd SS3 . . . . . **168** E8
BUMBLE'S GREEN **44** C6
Bumbles Green La EN9. . **44** B6
Bumfords La CM3, CM9 . . **35** A7
Bunces La IG8 . . . . . . **109** F3
Bundick's Hill CM11 . . **31** F3
Bungalows The
　Abbess Roding CM5. . **14** D1
　Grays RM20. . . . . . . **177** A8
　Redbridge IG6. . . . . **111** E2
Bunker's Hill DA17 . . . **169** A2

Bunters Ave SS3 . . . . 168 C6
Buntingbridge Rd
  IG2 . . . . 133 D6
Bunting Cl CM2 . . . . 54 B5
Bunting La CM11 . . . . 97 C1
Burches SS14 . . . . 119 E1
Burches Mead SS7 . . . . . . 145 A7
Burches Rd SS7 . . . . 144 F8
Burchett Way RM6 . . . . . . 134 C4
Burch Rd DA11 . . . . 178 F1
Burchwall Cl RM5 . . . . . . 113 C3
Burden Way E11 . . . . 132 B2
Burdett Ave SS0 . . . . 166 E8
Burdett Rd SS1 . . . . 167 C7
Burdetts Rd RM9 . . . . 153 F4
Bure RM18 . . . . 175 D3
Buren Ave SS8 . . . . 164 E3
Burfield Cl SS9 . . . . 146 F6
Burfield Rd SS9 . . . . 146 F6
Burford Cl
  Dagenham RM8 . . . . . . 134 C1
  Ilford IG6 . . . . 133 C7
Burford Gdns EN11 . . . . . . 21 B7
Burford Ho EN11 . . . . 21 B7
Burford Mews 9 EN11 . . . . 21 A7
Burford Pl 11 EN11 . . . . . . 21 A7
Burford St EN11 . . . . 21 A7
Burges Cl
  Hornchurch RM11 . . . . 136 F7
  Southend-on-S SS1 . . . 168 C6
Burges Rd
  Southend-on-S SS1 . . . 168 B6
  Wallend E6 . . . . 152 A5
Burgess Ave SS17 . . . . . . 160 E1
Burgess Ct
  Brentwood CM15 . . . . . . 94 D1
  Wallend E12 . . . . 152 A5
Burgess Field CM2 . . . . . . 32 F4
Burges Terr SS1 . . . . 167 F6
Burghley Rd RM16 . . . . . . 172 C3
Burghley Way SS4 . . . . 54 C8
Burghstead Cl CM12 . . . . . 97 A1
Burgoyne Hatch CM20 . . . . 11 A1
Burgundy Ct CM2 . . . . 32 C2
Burgundy Gdns 6
  SS13 . . . . 143 B8
Burland Rd
  Brentwood CM15 . . . . . . 94 D1
  Romford RM5 . . . . 113 C4
Burleigh Cl
  Billericay CM12 . . . . 97 B5
  Romford RM7 . . . . 135 B7
Burleigh Ct
  Southend-on-S SS0 . . . 166 C8
  Southend-on-S, Thorpe Bay
  SS1 . . . . 168 B8
Burleigh Sq SS1 . . . . 168 B8
Burlescoombe Cl SS1 . . . . 168 A8
Burlescoombe Leas
  SS1 . . . . 149 B1
Burlescoombe Rd
  SS1 . . . . 149 A1
Burley Cl E4 . . . . 109 A5
Burley Hill CM17 . . . . 24 D7
Burlington Ave RM7 . . . . . 135 B5
Burlington Ct SS13 . . . . . 143 B8
Burlington Gdns
  Dagenham RM6 . . . . . . 134 E4
  Hadleigh SS7 . . . . 145 F3
  Hullbridge SS5 . . . . . . 101 F1
Burlington Pl IG8 . . . . 110 A7
Burnaby Rd
  Gravesend DA11 . . . . . 178 E1
  Southend-on-S SS1 . . . 167 C7
Burne Ave SS12 . . . . 121 A6
Burnell Gate CM1 . . . . 33 A7
Burnell Wlk CM13 . . . . . . 116 C4
Burnels Ave E6 . . . . 152 A2
Burnett Pk CM19 . . . . 23 B3
Burnett Rd
  Erith DA8 . . . . 170 D1
  Redbridge IG6 . . . . . . 111 B3
Burney Ct IG7 . . . . 111 C5
Burney Dr IG10 . . . . 89 C6
Burnham Ave SS1 . . . . 81 A5
Burnham Bsns Pk
  CM0 . . . . 106 A6
Burnham Cres E11 . . . . . . 132 C7
BURNHAM-ON-CROUCH
  . . . . 106 D6
Burnham-on-Crouch &
  District Mus★ CM0 . . . 106 B4
Burnham-on-Crouch Prim
  Sch CM0 . . . . 106 D5
Burnham-on-Crouch Sta
  CM0 . . . . 106 B6
Burnham Rd
  Althorne CM3 . . . . 83 B1
  Battlesbridge SS11 . . . 100 E3
  Chelmsford CM1 . . . . . . 32 D5
  Dagenham RM9 . . . . . 153 B4
  Hullbridge SS5 . . . . . . 101 E2
  Latchingdon CM3 . . . . . 82 D5
  Mundon CM9 . . . . 81 C8
  Romford RM7 . . . . 135 D8
  Southend-on-S SS9 . . . 146 C1
  Southminster CM0 . . . . 84 C2
  Southminster CM0 . . . . 84 D3
  South Woodham Ferrers
  CM3 . . . . 79 D1
  Woodham Mortimer CM9,
  CM3 . . . . 57 E5
Burnley Rd RM20 . . . . 177 A6
Burns Ave
  Basildon SS13 . . . . . . 143 B5

Burns Ave continued
  Dagenham RM6 . . . . . . 134 C4
Burns Cl
  Billericay CM11 . . . . 97 B3
  Maldon CM9 . . . . 37 A1
Burns Cres CM2 . . . . 54 C8
Burnside
  Canvey Island SS8 . . . 164 A5
  Dagenham RM8 . . . . . 134 C2
  Sawbridgeworth CM21 . . . 1 D2
Burnside Ave E4 . . . . 109 A4
Burnside Cres CM1 . . . . . . 32 B7
Burnside Rd 6 RM1 . . . . . 135 F5
Burnside Ind Est IG6 . . . . 112 B5
Burnside Rd RM8 . . . . . . 134 C3
Burnside Terr CM17 . . . . . 11 F3
Burns Pl RM18 . . . . 179 B6
Burns Way CM13 . . . . 95 D3
Burnt Ho IG7 . . . . 89 F1
Burnthouse La
  Ingatestone CM4 . . . . . 73 F1
  Mountnessing CM4,
  CM13 . . . . 96 A8
Burntmill Cl CM20 . . . . . . 10 C3
Burntmill Cnr CM20 . . . . . 10 D4
Burnt Mill Comp Sch
  CM20 . . . . 10 E2
Burnt Mill Ind Est
  CM20 . . . . 10 C3
Burntmill La CM20 . . . . . . 10 D3
BURNT MILLS 121 B1
Burnt Mills Ind Est
  SS13 . . . . 121 C1
Burnt Mills Rd SS13 . . . . 121 C1
Burnt Oak Lo SS9 . . . . . . 146 A2
Burntwood CM14 . . . . 116 C7
Burntwood Ave RM11 . . . . 136 E5
Burntwood Cl
  Billericay CM12 . . . . 96 F2
  West Horndon CM13 . . . 139 D5
Burnway RM11 . . . . 136 E4
Burr Cl SS16 . . . . 140 E5
Burrow Cl IG7 . . . . 111 F5
Burrow Gn IG7 . . . . 111 F5
Burrow Rd IG7 . . . . 112 A5
Burrows Chase EN9 . . . . . 65 D4
Burrows Ho CM15 . . . . 71 F1
Burrows Way SS6 . . . . . . 123 C1
Burr's Way SS17 . . . . 161 B3
Burrswood Pl CM9 . . . . . . 37 E3
Burses Way SS15 . . . . 95 C2
Burslem Ave IG6 . . . . 112 A4
Burstead Dr CM11 . . . . . . 119 D7
Burstead Grange
  CM11 . . . . 119 D6
Burton Cl SS17 . . . . 160 F5
Burton Dr EN3 . . . . 65 A2
Burton Pl CM2 . . . . 32 F4
Burton Rd
  Loughton IG10 . . . . 89 C5
  Wanstead E18 . . . . . . 132 B8
Burtons Mill CM21 . . . . 1 F3
Burwell Ave SS8 . . . . 163 F5
Burwood Ct CM2 . . . . 32 C1
Burwood Gdns RM13 . . . . 154 F2
Bury Farm Cotts
  RM14 . . . . 138 E2
Bury Farm La CM11 . . . . . 120 D3
Bury La
  Epping CM16 . . . . 45 D2
  Great Waltham CM3 . . . 18 D8
Bury Rd
  Chingford E4 . . . . 87 E4
  Dagenham RM10 . . . . . 154 C7
  Epping CM16 . . . . 67 E8
  Harlow CM17 . . . . 11 D4
Buryside IG3 . . . . 133 F7
Bush Cl IG2 . . . . 133 D6
Bush Elms Rd RM11 . . . . . 136 A4
Bushey Cl
  Chingford E4 . . . . 109 C7
  South Woodham Ferrers
  CM3 . . . . 101 E7
Bushey Croft CM18 . . . . . 23 E7
BUSH FAIR 24 A6
Bush Fair CM18 . . . . 23 F6
Bushfields IG10 . . . . 89 A4
Bushgrove Rd RM8 . . . . . 134 D1
Bush Hall Rd CM12 . . . . . . 97 C5
Bush Ho CM18 . . . . 23 F6
Bush Rd
  Wanstead E11 . . . . . . 132 A4
  Woodford IG9 . . . . 110 D6
Bushway RM8 . . . . 134 D1
Bushwood E11 . . . . 132 A3
Bushy Lea CM5 . . . . 49 A2
Bushy Mead SS15 . . . . . . 141 B8
Business Ctr The
  RM3 . . . . 114 D3
Bute Rd IG6 . . . . 133 B6
Butler Ct 2 RM8 . . . . 135 A2
Butler Ho RM17 . . . . 178 B8
Butler Rd RM8 . . . . 153 B8
Butlers Cl CM1 . . . . 19 B2
Butlers Dr E4 . . . . 65 C1
Butlers Gr SS16 . . . . 141 B3
Butler Wlk RM17 . . . . 173 C2
Buttell Cl RM17 . . . . 173 D1
Butterbur Chase CM3 . . . . 101 C6
Buttercup Cl
  Billericay CM12 . . . . 97 A3
  Romford RM3 . . . . 114 D2
Buttercup Way CM0 . . . . . 84 C3
Butterfield Rd CM3 . . . . . . 33 E8

Butteridges Cl RM9 . . . . . 153 F4
Buttersweet Rise CM21 . . . 1 E1
Butterworth Gdns
  IG8 . . . . 110 A5
Butterys SS1 . . . . 167 E8
Buttfield Cl RM10 . . . . . . 154 B6
Butt La 37 A3
Button Rd RM17 . . . . 172 F2
Button's Hill CM3 . . . . 83 B4
Buttsbury CM4 . . . . 74 E1
Buttsbury Inf Sch
  CM12 . . . . 97 B5
Buttsbury Jun Sch The
  CM12 . . . . 97 B5
Buttsbury Rd IG1 . . . . . . 152 C7
Buttsbury Terr CM4 . . . . . 75 D1
Butts Green Rd RM11 . . . . 136 D5
Butt's Green Rd CM2 . . . . . 55 F3
Butts La
  Danbury CM3 . . . . 56 F7
  Stanford-le-H SS17 . . . 175 C8
Butts Paddock SS4 . . . . . 104 D2
Butts Rd SS17 . . . . 160 C5
Butts Way CM2 . . . . 53 E3
Buxton Ave SS9 . . . . 146 A3
Buxton Cl
  Southend-on-S SS9 . . . 146 A3
  Woodford IG8 . . . . 110 D4
Buxton Link SS15 . . . . . . 140 E6
Buxton Lo E11 . . . . 132 B2
Buxton Rd
  Chingford E4 . . . . 87 D2
  Grays RM16 . . . . 173 E4
  Ilford IG2 . . . . 133 E5
  Theydon Bois CM16 . . . . 67 E3
  Waltham Abbey EN9 . . . 66 A6
Buxton Sq SS9 . . . . 146 A3
Buyl Ave SS8 . . . . 164 B5
Byfield SS9 . . . . 146 F7
Byfield Ct CM13 . . . . 139 C5
Byfletts SS16 . . . . 142 F4
Byford Rd SS6 . . . . 123 E3
Bynghams CM19 . . . . 22 F6
By-Pass Rd SS17 . . . . . . 160 A2
Byrd Ct SS15 . . . . 141 C8
Byrd Mead CM15 . . . . 72 A6
Byrd Way SS17 . . . . 160 C3
Byrne Dr SS2 . . . . 147 E5
Byron Ave
  Southend-on-S SS2 . . . 148 B2
  Woodford E18 . . . . 109 F1
Byron Cl SS8 . . . . 164 C4
Byron Ct
  Basildon SS15 . . . . . . 141 B6
  11 Wanstead E11 . . . . 132 A4
  Woodford E18 . . . . 110 B2
Byron Gdns RM18 . . . . . . 179 C6
Byron Mans RM14 . . . . . . 137 C1
Byron Rd
  Brentwood CM13 . . . . . 95 D3
  Chelmsford CM2 . . . . . . 32 D2
  Dartford DA1 . . . . 176 B3
Byrons Ho CM16 . . . . 68 A8
Byron Way RM13 . . . . 114 C2
Byron Wks SS11 . . . . 121 F7
Bysouth Cl IG5 . . . . 111 B2
Bywater Rd CM3 . . . . 101 C6

C

Cabborns Cres SS17 . . . . 175 D8
Cabinet Way SS9 . . . . . . 146 C6
Cables Cl DA8 . . . . 169 C3
Cadiz Ct RM10 . . . . 154 D5
Cadiz Rd RM10 . . . . 154 C6
Cadmore La EN8 . . . . 43 A4
Cadogan Ave CM13 . . . . . 139 D5
Cadogan Gdns E18 . . . . . 132 B8
Cadogan Ho 17 IG8 . . . . . 111 A3
Cadogan Terr SS13 . . . . . 143 C7
Caernarvon Cl
  Hockley SS5 . . . . 124 D6
  Hornchurch RM11 . . . . 137 A3
Caernarvon Dr IG5 . . . . . . 111 A2
Cage End CM22 . . . . 3 F5
Cage End CM22 . . . . 3 F5
Cage Field Cotts SS4 . . . . 126 D4
Cagefield Rd SS4 . . . . . . 126 E4
Caidge Row CM0 . . . . 42 A2
Cairns Ave IG8 . . . . 110 F4
Caister Dr SS13 . . . . 143 B6
Caladonia La 9 SS12 . . . . 121 E5
Calbourne Ave RM12 . . . . 155 B7
Calcott Cl CM14 . . . . 94 B1
Calcroft Ave DA9 . . . . . . 177 B2
Calcutta Rd RM18 . . . . . . 178 F5
Caldbeck EN9 . . . . 65 D5
Calder RM18 . . . . 175 C2
Calder Ct 1 RM1 . . . . . . 135 D7
Caldwell Rd SS17 . . . . . . 160 B1
Caldy Rd DA17 . . . . 169 B3
Caledonia Cl 1 IG3 . . . . 134 B3
Caledon Rd E6 . . . . 152 A5
Calgary Ct RM7 . . . . 135 B7
Callan Gr RM15 . . . . 172 B6
Callow Ho RM13 . . . . 154 D2
Callowood Croft CM3 . . . . 58 D1
Calmore Cl RM12 . . . . . . 155 C7
Calmpatch 9 CM0 . . . . . . 106 C4
Calne Ave IG5 . . . . 111 B2
Calshot Ave RM16 . . . . . . 172 F4
Calshot Ct 28 DA2 . . . . . 176 B1
Calverley Cres RM10 . . . . 154 D5
Calvert Cl DA17 . . . . 169 B2
Calvert Dr SS13 . . . . 121 C1

Calverton Rd E6 . . . . 152 A4
Calvina Cl SS15 . . . . 119 F2
Cambell Jun & Inf Schs
  RM9 . . . . 153 D5
Cambeys Rd RM10 . . . . . 154 C7
Camborne Ave RM3 . . . . . 114 E3
Camborne Cl CM1 . . . . 32 E5
Camborne Way RM3 . . . . . 114 E3
Cambria SS8 . . . . 163 C3
Cambridge Ave RM2 . . . . 136 C8
Cambridge Cl
  Basildon SS16 . . . . . . 140 F5
  Stock CM4 . . . . 75 D2
Cambridge Ct SS1 . . . . . 166 F7
Cambridge Gdns
  Grays RM16 . . . . 174 B2
  Rochford SS4 . . . . 125 C5
Cambridge Ho
  Barking IG11 . . . . 152 C5
  Harlow CM17 . . . . 11 C5
Cambridge Park Rd
  E11 . . . . 132 A4
Cambridge Pk E11 . . . . . . 132 A5
Cambridge Rd
  Barking IG11 . . . . 152 C5
  Canvey Island SS8 . . . 163 F3
  3 Chingford E4 . . . . . . 87 D1
  Harlow CM20 . . . . 11 C6
  Ilford IG3 . . . . 133 E3
  Sawbridgeworth CM21 . . . 1 E4
  Southend-on-S SS1 . . . 166 F7
  Wanstead E11 . . . . . . 132 A4
CAMBRIDGE TOWN 168 C6
Camden Cl RM16 . . . . . . 174 B2
Camden Ct 10 DA17 . . . . 169 A1
Camden Rd
  Grays RM16 . . . . 172 F3
  Wanstead E11 . . . . . . 132 A4
Camelford Ho 1 RM3 . . . . 114 E6
Camelia Ct IG8 . . . . 109 E4
Camellia Cl
  2 Chelmsford CM1 . . . . 32 F6
  Romford RM3 . . . . 114 E2
Camelot Cl SS13 . . . . 31 F5
Camelot Gdns SS13 . . . . 143 C8
Cameron Cl
  Brentwood CM14 . . . . . 116 D6
  Ingatestone CM4 . . . . . 74 B3
  Southend-on-S SS9 . . . 146 C2
  Stanford-le-H SS17 . . . 160 E6
Cameron Pl SS12 . . . . . . 121 E5
Cameron Rd IG3 . . . . 133 E3
Cam Gn RM15 . . . . 172 B7
Camms Terr RM10 . . . . . . 154 C7
Camomile Dr SS11 . . . . . 121 E8
Camomile Rd RM7 . . . . . . 135 D2
Campbell Ave IG6 . . . . . . 133 C9
Campbell Cl
  Chelmsford CM2 . . . . . . 54 A7
  Harlow CM17 . . . . 24 B7
  Romford RM1 . . . . 113 E4
  4 Wickford SS12 . . . . 121 D5
Campden Cres RM8 . . . . . 153 C8
Campden Way RM8 . . . . . 153 B8
Camperdown Rd SS8 . . . . 164 C5
Camper Rd SS1 . . . . 167 D6
Campfield Rd SS3 . . . . . . 168 E6
Campion Cl RM7 . . . . 135 D2
Campion Ct CM17 . . . . . . 178 D8
Campion Gdns IG8 . . . . . 110 A5
Campions
  Epping CM16 . . . . 46 A3
  Harlow CM17 . . . . 11 F5
  Loughton IG10 . . . . 67 A1
Campion Sch The
  RM11 . . . . 136 F7
Campions The SS1 . . . . . 168 C8
Cample La RM15 . . . . . . 172 A6
Campsey Gdns RM9 . . . . . 153 B5
Campsey Rd RM9 . . . . . . 153 B5
Canal Basin DA12 . . . . . . 179 D1
Canal Rd DA12 . . . . 179 D1
Canal Road Ind Pk
  DA12 . . . . 179 D1
Canberra Cl
  Chelmsford CM1 . . . . . . 31 E5
  Dagenham RM10 . . . . . 154 D5
  Hornchurch RM12 . . . . 155 C8
Canberra Cres RM10 . . . . 154 D5
Canberra Sq RM18 . . . . . 179 A5
Can Bridge Way CM2 . . . . 32 C1
Cander Way RM15 . . . . . . 172 B6
Candlemakers The
  SS2 . . . . 148 A5
Candover Rd RM12 . . . . . 136 B3
Candy Terr 12 SS1 . . . . . 167 C7
Candytuft Rd CM1 . . . . . . 32 F6
Cane Hill RM3 . . . . 114 D1
Caneland Ct EN9 . . . . 65 F5
Canes La CM17 . . . . 24 E1
CANEWDON 104 E1
Canewdon CE Prim Sch
  SS4 . . . . 104 E1
Canewdon Cl SS11 . . . . . 99 D2
Canewdon Gdns SS11 . . . 99 D2
Canewdon Hall Cl
  SS4 . . . . 104 D2
Canewdon Rd
  Rochford SS4 . . . . 125 D8
  Southend-on-S SS0 . . . 166 D8
Canewdon View Rd
  SS4 . . . . 125 D6
Canfield Rd
  High Roding CM6 . . . . . . 5 E8
  Rainham RM13 . . . . . . 154 F4
  Woodford IG8 . . . . 110 E3
Canford Ave SS12 . . . . . . 120 F8

Canford Cl CM2 . . . . 54 E7
Canna Gdns SS12 . . . . . . 121 F5
Canney Rd CM0 . . . . 61 D4
Cannington Rd RM9 . . . . . 153 C6
Cannon Leys CM2 . . . . . . 54 D3
Cannon Mews 1 EN9 . . . . 65 B6
CANNON'S GREEN 27 E1
Cannons La
  Fyfield CM5 . . . . 27 E1
  Hatfield Broad Oak CM22 . 3 F5
Cannons Mead CM15 . . . . 72 A6
Cannons Villas CM22 . . . . . 3 F5
Canon Ave RM6 . . . . 134 C6
Canon Cl SS17 . . . . 160 F2
Canon Ct SS13 . . . . 121 A4
Canon Palmer RC High
  Sch IG3 . . . . 133 E3
Canons Brook CM19 . . . . . 23 B8
Canons Cl CM3 . . . . 56 E1
Canons Gate CM20 . . . . . 10 A2
Canonsleigh Cres
  SS9 . . . . 146 A5
Canonsleigh Rd RM9 . . . . 153 B5
Canopy La CM17 . . . . 11 C1
Canterbury Ave
  Redbridge IG1 . . . . . . 132 E4
  Southend-on-S SS2 . . . 148 A5
  Upminster RM14 . . . . . 137 F2
Canterbury Cl
  8 Basildon SS14 . . . . 142 F8
  Chigwell IG7 . . . . 111 F7
  Rayleigh SS6 . . . . 123 C5
Canterbury Ct CM15 . . . . . 93 F4
Canterbury Ho 2
  IG11 . . . . 153 A5
Canterbury Par RM15 . . . . 157 C2
Canterbury Pl RM17 . . . . 173 D1
Canterbury Way
  Brentwood CM13 . . . . . 116 C4
  Chelmsford CM1 . . . . . . 31 E4
  Dartford DA2 . . . . 176 D2
Canters The SS7 . . . . 145 B5
Cantley Gdns IG2 . . . . . . 133 C6
Canuden Rd CM1 . . . . . . 31 E2
Canute Cl SS4 . . . . 104 C2
Canvey Heights Ctry Pk★
  SS8 . . . . 164 C1
Canvey Inf Sch SS8 . . . . 163 F3
CANVEY ISLAND 164 E4
Canvey Jun Sch SS8 . . . . 163 F3
Canvey Rd
  Basildon SS13 . . . . . . 143 B6
  Canvey Island SS8 . . . 163 D6
  Southend-on-S SS9 . . . 146 B1
CANVEY VILLAGE 163 C2
Canvey Way SS7 . . . . . . 144 A3
Canvey Wlk CM1 . . . . 32 E6
Capability Way DA9 . . . . . 177 C3
Capadocia St SS1 . . . . . . 167 E6
Cape Cl IG11 . . . . 152 B5
Capel Cl
  Chelmsford CM1 . . . . . . 32 B7
  Stanford-le-H SS17 . . . 160 E2
Capel Gdns IG3 . . . . 152 F8
Capelston SS15 . . . . 141 F6
Capel Terr SS1 . . . . 167 A4
Capital Ind Est DA17 . . . . 169 B3
Capital Pl CM19 . . . . 23 A7
Capital Trad Est IG11 . . . . 153 A4
Capitol Ind Ctr 5
  SS11 . . . . 122 A5
Capon Cl CM14 . . . . 94 B1
Capons La CM3 . . . . 57 A5
Cappell La SG12 . . . . 8 D5
Capricorn Ctr
  Basildon SS14 . . . . . . 120 F1
  Dagenham RM8 . . . . . 134 F4
Capstan Cl RM6 . . . . 134 B5
Capstan Ct DA2 . . . . 176 C3
Capstan Ctr RM18 . . . . . 178 D7
Capstan Dr 9 RM13 . . . . 155 A1
Caravan Site The
  RM15 . . . . 171 D3
Caravel Ct RM16 . . . . . . 172 F3
Carbis Cl E4 . . . . 87 D1
Carbury Ct RM12 . . . . . . 155 C6
Cardamom Ct 1 E12 . . . . 152 A4
Cardigan Ave SS0 . . . . . . 147 C3
Cardigan Gdns IG3 . . . . . 134 A2
Cardigan Ho 4 RM3 . . . . 114 D5
Cardinal Dr IG6 . . . . 111 C4
Cardinal Rd RM16 . . . . . . 172 E4
Cardinal Way RM13 . . . . . 155 D3
Card's Rd CM2 . . . . 55 C6
Carew Cl RM16 . . . . 172 E3
Carew Ct 3 RM6 . . . . . . 134 B5
Carey Ho SS0 . . . . 166 E8
Carey Rd RM9 . . . . 153 E8
Carfax Rd RM12 . . . . 154 F8
Carisbrooke Cl
  Basildon SS13 . . . . . . 143 B6
  Hornchurch RM11 . . . . 137 A3
Carisbrooke Ct 20
  DA2 . . . . 176 B1
Carisbrooke Dr
  Corringham SS17 . . . . 161 B3
  South Woodham Ferrers
  CM3 . . . . 101 C7
Carisbrooke Rd SS0 . . . . 147 E1
Carisbrook Lo SS6 . . . . . 123 C1
Carisbrook Rd CM15 . . . . 94 B3
Carl Ho CM18 . . . . 23 E3
Carlina Gdns IG8 . . . . . . 110 B5
Carlingford Dr SS0 . . . . . 147 C3
Carlisle Gdns IG1 . . . . . . 132 E5
Carlisle Ho IG1 . . . . 132 E5
Carlisle Rd
  Dartford DA1 . . . . 176 A1

Car–Cha 191

Carlisle Rd *continued*
Romford RM1 136 A6
Carlisle Way SS13 143 B6
Carlton Ave
Greenhithe DA9 176 E1
Southend-on-S SS0 147 C4
Carlton Cl RM14 137 B2
Carlton Ct
Ilford IG6 133 D8
Southend-on-S SS2 148 A1
Carlton Dr
Hadleigh SS7 145 C4
Ilford IG6 133 D8
Southend-on-S SS9 146 F1
Carlton Ho [4] IG10 88 D4
Carlton Rd
Basildon SS13 143 E8
Grays RM16 173 F3
Romford RM2 136 A7
Wickford SS13 99 C2
Carlton Terr E11 132 B6
Carlton Villas SS2 148 A1
Carlyle Gdns
Billericay CM12 96 F5
Wickford SS12 121 E5
Carmania Cl SS3 149 F1
Carmelite Way CM9 36 F2
Carnach Gn RM15 172 B6
Carnanton Rd E17 109 D2
Carnarvon Rd
Southend-on-S SS2 147 F1
Woodford E18 109 F2
Carnation Cl
Chelmsford CM1 32 F5
Romford RM7 135 E2
Carnegie Cl EN3 65 B1
Carne Rasch Ct [2]
SS14 142 F5
Carnforth Gdns RM12 155 A7
Carnforth Ho [2] RM3 114 F4
Carnival Cl SS14 120 B1
Carnival Gdns SS9 146 D4
Carol Cl SS15 141 D7
Carol Ct SS15 141 D7
Caroline's Cl SS2 147 E5
Carolyn Ho IG3 134 A3
Caro Rd SS8 164 C3
Carousel Stps [8] SS1 167 C7
Carpenter Cl CM12 96 F3
Carpenter Path CM13 95 D4
Carpenters Arms La
CM16 46 C6
Carpenters Cl SS3 149 E6
Carpenters Ct [10]
RM10 154 B6
Carrack Ho DA8 169 E1
Carriage Dr CM1 32 E7
Carriage Mews IG1 133 C2
Carrick Dr IG6 111 C2
Carrington Rd DA1 176 A1
Carroll Gdns [7] SS12 121 D6
Carroll Hill IG10 88 F6
Carron Mead CM3 101 F6
Carrow Rd RM9 153 B5
Carr Rd E17 109 A1
Carruthers Cl SS11 99 D1
Carruthers Dr SS11 99 D1
Carsey Cl CM11 98 C4
Carson Rd CM11 97 D5
Carstone Pl CM1 31 F2
Carswell Cl
Brentwood CM13 95 D3
Redbridge IG4 132 D7
Carswell Gdns SS12 121 D5
Cartel Cl RM19 171 D2
Carte Pl SS16 141 A5
Carter Cl RM5 113 B3
Carter Dr RM5 113 B4
Cartersfield Rd EN9 65 C5
CARTER'S GREEN 12 E2
Carters La CM16 45 B7
Carters Mead CM17 24 C6
Carthagena Est EN9 21 C3
Cart La
Chingford E4 87 E1
Grays RM17 173 B1
Cartlodge Ave SS11 121 E8
Cartwright Rd
Dagenham RM9 153 F5
South Benfleet SS7 144 D7
Cartwright Wlk CM2 32 F2
Carvers Wood CM11 119 C7
Cascade Cl IG9 110 D8
Cascade Rd IG9 110 D8
Cascades [11] SS1 167 C7
Casey La CM0 63 E4
Cashiobury Terr SS1 166 F7
Cashmere Way SS16 142 D2
Caspian Cl RM19 171 A1
Caspian Way
Purfleet RM19 171 A1
Swanscombe DA10 177 E2
Cassel Ave SS8 164 C5
Cassell Cl RM16 174 A8
Cassino Rd CM1 31 E6
Cassis Ct IG10 89 C5
Castellan Ave RM2 136 B8
Castell Rd IG10 89 C8
Castle Ave
Chingford E4 109 D5
Hadleigh SS7 145 D1
Rainham RM13 154 E5
Castle Bank SS6 123 C2
Castle Cl
Hoddesdon EN11 8 C1
Rayleigh SS6 123 D2
Romford RM3 114 C7
Southend-on-S SS3 168 G8
Castle Cotts RM14 157 C6
Castle Ct
Dagenham RM9 153 E4
Hadleigh SS7 145 E2
Rayleigh SS8 123 C1
Castledon Rd CM11,
SS12 99 A2
Castledon Sch SS12 121 B5
Castle Dr
Rayleigh SS6 123 C3
Redbridge IG4 132 E5
Southend-on-S SS9 165 B8
CASTLE GREEN 153 C4
Castle Ho [3] E4 109 D5
Castle Hts RM9 153 B4
Castle La SS7 145 D1
Castle Mews SS6 123 C1
Castle Point Transport
Mus★ SS8 164 E3
Castle Rd
Dagenham RM9 153 B4
Grays RM17 177 F8
Hadleigh SS7 145 E2
Hoddesdon EN11 8 C1
Rayleigh SS6 123 D1
Swanscombe DA10 177 F1
Castle St
Chipping Ongar CM5 49 A2
Greenhithe DA9 177 A2
Swanscombe DA10 177 F1
Castle Terr SS6 123 C2
Castleton Rd
Chingford E17 109 D1
Ilford IG3 134 B3
Southend-on-S SS2 148 E1
Castleview Gdns IG1 132 F5
Castle View Rd SS8 164 A6
Castle View Sch SS8 164 B6
Castle Wlk
[11] Basildon SS13 143 C6
Canvey Island SS8 164 A5
Caswell Cl SS17 161 A3
Caswell Mews CM2 32 F2
Catalina Ave RM16 172 F4
Catalin Ct EN9 65 D6
Catcher Ct CM4 74 A2
Caterham Ave IG5 111 A1
Caterham Ct EN9 65 F5
Caterham High Sch
IG5 110 F1
Cater Mus The★ CM12 97 A2
Cater Wood CM12 97 B3
Catharine Cl RM16 172 F4
Cathedral CE Prim Sch
The CM1 32 C3
Cathedral Dr SS15 141 C7
Cathedral Pl CM14,
CM15 116 D8
Cathedral Wlk CM1 32 B3
Catherine Cl
East Hanningfield CM3 78 B7
Pilgrims Hatch CM15 94 A4
Catherine Ct [1] IG2 133 C5
Catherine Godfrey Ho
RM9 153 F4
Catherine Lo
[4] Southend-on-S
SS2 147 F1
Woodford E18 110 C2
Catherine Rd
Romford RM2 136 B6
South Benfleet SS7 144 E4
Cathrow Mews [3] EN11 8 A1
Catiline Ct RM2 136 A8
Cattawade End SS14 142 D7
Cattawade Link SS14 142 D7
Caulfield Rd
Southend-on-S SS3 168 D7
Wallend E6 152 A5
Causeway Cotts CM1 52 E8
Causeway The
Edney Common CM1 52 D7
Great Baddow CM2 54 F7
Maldon CM9 37 A4
Ulting CM9 35 D5
Causton Sq RM10 154 A5
Causton Way SS6 123 D4
Cautherly La SG12 8 A5
Cavalier Cl RM6 134 D7
Cavell Cres
Dartford DA1 176 B3
Romford RM3 114 E1
Cavell Rd CM11 97 C1
Cavendish Ave
Hornchurch RM12 155 B6
Woodford IG8 110 B3
Cavendish Cres RM12 155 B6
Cavendish Ct E4 87 E2
Cavendish Gdns
Aveley RM15 171 C4
Barking IG11 152 F7
Chelmsford CM2 32 E3
Dagenham RM6 134 E6
Ilford IG1 133 A3
Southend-on-S SS0 147 B2
Cavendish Rd
Chingford E4 109 C4
Hockley SS5 103 A1
Rochford SS5 103 A1
Cavendish Way SS15 119 D1
Cavenham Gdns
Hornchurch RM11 136 C6
Ilford IG1 133 D1
Caversham Ave SS3 149 E2
Caversham Park Ave
SS6 123 C4
Cawdor Ave RM15 172 B6
Cawdor Ho CM14 116 D6
Cawkwell Cl CM2 33 A4
Cawley Hatch CM19 22 F8
Caxton Rd EN11 8 B2
Caxton Way RM1 135 E7
Cazenove Rd E17 109 A2
Cecil Ave
Barking IG11 152 D5
Grays RM16 172 F4
Hornchurch RM11 136 E8
Cecil Ct
Harlow CM18 23 C5
Southend-on-S SS2 147 E3
Cecil Ho E17 109 A2
Cecil Jones Coll (Lower
Sch) SS2 148 B3
Cecil Jones Coll (Upper
Sch) SS2 148 D3
Cecil Rd
Chingford E17 109 A2
Dagenham RM6 134 D4
Hoddesdon EN11 21 C8
Ilford IG1 152 B8
Cecil Way SS6 123 F2
Cedar Ave
Chelmsford CM1 32 A3
Dagenham RM6 134 E6
Upminster RM14 156 A8
Wickford SS12 121 D5
Cedar Ave W CM1 32 A3
Cedar Chase CM9 37 C5
Cedar Cl
Brentwood CM13 95 D2
Buckhurst Hill IG9 110 D8
Rayleigh SS6 123 F1
Romford RM7 135 C7
Sawbridgeworth CM21 1 E1
Southend-on-S SS2 148 A2
Cedar Ct
Epping CM16 68 A8
Southend-on-S SS3 168 E7
[6] Wanstead E11 132 B6
[5] Woodford E18 110 A2
Cedar Dr
Hullbridge SS5 101 E2
Loughton IG10 89 B7
Cedar Gdns RM14 137 C1
Cedar Gn EN11 21 A5
Cedar Gr CM0 106 B6
Cedar Hall Gdns SS7 145 A6
Cedar Hall Sch SS7 145 B6
Cedar Mews SS5 124 C6
Cedar Park Cl SS7 145 A6
Cedar Park Gdns
RM6 134 D4
Cedar Pk IG7 111 A5
Cedar Rd
Brentwood CM13 95 D3
Canvey Island SS8 163 F4
Grays RM16 174 B3
Hornchurch RM12 136 C1
Romford RM7 135 C7
Thundersley SS7 145 A6
Cedar Rise RM15 157 D1
Cedars
Stanford-le-H SS17 160 E2
Waltham Abbey EN9 66 C4
Cedars The
Buckhurst Hill IG9 88 A1
Great Wakering SS3 150 B4
South Woodham Ferrers
CM3 101 D8
Cedar Terr [9] RM8 134 D4
Cedar Wlk
Canewdon SS4 104 D1
Waltham Abbey EN9 65 D5
Cedarwood Ct CM18 23 F6
Cedric Ave RM1 135 E8
Celandine Cl
Billericay CM12 96 F4
South Ockendon RM15 157 C1
Celandine Ct E4 109 B7
Celeborn St CM3 101 B6
Celedon Cl RM16 172 E4
Cement Block Cotts [10]
RM17 178 C8
Centaur Way CM9 59 A8
Central Ave
Althorne CM3 82 E2
Aveley RM15 171 C4
Basildon SS16 140 E4
Billericay CM12 97 C6
Canvey Island SS8 163 F5
Corringham SS17 161 A3
Grays RM20 171 F1
Hadleigh SS7 145 E5
Hullbridge SS5 101 F1
Hullbridge, Tower Park
SS5 101 E4
Rochford SS4 125 D5
Southend-on-S SS2 148 C1
Stanford-le-H SS17 160 E4
Tilbury RM18 179 A6
Central Cl SS7 145 E4
Central Ct [11] IG7 111 E5
Central Dr RM12 136 E1
Central Ho CM5 49 A3
Central Par IG2 133 D5
Central Park Ave
RM10 135 C1
Central Rd
Harlow CM20 11 A4
Stanford-le-H SS17 160 D1
Central Sq [7] CM1 32 B2
Central Wall SS8 164 A6
Central Wall Cotts
SS8 164 B5
Central Wall Rd SS8 164 B5
Centre Ave CM16 67 F7
Centre Dr CM16 67 F7
Centre Gn CM16 67 F7
Centre Pl [10] SS1 167 C7
Centre Rd
Dagenham RM10 154 B3
Wanstead E11 132 A2
Centre Reach SS2 148 A1
Centreway [4] IG1 133 C2
Centric Par IG10 88 E5
Centurion Cl SS3 168 F8
Centurion Ct RM1 135 D8
Centurion Lo [7]
RM10 154 B6
Centurion Way
Belvedere DA18 169 A3
Purfleet RM19 170 F2
Centurion Works
RM13 154 E2
Century Rd EN11 21 A7
Ceylon Rd SS0 166 D8
Chadacre Ave
Redbridge IG5 132 F8
Woodford IG5 110 F1
Chadacre Rd SS1 149 B1
Chadfields RM18 179 A7
Chadview Ct [2] RM6 134 D4
Chadville Gdns RM6 134 D6
Chadway RM8 134 C3
Chadwell Ave RM6 134 B4
Chadwell By-Pass
RM16 174 A1
CHADWELL HEATH 134 D5
Chadwell Heath
Foundation Sch The
RM6 134 B5
Chadwell Heath Ind Pk
RM8 134 D3
Chadwell Heath La
RM6 134 C5
Chadwell Heath Sta
RM6 134 D4
Chadwell Hill RM16 174 B1
Chadwell Prim Sch
RM6 134 C4
Chadwell Rd RM16,
RM17 173 D2
CHADWELL ST MARY
174 B1
Chadwell St Mary Prim
Sch RM16 174 B2
Chadwick Ave E4 109 D6
Chadwick Dr RM3 114 D1
Chadwick Rd
Ilford IG1 133 B1
Southend-on-S SS0 166 C8
South Woodham Ferrers
CM3 79 E1
Chaffinch Cl SS3 168 E8
Chaffinch Cres CM11 97 C1
Chafford CM14 94 B1
Chafford Gdns CM13 139 D5
Chafford Gorges Nature
Pk★ RM15 172 D3
CHAFFORD HUNDRED
172 E3
Chafford Hundred Bsns &
Ent Coll RM16 172 C1
Chafford Hundred Prim
Sch RM16 172 C1
Chafford Hundred Sta
RM16 172 B2
Chafford Sch The
RM13 170 C8
Chafford Way
Grays RM16 173 B5
Ilford RM6 134 C7
Chafford Wlk RM13 155 C3
Chaingate Ave SS2 148 E2
Chale Ct SS17 175 C8
Chalfont Cl SS9 146 D4
Chalfont Ct [3] DA17 169 A1
Chalford Ct IG2 133 B6
Chalforde Gdns RM2 136 B7
Chalford Wlk IG8 110 D3
Chalgrove Cres IG5 110 E1
Chalice Cl SS14 142 E6
Chalice Way DA9 176 F2
Chalk Ct RM17 178 A8
CHALK END 16 E2
Chalk End SS13 143 A7
Chalk La CM17 12 A2
Chalklands CM2 55 D3
Chalk Rd SS8 164 A6
Chalks Ave CM21 1 D3
Chalk St CM3 99 F7
Chalk Villas CM6 15 C7
CHALKWELL 166 B8
Chalkwell Ave SS0 166 B8
Chalkwell Bay Flats
SS9 166 A8
Chalkwell Espl SS0 166 B7
Chalkwell Hall Jun & Inf
Schs SS0 147 A1
Chalkwell Lo SS0 147 C1
Chalkwell Park Dr
SS9 146 F1
Chalkwell Sta SS9 166 A8
Challacombe SS1 149 C1
Challacombe Cl CM13 95 C1
Challinor CM17 24 E8
Challock Lees SS13 143 C5
CHALVEDON 143 B6
Chalvedon Ave SS13 143 B7
Chalvedon Sch SS13 143 B6
Chalvedon Sq [3]
SS13 143 A6
Chamberlain Ave
Canvey Island SS8 164 C4
Chamberlain Ave *continued*
Corringham SS17 161 A4
Chamberlain Cl
Harlow CM17 24 C8
Ilford IG1 133 C1
Chamberlains Ride
CM3 101 D6
Chambers Cl DA9 177 A2
Champion Cl
Stanford-le-H SS17 160 E3
Wickford SS12 121 D6
Champion Rd RM14 137 B2
Champions Gn EN11 8 A1
Champions Way
Hoddesdon EN11 8 A1
South Woodham Ferrers
CM3 101 C8
Champlain Ave SS8 163 F5
Champness Rd IG11 152 F5
Chance Cl RM16 172 F3
Chancel Cl
Basildon SS15 141 C7
South Benfleet SS7 144 C6
Tillingham CM0 63 E4
Chancellor Ave CM2 33 B4
Chancellor Rd SS1 167 B7
Chancery Pl CM1 31 B1
Chandler Rd IG10 89 B8
Chandlers CM0 106 A6
Chandlers Chase CM12 97 A2
Chandlers Cnr RM13 155 C1
Chandlers Dr DA8 169 E2
Chandlers Mews DA9 177 C3
Chandlers Quay CM9 37 A3
Chandlers Way
Romford RM1 135 E6
Southend-on-S SS2 148 A5
South Woodham Ferrers
CM3 101 E7
Chandlers Wlk CM15 71 E2
Chandos Ave E17 109 A1
Chandos Cl IG9 110 B8
Chandos Par SS7 146 A3
Chanlock Path RM15 172 B6
Channing Cl RM11 136 F4
Chanton Cl SS9 146 D7
Chantress Cl RM10 154 C4
Chantreywood CM13 117 B7
Chantry Cres SS17 160 C1
Chantry Ct [10] DA12 179 C1
Chantry Dr CM4 74 B3
Chantry Heritage Ctr★
DA12 179 C1
Chantry Ho RM13 154 D3
Chantry La SS15 141 C7
Chantry Prim Sch
DA12 179 C1
Chantry The
[3] Chingford E4 87 C1
Harlow CM20 11 A2
Chantry Way
Billericay CM11 97 B2
Rainham RM13 154 D3
Chapel Ave E12 132 D1
Chapel Cl RM20 177 B8
Chapel Croft CM4 74 B4
Chapel Ct
Billericay CM12 97 B2
Swanscombe DA10 177 E1
Chapel Dr CM3 19 B6
Chapel End EN11 21 A5
Chapel End Ho E17 109 B2
Chapel End Inf Sch
E17 109 B1
Chapel End Jun Sch
E17 109 B2
Chapelfields SG12 8 D4
Chapel Fields CM17 24 C6
Chapel High CM14 116 C8
Chapel La
Chigwell IG7 111 F7
[5] Dagenham RM6 134 D4
Great Wakering SS3 150 B4
Hadleigh SS7 145 C3
Harlow CM17 24 C6
Heybridge Basin CM9 37 E2
Little Baddow CM3 34 B3
Purleigh CM3 80 D8
Roxwell CM1 29 F1
Tillingham CM0 63 E4
Chapel Lo RM13 155 A1
Chapel Mews
Billericay CM12 97 B1
Chigwell IG8 111 A4
Chapel Pl SS3 168 F6
Chapel Rd
Burnham-on-C CM0 106 C4
Epping CM16 45 F1
Ilford IG1 133 B1
Southend-on-S SS3 168 F6
Chapel Row CM3 79 B5
Chapel St CM12 97 A2
Chapel Terr IG10 88 E5
Chapel The [5] RM11 136 B3
Chaplaincy Gdns
RM11 136 E3
Chaplemount Rd IG8 110 F4
Chaplin Cl
Basildon SS15 119 E1
Galleywood CM2 54 B2
Chaplin Rd RM9 153 E5
Chapman Ct SS8 163 C3
Chapman Rd
Belvedere DA17 169 B1
Canvey Island SS8 165 A3

Chapmans Cl SS9 . . . . 146 B1
Chapmans Wlk SS9 . . . . . . 146 B1
Charfleets Cl SS8 . . . . 163 D3
Charfleets Farm Ind Est
SS8 . . . . 163 D3
Charfleets Ho SS8 . . . . . . 163 C3
Charfleets Ind Est
SS8 . . . . 163 C3
Charfleets Rd SS8 . . . . . . 163 C3
Charfleets Service Rd
SS8 . . . . 163 D3
Charity Farm Chase
CM12 . . . . 96 F3
Charlbury Cl RM3 . . . . 114 C4
Charlbury Cres RM3 . . . . . 114 C4
Charlbury Gdns IG3 . . . . . 133 F2
Charlbury Ho
1 Ilford E12 . . . . 133 A1
8 Little Ilford E12 . . . . . 152 A8
Charlecote Rd RM8 . . . . . 134 E1
Charlemont Rd E6 . . . . . . 152 A2
Charles Church Wlk
IG1 . . . . 132 F5
Charles Cl SS0 . . . . 147 A5
Charles Ho
Billericay CM11 . . . . 97 B3
8 Hoddesdon EN11 . . . . 21 D8
Charles Rd
Dagenham RM10 . . . . 154 D6
Ilford RM6 . . . . 134 D5
Charles St
Epping CM16 . . . . 68 A7
Grays RM17 . . . . 178 C8
Greenhithe DA9 . . . . 177 A3
Greenhithe, Stone DA9 . . . 176 F2
Charleston Ave SS13 . . . . 121 C1
Charleston Ct SS13 . . . . . 121 C1
Charlotte Ave SS12 . . . . . 121 C7
Charlotte Cl IG6 . . . . 111 C2
Charlotte Ct
Hornchurch RM11 . . . . . . 136 D4
Ilford IG2 . . . . 133 A5
South Woodham Ferrers
CM3 . . . . 101 D6
Charlotte Gdns RM5 . . . . 113 B4
Charlotte Mews **5**
SS2 . . . . 147 F1
Charlotte Pl RM20 . . . . . . 177 B8
Charlotte Rd RM10 . . . . . 154 B6
Charlton Cl
Basildon SS13 . . . . 143 C7
Hoddesdon EN11 . . . . 21 A6
Charlton Cres IG11 . . . . . 152 F3
Charlton Mead La
EN11 . . . . 21 D5
Charlton St RM20 . . . . . . 177 D8
Charlton Way EN11 . . . . . 21 B6
Charnwood Ave CM1 . . . . 31 E1
Charnwood Dr E18 . . . . . . 132 B7
Charter Ave IG2 . . . . 133 D4
Charter Ho CM9 . . . . 37 A2
Charterhouse SS16 . . . . . 142 C5
Charterhouse Cotts
CM3 . . . . 80 F5
Charteris Rd IG8 . . . . 110 B4
Charter Rd The IG8 . . . . . 109 F4
Charters Cross CM18 . . . . 23 D5
Charters Ct SS11 . . . . 121 F8
Chartwell CI EN9 . . . . 65 E6
Chartwell Ct **2** IG8 . . . . 110 A3
Chartwell Pl RM1 . . . . 135 F7
Chartwell Sq **2** SS1 . . . . 167 A8
Chase Cl SS7 . . . . 144 F5
Chase Court Gdns
SS1 . . . . 167 C8
CHASE CROSS 113 D4
Chase Cross Rd RM5 . . . . 113 D3
Chase Ct SS1 . . . . 167 C8
Chase Dr CM3 . . . . 101 C8
Chase End
Basildon SS16 . . . . 142 F3
Rayleigh SS6 . . . . 123 F2
Chase Gdns
Chingford E4 . . . . 109 A6
Southend-on-S SS0 . . . . . 147 D3
Chase High Sch SS0 . . . . 147 C3
Chase House Gdns
RM11 . . . . 136 F6
Chase La
Chigwell IG7 . . . . 112 A7
Ilford IG6 . . . . 133 D6
Chase Nature Reserve
The★ RM7 . . . . 135 E1
Chase Rd
Brentwood CM14 . . . . 116 C7
Corringham SS17 . . . . 161 A2
Southend-on-S SS1 . . . . . 167 C8
Chaseside SS6 . . . . 145 E8
Chaseside Cl RM1 . . . . . . 113 E4
Chase Sq **4** DA11 . . . . . 179 B1
Chase The
Basildon, Langdon Hills
SS16 . . . . 141 E3
Basildon, Steeple View SS15,
CM12 . . . . 119 B2
Billericay CM11 . . . . 97 C2
Boreham CM3 . . . . 33 E8
Brentwood CM14 . . . . 116 D7
Brentwood, Warley
CM14 . . . . 116 B6
Brentwood, Warley
CM14 . . . . 116 D5
Chigwell IG7 . . . . 111 C6
Dagenham RM6 . . . . 134 E5
Dagenham RM7 . . . . 135 D1

Chase The *continued*
East Hanningfield CM3 . . . 78 B8
Foulness Island SS3 . . . . . 130 F7
Grays RM20 . . . . 177 D8
Great Amwell SG12 . . . . . 8 A1
Great Baddow CM2 . . . . . 54 F6
Hadleigh SS7 . . . . 145 B5
Harlow CM17 . . . . 11 C1
Hornchurch RM7, RM12 . . 135 F1
Ingrave CM13 . . . . 117 C5
Loughton IG10 . . . . 88 D2
Osea Island CM9 . . . . 39 A1
Rayleigh SS6 . . . . 123 F1
Rochford SS4 . . . . 125 C8
Romford RM1 . . . . 135 E8
Southminster CM0 . . . . . . 84 D4
South Woodham Ferrers
CM3 . . . . 101 C8
Upminster RM14 . . . . 137 D1
Wickford, Nevendon
SS12 . . . . 121 E4
Wickford, Runwell
SS12 . . . . 121 A6
Chaseway SS16 . . . . 142 F4
Chaseways SS21 . . . . 11 C8
Chatfield Way SS13 . . . . . 143 C7
Chatham Hall La CM3 . . . 19 B8
Chatham Pavement
SS13 . . . . 143 C7
Chatham Rd **1** E18 . . . . . 109 F1
Chatham Way CM14 . . . . . 116 C8
Chatsworth SS7 . . . . 144 F6
Chatsworth Gdns
SS5 . . . . 124 D6
Chatterford End SS14 . . . 142 B7
Chatteris Ave RM3 . . . . . . 114 D4
Chatton Cl **4** SS12 . . . . . 121 E5
Chaucer Cl
Maldon CM9 . . . . 59 A8
Tilbury RM18 . . . . 179 C5
Chaucer Ct EN11 . . . . 8 A1
Chaucer Rd
Chelmsford CM2 . . . . 32 D1
Chingford E17 . . . . 109 C1
Romford RM3 . . . . 114 B3
Wanstead E11 . . . . 132 A5
Chaucer Way
Dartford DA1 . . . . 176 A3
Hoddesdon EN11 . . . . 8 A2
Chaucer Wlk SS12 . . . . . . 121 D5
Cheapside E SS6 . . . . 123 C4
Cheapside W SS6 . . . . . . 123 B4
Cheddar Ave SS0 . . . . 147 A5
Chedington SS3 . . . . 149 C1
Cheelson Rd RM15 . . . . . 157 C3
Cheethams Rd E12 . . . . . . 132 E1
Cheldon Barton SS1 . . . . 168 C8
Chelmer Ave
Little Waltham CM3 . . . . . 19 B5
Rayleigh SS6 . . . . 123 C1
Chelmer Cres IG11 . . . . . 153 B3
Chelmer Ct E18 . . . . 110 B2
Chelmer Dr
Brentwood CM13 . . . . 95 E3
South Ockendon RM15 . . 172 C6
Chelmer Ho RM16 . . . . . . 174 A1
Chelmer Lea CM2 . . . . . . 54 E7
Chelmer Pl CM2 . . . . 32 D3
Chelmer Rd
Chelmsford CM2 . . . . 32 E2
Grays RM16 . . . . 174 A1
Upminster RM14 . . . . 137 D5
Chelmer Terr CM9 . . . . . . 37 B2
Chelmerton Ave CM2 . . . . 54 E7
Chelmer Valley High Sch
CM1 . . . . 19 A2
Chelmer Valley Rd
CM1 . . . . 32 B5
CHELMER VILLAGE 33 B4
Chelmer Village Ret Pk
CM2 . . . . 32 E2
Chelmer Village Way
CM2 . . . . 33 A3
Chelmer Way
Burnham-on-C CM0 . . . . . 106 A6
Southend-on-S SS3 . . . . . 168 D7
CHELMSFORD 32 C4
Chelmsford Ave
Romford RM5 . . . . 113 D4
Southend-on-S SS2 . . . . . 147 F1
Chelmsford Coll
Chelmsford CM2 . . . . 54 A8
Chelmsford CM2 . . . . 54 C7
Chelmsford Cty High Sch
for Girls CM1 . . . . 32 A4
Chelmsford Dr RM14 . . . . 136 F1
Chelmsford Gdns IG1 . . . 132 F4
Chelmsford Rd
Battlesbridge SS11 . . . . . 100 E1
Brentwood CM15 . . . . 95 B5
Great Waltham CM3 . . . . . 19 A6
Hatfield Heath CM22 . . . . 3 C3
High Ongar CM4, CM5 . . . 49 D4
Margaret Roding CM6,
CM5 . . . . 15 E4
Mountnessing CM15 . . . . 95 C6
Purleigh CM3 . . . . 58 C3
Rawreth SS11 . . . . 122 E6
Shenfield CM15 . . . . 94 F3
Woodford IG8 . . . . 109 F2
Woodham Mortimer
CM9 . . . . 57 C6
Writtle CM1 . . . . 31 C1
Chelmsford Sta CM1 . . . . 32 B3
Chelsea Ave SS1 . . . . 167 D6

Chelsea Ct
6 Chingford E4 . . . . 87 C1
Rochford SS4 . . . . 125 E2
Southend-on-S SS1 . . . . . 167 C8
Chelsea Fields EN11 . . . . 8 B2
Chelsea Gdns CM17 . . . . 24 E7
Chelsea Mews **4**
RM11 . . . . 136 B3
Chelston Ct **2** E11 . . . . . 132 B6
Chelsworth Cl
Romford RM3 . . . . 114 F2
Southend-on-S SS1 . . . . . 167 F8
Chelsworth Cres SS1 . . . . 167 F8
Chelsworth Dr RM3 . . . . . 114 F2
Cheltenham Dr
Southend-on-S SS9 . . . . . 146 F2
Thundersley SS7 . . . . 145 B7
Cheltenham Gdns
IG10 . . . . 88 E3
Cheltenham Ho IG8 . . . . . 111 A4
Cheltenham Rd
Hockley SS5 . . . . 124 F7
Southend-on-S SS1 . . . . . 167 C8
Chelwater CM2 . . . . 54 D8
Chelwood Cl E4 . . . . 87 B3
Chenies Dr SS15 . . . . 119 B1
Chepstow Ave RM12 . . . . 136 E1
Chepstow Cl RM11 . . . . . 97 D5
Chepstow Cres IG3 . . . . . 133 E5
Chepstow Ho RM3 . . . . . . 115 A5
Chequers
Buckhurst Hill IG9 . . . . . . 88 B1
Ingatestone CM4 . . . . 74 B4
Chequers La
Dagenham RM9 . . . . 154 A2
Maldon CM9 . . . . 37 A2
Chequers Par RM9 . . . . . 154 A4
Chequers Rd
Brentwood CM14, RM3 . . 92 F1
Loughton IG10 . . . . 89 B4
Hockley SS5 . . . . 124 F6
Writtle CM1 . . . . 30 F1
Chequers Wlk EN9 . . . . . . 65 F4
Cheriton Ave IG5 . . . . 111 A1
Cherries The SS8 . . . . 164 B1
Cherry Ave CM13 . . . . 116 F7
Cherry Blossom Cl **3**
CM17 . . . . 11 C4
Cherry Blossom La
CM3 . . . . 80 F6
Cherrybrook SS1 . . . . 149 C1
Cherry Cl
Canvey Island SS8 . . . . . . 163 F4
Hockley SS5 . . . . 124 E7
Cherry Ct
Canvey Island SS8 . . . . . . 164 B1
Ilford IG6 . . . . 133 B8
Cherrydene Cl SS5 . . . . . 101 E2
Cherrydown
Grays RM16 . . . . 173 D5
Rayleigh SS6 . . . . 123 D4
Cherrydown Ave E4 . . . . . 109 A7
Cherrydown Cl E4 . . . . . . 109 A7
Cherrydown E SS14 . . . . . 142 A5
Cherrydown W SS16 . . . . 142 A5
Cherrydown Wlk RM7 . . . 113 B1
Cherrygarden La **1**
CM2 . . . . 54 A8
Cherry Garden La CM3 . . 57 B7
Cherry Garden Rd
Great Waltham CM3 . . . . . 18 E7
Maldon CM9 . . . . 36 E2
Cherry Gdns
Billericay CM12 . . . . 96 E4
Dagenham RM9 . . . . 153 F7
Sawbridgeworth CM21 . . . 1 E4
Cherry La SS11 . . . . 122 A7
Cherrymeade SS7 . . . . . . 145 A4
Cherry Orch CM0 . . . . 84 E4
Cherry Orchard La
SS4 . . . . 147 B8
Cherry Orchard Way
Rochford SS4 . . . . 125 B1
Southend-on-S SS2,
SS4 . . . . 147 B8
Cherry St RM7 . . . . 135 D6
Cherrytree Chase
SS3 . . . . 150 C1
Cherry Tree Cl
Grays RM17 . . . . 178 D8
Rainham RM13 . . . . 155 A3
Cherry Tree Ct **3**
E18 . . . . 109 F1
Cherry Tree Dr RM15 . . . . 157 D1
Cherry Tree La
Harlow CM20 . . . . 10 B1
Rainham RM13 . . . . 154 F2
Cherry Tree Prim Sch
SS16 . . . . 142 D5
Cherry Tree Rd EN11 . . . . 21 A7
Cherry Tree Rise IG9 . . . . 110 D6
Cherrytrees CM12 . . . . . . 118 F8
Cherry Trees CM4 . . . . . . 74 B4
Cherry Wlk
Grays RM16 . . . . 174 A3
Rainham RM13 . . . . 154 F3
Cherston Gdns IG10 . . . . 89 A5
Cherston Rd IG10 . . . . . . 89 A5
Chertsey Cl SS3 . . . . 149 D1
Chertsey Rd IG1 . . . . 152 D8
Cherwell Dr CM1 . . . . 31 C5
Cherwell Gr RM15 . . . . . . 172 B6
Chesham Cl RM7 . . . . 135 D7
Chesham Dr SS15 . . . . . . 119 B1
Chesham Ho **9** RM3 . . . 114 E4
Cheshire Cl
Chingford E4 . . . . 109 B2
Hornchurch RM11 . . . . . . 137 A6
Cheshunt Dr SS6 . . . . 123 B6

Cheshunt Rd DA17 . . . . . 169 A1
Cheshunts SS13 . . . . 143 A7
Chester Ave
Southend-on-S SS1 . . . . . 167 D6
Upminster RM14 . . . . 137 E2
Chester Cl
Grays RM16 . . . . 172 E3
Loughton IG10 . . . . 89 C8
Chesterfield Ave SS7 . . . . 144 D6
Chesterfield Cres
SS9 . . . . 146 D6
Chesterfield Gdns **3**
SS14 . . . . 142 F8
Chesterford Gn SS14 . . . . 142 F8
Chesterford Rd E12 . . . . . 152 A7
Chester Gn IG10 . . . . 89 C8
Chester Hall La CM20 . . . 120 A1
Chesterman Rd SS3 . . . . 168 F6
Chester Mews CM17 . . . . 109 A1
Chester Path IG10 . . . . . . 89 C8
Chester Pl CM1 . . . . 32 A5
Chester Rd
Chigwell IG7 . . . . 111 A7
Ilford IG3 . . . . 133 F4
Loughton IG10 . . . . 89 C8
Wanstead E11 . . . . 132 B5
Chesterton Way
RM18 . . . . 179 C5
Chester Way **9** SS14 . . . 142 F8
Chestnut Ave
Billericay CM12 . . . . 97 A2
Buckhurst Hill IG9 . . . . . . 110 D7
Grays RM16 . . . . 173 B4
Heybridge CM9 . . . . 37 C6
Hornchurch RM12 . . . . . . 136 A2
Chestnut Cl
Buckhurst Hill IG9 . . . . . . 110 D8
Burnham-on-C CM0 . . . . . 106 A5
Gravesend DA11 . . . . 178 F1
Hockley SS5 . . . . 124 F6
Hornchurch RM12 . . . . . . 155 C8
Chestnut Cotts CM16 . . . 67 E2
Chestnut Ct
Basildon SS16 . . . . 143 A4
Ingatestone CM4 . . . . 74 A4
Southend-on-S SS3 . . . . . 168 F7
Chestnut Dr
Hatfield Heath CM22 . . . . 2 F3
Wanstead E11 . . . . 132 A5
Chestnut Farm Dr CM3 . . 82 E2
Chestnut Glen CM12 . . . . 136 A2
Chestnut Gr
Brentwood CM14 . . . . 116 C8
Epping Green CM16 . . . . . 45 B7
Little Baddow CM3 . . . . . . 34 E1
Woodford IG8 . . . . 110 A5
Chestwood Cl CM12 . . . . 97 B5
Chestnuts The
Abridge RM4 . . . . 90 B6
2 Loughton IG10 . . . . . 88 E4
Rayleigh SS6 . . . . 123 E4
Southminster CM0 . . . . . . 84 D4
Willingale CM5 . . . . 28 D4
Chestnut Wlk
Canvey Island SS8 . . . . . . 163 E3
Chelmsford CM1 . . . . 32 A5
Epping Green CM16 . . . . . 45 B7
Little Baddow CM3 . . . . . . 34 E1
Woodford IG8 . . . . 110 A5
Chetwood Cl CM12 . . . . . 97 B5
Chetwood Prim Sch The
CM3 . . . . 101 D6
Cheveley Cl RM3 . . . . 114 F2
Chevely Cl RM3 . . . . 46 D2
Chevening Gdns SS5 . . . . 124 C6
Chevers Pawen SS13 . . . . 143 A5
Chevington Pl RM12 . . . . 155 D7
Chevington Way
RM12 . . . . 155 D8
Cheviot Dr CM1 . . . . 31 D6
Cheviot Ho DA11 . . . . 178 D1
Cheviot Rd RM11 . . . . 136 A4
Cheviot Way IG2 . . . . 133 D7
Chevron Ho RM17 . . . . . . 178 B7
Cheyne Ct **8** SS12 . . . . . 121 E5
Chichester Cl
Aveley RM15 . . . . 171 C5
Basildon SS14 . . . . 142 F8
Canvey Island SS8 . . . . . . 164 A2
Grays RM16 . . . . 172 D2
Chichester Dr CM1 . . . . . 32 C4
Chichester Gdns IG1 . . . . 132 C4
Chichester Ho **1**
CM14 . . . . 116 C8
Chichester Rd
Greenhithe DA9 . . . . 176 F1
Southend-on-S SS1 . . . . . 167 A8
Chichester Way CM9 . . . . 59 B8
Chichester Wharf
DA8 . . . . 169 E1
Chieftan Dr RM19 . . . . . . 171 A2
Chigborough Rd CM9 . . . 37 F6
Chignal Ho SS6 . . . . 123 B3
Chignal Rd CM1 . . . . 31 D5
CHIGNALL ST JAMES . . . 31 A8
CHIGNALL SMEALY 17 F4
Chignalls The **4**
SS15 . . . . 141 A6
CHIGWELL 111 B8
Chigwell Cty Prim Sch
IG7 . . . . 111 C8

Chigwell La IG10 . . . . 89 C5
Chigwell Park Dr IG7 . . . . 111 A6
Chigwell Pk IG7 . . . . 111 B6
Chigwell Rd
Wanstead E18 . . . . 132 B8
Woodford IG8 . . . . 110 B3
Chigwell Rise IG7 . . . . . . 111 A8
CHIGWELL ROW 112 B8
Chigwell Row Inf Sch
IG7 . . . . 112 B8
Chigwell Sch IG7 . . . . 111 B8
Chigwell Sta IG7 . . . . 111 B7
Chigwell View RM5 . . . . . 113 A5
Childerditch Hall Dr
CM13 . . . . 139 A7
Childerditch Ind Pk
CM13 . . . . 138 F8
Childerditch La
Little Warley CM13 . . . . . . 116 C2
West Horndon CM13 . . . . 139 A5
Childerditch St CM13 . . . 139 B8
Childers The IG8 . . . . 110 F5
Childs Cl RM11 . . . . 136 C5
Childs Cres DA10 . . . . 177 C3
Chilham Cl SS13 . . . . 143 C5
Chiltern **1** SS1 . . . . 167 B8
Chiltern App SS8 . . . . 163 E4
Chiltern Cl SS6 . . . . 123 D3
Chiltern Gdns RM12 . . . . 136 C5
Chiltern Rd IG2 . . . . 133 E6
Chilterns The SS8 . . . . . . 163 F4
Chiltern Way IG8 . . . . 110 A7
Chilton Cl CM2 . . . . 54 D7
Chilton Rd RM16 . . . . 174 A3
Chiltons The **4** E18 . . . . 110 A1
Chimes The SS7 . . . . 144 E4
Chimney Pot La CM3 . . . . 57 E3
China La CM14 . . . . 139 C4
Chinchilla Rd SS1 . . . . . . 167 D8
Chindits La CM14 . . . . . . 116 C5
Chinery Cl CM1 . . . . 32 C4
Ching Ct E4 . . . . 109 E7
Chingdale Rd E4 . . . . 109 F7
CHINGFORD 87 E1
Chingford Ave E4 . . . . 109 E6
Chingford CE Inf Sch
E4 . . . . 87 D1
Chingford CE Jun Sch
E4 . . . . 87 D1
Chingford Foundation Sch
E4 . . . . 87 B1
CHINGFORD GREEN 87 C4
CHINGFORD HATCH 109 D6
Chingford La IG8 . . . . 109 F5
Chingford Mount Rd
E4 . . . . 109 A5
Chingford Rd
Chingford E4 . . . . 109 A3
Chingford E17 . . . . 109 A1
Chingford Sta E4 . . . . 87 E2
Chippenham Cl RM3 . . . . 114 C5
Chippenham Gdns
RM3 . . . . 114 C5
Chippenham Rd RM3 . . . 114 C5
Chippenham Wlk
RM3 . . . . 114 C5
Chipperfield Cl RM17 . . . 137 E3
Chippingfield CM17 . . . . 11 C3
Chipping Lo RM1 . . . . 135 F6
CHIPPING ONGAR 48 F4
Chipping Ongar Prim Sch
CM5 . . . . 48 F4
Chipping Row **5**
CM3 . . . . 101 E7
Chisholm Ct **11** SS12 . . . 121 E5
Chislett Row CM2 . . . . . . 54 C8
Chittenden Ct **5** EN11 . . 8 B1
Chittock Gate SS14 . . . . . 142 E6
Chittock Mead SS14 . . . . 142 E6
Chitty's La RM8 . . . . 134 C2
Chivers Rd
Chingford E4 . . . . 109 E6
Stondon Massey CM15 . . . 71 A7
Choats Manor Way
RM9 . . . . 153 E2
Choats Rd IG11 . . . . 153 E2
Choice View **5** IG1 . . . . 133 C2
Chorley Cl SS16 . . . . 140 F5
Christchurch Ave
Rainham RM13 . . . . 154 F2
Wickford SS12 . . . . 121 A8
Christchurch Prim Sch
IG1 . . . . 133 C3
Christchurch Rd
Ilford IG1 . . . . 133 C3
Southend-on-S SS2 . . . . . 148 C1
Tilbury RM18 . . . . 179 A6
Christian Ct EN11 . . . . . . 8 A2
Christie Ct **12** CM14 . . . . 116 C7
Christie Gdns RM6 . . . . . 134 B4
Christie Rd EN9 . . . . 65 B4
Christies Ct **5** EN11 . . . . 21 A6
Christine Ct **7** RM13 . . . 155 A1
Christopher Cl RM12 . . . . 155 D7
Christopher Gdns
RM9 . . . . 153 D7
Christopher Martin Pl
CM11 . . . . 97 C2
Christopher Martin Rd
SS14 . . . . 120 F3
Christy Ave CM1 . . . . 31 F4
Christy Cl SS15 . . . . 140 E7
Christy Ct SS15 . . . . 140 E7
Christy Way SS15 . . . . . . 140 E7
Chudleigh Cres IG3 . . . . . 152 E8
Chudleigh Rd RM3 . . . . . 114 E6
Chulmleigh Ct CM15 . . . . 95 A1
Churchall Terr IG6 . . . . . . 111 F5

Church Ave
Broomfield CM1 . . . . 19 A2
Chingford E4 . . . . 109 D4
Wanstead E12 . . . . 132 D1
Church Chase CM3 . . . . 100 C5
Church Cl
Canvey Island SS8 . . . . . 163 F3
Horndon on t H SS17 . . . 159 F3
Kelvedon Hatch CM14 . . . . 71 D2
Loughton IG10 . . . . 88 F7
Mountnessing CM15 . . . . . 95 E8
Southend-on-S SS3 . . . . 168 D6
Church Cnr
South Benfleet SS7 . . . . . 144 D1
Woodham Walter CM9 . . . . 35 D2
Church Cotts
Gilston CM20 . . . . 10 C7
Stanford Rivers CM5 . . . . . 70 C7
Church Cres
Mountnessing CM15 . . . . . 95 E8
Sawbridgeworth CM21 . . . . . 1 F2
South Ockendon RM15 . . 157 C2
Church Ct EN10 . . . . 21 A3
Church Elm La RM10 . . 154 A6
CHURCHEND 130 B6
Church End CM19 . . . . . 23 A6
Church End Ave SS11 . . 99 E2
Church End La SS11 . . . 99 E2
Churchfield CM20 . . . . . 11 B2
Church Field RM16 . . . . 46 A2
Churchfield Cotts
SS3 . . . . 130 B7
Churchfields
Hoddesdon EN10 . . . . 21 A3
Loughton IG10 . . . . 88 E5
Southend-on-S SS3 . . . . 149 E4
Woodford E18 . . . . 110 A4
Churchfields Inf Sch
E18 . . . . 110 A4
Churchfields Jun Sch
E18 . . . . 110 A4
Churchfields La EN10 . . 21 A3
Churchgate SS0 . . . . . . 147 C1
Churchgate CE Prim Sch
CM17 . . . . 11 F3
Churchgate St CM17 . . . 11 E4
CHURCHGATE STREET
. . . . 11 F3
Church Grn
Boreham CM3 . . . . 33 F8
Broomfield CM1 . . . . 19 B1
Canewdon SS4 . . . . 104 D2
Roxwell CM1 . . . . 30 B5
Church Hill
Basildon SS15 . . . . 141 D8
Epping CM16 . . . . 46 A2
Greenhithe DA9 . . . . 176 E2
Little Waltham CM3 . . . . . 19 C6
Loughton IG10 . . . . 88 F6
Purleigh CM3 . . . . 58 E1
Southend-on-S SS9 . . . . 165 E8
Stanford-le-H SS17 . . . . 160 C1
Woodham Walter CM9 . . . 35 D2
Church Hollow RM19 . . 171 A1
Church Housen CM3 . . . 58 F7
Churchill Cl CM5 . . . . . . 49 A4
Churchill Cres SS7 . . . 160 E4
Churchill Ct 8 IG1 . . . 133 B1
Churchill Lo
Ilford IG6 . . . . 133 C7
Woodford IG8 . . . . 109 F4
Churchill Mews IG8 . . . 109 F4
Churchill Pk DA1 . . . . . 176 A2
Churchill Rd RM17 . . . 178 D8
Churchill Rise CM1 . . . . 32 E7
Churchill Sq 3 SS1 . . 167 A8
Churchill Terr E4 . . . . . 109 A7
Church La
Abridge RM4 . . . . 90 E6
Basildon, Burnt Mills
SS13 . . . . 121 A2
Brentwood CM13 . . . . 95 F2
Bulphan RM14 . . . . 158 F7
1 Chelmsford, Moulsham
CM1 . . . . 32 B2
Chelmsford, Springfield
CM1 . . . . 32 D4
Chipping Ongar CM5 . . . . 49 B7
Crays Hill CM11 . . . . 120 B6
Dagenham RM10 . . . . . . 154 C5
Doddinghurst CM15 . . . . . 72 B2
Great Warley CM13 . . . . 138 D5
Loughton IG10 . . . . 88 F6
Margaretting CM4 . . . . . . 74 E6
North Ockendon RM14 . . 157 B7
North Weald Bassett
CM16 . . . . 47 A6
Purfleet RM19 . . . . 171 A1
Romford RM1 . . . . 135 E7
Sheering CM22 . . . . 12 D7
South Hanningfield CM3 . . 99 C8
Stapleford Abbotts RM4 . . 91 C5
Stow Maries CM3 . . . . . . 80 D3
Wennington RM13 . . . . . 170 D7
West Hanningfield CM2 . . . 77 A4
White Roothing or White
Roding CM6 . . . . 14 C7
Writtle CM1 . . . . 31 B1
Church Lane Cotts
Doddinghurst CM15 . . . . . 72 B2
Rainham RM13 . . . . 170 D7
CHURCH LANGLEY 24 D8
**Church Langley Com Prim
Sch** CM17 . . . . 24 C8
Church Langley Way
CM17 . . . . 24 D8
Church Leys CM18 . . . . 23 F7

Church Manorway
DA8 . . . . 169 D3
Church Mead CM19 . . . . . 9 B1
Church Mews SS15 . . . 141 B7
Church Mill Grange
CM17 . . . . 11 E4
Church Par SS8 . . . . . . 163 E5
Church Park Rd SS13 . . 143 B5
Church Path
Greenhithe DA9 . . . . 176 F2
Northfleet DA11 . . . . 178 C1
Wanstead E11 . . . . 132 A6
Church Rd
Barking E12 . . . . 152 C6
Barling SS3 . . . . 149 E8
Basildon, Barstable SS14,
SS16 . . . . 142 C6
Basildon, Bowers Gifford
SS13 . . . . 143 F6
Basildon, Great Berry
RM14 . . . . 140 D5
Basildon, Noak Bridge
SS15 . . . . 119 E1
Basildon, Pipps Hill
SS15 . . . . 141 E8
Buckhurst Hill IG9 . . . . . . 88 B1
Bulphan RM14 . . . . 158 F8
Burnham-on-C CM0 . . . . 106 B6
Corringham SS17 . . . . . . 161 B2
Erith DA8 . . . . 169 D1
Greenhithe DA9 . . . . 176 F2
Hadleigh SS7 . . . . 145 F2
Harlow CM17 . . . . 24 C5
High Beach IG10 . . . . 88 A7
Hockley SS5 . . . . 124 B7
Ilford IG2 . . . . 133 E5
Kelvedon Hatch CM14 . . . 71 C2
Little Baddow CM3 . . . . . 34 A6
Little Ilford E12 . . . . 152 A7
Moreton CM5 . . . . 26 D2
Mountnessing CM15 . . . . 95 F7
Navestock Heath RM4 . . . 92 D8
North Fambridge CM3 . . 103 A7
Ramsden Heath CM11, SS14,
SS16, SS13 . . . . 98 D2
Rawreth SS11 . . . . 122 D7
Rayleigh SS6 . . . . 123 F2
Rochford SS4 . . . . 125 C7
Romford, Harold Park
RM3 . . . . 115 A3
Romford RM4 . . . . 92 C1
South Benfleet, New
Thundersley SS7 . . . . 144 D6
Southend-on-S, Cambridge
Town SS3 . . . . 168 D6
Southend-on-S SS1 . . . . 167 A7
Stanford Rivers CM5 . . . . 70 D6
Swanscombe DA10 . . . . 177 F1
Tilbury RM18 . . . . 178 F6
Ulting CM9 . . . . 35 C6
West Hanningfield CM2 . . . 77 A4
West Tilbury RM18 . . . . . 179 E8
Church Row RM16 . . . . 159 A1
Church St
Billericay CM11 . . . . 119 C6
Blackmore CM4 . . . . 72 E8
Chelmsford CM1 . . . . 32 B2
Dagenham RM10 . . . . . . 154 B6
Goldhanger CM9 . . . . 38 E7
Gravesend DA11 . . . . . . 179 B1
Grays RM17 . . . . 178 C8
Great Baddow CM2 . . . . . 55 A6
Maldon CM9 . . . . 37 B2
Rayleigh SS6 . . . . 123 D2
Sawbridgeworth CM21 . . . . 1 E2
Waltham Abbey EN9 . . . . 65 C6
Church Terr RM4 . . . . . . 91 C5
Church View
Aveley RM15 . . . . 171 D4
Steeple CM0 . . . . 61 E2
Upminster RM14 . . . . . . 137 B2
Church View Cl SS2 . . 148 B2
Church View Rd SS7 . . 144 E6
Churchway SS7 . . . . . . 145 F2
Church Wlk
2 Basildon SS14 . . . . . 142 A6
Brentwood CM15 . . . . 94 B2
Maldon CM9 . . . . 37 B2
Sawbridgeworth CM21 . . . . 1 F2
Churchwood Gdns
IG8 . . . . 110 A6
Chuzzlewit Dr CM1 . . . . 31 E7
Cillocks Cl EN11 . . . . . . 21 A7
Cimarron Cl CM3 . . . . . 101 D7
Cinema Par RM8 . . . . . 134 F2
Circle The RM18 . . . . . 179 A6
City View 3 IG1 . . . . . 133 C2
Civic Sq RM18 . . . . 179 A5
Civic Way IG6 . . . . 133 C7
Clachar Cl CM2 . . . . 33 A3
Claire Cl CM13 . . . . 116 F6
Claire Ho
Ilford IG1 . . . . 152 B8
Woodford IG5 . . . . 110 F2
Clairvale RM11 . . . . 136 E4
Clandon Rd IG3 . . . . . . 133 E2
Claps Gate La E6 . . . . . 152 B1
Clare Ave SS11 . . . . 99 D2
Clare Cswy DA2 . . . . . . 176 F3
Clare Ct RM15 . . . . 171 C4
Clare Gdns IG11 . . . . . . 153 A5
Clare James Cotts 4
SS8 . . . . 164 A3
Clare Mews CM5 . . . . . . 49 A5
Claremont Cl
Grays RM17 . . . . 173 C3
Southend-on-S SS0 . . . . 147 E1
Claremont Dr SS16 . . . 143 A4

Claremont Gdns
Ilford IG3 . . . . 133 E2
Upminster RM14 . . . . . . 137 D3
Claremont Gr IG8 . . . . . 110 C4
Claremont Pl IG7 . . . . . 111 B7
Claremont Rd
Basildon SS15 . . . . 141 C8
Hornchurch RM11 . . . . . 136 A5
Southend-on-S SS0 . . . . 147 D1
Clarence Ave
Ilford IG2 . . . . 133 A5
Redbridge IG1 . . . . 132 F5
Upminster RM14 . . . . . . 137 A2
Clarence Cl
Chelmsford CM2 . . . . 33 A4
South Benfleet SS7 . . . . 144 D4
Clarence Gate IG8 . . . . 111 A4
Clarence Lo 8 EN11 . . . 21 A6
Clarence Rd
Basildon SS13 . . . . 143 F7
Canvey Island SS8 . . . . 164 B2
Grays RM17 . . . . 173 B1
Pilgrims Hatch CM15 . . . . 94 B3
Rayleigh SS6 . . . . 124 A1
South Benfleet SS7 . . . . 144 D3
Southend-on-S SS1 . . . . 167 A4
Clarence Rd N SS7 . . . 144 E4
Clarence St SS1 . . . . . . 167 A7
Clarendon Gdns
Ilford IG1 . . . . 133 A4
Redbridge IG1 . . . . 132 F4
Clarendon Rd
Basildon SS13 . . . . 143 C7
Canvey Island SS8 . . . . 164 C4
Gravesend DA12 . . . . . . 179 C1
Hockley SS5 . . . . 102 F1
Wanstead E18 . . . . 132 A8
Clare Rd SS7 . . . . 144 A6
Claridge Rd RM8 . . . . . 134 D3
Clarissa Rd RM6 . . . . . 134 D4
Clarkbourne Dr RM17 . . 178 D8
Clarke Mans 9 IG11 . . . 152 F5
Clarke Rise CM3 . . . . . . 80 F5
Clarklands Ind Est CM21 . . 1 E5
Clarks Cotts SS11 . . . . 122 F7
Clarks Farm Rd CM3 . . . 56 F8
Clarks Field Cotts CM3 . . 57 E2
Clarks La CM16 . . . . 67 F8
Clarksons The SS11 . . . 152 C3
Clark's Rd IG1 . . . . 133 D2
Clark Way CM1 . . . . 19 A1
Claters Cl SS2 . . . . 148 F2
Clatterfield Gdns SS0 . . 147 B3
CLATTERFORD END
Fyfield 27 C2
Leaden Roding 16 B7
Toot Hill 48 A1
Claudian Way RM16 . . . 174 B3
Claughton Way CM13 . . . 95 D3
CLAVERHAMBURY 44 B4
Claverhambury Rd
EN9 . . . . 44 A3
Clavering SS16 . . . . 142 F4
Clavering Ct SS6 . . . . . 123 B3
Clavering Gdns CM13 . . 139 D5
Clavering Rd E12 . . . . . 132 D2
Clavering Way CM13 . . . 95 C3
Claybrick Ave SS5 . . . . 124 D5
Clayburn Circ SS14 . . . 142 D6
Clayburn End SS14 . . . 142 D6
Clayburn Gdns RM15 . . 172 B6
Clayburn Side SS14 . . . 142 D6
Claybury Broadway
IG5 . . . . 132 E8
Claybury Rd IG8 . . . . . . 110 E3
Claydon Cres SS14 . . . 142 C7
Claydon Ct RM12 . . . . . 154 F8
Claydons La SS6 . . . . . 145 C7
Claygate Cl RM12 . . . . . 155 A8
CLAYHALL 110 F1
Clayhall Ave
Redbridge IG5 . . . . 111 A1
Woodford IG5 . . . . 110 E1
Clay Hill Rd SS16 . . . . . 142 C4
Claypit Hill EN9 . . . . 66 C2
Claypits Rd CM3 . . . . . . 20 F1
Clayside IG7 . . . . 111 C5
Clay's La IG10 . . . . 89 A8
Clayspring Cl SS5 . . . . 124 D7
Clayswell Ct SS5 . . . . . 124 E6
Clayton Ave RM14 . . . . 156 B7
Clayton Hill Ctry Pk★
EN9 . . . . 43 D8
Clayton Rd RM7 . . . . . . 135 C3
Claytonville Terr
DA17 . . . . 169 C4
Clayton Way CM9 . . . . . 59 A8
Clay Tye Rd
North Ockendon
RM14 . . . . 157 C8
Upminster RM14 . . . . . . 138 C1
Cleall Ave EN9 . . . . 65 C5
Clear Ct CM3 . . . . 82 B5
Cleland Path IG10 . . . . . 89 B8
Clemantine Wlk IG8 . . . 109 F3
Clematis Cl RM3 . . . . . . 114 C3
Clematis Gdns IG8 . . . . 110 A5
Clematis Tye 3 CM1 . . . 32 E7
Clemence Rd RM10 . . . 154 C4
Clementhorpe Rd
RM9 . . . . 153 D6
Clementine Wlk 4
IG8 . . . . 110 A3
Clements Cl CM2 . . . . . . 33 B3
Clements Ct 6 IG1 . . . 133 B1
Clements Gdns SS5 . . . 125 A5

Clements Green La
SS5 . . . . 101 D8
Clements Hall La SS5 . . 125 A5
Clements Hall Way
SS5 . . . . 125 A4
Clements La IG1 . . . . . . 133 B1
Clements Pl CM3 . . . . . 101 D8
Clements Rd
Ilford IG1 . . . . 133 B1
Wallend E6 . . . . 152 A5
Clement Way RM14 . . . 136 F1
Clerks Piece IG10 . . . . . 88 F6
Cleveden Ho SS7 . . . . . 144 F6
Cleveland Dr SS0 . . . . . 147 E3
Cleveland Ho DA11 . . . 178 D1
Cleveland Jun & Inf Sch
IG1 . . . . 133 B1
Cleveland Rd
Basildon SS14 . . . . 142 C6
Canvey Island SS8 . . . . 164 B2
Ilford IG1 . . . . 133 B1
Wanstead E18 . . . . 132 A8
Cleves Ave CM14 . . . . . . 94 A3
Cleves Cl IG10 . . . . 88 E3
Cleves Ct CM3 . . . . 20 E1
Cleves Wlk IG6 . . . . 111 C3
Clevis Dr CM3 . . . . 101 E5
Clieveden Rd SS1 . . . . . 167 F6
Cliff Ave
Southend-on-S, Chalkwell
SS9 . . . . 166 A8
Southend-on-S SS0 . . . . 147 A8
Cliff Gdns SS9 . . . . 166 A8
Clifford Ave IG5 . . . . . . 111 B1
Clifford Cl SS15 . . . . . . 141 D5
Clifford Rd
Chingford E17 . . . . 109 C1
Grays RM16 . . . . 172 F1
Cliff Par SS9 . . . . 165 E8
Cliff Pl RM15 . . . . 157 D2
Cliff Rd SS9 . . . . 166 A8
Cliff Reach DA9 . . . . . . 176 F1
Cliffsea Gr SS9 . . . . 146 F1
Cliffside Ind Est
RM17 . . . . 172 E1
CLIFFTOWN 166 E7
Clifftown Par SS1 . . . . . 166 F7
Clifftown Rd SS1 . . . . . 167 A7
Clifton Ave SS7 . . . . . . 144 C4
Clifton Cl SS7 . . . . 144 D4
Clifton Ct 3 IG8 . . . . . 110 A4
Clifton Dr SS0 . . . . 166 D7
Clifton Hatch CM18 . . . . 24 A5
Clifton Marine Par
DA11 . . . . 178 F1
Clifton Mews SS1 . . . . . 167 A7
Clifton Rd
Basildon SS13 . . . . 143 F7
Canvey Island SS8 . . . . 164 B3
Gravesend DA11 . . . . . . 179 A1
Hornchurch RM11 . . . . . 136 A5
Ilford IG2 . . . . 133 D5
Loughton IG10 . . . . 88 E5
Rochford SS4 . . . . 125 C7
Clifton Terr
1 Ingatestone CM4 . . . . 74 C4
Southend-on-S SS1 . . . . 167 A7
Clifton Way
Brentwood CM13 . . . . 95 D1
South Benfleet SS7 . . . . 144 C4
Clifton Wlk
22 Dartford DA2 . . . . . . 176 B1
South Benfleet SS7 . . . . 144 B1
Climmen Rd SS8 . . . . . 164 B5
Clinton Cl CM3 . . . . 78 B7
Clinton Cres IG6 . . . . . . 111 E4
Clinton Rd SS8 . . . . 163 D3
Clipped Hedge CM22 . . . . 3 B3
Clipper Bvd DA2 . . . . . . 176 E3
Clipper Bvd W DA2 . . . . 176 D4
Clitheroe Rd RM5 . . . . . 113 C5
Cliveden Cl
Chelmsford CM1 . . . . 31 E3
Shenfield CM15 . . . . 94 F2
Clivedon Rd E4 . . . . 109 E5
Clive Rd
Belvedere DA17 . . . . 169 A2
Brentwood CM13 . . . . . . 116 C3
17 Gravesend DA11 . . . 179 B1
Romford RM2 . . . . 136 B6
Clobbs Yd CM1 . . . . 32 B8
Clock Ct 2 E11 . . . . . . 132 B7
Clock Ho SS15 . . . . 141 B6
Clockhouse Ave IG11 . . 152 C4
Clockhouse Jun & Inf Sch
RM5 . . . . 113 B4
Clockhouse La
Grays RM16 . . . . 172 E1
Romford RM5 . . . . 113 C4
South Ockendon RM16 . . 172 E5
Clock House Par 1
E11 . . . . 132 B5
Clock House Rd CM12 . . 118 F5
Clockhouse The
RM14 . . . . 137 C2
Cloister Cl RM13 . . . . . . 155 B1
Cloisters
1 Hornchurch RM13 . . . 155 A6
Stanford-le-H SS17 . . . . 160 E2
Cloisters The SS15 . . . 141 C6
Clopton Gn SS14 . . . . . 142 B7
Clore Tikva Sch IG6 . . . 111 C1
Close The
Brentwood CM14 . . . . . . 116 D7

Close The continued
Chingford E4 . . . . 109 C3
Dagenham RM6 . . . . 134 C5
Grays RM16 . . . . 173 C4
Hatfield Heath CM22 . . . . . 3 A3
Ilford IG2 . . . . 133 E5
South Benfleet, Hope's Green
SS7 . . . . 144 D1
Thundersley SS7 . . . . . . 145 B8
Cloudberry Rd RM3 . . . 114 D4
Clova Rd SS9 . . . . 146 F2
Clovelly Ct RM11 . . . . . 136 F2
Clovelly Gdns
Romford RM7 . . . . 113 B2
2 Wickford SS11 . . . . . 121 C8
Clover Cl SS16 . . . . 142 E3
Clover Ct RM17 . . . . . . 178 C8
Clover Field CM18 . . . . . 24 A5
Clover Leas CM16 . . . . . 45 F2
Cloverley Rd CM5 . . . . . 49 A1
Cloverleys IG10 . . . . 88 D4
Clover Villas SS1 . . . . . 167 B7
Clover Way SS16 . . . . . 142 E3
Cluff Cl CM14 . . . . 116 C6
Clunas Gdns RM2 . . . . . 136 D8
Clune Ct CM15 . . . . 95 A2
Clunford Pl CM1 . . . . 32 F7
Cluny Sq SS2 . . . . 148 C3
Clusters The 3 SS2 . . 147 F1
Clyde RM18 . . . . 175 C2
Clyde Cres
Chelmsford CM1 . . . . 31 D4
Rayleigh SS6 . . . . 145 D8
Upminster RM14 . . . . . . 137 E5
Clyde Rd EN11 . . . . 21 D5
Clydesdale Rd RM11 . . 135 F4
Clyde Way RM1 . . . . . . 113 E2
Clynes Ho 6 RM10 . . . . 135 A1
Coach Ho The CM5 . . . . 49 F6
Coach La CM9 . . . . 36 F3
Coach Mews CM11 . . . . . 97 D5
Coal Ct RM17 . . . . 178 A8
COALHILL 99 E7
Coalhouse Fort★
RM18 . . . . 180 E6
Coalport Cl CM17 . . . . . 24 D7
Coaster Stps 4 SS1 . . 167 C7
Coastguard Cotts
Bradwell on S CM0 . . . . . 63 E8
Canvey Island SS8 . . . . 163 C1
Coates Cl CM9 . . . . 37 B4
Coates Quay CM2 . . . . . 32 C2
Cobbets Ave IG4 . . . . . 132 D6
Cobbinsbank EN9 . . . . . . 65 D6
Cobbins Chase CM0 . . . 106 B8
Cobbins Cl CM0 . . . . . . 106 B8
Cobbinsend Rd EN9 . . . . 44 D2
Cobbins Gr CM0 . . . . . . 106 B8
Cobbins The
Burnham-on-C CM0 . . . . 106 B8
Waltham Abbey EN9 . . . . 65 E6
Cobbins Way CM17 . . . . 11 E4
Cobbles The
Brentwood CM15 . . . . . . 116 B8
Upminster RM14 . . . . . . 137 F4
Cobbs Pl CM1 . . . . 32 D3
Cobdens Ho IG7 . . . . . . 111 D4
Cobden Wlk SS13 . . . . . 143 C7
Cobham RM16 . . . . 173 B4
Cobham Cl DA9 . . . . 177 B1
Cobham Ho IG11 . . . . . 152 C4
Cobham Rd
Chingford E17 . . . . 109 C2
Ilford IG3 . . . . 133 E1
Southend-on-S SS0 . . . . 166 C7
Cobham Terr 1 DA9 . . . 177 B1
Cobill Cl RM11 . . . . 136 C7
Coburg Gdns
Woodford IG5 . . . . 110 E1
Woodford IG5 . . . . 110 E1
Coburg La SS16 . . . . . . 140 F4
Coburg Pl CM3 . . . . 101 D6
Cockbourne Ct RM3 . . . 115 A1
COCK CLARKS 57 F2
Cockerell Cl SS13 . . . . . 121 B1
Cockethurst Cl SS0 . . . 147 A4
Cock Gn CM19 . . . . 23 B6
Cock La
Blackmore CM1 . . . . 51 F2
Edney Common CM1 . . . . 52 A3
Hoddesdon EN11 . . . . . . 21 A5
Cockle Sheds SS9 . . . . 165 D8
Cockridden Farm Ind Est
CM13 . . . . 139 F8
Cockrobin La CM20 . . . . 10 A7
Codenham Gn SS16 . . . 142 B5
Codenham Straight
SS16 . . . . 142 B4
Codham Hall La
CM13 . . . . 138 C7
Cokefield Ave SS2 . . . . 148 D3
Coker Rd SS8 . . . . 163 D2
Colam La CM3 . . . . 34 C3
Colbert Ave SS1 . . . . . . 167 E4
Colbourne Cl SS17 . . . . 160 F3
Colchester Ave E12 . . . 132 F1
Colchester Cl SS2 . . . . 147 F2
Colchester Rd
Chelmsford CM2 . . . . 33 A6
Heybridge CM9 . . . . 37 B5
Romford RM3 . . . . 114 C2
Southend-on-S SS2 . . . . 147 B4
Coldharbour La RM19 . . 170 A4
Coldharbour Rd CM19 . . 23 A7
COLD NORTON 80 E6

Cold Norton Prim Sch
CM3 . . . . 80 F5
Cold Norton Rd CM3 . . . . 81 D5
Cole Ave RM16 . . . . 174 C2
Colebrooke Dr E11 . . . . . . 132 C4
Colebrook Gdns IG10 . . . . 89 B7
Colebrook La IG10 . . . . . . 89 B7
Colebrook Path IG10 . . . . . 89 B7
Cole Ct RM3 . . . . 114 D5
Coleford Ho **7** RM3 . . 114 E4
Coleman Rd
  Belvedere DA17 . . . . 169 A2
  Dagenham RM9 . . . . 153 E6
Colemans Ave SS0 . . . . . . 147 D4
Colemans La CM3 . . . . 56 D7
Coleman St SS2 . . . . 148 A1
Colenso Rd IG2 . . . . 133 E4
Coleridge Rd
  Dartford DA1 . . . . 176 B3
  Maldon CM9 . . . . 37 A1
  Romford RM3 . . . . 114 B3
  Tilbury RM18 . . . . 179 C5
Coleridge Wlk CM13 . . . . . 95 D2
Coles Cl CM5 . . . . 49 A5
Coles Gn IG10 . . . . 89 A8
Colet Rd CM13 . . . . 95 D4
Coley Ct SS7 . . . . 144 B4
Colgate Pl EN3 . . . . 65 A2
Colin Cl DA2 . . . . 176 B1
Colin Pond Ct RM6 . . . . . 134 D8
Colinton Rd IG3 . . . . 134 B2
Collard Ave IG10 . . . . 89 C7
Collard Gn IG10 . . . . 89 C7
College Ave
  Chingford E4 . . . . 87 B2
  Redbridge IG4 . . . . 132 E6
College Pl DA9 . . . . 177 C3
College Rd
  Grays RM17 . . . . 173 C2
  Northfleet DA11 . . . . 178 B2
College Sq CM20 . . . . 23 D8
College Way SS1 . . . . 167 A8
Colley Rd CM2 . . . . 55 A6
Collier Ct RM16 . . . . 173 B5
COLLIER ROW 113 B2
Collier Row La RM5 . . . . . 113 C1
Collier Row Rd
  Dagenham RM5 . . . . 112 F2
  Romford RM5 . . . . 113 B3
COLLIERS HATCH 47 C1
Colliers The CM9 . . . . 37 E3
Collier Way SS1 . . . . 167 D7
Collindale Cl SS8 . . . . . . 164 D4
Collingdale SS7 . . . . 144 E4
Collingwood Ho
  Greenhithe DA9 . . . . 177 D2
  Southend-on-S SS0 . . . . . 147 D2
Collingwood Prim Sch
CM3 . . . . 101 E6
Collingwood Rd
  Basildon SS16 . . . . 142 D4
  Rainham RM13 . . . . 155 A3
  South Woodham Ferrers
  CM3 . . . . 101 F6
Collingwood Terr
SS16 . . . . 142 D5
Collingwood Way
SS3 . . . . 149 E1
Collingwood Wlk
SS16 . . . . 142 D5
Collins Cl SS17 . . . . 160 E2
Collins Ct **5** IG10 . . . . 88 D4
Collins Ho **8** IG11 . . . . 152 B5
Collins Mdw CM19 . . . . . . 23 B7
Collins Way
  Brentwood CM13 . . . . . . 95 F4
  Southend-on-S SS9 . . . . . 147 A6
Collinwood Gdns
  Ilford IG5 . . . . 133 A7
  Redbridge IG5 . . . . 132 F6
Colman Cl SS17 . . . . 160 D3
Colne RM18 . . . . 175 C3
Colne Cl
  South Ockendon
  RM15 . . . . 172 C6
  South Woodham Ferrers
  CM3 . . . . 101 E7
Colne Ct RM18 . . . . 175 C2
Colne Dr
  Romford RM3 . . . . 114 F4
  Southend-on-S SS3 . . . . . 149 E1
Colne Ho **5** IG11 . . . . 152 B6
Colne Pl SS16 . . . . 142 C5
Colne Valley RM14 . . . . . 137 E5
Colney Rd DA1 . . . . 176 A1
Colombo Rd IG1 . . . . 133 C4
Colson Gdns IG10 . . . . . . 89 B5
Colson Gn IG10 . . . . 89 B4
Colson Path IG10 . . . . 89 A5
Colson Rd IG10 . . . . 89 B5
Colt Hatch CM20 . . . . 10 B1
Colthurst Gdns EN11 . . . . 21 D8
Coltishall Cl SS11 . . . . . . 122 B6
Coltishall Rd RM12 . . . . . 155 C6
Colt Mews EN3 . . . . 65 A2
Coltsfoot Ct RM17 . . . . . 178 D8
Coltsfoot Path RM3 . . . . . 114 D4
Columbia Wharf Rd
RM17 . . . . 178 A8
Columbine Way RM3 . . . . 114 E2
Colvers CM17 . . . . 13 C2

Colville Cl SS17 . . . . 160 F5
Colville Mews CM12 . . . . . 96 F5
Colvin Chase CM2 . . . . . . 54 B1
Colvin Gdns
  Chingford E4 . . . . 109 C7
  Redbridge IG6 . . . . 111 C3
  Wanstead E11 . . . . 132 B7
Colwall Gdns IG8 . . . . . . 110 A5
Colworth Rd IG3 . . . . 145 D4
Colyers Reach CM2 . . . . . 33 A2
Combes Rd RM9 . . . . 153 F5
Comet Cl RM19 . . . . 171 A2
Comet Way SS2 . . . . 147 B6
Comfrey Ct RM17 . . . . . . 178 D8
Commerce Est E18 . . . . 110 C1
Commercial Ho IG2 . . . . . 133 A5
Commercial Pl DA12 . . . . 179 C1
Commercial Rd SS0 . . . . . 147 D4
Commercial Way
SS15 . . . . 140 E7
Commodore Ho SS14 . . . . 142 E6
Common App SS7 . . . . . . 145 A7
Commonfields CM20 . . . . . 10 E1
Commonhall La SS7 . . . . 145 D3
Common La
  Little Baddow CM3 . . . . . 34 E2
  Stock CM4 . . . . 75 E2
  Thundersley SS7 . . . . . . 145 B7
  Woodham Walter CM9 . . . 35 B3
Common Rd
  Great Wakering SS3 . . . . 150 B4
  Harlow EN9 . . . . 22 E2
  Ingrave CM13 . . . . 117 C5
  Stock CM4 . . . . 75 E3
Commonside Rd CM18 . . . 23 F4
Common The
  Danbury CM3 . . . . 56 E6
  East Hanningfield CM3 . . . 78 B7
  Thundersley SS7 . . . . . . 145 A7
Commonwealth Ho
RM18 . . . . 179 A5
Como St RM7 . . . . 135 D7
Compass Ct DA11 . . . . . . 178 E1
Compass Gdns CM0 . . . . 106 A6
Compton Ave
  Brentwood CM13 . . . . . . 95 C1
  Romford RM2 . . . . 136 C8
Compton Ct
  Canvey Island SS8 . . . . . 164 D2
  Southend-on-S SS9 . . . . . 146 B1
  Wickford SS11 . . . . 121 E7
Compton Terr SS11 . . . . . 121 E7
Compton Wlk SS15 . . . . . 141 B7
Comroston **13** EN11 . . . 21 A6
Comyns Pl CM1 . . . . 31 B1
Comyns Rd RM9 . . . . 154 A5
Concorde Ho 1
RM12 . . . . 155 B6
Concord Rd SS8 . . . . 163 F5
Condor Wlk RM12 . . . . . . 155 B5
Condovers Cotts
RM18 . . . . 179 F8
Conduit La
  Hoddesdon EN11 . . . . . . 21 A6
  Woodham Mortimer CM9 . . 57 E6
Conduit La E EN11 . . . . . . 21 B6
Coney Burrows E4 . . . . . . 109 E8
Coney Gree CM21 . . . . . . 1 D3
Conference St **3** E4 . . . 109 C8
Congreve Rd EN9 . . . . . . 65 E6
Conifer Ave RM5 . . . . 113 B5
Conifer Ct IG1 . . . . 152 B6
Conifer Dr CM14 . . . . 116 D5
Conifers SS7 . . . . 145 E3
Coningsby Gdns E4 . . . . . 109 B4
Conisborough Ct 12
DA2 . . . . 176 B1
Coniston SS2 . . . . 147 A7
Coniston Ave
  Barking IG11 . . . . 152 E5
  Purfleet RM19 . . . . 171 C1
  Upminster RM14 . . . . . . 156 C8
Coniston Cl
  Barking IG11 . . . . 152 E5
  Rayleigh SS6 . . . . 123 E2
Coniston Ct IG6 . . . . 68 A8
Coniston Gdns IG4. . . . . . 132 E7
Coniston Rd
  Canvey Island SS8 . . . . . 164 A3
  South Benfleet SS7 . . . . . 144 E8
Coniston Way RM12 . . . . 155 A7
Connaught Ave
  Chingford E4 . . . . 87 D2
  Grays RM16 . . . . 173 C3
  Loughton IG10 . . . . 88 D5
Connaught Ct E4 . . . . 87 E2
Connaught Dr CM3 . . . . . 101 C2
Connaught Gdns SS3.. . . 168 C6
Connaught Hill IG10 . . . . 88 D5
Connaught La IG1 . . . . . . 133 D2
Connaught Mews
  Ilford IG1 . . . . 133 D2
  Loughton IG10 . . . . 88 E5
Connaught Rd
  Chingford E4 . . . . 87 E1
  Hornchurch RM12 . . . . . . 136 D1
  Ilford IG1 . . . . 133 D2
  Rayleigh SS6 . . . . 146 A8
Connaught Way CM12. . . . 97 A5
Connaught Wlk SS6 . . . . . 146 A8
Connect La IG11 . . . . 111 C1
Connington Cres E4 . . . . . 109 D7
Connor Cl IG6 . . . . 111 C2
Connor Rd RM9 . . . . 153 F8
Conrad Ct RM16 . . . . 173 B4
Conrad Gdns RM16 . . . . . 173 B4
Conrad Rd SS17 . . . . 160 E1

Consort Cl CM14 . . . . 116 C5
Constable Mews **3**
RM8 . . . . 153 B8
Constable View CM1 . . . . . 32 F6
Constable Way SS3 . . . . . 168 G8
Constance Cl CM1 . . . . . . 19 A3
Constitution Hill SS7. . . . 144 D3
Consul Ave RM13 . . . . . . 154 D2
Convent Cl SS15 . . . . 141 C6
Convent Rd SS8 . . . . 164 B3
Con Way SS7 . . . . 144 D3
Conway Ave SS3 . . . . 150 B3
Conway Cl RM13 . . . . 155 A5
Conway Cres RM6 . . . . . . 134 C5
Conway Gdns RM17 . . . . . 178 B7
Conway's Rd RM16 . . . . . 159 A3
Conybury Cl EN9 . . . . 66 A7
Conybury Ct EN9 . . . . 66 A7
Conyer Cl CM9 . . . . 58 F8
Cooke Cl RM16 . . . . 172 E3
Cooke St **3** IG11 . . . . 152 C4
Cookham Ct SS3 . . . . 149 E2
Cook Pl CM2 . . . . 32 F3
Cook's Cl RM5 . . . . 113 C2
Cooks Gn SS13 . . . . 121 C1
COOKSMILL GREEN 29 F1
Cooks Spinney CM20 . . . . 11 A3
Coolgardie Ave
  Chigwell IG7 . . . . 111 A7
  Chingford E4 . . . . 109 D5
Coombe Dr SS16 . . . . . 141 C1
Coombe Rd
  Romford RM3 . . . . 136 F8
  Southminster CM0 . . . . . 84 D5
Coombe Rise
  Chelmsford CM1 . . . . 32 B7
  Shenfield CM15 . . . . 94 F1
  Stanford-le-H SS17 . . . . . 160 E2
Coombes Cl CM12 . . . . . . 96 F4
Coombes Gr SS4. . . . . . . 126 B3
Coombes Rd RM9. . . . . . 153 F4
Coombewood Dr
  Dagenham RM6 . . . . 134 F5
  Thundersley SS7 . . . . . . 144 F5
Cooper Cl DA9 . . . . 176 F2
Coopers CM3 . . . . 33 E8
COOPERSALE 46 C2
Coopersale Cl **3** IG8 . . 110 C3
Coopersale Comm
CM16 . . . . 46 D3
Coopersale Hall Sch
CM16 . . . . 68 B5
Coopersale La CM16 . . . . 68 B3
Coopersales SS15 . . . . . . 141 A6
Coopersale St CM16 . . . . 68 D7
COOPERSALE STREET
. . . . 68 C8
Coopersale & Theydon
Garnon CE Prim Sch
CM16 . . . . 46 D2
Coopers Ave CM9 . . . . . . 37 D5
Coopers Cl
  Chigwell IG7 . . . . 112 B8
  Dagenham RM10 . . . . . . 154 B6
Coopers' Company &
Coborn Sch The
RM14 . . . . 137 D2
Coopers Ct RM2 . . . . 136 C8
Coopers Dr CM11 . . . . . . 119 C6
Cooper Shaw Rd
RM18 . . . . 179 E7
Coopers Hill CM5 . . . . . . 49 A1
Coopers Mews CM5 . . . . . 49 A2
Cooper's Row CM1. . . . . . 32 A5
Coopers Way SS2 . . . . . . 148 A5
Coote Gdns **2** RM8 . . . 134 F1
Coote Rd RM8 . . . . 134 F1
Copdock SS14 . . . . 142 C4
Copeland Ho 7
CM14 . . . . 116 C6
Copelands SS4 . . . . 125 D6
Copeman Rd CM13 . . . . . 95 D2
Copford Ave SS6. . . . . . . 123 F1
Copford Cl
  Billericay CM11 . . . . 97 C2
  Woodford IG8 . . . . 110 E4
Copford Rd CM11 . . . . . . 97 C2
Copland Cl
  Broomfield CM1. . . . . 19 A1
  Great Baddow CM2 . . . . . 54 F8
Copland Rd SS17 . . . . . . 160 D1
Coppen Rd RM8 . . . . 134 F4
Coppens Gn SS12 . . . . . . 121 E6
Copper Beech Cl IG5 . . . . 111 A2
Copper Beech Ct IG10 . . . 89 A8
Copper Beeches
  Brentwood CM14. . . . . . . 116 C6
  Thundersley SS7 . . . . . . 145 B7
Copper Beech Rd
RM15 . . . . 157 C2
Copper Ct CM21 . . . . 1 E2
Copperfield
  Billericay CM11 . . . . 119 D6
  Chigwell IG7 . . . . 111 D4
Copperfield Ct IG6. . . . . . 133 C8
Copperfield Gdns
CM14 . . . . 94 C1
Copperfield Rd CM1 . . . . . 31 E7
Copperfields SS15 . . . . . . 141 C7
Copperfields Way
RM3 . . . . 114 D2
Coppergate Ct EN9 . . . . . 66 A5
Coppice Hatch CM18 . . . . 23 D6
Coppice La
  Basildon SS15 . . . . 119 F1

Coppice La continued
  Pleshey CM6 . . . . 7 E8
Coppice Path IG7. . . . . . . 112 B6
Coppice Prim Sch
IG7 . . . . 112 A5
Coppice Row CM16 . . . . . 67 D3
Coppice The CM15 . . . . . 71 E2
Coppid Hall RM16. . . . . . 172 F5
Coppings The EN11 . . . . . 8 A1
Coppins Cl CM2.. . . . . . . 32 E4
Coppins The **2** RM6 . . 134 B4
Copse Hill CM19 . . . . 23 B5
Copse The
  Billericay CM12 . . . . 97 B4
  Chingford E4 . . . . 87 F1
Copsfield Ct E18 . . . . 132 A8
Copshall Cl SS1 . . . . 23 E4
Coptfold Cl SS1. . . . . 148 E8
Coptfold Rd CM14 . . . . . . 116 D8
COPTHALL GREEN 66 E6
Copt Hill CM16 . . . . 56 E6
Copthorne Ave IG6 . . . . . 111 B4
Copthorne Gdns
RM11 . . . . 137 A6
Coral Cl
  Ilford RM6 . . . . 134 D8
  South Woodham Ferrers
  CM3 . . . . 101 C8
Coral Ho CM20 . . . . 10 A1
Coram Gn CM13 . . . . 95 D4
Corasway SS7 . . . . 145 C5
Corbets Ave RM14 . . . . . 156 B7
CORBETS TEY 156 B7
Corbets Tey Rd RM14 . . . 156 B8
Corbets Tey Sch
RM14 . . . . 156 C7
Corbett Rd E11 . . . . 132 C5
Corbett Villas RM8. . . . . . 134 C3
Corbridge Mews 6
RM1 . . . . 135 F6
Corcorans CM15 . . . . 94 C3
Cordelia Cres SS6 . . . . . . 123 C3
Cordwainers The SS2 . . . 148 A5
Corfe Ct **2** SS13 . . . . . 143 B5
Cories Cl RM8 . . . . 134 D2
Corinth Ho IG3 . . . . 134 A4
Corinthian Manorway
DA8 . . . . 169 D2
Corinthian Rd DA8 . . . . . 169 D2
Cormorant Wlk
  Chelmsford CM2 . . . . . . 54 C5
  8 Hornchurch RM12 . . 155 B6
Cornec Ave SS9 . . . . 146 B6
Cornec Chase SS9 . . . . . . 146 C6
Cornelius Vale CM2 . . . . . 33 B4
Cornelius Vermuyden Sch
& Arts Coll The SS8. . . 163 E5
Cornell Way RM5 . . . . . . 113 B5
Corner Ho CM18 . . . . 23 F6
Corner Mdw CM18 . . . . . 24 A4
Corner Rd CM11 . . . . 120 D6
Cornfield Ct CM1. . . . . . . 32 F6
Cornfields CM3 . . . . 101 C8
Cornflower Dr CM1 . . . . . 32 F6
Cornflower Gdns CM12. . . 96 F4
Cornflower Way RM3 . . . . 114 C2
Cornhill **4** CM1. . . . . . . 32 B2
Cornhill Ave SS5. . . . . . . 124 E7
Cornhouse Bldgs 145 C8
Cornish Gr CM3. . . . . 101 E6
Cornmill EN9 . . . . 65 B6
Cornshaw Rd RM8 . . . . . . 134 D3
Cornsland CM14 . . . . 116 D7
Cornsland Cl RM14 . . . . . 137 C8
Cornsland Ct 10
CM14 . . . . 116 C7
Cornwall Cl
  Barking IG11 . . . . 152 F6
  Hornchurch RM11 . . . . . . 137 A7
Cornwall Cres CM1 . . . . . 32 A7
Cornwall Gate RM19 . . . . 171 A2
Cornwall Gdns SS4 . . . . . 125 C5
Cornwallis Dr CM3. . . . . . 101 F7
Cornwallis Ho SS14 . . . . . 142 A8
Cornwallis Rd RM9. . . . . . 153 E8
Cornwall Rd
  Basildon SS13 . . . . 143 F7
  Dartford DA1. . . . . 176 A4
  Pilgrims Hatch CM15 . . . . 94 B4
Cornwell Cres SS17. . . . . 160 E3
Cornworthy SS3 . . . . 168 C8
Cornworthy Rd RM8 . . . . 153 C7
Corona Rd
  Basildon SS16 . . . . 141 B3
  Canvey Island SS8 . . . . . 164 D5
Coronation Ave RM18 . . 175 C2
Coronation Cl
  Great Wakering SS3 . . . . 149 F2
  Ilford IG6 . . . . 133 C7
Coronation Cotts
CM15 . . . . 116 E8
Coronation Ct RM18 . . . . 175 C2
Coronation Dr RM12 . . . . 155 B7
Coronation Hill CM16 . . . . 45 F2
Coronation Rd CM0 . . . . . 106 B4
Corporation Rd CM1 . . . . . 32 A4
Corral Hts DA8 . . . . 169 E1
Corran Way RM15. . . . . . 172 B6
CORRINGHAM 161 A4
Corringham Prim Sch
SS17 . . . . 161 C3
Corringham Rd
  Corringham SS17 . . . . . . 161 A2
  Stanford-le-H, Balstonia
  SS17 . . . . 160 F2
  Stanford-le-H SS17 . . . . . 160 E3
Corsel Rd SS8 . . . . 164 E3
Cortina Dr RM13 . . . . 154 C3
Corton Trad Est SS7. . . . . 144 D7

Corve La RM15. . . . . 172 B6
Cory Dr CM13.. . . . . 95 B2
Cosgrove Ave SS9 . . . . . . 146 B3
Cosgrove Rd RM20 . . . . . 176 F2
Cossington Ct SS0 . . . . . 166 E8
Cossington Rd SS0 . . . . . 166 E8
Costead Manor Rd
CM14 . . . . 94 B3
Coteford Cl SS17 . . . . 89 B7
Cotelands SS16 . . . . 142 F3
Cotleigh Rd RM7. . . . . . . 135 D5
Cotman Lo CM1. . . . . 32 F6
Cotman Mews RM8 . . . . . 153 B7
Cotswold Ave SS6 . . . . . . 123 D4
Cotswold Cres CM1 . . . . . 31 D6
Cotswold Gdns
  Brentwood CM13. . . . . . . 95 E2
  Ilford IG2 . . . . 133 D4
Cotswold Rd
  Romford RM3 . . . . 114 F1
  Southend-on-S SS0 . . . . . 147 D1
Cottage Pl CM1 . . . . 32 B3
Cottages The SS3 . . . . . . 168 F4
Cottesmore Ave IG5 . . . . 111 A1
Cottesmore Ct SS8. . . . . 164 B2
Cottesmore Ct SS9. . . . . 146 A2
Cottesmore Gdns
SS9 . . . . 146 A1
Cottey Ho CM2 . . . . 54 B2
Cottis Cl SS16 . . . . 141 A3
Cotton Cl RM9 . . . . 153 C5
Cotton La DA2, DA9 . . . . . 176 C2
Cottons App RM7. . . . . . . 135 D5
Cottons Ct **3** RM7 . . . . 135 D6
Couchmore Ave IG5 . . . . 110 F1
Coulde Dennis **2** 78 B7
Coulson Ct RM8 . . . . 134 C3
Coulter Ho DA9 . . . . 177 C2
Coulter Mews CM11. . . . . 97 B3
Council Ave DA11 . . . . . 178 C1
Council Bglws SS17 . . . . . 161 D4
Council Hos
  Bicknacre CM3. . . . . 56 F1
  Bradwell on S CM0 . . . . . 63 E8
  Corringham SS17. . . . . . 161 D4
County Chambers
SS1 . . . . 167 A7
County Pl CM2 . . . . 32 B1
Courage Ct 7 CM13 . . . 95 C3
  8 Hornchurch RM12 . . 155 B6
Courage Wlk CM13. . . . . . 95 D3
Courtauld Rd SS13 . . . . . 121 C2
Court Ave RM3 . . . . 115 A3
Courtenay Dr RM16 . . . . . 172 F3
Courtenay Gdns
RM14 . . . . 137 C3
Courtfield SS7. . . . . 144 D1
Courtfield Cl EN10 . . . . . . 21 A3
Court Gdns RM3 . . . . 115 A3
Court Ind Est CM2 . . . . . . 32 C2
Courtland Ave
  Chingford E4 . . . . 109 F8
  Ilford IG1 . . . . 133 C3
  Redbridge IG4 . . . . 132 F2
Courtland Dr IG7 . . . . 111 C9
Courtland Mews CM9 . . . . 58 F8
Courtland Pl CM9 . . . . . . 58 F8
Courtlands
  Billericay CM12 . . . . 96 E2
  Chelmsford CM1 . . . . 32 A6
  Southend-on-S SS9 . . . . . 146 B7
Court Lo **12** DA17 . . . . 169 A1
Court Mews DA11 . . . . . . 178 B1
Court Needham EN3 . . . . 65 A2
Courtney Park Rd
SS16 . . . . 141 B5
Courtney Rd RM16 . . . . . 174 C4
Courtney Twrs IG2. . . . . . 133 D5
Court Rd CM1 . . . . 19 A3
COURTSEND 130 F8
Courts The SS6 . . . . 123 E3
Court View CM4 . . . . 73 F1
Courtway IG8 . . . . 110 C5
Court Way
  Ilford IG6 . . . . 133 C8
  Romford RM3 . . . . 114 F1
Courtway Cotts SS17 . . . . 161 D4
Courtyard Mews 1
DA9 . . . . 177 A1
Courtyard The
  Basildon SS14 . . . . 142 D7
  Billericay CM11 . . . . 97 C1
  Brentwood CM15. . . . . . . 94 B2
  Harlow CM17. . . . . 11 D4
  Maldon CM9. . . . . 36 F2
  Mayland CM3. . . . . 60 F1
Coval Ave CM1 . . . . 32 A3
Coval La CM1 . . . . 32 A2
Coval Wells CM1 . . . . 32 A2
Covenbrook CM13 . . . . . . 117 B7
Coventry Cl SS5 . . . . 101 F1
Coventry Rd IG1 . . . . 133 B3
Coverdales The IG11. . . . . 152 D3
Coverley Cl CM13 . . . . . . 116 C4
Covert Rd IG6 . . . . 111 F4
Coverts The
  Brentwood CM13. . . . . . . 95 A1
  Writtle CM1 . . . . 31 B1
Cowan Cl **1** IG8 . . . . . 110 C4
Cowbridge La IG11 . . . . . 152 B5
Cowdray Way RM12 . . . . . 155 A8
Cowdrie Way CM2 . . . . . . 33 B4
Cowell Ave CM1 . . . . 31 E5
Cowell Lo IG8 . . . . 109 F5
COW GREEN 94 A5
Cowley Ave DA9 . . . . 177 A2
Cowley Ct **3** E18 . . . . . 110 A1

Cowley Rd
 Ilford IG1 ....133 A4
 Redbridge IG1 ....132 F4
 Romford RM3 ....114 B3
 Wanstead E11 ....132 B6
Cowlins CM17 ....11 D4
Cowper Ave RM18 ....179 B6
Cowper Rd
 6 Belvedere DA17 ....169 A2
 Rainham RM13 ....155 A1
Cowslip Mead SS14 ....142 B6
Cowslip Rd E18 ....110 B1
Cow Watering La CM1 ....30 E2
Coxbridge Ct CM12 ....97 A2
Coxes Cl SS17 ....160 D3
Coxes Farm Rd CM11 ....119 E7
Cox Ley CM22 ....3 A3
Coxon Dr RM16 ....172 E3
Coxs Cl CM3 ....101 E8
COXTIE GREEN 93 C4
Coxtie Green Rd
 Pilgrims Hatch CM14 ....93 C5
 South Weald CM14 ....93 A2
Crabtree Ave RM6 ....134 D7
Crabtree Manorway N
 DA17 ....169 C5
Crabtree Manorway S
 DA17 ....169 C3
Craftsmans Sq SS2 ....148 A5
Craigdale Rd RM11 ....135 F4
Craig Gdns E18 ....109 F1
Craiston Way CM2 ....54 F5
Crammavill St RM16 ....173 A5
Crammerville Wlk 2
 RM13 ....155 B1
Cramphorn Wlk CM1 ....31 F3
Cranborne Gdns
 RM14 ....137 B2
Cranborne Rd
 Barking IG11 ....152 D4
 Hoddesdon EN11 ....21 C7
Cranbourne Ave E11 ....132 B7
Cranbourne Ct E18 ....132 B7
Cranbourne Dr EN11 ....8 C2
Cranbourne Gdns
 IG6 ....133 C8
Cranbourne Ho EN11 ....8 C2
Cranbourne Prim Sch The
 EN11 ....8 B2
Cranbrook Ave SS7 ....145 C4
Cranbrook Coll (Boys)
 IG1 ....133 A2
Cranbrook Dr RM2 ....136 C7
Cranbrook Lo SS7 ....145 C4
Cranbrook Rd IG1,
 IG2 ....133 A5
Cranbrook Rise
 Ilford IG1 ....133 A4
 Redbridge IG1 ....132 F5
Crane Cl RM10 ....154 A6
Cranell Gn RM15 ....172 B5
CRANES 120 F2
Cranes Cl SS13 ....120 F1
Cranes Ct SS14 ....142 C8
Cranes Farm Rd SS14 ....120 D1
Cranes La SS14 ....142 C8
Cranfield Ct
 4 Wickford SS12 ....121 C8
 2 Woodford IG8 ....110 A6
Cranfield Park Ave
 SS12 ....121 F2
Cranfield Park Ct 5
 SS12 ....121 D5
Cranfield Park Rd
 SS12 ....121 D4
CRANHAM 137 F4
Cranham Gdns RM14 ....137 F4
Cranham Pl RM14 ....157 A7
Cranham Rd RM11 ....136 B5
Cranleigh Dr SS9 ....146 E1
Cranleigh Gdns
 Barking IG11 ....152 D6
 Hullbridge SS5 ....101 D1
 Loughton IG10 ....88 F3
Cranley Ave SS0 ....147 D1
Cranley Dr IG2 ....133 C4
Cranley Gdns SS3 ....168 C6
Cranley Rd
 Ilford IG2 ....133 C4
 Southend-on-S SS7 ....147 D1
Cranmer Cl CM12 ....97 B6
Cranmer Ct RM14 ....137 C2
Cranmer Gdns RM10 ....154 C8
Cranmer Ho CM2 ....53 F7
Cranston Ave SS0 ....147 D5
Cranston Gdns E4 ....109 B4
Cranston Park Ave
 RM14 ....156 C8
Cranworth Cres 7 E4 ....87 D1
Craven Ave SS8 ....164 A3
Craven Cl SS4 ....125 D5
Craven Ct RM6 ....134 E5
Craven Gdns
 Barking IG11 ....152 E3
 Ilford IG6 ....133 D8
 Redbridge IG6 ....111 D1
 Romford, Harold Park
  RM3 ....115 C4
 Romford, Willoughby's Hill
  RM5 ....113 A5
Crawford Ave RM3 ....173 B5
Crawford Chase SS12 ....121 C6
Crawford Cl CM12 ....97 C5
Crawford Compton Cl
 RM12 ....155 C6
Crawley Cl SS17 ....161 A4
Crawley Ct 6 DA11 ....179 B1
Crayford Cl CM9 ....58 E8

Craylands SS14 ....142 F7
Craylands La DA10 ....177 D2
Craylands Sch The
 DA10 ....177 D2
Craylands Sq DA10 ....177 D2
CRAYS HILL 120 D5
Crays Hill CM11 ....120 C5
Crayshill Pk CM11 ....120 C5
Crays Hill Prim Sch
 CM11 ....120 D6
Crays Hill Rd CM11 ....120 D4
Crays View CM12 ....119 B8
Crealock Gr IG8 ....109 F5
Creance Ct CM2 ....32 A2
Creasen Butt Cl CM9 ....37 A4
Creasey Cl RM11 ....136 B2
Creasy Ct SS14 ....142 E6
Crediton Ho 4 RM3 ....114 D4
Credo Way RM20 ....177 B8
Creeds Cotts CM16 ....67 E7
Creeds Farm CM16 ....67 E7
Creekmouth Ind Pk
 IG11 ....152 F1
Creek Rd
 Barking IG11 ....152 F2
 Canvey Island SS8 ....164 D4
CREEKSEA 105 F5
Creeksea Ferry Rd
 SS4 ....105 C2
Creeksea La CM0 ....105 F6
Creekside RM13 ....154 F1
Creek The DA11 ....178 B2
Creek View SS16 ....142 E3
Creek View Ave SS5 ....101 D3
Creekview Rd CM3 ....101 F7
Cree Way RM1 ....113 E3
Creephedge La CM3 ....78 E5
Crescent Ave
 Grays RM17 ....178 D8
 Hornchurch RM12 ....135 F2
Crescent Cl CM12 ....96 F4
Crescent Ct
 Billericay CM12 ....97 A2
 Grays RM17 ....173 D1
 Heybridge CM9 ....36 F5
Crescent Dr CM15 ....94 E1
Crescent Gdns CM12 ....96 F4
Crescent Rd
 Aveley RM15 ....171 C4
 Billericay CM12 ....96 F4
 Brentwood CM14 ....116 B6
 Canvey Island SS8 ....164 D2
 Chingford E4 ....87 E2
 Dagenham RM10 ....135 B1
 Great Baddow CM2 ....55 A7
 Heybridge CM9 ....36 F5
 South Benfleet SS7 ....144 D2
 Southend-on-S SS9 ....146 B1
 Woodford E18 ....110 C2
Crescent The
 Epping CM16 ....67 F7
 Greenhithe DA9 ....177 C2
 Hadleigh SS7 ....145 F3
 Harlow CM17 ....11 C6
 Ilford IG2 ....133 A5
 Loughton IG10 ....88 D3
 Upminster RM14 ....137 F4
Crescent Way IG10 ....88 D4
Crescent Way RM15 ....171 D5
Crescent Wlk RM15 ....171 C4
Cressells SS15 ....141 F6
Cresset Cl SG12 ....8 C3
Cressingham Ct 1
 DA17 ....169 A3
Crest Ave
 Basildon SS13 ....143 C6
 Grays RM17 ....178 B7
Cresthill Ave RM17 ....173 C2
Crest The
 Sawbridgeworth CM21 ....1 D2
 Southend-on-S SS9 ....146 D6
Crest View DA9 ....177 A3
Creswick Ave SS6 ....123 C3
Creswick Ct SS6 ....123 C3
Crete Hall Rd DA11 ....178 E1
Crick Ct 3 IG11 ....152 C3
Cricket Ct E6 ....152 A2
Cricketers Cl
 Broomfield CM1 ....19 C1
 Erith DA8 ....169 E1
Cricketers La CM13 ....117 D3
Cricketers Ret Pk
 SS13 ....121 A2
Cricketers Row CM13 ....117 D3
Cricketers Way SS13 ....121 A2
Cricketfield Gr SS9 ....146 F2
Crickhollow CM3 ....101 C5
Cricklade Ave RM3 ....114 D4
Cringle Lock CM3 ....101 E5
Cripplegate CM0 ....84 E5
Cripsey Ave SS5 ....48 F5
Crispe Ho 4 IG11 ....152 D3
Crispins SS1 ....168 A8
Crispin Terr IG8 ....110 D4
Critchett Terr 1 CM1 ....32 A3
Crocus Way CM1 ....32 E7
Croft Cl
 South Benfleet SS7 ....144 C5
 Southend-on-S SS9 ....146 E4
Croft Ct CM1 ....32 E8
Crofters CM21 ....1 E3
Crofters End CM21 ....1 E3
Croft Lodge Cl IG8 ....110 B4
Crofton Ave SS17 ....160 F4
Crofton Gr E4 ....109 D6
Crofton Rd RM16 ....173 E4
Croft Rd SS7 ....144 C5

Crofts The SS3 ....149 E4
Croft The
 Chingford E4 ....109 E8
 Loughton IG10 ....89 A7
 Rayleigh SS6 ....145 F8
Cromarty Ho CM14 ....116 D6
Cromar Way CM1 ....31 F1
Crombie Cl IG4 ....132 F6
Cromer Cl SS15 ....141 B8
Cromer Rd
 Dagenham RM6 ....134 E5
 Hornchurch RM11 ....136 D4
 Romford RM7 ....135 C5
 Southend-on-S SS1 ....167 B8
 Woodford IG8 ....110 A6
Cromer Terr 3 RM6 ....134 B6
Crompton Cl SS14 ....141 F8
Crompton Pl 8 EN3 ....65 A1
Crompton St CM1 ....31 F1
Cromwell Ave CM12 ....97 A3
Cromwell Cl CM3 ....33 D8
Cromwell Ctr
 Barking IG11 ....153 A1
 Redbridge IG6 ....112 B5
Cromwell Ctr The
 RM8 ....134 F4
Cromwell Hill CM9 ....36 F3
Cromwell La CM9 ....36 F3
Cromwell Lo IG11 ....152 E7
Cromwell Rd
 Brentwood CM14 ....116 B6
 Grays RM17 ....173 A1
 Hockley SS5 ....124 E6
 Southend-on-S SS2 ....148 B3
Cromwells Mere RM5 ....113 D4
Cromwell Trad Ctr
 IG11 ....152 E2
Crondon Park La CM4 ....75 E4
Crooked La DA11,
 DA12 ....179 B1
Crooked Mile
 Waltham Abbey EN9 ....65 C6
 Waltham Abbey EN9 ....65 C2
Crooked Way EN9 ....21 E1
Cropenburg Wlk SS8 ....164 B5
Croppath Rd RM10 ....154 A8
Crosby Ct IG7 ....112 A7
Crosby Rd
 Dagenham RM10 ....154 B4
 Southend-on-S SS0 ....166 C8
Cross Ave SS12 ....121 C6
Cross Cl SS16 ....141 F5
Crossbow Ct CM5 ....49 A2
Crossbow Rd IG7 ....111 F5
Crosby Cl CM15 ....95 E8
Crosse Cts SS15 ....141 C5
Crossfell Rd SS7 ....144 F7
Crossfield Rd
 Hoddesdon EN11 ....21 B8
 Southend-on-S SS2 ....148 D2
Crossfields IG10 ....89 B4
Cross Gn SS16 ....141 F5
Crossing Rd CM16 ....68 A6
Crossness Rd IG11 ....152 F2
Cross Rd
 Basildon SS13 ....143 F7
 Chingford E4 ....87 E1
 Dagenham RM6 ....134 C4
 Gravesend DA11 ....178 F1
 Hadleigh SS7 ....145 B4
 Maldon CM9 ....37 A1
 Romford RM7 ....135 B8
 Woodford IG8 ....110 F4
Cross Roads IG10 ....88 C7
Cross St 16 DA11 ....179 B1
Crossway
 Dagenham RM8 ....134 C1
 6 Stanford-le-H SS17 ....160 F3
 Woodford IG8 ....110 C6
Cross Way 3 CM17 ....11 D1
CROSSWAYS 176 D4
Crossways
 Canvey Island SS8 ....163 E4
 Chelmsford CM2 ....54 C7
 Loughton IG10 ....89 A4
 Romford RM2 ....136 B8
 Shenfield CM15 ....95 A3
Crossways Bvd DA2 ....176 C3
Crossways The SS0 ....166 A8
Crossway The CM11 ....97 D3
Crouch Ave
 Barking IG11 ....153 B3
 Hullbridge SS5 ....101 E1
Crouch Beck CM3 ....101 E2
Crouch Ct CM20 ....10 C3
Crouch Dr SS11 ....121 D8
Crouchman Cl RM16 ....173 C4
Crouchmans Ave SS3 ....150 A4
Crouchman's Farm Rd
 CM9 ....35 C7
Crouch Mdw SS5 ....101 E4
Crouch Pk SS5 ....101 E4
Crouch Rd
 Burnham-on-C CM0 ....106 C3
 Grays RM16 ....174 A1
Crouch St SS15 ....119 E2
Crouch Valley RM14 ....137 E4
Crouchview Cl SS11 ....122 B7
Crouch View Cotts
 CM3 ....100 C5
Crouch View Cres
 SS5 ....125 A8
Crouch View Gr SS5 ....101 D3
Crouch View Villas
 SS4 ....104 E2

Crouch Way SS3 ....168 E7
Crough Rd CM3 ....103 A7
Crowborough Rd SS2 ....148 A2
Crow Gn SS5 ....94 A5
Crow Green La CM15 ....94 A5
Crow Green Rd CM15 ....94 A5
Crow La RM7 ....135 B4
Crowlands Ave RM7 ....135 B5
Crowlands Jun & Inf Schs
 RM7 ....135 C5
Crown Ave SS13 ....143 C7
Crown Bldgs 4 E4 ....87 D1
Crown Cl
 Basildon SS13 ....143 C6
 Sheering CM22 ....12 C8
Crown Ct RM18 ....179 A5
Crownfield Ave IG2 ....133 E6
Crownfield Jun & Inf Schs
 RM7 ....113 A1
Crown Gate CM20 ....23 D8
Crown Gdns SS6 ....123 C2
Crown Hill
 Loughton IG16 ....67 A5
 Rayleigh SS6 ....123 C2
 Waltham Abbey EN9,
  CM20 ....66 F6
Crownhill Rd IG8 ....110 E3
Crown Hts SS6 ....123 D2
Crownmead Way
 RM7 ....135 B7
Crown Par RM13 ....155 B1
Crown Rd
 Billericay CM11 ....97 B2
 Cold Norton CM3 ....80 F6
 Grays RM17 ....178 A8
 Hockley SS5 ....124 B5
 Ilford IG6 ....133 D7
 Kelvedon Hatch CM14 ....93 D8
Crown St
 Brentwood CM14 ....116 C8
 Dagenham RM10 ....154 C6
Crown Way CM0 ....84 C4
Crowsfield Cotts CM4 ....76 F4
Crowsheath La CM11 ....98 E6
Crows La CM3 ....79 D5
Crowsnest The CM0 ....106 C3
Crows Rd
 Barking IG11 ....152 B6
 Epping CM16 ....45 F1
Crowstone Ave SS0 ....166 C8
Crowstone Cl SS0 ....147 D1
Crowstone Prep Sch
 SS0 ....166 C8
Crowstone Rd
 Grays RM16 ....173 C4
 Southend-on-S SS0 ....166 C8
Crowstone (Sutton) Prep
 Sch SS4 ....148 B8
Croxford Way RM7 ....135 D3
Croxon Way CM0 ....106 B7
Crozier Terr CM2 ....33 B4
Crucible Cl RM6 ....134 B5
Cruick Ave RM15 ....172 C6
Crusader Ct RM19 ....171 A2
Crushes Cl CM13 ....95 E3
Crushton Pl CM1 ....31 F6
Crusoe Rd DA8 ....169 D1
Crystal Ave RM12 ....136 E1
Crystal Cl 1 RM13 ....155 A1
Crystal Stps 15 SS1 ....167 C7
Crystal Way RM8 ....134 C3
Cuckoo Cnr SS2 ....147 E4
Cuckoo La RM16 ....172 F5
Culford Rd RM16 ....173 C4
Cullen Sq RM15 ....172 C5
Cullings Ct EN9 ....65 F6
Culverdown SS14 ....142 A6
Culver Rise CM3 ....101 E6
Cumberland Ave
 Hornchurch RM12 ....136 E1
 Maldon CM9 ....36 E1
 South Benfleet SS7 ....144 C3
 Southend-on-S SS2 ....148 D2
Cumberland Cl
 Hornchurch RM12 ....136 E1
 Redbridge IG6 ....111 C2
Cumberland Cres CM1 ....32 A7
Cumberland Ct
 2 Hoddesdon EN11 ....21 A7
 Woodford IG8 ....110 B3
Cumberland Dr SS15 ....141 A6
Cumberland Ho
 Romford RM7 ....113 A1
 Southend-on-S SS2 ....147 F1
Cumberland Rd RM16 ....172 E3
Cumbrae Mews SS12 ....121 F5
Cumley Rd CM5 ....47 C3
Cumming Rd CM11 ....99 A2
Cummings Hall La
 RM3 ....114 D7
Cunningham Cl
 Ilford RM6 ....134 C6
 Southend-on-S SS3 ....168 F8
Cunningham Dr SS12 ....121 F5
Cunningham Rise
 CM16 ....47 D6
Cupids Chase SS3 ....150 C2
Cupid's Cnr SS3 ....150 C2
Curlew Ave CM3 ....83 A4
Curlew Cl CM9 ....37 C5
Curlew Cres SS16 ....142 B3
Curlew Ho
 1 Burnham-on-C
  CM0 ....106 C4
 Rainham RM13 ....170 A8

Curlew Terr IG5 ....133 A8
Curling La RM17 ....172 F1
Curling Tye SS14 ....142 D7
CURLING TYE GREEN 36 A3
Curling Tye La
 Maldon CM9 ....36 A3
 Woodham Walter CM9 ....35 F3
Curling Wlk SS14 ....142 D7
Curteys CM17 ....11 D5
Curtis Mill La RM4 ....91 F4
Curtis Rd RM11 ....136 F4
Curtisway SS6 ....123 E4
Curzon Cres IG11 ....152 F2
Curzon Dr RM17 ....178 C7
Curzon Way CM2 ....33 A2
Cusak Rd CM2 ....32 F3
Cut-A-Thwart La CM9 ....36 C4
Cutforth Rd CM21 ....1 E3
Cuthberga Cl 2 IG11 ....152 C5
Cutlers Ct CM3 ....101 E8
Cutmore Pl CM2 ....53 F8
Cuton Hall La CM2 ....33 A5
Cutter Ho DA8 ....169 E1
Cutty Sark Ct DA9 ....177 A2
Cygnet Cl
 Kelvedon Hatch CM15 ....71 E2
 Wickford SS12 ....121 D8
Cygnet View RM20 ....171 F2
Cygnet Way CM19 ....9 A1
Cyna Ct 6 E11 ....132 A5
Cypress Cl
 Basildon SS15 ....119 C1
 Waltham Abbey EN9 ....65 D5
Cypress Dr CM2 ....54 C6
Cypress Gr IG6 ....111 E4
Cypress Path RM3 ....114 D3
Cyril Dowsett Ct CM9 ....36 E2
Cyril Hall Ct DA11 ....178 F1
Czarina Rise SS15 ....141 E8

D

Daarle Ave SS8 ....164 A4
Dacre Ave
 Aveley RM15 ....171 D5
 Redbridge IG5 ....111 A1
Dacre Cl IG7 ....111 C6
Dacre Cres RM15 ....171 D5
Dacre Gdns IG7 ....111 C6
Dacres Gate CM5 ....27 E4
Dads Wood CM20 ....23 C8
Daen Ingas CM3 ....56 D7
Daffodil Ave CM15 ....94 B4
Daffodil Gdns IG1 ....152 B7
Daffodil Way CM1 ....32 E7
DAGENHAM 154 C4
Dagenham Ave RM9 ....153 E4
Dagenham Dock Sta
 RM9 ....153 F3
Dagenham East Sta
 RM10 ....154 C7
Dagenham Heathway Sta
 RM9 ....153 F6
Dagenham Park Com Sch
 RM10 ....154 B4
Dagenham Rd
 Dagenham RM10,
  RM7 ....135 D2
 Rainham RM13 ....154 E5
Dagmar Rd RM10 ....154 C5
Dagnam Park Cl RM3 ....115 A5
Dagnam Park Dr RM3 ....114 F5
Dagnam Park Gdns
 RM3 ....115 A4
Dagnam Park Sq RM3 ....115 B4
Dagwood La CM15 ....72 B1
Dahlia Cl 2 CM1 ....32 F5
Dahlia Gdns IG1 ....152 B6
Daiglen Dr SS15 ....172 B7
Daiglen Sch The IG9 ....110 C8
Daines Cl
 Little Ilford E12 ....132 F1
 Southend-on-S SS1 ....168 B8
 South Ockendon RM15 ....157 A1
Daines Way CM11 ....97 C2
Daines Way SS1 ....168 B8
Dairy Ct CM3 ....101 C8
Dairy Farm Rd CM3 ....83 D3
Dairy Rd CM2 ....32 F4
Daisy Ct CM1 ....33 A6
Daisy Ho IG3 ....134 A3
Daisy Rd E18 ....110 B1
Dakyn Dr CM4 ....75 D3
Dale Ct RM15 ....172 A7
Dale Ct
 Sawbridgeworth CM21 ....1 D1
 Woodford E18 ....110 A1
Dalefield IG9 ....88 D1
Dale Gdns IG8 ....110 B6
Dalen Ave SS8 ....164 A3
Dale Rd SS9 ....146 B1
Dales The SS4 ....125 D3
Dalestone Mews RM3 ....114 B4
Dale The
 Thundersley SS7 ....145 A4
 Waltham Abbey EN9 ....65 C5
Dale View Ave E4 ....109 C8
Dale View Cres E4 ....109 C7
Dale View Gdns E4 ....109 D7
Dalewood Cl RM11 ....136 E4
Dalkeith Rd IG1 ....133 C1
Dalmatia Rd SS1 ....167 D8
Dalmeney SS16 ....141 B4

Dalroy Cl RM15 . . . . .172 A7
Dalrymple Cl CM1 . . . . .32 D3
Dalton Holme IG8 . . . . . . .110 F4
Daltons Fen SS3 . . . . .143 C8
Daltons Shaw RM16 . . . . .174 A8
Dalwood SS3 . . . . .149 D1
Dalwood Gdns SS7 . . . . . .145 E4
Dalys Rd SS4 . . . . .125 E2
Dame Elizabeth Ct
  CM1 . . . . .18 F3
Dames Rd E7 . . . . .132 A1
Dame Tipping CE Prim
  Sch RM4 . . . . .113 E7
Dammer Wick CM0 . . . . . .106 E6
Dammerwick Cotts
  CM0 . . . . .106 D6
Damon Pl 16 CM14 . . . . . .116 C7
Danacre SS15 . . . . .141 C7
DANBURY 56 D7
Danbury Cl
  Ilford RM6 . . . . .134 D8
  Pilgrims Hatch CM15 . . . .93 F4
  Southend-on-S SS9 . . . . .146 F4
Danbury Cres RM15 . . . . .172 B7
Danbury Ctry Pk★
  CM3 . . . . .56 B7
Danbury Down SS14 . . . . .142 E8
Danbury Lo IG10 . . . . .88 E3
Danbury Mans 3
  IG11 . . . . .152 B5
Danbury Park Com Prim
  Sch CM3 . . . . .56 C7
Danbury Rd
  Loughton IG10 . . . . .88 E3
  Rainham RM13 . . . . .154 F4
  Rayleigh SS6 . . . . .123 B3
Danbury Vale CM3 . . . . . . .57 A6
Danbury Way IG8 . . . . . . .110 C4
Dandelion Cl RM7 . . . . . . .135 E2
Dandies Chase SS9 . . . . .146 E7
Dandies Cl SS9 . . . . .146 D7
Dandies Dr SS9 . . . . .146 D7
Danehurst Gdns IG4 . . . . .132 F6
Danemead EN11 . . . . .8 A1
Dane Rd
  Chelmsford CM1 . . . . .31 E2
  Ilford IG1 . . . . .152 C7
Dane's Ave SS3 . . . . .168 F5
Danescroft Cl SS9 . . . . . .146 E4
Danescroft Dr SS9 . . . . . .146 D4
Danesfield SS7 . . . . .144 C2
Danesleigh Gdns SS9 . . . .146 D4
Danes Rd RM7 . . . . .135 C4
Dane St SS3 . . . . .168 G6
Danes Way CM15 . . . . .94 A4
Danette Gdns RM8 . . . . . .134 F2
Dangan Rd E11 . . . . .132 A5
Daniel Cl
  Grays, Chafford Hundred
    RM16 . . . . .172 E4
  Grays, Orsett Heath
    RM16 . . . . .174 B3
Danyon Cl RM13 . . . . .155 C3
Daphne Gdns E4 . . . . .109 C7
Darby Dr EN9 . . . . .65 C6
D'arcy Ave CM9 . . . . .37 B1
D'arcy Cl CM13 . . . . .95 B2
D'arcy Cl CM0 . . . . .106 C6
D'arcy Gdns RM9 . . . . . . .153 F4
Darcy Rise CM3 . . . . .34 E1
Dare Gdns RM8 . . . . .134 E1
Darell Way CM11 . . . . .97 D1
Darenth La RM15 . . . . . . .172 A7
Darenth Rd SS9 . . . . .146 B1
Darent Ind Pk DA8 . . . . . .170 D1
Dark La
  Brentwood CM14 . . . . . . .115 F5
  Great Warley CM14 . . . . .116 A3
  Thundersley SS7 . . . . . . .145 A6
Darlinghurst Gr SS9 . . . . .147 A2
Darlinghurst Prim Sch
  SS9 . . . . .146 F2
Darlington Ct
  6 Harlow CM17 . . . . .11 C4
  Pilgrims Hatch CM15 . . . .94 A3
Darlington Gdns RM3 . . . .114 D5
Darlington Path 16
  RM3 . . . . .114 D5
Darnay Rise CM1 . . . . .31 D6
Darnley Rd
  Gravesend DA11 . . . . . . .179 B1
  Grays RM17 . . . . .178 B8
  Woodford IG8 . . . . .110 B2
Darrell Cl CM1 . . . . .32 B6
Dart Cl RM14 . . . . .137 D5
Dartfields RM3 . . . . .114 D4
DARTFORD 176 B2
Dartford Gdns RM6 . . . . . .134 B6
Dart Gn RM15 . . . . .172 B7
Dartmouth Cl SS6 . . . . . . .123 C5
Dartmouth Rd CM1 . . . . . . .32 E6
Dartview Ct RM17 . . . . . . .173 E2
Darwell Cl E6 . . . . .152 A3
Darwin Rd RM18 . . . . .178 F6
Dashes The CM20 . . . . .10 E1
Datchet Dr SS3 . . . . .149 E2
Davall Ho RM17 . . . . .178 B8
Davenant Foundation Sch
  Loughton IG10 . . . . .67 C1
  Loughton IG10 . . . . .89 C8
Davenants SS13 . . . . .143 B8
Davenport CM17 . . . . .24 E7
Davenport Ctr IG11 . . . . . .153 B3
Daventry Gdns RM3 . . . . .114 C5
Daventry Gn RM3 . . . . . . .114 C5

Daventry Rd RM3 . . . . . . .114 C5
David Ave SS11 . . . . .99 D2
David Coffer Ct DA17 . . . .169 B2
David Dr RM3 . . . . .115 A3
David Rd RM8 . . . . .134 E2
Davidson Gdns SS12 . . . .121 E5
Davidson Ho RM7 . . . . . . .177 C2
Davidson Way RM7 . . . . . .135 E5
Davids Way IG6 . . . . .111 E3
David Terr RM3 . . . . .115 A4
Davies Cl RM13 . . . . .155 C2
Davington Gdns RM8 . . . . .153 B7
Davington Rd RM8 . . . . . . .153 B7
Davinia Cl IG8 . . . . .110 F4
Davis Rd
  Aveley RM15 . . . . .171 D5
  Grays RM17 . . . . .172 F3
Dawberry Pl CM3 . . . . . . .101 D5
Dawes Ave RM12 . . . . . . .136 E1
Dawes Cl DA9 . . . . .176 F2
Dawley Gn RM15 . . . . . . .172 A7
Dawlish Cres SS6 . . . . . . .123 D5
Dawlish Dr
  Ilford IG3 . . . . .152 F8
  Southend-on-S SS9 . . . . .146 E1
Dawlish Wlk RM3 . . . . . . .114 C4
Dawn Cl CM7 . . . . .59 B8
Dawnings The CM3 . . . . . .101 C8
Daws Cl CM1 . . . . .30 F1
Daws Hill E4 . . . . .87 C6
DAWS HEATH 145 E5
Daws Heath Rd
  Hadleigh SS7 . . . . .145 E4
  Rayleigh SS6 . . . . .145 E8
  Thundersley SS7 . . . . . . .145 D6
Dawson Ave IG11 . . . . . . .152 F5
Dawson Dr RM13 . . . . . . .155 B5
Dawson Gdns 10 IG11 . . .152 F5
Dawson Mews CM11 . . . . .97 B3
Daylop Dr IG7 . . . . .112 B7
Days Cl CM1 . . . . .32 B8
Days La
  Doddinghurst CM15 . . . . .72 C1
  Pilgrims Hatch CM15 . . . .94 B7
Dayton Dr DA8 . . . . .170 D1
Deacon Dr SS15 . . . . .141 C7
Deacon Way IG8 . . . . .110 F4
Deadman's La CM2 . . . . . . .54 C4
Dealtree Cl CM15 . . . . .72 B4
Dean Ct RM7 . . . . .135 D5
Deanes Sch The SS7 . . . . .145 C6
Deans Ct CM14 . . . . .116 B6
Deans Ind Est RM13 . . . . .155 D1
Deans Rd CM14 . . . . .116 B6
Dean Way CM1 . . . . .31 E1
Dearsley Ho RM13 . . . . . .154 D3
DEBDEN 89 C7
Debden Cl IG8 . . . . .110 D3
Debden Gn SS16 . . . . .141 C4
DEBDEN GREEN 67 B1
Debden La
  IG10 . . . . .89 D7
Debden Park High Sch
  IG10 . . . . .89 D7
Debden Rd IG10 . . . . .67 B1
Debden Sta IG10 . . . . .89 C5
Debden Way CM0 . . . . . . .106 A6
Debden Wlk 4 RM12 . . . . .155 B6
De Beauvoir Chase
  CM11 . . . . .98 E3
Deben RM18 . . . . .175 C3
Deborah Ct 7 E18 . . . . . . .132 B8
Dedham Cl CM11 . . . . .97 C2
Dedham Rd CM11 . . . . .97 C2
Dee Cl RM14 . . . . .137 E5
Deepdale SS7 . . . . .144 F6
Deepdene
  Basildon SS16 . . . . .142 B5
  Ingatestone CM4 . . . . . . .74 B3
Deepdene Ave SS6 . . . . . .123 D4
Deepdene Cl E11 . . . . .132 A7
Deepdene Path IG10 . . . . . .89 B5
Deepdene Rd IG10 . . . . . . .89 A5
Deeping 5 SS1 . . . . .167 A8
Deepwater Rd SS8 . . . . . .163 E3
Deerbank Rd CM11 . . . . . . .97 C3
Deere Ave RM13 . . . . .155 A6
Deerhurst SS7 . . . . .145 B7
Deerhurst Chase CM3 . . . . .56 F1
Deerhurst Cl SS7 . . . . . . .145 B7
Deerleap Gr E4 . . . . .87 B4
Deer Mead Ct 1 RM2 . . . .135 F6
Deer Park Way EN9 . . . . . . .65 B4
Deer Pk CM19 . . . . .23 B5
Deeside Wlk 3 SS12 . . . . .121 E6
Dee Way RM1 . . . . .113 E2
Defoe Par RM16 . . . . .174 B3
Defoe Way RM5 . . . . .113 B4
De Havilland Sq IG1 . . . . .133 D3
Deidre Chapman Ho
  DA10 . . . . .177 E1
Deirdre Ave SS12 . . . . . . .121 B7
Deirdre Cl SS12 . . . . .121 B7
Delafield Rd RM17 . . . . . .173 D1
Delamere Rd CM1 . . . . .31 E1
Delargy Cl RM16 . . . . .174 B3
De La Salle Sch SS14 . . . .142 C8
Delaware Cres SS3 . . . . . .168 D7
Delaware Rd SS3 . . . . . . .168 D7
Delder Ave SS8 . . . . .164 D2
Delderfield Ho RM1 . . . . . .113 D1
Delft Rd SS8 . . . . .164 A4
Delfzul Rd SS8 . . . . .164 A4
Delgada Rd SS8 . . . . .164 A4
Delhi Rd SS13 . . . . .143 C6
Delimands SS15 . . . . .141 F6
Delius Way SS17 . . . . .160 C3
Dell Cl IG8 . . . . .110 B7

Dell Ct
  Grays RM17 . . . . .173 B2
  Hornchurch RM12 . . . . . .136 E2
Dellfield Ct 4 CM17 . . . . . .11 C4
Dell La IG2 . . . . .2 A8
Dellow Cl IG2 . . . . .133 D4
Dell Rd RM17 . . . . .173 B2
Dell The
  Basildon SS16 . . . . .142 B3
  Brentwood CM13 . . . . . .116 B4
  Great Baddow CM2 . . . . . .54 F6
  5 Greenhithe DA9 . . . . . .177 B2
  Waltham Abbey EN9 . . . . .65 C3
  Wickford SS11 . . . . .121 E7
  Woodford IG8 . . . . .110 B7
Dellwood Gdns IG5 . . . . . .133 A8
Delmar Gdns SS11 . . . . . . .99 C2
Delmores SS16 . . . . .141 C3
Delta Rd CM13 . . . . .95 D3
De Luci Rd DA8 . . . . .169 C1
Delvers Mead RM10 . . . . .154 C8
Delview SS8 . . . . .163 F5
Delvins SS13 . . . . .143 B8
Denbar Par RM7 . . . . .135 C2
Denbigh Cl RM11 . . . . . . .137 A7
Denbigh Ho 8 RM3 . . . . . .114 E4
Denbigh Rd SS15 . . . . . . .141 B5
Denby Grange CM17 . . . . . .24 E8
Dencourt Cres SS14 . . . . .142 F5
Dene Cl SS6 . . . . .123 D4
Dene Ct CM1 . . . . .31 D5
Dene Gdns SS16 . . . . .123 D4
Denecroft Gdns
  RM17 . . . . .173 D3
Denehurst Gdns
  Basildon SS16 . . . . .140 E4
  Woodford IG8 . . . . .110 B6
Dene Path RM15 . . . . .172 A7
Dene Rd IG9 . . . . .88 E1
Denesmere SS7 . . . . .144 C4
Deneway SS16 . . . . .142 D2
Dengayne SS14 . . . . .142 D6
DENGIE 63 D1
Dengie Hundred Sports
  Ctr CM0 . . . . .106 B4
Denham Dr IG2 . . . . .133 C5
Denham Rd SS8 . . . . .164 A4
Denham Vale SS6 . . . . . . .123 A3
Denham Way IG11 . . . . . . .152 F4
Denholme Wlk RM13 . . . . .154 F6
Denmark Ho CM2 . . . . .54 D8
Denner Rd E4 . . . . .109 A8
Dennis Ct E17 . . . . .109 D1
Dennises La RM14 . . . . . .156 E5
Dennis Rd RM15 . . . . .157 A4
Denny Ave EN9 . . . . .65 D5
Denny Ct 2 DA2 . . . . .176 B1
Denny Gdns RM9 . . . . . . .153 B5
Dent Cl RM15 . . . . .172 A7
Denton App SS0 . . . . .147 C5
Denton Ave SS0 . . . . .147 C5
Denton Cl SS0 . . . . .147 C5
Denton Cl SS0 . . . . .147 C5
Denver SS13 . . . . .121 C1
Denver Ind Est RM13 . . . .169 F8
Denys Dr SS14 . . . . .120 F1
Derby Ave
  Romford RM7 . . . . .135 C5
  Upminster RM14 . . . . . . .137 A1
Derby Cl
  Basildon SS16 . . . . .140 F4
  Billericay CM11 . . . . .97 D5
  Mayland CM3 . . . . .61 A1
Derby Ct E18 . . . . .109 F2
Derbydale SS4 . . . . .125 C6
Derby Rd
  Basildon SS16 . . . . .140 F4
  Hoddesdon EN11 . . . . . . .21 D5
  Woodford E18 . . . . .109 F2
Derby Road Bridge
  RM17 . . . . .178 B8
Dereham Pl RM5 . . . . .113 B4
Dereham Rd IG11 . . . . . . .152 F7
Derek Gdns SS2 . . . . .147 E5
Derham Gdns RM14 . . . . .137 C1
Deri Ave RM13 . . . . .155 B1
Dering Cres SS9 . . . . .146 D7
Derry Ave RM15 . . . . .172 A7
Dersingham Ave E12 . . . . .152 A8
Dersingham Inf Sch
  E12 . . . . .152 A7
Derventer Ave SS8 . . . . . .164 A6
Derwent Ave SS6 . . . . . . .123 E2
Derwent Gdns IG4 . . . . . . .132 E7
Derwent Par RM15 . . . . . .172 B7
Derwent Way
  Chelmsford CM1 . . . . .31 D4
  Hornchurch RM12 . . . . . .155 B7
Desborough Path CM2 . . . .32 F8
Dessons Ct SS17 . . . . .160 F4
Detling Rd RM12 . . . . .155 C7
De Vere Ave CM9 . . . . .37 B1
De Vere Ct SS9 . . . . .146 C6
De Vere Gdns
  Ilford IG1 . . . . .133 A3
  Redbridge IG1 . . . . .132 F3
Devereux Rd
  Grays RM16 . . . . .172 F3
  Southend-on-S SS1 . . . . .167 A7
Devereux Way CM12 . . . . . .97 A5
Deverill Cl CM1 . . . . .19 B2
Deveron Gdns RM15 . . . . .172 A8
Deveron Way RM1 . . . . . . .113 E2
Devizes Rd 6 RM3 . . . . . .114 D5
Devon Cl IG9 . . . . .110 B8
Devon Gdns SS4 . . . . .125 C5

Devon Ho
  Romford RM7 . . . . .113 A1
  6 Wanstead E11 . . . . . . .132 A6
Devonport Gdns IG1 . . . . .132 F5
Devon Rd IG11 . . . . .152 E4
Devonshire Cl SS15 . . . . .141 A8
Devonshire Gdns
  SS17 . . . . .175 A3
Devonshire Ho IG6 . . . . . .111 B3
Devonshire Rd
  Basildon SS15 . . . . .141 A7
  Burnham-on-C CM0 . . . . .106 C5
  Grays RM16 . . . . .172 E2
  Hornchurch RM12 . . . . . .136 D2
  Ilford IG2 . . . . .133 C4
  Southminster CM0 . . . . . .84 C4
Devon Way SS8 . . . . .164 B5
De Warren Ho DA11 . . . . .178 D1
Dewey Path RM12 . . . . . . .155 C6
Dewey Rd RM10 . . . . .154 C6
Dewlands SS14 . . . . .142 A7
Dewsbury Cl RM3 . . . . . . .114 E4
Dewsbury Gdns RM3 . . . .114 E4
Dewsbury Rd RM3 . . . . . .114 E4
Dewsgreen SS16 . . . . .142 E4
Dewyk Rd SS8 . . . . .164 C5
Dexter Cl RM17 . . . . .173 A3
Deyncourt Gdns
  RM14 . . . . .137 C2
Deyncourt Gdns E11 . . . . .132 C7
Dial Cl DA9 . . . . .177 D2
Diamond Cl
  Dagenham RM8 . . . . . . .134 C3
  Grays RM16 . . . . .172 F3
Diamond Ct RM11 . . . . . . .136 A3
Diana Cl
  Grays RM16 . . . . .172 F3
  Woodford E18 . . . . .110 B2
Diban Ave RM12 . . . . .155 B8
Diban Ct RM12 . . . . .155 B8
Dickens Ave
  Dartford DA1 . . . . .176 A3
  Tilbury RM18 . . . . .179 B6
Dickens Cl SS2 . . . . .148 B2
Dickens Ct
  Basildon SS15 . . . . .141 D7
  10 Wanstead E11 . . . . . .132 A7
Dickens Dr SS15 . . . . .141 D7
Dickens Pl CM1 . . . . .31 D7
Dickens Rise IG7 . . . . .111 B7
Dickens Way RM1 . . . . . . .135 E7
Dicky Moors CM3 . . . . .18 F7
Digby Gdns RM10 . . . . . . .154 A4
Digby Rd
  Barking IG11 . . . . .152 F5
  Corringham SS17 . . . . . .161 C4
Digby Wlk 1 RM12 . . . . . .155 C7
Diggens Ct IG10 . . . . .88 E6
Dilkes Prim Sch
  RM15 . . . . .171 F7
Dilliway Ct CM0 . . . . .106 B4
Dilston CM3 . . . . .57 A6
Dinant Ave SS8 . . . . .163 E4
Dinant Link Rd EN11 . . . . .21 B7
Disney Cl CM4 . . . . .74 B4
Disraeli Rd SS6, SS9 . . . .146 B8
District Ctr SS3 . . . . .149 D1
Ditchfield Rd EN11 . . . . . . .8 A1
Ditton Court Rd SS0 . . . . .166 D8
Dixon Ave CM1 . . . . .31 F4
Dixon Ct SS13 . . . . .143 B6
Dobb's Weir Rd EN11 . . . . .21 D5
Dobsons Cl SS6 . . . . .123 E1
Dock Approach Rd RM16,
  RM17 . . . . .173 E2
Docklands Ave CM4 . . . . . .74 C4
Dock Rd
  Grays RM17, RM18 . . . . .178 E7
  Mayland CM3 . . . . .61 B1
  Tilbury RM18 . . . . .178 F5
Dockwra La CM3 . . . . .57 A7
DODDINGHURST 72 C2
Doddinghurst CE Jun Sch
  CM15 . . . . .72 B2
Doddinghurst Ct CM15 . . . .94 C2
Doddinghurst Inf Sch
  CM15 . . . . .72 B2
Doddinghurst Rd
  Brentwood CM15 . . . . . . .94 D5
  Doddinghurst CM15 . . . . .72 C1
Doesgate La RM14 . . . . . .140 C1
Doeshill Dr SS12 . . . . .121 E7
Doggetts Chase SS4 . . . . .126 A4
Doggett's Cnr RM11 . . . . .136 F2
Doggetts Prim Sch
  SS4 . . . . .125 F3
Dog Kennel La CM4 . . . . . .74 C7
Dolby Rise CM2 . . . . .32 F2
Dollant Ave SS8 . . . . .164 A3
Dolphin App RM1 . . . . . . .135 F7
Dolphin Cl IG7 . . . . .111 B7
Dolphin Gdns SS2 . . . . . . .96 F5
Dolphin Motorway Est
  RM19 . . . . .171 E1
Dolphin Point RM19 . . . . . .171 E1
Dolphins SS0 . . . . .147 D4
Dolphin Way RM19 . . . . . . .171 E1
Dombey Cl CM1 . . . . .31 F7
Dome Cvn Pk SS5 . . . . . . .102 C2
Dominic Ct EN9 . . . . .65 B6
Dominion Dr RM5 . . . . . . .113 C4
Dominion Way RM13 . . . . .155 A2
Dominion Wks RM8 . . . . . .134 E4
Domsey La CM3 . . . . .19 F5
Donald Dr RM6 . . . . .134 C6
Donald Thorn Cl
  SS12 . . . . .121 D6
Donald Way CM2 . . . . .54 C7

Doncaster Way RM14 . . . .136 F1
Doncel Ct E4 . . . . .87 D2
Doncella Cl RM16 . . . . . . .172 D3
Donington Ave IG6 . . . . . .133 C6
Donne Rd RM8 . . . . .134 C2
Donnington Ct 1
  DA2 . . . . .176 B1
Donovan's Gdn CM13 . . . .117 E3
Don Way RM1 . . . . .113 E3
Dorchester Ave EN11 . . . . .21 A3
Dorchester Ct 2 E18 . . . . .109 F2
Dorchester Gdns E4 . . . . .109 A6
Dorchester Rd CM12 . . . . .97 A5
Dordells SS15 . . . . .141 E6
Dore Ave E12 . . . . .152 A7
Dorian Rd RM12 . . . . .136 A3
Doric Ave SS4 . . . . .125 D5
Doric Lo SS0 . . . . .166 E7
Dorking Rd RM3 . . . . .114 D6
Dorking Rise RM3 . . . . . . .114 D6
Dorking Wlk
  Great Baddow CM2 . . . . . .54 E7
  Romford RM3 . . . . .114 D5
Dorkins Way RM14 . . . . . .137 E4
Dorothy Barley Jun & Inf
  Sch RM8 . . . . .153 B7
Dorothy Farm Rd SS6 . . . .124 A1
Dorothy Gdns
  Dagenham RM8 . . . . . . .153 B8
  Thundersley SS7 . . . . . . .144 F5
Dorrington Gdns
  RM12 . . . . .136 D3
Dorset Ave
  Great Baddow CM2 . . . . . .54 E6
  Romford RM1 . . . . .135 D8
Dorset Cl CM2 . . . . .54 E6
Dorset Gdns
  Linford SS17 . . . . .175 A4
  Rochford SS4 . . . . .125 C5
Dorset Rd
  Burnham-on-C CM0 . . . . .106 C4
  Maldon CM9 . . . . .58 F8
Dorset Way
  Billericay CM12 . . . . .97 A5
  Canvey Island SS8 . . . . .164 A5
Doubleday Dr CM9 . . . . . . .36 F5
Doubleday Rd IG10 . . . . . . .89 C6
Doublegate La SS11 . . . . .122 B5
Doublet Mews CM11 . . . . . .97 D5
Douglas Ave
  Chingford E17 . . . . .109 A2
  Romford RM3 . . . . .114 A1
Douglas Cl
  Galleywood CM2 . . . . .54 D3
  Grays RM16 . . . . .172 E3
  Redbridge IG6 . . . . .111 B3
Douglas Dr SS12 . . . . . . .121 D5
Douglas Matthew Ho 1
  CM14 . . . . .116 C7
Douglas Rd
  Chingford E4 . . . . .87 E1
  Hadleigh SS7 . . . . .145 F3
  Ilford IG3 . . . . .134 A5
  Romford RM11 . . . . .135 F5
Douglas Wlk 3 CM2 . . . . . .54 A8
Doug Siddons Ct
  RM17 . . . . .178 C8
Doulton Cl CM17 . . . . .24 E7
Doulton Way SS4 . . . . . . .125 C6
Dounsell Ct CM15 . . . . . . .94 A3
Dove Cl RM16 . . . . .172 E3
Dovecote SS3 . . . . .149 E1
Dove Crofts CM6 . . . . .5 E7
Dovedale SS8 . . . . .164 E5
Dovedale Ave IG5 . . . . . . .111 A1
Dovedale Cl
  Basildon SS16 . . . . .141 A4
  Ramsden Heath CM11 . . .98 C4
Dove Dr SS7 . . . . .144 B2
Dovehouse Croft CM20 . . .11 A2
Dove House Gdns E4 . . . .109 A8
Dovehouse Mead
  IG11 . . . . .152 D3
Dove La CM2 . . . . .54 A6
Dover Cl RM5 . . . . .113 C4
Dovercliff Rd SS8 . . . . . . .164 E2
Dover Rd
  Dagenham RM6 . . . . . . .134 E5
  Northfleet DA11 . . . . . . .178 D1
  Wanstead E12 . . . . .132 C2
Dovers Corner Ind Pk
  RM13 . . . . .154 F1
Dovervelt Rd SS8 . . . . . . .164 C5
Dover Way SS13 . . . . .143 B4
Dovesgate SS7 . . . . .144 B4
Doves Mews SS15 . . . . . . .119 C1
Dovetree Ct RM3 . . . . . . .114 D6
Dove Wlk 7 RM12 . . . . . . .155 B6
Dow Ct CM0 . . . . .84 C4
Dowding Way
  Hornchurch RM12 . . . . . .155 B5
  Waltham Abbey EN9 . . . . .65 E3
Dowland Cl SS17 . . . . .160 C3
Dowland Wlk SS15 . . . . . .141 C7
Downer Rd SS7 . . . . .144 D5
Downer Rd N SS7 . . . . . . .144 E6
Downesway SS7 . . . . .144 D3
Downey Cl SS14 . . . . .142 C7
Downhall Cl SS6 . . . . .123 D4
Downhall Park Way
  SS6 . . . . .123 D5
Down Hall Prim Sch
  SS6 . . . . .123 D5
Downhall Rd CM17,
  CM22 . . . . .13 C5
Down Hall Rd SS6 . . . . . . .123 D4
DOWNHAM 98 E4

Downham CE Prim Sch
CM11 . . . . .98 C4
Downham Cl RM5 . . . . .113 A3
Downham Rd
Canvey Island SS8 . . . . .164 A3
Ramsden Heath CM11 . . .98 D5
Stock CM4 . . . . .76 B1
Stock CM4, CM11 . . . . . .98 D7
Wickford SS11 . . . . .99 C3
Downing Rd RM9 . . . . .153 F5
Downlands EN9 . . . . .65 E5
Downleaze CM3 . . . . . .101 E8
Downs Gr SS16 . . . . . . .142 E3
Downshall Ave IG3 . . . .133 F5
Downshall Ct IG3 . . . . .133 E5
Downshall Prim Sch
IG3 . . . . .133 E4
Downsland Dr CM14 . . .116 C7
Downs Prim Sch The
CM20 . . . . .23 E8
Downs Rd CM9 . . . . .37 B3
Downs The CM20 . . . . . .23 E8
Downsway CM1 . . . . .32 D6
Dowsetts La CM11 . . . . .98 C6
Doyle Way RM18 . . . . . .179 C5
Dragon Cl CM0 . . . . . . .106 A5
Drake Ave CM3 . . . . .83 A8
Drake Cl
Brentwood CM14 . . . . . .116 D5
Hadleigh SS7 . . . . .145 C5
Drake Ct 4 SS14 . . . . .142 F5
Drake Mews RM12 . . . .155 A6
Drake Point DA8 . . . . . .169 E1
Drake Rd
Basildon SS15 . . . . .141 D6
Grays RM16 . . . . .172 D3
Grays RM16 . . . . .172 E4
Southend-on-S SS0 . . . .147 C1
Drakes La
Boreham CM3 . . . . .20 B7
Little Waltham CM3 . . . . .19 F7
Drakes Mdw CM17 . . . . .11 E4
Drakes The SS3 . . . . . . .168 E8
Drakes Way SS6 . . . . . .123 E4
Drapers Chase CM9 . . . .37 D4
Drapers Ct RM12 . . . . .136 E2
Drapers Rd CM3 . . . . . .101 E8
Draycot El RM18 . . . . . .132 B4
Drayson Cl EN9 . . . . .65 E7
Drayton Ave IG10 . . . . . .88 F3
Drayton Cl
Ilford IG1 . . . . .133 D3
4 Maldon CM9 . . . . . . .37 A1
Drayton Lo E17 . . . . . . .109 B1
Drewsteignton SS3 . . . .168 D8
Driberg Ct RM8 . . . . . . .153 B6
Driftway SS16 . . . . .142 F4
Drive The
Barking IG11 . . . . .152 F5
Brentwood CM13 . . . . . .116 C4
Buckhurst Hill IG9 . . . . . .88 C2
Chelmsford CM1 . . . . . . .32 A6
Chingford E4 . . . . .87 D2
Harlow CM20 . . . . .10 E1
Hoddesdon EN11 . . . . . . .21 A8
Hullbridge SS5 . . . . .101 D3
Ilford IG1 . . . . .133 A3
Loughton IG10 . . . . .88 E5
Mayland CM3 . . . . .82 F8
Rayleigh SS6 . . . . .146 B8
Redbridge E18 . . . . .132 F4
Rochford SS4 . . . . .125 F3
Romford, Collier Row
RM5 . . . . .113 D3
Romford, Harold wood
RM3 . . . . .114 F2
Sawbridgeworth CM21 . . . .1 E2
Southend-on-S SS0 . . . .166 B8
Wanstead E18 . . . . .132 A8
Driveway The SS8 . . . . .164 B3
Droitwich Ave SS13 . . . .148 D1
Dronfield Gdns RM8 . . .153 D7
Drood Cl CM1 . . . . .31 F7
Drovers Mead CM14 . . .116 B6
Droveway IG10 . . . . .89 B7
Drummond Ave RM7 . . .135 D7
Drummond Ct CM15 . . . .94 C2
Drummond Pl 7
SS12 . . . . .121 E5
Drummond Rd
Romford RM7 . . . . .135 D7
Wanstead E11 . . . . .132 C5
Drummonds The
Buckhurst Hill IG9 . . . . . .110 B8
Epping CM16 . . . . .46 A1
Drury La CM6 . . . . .5 C2
Dryden Ave SS2 . . . . . .148 B2
Dryden Cl
Maldon CM9 . . . . .59 A8
Redbridge IG6 . . . . .111 F4
Dryden Pl RM18 . . . . . .179 B6
Dryden Twrs RM3 . . . . .114 B3
Drysdale Ave E4 . . . . . . .87 B3
Dry St SS16 . . . . .141 E1
Drywoods CM3 . . . . . . .101 D5
Duarte Pl RM16 . . . . . . .172 F3
Dubarry Cl SS7 . . . . . . .144 F5
Duchess Gr IG9 . . . . . . .110 B8
Ducker's La CM1 . . . . . . .17 C7
Ducketts Mead
Canewdon SS4 . . . . .104 D2
Roydon CM19 . . . . .9 B1
Ducking Stool Ct
RM1 . . . . .135 E7
Duck La CM16 . . . . .46 C6
Duckling La CM21 . . . . . .1 E2
Dudbrook Rd CM14 . . . . .71 B1

Dudley Cl
Boreham CM3 . . . . .20 E1
Grays RM16 . . . . .172 E4
Dudley Ct 14 E11 . . . . .132 A6
Dudley Gdns RM3 . . . . .114 D4
Dudley Rd
Chingford E17 . . . . .109 A1
Ilford IG1 . . . . .152 B8
Romford RM3 . . . . .114 D4
Duffield Cl RM16 . . . . . .172 F3
Duffield Rd CM2 . . . . . . .54 D6
Duffries Cl CM3 . . . . .18 E7
Duke Gdns IG6 . . . . . . .133 D7
Duke Pl SS15 . . . . .141 E8
Duke Rd IG6 . . . . .133 D7
Dukes Ave
Grays RM17 . . . . .173 A4
Southminster CM0 . . . . . .84 D3
Theydon Bois CM16 . . . . .67 E4
Dukes Cl CM16 . . . . .47 B4
Dukes Ct E6 . . . . .152 A4
Dukes Farm Cl CM12 . . .97 C5
Dukes Farm Rd CM12 . . .97 B5
Dukes La
5 Chelmsford CM2 . . . . .32 F4
Willingale CM5 . . . . .28 C5
Dukes Orch
Hatfield Broad Oak
CM22 . . . . .3 C1
Writtle CM1 . . . . .31 B1
Dukes Park Ind Est
CM2 . . . . .32 F4
Dukes Pl CM14 . . . . .94 C1
Dukes Priory Hospl The
CM1 . . . . .32 D4
Dukes Rd
Billericay CM11 . . . . .97 C4
Wallend E6 . . . . .152 A4
Duke St
Chelmsford CM1 . . . . . . .32 B2
Hoddesdon EN11 . . . . . . .21 A7
Dulverton Ave SS0 . . . .147 A5
Dulverton Cl SS0 . . . . . .147 A5
Dulverton Rd RM3 . . . . .114 D4
Dumbarton Way CM3 . . .37 D4
Dunbar Ave RM10 . . . . .135 A1
Dunbar Gdns RM10 . . . .154 B7
Dunbar Pl SS12 . . . . . . .121 E5
Duncan Cl SS12 . . . . . .121 F5
Duncannon Pl DA9 . . . .177 C3
Dunchurch Ho RM10 . . .154 A5
Duncombe Ct 4
RM19 . . . . .171 B1
Dundas Mews EN3 . . . . .65 A2
Dundee Ave SS9 . . . . . .146 B2
Dundee Cl SS9 . . . . . . .146 C2
Dundee Ct SS14 . . . . . .142 F8
Dundonald Dr SS9 . . . .146 F1
Dunedin Ho RM18 . . . . .179 A5
Dunedin Rd
Ilford IG1 . . . . .133 C3
Rainham RM13 . . . . .154 F2
Dunfane CM11 . . . . .97 C5
Dungannon Chase
SS1 . . . . .168 B6
Dungannon Dr SS1 . . . .168 B6
Dunkeld Rd RM8 . . . . . .134 C2
Dunkellin Gr RM15 . . . .172 A7
Dunkellin Way RM15 . . .172 A7
Dunkin Rd DA1 . . . . . . .176 A4
Dunkirk Rd CM0 . . . . . .106 C5
Dunlin Cl
Heybridge CM9 . . . . .37 C5
South Woodham Ferrers
CM3 . . . . .79 D1
Dunlop Cl RM18 . . . . . .178 F5
Dunlop Rd RM18 . . . . . .178 F6
Dunmore Rd CM2 . . . . . .33 A3
Dunmow Cl
Ilford RM6 . . . . .134 C6
Loughton IG10 . . . . .88 E3
Dunmow Dr RM13 . . . . .154 F4
Dunmow Gdns CM13 . . .139 D5
Dunmow Ho RM9 . . . . .153 B4
Dunmow Rd
Fyfield CM5 . . . . .27 E6
Hatfield Broad Oak CM22 . .3 F6
High Roding CM6 . . . . . . .5 D5
Leaden Roding CM6 . . . . .15 A4
Dunning Cl RM15 . . . . .172 A7
Dunningford Pl RM12 . .154 F7
Dunningford Prim Sch
RM12 . . . . .154 F7
Dunnings La RM13 . . . .139 B2
Dunnose Ct 16 RM19 . .171 B1
Dunspring La IG5 . . . . .111 B2
Dunstable Cl RM3 . . . . .114 D4
Dunstable Rd
Romford RM3 . . . . .114 D4
Stanford-le-H SS17 . . . .160 D3
Dunstalls CM19 . . . . . . .23 A4
Dunster Ave SS0 . . . . . .147 A5
Dunster Cl RM5 . . . . . . .113 C1
Dunster Cres RM11 . . . .137 E2
Dunster Ct 24 DA2 . . . .176 B1
Dunster Ho SS7 . . . . . . .144 F6
Dunton Park Cvn Pk
CM13 . . . . .140 E5
Dunton Rd
Basildon CM12, SS15 . . .119 B1
Romford RM1 . . . . .135 E7
Dunton View CM13 . . . .140 E5
DUNTON WAYLETTS . . .118 C1
Dunwich Ct 2 RM6 . . . .134 B6
Dupre Cl RM16 . . . . . . .172 E3
Durants Wlk 4 SS12 . . .121 D6
Durban Gdns RM10 . . . .154 C5
Durban La SS15 . . . . . . .119 F2

Durban Rd IG2, IG3 . . . .133 E3
Durdans The SS16 . . . . .141 B4
Durell Gdns RM9 . . . . . .153 D7
Durell Rd RM9 . . . . .153 D7
Durham Ave
Romford RM2 . . . . .136 C7
Woodford IG8 . . . . .110 D5
Durham Cl
Sawbridgeworth CM21 . . . .1 C1
Stanstead Abbotts SG12 . . .8 B5
Durham Ho
3 Barking IG11 . . . . . . .153 A5
Romford RM7 . . . . .113 A1
Durham Pl IG1 . . . . .152 C8
Durham Rd
Basildon SS15 . . . . .140 E6
Dagenham RM10 . . . . . .154 C7
Rochford SS4 . . . . .125 B6
Southend-on-S SS2 . . . .148 D2
Durham Way SS6 . . . . . .123 D5
Durley Ave SS12 . . . . . .120 F8
Durley Cl SS7 . . . . .144 E4
Durnell Way IG10 . . . . . .89 A6
Durninge Wlk RM16 . . .173 B6
Durrants Cl RM13 . . . . .155 C3
Durrington Cl SS16 . . . .142 C5
Dury Falls Cl RM11 . . . .137 A3
Dutch Cottage Mus★
 . . . . .163 C4
DUTCH VILLAGE 163 C4
Duxford SS11 . . . . .122 A6
Duxford Cl RM12 . . . . . .155 C6
Dycorts Sch RM3 . . . . . .115 A6
Dyer Ct EN3 . . . . .65 A2
Dyer's Rd CM9 . . . . .37 A2
Dyers Way RM3 . . . . . . .114 B3
Dyke Cres SS8 . . . . .163 D4
Dykes Chase CM9 . . . . . .36 F3
Dylan Rd DA17 . . . . . . .169 A3
Dymchurch Cl IG5 . . . . .111 A1
Dymoke Rd RM11 . . . . .135 F4
Dymokes Way 8 SS16 . . . .8 A1
Dynevor Gdns SS9 . . . .146 B1
Dytchleys La CM14 . . . . .93 A5
Dytchleys The CM14 . . . .92 F5

E

Eagle Ave
Hornchurch RM12 . . . . .155 B6
Waltham Abbey EN9 . . . .66 A5
Eagle Ct 6 E11 . . . . . . .132 A7
Eagle Ho RM17 . . . . . . .177 F8
Eagle La
Kelvedon Hatch CM15 . . .71 E2
Wanstead E11 . . . . .132 A7
Eagles Rd DA9 . . . . .177 B2
Eagle Terr IG8 . . . . .110 B3
Eagle Way
Great Warley CM13 . . . .116 D4
Northfleet DA11 . . . . . . .178 A2
Southend-on-S SS3 . . . .168 F8
Eardley Rd DA17 . . . . . .169 A1
Earl Mountbatten Dr
CM12 . . . . .96 F4
Earlsdown Ho 6
IG11 . . . . .152 D3
Earlsfield Dr 7 CM2 . . . .32 F3
Earls Hall Ave SS2 . . . .147 E5
Earls Hall Inf Sch
SS0 . . . . .147 D4
Earls Hall Jun Sch
SS0 . . . . .147 D4
Earls Hall Par SS2 . . . .147 E4
Earl's Path IG10 . . . . . . .88 C6
Earls Wlk RM8 . . . . . . .153 B8
Earlswood SS7 . . . . . . .144 D4
Earlswood Gdns IG5 . . .133 A8
Easebourne Rd RM8 . . .153 C7
Easedale Dr RM12 . . . . .155 B7
Easington Way RM15 . . .172 A8
East Av see CM3 . . . . . . .82 E2
Eastbourne Gr SS0 . . . .147 C3
Eastbourne Rd E6 . . . . .152 A2
East Bridge Rd CM3 . . .101 E8
Eastbrook Ave RM10 . . .154 C8
Eastbrook Comp Sch
RM10 . . . . .154 C8
Eastbrook Rd EN9 . . . . .65 E6
Eastbrooks SS13 . . . . . .143 B7
Eastbrooks Mews
SS13 . . . . .143 B7
Eastbrooks Pl SS13 . . . .143 B7
Eastbury Ave
Barking IG11 . . . . .152 E4
Rochford SS4 . . . . .125 D4
Eastbury Comp Sch
Barking IG11 . . . . .152 E6
Barking IG11 . . . . .152 F5
Eastbury Ct IG11 . . . . . .152 E4
Eastbury Inf Sch IG11 . .152 F5
Eastbury Rd
Romford RM7 . . . . .135 D5
Wallend E6 . . . . .152 A1
Eastbury Sq IG11 . . . . .152 F4
East Canney Cotts CM3 . .80 F5
Eastcheap SS6 . . . . .123 C4
East Cl RM13 . . . . .155 B1
Eastcote Gr SS2 . . . . . .148 D3
Eastcourt Ind Est
IG3 . . . . .134 A3
East Cres SS8 . . . . .163 F4

East Crescent Rd 5
DA2 . . . . .179 C1
East Dene Dr RM3 . . . . .114 D5
East Dr CM21 . . . . .1 E1
EASTEND 9 E1
Eastend Cotts CM19 . . . . .9 D1
East End Rd CM0 . . . . . .42 C3
East Entrance RM10 . . .154 B3
Eastern App IG11 . . . . .153 A3
Eastern App CM2 . . . . . .32 F5
Eastern Ave
Aveley RM15 . . . . .171 C4
Grays RM20 . . . . .176 F8
Ilford IG2 . . . . .133 D5
South Benfleet SS7 . . . .144 C5
Southend-on-S SS2 . . . .148 B3
Wanstead E11 . . . . .132 C5
Eastern Ave E RM1, RM2,
RM3 . . . . .113 E1
Eastern Avenue Ret Pk
RM7 . . . . .135 C2
Eastern Avenue W
RM7 . . . . .135 B7
Eastern Cl SS2 . . . . . . .148 A3
Eastern Cres CM1 . . . . . .31 F5
Eastern Espl
Canvey Island SS8 . . . . .164 D2
Southend-on-S SS1 . . . .167 D6
Eastern Rd
Burnham-on-C CM0 . . . .106 C5
Grays RM17 . . . . .173 D2
Rayleigh SS6 . . . . .123 B1
Romford RM1 . . . . .135 F6
Easternville Gdns
IG2 . . . . .133 C5
Eastern Way
Belvedere DA18 . . . . . . .169 A4
Grays RM17 . . . . .173 A1
Eastfield Gdns RM10 . . .154 A8
Eastfield Rd
Basildon SS15 . . . . .119 F2
Brentwood CM14 . . . . . .116 D8
Canvey Island SS8 . . . . .164 D5
Dagenham RM9 . . . . . . .153 F8
Dagenham RM9, RM10 . .154 A8
Eastgate SS14 . . . . .142 B5
East Gate SS14 . . . . .10 D1
Eastgate Bsns Ctr 2
SS14 . . . . .142 B6
East Hall La RM13 . . . . .170 D7
Eastham Cres CM3 . . . .117 A7
EAST HANNINGFIELD . . .78 B7
East Hanningfield CE Prim
Sch CM3 . . . . .78 B7
East Hanningfield Ind Est
CM3 . . . . .78 C6
East Hanningfield Rd
Howe Green CM2 . . . . . . .55 E2
Rettendon CM3 . . . . .78 C4
EAST HORNDON 139 E7
East Kent Ave E16 . . . . .152 A1
Eastleigh Rd SS7 . . . . . .144 E1
Eastley SS16 . . . . .141 F4
East Mayne SS13 . . . . . .121 A2
Eastmead IG3 . . . . .134 A4
East Mill DA11 . . . . .179 A1
Easton End SS15 . . . . . .141 A6
East Park Cl RM6 . . . . . .134 E6
East Pk
Harlow CM17 . . . . .11 C3
Sawbridgeworth CM21 . . . .1 E1
East Rd
Dagenham, Chadwell Heath
RM6 . . . . .134 C6
Harlow CM20 . . . . .11 B4
Romford RM7 . . . . .135 D4
East Row E11 . . . . .132 A5
East Sq SS14 . . . . .142 B6
East St
Barking IG11 . . . . .152 C5
Grays RM17 . . . . .178 C4
Grays, West Thurrock
RM20 . . . . .177 E8
Rochford SS4 . . . . .125 F2
Southend-on-S, Leigh Cliffs
SS9 . . . . .165 E8
Southend-on-S SS2 . . . .147 F2
East Terr DA12 . . . . .179 C1
East Thorpe SS14 . . . . .142 C6
East Thurrock Rd
RM17 . . . . .178 C4
EAST TILBURY 175 C1
East Tilbury Inf Sch
RM18 . . . . .175 C1
East Tilbury Jun Sch
RM18 . . . . .175 C1
East Tilbury Rd SS17 . . .175 A4
East Tilbury Sta
RM18 . . . . .175 B2
East View
Chingford E4 . . . . .109 C5
Writtle CM1 . . . . .30 F1
Eastview Dr SS6 . . . . . . .123 E5
Eastway E11 . . . . .132 B6
Eastways SS8 . . . . .163 F5
EASTWICK 10 A4
Eastwick Hall La CM20 . .10 A5
Eastwick Rd
Eastwick CM20 . . . . .10 B4
Gilston CM20 . . . . .10 E6
East Wlk
Basildon SS14 . . . . .142 B6
Harlow CM20 . . . . .10 D1
EASTWOOD 146 E5
Eastwoodbury Cl SS2 . .147 E6
Eastwoodbury Cres
SS2 . . . . .147 E6
Eastwoodbury La SS2 . .147 C6

Eastwood Bvd SS0 . . . . .147 A2
Eastwood Cl E18 . . . . . .110 A1
Eastwood Dr RM13 . . . .170 B7
Eastwood Ind Est SS9 . .146 C6
Eastwood La S SS0 . . . .147 B2
Eastwood Old Rd SS9 . .146 B6
Eastwood Park Cl
SS9 . . . . .146 E6
Eastwood Park Dr
SS9 . . . . .146 E7
Eastwood Prim Sch
SS9 . . . . .146 F6
Eastwood Rd
Ilford IG3 . . . . .134 A4
Rayleigh SS6 . . . . .123 E1
Southend-on-S SS9 . . . .146 D3
Woodford E18 . . . . .110 A1
Eastwood Rd N SS9 . . . .146 D4
Eastwood Rise
Rayleigh SS9 . . . . .124 C1
Southend-on-S SS9 . . . .146 C8
Eastwood Sch The
SS9 . . . . .146 F5
Eaton Cl CM12 . . . . .97 A5
Eaton Ct RM10 . . . . . . .154 C6
Eaton Gdns RM9 . . . . . .153 E5
Eaton Rd
Southend-on-S SS9 . . . .146 C2
Upminster RM14 . . . . . .137 E2
Eaton Rise E11 . . . . . . .132 C6
Eatons Mead E4 . . . . . .109 A8
Ebbsfleet Ind Est
DA11 . . . . .178 A2
Ebbsfleet Int Sta
DA10 . . . . .178 A1
Ebbsfleet Wlk DA11 . . . .178 B1
Ebenezer Terr CM2 . . . . .54 E7
Eccles Ho 2 RM3 . . . . .114 D4
Eccleston Cres RM6 . . . .134 B4
Eccleston Gdns CM12 . . .97 A5
Echo Hts E4 . . . . .87 B1
Eckersley Rd CM1 . . . . . .32 C3
Eddy Cl RM7 . . . . .135 B5
Eden Cl EN3 . . . . .65 A1
Eden Gn RM15 . . . . . . .172 B8
Edenhall Cl RM3 . . . . . .114 C5
Edenhall Glen RM3 . . . .114 C5
Edenhall Rd RM3 . . . . . .114 C5
Edens Mount CM21 . . . . .1 F4
Eden Way CM1 . . . . .31 C5
Edgar Ho E11 . . . . .132 C6
Edgar Rd RM6 . . . . .134 D4
Edgecotts SS16 . . . . . . .141 E4
Edgefield Ave IG11 . . . .152 F5
Edgefield Ct 3 IG11 . . .152 F5
Edgehill Gdns RM10 . . .154 A8
Edinburgh Ave
Corringham SS17 . . . . . .160 F4
Southend-on-S SS9 . . . .146 B2
Edinburgh Cl SS6 . . . . .123 B5
Edinburgh Gate CM20 . .10 D3
Edinburgh Ho 1
RM2 . . . . .136 C7
Edinburgh Mews
RM18 . . . . .179 B5
Edinburgh Pl CM20 . . . .11 A4
Edinburgh Way
Basildon SS13 . . . . .143 B6
Harlow CM20 . . . . .10 E3
Edison Ave RM12 . . . . . .135 F3
Edison Cl RM12 . . . . . . .135 F3
Edisons Pk DA2 . . . . . . .176 D4
Edith Cl SS8 . . . . .163 C3
Edith Rd
Canvey Island SS8 . . . . .163 D3
Dagenham RM6 . . . . . . .134 D4
Southend-on-S SS2 . . . .147 E2
Edith Way SS17 . . . . . . .161 A4
Edmund Rd
Grays RM16 . . . . .172 D4
Rainham RM13 . . . . .154 E2
Edmunds Ho RM16 . . . . .67 F8
Edmund's Twr CM19 . . . .23 C8
EDNEY COMMON 52 D5
EDRIDGE Cl RM12 . . . . .155 D7
Edridge Cl RM12 . . . . . .155 D7
Edward Ave E4 . . . . . . .109 B4
Edward Bright Cl CM9 . .37 A2
Edward Cl
Billericay CM12 . . . . .96 F5
Grays RM16 . . . . .172 D4
Rochford SS4 . . . . .125 C6
Romford RM2 . . . . .136 C8
Edward Ct EN9 . . . . .65 F6
Edward Dr CM2 . . . . .54 C7
Edward Francis Jun Sch
SS6 . . . . .123 E3
Edward Gdns SS11 . . . .121 D8
Edward Mans 8 IG11 . .152 F5
Edward Rd RM6 . . . . . . .134 C5
Edwards Cl CM13 . . . . . .95 E4
Edwards Hall Prim Sch
SS9 . . . . .146 C7
Edwards Rd DA17 . . . . .169 A2
Edwards Way CM13 . . . .95 E4
Edwards Wlk CM9 . . . . . .36 F3
Edwina Gdns IG4 . . . . . .132 E6
Edwin Ave E6 . . . . .152 A3
Edwin Cl RM13 . . . . . . .154 F2
Edwin Hall View CM3 . . .79 C3
Edwin Lambert Sch
RM11 . . . . .136 A4
Edwin's Hall Rd CM3 . . .79 D3
Edwin St DA12 . . . . . . .179 B1
Egbert Gdns SS11 . . . . . .99 D1

Egerton Dr SS16 . . . . . . 140 E5
Egerton Gdns IG3 . . . . 133 F1
Egg Hall CM16 . . . . 46 A2
Eglington Rd E4 . . . . 87 D2
Eglinton Dr CM2 . . . . 33 B4
Eglinton Rd DA10 . . . . . 177 F1
Eisenhower Rd SS15 . . . 141 A6
Elan Rd RM15 . . . . 172 A8
Elbourne Trad Est
DA17 . . . . 169 B3
Elbury Ct IG8 . . . . 110 E3
Eldan Ho RM4 . . . . 113 E7
Eldbert Cl SS2 . . . . 148 E2
Eldeland SS15 . . . . 141 E7
Elder Ave SS12 . . . . 121 C6
Elderberry Cl
Basildon SS16 . . . . 141 B5
Redbridge IG6 . . . . 111 B3
Elderfield CM17 . . . . 11 D3
Elderfield Wlk E11 . . . . . 132 B6
Elderstep Ave SS8 . . . . . 164 E3
Elderton Rd SS0 . . . . . . 147 D1
Elder Tree Rd SS8 . . . . . 164 C4
Elder Way
Rainham RM13 . . . . 155 D2
Wickford SS12 . . . . 121 C6
Eldon Rd EN11 . . . . 21 D4
Eldonwall Est RM8 . . . . 134 F3
Eldon Way SS5 . . . . 124 E6
Eldon Way Ind Est
SS5 . . . . 124 D6
Eldred Gdns RM14 . . . . . 137 E4
Eldred Rd IG11 . . . . 152 E4
Eldridge Ct 2 RM10 . . . 154 B6
Eleanor Chase SS15 . . . 121 C7
Eleanor Ct RM11 . . . . . . 136 D4
Eleanor Gdns RM8 . . . . . 134 D2
Eleanor Way CM14 . . . . 116 C5
Eleanor Wlk 3 DA9 . . . . 177 C3
Electric Ave SS0 . . . . . . 147 C2
Electric Ho 9 E4 . . . . 87 D1
Electric Par
Ilford IG3 . . . . 133 F2
Woodford E18 . . . . 110 A1
Eleven Acre Rise IG10 . . 88 F6
Elgar Cl
Basildon SS15 . . . . 141 D8
Buckhurst Hill IG9 . . . . . 110 D8
South Benfleet SS7 . . . . 144 B6
Elgar Gdns RM18 . . . . . 179 B6
Elgin Ave
Chelmsford CM1 . . . . . . 32 A2
Romford RM3 . . . . 115 B4
Elgin Ho CM14 . . . . 116 D6
Elgin Rd IG3 . . . . 133 E4
Elham Dr SS13 . . . . 143 C6
Eliot Cl SS12 . . . . 121 C5
Eliot Mews SS2 . . . . 148 A2
Eliot Rd
Dagenham RM9 . . . . . . 153 D8
Dartford DA1 . . . . 176 B2
Eliot Way CM9 . . . . 37 A1
Elizabeth Ave
Ilford IG1 . . . . 133 D2
Rayleigh SS6 . . . . 123 C1
Elizabeth Cl
Hockley SS5 . . . . 124 E4
Lower Nazeing EN9 . . . . 43 D8
Romford RM7 . . . . 113 B2
Tilbury RM18 . . . . 179 B5
Elizabeth Ct
Buckhurst Hill IG9 . . . . . 88 B1
6 Gravesend DA11 . . . 179 A1
6 Woodford E18 . . . . . 110 A2
2 Woodford IG8 . . . . . 110 C3
Elizabeth Dr
Theydon Bois CM16 . . . . 67 E3
Wickford SS12 . . . . 121 B8
Elizabeth Garrett
Anderson Ho 9
DA17 . . . . 169 A3
Elizabeth Ho
Pilgrims Hatch CM15 . . . 94 B3
3 Romford RM2 . . . . . 136 C7
Southend-on-S SS9 . . . 146 D7
Elizabeth Rd
Grays RM16 . . . . 172 F4
Pilgrims Hatch CM15 . . . 94 B3
Rainham RM13 . . . . 170 B8
Southend-on-S SS1 . . . 167 D6
Elizabeth St DA9 . . . . . . 176 E2
Elizabeth Way 5 SS2 . . 147 F1
Elizabeth Way
Basildon SS15 . . . . 141 D5
Hadleigh SS7 . . . . 145 C4
Harlow CM20 . . . . 10 B2
Heybridge CM9 . . . . 37 A5
Eliza Cook Cl DA9 . . . . . 177 B3
Elkins The RM1 . . . . 113 E1
Ellenbrook Cl SS9 . . . . . 146 E3
Ellen Ct 5 E4 . . . . 87 C1
Ellen Wilkinson Ho 12
RM10 . . . . 135 A1
Ellerman Rd RM18 . . . . . 178 F5
Ellerton Gdns RM9 . . . . 153 C5
Ellerton Rd RM9 . . . . . . 153 C5
Ellesmere Gdns IG4 . . . . 132 E5
Ellesmere Rd
Canvey Island SS8 . . . . 163 E3
Rochford SS4 . . . . 103 C1
Ellie Cl SS17 . . . . 160 C2
Elliot Cl
South Woodham Ferrers
CM3 . . . . 101 F6

Elliot Cl continued
Woodford IG8 . . . . 110 D4
Elliott Gdns RM3 . . . . . . 114 B3
Ellis Ave RM13 . . . . 170 A4
Ellis Cl RM16 . . . . 174 E7
Ellmore Cl RM3 . . . . 114 B2
Ellswood SS15 . . . . 119 D1
Elm Ave
Heybridge CM9 . . . . 37 C5
Upminster RM14 . . . . . . 159 B4
Elm Bank Pl SS17 . . . . . 159 F4
Elmbourne Dr DA17 . . . . 169 B2
Elmbridge CM17 . . . . 11 F3
Elmbridge Hall CM5 . . . . 27 C1
Elmbridge Rd IG6 . . . . . 112 A4
Elmbrook 3 E18 . . . . . . 132 A8
Elm Cl
Buckhurst Hill IG9 . . . . . 110 D8
Chelmsford RM1 . . . . . . 32 A8
Epping Green CM16 . . . . 45 B7
Great Baddow CM2 . . . . 54 F6
Rayleigh SS6 . . . . 123 C3
Romford RM7 . . . . 113 B1
Southend-on-S SS3 . . . . 168 E7
Waltham Abbey EN9 . . . 65 D5
Wanstead E11 . . . . 132 B5
Elm Cotts
Billericay CM11 . . . . . . 119 E7
Southend-on-S SS2 . . . 147 E2
Waltham Abbey EN9 . . . 65 D1
Elm Court Pk CM4 . . . . . . 50 F1
Elmcroft Ave E11 . . . . . . 132 B7
Elmcroft Cl E11 . . . . 132 B7
Elm Ct
Chingford E4 . . . . 109 C4
Theydon Bois CM16 . . . . 67 E2
Woodford IG8 . . . . 110 F4
Elmdene Ave RM11 . . . . 136 F6
Elmdon Rd RM15 . . . . . . 172 A8
Elm Dr SS6 . . . . 123 D3
Elmer App SS1 . . . . 167 A8
Elmer Ave
Romford RM4 . . . . 113 E7
Southend-on-S SS1 . . . 167 A8
Elmer Cl RM13 . . . . 155 A5
Elmer Gdns RM13 . . . . . 155 A5
Elmfield Rd E4 . . . . 109 D8
Elm Gdns CM16 . . . . 47 B5
Elm Gn
Basildon SS13 . . . . 143 A5
Billericay CM11 . . . . 97 E2
Elm Gr
Hornchurch RM11 . . . . . 136 E5
Hullbridge SS5 . . . . 101 D2
Southend-on-S SS1 . . . 168 A8
Woodford IG8 . . . . 109 F5
Elm Green La CM3 . . . . . 56 C8
Elm Green Prep Sch
CM3 . . . . 34 D3
Elm Hall Gdns E11 . . . . . 132 B5
Elm Ho SS8 . . . . 164 B1
Elmhurst
2 Greenhithe DA9 . . . 177 B1
Hoddesdon EN10 . . . . . . 21 A4
Elmhurst Ave SS7 . . . . . 144 B4
Elmhurst Dr
Hornchurch RM11 . . . . . 136 C4
Woodford E18 . . . . 110 A1
Elmhurst Way IG10 . . . . . 88 F2
Elmores IG10 . . . . 89 A6
Elm Par RM12 . . . . 155 B8
ELM PARK 155 B7
Elm Park Ave
Hornchurch RM12 . . . . . 155 A8
Rainham RM12 . . . . 154 F8
Elm Park Sta RM12 . . . . 155 A8
Elm Rd
Aveley RM15 . . . . 171 D5
Basildon SS13 . . . . 121 E1
Canvey Island SS8 . . . . 164 C3
Chelmsford CM2 . . . . . . 54 D8
Grays RM17 . . . . 178 C8
Greenhithe DA9 . . . . . . 176 E1
Hadleigh SS7 . . . . 145 D2
Romford RM7 . . . . 113 B1
Southend-on-S, Leigh-on-S
SS9 . . . . 146 E1
Southend-on-S, Shoeburyness
SS3 . . . . 168 E8
South Woodham Ferrers
CM3 . . . . 101 C8
Wickford SS11 . . . . 121 D8
Elms EN9 . . . . 66 C4
Elms Dr CM1 . . . . 32 A4
Elms Farm Rd RM12 . . . 155 C7
Elms Gdns RM9 . . . . 153 F8
Elms Ind Est RM3 . . . . . 115 B3
Elmsleigh Dr SS9 . . . . . 146 E3
Elmslie Cl IG8 . . . . 110 F4
Elmslie Lo IG6 . . . . 133 C8
Elms Rd CM1 . . . . 29 F6
Elmstead Cl SS17 . . . . . 161 B4
Elmstead Rd IG3 . . . . . . 133 F2
Elms The CM5 . . . . 49 A1
Elmswood IG7 . . . . 111 D4
Elm Terr RM20 . . . . 177 B8
Elmtree Ave CM15 . . . . . 71 F2
Elmtree Rd SS16 . . . . . . 143 A4
Elm View Rd SS7 . . . . . . 144 B3
Elmway RM16 . . . . 173 C5
Elm Way
Boreham CM3 . . . . 20 E1
Brentwood CM14 . . . . . 116 A6
Elm Wlk RM2 . . . . 136 A8
Elmwood
Sawbridgeworth CM21 . . . 1 F1
Woodford IG8 . . . . 110 B2
Elmwood Ave SS5 . . . . . 124 F4

Elmwood Ct SS5 . . . . . . 124 E6
Elmwood Prim Sch
CM3 . . . . 101 D7
Elounda Ct SS7 . . . . 144 D4
Elrington Rd IG8 . . . . . . 110 A5
Elronds Rest CM3 . . . . . 101 C6
Elsden Chase CM0 . . . . . 84 D4
Elsenham Cres SS14 . . . 142 F6
Elsenham Ct SS6 . . . . . . 123 B3
Elsenham Mews SS14 . . 142 F6
Elsenham Rd E12 . . . . . 152 A7
Elsinor Ave SS14 . . . . . . 164 A6
Elstow Gdns RM9 . . . . . 153 E4
Elstow Rd RM9 . . . . 153 E4
Elstree Cl RM12 . . . . 155 B5
Elstree Gdns IG1 . . . . . . 152 C7
Eltisley Rd IG1 . . . . 152 B8
Elverston Cl SS15 . . . . . 141 D8
Elvet Ave RM2 . . . . 136 C7
Elvin Ct RM2 . . . . 136 B8
Elvin Dr RM15 . . . . 172 D5
Elwick Rd RM15 . . . . . . 172 C7
Elwood CM17 . . . . 24 E8
Ely Cl CM0 . . . . 84 D4
Ely Gdns
Dagenham RM10 . . . . . 135 C1
Redbridge IG1 . . . . 132 E4
Ely Pl IG8 . . . . 111 A5
Ely Rd SS2 . . . . 148 C2
Ely Way
Basildon SS14 . . . . 142 E7
Rayleigh SS6 . . . . 123 C4
Emanuel Rd SS16 . . . . . 141 B4
Embassy Ct
Maldon CM9 . . . . 37 A2
8 Wanstead E18 . . . . . 132 A8
Emberson Ct CM2 . . . . . . 32 F4
Emberson Way CM16 . . . 47 C5
Ember Way CM0 . . . . . . 106 A6
Emerald Gdns RM8 . . . . 135 A3
Emerald Ho 2 RM13 . . . 155 A1
Emerson Dr RM11 . . . . . 136 D4
Emerson Ho RM11 . . . . . 136 D5
EMERSON PARK 136 E5
Emerson Park Ct
RM11 . . . . 136 D4
Emerson Park Sch
RM11 . . . . 137 B4
Emerson Park Sta
RM11 . . . . 136 E4
Emerson Rd IG1 . . . . . . 133 A4
Emerson Terr IG1 . . . . . 110 D4
Emily White Ct SS11 . . . 121 F8
Emma's Cres SG12 . . . . . 8 B4
Emmaus Way IG7 . . . . . 111 A5
Emmott Ave IG6 . . . . . . 133 C4
Empire Wlk
2 Chelmsford CM2 . . . 32 C2
Greenhithe DA9 . . . . . . 177 C3
Empress Ave
Chingford E4 . . . . 109 B3
Ilford IG1 . . . . 133 A2
Redbridge IG1 . . . . 132 F2
Wanstead E12 . . . . 132 D2
Woodford IG8 . . . . 109 F3
Empress Par E4 . . . . . . 109 A3
Emsworth Rd IG6 . . . . . 111 B1
Enborne Gn RM15 . . . . . 172 A8
Endeavour Dr SS14 . . . . 120 B1
Endeavour Sch The
CM15 . . . . 116 F7
Endeavour Way IG11 . . . 153 A4
Endey Gdns CM1 . . . . . . 52 E5
Endlebury Ct E4 . . . . . . 109 D8
Endlebury Rd E4 . . . . . . 109 C8
Endsleigh Gdns IG1 . . . . 132 F3
Endway SS7 . . . . 145 E2
End Way Cotts CM0 . . . . 85 A7
Endways Ct CM15 . . . . . 94 C1
Endway The CM3 . . . . . . 83 D2
Enfield Ho 6 RM3 . . . . . 114 E3
ENFIELD ISLAND VILLAGE
. . . . 65 B2
Enfield Rd SS11 . . . . . . 122 C7
Engayne Gdns RM14 . . . 137 B3
Engayne Prim Sch
RM14 . . . . 137 E5
England's La IG10 . . . . . . 89 B7
Englefield Cl SS5 . . . . . 125 A4
Englefields CM0 . . . . 63 E3
Ennerdale Ave RM14 . . . 155 A7
Ennerdale Ct E11 . . . . . 132 A4
Ennismore Gdns SS2 . . 148 A3
Ensign Cl SS9 . . . . 147 A1
Ensign Ct DA11 . . . . . . 178 E1
Ensign Ho RM17 . . . . . . 177 F8
Enterprise Ctr The
SS14 . . . . 120 E2
Enterprise Ho IG11 . . . . 152 F2
Enterprise Ho E4 . . . . . . 87 C2
Enterprise Way SS11 . . 121 F6
EPPING 46 A3
Epping Cl
Chelmsford CM1 . . . . . . 31 E1
Romford RM7 . . . . 135 B8
Southend-on-S SS9 . . . 146 E7
Epping Forest Coll
IG10 . . . . 89 B5
Epping Forest District
Mus* IG10 . . . . 65 C6
Epping Forest Visitor Ctr*
IG10 . . . . 66 C1
Epping Forest YH*
IG10 . . . . 66 B1
Epping Glade E4 . . . . . . 87 C3
EPPING GREEN 45 A7
Epping Inf Sch CM16 . . . 45 F1
Epping Jun Sch CM16 . . 45 F1

Epping La
Chipping Ongar RM4 . . . 69 A1
Stapleford Abbotts RM4 . . 91 B8
Theydon Bois RM4 . . . . . 68 D1
Epping New Rd
Buckhurst Hill IG9,
IG10 . . . . 88 B4
Loughton IG10, CM16 . . 66 E2
Epping Ongar Rly*
CM16 . . . . 47 D4
Epping Rd
Chipping Ongar CM5 . . . 48 D6
Coopersale CM16 . . . . . 46 D4
Epping Green CM16 . . . . 23 A1
Loughton CM16 . . . . . . 67 A4
Roydon CM19 . . . . 22 D5
Toot Hill CM5 . . . . 47 D1
Epping Sta CM16 . . . . . . 68 A8
EPPING UPLAND 45 C5
Epping Upland CE Prim
Sch CM16 . . . . 45 B7
Epping Way E4 . . . . 87 B3
Epsom Cl CM11 . . . . 97 D5
Epsom Ho 15 RM3 . . . . 114 E5
Epsom Mews CM0 . . . . . 84 D4
Epsom Rd IG3 . . . . 133 F5
Epsom Way RM12 . . . . . 155 F8
Equinox Ho 7 IG11 . . . . 152 C6
Eric Clarke La IG11 . . . . 152 C2
Erick Ave CM1 . . . . 32 B7
Eric Rd
Basildon SS13 . . . . 143 F6
Dagenham RM6 . . . . . . 134 D4
Eridge Cl CM1 . . . . 32 D7
Erin Cl IG3 . . . . 134 A5
ERITH 169 E2
Erith Cres RM5 . . . . 113 C2
Erith Ct RM19 . . . . 171 A2
Erith High St DA8 . . . . . 169 E1
Erith Mus* DA8 . . . . . . 169 E1
Erith Rd DA17 . . . . 169 B1
Erith Sta DA8 . . . . 169 E1
Ernan Cl RM15 . . . . 172 A8
Ernan Rd RM15 . . . . 172 A8
Ernest Rd RM11 . . . . . . 136 F5
Erriff Dr RM15 . . . . 172 A8
Errington Rd RM16 . . . . 174 B3
Erroll Rd RM1 . . . . 135 F7
Erskine Pl 2 SS12 . . . . 121 E6
Esdaile Gdns RM14 . . . . 137 D4
Esdaile La EN11 . . . . 21 A5
Esgors Farm CM16 . . . . . 46 B7
Esher Ave RM7 . . . . 135 C5
Esher Rd IG3 . . . . 133 E1
Eskley Gdns
South Ockendon
RM15 . . . . 157 B1
South Ockendon RM15 . . 172 B8
Esk Way RM1 . . . . 113 E3
Esmond Ct RM13 . . . . . 155 B3
Esplanade Ct SS1 . . . . . 167 E6
Esplanade Gdns SS9 . . . 166 B8
Esplanade Ho SS0 . . . . . 166 B8
Esplanade The SS5 . . . . 101 D3
Essenden Rd DA17 . . . . 169 A1
Essex Ave CM1 . . . . 32 A7
Essex Cl
Basildon SS15 . . . . 141 B6
Canvey Island SS8 . . . . 164 A2
Rayleigh SS6 . . . . 123 F2
Romford RM7 . . . . 135 B7
Essex County Cricket
Club* CM2 . . . . 32 B2
Essex Gdns
Hornchurch RM11 . . . . . 137 A6
Linford SS17 . . . . 175 A4
Southend-on-S SS9 . . . 146 E4
Essex Ho EN9 . . . . 65 C5
Essex Nuffield Hospl The
CM15 . . . . 94 E1
Essex Rd
Barking IG11 . . . . 152 D5
Burnham-on-C CM0 . . . 106 C5
Canvey Island SS8 . . . . 164 C4
Chingford E4 . . . . 87 E3
Dagenham, Goodmayes
RM6 . . . . 134 C4
Dagenham RM10 . . . . . 154 C7
Grays RM20 . . . . 177 A8
Hoddesdon EN11 . . . . . 21 C6
Maldon CM9 . . . . 36 F1
Romford RM7 . . . . 135 B7
Woodford E18 . . . . 110 B1
Essex Regiment Way
CM3 . . . . 19 D5
Essex St SS1 . . . . 167 A8
Essex Way
Brentwood CM13 . . . . . 116 C4
South Benfleet SS7 . . . . 144 F1
Estate Rd SS7 . . . . 145 F3
Estella Mead CM1 . . . . . . 31 E7
Estfeld Cl 4 EN11 . . . . . 8 B1
Eston Ct 1 E18 . . . . 110 A1
Estuary Cl IG11 . . . . 153 B2
Estuary Cotts RM18 . . . 180 D7
Estuary Ct SS9 . . . . 165 F8
Estuary Gdns SS3 . . . . . 150 C2
Estuary Lo SS1 . . . . 167 E8
Estuary Mews SS3 . . . . . 168 E6
Ethelbert Gdns IG2 . . . . 133 A6
Ethelbert Rd SS4 . . . . . 103 C1
Ethelburga Rd RM3 . . . . 114 F2
Ethel Cotts RM6 . . . . . . 134 D8
Etheldore Ave SS5 . . . . 124 E8
Ethel Rd SS6 . . . . 146 B8
Ethelred Gdns SS11 . . . . 99 E1
Etheridge Gn IG10 . . . . . 89 C6

Etheridge Rd IG10 . . . . . 89 C6
Eton Cl SS8 . . . . 164 B5
Eton Rd IG1 . . . . 152 D8
Eton Wlk SS3 . . . . 149 E2
Etton Cl RM12 . . . . 136 E2
Eugene Cl RM2 . . . . 136 C7
Europa Pk RM20 . . . . . . 177 C8
Europa Trad Est DA8 . . 169 D1
Eustace Rd RM6 . . . . . . 134 C5
Evans Cl DA9 . . . . 177 A2
Evansdale RM13 . . . . . . 154 F2
Evanston Ave E4 . . . . . . 109 C3
Evanston Gdns IG4 . . . . 132 E5
Eva Rd RM6 . . . . 134 D4
Evelyn Pl CM1 . . . . 31 F1
Evelyn Rd SS5 . . . . 124 E6
Evelyn Sharp Cl RM2 . . 136 D8
Evelyn Sharp Ho RM2 . . 136 D8
Evelyn Wlk CM13 . . . . . 116 C4
Everard Rd SS14 . . . . . . 143 A8
Everest SS6 . . . . 123 D5
Everest Rise CM12 . . . . . 96 F1
Everest Way CM9 . . . . . . 37 B3
Everglades The SS7 . . . . 145 F2
Evergreen Ct SS12 . . . . 121 C6
Evergreens The SS3 . . . 149 E6
Everik Bsns Ctr CM13 . . 95 C4
Eversleigh Gdns
RM14 . . . . 137 D3
EVERSLEY 143 C6
Eversley Cl IG10 . . . . 89 C6
Eversley Ct SS7 . . . . . . 144 C7
Eversley Lo 11 EN11 . . . 21 A6
Eversley Prim Sch
SS13 . . . . 143 C6
Eversley Rd
Basildon SS13 . . . . 143 D6
South Benfleet SS7 . . . . 144 C7
Eves Cnr
Burnham-on-C CM0 . . . 106 B7
Danbury CM3 . . . . 56 E7
Eves Cres CM1 . . . . 32 A5
Evesham Ave E17 . . . . . 109 A1
Evesham Way IG5 . . . . . 133 A8
Ewan Cl SS9 . . . . 146 A3
Ewan Rd RM3 . . . . 114 C1
Ewanrigg Terr IG8 . . . . . 110 C5
Ewan Way SS9 . . . . 146 A3
Ewellhurst Rd IG5 . . . . . 110 E1
Exchange St
Romford RM1 . . . . 135 E6
Romford RM1, RM7 . . . 135 E5
Exchange The IG1 . . . . . 133 E4
Exchange Way 5 CM1 . . 32 B2
Exeter Cl
Basildon SS14 . . . . 142 F7
Southend-on-S SS3 . . . 149 F1
Exeter Gdns IG1 . . . . . . 132 F3
Exeter Ho
7 Barking IG11 . . . . . . 153 A5
Southend-on-S SS3 . . . 149 F1
Exeter Rd
Chelmsford CM1 . . . . . . 32 E5
Dagenham RM10 . . . . . 154 B7
Exford Ave SS0 . . . . 147 B5
Exley Cl CM4 . . . . 74 B4
Exmoor Cl
Chelmsford CM1 . . . . . . 31 D1
Redbridge IG6 . . . . 111 C2
Exmouth Dr SS6 . . . . . . 123 D5
Exmouth Rd RM17 . . . . 178 B8
Express Dr IG3 . . . . 134 B3
Exton Gdns RM8 . . . . . . 153 C7
Eyhurst Ave RM12 . . . . . 136 B1
Eynesham Way 1
SS13 . . . . 121 A1
Eynsford Rd
Greenhithe DA9 . . . . . . 177 C2
Ilford IG3 . . . . 133 E2
Eyre Cl RM2 . . . . 136 B7

F

Factory Rd DA11 . . . . . . 178 C1
Faggotters La CM17 . . . . 12 F1
Fagus Ave RM13 . . . . . . 155 D2
Failand Mews SS17 . . . . 160 D4
Fairbank Cl CM5 . . . . 48 F2
Fairburn Cl 2 SS1 . . . . 167 C8
Fairburn Ct 4 SS1 . . . . 167 C8
Faircroft CM17 . . . . 11 C4
FAIR CROSS 152 F7
Fair Cross IG11 . . . . 152 E7
Faircross Ave
Barking IG11 . . . . 152 C6
Romford RM5 . . . . 113 D3
Faircross Par IG11 . . . . . 152 E7
Fairfax Ave SS13 . . . . . . 143 C8
Fairfax Mead CM2 . . . . . 33 A2
Fairfax Rd
Grays RM17 . . . . 173 C6
Tilbury RM18 . . . . 178 F6
Fairfield
Great Wakering SS3 . . . 150 A3
Ingatestone CM4 . . . . . . 74 C4
Fairfield Ave
Grays RM16 . . . . 173 C6
Upminster RM14 . . . . . . 137 C1
Fairfield Cl RM12 . . . . . . 136 A2
Fairfield Cres SS9 . . . . . 146 F6
Fairfield Ct 8 IG8 . . . . . 110 A4
Fairfield Gdns SS9 . . . . . 146 F7
Fairfield Rd
Brentwood CM14 . . . . . 116 C7
Chelmsford CM1 . . . . . . 32 A3

Fairfield Rd continued
Chipping Ongar CM5 . . . . . . **48** F2
Epping CM16 . . . . **46** B2
Hoddesdon EN11 . . . . **21** A8
Ilford IG1 . . . . **152** B6
Southend-on-S SS9 . . . . . . **146** E7
Woodford IG8 . . . . **110** A4
Fairfield Rise CM12 . . . . . . **118** F8
Fairfields CM3 . . . . **58** D1
Fairfield Sq 3 DA11 . . . . . **179** A1
Fairford Cl RM3 . . . . **115** B4
Fairford Way RM3 . . . . . . **115** B4
Fairham Ave RM15 . . . . . . **172** A6
Fairholme Ave RM2 . . . . . **136** B7
Fairholme Gdns
RM14 . . . . **137** F4
Fairholme Rd
Ilford IG1 . . . . **133** A4
Redbridge IG1 . . . . **132** F4
Fairhouse Com Jun & Inf
Sch SS14 . . . . **142** D6
Fairhouse Ct SS14 . . . . **142** D6
Fairings Ct SS0 . . . . **147** D2
Fairkytes Ave RM11 . . . . . **136** D3
Fairland Cl SS6 . . . . **123** E5
Fairlands Ave IG9 . . . . **110** A8
Fairlawn Dr IG8 . . . . **110** A3
Fairlawn Gdns SS2 . . . . . . **147** C5
Fairlawns
Brentwood CM14 . . . . **116** A7
10 Chingford E4 . . . . **109** C8
Epping CM16 . . . . **46** B2
Southend-on-S SS1 . . . . . . **167** F7
Fairlawns Cl RM11 . . . . . . **136** F4
Fairleads CM3 . . . . **56** F8
Fairleigh Ave SS13 . . . . . . **143** D5
Fairleigh Cl SS9 . . . . **146** D1
Fairleigh Dr SS9 . . . . **146** D1
Fairleigh Rd SS13 . . . . . . **143** D5
Fairlight Ave
Chingford E4 . . . . **109** D8
Woodford IG8 . . . . **110** A4
Fairlight Cl E4 . . . . **109** D8
Fairlight Rd SS7 . . . . **145** C3
Fairlight Villas RM4 . . . . . **113** E7
FAIRLOP **111** E2
Fairlop Ave SS8 . . . . **164** A4
Fairlop Cl RM12 . . . . **155** B6
Fairlop Gdns
Basildon SS14 . . . . **142** D6
Redbridge IG6 . . . . **111** C3
FAIRLOP PLAIN **111** F1
Fairlop Prim Sch IG6 . . . **111** C2
Fairlop Rd IG6 . . . . **111** C1
Fairlop Sta IG6 . . . . **111** D2
Fairlop Waters Ctry Pk ★
IG6 . . . . **111** C3
Fairmead SS6 . . . . **123** B4
Fair Mead SS14 . . . . **142** C8
Fairmead Ave
Hadleigh SS7 . . . . **145** E6
Southend-on-S SS0 . . . . . . **147** C2
Fairmead Ct E4 . . . . **87** C2
Fairmead Gdns IG4 . . . . . **132** E6
Fairmead Ho SS0 . . . . **147** C2
Fairmead Rd IG10 . . . . **88** B6
Fairmeads IG10 . . . . **89** B7
Fairmeadside IG10 . . . . **88** C4
Fairoak Gdns RM1 . . . . . . **113** E1
Fair Oak Pl IG6 . . . . **111** C1
Fairstead SS14 . . . . **142** A6
Fairstead Lo 4 IG8 . . . . . **110** A4
Fairview
Billericay CM12 . . . . **97** A1
Canvey Island SS8 . . . . . . **163** F5
Fairview Ave
Brentwood CM13 . . . . **95** C3
Rainham RM13 . . . . **155** D2
Stanford-le-H SS17 . . . . . . **160** C1
Fairview Chase SS17 . . . . **175** C8
Fairview Cl
Chigwell IG7 . . . . **111** E6
South Benfleet SS7 . . . . . . **144** C7
Fairview Cres SS7 . . . . . . **144** C7
Fairview Dr
Chigwell IG7 . . . . **111** E5
Southend-on-S SS0 . . . . . . **147** C4
Fairview Est EN11 . . . . **21** C7
Fairview Gdns
Southend-on-S SS9 . . . . . . **146** C2
Woodford IG8 . . . . **110** B2
Fairview Ind Pk
RM13 . . . . **169** D8
Fair View Lo SS9 . . . . **146** C2
Fairview Par RM7 . . . . **135** D6
Fairview Rd
Basildon SS14 . . . . **142** F5
Chigwell IG7 . . . . **111** E6
Fairview Wlk SS7 . . . . **144** C7
Fairville Mews SS0 . . . . . . **147** C2
Fairway
Chelmsford CM2 . . . . **54** D7
Grays RM16 . . . . **173** B5
Sawbridgeworth CM21 . . . . .**1** F2
Wickford SS12 . . . . **121** E3
Woodford IG8 . . . . **110** C5
Fairway Dr CM0 . . . . **106** B5
Fairway Gardens Cl
SS9 . . . . **146** C5
Fairway Gdns
Ilford IG1 . . . . **152** C7
Southend-on-S SS9 . . . . . . **146** C5
Fairways
11 Chingford E4 . . . . **87** C1
Southend-on-S SS1 . . . . . . **167** F8
Waltham Abbey EN9 . . . . . . **65** E5
Fairways Prim Sch
SS9 . . . . **146** C4

Fairways The
Cold Norton CM3 . . . . **80** F5
South Benfleet ss7 . . . . . . **144** D2
Fairway The
Harlow CM18 . . . . **24** A6
South Benfleet SS7 . . . . . . **144** C7
Southend-on-S SS9 . . . . . . **146** C5
Upminster RM14 . . . . **137** D4
Falbro Cres SS7 . . . . **145** D4
Falcon Ave RM17 . . . . **178** C8
Falcon Cl
Rayleigh SS6 . . . . **123** B3
Sawbridgeworth CM21 . . . . .**1** C1
Southend-on-S SS9 . . . . . . **146** F5
Waltham Abbey EN9 . . . . . . **66** A5
Falcon Ct 6 E18 . . . . **132** B8
Falconer Rd IG6 . . . . **112** C5
Falconers Pk CM21 . . . .**1** D1
Falcon Fields CM9 . . . . **58** F8
Falcon Mews CM9 . . . . **58** F8
Falcon Pk SS14 . . . . **141** F8
Falcon Rd CM0 . . . . **84** C4
Falcons Mead CM2 . . . . **32** A1
Falcon Way
Basildon SS16 . . . . **142** C4
Chelmsford CM2 . . . . **54** A6
Rainham RM13 . . . . **155** A5
Southend-on-S SS3 . . . . . . **149** E1
Wanstead E11 . . . . **132** A7
Falkenham End SS14 . . . . **142** C7
Falkenham Path 1
SS14 . . . . **142** C7
Falkenham Rise SS14 . . . . **142** C7
Falkenham Row SS14 . . . . **142** C7
Falkirk Rd RM11 . . . . **137** A3
Falkland Cl CM3 . . . . **33** E8
Falkland Gn CM9 . . . . **57** E6
Falklands Rd CM0 . . . . . . **106** B5
Falkner Cl 6 RM8 . . . . . . **134** D4
Fallaize Ave IG1 . . . . **152** B8
Fallow Cl IG7 . . . . **111** F5
Fallowfield SS3 . . . . **149** D1
Fallow Fields IG10 . . . . **88** C2
Fallows The SS8 . . . . **163** F6
Falmouth Ave E4 . . . . **109** E5
Falmouth Gdns IG4 . . . . . **132** E6
Falmouth Rd CM1 . . . . **32** E5
Falstaff Pl SS16 . . . . **141** A5
Falstones SS15 . . . . **141** E5
Fambridge Cl CM9 . . . . **37** A1
Fambridge Ct 2 RM7 . . . **135** D6
Fambridge Dr SS12 . . . . . **121** E6
Fambridge Rd
Althorne CM3 . . . . **82** F2
Cold Norton CM9, CM3 . . . . **81** C5
Dagenham RM8 . . . . **135** A3
Maldon CM9 . . . . **36** F2
Rochford SS4, CM3 . . . . . . **103** C3
Fambridge Sta CM3 . . . . . **103** B8
Fane Rd SS7 . . . . **144** D8
FANNER'S GREEN **18** C5
Fanner's Green Cotts
CM3 . . . . **18** C5
Fanns Rise RM19 . . . . **171** A2
Fanshawe Ave IG11 . . . . . **152** C6
Fanshawe Cres
Dagenham RM9 . . . . **153** F7
Hornchurch RM11 . . . . **136** D5
Fanshawe Rd RM16 . . . . . **174** A3
Fanshawe The RM9 . . . . . **153** D5
Fantasia Ct CM14 . . . . **116** B5
Fanton Ave SS11 . . . . **121** F3
Fanton Chase SS11 . . . . . **122** A6
Fanton Gdns SS11 . . . . . . **122** B6
Fanton Wlk SS11 . . . . **122** B6
Faraday Ho 4 DA17 . . . . . **169** A3
Faraday Rd SS9 . . . . **146** C6
Faringdon Ave RM3 . . . . . **114** D3
Faringdon Gr RM3 . . . . . . **114** D3
Farley Dr IG3 . . . . **133** E3
FARMBRIDGE END **16** D3
Farmbridge End Rd
CM1 . . . . **16** D4
Farm Cl
Brentwood CM13 . . . . **95** C2
Buckhurst Hill IG9 . . . . . . **110** C7
Dagenham RM10 . . . . **154** C5
Roydon CM19 . . . .**9** B1
Farm Cres SS11 . . . . **100** E4
Farm Dr RM16 . . . . **173** C6
Farm End E4 . . . . **87** E4
Farmer Ct EN9 . . . . **66** A6
Farm Hill Rd EN9 . . . . **65** D6
Farm La EN11 . . . . **21** C8
Farm Rd
Canvey Island SS8 . . . . . . **164** B5
Chadwell St M RM16 . . . . . **173** F4
East Tilbury RM18 . . . . . . **175** C2
Rainham RM13 . . . . **155** C4
Wanstead E12 . . . . **132** E2
Farm View SS6 . . . . **123** D5
Farmway RM8 . . . . **134** C1
Farm Way
Buckhurst Hill IG9 . . . . . . **110** C6
Hornchurch RM12 . . . . **155** C8
Thundersley SS7 . . . . **145** B6
Farnaby Way SS17 . . . . . . **160** C3
Farnan Ave E17 . . . . **109** B1
Farne Dr SS12 . . . . **121** F5
Farnes Ave SS12 . . . . **121** C1
Farnes Dr RM2 . . . . **114** C1
Farnham Cl SS11 . . . .**1** C1
Farnham Green Prim Sch
IG3 . . . . **134** A5
Farnham Rd
Ilford IG1 . . . . **133** F4
Romford RM3 . . . . **114** D5
Farnley Rd E4 . . . . **87** E2

Farnol Rd DA1 . . . . **176** A3
Farrance Rd RM6 . . . . **134** E4
Farr Ave IG11 . . . . **153** A3
Farriers
Great Amwell SG12 . . . .**8** A6
Sawbridgeworth CM21 . . . . .**1** E3
Farriers Dr CM12 . . . . **97** B5
Farriers Sq CM11 . . . . **98** C4
Farriers Way SS2 . . . . **147** F5
Farringdon Service Rd 8
SS1 . . . . **167** A8
Farrow Gdns RM16 . . . . . **173** C5
Farrow Ho CM15 . . . . **94** C1
Farr Rd N1 . . . . **53** E7
FARTHER HOWEGREEN
. . . . **80** E7
Farthingale Ct EN9 . . . . **66** A5
Farthingale La EN9 . . . . **66** A5
Farthings CM4 . . . . **109** E7
Fastnet SS2 . . . . **147** A7
Faulkner Cl 6 RM8 . . . . . **134** D4
Fauna Cl RM6 . . . . **134** C5
Fauners SS15 . . . . **142** A5
Faversham Ave E4 . . . . **87** F1
Faversham Cl IG7 . . . . **112** B8
Fawbert & Barnards Prim
Sch CM21 . . . .**11** C3
Fawbert & Bernard Inf Sch
CM21 . . . .**1** E2
Fawcett Dr SS15 . . . . **119** E1
Fawkner Cl CM2 . . . . **32** F2
Fawkon Wlk EN11 . . . . **21** A6
Fawn Rd IG7 . . . . **111** F5
Faymore Gdns RM15 . . . . **172** A4
Fazal Laj IG1 . . . . **133** C2
Fearns Mead CM14 . . . . . . **116** C5
Featherby Way SS4 . . . . . **126** A1
Featherston Ct RM6 . . . . . **134** F5
Fetherston Rd SS13 . . . . . **160** D1
Fetherton Ct 5 IG11 . . . . **152** C3
Fews Lo RM6 . . . . **134** D7
Fiddlers Cl E18 . . . . **177** B3
FIDDLERS HAMLET **68** C7
Field Cl
Abridge RM4 . . . . **90** B6
Buckhurst Hill IG9 . . . . . . **110** C7
Chingford E4 . . . . **109** B4
Fielders Ct 14 CM14 . . . . **116** C8
Fielders The SS8 . . . . **164** A2
Fieldfare CM11 . . . . **119** C8
Fieldhouse Ct E18 . . . . . . **110** B2
Fielding Ave RM18 . . . . . . **179** C6
Fielding Way
Brentwood CM13 . . . . **95** C3
Southend-on-S SS0 . . . . . . **147** D2
Field Rd RM15 . . . . **171** C5
Fields Park Cres RM6 . . . . **134** D6
Field View RM16 . . . . **174** A3
Field View Cl RM7 . . . . . . **135** A8
Fieldway
Basildon SS13 . . . . **143** C4
Dagenham RM8 . . . . **153** C8
Grays RM20 . . . . **173** A5
Stanstead Abbotts SG12 . . . .**8** B4
Wickford SS12 . . . . **121** D3
Field Way EN11 . . . .**8** C2
Fiennes Cl RM8 . . . . **134** C3
Fiesta Dr RM9, RM13 . . . . **154** C1
Fifth Ave
Canvey Island SS8 . . . . . . **163** E4
Chelmsford CM1 . . . . **32** B6
Grays RM20 . . . . **177** A8
Thundersley SS7 . . . . **145** A6
Wickford SS11 . . . . **122** A6
Fifth Ave / Allende Ave
CM20 . . . . **10** C3
Filey Rd CM0 . . . . **84** A3
Fillebrook Ave SS9 . . . . . . **147** A2
Fillebrook Ct SS9 . . . . **147** A2
Filliol Cl CM3 . . . . **78** B6
Filston Rd DA8 . . . . **169** C1
Finch Ct CM5 . . . . **49** D3
Finches Cl SS17 . . . . **161** C4
Finches The SS7 . . . . **145** A7
Finchfield SS6 . . . . **123** D1
Finch Gdns E4 . . . . **109** A5
Finchingfield Ave
IG8 . . . . **110** C3
Finchingfields The
CM15 . . . . **71** E2
Finchingfield Way 7
SS12 . . . . **121** C5
Finchland View CM3 . . . . **101** D6
Finchley Ave CM2 . . . . **54** D7
Finchley Cl DA1 . . . . **176** A1
Finchley Rd
Grays RM17 . . . . **178** B8
Southend-on-S SS0 . . . . . . **166** D8
Finchmoor CM18 . . . . **23** D5
Findon Gdns RM13 . . . . . . **170** B8
Fingrith Hall Cotts
CM4 . . . . **50** F3
Fingrith Hall La CM4 . . . . . **50** F3
Finnymore Rd RM9 . . . . . **153** E5
Finucane Gdns RM13 . . . . **155** A6
Firbank Rd RM5 . . . . **113** B5
Fir Ct SS15 . . . . **119** C1
Firecrest Rd CM2 . . . . **54** C5
Firfield Rd SS7 . . . . **145** C4
Firham Park Ave
RM3 . . . . **115** A3
Firle The SS16 . . . . **141** C4
Firmans SS16 . . . . **141** B3

Fernden Way RM7 . . . . . . **135** B5
Ferndown
Hornchurch RM11 . . . . **136** F5
7 Wanstead E18 . . . . . . **132** A8
Ferndown Cl SS2 . . . . **167** C8
Fernhall Dr IG4 . . . . **132** D6
Fernhall La EN9 . . . . **66** D8
Fern Hill SS16 . . . . **141** C4
Fernhill Ct E17 . . . . **109** D1
Fern Hill La CM18 . . . . **23** F3
Fernie Cl IG7 . . . . **112** A5
Fernlea Rd
Burnham-on-C CM0 . . . . . **106** B5
South Benfleet SS7 . . . . . . **144** E3
Fernleigh Ct
Romford RM7 . . . . **135** C6
Southend-on-S SS0 . . . . . . **147** A3
Fernleigh Dr SS9 . . . . **147** A1
Fernside IG9 . . . . **88** B1
Fernside Cl SS17 . . . . **161** B4
Fernways IG1 . . . . **152** B8
Fern Wlk
Basildon SS16 . . . . **140** E4
Canvey Island SS8 . . . . . . **163** F3
Fernwood SS7 . . . . **145** E4
Ferrers Rd CM3 . . . . **101** D6
Ferris Ave CM3 . . . . **80** F5
Ferris Stps 13 SS1 . . . . . **167** C7
Ferro Rd RM13 . . . . **155** A5
Ferry La RM13 . . . . **169** E7
Ferrymead SS8 . . . . **163** F5
Ferry Rd
Burnham-on-C CM0 . . . . . **105** E6
Hullbridge SS5 . . . . **101** D2
North Fambridge CM3 . . . . **103** A6
South Benfleet SS7 . . . . . . **163** D8
Tilbury RM18 . . . . **179** A4
Feryby Rd RM16 . . . . **174** B3
Feryngs Cl CM17 . . . . **11** D4
Fesants Croft CM20 . . . . . . **11** B3
Festival Link SS14 . . . . . . **142** B8
Festival Way SS14 . . . . . . **120** B1
Fetherston Ct RM6 . . . . . . **134** F5
Fetherston Rd SS13 . . . . . **160** D1
Fetherton Ct 5 IG11 . . . . **152** C3
Fews Lo RM6 . . . . **134** D7
Fiddlers Cl E18 . . . . **177** B3
FIDDLERS HAMLET **68** C7
Field Cl
Abridge RM4 . . . . **90** B6
Buckhurst Hill IG9 . . . . . . **110** C7
Chingford E4 . . . . **109** B4

Fir Pk CM19 . . . . **23** B5
Firs EN9 . . . . **66** C4
Firs Ct SS16 . . . . **142** F4
Firs Dr
Loughton IG10 . . . . **89** A8
Writtle CM1 . . . . **31** B1
Firsgrove Cres CM14 . . . . **116** B6
Firsgrove Rd CM14 . . . . . . **116** C6
First Ave
Basildon RM14, SS16 . . . . **140** E4
Billericay CM12 . . . . **118** F7
Canvey Island SS8 . . . . . . **163** E4
Chelmsford CM1 . . . . **32** B5
Dagenham RM10 . . . . **154** B3
Grays RM20 . . . . **177** A8
Hook End CM15 . . . . **72** C5
Hullbridge SS5 . . . . **101** F1
Ilford RM6 . . . . **134** C6
Southend-on-S SS0 . . . . . . **166** B8
Stanford-le-H SS17 . . . . . . **160** D3
Wickford SS11 . . . . **122** A6
First Ave / Mandela Ave
CM20 . . . . **10** F2
Firs The
Canvey Island SS8 . . . . . . **163** F5
Grays RM16 . . . . **173** C5
Pilgrims Hatch CM15 . . . . . **94** A3
Woodford IG8 . . . . **110** C5
Firs Wlk IG8 . . . . **110** A5
Fir Tree Cl
Grays RM17 . . . . **178** D8
Romford RM1 . . . . **135** D8
Fir Tree La CM3 . . . . **34** E1
Fir Tree Rise CM2 . . . . **54** B6
Fir Trees
Abridge RM4 . . . . **90** B6
Epping CM16 . . . . **46** B2
Fir Tree Wlk
Dagenham RM10 . . . . **135** C1
Heybridge CM9 . . . . **37** C5
Fir Wlk SS8 . . . . **163** F5
Fisgard Ct 9 DA12 . . . . . . **179** D1
Fisher Cl EN3 . . . . **65** B2
Fisher Ct CM14 . . . . **116** B5
Fishermans Way EN11 . . . . **21** D8
Fishermen's Hill
DA1 . . . . **178** B2
Fishers Cl EN8 . . . . **65** A5
Fishers Hatch CM20 . . . . . **10** E1
Fisher's Way DA17 . . . . . . **169** C5
Fish St CM9 . . . . **38** E6
Fiske Ct IG11 . . . . **152** D3
Fitches Cres CM9 . . . . **37** B1
Fitches Mews CM9 . . . . **37** B1
Fitzgerald Rd E11 . . . . **132** A6
Fitzilian Ave RM3 . . . . **114** F2
Fitzroy Cl CM12 . . . . **97** A4
Fitzstephen Rd RM8 . . . . . **153** C7
Fitzwalter La CM3 . . . . **56** D6
Fitzwalter Pl CM1 . . . . **31** E3
Fitzwalter Rd CM3 . . . . **33** F8
Fitzwarren SS3 . . . . **149** D1
Fitzwilliams Ct CM17 . . . . . **11** E4
Fitzwimarc Sch The
SS6 . . . . **123** E3
Five Acres
Bicknacre CM3 . . . . **56** F3
Harlow CM18 . . . . **23** E5
Five Elms Prim Sch
RM8 . . . . **134** F1
Five Elms Rd RM9 . . . . . . **134** F1
Five Oaks SS7 . . . . **145** B4
Five Oaks La IG7 . . . . **112** E5
Flagstaff Cl E4 . . . . **65** B6
Flagstaff Rd EN9 . . . . **65** B6
Flambird's Chase
Purleigh CM3 . . . . **80** A7
Stow Maries CM3 . . . . **79** F6
Flamboro Cl SS9 . . . . **146** D6
Flamboro Wlk SS9 . . . . . . **146** D6
Flamingo Wlk 4
RM13 . . . . **155** A6
Flamstead Gdns RM9 . . . . **153** C5
Flamstead Rd RM9 . . . . . . **153** C5
Flanders Rd E6 . . . . **152** A3
Flandrian Cl EN3 . . . . **65** B1
Flats The
Grays RM17 . . . . **173** D2
Greenhithe DA9 . . . . **177** C2
Flaxen Cl E4 . . . . **109** B7
Flaxen Rd E4 . . . . **109** B7
Flaxman Ct 13 DA17 . . . . **169** A1
Fleet Ave RM14 . . . . **137** D5
Fleet Cl RM14 . . . . **137** D5
Fleet Hall Cotts SS4 . . . . . **148** B8
Fleethall Gr RM16 . . . . **173** A5
Fleethall Rd SS4 . . . . **148** A8
Fleet Rd SS7 . . . . **144** E3
Fleetway SS16 . . . . **142** F4
Fleetwood SS8 . . . . **164** E2
Fleetwood Ave SS0 . . . . . . **147** C2
Fleming Gdns
Romford RM3 . . . . **114** D1
Tilbury RM18 . . . . **179** C6
Fleming Ho RM3 . . . . **114** E1
Fleming Rd
Grays RM16 . . . . **172** C3
Waltham Abbey EN9 . . . . . . **65** B4
Flemings CM13 . . . . **116** C4
Flemings Farm Rd
SS9 . . . . **146** D8
Flemming Ave SS9 . . . . . . **146** D3
Flemming Cres SS9 . . . . . **146** D4
Fletcher Cl CM11 . . . . **97** D2
Fletcher Dr SS12 . . . . **121** E6

Fletcher Rd IG7 . . . . **111** F5
Fletchers SS16 . . . . **141** E3
Fletchers Sq SS2 . . . . **148** A5
Flex Mdw CM19 . . . . **22** F7
Flint Cl SS16 . . . . **140** F5
Flint St RM20 . . . . **177** B8
Flintwich Manor CM1 . . . **31** E7
Flora Gdns RM6 . . . . **134** C5
Florence
  Grays RM20 . . . . **177** E8
  Hadleigh SS7 . . . . **145** D3
  Harlow CM17 . . . . **24** C6
  Hornchurch RM12 . . . . . **136** E2
Florence Ct E11 . . . . **132** C7
Florence Elson Cl
  E12 . . . . **152** A8
Florence Gdns
  Dagenham RM6 . . . . **134** C4
  Hadleigh SS7 . . . . **145** D3
Florence Ho RM3 . . . . . . **114** E1
Florence Neale Ho [2]
  SS8 . . . . **164** A3
Florence Rd SS8 . . . . **164** D3
Florence Root Ho [3]
  IG4 . . . . **132** F6
Florence Terr SS17 . . . . . **159** F4
Florence Way SS16 . . . . . **141** B5
Florentine Ho [3] IG1 . . . **133** B2
Flux's La CM16 . . . . **68** A6
FOBBING **161** D5
Fobbing Farm Cl
  SS16 . . . . **142** A3
Fobbing Rd SS17 . . . . **161** C3
Fodderwick [1] SS14 . . . . **142** A5
Fogerty Cl EN3 . . . . **65** B2
Foksville Rd SS8 . . . . **164** C4
Fold Croft CM20 . . . . **10** A1
Fold The SS14 . . . . **142** B6
Folkes La RM14, CM13 . . . **137** F7
Folly Chase SS5 . . . . **124** B6
Folly La SS5 . . . . **124** C6
Folly View SG12 . . . . **8** B4
Fontayne Ave
  Chigwell IG7 . . . . **111** C6
  Rainham RM13 . . . . **154** E3
  Romford RM1 . . . . **113** E1
Font Cl SS15 . . . . **141** C6
Fonteyn Cl SS15 . . . . **141** C8
Fonteyne Gdns IG8 . . . . . **110** D1
Fontwell Park Gdns
  RM12 . . . . **155** E8
Forbes Cl RM11 . . . . **136** B3
Ford Cl
  Basildon SS15 . . . . **141** A6
  Rainham RM13 . . . . **154** F5
Ford End IG8 . . . . **110** B4
Fordham Cl RM11 . . . . . . **137** A4
Fordhams Row RM16 . . . **174** B8
Ford Ho SS3 . . . . **168** F6
Ford La RM13 . . . . **154** F5
Ford Rd
  Dagenham RM10 . . . . . . **154** A5
  Northfleet DA11 . . . . . . **178** B2
Fordson Rd CM2 . . . . **33** B6
Fordview Ind Est
  RM13 . . . . **154** D2
Fordyce Cl RM11 . . . . **137** A4
Fordyke Rd RM8 . . . . **134** F2
Forebury Ave CM21 . . . . **1** F2
Forebury Cres CM21 . . . . . . **1** F2
Forebury The CM21 . . . . **1** F2
Forefield Gn CM1 . . . . **32** F7
Forelands Pl CM21 . . . . **1** E2
Foremans CM1 . . . . **31** E3
Foremark Cl IG6 . . . . **111** F4
Fore St
  Basildon SS15 . . . . **119** C2
  Harlow CM17 . . . . **11** C4
Forest App
  Chingford E4 . . . . **87** E2
  Woodford IG8 . . . . **110** A3
Forest Ave
  Chigwell IG7 . . . . **111** A5
  Chingford E4 . . . . **87** E2
Forest Cl
  Waltham Abbey EN9 . . . . **66** B2
  Wanstead E11 . . . . **132** A6
  Woodford IG8 . . . . **110** B6
Forest Ct
  Chingford E4 . . . . **87** F1
  Loughton IG10 . . . . **88** D6
Forest Dr
  Chelmsford CM1 . . . . **31** E1
  Chingford IG8 . . . . **109** E3
  Fyfield CM5 . . . . **27** C1
  Theydon Bois CM16 . . . . **67** E3
  Wanstead E12 . . . . **132** D1
Forest Edge IG9 . . . . **110** D7
Forester Ct CM12 . . . . **96** F3
Foresters Ct IG10 . . . . **89** A7
Forest Farm Cotts
  IG6 . . . . **111** E2
Forest Glade
  Basildon SS16 . . . . **140** F4
  Chingford E4 . . . . **109** C5
  Epping CM16 . . . . **46** E4
Forest Gr CM16 . . . . **46** C5
Forest Ho E4 . . . . **87** E2
Forest Hts IG9 . . . . **110** A8
Forest Ind Pk IG6 . . . . . . **111** E2
Forest La IG7 . . . . **111** A5
Forest Mount Rd IG8 . . . **109** D3
Forest Rd
  Chingford E17 . . . . **109** D1

Forest Rd *continued*
  Loughton IG10 . . . . **88** E5
  Redbridge IG6 . . . . **112** B4
  Romford RM7 . . . . **135** B8
  Woodford IG8 . . . . **110** A7
Forest Side
  Buckhurst Hill IG9 . . . . . . **88** C1
  Chingford E4 . . . . **87** F1
  Epping CM16 . . . . **67** D6
Forest Terr IG7 . . . . **111** A5
Forest View E4 . . . . **87** D2
Forest View Dr SS9 . . . . . **146** A3
Forest View Rd
  Chingford E17 . . . . **109** C2
  Loughton IG10 . . . . **88** D5
Forest Way
  Loughton IG10 . . . . **88** E6
  Woodford IG8 . . . . **110** B6
Forfar CI SS9 . . . . **146** B2
Forge Cotts CM22 . . . . **2** F3
Forges Rd E12 . . . . **132** D2
Forres CI EN11 . . . . **21** A8
Forres Ho CM14 . . . . **116** D6
Forres Prim Sch EN11 . . . . . **8** B1
Forrest Cl CM3 . . . . **101** C7
Forster Cl E4 . . . . **109** D3
Forsters Cl RM6 . . . . **134** F5
Forsyth St [1] RM10 . . . . . **154** B6
Forsythia Cl
  Chelmsford CM1 . . . . **32** E7
  Ilford IG1 . . . . **152** B7
Forterie Gdns IG3 . . . . . . **153** A8
Fortescue Chase SS1 . . . **148** F1
Forth Rd RM14 . . . . **137** D5
Fortinbras Way CM2 . . . . . **54** B8
Fortin Cl RM15 . . . . **172** A6
Fortin Path RM15 . . . . . . **172** A6
Fortin Way RM15 . . . . . . **172** A6
Fort Rd RM18 . . . . **179** C5
Fortune Ct IG11 . . . . **153** C3
Fortunes The CM18 . . . . . . **23** E4
Fortune Stps [2] SS1 . . . . **167** C7
Fort William Rd SS16 . . . **142** B2
Forum The SS2 . . . . **148** A5
Fosbery Ct EN3 . . . . **65** A2
Fossetts Way SS2 . . . . . . **148** C4
Fossway RM8 . . . . **134** C2
Fostal Cl SS9 . . . . **146** E3
Foster Rd SS8 . . . . **164** C4
Fosters Cl
  Woodford E18 . . . . **110** B2
  Writtle CM1 . . . . **30** F1
FOSTER STREET **24** F7
Foulgar Cl CM3 . . . . **101** E8
FOULNESS ISLAND **130** C5
Founders Rd EN11 . . . . **8** B1
Foundry SS5 . . . . **124** E6
Foundry Bsns Pk SS5 . . . **124** E6
Foundry La CM0 . . . . **106** B5
Founes Dr RM16 . . . . **172** E3
Fountain Farm CM18 . . . . **23** F6
Fountain La SS5 . . . . **124** B6
Fountain Pl EN9 . . . . **65** C5
Fountain Rd CM1 . . . . **16** C4
Fountains The IG10 . . . . . . **88** D2
Fountain Wlk DA11 . . . . . **178** F1
Four Acres The CM1 . . . . . . **2** A2
Four Sisters Cl SS9 . . . . . **146** F5
Four Sisters Way SS9 . . . **146** F5
Fourth Ave
  Basildon SS16 . . . . **140** E3
  Chelmsford CM1 . . . . **32** B5
  Grays RM20 . . . . **177** A8
  Harlow CM19 . . . . **23** B8
  Romford RM7 . . . . **135** D3
  Stanford-le-H SS17 . . . . **160** E5
  Thundersley SS7 . . . . . . **145** A6
  Wickford SS11 . . . . **122** A6
Fourth Wlk SS8 . . . . **163** E4
Four Wantz The CM5 . . . . **49** A4
Fourways Ct [1] CM1 . . . . . **21** A7
Four Wents The E4 . . . . . **109** D8
Fowey Ave IG4 . . . . **132** D6
Fowler Cl SS1 . . . . **167** C8
Fowler Ct CM2 . . . . **54** A4
Fowler Rd IG6 . . . . **112** C5
Fowley Mead Pk EN8 . . . . **65** A5
Foxborough Chase
  CM4 . . . . **76** B3
Fox Burrow Rd IG7 . . . . . **112** D6
Fox Burrows La CM1 . . . . . **31** B2
Fox Cl
  Romford RM5 . . . . **113** B5
  Thundersley SS7 . . . . . . **144** F6
Fox Cres CM1 . . . . **31** F4
Foxes Gn RM16 . . . . **174** A4
Foxes Gr CM13 . . . . **96** C2
Foxes Par EN9 . . . . **65** C6
Foxfield Chase CM3 . . . . . **83** A8
Foxfield Cl SS5 . . . . **125** A6
Foxfield Dr SS17 . . . . **160** E5
Foxglove Cl EN11 . . . . **8** C1
Foxglove Ct SS15 . . . . . . **141** C5
Foxglove Gdns E11 . . . . . **132** C7
Foxglove Ho DA1 . . . . **176** A2
Foxglove Rd
  Romford RM7 . . . . **135** E2
  South Ockendon RM15 . . **172** C2
Foxgloves The CM12 . . . . . **96** F4
Foxglove Way CM1 . . . . . . **32** F6
Foxhall Rd
  Mayland CM0 . . . . **83** D7
  Steeple CM0 . . . . **84** B7
  Upminster RM14 . . . . . . **156** C7
Foxhatch CM15 . . . . **121** F6
Fox Hatch CM15 . . . . **71** E1
Foxhills Rd RM16 . . . . . . **173** D5

Foxholes Rd CM2 . . . . **54** F6
Fox House Rd SS4 . . . . . . **169** B1
Foxhunter Wlk CM11 . . . . . **97** D6
Foxlands Cres RM10 . . . . **154** C2
Foxlands Rd RM10 . . . . . . **154** C7
Foxleigh CM12 . . . . **119** A8
Foxleigh Cl CM12 . . . . **119** A8
Foxley Cl IG10 . . . . **89** B7
Fox Manor Way RM20 . . . **177** B8
Foxmeadows SS7 . . . . . . **144** F6
Foxton Rd
  Grays RM20 . . . . **177** D8
  Hoddesdon EN11 . . . . . . **21** A6
Foxwood Chase EN9 . . . . . **65** C4
Foxwood Cl SS9 . . . . **146** D2
Foxwood Pl SS9 . . . . **146** D2
Foyle Dr RM15 . . . . **172** A7
Foys Wlk CM11 . . . . **119** C7
Frame The SS15 . . . . **141** E7
Framlingham Ct
  [5] Ilford RM6 . . . . **134** B6
  Rayleigh SS6 . . . . **123** C1
Frampton Rd
  [5] Basildon SS13 . . . . . **121** A1
  Epping CM16 . . . . **46** A3
Frances Ave RM14 . . . . . . **172** C2
Frances Bardsley Sch for
  Girls RM1 . . . . **136** A5
Frances Cottee Lo
  SS6 . . . . **146** A8
Frances Ct E4 . . . . **109** A4
Frances Gdns RM15 . . . . **171** F7
Frances Gn CM1 . . . . **33** A7
Frances Rd E4 . . . . **109** A4
Francis Ave IG1 . . . . **133** D2
Francis Cl SS17 . . . . **159** F3
Francisco Cl RM16 . . . . . **172** C3
Francis Ct
  [3] Basildon SS14 . . . . . **142** F5
  Erith DA8 . . . . **169** E1
Francis Green Ho [7]
  EN9 . . . . **65** B6
Francis Mews CM9 . . . . . . **59** B8
Francis Rd IG1 . . . . **133** D2
Francis St IG1 . . . . **133** D2
Francis Wks EN11 . . . . **21** B6
Francis Wlk SS6 . . . . **123** D2
Francombe Gdns
  RM1 . . . . **136** A5
Frank Bailey Wlk E12 . . . . **152** A6
Frank Bretton Ho CM5 . . . **49** A3
Frankland Cl IG8 . . . . **110** C5
Frankland Rd E4 . . . . **109** A4
Franklin Rd
  Hornchurch RM12 . . . . . **155** C6
  North Fambridge CM3 . . **103** B8
Franklins RM15 . . . . **171** D7
Franklins Way SS11 . . . . **121** E8
Franklyn Gdns IG6 . . . . . **111** D4
Franks Cotts RM14 . . . . . **138** B3
Frank Slater Ho [4]
  IG3 . . . . **134** B3
Franmil Rd RM12 . . . . . . **136** A3
Fraser Cl
  Basildon SS15 . . . . **140** F6
  Chelmsford CM2 . . . . **54** C8
  Southend-on-S SS3 . . . . **168** F8
Fraser Rd DA8 . . . . **169** D1
Frating Cres IG8 . . . . **110** B4
Frayes Chase CM5 . . . . . . **15** A3
Frazer Cl RM1 . . . . **135** F4
Frederica Rd E4 . . . . **87** D2
Frederick Andrews Ct
  RM17 . . . . **178** D8
Frederick Rd RM13 . . . . . **154** E3
Fred Leach Ho [1]
  SS8 . . . . **164** A3
Fredrick J French Meml
  Homes CM1 . . . . **32** B6
Fred Tibble Ct RM9 . . . . . **153** E8
Freeborne Gdns
  RM13 . . . . **155** A6
Freeman Ct SS17 . . . . . . **160** F3
Freemantle Ho RM18 . . . **178** F6
Freeman Way RM11 . . . . **136** F5
Freightmaster Est
  RM13 . . . . **170** A2
Freightways SS3 . . . . **168** D5
Fremantle Cl CM3 . . . . **79** D1
Fremantle Rd
  Belvedere DA17 . . . . . . **169** A2
  Ilford IG6 . . . . **111** C1
  Redbridge IG6 . . . . **111** C1
Fremnells The SS14 . . . . . **142** D7
French Rd CM3 . . . . **80** F1
French's Cl SG12 . . . . **8** B4
French's Wlk [4] CM2 . . . . **32** C2
Frerichs Cl SS12 . . . . **121** D5
Freshfields Ave RM14 . . . **156** C7
Freshwater Cres CM9 . . . . **37** B4
Freshwater Dr SS16 . . . . **142** F4
Freshwater Rd RM8 . . . . . **134** E3
Freshwaters CM20 . . . . . . **10** E1
Freshwell Ave RM6 . . . . . **134** C7
Freshwell Gdns CM13 . . . **139** D5
Fresh Wharf Est IG11 . . . **152** B4
Fresh Wharf Rd IG11 . . . . **152** B3
Frettons SS14 . . . . **142** E6
Friar's Ave CM15 . . . . **95** A2
Friars Cl
  Basildon SS15 . . . . **141** C6
  Chingford E4 . . . . **109** C7
  Ilford IG1 . . . . **133** D3
Friar's Cl CM15 . . . . **95** A2
Friarscroft EN10 . . . . **21** A3
Friars Gate Cl IG8 . . . . . . **110** A6

Friars La
  Hatfield Heath CM22 . . . . . **3** C1
  Maldon CM9 . . . . **36** F2
Friars Prim Sch SS3 . . . . **168** F8
Friars St SS3 . . . . **168** F7
Friars The
  Chigwell IG7 . . . . **111** E6
  Harlow CM19 . . . . **23** A6
Friars Wlk CM2 . . . . **32** B1
Friary Fields CM9 . . . . **37** A2
Friary La IG8 . . . . **110** A6
FRIDAY HILL **109** E7
Friday Hill E4 . . . . **109** E7
Friday Hill E E4 . . . . **109** E7
Friday Hill W E4 . . . . **109** E8
Friday Rd DA8 . . . . **169** D1
Friern Gdns SS12 . . . . . . **121** B7
Friern Pl SS12 . . . . **121** B6
Friern Wlk SS12 . . . . **121** B7
Frimley Ave RM11 . . . . . . **137** A3
Frimley Rd IG3 . . . . **133** E1
Frinton Dr IG8 . . . . **109** D3
Frinton Mews IG2 . . . . . . **133** A5
Frinton Rd RM5 . . . . **113** A3
Friston Path [4] IG6 . . . . **111** E5
Frithwood Cl CM12 . . . . . **118** F7
Frithwood La CM12 . . . . . **118** F7
Frizlands La RM10 . . . . . . **135** B2
Frobisher Cl
  Basildon SS15 . . . . **141** D6
  Maldon CM9 . . . . **59** A8
Frobisher Gdns RM16 . . . **172** E3
Frobisher Way
  Greenhithe DA9 . . . . . . **177** B3
  Southend-on-S SS3 . . . . **149** E1
Froden Brook CM11 . . . . . **119** C7
Froden Cl CM11 . . . . **119** C7
Froden Ct CM11 . . . . **119** C6
Froghall La IG7 . . . . **111** D6
Frog La RM13 . . . . **169** D8
Frogmore Est RM20 . . . . **172** A1
Frog St CM15 . . . . **93** E8
Frome RM18 . . . . **175** C2
Front La RM14 . . . . **137** E4
Fry Cl RM5 . . . . **113** A4
FRYERNING **74** A5
Fryerning La CM4 . . . . **74** B4
FRYERNS **142** E8
Fryerns Terr SS14 . . . . . . **142** F8
Fryth The SS14 . . . . **142** E8
Fuchsia Cl RM7 . . . . **135** E2
Fulbourne Rd E17 . . . . . . **109** C1
Fulbrook La RM15 . . . . . . **171** F6
Fulcher Ave CM2 . . . . **32** F3
Fulford Dr SS9 . . . . **147** A6
Fullarton Cres RM15 . . . . **171** F7
Fullbridge CM9 . . . . **37** A3
Fuller Rd RM8 . . . . **153** C8
Fuller's Ave IG8 . . . . **109** F3
Fullers Cl
  Romford RM5 . . . . **113** C3
  Waltham Abbey EN9 . . . . **66** A6
Fuller's La RM5 . . . . **113** C3
Fullers Mead CM17 . . . . . **24** C7
Fuller's Rd E18 . . . . **109** F3
Fuller Terr IG1 . . . . **152** D7
Fullman Ind Pk SS8 . . . . . **163** C3
Fullwell Ave IG5 . . . . **111** B2
FULLWELL CROSS **111** C2
Fullwell Ct IG5 . . . . **111** A2
Fullwell Par IG5 . . . . **111** A2
Fullwood Prim Sch
  IG6 . . . . **133** C7
Fulmar Rd RM12 . . . . **155** B6
Fulmar Way SS11 . . . . . . **122** A5
Fulton Ct [3] EN3 . . . . **65** A1
Fulton Rd SS7 . . . . **144** D7
Fulwich Rd DA1 . . . . **176** A1
Furlongs SS16 . . . . **142** D4
Furlongs The CM4 . . . . **74** B3
Furlong Way SG12 . . . . **8** A7
Furness Cl RM16 . . . . **174** B1
Furness Way RM12 . . . . . **155** A2
Furrowfelde SS16 . . . . . . **142** A4
Further Mdw CM1 . . . . **53** A8
Furrwick Park Sch
  SS8 . . . . **164** C3
Furtherwick Rd SS8 . . . . . **164** C2
Furze Farm Cl RM6 . . . . . **112** C1
Furze Glade SS16 . . . . . . **141** B4
Furze Inf Sch RM6 . . . . . **134** C5
Furze La CM4 . . . . **76** A1
Fuschia Cl IG8 . . . . **109** E4
Fusedale Way RM15 . . . . **171** F6
Fyefields SS13 . . . . **143** C7
FYFIELD **27** D2
Fyfield Ave SS12 . . . . **121** C5
Fyfield Bsns & Research
  Pk CM5 . . . . **49** B6
Fyfield Cl CM13 . . . . **139** D5
Fyfield Dr RM15 . . . . **171** F7
Fyfield Dr Walker's CE
  Prim Sch CM5 . . . . **27** D2
Fyfield Ho RM9 . . . . **153** B5
Fyfield Path SS6 . . . . **123** A3
Fyfield Rd
  Chipping Ongar CM5 . . . . **49** A5
  Moreton CM5 . . . . **26** F3
  Rainham RM13 . . . . **154** F4
  Willingale CM5 . . . . **28** C3
  Woodale IG8 . . . . **110** C3

Gabion Ave RM19 . . . . . . **171** D2
Gablefields CM2 . . . . **55** D6
Gable Hall Sch SS17 . . . . **161** A4
Gables The
  Barking IG11 . . . . **152** C6
  Basildon SS13 . . . . **143** B8
  Brentwood CM13 . . . . . . **116** C4
  Chipping Ongar CM5 . . . . **49** A5
  Sawbridgeworth CM21 . . . . **1** E2
  Southend-on-S, Eastwood
   SS9 . . . . **146** B6
  Southend-on-S SS9 . . . . **146** D1
Gabriel Cl
  Grays RM20 . . . . **172** C3
  Romford RM5 . . . . **113** C3
Gadsden Cl RM14 . . . . . . **137** E5
Gafzelle Dr SS8 . . . . **164** E3
Gaiger Cl CM1 . . . . **32** D7
Gainsborough Ave
  Canvey Island SS8 . . . . . **164** E3
  Little Ilford E12 . . . . **152** A7
  Tilbury RM18 . . . . **179** B6
Gainsborough Cl RM11 . . . **97** B1
Gainsborough Cres
  CM2 . . . . **32** E3
Gainsborough Ct [4]
  CM14 . . . . **116** C6
Gainsborough Dr SS0 . . . **147** C2
Gainsborough Ho
  [2] Barking RM8 . . . . . . **153** B8
  Redbridge IG8 . . . . **111** B4
Gainsborough Pl
  Brentwood CM13 . . . . . . **95** D1
  Chigwell IG7 . . . . **111** F7
Gainsborough Rd
  Dagenham RM8 . . . . **134** B1
  Rainham RM13 . . . . **155** A4
  Woodford IG8 . . . . **110** A4
Gains Cl SS8 . . . . **164** D4
Gainsthorpe Rd CM5 . . . . . **48** D8
Gaitskell Ho RM16 . . . . . . **173** B5
Galadriel Spring CM3 . . . **101** C6
Galahad Cl CM0 . . . . **106** B5
Galaxie Lo SS7 . . . . **144** D2
Galeborough Ave
  IG8 . . . . **109** D3
Gale St RM9 . . . . **153** D5
Gales Way IG8 . . . . **110** E3
Galey Gn RM15 . . . . **172** B8
Galleon Bvd DA2 . . . . **176** D3
Galleon Cl DA8 . . . . **169** D2
Galleon Rd RM16 . . . . . . **172** C2
Galleons Dr IG11 . . . . **153** A2
Galleydene SS7 . . . . **145** C3
Galleydene Ave CM2 . . . . . **54** C3
GALLEYEND **54** D4
Galley Gn SG13 . . . . **8** A3
Galleyhill Rd EN9 . . . . **65** E7
Galley Hill Rd
  Northfleet DA11 . . . . . . **178** A2
  Swanscombe DA10 . . . . **177** F2
Galley Hill Trad Est
  DA10 . . . . **177** F2
GALLEYWOOD **54** D2
Galleywood Cres
  RM5 . . . . **113** D4
Galleywood Inf Sch
  CM2 . . . . **54** C2
Galleywood Rd
  Chelmsford CM2 . . . . **54** E5
  Great Baddow CM2 . . . . . **54** E5
Galliford Rd CM9 . . . . **37** A4
Galliford Road Ind Est
  CM9 . . . . **37** A4
Gallions Cl IG11 . . . . **153** A2
Gallops The SS16 . . . . . . **141** B5
Gallows Cnr RM3 . . . . **114** C2
Galsworthy Ave RM6 . . . . **134** B5
Galsworthy Rd RM18 . . . . **179** C6
Galt Cl SS12 . . . . **121** D4
Galton Rd SS0 . . . . **166** C8
Gambleside SS16 . . . . . . **142** B3
Gammon Field RM16 . . . . **173** E5
Gandalf's Ride CM3 . . . . . **101** D6
Ganels Cl CM11 . . . . **119** C7
Ganels Rd CM11 . . . . **119** C7
Gangies Hill CM21 . . . . **1** A4
Ganley Ct [6] CM11 . . . . . **97** B2
Gant Ct EN9 . . . . **65** C5
GANTS HILL **133** A5
Gantshill Cres IG2 . . . . . . **133** A5
Gants Hill Sta IG2 . . . . . . **133** A5
Garbutt Rd RM14 . . . . . . **137** C2
Garden Cl
  Althorne CM3 . . . . **82** F4
  Chingford E4 . . . . **109** A5
  Steeple CM0 . . . . **61** F3
Garden Ct RM14 . . . . **137** E4
Garden End CM4 . . . . **75** F2
Gardeners CM2 . . . . **54** D5
Gardeners La SS4 . . . . . . **104** F1
Garden Fields CM0 . . . . . . **61** F3
Garden Hos The CM21 . . . . . **2** B1
Gardenia Way IG8 . . . . . . **110** A5
Gardens Fields CM5 . . . . . **70** E5
Gardens The
  Doddinghurst CM15 . . . . **72** B3
  Southend-on-S SS9 . . . . **165** B1
Garden Terrace Rd [2]
  CM17 . . . . **11** C4
Garden Way IG10 . . . . **67** A1
Garden Wharf DA8 . . . . . . **169** D1
Gardiner Cl RM8 . . . . **153** D8
Gardiners Cl SS14 . . . . . . **120** D1
Gardiners La N CM11 . . . . **120** E4

Gardiners La S SS14	120 E2
Gardiners Link SS14	120 D2
Gardiners The CM17 ..	24 B8
Gardiners Way SS14	120 D2
Gardner Ave SS17.....	161 A3
Gardner Cl E11	132 B5
Gardners Ct RM7	135 C6
Garenne Ct **8** E4......	87 C1
Garfield Rd E4........	87 D1
Garland Way RM11	136 E7
Garner Cl RM8	134 D3
Garner Rd E17	109 C2
Garners The SS4	125 F2
Garnon Mead CM16	46 D3
Garrettlands CM2.....	55 F6
Garrick Ho RM12......	136 A2
Garrick St DA11......	179 B1
Garrison Par RM19...	171 A2
Garron La	
South Ockendon	
RM15	171 F7
South Ockendon RM15 .	172 A6
Garry Cl RM1	113 E3
Garry Way RM1	113 E3
Garth Rd RM15	157 C1
Gartmore Rd IG3	133 F2
Gascoigne Gdns IG8	109 E3
Gascoigne Prim Sch	
IG11 ....52 C4	
Gascoigne Rd IG11 ...	152 C3
Gascoigne Way CM11 ..	97 D2
Gascoyne Rd RM3	114 D2
Gasson Rd DA10	177 E1
GASTON GREEN	2 B7
Gatehope Dr RM15....	171 F7
Gatehouse Mews CM4..	74 B3
Gatehouse The **4**	
RM1................	135 E6
Gate House The **2**	
CM4...............	74 B3
Gate Lodge Sq SS15	119 F2
Gate Lodge Way SS15 ...	119 F2
Gate St CM9	36 F3
Gate Street Mews CM9 ..	36 F3
Gateway SS14	142 B6
Gateway Acad The	
RM16..............	173 F4
Gateway Ho **4** IG11 ..	152 C4
Gateway Prim Sch The	
DA1...............	176 B1
Gateway Ret Pk E6 ..	152 B1
Gatscombe Cl SS15...	124 D6
Gattens The SS6	123 F4
Gatwick View CM12 ..	119 B8
Gatwick Way RM12....	136 F1
Gavenny Path RM15...	171 F7
GAY BOWERS	57 A5
Gay Bowers	
Basildon SS14......	142 D7
Hockley SS5........	124 B6
Gay Bowers La CM3...	56 F6
Gay Bowers Rd CM3...	56 F4
Gayfere Rd IG5	132 F8
Gay Gdns RM10	154 C7
Gayleighs SS6	123 D4
Gay Links SS14	142 B7
Gaylor Rd RM18......	178 F6
Gaynes Ct RM14	156 B8
Gaynesford SS16.....	141 E4
Gaynes Hill Rd IG8...	110 E3
Gaynes Park Rd	
RM14...............	156 B8
Gaynes Rd RM14	137 E2
Gaynes Way SS14....	156 C7
Gaysham Ave IG2.....	133 E5
Gaysham Hall IG5 ...	133 B8
Gays La SS4	104 E2
Gayton Rd SS2.......	148 A2
Gaywood SS15	141 A7
Gearies Inf Sch IG2..	133 B6
Gearies Jun Sch IG2..	133 B6
Geariesville Gdns	
IG6................	133 B7
Geary Ct CM14	94 C1
Geary Dr CM14	94 C1
Geddings Rd EN11 ...	21 B6
Geddy Ct RM2	136 B7
Geerings The SS17....	161 A2
Geesh Rd SS8	164 C5
Geffrey Cl CM3	78 B6
Geisthorp Ct EN9	66 A6
Gelsthorpe Rd RM5 ..	113 D3
General Hospl SS0...	147 C3
Generals La CM3.....	20 B2
Genesta Rd SS0......	166 B8
Geneva Gdns RM6 ...	134 E6
Genever Cl E4.......	109 A5
Genk Cl SS8	164 B5
Gennep Rd SS8	164 B5
Gennep Rd S SS8 ...	164 B5
Genotin Mews **3**	
RM12..............	155 C7
Gentry Cl SS17.......	160 C2
Geoffrey Ave RM3....	115 B3
George Avey Croft	
CM16..............	47 B5
George Cardnell Way	
CM3...............	60 E1
George Cl SS18	163 F6
George Comberton Wlk **3**	
E12...............	152 A7
George Crooks Ho	
RM17..............	178 B8
George Ct	
8 Buckhurst Hill IG9 ..	110 D8
Chelmsford CM2 ...	32 B1
George Davies Lo	
IG6................	133 C6

George Green Villas	
CM22................	2 B8
George La	
Wanstead E18	132 B8
Woodford E18	110 A1
George Lovell Dr EN3 ..	65 A2
George Rd E4	109 A4
Georges Dr CM15	93 F4
George St	
Barking IG11	152 C5
Chelmsford CM2 ...	32 B1
Grays RM17........	178 A8
Romford RM1	135 F5
Southend-on-S SS3 ..	168 G6
George Tilbury Ho	
RM16..............	174 B4
Georgeville Gdns IG6 ..	133 B7
George Williams Ho	
RM7...............	135 F4
Gepp Pl CM2	33 B4
Gepps Cl CM1	6 D2
Gerald Rd RM8	134 F3
Gerard Gdns RM14...	154 E3
Gerboa Ct **7** E4....	109 D5
Gernon Cl	
Broomfield CM1....	19 B3
Rainham RM13	155 D3
Gernons SS16	141 F4
Gerpins La RM14....	156 A4
Gerrard Cres CM14...	116 C2
Gertrude Rd DA17...	169 A2
Geylen Rd SS8......	164 E4
GHYLLGROVE ....!...	142 B7
Ghyllgrove SS14	142 B7
Ghyllgrove Com Jun Sch	
SS14..............	142 A7
Gibbards Cott **1**	
IG11..............	152 F5
Gibb Croft CM18	23 F4
Gibbfield Cl RM6....	134 E8
Gibcracks SS14	142 E6
Gibraltar Cl CM13...	116 C4
Gibraltar Ho CM13...	116 C4
Gibson Cl CM16	47 C6
Gibson Ct	
Harlow CM18.......	23 E5
7 Romford RM1 ...	135 E5
Gibson Rd RM8	134 C3
Gibson Vale CM1....	32 B8
Gidea Ave RM2	136 A8
Gidea Cl	
Romford RM2	136 A8
South Ockendon RM15 ..	157 C2
Gidea Lo RM2.......	136 B8
Gidea Park Coll RM2..	136 A8
Gidea Park Prim Sch	
RM2...............	136 A8
Gidea Park Sta RM2..	136 B7
Gideon Cl DA17.....	169 B2
Gideons Way SS17...	160 E3
Giffards Prim Sch	
SS17..............	160 F4
Gifford Gn SS13	143 B5
Gifford Pl CM14.....	116 D5
Gifford Rd SS7......	144 D5
Giffords Cross Ave	
SS17..............	161 A3
Giffords Cross Rd	
SS17..............	161 B2
Giffordside RM16....	174 B1
Gifhorn Rd SS8	164 E3
Gilbert Calvin Prim Sch	
IG5................	111 A1
Gilbert Cl	
Rayleigh SS6......	123 F2
Swanscombe DA10..	177 D1
Gilbert Dr SS16......	141 E3
Gilbert Rd	
Belvedere DA17.....	169 A3
Grays RM16.......	172 C3
Romford RM1	135 F7
Gildborne Cl SS17...	161 D4
Gilden Cl CM17	11 E4
Gilden Way CM17 ...	11 D3
Gilders CM21	1 D5
Giles Cl RM13.......	155 D3
Gilford Ho **5** IG1....	133 B1
Gillam Way RM13 ...	155 A6
Gill Cl CM9	36 F6
Gillian Cres RM2 ...	114 C1
Gilliflower Ho EN11 ..	21 A5
Gillingham Ho **14**	
RM3...............	114 E5
Gills Ave SS8	164 C4
Gill The SS7	145 D5
Gilmore Way CM2...	55 B6
Gilmour Rise CM17 ..	96 F1
Gilpin's Gallop SG12...	8 B4
Gilroy Cl RM13......	154 F6
Gilsland EN9	65 C4
Gilson Cl CM2	32 F2
Gilstead Hall Mews Cotts	
CM14..............	93 A4
Gilstead Ho **1** IG11..	153 B3
GILSTON	10 E5
Gilston Park Ho CM20..	10 C6
Gilston Pk CM20	10 C7
Gilwell Cl E4........	87 B5
Gilwell La E4.......	87 D5
Gimli Watch CM3 ...	101 D6
Gippeswyk SS14....	142 C7
Gipson Park Cl SS9..	146 D6
Gipsy La RM17......	178 C8
Girona Cl RM16.....	172 C3
Gisborne Gdns RM13..	154 F2
Gladden Ct CM18....	23 E4
Gladden Fields CM3...	101 C6

Glade Bsns Ctr The	
RM20..............	171 F1
Glade Ct IG5	110 F2
Glade Prim Sch IG5 ...	110 F1
Gladeswood Rd DA17..	169 B2
Glade The	
Basildon SS16......	142 C4
Brentwood CM13....	95 A1
Upminster RM14 ...	156 C7
Woodford, Clayhall IG5 ..	110 C7
Woodford, Woodford Wells	
IG8...............	110 B7
Gladeway The EN9 ...	65 D6
Gladstone Ct	
Buckhurst Hill IG9 ..	88 C1
Hockley SS5........	124 E6
Hoddesdon EN1 ...	21 B7
Gladstone Gdns SS6..	123 C1
Gladstone Rd	
Buckhurst Hill IG9 ..	88 C1
Hockley SS5........	124 E6
Hoddesdon EN1 ...	21 B7
Gladwyns SS15	141 E7
Glamis SS13	136 E3
Glamis Ho CM14 ...	116 C6
Glan Avon Mews CM17..	24 C7
Glandford Way RM6...	134 B6
Glanmead CM15	94 E1
Glanmire CM11	97 D6
Glanthams Cl CM15..	116 F8
Glanthams Rd CM15..	116 F8
Glanville Dr RM11...	136 F3
Glasseys La SS6	145 C8
Glastonbury Ave IG8..	110 D4
Glastonbury Chase	
SS0...............	147 B5
Glebe Ave IG8.......	110 A4
Glebe Cl	
Great Wakering SS3 ..	150 D3
Rayleigh SS6......	123 C3
Southend-on-S SS1 ..	167 E8
Glebe Cres CM1	19 B1
Glebe Dr SS6	123 C3
Glebe Field SS14....	142 C8
Glebe Gdns SS13...	117 E3
Glebe Jun & Inf Sch	
SS6...............	123 C3
Glebe La CM0.......	63 D1
Glebelands	
Chigwell IG7.......	112 B7
Harlow CM20.......	10 F3
South Benfleet SS7..	144 B7
Glebelands Ave	
Ilford IG2..........	133 D5
Woodford E18	110 A1
Glebe Mdw CM3 ...	18 E7
Glebe Rd	
Chelmsford CM1 ...	32 B3
Chipping Ongar CM5 ..	48 F2
Dagenham RM10 ...	154 B6
Heybridge CM9	37 C5
Rainham RM13	155 C2
Ramsden Bellhouse	
CM11..............	98 F1
Wickford SS11.....	121 E7
Glebe The	
Harlow CM20.......	10 E1
Magdalen Laver CM5...	25 D5
Purleigh CM3......	58 D1
Glebe View CM2	54 B3
Glebe Way	
Burnham-on-C CM0 ..	106 C6
Hadleigh SS7......	145 F3
Hornchurch RM11..	136 E3
Woodford IG8	110 C5
Glenarm Coll IG1 ...	133 B2
Glenavon Lo **6** E18 ..	132 A8
Glenbervie Dr SS9...	146 F2
Glencoe Ave IG2.....	133 E4
Glencoe Dr	
Dagenham RM10 ...	154 A8
Wickford SS11.....	122 A8
Glencree CM11	97 D6
Glen Cres IG8	110 B4
Glencrofts SS5	124 F6
Glen Ct SS7	145 B4
Glendale Ave RM6...	134 C4
Glendale Cl	
Burnham-on-C CM0 ..	106 C6
Shenfield CM15....	94 E1
Glendale Gdns SS9..	146 D1
Glendale Ho CM15 ..	94 E2
Glendale Rd	
Burnham-on-C CM0 ..	106 C6
Erith DA8.........	169 C2
Glendower Rd E4....	87 D1
Gleneagles CM3 ...	79 E1
Gleneagles Cl RM3...	114 F3
Gleneagles Rd SS9..	146 C5
Glenester Cl EN11 ...	8 A1
Glen Faba CM19	21 E7
Glen Faba Rd CM19..	21 F6
Glenfield Rd SS17...	161 B4
Glengall Rd IG8	110 B4
Glenham Dr IG2.....	133 B6
Glen Hazel CM15 ...	72 D4
Glenhurst Mans SS1..	167 B8
Glenhurst Rd SS2...	148 A2
Glenmead CM9	88 C1
Glenmere SS16	142 D2
Glenmere Park Ave	
SS7...............	145 B4
Glenmere Terr SG12...	8 B4
Glenmore Ho CM15..	94 F2
Glenmore St SS2....	148 D1
Glenmore Way IG11..	153 A9
Glenny Rd IG11.....	152 C5
Glen Rd	
South Benfleet SS7..	144 E5
Southend-on-S SS9..	166 A8

Glenridding SS7.....	144 D5
Glen Rise IG8	110 B4
Glenside	
Billericay CM11....	97 D2
Chigwell IG7.......	111 B4
Glen The	
Basildon SS16......	143 A4
Hullbridge SS5.....	101 E4
Rainham RM13	155 C1
Rayleigh SS6......	145 E8
Stanford-le-H SS17..	160 F3
Glenthorne Gdns IG6..	133 B7
Glenton Cl RM1.....	113 E3
Glenton Way RM1...	113 E3
Glenwood SS8......	163 F5
Glenwood Ave	
Hockley SS5........	124 F5
Rainham RM13	155 B1
Southend-on-S, Eastwood	
SS9...............	146 B7
Southend-on-S, Prittlewell	
SS0...............	147 D2
Glenwood Ct **6** E18..	132 A8
Glenwood Dr RM2 ..	136 A7
Glenwood Gdns	
Basildon SS16......	140 E8
Ilford IG2..........	133 A6
Glenwood Sch SS7...	144 B7
Gleten Rd SS8......	164 D4
Globe Ind Est RM17..	173 C1
Globe Rd	
Hornchurch RM11..	136 A5
Woodford IG8	110 A5
Glossop Ho **13** RM3..	114 E5
Gloucester Ave	
Chelmsford CM2 ...	54 C6
East Tilbury RM18..	175 C1
Grays RM16........	173 C4
Hornchurch RM11..	137 A7
Maldon CM9.......	36 F1
Rayleigh SS6......	146 A8
Gloucester Bsns Pk	
SS15..............	141 E8
Gloucester Cres CM1..	32 A5
Gloucester Ct	
Redbridge IG1.....	132 F4
Tilbury RM18......	178 F5
Gloucester Gdns IG1..	132 E4
Gloucester Pl CM12..	97 A5
Gloucester Rd	
Little Ilford E12....	132 F1
Pilgrims Hatch CM15..	94 B4
Romford RM1	135 F5
Wanstead E11	132 C6
Gloucester Terr SS1..	168 A6
Glovers Field CM15 ..	71 F2
Glovers La CM17....	24 E3
Glyders SS7........	144 E1
Glynde Way SS2....	148 F1
Glynn Rd CM4	106 B5
Goat Hall La	
Chelmsford CM2 ...	53 F3
Galleywood CM2 ...	54 A3
Goat House La CM3..	57 F4
Goatsmoor La	
Billericay CM4, CM11..	97 F6
Stock CM4.........	98 A8
Goatswood La RM4...	92 B2
Gobions SS16.......	142 A4
Gobions Ave RM5...	113 D3
Goddard Rd RM16...	173 A5
Goddards Way IG11..	133 D3
Goddard Way CM2 ..	32 F2
Godfreys Mews CM2..	32 B1
Godman Rd RM16...	174 B3
Godsafe CM17	11 E4
Godwin Cl E4.......	65 C1
Godwin Prim Sch	
RM9...............	153 E5
Goirle Ave SS8	164 C4
Goldace RM17	177 F8
Gold Berry Mead	
CM3...............	101 C6
Goldcrest Dr CM11 ..	97 C2
Goldenacres CM1...	32 F8
Golden Cross SS4...	125 D4
Golden Cross Mews	
SS4...............	125 C5
Golden Cross Par	
SS4...............	125 C5
Golden Cross Rd SS4..	125 D6
Golden Jubilee Ct	
RM12..............	136 A3
Golden Manor Dr SS7..	144 F5
Goldfinch La SS7....	145 A8
GOLDHANGER	38 F7
Goldhanger Cl SS6...	123 A3
Goldhanger Cross	
SS14..............	142 E7
Goldhanger Rd CM9..	37 D4
Goldhaze Cl IG8....	110 D3
Golding Cres SS17...	160 E3
Golding Ct **6** IG1....	133 A1
Goldingham Ave IG10..	89 C7
Goldings Cotts CM13..	116 B1
Goldings Cres SS16..	142 E3
Goldings Hill IG10,	
CM16..............	66 F2
Goldings Rd IG10...	89 A8
Goldings Rise IG10..	89 A8
Golding Thoroughfare	
CM2...............	32 F3
Goldington Cres CM12..	96 F5
Goldlay Ave CM2....	54 C8
Goldlay Gdns CM2 ..	32 C1
Goldlay Rd CM2.....	32 C1
Goldmer Cl SS3.....	168 C8
Goldsands Rd CM0...	84 E2

Goldsborough Cres	
E4................	109 C8
Goldsmere Ct RM11..	136 E3
Goldsmith RM17	177 F8
Goldsmith Ave RM7..	135 A4
Goldsmith Dr SS6...	123 D7
Goldsmith Ho IG8 ..	111 B4
Goldsmiths	
Corringham SS17...	161 A2
4 Stanford-le-H SS17..	160 F3
Goldsworthy Dr SS3..	150 C2
Golfe Ho IG1	133 D1
Golfe Rd IG1	133 D1
Golf Ride SS7.......	144 D3
GOOD EASTER	16 C5
Gooderham Ho RM16..	174 B4
Goodey Rd IG11.....	152 F5
Goodier Rd CM1	31 F4
Goodmans SS3	150 B3
GOODMAYES	134 B3
Goodmayes Ave IG3..	134 A3
Goodmayes Hospl	
IG3...............	134 A6
Goodmayes La IG3...	134 A1
Goodmayes Rd IG8..	153 A8
Goodmayes Prim Sch	
IG3...............	134 B3
Goodmayes Rd IG3..	134 B3
Goodmayes Ret Pk	
IG3...............	134 B3
Goodmayes Sta IG3..	134 A3
Goodmayes Wlk **1**	
SS12..............	121 D6
Goodridge Ho E17 ..	109 C3
Goodrington Sch	
RM11..............	136 D5
Goodview Rd SS14..	120 E2
Goodwin Cl CM2....	54 D8
Goodwood Ave	
Brentwood CM13....	95 F3
Hornchurch RM12..	155 E8
Goodwood Cl	
Hoddesdon EN11 ..	21 A7
Thundersley SS7...	145 B4
GOOSEBERRY GREEN..	97 A1
Goose Cotts SS11...	100 E1
Goose La CM22	2 E7
Gooseley La E6	152 A2
Gooshays Dr RM3...	114 E4
Gooshays Gdns RM3..	114 E4
Gordon Ave	
Chingford E4......	109 E4
Hornchurch RM12..	135 F2
Gordon Cl	
Billericay CM12....	96 F3
East Tilbury RM18..	180 D7
Gordon Cotts RM4...	91 B5
Gordon Inf Sch IG1..	133 D1
Gordon Pl	
9 Gravesend DA12..	179 C1
Southend-on-S SS1..	166 F8
Gordon Prom E DA12..	179 C1
Gordon Rd	
Barking IG11.......	152 E4
Basildon SS14.....	142 D4
Belvedere DA17....	169 C2
Brentwood CM15...	95 A1
Chelmsford CM2 ...	54 A6
Chingford E4......	87 E2
Corringham SS17...	160 F3
Dagenham RM6 ...	134 F5
Gravesend DA11...	178 E1
Grays RM16........	173 F3
Holdbrook EN9....	65 A5
Horndon on t H SS17..	159 F3
Ilford IG1..........	133 D1
Southend-on-S SS9..	146 B2
Southend-on-S, Westcliff-S	
SS1...............	166 F8
Wanstead E11	132 A5
Woodford E18	110 B2
Gordon Roughley Ct	
SS6...............	123 C1
Gordons SS13	143 A5
Gore Rd SS4	126 E6
Gore The SS14......	142 A7
Goring Cl RM5......	113 C2
Goring Gdns RM8 ..	153 C8
Goring Rd RM10 ...	154 D6
Gorseway RM7	135 C3
Gosfield Cl SS6	123 A3
Gosfield Rd RM8....	135 A3
Gosford Gdns IG4 ..	132 F6
Goshawk Dr CM2 ...	54 B5
Goslings The SS3...	168 G7
Gosport Dr RM12...	155 C6
Gossetts The CM6...	15 E4
Gould Cl CM5.......	26 C2
Goulds Cotts RM4...	90 B6
Goulton Rd CM1 ...	19 A1
Gourney Gr RM16...	173 B6
Government Row EN3..	65 A2
Gowan Brae SS7....	144 B5
Gowan Cl SS7	144 B5
Gowan Ct SS7	144 B5
Gowan Lea **4** E18...	132 A7
Gower Chase SS15..	141 D5
Gower Ho **3** IG11 ..	152 C5
Gower Pl **1** RM16..	172 B3
Gowers Ave CM3....	54 E6
Gowers La RM16....	174 A4
Gowers The CM20...	11 B2
Goya Rise SS3	168 G8
Grace Cl IG6	111 F4

Grace Rd SS13 . . . . **121** A2
Grace's Cross CM2 . . . . **55** C7
Graces La CM3 . . . . **34** B1
Grafton Gdns RM8 . . . . . **134** E2
Grafton Inf Sch RM8 . . . . **134** F2
Grafton Jun Sch RM8 . . . . **134** F2
Grafton Pl CM2 . . . . **33** A4
Grafton Rd
  Canvey Island SS8 . . . . . . **164** C2
  Dagenham RM8 . . . . **134** E2
Graham Cl
  Billericay CM12 . . . . **97** C5
  Brentwood CM13 . . . . **95** C4
  Hockley SS5 . . . . **124** C7
  Stanford-le-H SS17 . . . . . **160** E4
Grahame Ct **3** SS12 . . . . **121** D5
Grahame Ho SS2 . . . . **148** C3
Graham James Prim Sch
SS17 . . . . **160** F3
Graham Mans **11**
  IG11 . . . . **153** A5
Grainger Cl SS2 . . . . **148** A1
Grainger Rd SS2 . . . . **148** A1
Grainger Road Ind Est
SS2 . . . . **148** A1
Grampian SS0 . . . . **147** E1
Grampian Gr CM1 . . . . **31** D6
Granaries The EN9 . . . . . . **65** E5
Granary Cl CM3 . . . . **82** B5
Granary Ct
  3 Dagenham RM6 . . . . . **134** D4
  Sawbridgeworth CM21 . . . . . **1** E2
Granary Mdw CM15 . . . . . . **72** E3
Granary The
  Roydon CM19 . . . . **9** B1
  Stansted Abbotts SG12 . . . **8** C3
Granby Rd DA11 . . . . **178** D1
Grand Court W SS9 . . . . . **165** F8
Grand Ct RM8 . . . . **134** E1
Grand Dr SS9 . . . . **165** F8
Grand Par SS9 . . . . **165** F8
Grandview Rd SS7 . . . . . . **144** F7
Grange Ave
  Mayland CM3 . . . . **83** C7
  South Benfleet SS7 . . . . . **146** A5
  Wickford SS12 . . . . **121** C6
  Woodford IG8 . . . . **110** A3
Grange Cl
  Ingrave CM13 . . . . **117** C5
  Southend-on-S SS9 . . . . . **146** E3
  Woodford IG8 . . . . **110** A3
Grange Cres
  Chigwell IG7 . . . . **111** D5
  28 Dartford DA2 . . . . . . **176** B1
Grange Ct
  Chelmsford CM2 . . . . **53** F7
  Ilford IG3 . . . . **133** C8
  Loughton IG10 . . . . **88** D4
  Waltham Abbey EN9 . . . . . . **65** C5
Grange Gdns
  Rayleigh SS6 . . . . **123** B3
  Southend-on-S SS1 . . . . . **167** B8
GRANGE HILL **111** D5
Grange Hill Sta IG7 . . . . . **111** D6
Grange Ho **6** IG11 . . . . . **152** D4
Grange La CM19 . . . . **22** C8
Grange Par CM11 . . . . **119** C7
Grange Park Dr SS9 . . . . . **146** F2
Grange Prim Sch
SS12 . . . . **121** B6
Granger Ave CM9 . . . . **36** F1
Granger Row CM1 . . . . **31** F6
Granger Way RM1 . . . . . . **136** A5
Grange Rd
  Aveley RM15 . . . . **171** C5
  Basildon SS13 . . . . **143** E8
  Billericay CM11 . . . . **119** D7
  Grays RM17 . . . . **178** B8
  Ilford IG1 . . . . **152** C8
  Pleshey CM3 . . . . **7** E2
  Romford RM3 . . . . **114** B4
  Southend-on-S SS9 . . . . . **146** D1
  Thundersley SS7 . . . . **144** F7
  Tillingham CM0 . . . . **64** A1
  Wickford SS11 . . . . **99** C2
Grange The
  Hoddesdon EN11 . . . . **21** A5
  Waltham Abbey EN9 . . . . . . **65** D2
  4 Wanstead E18 . . . . . . **132** A8
Grangeway
  Thundersley SS7 . . . . **145** A6
  Woodford IG8 . . . . **110** C6
Grangeway Gdns IG4 . . . . **132** E6
Grangewood SS7 . . . . **144** D5
Grangewood Ave
  Grays RM16 . . . . **173** E3
  Rainham RM13 . . . . **155** C1
Grangewood Cl CM13 . . . . **117** A7
Granites Chase CM11 . . . . **119** F5
Grant Cl **12** SS12 . . . . . **121** D5
Grant Ct **2** E4 . . . . **87** C1
Grantham Ct RM6 . . . . . . **134** F4
Grantham Gdns RM6 . . . . **134** F4
Grantham Lo SS9 . . . . . . **146** D1
Grantham Rd
  Ilford E12 . . . . **133** A1
  Little Ilford E12 . . . . **152** A8
Grantham Way RM16 . . . . **173** A5
Grantock Rd E17 . . . . **109** D2
Granton Ave IG3 . . . . **134** A3
Granville Cl
  Billericay CM12 . . . . **96** F5
  South Benfleet SS7 . . . . . **144** E4
Granville Gdns EN11 . . . . . . **8** A2

Granville Rd
  Epping CM16 . . . . **46** B2
  Hockley SS5 . . . . **102** F1
  Ilford IG1 . . . . **133** B2
  Woodford E18 . . . . **110** B1
Granville Terr **4**
  CM0 . . . . **106** C4
Grapnells SS16 . . . . **142** F4
Grapnells Farm Cotts
SS4 . . . . **106** A2
Grasmead Ave SS9 . . . . . **146** F2
Grasmere Ave SS5 . . . . . **101** D3
Grasmere Cl IG10 . . . . **88** F7
Grasmere Gdns IG4 . . . . . **132** F6
Grasmere Ho SS6 . . . . . . **123** D2
Grasmere Rd
  Canvey Island SS8 . . . . . . **163** E3
  Thundersley SS7 . . . . **144** E6
Grass Croft RM17 . . . . . . **173** B3
Grassmere Rd RM11 . . . . **136** F7
Gratmore Gn SS16 . . . . . . **142** F3
Gravel Cl IG7 . . . . **112** A8
Gravel Hill IG10 . . . . **66** A1
Gravel La IG7 . . . . **90** A3
Gravelly La CM1 . . . . **30** C3
Gravel Pit Farm CM19 . . . . **23** C6
Gravel Rd SS9 . . . . **146** C8
GRAVESEND **179** C2
Gravesend Sta DA11 . . . . **179** B1
Gravesham Com Hospl
DA11 . . . . **179** A1
Gravesham Mus★
  DA11 . . . . **179** B1
Gray Ave RM8 . . . . **134** F3
Gray Gdns RM13 . . . . **155** A6
Graylands
  Grays RM17 . . . . **177** E8
  Theydon Bois CM16 . . . . . . **67** D2
GRAYS **178** A7
Grays Ave SS16 . . . . **141** C1
Grays Convent High Sch
RM17 . . . . **173** B2
Grays Cotts RM14 . . . . . . **137** D7
Grays Court Hospl
RM10 . . . . **154** B5
Grays End Cl RM17 . . . . . **173** A3
Graysons Cl SS6 . . . . **123** E2
Grays Sch Media Arts Coll
  The RM17 . . . . **173** B3
Grays Sh Ctr RM17 . . . . . **178** A8
Grays Sta RM17 . . . . **178** A8
Grays Wlk CM13 . . . . **95** D2
Great Augur St **4**
  CM17 . . . . **11** D1
GREAT BADDOW **54** E7
Great Baddow High Sch
CM2 . . . . **54** D6
GREAT BERRY **140** F4
Great Berry Farm Chase
SS16 . . . . **141** A4
Great Berry La SS16 . . . . **141** A5
Great Berry Prim Sch
SS16 . . . . **140** F4
Great Brays CM18 . . . . **24** A7
Great Burches Rd
SS7 . . . . **145** A7
GREAT BURSTEAD **119** C5
Great Cob CM1 . . . . **32** E5
Great Cullings RM7 . . . . . **135** E2
Great Eastern Ave
SS2 . . . . **148** A1
Great Eastern Rd
  Brentwood CM14 . . . . . . **116** C6
  Hockley SS5 . . . . **124** E6
Greatfields Rd IG11 . . . . . **152** D3
Great Fleete Way
  IG11 . . . . **153** C3
Great Fox Mdw CM15 . . . . **71** F1
Great Galley Cl IG11 . . . . **153** C2
Great Gardens Rd
RM11 . . . . **136** C5
Great Gibcracks Chase
CM2 . . . . **56** A2
Great Godfreys CM1 . . . . . **30** F1
Great Gregorie SS16 . . . . **141** F5
Great Gregories La
CM16 . . . . **67** E6
Great Hall The **1** E11 . . **132** B7
Great Hays SS9 . . . . **146** C5
Greathouse Chase
SS17 . . . . **161** C5
Great Hyde Hall CM21 . . . . **2** B3
Great Knightleys
SS15 . . . . **141** E6
Great Lawn SS5 . . . . **49** A4
Great Leighs Way
SS13 . . . . **121** C1
Great Leylands CM18 . . . . **24** A7
Great Mdw EN10 . . . . **21** A1
Great Mead SS3 . . . . **149** E1
Great Mistley SS16 . . . . . **142** C5
Great Nelmes Chase
RM11 . . . . **136** F6
Great Oaks
  Basildon SS14 . . . . **142** A6
  Brentwood CM13 . . . . **95** B3
  Chigwell IG7 . . . . **111** C6
Great Owl Rd IG7 . . . . . . **111** A7
Great Oxcroft SS15 . . . . . **141** B6
GREAT OXNEY GREEN
  . . . . **30** E1
GREAT PARNDON **23** B6
Great Pettits Ct RM1 . . . . **113** E1
Great Plumtree CM20 . . . . **10** F2
Great Ranton SS13 . . . . . **143** C8
Great Ropers La
CM13 . . . . **116** B4
Great Saling SS11 . . . . . . **122** A6

Great Smials CM3 . . . . . . **101** C6
Great Spenders SS14 . . . . **142** D8
GREAT STAMBRIDGE
  . . . . **126** D4
Great Stony Pk CM5 . . . . . **49** A4
GREAT WAKERING **150** A3
Great Wakering Prim Sch
SS3 . . . . **150** A3
GREAT WALTHAM **18** E7
Great Waltham CE Prim
  Sch CM3 . . . . **18** E7
GREAT WARLEY **116** A2
Great Warley St
CM13 . . . . **116** B1
Great Wheatley Rd
SS6 . . . . **123** B1
Greaves Cl IG11 . . . . **152** E5
Grebe Cl
  Barking IG11 . . . . **153** A1
  Mayland CM3 . . . . **83** A3
Grebe Crest RM20 . . . . . . **172** A2
Greding Wlk CM13 . . . . . **117** B8
Greenacre La CM14 . . . . . **97** E8
Greenacre Mews SS9 . . . . **146** E2
Greenacres
  Epping CM16 . . . . **45** F3
  Hadleigh SS7 . . . . **145** E3
Greenacres CM13 . . . . . . **155** E2
Green Ave SS8 . . . . **163** E3
Greenbank Cl
  Chingford E4 . . . . **109** C8
  Romford RM3 . . . . **114** D7
Greenbanks
  Southend-on-S SS9 . . . . . **147** A2
  Upminster RM14 . . . . **137** E2
Green Cl
  Chelmsford CM1 . . . . **32** D4
  Epping Green CM16 . . . . . **45** B7
  Writtle CM1 . . . . **31** B1
Greendyke SS8 . . . . **163** F5
Greener Ct EN3 . . . . **65** A2
Greenfield Gdns RM9 . . . . **153** C4
Greenfield Rd RM9 . . . . . **153** C4
Greenfields
  Billericay CM12 . . . . **119** A8
  Galleywood CM2 . . . . **54** C2
  Loughton IG10 . . . . **89** A5
Greenfields Cl
  Billericay CM12 . . . . **119** A8
  Brentwood CM13 . . . . . . **116** C4
  Loughton IG10 . . . . **89** A5
Greenfield St EN9 . . . . **65** C5
Green Glade EN6 . . . . **67** E2
Green Glades RM11 . . . . . **137** A5
Greenheys Dr E18 . . . . . . **109** F1
Greenhill IG9 . . . . **88** C1
Greenhills CM20 . . . . **23** E8
GREENHITHE **177** A3
Greenhithe for Bluewater
  Sta DA9 . . . . **177** A2
Green La
  Basildon, Lee Chapel South
    SS16 . . . . **141** E4
  Basildon, Steeple View
    CM12 . . . . **119** A2
  Brentwood CM14 . . . . **94** A1
  Burnham-on-C CM0 . . . . . **106** A7
  Canvey Island SS8 . . . . . . **163** F3
  Chigwell, Grange Hill
    IG7 . . . . **111** E7
  Chigwell IG7 . . . . **89** C1
  Dagenham IG3, RM8 . . . . **134** C2
  Great Warley CM13,
    CM14 . . . . **116** A3
  Hoddesdon EN10 . . . . **43** B8
  Ilford IG1, IG3 . . . . **133** E2
  Kelvedon Hatch CM14 . . . . **93** D8
  Mayland CM3 . . . . **83** B6
  Orsett RM16 . . . . **173** C8
  Pilgrims Hatch CM15 . . . . . **94** C3
  Roxwell CM1 . . . . **30** A4
  Southend-on-S SS9 . . . . . **146** E7
  South Woodham Ferrers
    CM3 . . . . **101** D8
  Threshers Bush CM17 . . . . **25** A6
  Waltham Abbey EN9 . . . . . **66** D4
Greenlands SS4 . . . . **125** D4
Greenleafe Dr IG6 . . . . . . **133** B8
Greenleas
  Thundersley SS7 . . . . **145** B6
  Waltham Abbey EN9 . . . . . . **65** E5
Greenleaves Cvn Pk
EN9 . . . . **22** A2
Green Man Ct CM20 . . . . . **10** A4
Green Mdws CM3 . . . . **57** A6
Green Mead CM3 . . . . **101** C8
Greenoaks SS7 . . . . **144** E3
Greenock Way RM1 . . . . . **113** C3
Green Pk CM20 . . . . **23** E8
Green Rd SS7 . . . . **144** D1
Greens Cl The IG10 . . . . . . **89** A7
Greens Farm La CM11 . . . . **97** C1
Greenshaw CM15 . . . . **94** B2
Greenside RM8 . . . . **134** C3
Greenslade Rd IG11 . . . . . **152** D5
Greensleeves Dr
CM14 . . . . **116** B5
Green St
  2 Harlow CM17 . . . . . . **11** D1
  Ingatestone CM4 . . . . **73** C4
Greenstead CM21 . . . . **1** E1
Greenstead Ave IG8 . . . . . **110** C4
Greenstead Cl
  Brentwood CM13 . . . . **95** E2
  Woodford IG8 . . . . **110** C4
Greenstead Gdns IG8 . . . **110** C4
Greenstead Jun & Inf Schs
SS14 . . . . **142** F6

Greenstead Rd CM5 . . . . . **48** F2
GREENSTED **48** D2
Greensted Cl SS14 . . . . . **142** F5
GREENSTED GREEN **48** B3
Greensted Log Church★
CM5 . . . . **48** D2
Greensted Rd
  Chipping Ongar CM5 . . . . . **48** D2
  Loughton IG10 . . . . **88** F2
Greensted The SS14 . . . . **142** F5
Greenstone Mews
E11 . . . . **132** A5
GREEN STREET **73** D4
Greensward Coll The
SS5 . . . . **124** F7
Greensward La SS5 . . . . . **124** F7
Green The
  Blackmore CM4 . . . . **72** E8
  Buckhurst Hill IG9 . . . . . . **88** B1
  Chelmsford CM1 . . . . **31** F4
  Chingford E4 . . . . **87** D1
  Orsett RM16 . . . . **174** A8
  Romford RM3 . . . . **114** C7
  Southend-on-S SS9 . . . . . **146** E7
  South Ockendon RM15 . . . **157** D2
  Stanford-le-H SS17 . . . . . **160** D1
  Theydon Bois CM16 . . . . . . **67** D3
  Theydon Bois CM16 . . . . . . **67** E2
  Waltham Abbey EN9 . . . . . . **65** C5
  Wanstead E11 . . . . **132** B5
  Wennington RM13 . . . . . . **170** E6
  West Tilbury RM18 . . . . . **179** D8
  Woodford IG8 . . . . **110** A5
  Writtle CM1 . . . . **31** B1
Green Trees CM16 . . . . . . **68** A8
Green Trees Ave CM3 . . . . **80** F5
Greenview SS8 . . . . **163** F5
Green View CM16 . . . . **67** E2
Greenway
  Billericay CM11 . . . . **97** D2
  Brentwood CM13 . . . . **95** A2
  Dagenham RM8 . . . . **134** C3
  Harlow CM19 . . . . **22** E8
  Romford RM3 . . . . **115** B4
  Woodford IG8 . . . . **110** C5
Greenway Bsns Ctr
CM19 . . . . **22** E8
Greenway Ct IG1 . . . . **133** B3
Greenways
  Canvey Island SS8 . . . . . . **163** F5
  Chelmsford CM1 . . . . **32** B6
  Maldon CM9 . . . . **36** F2
  Rochford SS4 . . . . **125** F2
  South Benfleet SS7 . . . . . **144** C2
  Southend-on-S SS1 . . . . . **167** E7
Greenways Ct RM11 . . . . **136** D5
Greenway The SS11 . . . . . **99** C3
Greenwich Way EN9 . . . . . **65** C3
Green Wlk
  Chipping Ongar CM5 . . . . . **49** A1
  Woodford IG8 . . . . **110** E4
Green Wlk The E4 . . . . **87** D1
Greenwood **3** IG8 . . . . . **110** A3
Greenwood Ave
  Dagenham RM10 . . . . **154** B8
  South Benfleet SS7 . . . . . **144** E1
Greenwood Dr E4 . . . . . . **109** D5
Greenwood Gdns IG6 . . . . **111** C3
Greenwood Ho RM17 . . . . **178** B8
Greenwood Mans **9**
IG11 . . . . **153** A5
Greenwood Rd IG7 . . . . . **112** B6
Greenyard EN9 . . . . **65** C6
Gregory Cl SS5 . . . . **124** F4
Gregory Mews EN9 . . . . . . **65** B7
Gregory Rd RM6 . . . . **134** D7
Grenfell Ave RM12 . . . . . **135** F3
Grenfell Gdns IG2 . . . . . . **133** F6
Grennan Cl CM13 . . . . . . **117** D4
Grenville Gdns IG8 . . . . . **110** C3
Grenville Rd RM16 . . . . . **172** B1
Gresham Cl CM14 . . . . . . **116** C7
Gresham Ct **6** CM14 . . . **116** C7
Gresham Dr RM6 . . . . **134** B5
Gresham Rd CM14 . . . . . **116** C7
Grested Ct SS4 . . . . **125** F2
Grevatt Lo SS13 . . . . **143** C5
Greyfriars CM13 . . . . **95** B2
Greygoose Pk CM19 . . . . . **23** A5
Greyhound La RM16 . . . . . **174** A4
Greyhound Pk SS2 . . . . . . **148** A1
Greyhound Way SS2 . . . . **148** A1
Grey Gdn Pl CM11 . . . . . . **97** B3
Grey Ladys CM2 . . . . **54** B2
Greystone Gdns IG6 . . . . **111** C1
Grey Towers Ave
RM11 . . . . **136** D3
Grey Towers Gdns
RM11 . . . . **136** C3
Gridiron Pl RM14 . . . . **137** B2
Griffin Ave
  Canvey Island SS8 . . . . . . **164** C5
  Upminster RM14 . . . . **137** E5
Griffins The RM16 . . . . . . **173** B4
Griffin's Wood Cotts
CM16 . . . . **67** D7
Griffin Wlk DA9 . . . . **176** F2
Griffith Cl RM8 . . . . **134** C3
Grifon Cl RM16 . . . . **172** C3
Grifon Rd RM16 . . . . **172** C3
Griggs App IG1 . . . . **133** C2
Griggs Gdns RM12 . . . . . **155** C7
Grimshaw Way RM1 . . . . . **135** F6
Grimstone Cl RM5 . . . . . . **113** B4
Grimston Rd SS14 . . . . . . **142** F8
Grinstead La CM22 . . . . **2** C6
Grosvenor Cl
  Chelmsford CM2 . . . . **54** D7

Grosvenor Cl *continued*
  Loughton IG10 . . . . **89** B8
Grosvenor Ct
  Southend-on-S SS0 . . . . . **166** C7
  3 Wanstead E11 . . . . . **132** B6
Grosvenor Dr
  Hornchurch RM11 . . . . . . **136** C4
  Loughton IG10 . . . . **89** B8
Grosvenor Gdns
  Billericay CM12 . . . . **97** A4
  Upminster RM14 . . . . **137** D3
  Woodford IG8 . . . . **110** B4
Grosvenor Hts E4 . . . . **87** E2
Grosvenor Cl **4** E18 . . . . **109** F1
Grosvenor Mans SS0 . . . . **166** C8
Grosvenor Mews SS0 . . . . **166** C7
Grosvenor Path IG10 . . . . . **89** B8
Grosvenor Rd
  Dagenham RM8 . . . . **134** F3
  Ilford IG1 . . . . **133** C1
  Orsett RM16 . . . . **174** D7
  Rayleigh SS6 . . . . **123** B5
  Romford RM7 . . . . **135** D4
  South Benfleet SS7 . . . . . **163** E8
  Southend-on-S SS0 . . . . . **166** C7
  Wanstead E11 . . . . **132** B6
Grove Ave SS16 . . . . **141** B3
Grove Cl SS6 . . . . **123** F2
Grove Cotts IG7 . . . . **111** F7
Grove Cres E18 . . . . **109** F1
Grove Ct
  Hornchurch RM11 . . . . . . **136** A3
  Rayleigh SS6 . . . . **124** B1
  Southend-on-S SS0 . . . . . **147** B3
  Upminster RM14 . . . . **156** A8
  Waltham Abbey EN9 . . . . . . **65** B6
Grove End E18 . . . . **109** F1
Grove Gdns RM10 . . . . . . **135** C1
Grove Hill
  Southend-on-S SS9 . . . . . **146** B7
  Woodford E18 . . . . **109** F1
Grove Ho CM14 . . . . **116** B6
Grove La
  Chigwell IG7 . . . . **111** F7
  Epping CM16 . . . . **46** A1
Grovelands SS2 . . . . **148** D2
Grovelands Rd SS12 . . . . **121** D6
Grovelands Way
RM17 . . . . **172** F1
Grove Lo SS3 . . . . **168** G7
Grove Park Ave E4 . . . . . **109** B3
Grove Park Rd RM13 . . . . **155** A4
Grove Pk E11 . . . . **132** B6
Grove Prim Sch RM6 . . . . **134** C6
Grove Rd
  Billericay CM12 . . . . **96** F2
  Canvey Island SS8 . . . . . . **164** C4
  Chelmsford CM2 . . . . **32** B1
  Chingford E4 . . . . **109** C7
  Grays RM17 . . . . **178** C8
  Ilford RM6 . . . . **134** C5
  Northfleet RM17 . . . . **178** B2
  Rayleigh SS6 . . . . **123** F2
  South Benfleet SS7 . . . . . **144** D2
  Stanford-le-H SS17 . . . . . **175** D8
  Woodford E18 . . . . **109** F1
Grover Wlk SS17 . . . . **160** F3
Groves Cl RM15 . . . . **171** F6
Groveside Rd E4 . . . . **109** E7
Grove Terr SS1 . . . . **167** A7
Grove The
  Bicknacre CM3 . . . . **56** F1
  Billericay CM11 . . . . **97** C4
  Brentwood CM14 . . . . . . **115** F6
  3 Gravesend DA12 . . . . **179** C1
  Southend-on-S SS2 . . . . . **148** C2
  Stanford-le-H SS17 . . . . . **175** D8
  Swanscombe DA10 . . . . . **177** F2
  Upminster RM14 . . . . **156** B7
Groveway RM8 . . . . **153** D6
Grove Wlk SS3 . . . . **168** E7
Grovewood Ave SS9 . . . . **146** B7
Grovewood Cl SS9 . . . . . **146** B7
Grovewood Pl IG8 . . . . . . **110** E4
Grove Wood Prim Sch
SS6 . . . . **124** A1
Guardian Ave RM16 . . . . . **172** D4
Guardian Bsns Ctr
RM3 . . . . **114** D3
Guardian Cl RM11 . . . . . . **136** B2
Guardsman Cl CM14 . . . . **116** D5
Gubbins La RM3 . . . . **114** F2
Guernsey Ct CM9 . . . . **36** F2
Guernsey Gdns SS11 . . . . . **99** C3
Guildford Ct SS2 . . . . **148** A1
Guildford Gdns RM3 . . . . **114** E4
Guildford Rd
  Chingford E17 . . . . **109** C2
  Ilford IG3 . . . . **133** E2
  Romford RM3 . . . . **114** E4
  Southend-on-S SS2 . . . . . **148** A1
Guild Way **3** CM3 . . . . . **101** E7
Guilford Lo **5** CM14 . . . **116** C7
Guilfords CM17 . . . . **11** D5
Gull Wlk RM12 . . . . **155** B5
Gumley Rd RM20 . . . . **177** E8
Gunfleet SS3 . . . . **168** C7
Gun Hill RM18 . . . . **179** D1
Gun Hill Pl SS16 . . . . **142** C4
Gunnels Ct & Hastingwood
  Ct **8** IG9 . . . . **110** C8
Gunner Dr EN3 . . . . **65** A2
Gunners Gr E4 . . . . **109** C7
Gunners Rd SS3 . . . . **168** G7
Gunning Rd RM17 . . . . . . **173** D1
Gunn Rd DA10 . . . . **177** E1
Gunpowder Pk★ EN9 . . . . **65** B3
Gunson Gate CM2 . . . . . . **54** D7

- Gurney Cl IG11 152 B6
- Guru Gobind Singh Khalsa Coll IG7 88 F1
- Gustedhall La SS5 124 E3
- Gutteridge La RM4 91 C3
- Gutters La CM1 32 C7
- Guys Farm CM1 31 B1
- Guys Farm Rd CM3 101 D7
- Guysfield Cl RM13 155 A4
- Guysfield Dr RM13 155 A4
- Guy's Retreat IG9 88 C2
- Gwend Alen Ave SS8 164 D4
- Gwyn Cl CM3 20 E1
- Gwynne Ho 3 E11 132 A6
- Gwynne Park Ave IG8 110 F4
- Gyllyngdune Gdns IG3 133 F1

H

- Haarlem Rd SS8 163 D4
- Haarle Rd SS8 164 D2
- Haase Cl SS8 164 A6
- Habgood Rd IG10 88 E6
- Hackamore SS7 145 B5
- Hackmans La
  - Cock Clarks CM3 57 E2
  - Cold Norton CM3 80 B6
- Hacton Dr RM12 155 E8
- Hacton La RM14 155 F8
- Hacton Par RM12 136 F1
- Hacton Prim Sch RM12 155 E8
- Haddon Cl SS6 123 A4
- Haddon Mead CM3 101 D5
- Hadfield Rd SS17 160 D1
- HADLEIGH 145 E3
- Hadleigh Bsns Ctr SS7 145 E2
- Hadleigh Castle★ SS7 145 D1
- Hadleigh Castle Ctry Pk★ SS7 145 B1
- Hadleigh Ct
  - Brentwood CM14 116 A7
  - Chingford E4 87 E2
- Hadleigh Hall Ct SS9 146 C1
- Hadleigh Inf Sch SS7 145 E3
- Hadleigh Jun Sch SS7 145 E3
- Hadleigh Lo 5 IG8 110 A4
- Hadleigh Park Ave SS7 145 C3
- Hadleigh Rd
  - Southend-on-S SS9 146 C1
  - Southend-on-S, Westcliff-on-S SS0 166 E7
- Hadley Grange CM17 24 C7
- Hadrians Way CM9 37 A4
- Hagg Hill CM3 80 D5
- Haig Ct CM2 32 A1
- Haig Rd RM16 174 A3
- Haigville Gdns IG6 133 B7
- Hailey Ave EN11 8 A2
- Hailey La SG13 8 A2
- Hailey Rd DA18 169 A4
- Hailey Road Bsns Pk DA18 169 A4
- Hailsham Cl RM3 114 C5
- Hailsham Gdns RM3 114 C5
- Hailsham Rd RM3 114 C5
- HAINAULT 111 F3
- Hainault Ave
  - Rochford SS4 125 D4
  - Southend-on-S SS0 147 D2
- Hainault Bridge Par 5 IG1 133 B2
- Hainault Cl SS7 145 E4
- Hainault Forest Ctry Pk★ IG7 112 C7
- Hainault Forest High Sch IG6 112 B5
- Hainault Gore RM6 134 E6
- Hainault Gr
  - Chelmsford CM1 31 E1
  - Chigwell IG7 111 C6
- Hainault Rd
  - Chigwell IG7 111 C6
  - Dagenham RM6 134 F5
  - Ilford RM6 134 B8
  - North Fambridge CM3 81 A1
  - Redbridge RM6 112 B2
  - Romford RM5 135 C8
- Hainault St IG1 133 B2
- Hainault Sta IG6 111 E3
- Halbutt Gdns RM9 134 F1
- Halbutt St RM9 153 F7
- Halcyon Cvn Pk SS5 101 F4
- Halcyon Way RM11 136 F3
- Haldane Cl EN3 65 B1
- Haldan Rd E4 109 C4
- Haldon Cl 3 IG7 111 E5
- Hale Cl E4 109 C7
- Hale Cotts DA9 177 C2
- HALE END 109 D4
- Hale End RM3 114 B4
- Hale End Rd E17 109 D2
- Hale Ho RM11 136 A5
- Halesworth Cl RM3 114 E3
- Halesworth Rd RM3 114 E4
- Hale The E4 109 D3
- Hale Way SS3 168 F6
- Half Acre 2 E18 132 A8
- Halfhides
  - Brentwood CM14 116 C6
  - Waltham Abbey EN9 65 D6
- Half Moon Cotts CM21 1 B1
- Half Moon La CM16 67 F8
- Halfway Ct RM19 171 A2
- Halidon Rise RM3 115 B4
- Halifax Ho 12 RM3 114 E5
- Hallam Cl CM15 72 B3
- Hallam Ct CM12 96 F4
- Hall Ave RM15 171 C5
- Hall Barns The CM5 70 C6
- Hall Bridge Rise CM9 37 C4
- Hall Cl
  - Great Baddow CM2 55 A6
  - Stanford-le-H SS17 160 E4
- Hall Cotts CM3 100 B6
- Hall Cres
  - Aveley RM15 171 C4
  - Hadleigh SS7 145 D3
- Hall Est CM9 38 E7
- Hallet Rd SS8 164 E3
- Halley Rd EN9 65 B3
- Hall Farm Cl SS7 144 D1
- Hall Farm Rd SS7 144 D1
- Hall Green La CM13 95 D2
- Hallingbury Rd CM21 2 A4
- Halling Hill CM20 10 F2
- Hall La
  - Brentwood CM15 95 A6
  - Chelmsford CM2 55 C6
  - Chingford E4 109 A6
  - Ingatestone CM4 74 C1
  - Romford RM14 115 C1
  - Shenfield CM15 94 F4
  - Shenfield CM15 94 F6
  - South Ockendon RM15 157 D3
  - Upminster RM14 137 D5
  - West Hanningfield CM2 76 D6
- Hall Mead Sch RM14 137 D3
- Hallmores EN10 21 A4
- Hallowell Down CM3 101 E6
- Hall Park Ave SS0 166 B8
- Hall Park Rd RM14 156 C7
- Hall Rd
  - Asheldham CM0 85 C7
  - Aveley RM15 171 C4
  - Hockley SS5 125 A2
  - Ilford RM6 134 D5
  - Maldon CM9 37 B4
  - Rochford SS4 125 D1
  - Romford RM2 136 B8
  - Southminster CM0 84 E4
- Hall Road Ind Est CM0 84 E4
- Hallsford Bridge Ind Est CM5 71 C8
- HALLS GREEN 22 C5
- Hall St CM2 32 B1
- Hall Terr
  - Aveley RM15 171 D4
  - Romford RM3 115 A3
- Hallwood Cres CM15 94 E2
- Halsham Cres IG11 152 F7
- Halstead Ct 5 SS12 121 C5
- Halstead Ho 15 RM3 114 D4
- Halstead Rd E11 132 B6
- Halstead Way CM13 95 C3
- Halston Ct SS17 161 B3
- Halston Pl CM9 58 F8
- Halstow Way SS13 143 C5
- Halt Dr SS17 175 B2
- Halton Rd RM16 174 C3
- Halt Robin La DA17 169 B2
- Halt Robin Rd DA17 169 B2
- Haltwhistle Rd CM3 101 C8
- Halyard Reach CM3 101 E5
- Hamberts Rd CM3 79 E1
- Hamble La RM15 171 F8
- Hamble Way CM0 106 A6
- Hamboro Gdns SS9 146 B1
- Hambro Ave SS6 123 D4
- Hambro Cl SS6 123 E4
- Hambro Hill SS6 123 E4
- Hamden Cres RM10 135 B1
- Hamerton Rd DA11 178 B2
- Hameway E6 152 A1
- Hamilton Ave
  - Hoddesdon EN11 21 A8
  - Ilford IG6 133 C6
  - Romford RM1 113 D1
- Hamilton Cl SS9 146 A2
- Hamilton Cres CM14 116 C6
- Hamilton Ct
  - Althorne CM3 82 F4
  - 3 Burnham-on-C CM0 106 C4
  - Chelmsford CM1 31 D6
- Hamilton Dr RM3 114 E1
- Hamilton Gdns SS5 124 E7
- Hamilton Grange SS0 166 C7
- Hamilton Mews SS6 123 F3
- Hamilton Rd
  - Ilford IG1 152 B8
  - Romford RM2 136 B6
- Hamlet Cl RM5 113 A3
- Hamlet Court Mews SS0 147 E1
- Hamlet Court Rd SS0 166 E8
- Hamlet Ct CM14 115 E6
- Hamlet Hill CM19 22 B4
- Hamlet International Ind Est DA8 169 D1
- Hamleton Terr RM9 153 C5
- Hamlet Rd
  - Chelmsford CM2 32 B1
  - Romford RM5 113 A3
  - Southend-on-S SS1 166 F7
- Hamley Cl SS7 144 B6
- Hammarskjold Rd CM20 10 D2
- Hammond Ct RM12 135 F3
- Hammonds Cl RM8 134 C1
- Hammonds La
  - Billericay CM11 119 C7
  - Brentwood CM13 116 B4
- Hammonds Rd
  - Hatfield Broad Oak CM22 4 A6
  - Little Baddow CM3 33 E3
- Hampden Cl CM16 47 A4
- Hampden Cres CM14 116 C5
- Hampden Rd
  - Grays RM17 173 B1
  - Romford RM5 113 B3
- Hampshire Gdns SS17 175 A4
- Hampshire Rd RM11 137 A7
- Hampshire Villas SS2 167 B8
- Hampstead Ave 8 IG8 111 A3
- Hampstead Gdns
  - Hockley SS5 124 F7
  - Ilford RM6 134 B6
- Hampton Cl
  - Grays RM16 172 C3
  - Southend-on-S SS2 147 E4
- Hampton Ct
  - Hockley SS5 124 D6
  - Southend-on-S, Chalkwell SS9 165 F8
  - Southend-on-S SS9 146 E1
- Hampton Gdns
  - Sawbridgeworth CM21 11 C7
  - Southend-on-S SS2 147 E4
- Hampton Mead IG10 89 B6
- Hampton Rd
  - Chingford E4 109 A5
  - Great Baddow CM2 54 E6
  - Ilford IG1 152 C8
- Hamstel Inf Sch SS2 148 D2
- Hamstel Jun Sch SS2 148 D2
- Hamstel Mews SS2 148 D1
- Hamstel Rd
  - Harlow CM20 10 C1
  - Southend-on-S SS2 148 D2
- Hanbury Rd CM1 53 E8
- Handel Cres RM18 179 B7
- Handel Rd SS8 164 D2
- Handforth Rd 7 IG1 133 B1
- Hand La CM21 1 C1
- HANDLEY GREEN 74 D8
- Handleys Chase SS15 119 F2
- Handleys Ct SS15 119 F2
- Handsworth Ave E4 109 D4
- Handsworth Prim Sch E4 109 D4
- Handtrough Way IG11 152 B3
- Hanford Rd RM15 171 C5
- Hanging Hill CM13 95 C2
- Hanging Hill La CM13 117 B8
- Hanlee Brook CM2 54 F6
- Hannah Cl SS8 164 A6
- Hannards Way IG6 112 B5
- Hannett Rd SS8 164 E3
- Hanningfield Cl SS6 123 A3
- Hanningfield Nature Reserve★ CM11 99 A7
- Hanningfield Nature Trail★ CM3 99 B8
- Hanningfield Reservoir Visitor Ctr★ CM11 98 F7
- Hanover Cl SS14 142 E5
- Hanover Ct
  - Hoddesdon EN11 21 A7
  - Rayleigh SS6 123 D3
  - Sawbridgeworth CM21 1 F1
  - Waltham Abbey EN9 65 C6
- Hanover Dr SS14 142 E6
- Hanover Gdns IG6 111 C3
- Hanover Mews SS5 124 D6
- Hanover Pl CM14 116 B5
- Hansells Mead CM19 22 B8
- Hanson Cl IG10 89 C7
- Hanson Dr IG10 89 C7
- Hanson Gn IG10 89 C7
- Harberts Rd CM19 23 B8
- Harberts Way SS6 123 C5
- Harbourer Cl IG6 112 B5
- Harbourer Rd IG6 112 B5
- Harcourt Ave SS2 147 F1
- Harcourt Ho 6 E4 109 D5
- Harcourt Mews 2 RM2 135 F6
- Hard Ct IG8 110 C4
- Hardie Rd
  - Dagenham RM10 135 C1
  - Stanford-le-H SS17 160 D2
- Harding Ho CM16 68 A8
- Harding Rd RM16 174 A3
- Harding's Elms Rd CM11 120 B4
- Harding's La CM4 74 A7
- Hardings Reach 8 CM0 106 C4
- Hardley Cres RM11 136 D7
- Hardwick Cl SS6 123 D1
- Hardwick Cres 27 DA2 176 B1
- Hardwick Ct
  - Southend-on-S SS2 147 E3
  - 9 Wanstead E11 132 A5
- Hardwick St IG11 152 C4
- Hardwick Ho SS6 123 E1
- Hardy SS3 168 D5
- Hardy Ct 9 E11 132 A7
- Hardy Gr DA1 176 A3
- Hardy Rd SS14 142 E8
- Hardys Way SS8 164 A6
- Harebell Cl CM12 96 F4
- Harebell Way RM3 114 D3
- Hare Bridge Cres CM4 74 A2
- Harefield CM20 11 A1
- Hare Hall La RM2 136 B7
- Hares Chase CM12 96 F3
- Haresfield Rd RM10 154 A6
- Haresland Cl SS7 145 F6
- Hare St
  - Harlow CM19 23 B8
  - Stanford Rivers CM5 70 E5
- HARE STREET 23 B7
- Hare Street Com Prim Sch CM19 23 C8
- Hare Street Springs CM19 23 B8
- Hare Terr RM20 172 D1
- Harewood Ave SS4 125 D5
- Harewood Dr IG5 110 F1
- Harewood Hill CM16 67 E4
- Harewood Rd
  - Chelmsford CM1 31 E1
  - Pilgrims Hatch CM15 94 B3
- Harford Cl E4 87 B2
- Harford Rd E4 87 B2
- Harfred Ave CM9 37 E3
- Harkness Cl RM3 114 F5
- HARKNETT'S GATE 22 E2
- Harlech Rd 1 SS13 143 B5
- Harlequin Stps 16 SS1 167 C7
- Harlesden Cl RM3 114 F4
- Harlesden Rd RM3 114 F4
- Harlesden Wlk RM3 114 F3
- Harley Ct E11 132 A4
- Harley St SS9 146 C1
- Harlings Gr CM1 32 C3
- HARLOW 11 C2
- Harlow Bsns Pk CM19 22 E8
- Harlowbury Prim Sch CM17 11 D4
- Harlow Coll CM20 10 D1
- Harlow Comm CM17 24 D6
- Harlow Fields Sch CM18 23 E6
- Harlow Gdns RM5 113 C4
- Harlow Mans 2 IG11 152 B5
- Harlow Mill Sta CM20 11 C5
- Harlow Rd
  - Moreton CM5 26 C3
  - Rainham RM13 154 F4
  - Roydon CM19 9 C1
  - Sawbridgeworth CM21 11 C8
  - Sheering CM22, CM17 12 B8
  - Sheering, Matching Tye CM22 12 F3
- Harlow Ret Pk CM20 10 F4
- Harlow Seedbed Ctr CM19 23 A7
- Harlow Stad (Greyhounds) CM19 9 E1
- Harlow Town Sta CM20 10 D3
- HARLOW TYE 12 B3
- Harlton Ct EN9 65 F5
- Harman Ave IG8 109 F4
- Harman Cl E4 109 D6
- Harmer Ct DA10 177 F1
- Harmer Rd DA10 177 F1
- Harmer St DA12 179 C1
- Harness Cl CM1 32 E7
- Harold Cl CM19 22 F7
- Harold Court Prim Sch RM3 115 A3
- Harold Court Rd RM3 115 B3
- Harold Cres EN9 65 C7
- Harold Ct RM3 115 B3
- Harold Gdns SS11 99 E1
- HAROLD HILL 114 E5
- HAROLD PARK 115 B3
- Harold Rd
  - Chingford E4 109 C7
  - Woodford IG8 110 A2
- Harold Rise CM9 36 F5
- Harolds Rd CM19 22 F7
- Harold View RM3 114 F1
- HAROLD WOOD 114 F2
- Harold Wood Hall RM3 114 D2
- Harold Wood Hospl RM3 114 E2
- Harold Wood Prim Sch RM3 137 A8
- Harold Wood Sta RM3 114 F2
- Haron Cl SS8 164 B3
- Harpenden Rd E12 132 C2
- Harper Cl RM16 172 C1
- Harpers La CM15 72 D2
- Harper Way SS6 123 C3
- Harpour Rd IG11 152 C6
- Harrap Chase RM17 172 F1
- Harridge Cl SS9 146 E3
- Harridge Rd SS9 146 E3
- Harrier Ave E11 132 B5
- Harrier Cl
  - Hornchurch RM12 155 B6
  - Southend-on-S SS3 149 E1
- Harrier Way EN9 66 A5
- Harriescourt EN9 66 A7
- Harrington Cres RM16 172 D5
- Harris Cl
  - Corringham SS17 161 B4
  - Romford RM3 114 E3
  - Wickford SS12 121 F5
- Harris Ct SS5 124 E5
- Harrison Cl CM13 95 D4
- Harrison Ct CM1 31 F3
- Harrison Dr CM16 47 B5
- Harrison Gdns SS5 101 D2
- Harrison Rd
  - Dagenham RM10 154 B6
  - Waltham Abbey EN9 65 C4
- Harrisons Wharf RM19 171 A1
- Harris Rd RM9 153 F7
- Harrods Ct CM11 97 E2
- Harrogate Dr SS5 124 F8
- Harrogate Rd SS5 124 F7
- Harrold Rd RM8 153 B7
- Harrowband Rd 7 CM17 11 C1
- Harrow Cl
  - Hockley SS5 125 A5
  - 3 Hornchurch RM11 136 B3
- Harrow Cres RM3 114 B2
- Harrow Dr RM11 136 C4
- Harrow Gdns SS5 125 A5
- Harrow La RM14 158 C6
- Harrow Lo RM11 136 C3
- Harrow Rd
  - Barking IG11 152 E4
  - Basildon SS12 122 A2
  - Bulphan RM14 158 C7
  - Canvey Island SS8 164 B5
  - Ilford IG1 152 C8
  - North Benfleet SS12 121 F2
- Harrow Way CM2 55 A6
- Harston Dr EN3 65 A1
- Hart Cl SS7 145 A6
- Hart Cnr RM20 172 D1
- Hart Cres IG7 111 F5
- Hart Ct E12 152 A5
- Hartford Cl SS6 123 B4
- Hartford End SS13 143 A5
- Hartington Ct SS1 167 B7
- Hartington Pl SS1 167 B7
- Hartington Rd SS1 167 B7
- Hartland Cl SS9 146 D7
- Hartland Rd
  - Epping CM16 46 A1
  - Hornchurch RM12 136 A2
- Hartley Cl CM2 33 A4
- Hart Rd
  - Harlow CM17 11 C6
  - Thundersley SS7 145 B6
- Harts Gr IG8 110 A5
- Hartshorn Gdns E6 152 A1
- Harts La IG11 152 B6
- Hart St
  - Brentwood CM14 116 C8
  - Chelmsford CM2 32 A1
- Hartswood Cl CM14 116 E6
- Hartswood Hospl CM13 116 B4
- Hartswood Rd CM14 116 E5
- Hartwell Dr E4 109 C4
- Harty Cl RM16 173 B5
- Harvard Ct SS6 123 B4
- Harvard Wlk RM12 155 A8
- Harvest Cl CM3 101 D7
- Harvest La IG10 88 D2
- Harvest Rd SS8 164 B5
- Harvest Way CM9 36 F5
- Harvey RM16 173 B4
- Harvey Cl SS13 121 B1
- Harvey Ctr CM20 23 D8
- Harveyfields EN9 65 C5
- Harvey Gdns IG10 89 B6
- Harvey Ho
  - 4 Barking IG11 152 C5
  - Ilford RM6 134 D7
- Harvey Rd
  - Basildon SS13 121 C1
  - Ilford IG1 152 B7
- Harvey's La RM7 135 E2
- Harwater Dr IG10 88 F7
- Harwood Ave RM11 136 E8
- Harwood Ct 7 RM17 178 C8
- Harwood Hall La RM14 156 B6
- Haselfoot Rd CM3 33 F8
- Haskard Rd RM9 153 D7
- Haskins SS17 160 F2
- Haslemere Est The EN11 21 D6
- Haslemere Pinnacles Est The CM19 23 A7
- Haslemere Rd
  - Ilford IG3 133 F2
  - Wickford SS12 99 C2
- Haslers Ct CM4 74 C4
- Haslewood Ave EN11 21 A6
- Haslingden Ho 11 RM3 114 E5
- Hassell Rd SS8 164 D3
- Hassenbrook Ct SS17 160 E1
- Hassenbrook Ho SS17 160 D1
- Hassenbrook Rd SS17 160 E1
- Hassenbrook Sch SS17 160 E2
- Hasted Cl DA9 177 C1
- Hastings Ave IG6 133 C7
- Hastings Cl RM17 177 E8
- Hastings Rd
  - Romford RM2 136 B6
  - Southend-on-S SS1 167 B8
- Hastings The SS11 99 D1
- Hastingswood Bsns Ctr CM17 25 A5
- HASTINGWOOD 24 F4

Hastingwood Ct
Chipping Ongar CM5 . . . . . . **48** F5
Ilford IG2 . . . . **133** D5
Hastingwood Rd RM17 . . **24** E4
Hatches Farm Rd
CM12 . . . . **118** D5
Hatchfields CM3 . . . . **18** F7
Hatch Gn CM22 . . . . **2** B8
Hatch Gr RM6 . . . . **134** E7
Hatch La E4 . . . . **109** E7
Hatch Rd CM15 . . . . **94** B4
Hatch Side IG7 . . . . **111** A5
Hatchwoods IG8 . . . . **109** F6
HATFIELD BROAD OAK **3** F5
Hatfield Cl
Brentwood CM13 . . . . **95** D2
Hornchurch RM12 . . . . . . **155** D7
Ilford IG6 . . . . **133** B8
Redbridge IG6 . . . . **111** B1
Hatfield Dr CM11 . . . . **97** D2
Hatfield Gr CM1 . . . . **31** D1
HATFIELD HEATH **3** B3
Hatfield Heath Com Prim
Sch CM22 . . . . **3** A3
Hatfield Ho SS4 . . . . **125** F2
Hatfield Lo IG6 . . . . **133** B8
Hatfield Mews RM9 . . . . . **153** E5
Hatfield Rd
Dagenham RM9 . . . . **153** E5
Grays RM16 . . . . **172** D1
Langford CM9 . . . . **36** B7
Rayleigh SS6 . . . . **123** B3
Hatfields IG10 . . . . **89** B6
Hathaway Cl IG6 . . . . **111** B4
Hathaway Cres E12 . . . . . **152** A6
Hathaway Gdns
Grays RM17 . . . . **173** A3
Ilford RM6 . . . . **134** D6
Hathaway Rd RM17 . . . . . **173** B2
Hatherleigh Way
RM3 . . . . **114** D2
Hatherley The SS14 . . . . . **142** D7
Hatley Ave IG6 . . . . **133** C7
Hatley Gdns SS7 . . . . **144** C5
Hatterill SS15 . . . . **141** D5
Hatton Cl RM16 . . . . **172** C3
Hatton Mews DA9 . . . . . . **177** C3
Hatton Sch IG8 . . . . **132** D8
Havalon Cl SS14 . . . . **142** D7
Havana Cl RM1 . . . . **135** E6
Havana Dr SS6 . . . . **123** B7
Havant Ho 9 RM3 . . . . . . **114** E3
Havelock Ho 8 E4 . . . . . **109** D5
Havelock St IG1 . . . . **133** B2
Haven Cl
Basildon SS16 . . . . **142** E3
Canvey Island SS8 . . . . . **163** E3
Hadleigh SS7 . . . . **145** D3
Havencourt CM1 . . . . **32** B3
Havengore
Basildon SS13 . . . . **143** C8
Chelmsford CM1 . . . . **32** F5
Havengore Cl SS3 . . . . . . **150** C3
Havengore Ho SS9 . . . . . **146** E1
Haven Pl RM16 . . . . **173** C4
Haven Quays SS8 . . . . . . **163** C1
Haven Rd SS8 . . . . **163** D2
Haven Rise RM11 . . . . . . **119** D6
Havenside SS3 . . . . **149** E5
Haven The RM16 . . . . **173** F2
Havenwood Cl CM13 . . . . **116** C4
Haverhill Rd E4 . . . . **87** C1
HAVERING-ATTE-BOWER
. . . . **113** E7
Havering Cl SS3 . . . . **150** B4
Havering Coll, Ardleigh
Green Campus
RM11 . . . . **136** E7
Havering Coll of F & H Ed
RM3 . . . . **114** E6
Havering Ctry Pk★
RM4 . . . . **113** C6
Havering Dr RM1 . . . . **135** E8
Havering Gdns RM6 . . . . **134** D6
Havering Music Sch
RM11 . . . . **136** F2
Havering Rd RM1 . . . . . . **113** D3
HAVERING'S GROVE **96** B2
Havering Sixth Form Coll
RM11 . . . . **136** F3
Havering Way IG11 . . . . . **153** B2
Haverstock Pl 6 RM2 . . **136** B6
Havisham Way CM1 . . . . . **31** E7
Havis Rd SS17 . . . . **160** E4
Haward Rd EN11 . . . . **21** C8
Hawbush Gn SS13 . . . . . **121** B1
Hawes La E4 . . . . **65** C1
Hawfinch Wlk CM2 . . . . . . **54** B5
Hawk Cl EN9 . . . . **66** A5
Hawk Cnr RM20 . . . . **172** D1
Hawkdene E4 . . . . **87** C3
Hawkenbury CM19 . . . . . . **23** B6
Hawkesbury Bush La
SS16 . . . . **142** B2
Hawkesbury Cl
Canvey Island SS8 . . . . . **163** F2
3 Redbridge IG7 . . . . **112** B6
Hawkesbury Rd SS8 . . . . **163** E2
Hawkes Cl RM17 . . . . **178** B8
Hawk Hill SS11 . . . . **100** D2
Hawkhurst Cl CM1 . . . . . . **31** E2
Hawkhurst Gdns RM5 . . **113** D4
Hawkinge Way RM12 . . . **155** C6
Hawkins SS3 . . . . **168** D5

Hawkins Cl
Cock Clarks CM3 . . . . **57** E2
Wickford SS11 . . . . **121** F7
Hawkins Dr RM16 . . . . . . **172** D4
Hawk La SS11 . . . . **100** D2
Hawkley Ct 9 CM12 . . . . . **97** B2
Hawkridge SS3 . . . . **168** C8
Hawkridge Cl RM6 . . . . . **134** C5
Hawkridge Dr RM17 . . . . **173** D1
Hawks Cl CM3 . . . . **57** A6
Hawks Hill CM16 . . . . **47** A4
Hawks La SS5 . . . . **124** E5
Hawksmoor Gn CM13 . . . . **95** D4
Hawksmouth E4 . . . . **87** C2
Hawksway SS16 . . . . **142** B4
Hawkswood Rd CM11,
SS11 . . . . **99** A6
Hawk Terr IG5 . . . . **133** A8
HAWKWELL **125** A4
Hawkwell Chase SS5 . . . **124** E4
Hawkwell Ct E4 . . . . **109** C7
Hawkwell Ho 1 RM8 . . . . **135** A2
Hawkwell Park Dr
SS5 . . . . **124** F5
Hawkwell Rd SS5 . . . . . . **124** F6
Hawkwood Cl CM3 . . . . . . **79** E1
Hawkwood Cres E4 . . . . . . **87** B3
Hawsted IG9 . . . . **88** B2
Hawthorn Ave
Brentwood CM13 . . . . **116** F6
Rainham RM13 . . . . **155** B1
Hawthorn Cl
Chelmsford CM2 . . . . **54** C6
Hockley SS5 . . . . **124** F5
Hawthorn Ct IG5 . . . . **132** F8
Hawthorne Ct E4 . . . . **109** B4
Hawthorne Gdns SS5 . . . **124** B6
Hawthorne Rd SS17 . . . . **160** F4
Hawthornes CM3 . . . . **58** D1
Hawthorn Pl DA8 . . . . **169** C1
Hawthorn Rd
Canvey Island SS8 . . . . . **164** C3
Hoddesdon EN11 . . . . **21** B8
Woodford IG9 . . . . **110** D6
Hawthorns
Harlow CM18 . . . . **23** F4
South Benfleet SS7 . . . . . **144** C4
Southend-on-S SS9 . . . . **146** E4
Woodford IG8 . . . . **110** A7
Hawthorns The
Burnham-on-C CM0 . . . . . **106** A7
Corringham SS17 . . . . . . **161** C3
Danbury CM3 . . . . **57** A7
Hadleigh SS7 . . . . **145** E2
Loughton IG10 . . . . **89** A5
Hawthorn Way SS6 . . . . . **123** F1
Hawthorn Wlk CM3 . . . . . . **79** E1
Hawtree Cl SS1 . . . . **167** C7
Hayburn Way RM12 . . . . **135** F3
Hayden Rd EN9 . . . . **65** C4
Haydens Rd CM20 . . . . . . **23** C8
Hayden Way RM5 . . . . . . **113** C1
Haydock Cl RM12 . . . . . . **155** F8
Haydon Cl RM3 . . . . **114** B3
Haydon Rd RM8 . . . . **134** C2
Hayes Barton SS1 . . . . . . **168** C8
Hayes Chase SS11 . . . . . **101** A4
Hayes Cl
Chelmsford CM2 . . . . **32** B1
Grays RM20 . . . . **177** C8
Hayes Dr RM13 . . . . **155** B5
Hayes Farm Cvn Pk
SS11 . . . . **101** A4
Hayes Hill Farm★ EN9 . . . **43** C3
Hayes La SS8 . . . . **163** F3
Hayes Rd DA9 . . . . **176** E1
Hay Gn
Danbury CM3 . . . . **56** F8
Hornchurch RM11 . . . . . . **137** A5
Hay Green La CM15 . . . . . **72** A4
Hayle RM18 . . . . **175** C3
Hayley Cl RM16 . . . . **172** C3
Hayling Gr SS12 . . . . **122** A5
Haynes Park Ct RM11 . . . **136** C6
Haynes Rd RM11 . . . . . . **136** D6
Hayrick Cl SS16 . . . . **141** A4
Hayron's La CM1 . . . . **16** D8
Haysoms Cl RM1 . . . . **135** E7
Hayter Ct E11 . . . . **132** B2
Hay Terr RM20 . . . . **172** D1
Haywards RM15 . . . . **171** D7
Haywards Cl
Brentwood CM13 . . . . **95** E3
Ilford RM6 . . . . **134** C6
Haywards Ct 21 CM14 . . **116** C7
Haywood Ct EN9 . . . . **65** F5
Hazard Ho 2 DA11 . . . . . **179** A1
Hazelbrouck Gdns
IG6 . . . . **111** D3
Hazel Cl
Basildon SS15 . . . . **119** F2
Hadleigh SS7 . . . . **145** F3
Hornchurch RM12 . . . . . . **136** B1
Southend-on-S SS9 . . . . **146** C2
Hazel Ct
7 Chigwell IG6 . . . . **111** E5
Loughton IG10 . . . . **88** F6
Hazeldene Rd IG3 . . . . . . **134** B2
Hazeldon Cl CM3 . . . . **19** C6
Hazel Dr RM15 . . . . **157** D2
HAZELEIGH **58** A4
Hazeleigh CM13 . . . . **117** B7
Hazeleigh Gdns IG8 . . . . **110** E5
Hazeleigh Hall La CM3 . . . **58** C4
Hazel Gdns
Grays RM16 . . . . **173** E3
Sawbridgeworth CM21 . . . . **1** F1

Hazel Gr RM6 . . . . **134** E8
Hazel La IG6 . . . . **111** B3
Hazell Cres RM5 . . . . **113** B2
Hazelmere SS13 . . . . **143** B4
Hazelmere Gdns
RM11 . . . . **136** C6
Hazel Rise RM11 . . . . **136** C5
Hazelwood
Hockley SS5 . . . . **124** F4
Linford SS17 . . . . **175** A2
Loughton IG10 . . . . **88** D4
South Benfleet SS7 . . . . . **144** B7
Hazelwood Ct CM9 . . . . . . **37** B6
Hazelwood Gdns CM15 . . **94** A3
Hazelwood Gr SS9 . . . . . **146** E5
Hazelwood Ho E4 . . . . **87** D2
Hazelwood Park Cl 5
IG7 . . . . **111** E5
Hazlemere Rd SS7 . . . . . **144** D6
Headcorn Cl SS13 . . . . . . **143** C5
Headingham Ho SS6 . . . . **123** C1
Headingley Cl
Basildon SS13 . . . . **121** A2
Redbridge IG6 . . . . **111** F4
Headley App IG2 . . . . **133** B6
Headley Chase CM14 . . . **116** D6
Headley Comm CM13 . . . **116** B3
Headley Dr IG2 . . . . **133** B5
Headley Rd CM11 . . . . **97** C4
Head St CM9 . . . . **38** E6
Healey Ho RM6 . . . . **134** E7
Heard's La CM15 . . . . **94** F6
Hearn Rd RM1 . . . . **135** F5
Hearsall Ave
Chelmsford CM1 . . . . **32** B7
Stanford-le-H SS17 . . . . . **160** E2
Heath Cl
Billericay CM12 . . . . **96** F1
Romford RM2 . . . . **136** A8
Heathcote Ct IG5 . . . . **110** F1
Heathcote Gdns CM17 . . . . **24** E8
Heathcote Gr E4 . . . . **109** C8
Heathcote Sch
Chingford E4 . . . . **109** E8
Danbury CM3 . . . . **56** E7
Heathcroft Gdns E17 . . . **109** D2
Heathdene Dr DA17 . . . . **169** B2
Heath Dr
Chelmsford CM2 . . . . **54** B6
Romford RM2 . . . . **114** A1
Theydon Bois CM16 . . . . . . **67** C4
Heather Ave RM1 . . . . . . **113** D1
Heather Bank RM11 . . . . . **97** C2
Heather Cl
Canvey Island SS8 . . . . . **163** F2
Pilgrims Hatch CM15 . . . . **94** B4
Romford RM1 . . . . **113** D2
Heathercroft Rd SS11 . . . **122** A6
Heather Ct 10 CM1 . . . . . **32** F6
Heather Dr
Romford RM1 . . . . **113** E1
South Benfleet SS7 . . . . . **146** A2
Heather Gdns
Romford RM1 . . . . **113** E2
Waltham Abbey EN9 . . . . . . **65** C3
Heather Glen RM1 . . . . . . **113** D1
Heatherley Dr IG5 . . . . . . **132** F8
Heather Way RM1 . . . . . . **113** D1
Heatherwood Cl E12 . . . . **132** C2
Heathfield
Chingford E4 . . . . **109** C7
Rayleigh SS6 . . . . **123** C1
Thundersley SS7 . . . . **145** C6
Heathfield Park Dr
RM6 . . . . **134** B6
Heathfield Rd CM1 . . . . **32** B7
Heathlands RM2 . . . . **136** B6
Heathleigh Dr SS16 . . . . . **141** B4
HEATH PARK **136** C5
Heath Park Ct RM2 . . . . . **136** A6
Heath Park Ind Est
RM8 . . . . **134** E3
Heath Park Rd RM2 . . . . . **136** B6
Heath Rd
Billericay CM11 . . . . **97** F4
Chadwell St M RM16 . . . . **173** F1
Dagenham RM6 . . . . **134** E4
Grays RM16 . . . . **174** A3
Ramsden Heath CM11 . . . . **98** B4
Heathside Cl IG2 . . . . **133** B6
Heath Terr RM6 . . . . **134** D4
Heath View Gdns
RM16 . . . . **173** C3
Heath View Rd RM16 . . . . **173** C4
Heathway
Dagenham RM9,
RM10 . . . . **154** A6
Woodford IG8 . . . . **110** C5
Heaton Ave RM3 . . . . **114** B3
Heaton Cl
Chingford E4 . . . . **109** C7
Romford RM3 . . . . **114** C3
Heaton Grange Rd
RM2 . . . . **113** F1
Heaton Way RM3 . . . . . . **114** C3
Heavitree Cl E17 . . . . **109** B2
Heberden Ct 5 RM19 . . . **171** B1
Hedgehope Ave SS6 . . . . **123** D4
Hedge La SS7 . . . . **145** D4
Hedgeley IG4 . . . . **132** F7
Hedgemans Rd RM9 . . . . **153** E6
Hedgemans Way RM9 . . . **153** E6
Hedgemoor Ct 1 E4 . . . . **109** D5
Hedge Place Rd DA9 . . . . **176** F1

Hedgerow Ct SS15 . . . . . **119** F2
Hedgerows
Brentwood CM13 . . . . **95** E3
Sawbridgeworth CM21 . . . . **1** F2
Hedgerows Bsns Pk
CM2 . . . . **33** A6
Hedgerow The SS16 . . . . **142** E4
Hedgers Cl IG10 . . . . **89** A6
Hedgewood Gdns IG2,
IG5 . . . . **133** A6
Hedingham Dr SS12 . . . . **121** F6
Hedingham Pl SS4 . . . . . **125** D4
Hedingham Rd
Dagenham RM8 . . . . **153** B7
Grays RM16 . . . . **172** C1
Hornchurch RM11 . . . . . . **137** A3
Hedley Ave RM20 . . . . . . **177** C8
Hedley Cl 1 RM1 . . . . . . **135** E6
Heenan Cl 1 IG11 . . . . . . **152** C6
Heeswyk Rd SS8 . . . . **164** D5
Heideburg Rd SS8 . . . . . **164** D5
Heideck Gdns CM13 . . . . **117** B8
Heighams CM19 . . . . **22** F5
Heilsburg Rd SS8 . . . . . . **164** D5
Helena Ave SS8 . . . . **164** B5
Helena Cl SS5 . . . . **124** F5
Helena Ct CM3 . . . . **101** D6
Helena Rd SS6 . . . . **123** E3
Helen Ho 14 CM14 . . . . . **116** C7
Helen Rd RM11 . . . . **136** D8
Helford Ct RM15 . . . . **172** B6
Helford Way RM14 . . . . . **137** D5
Helions Rd CM19 . . . . **23** B8
Helleborine RM17 . . . . . . **172** F1
Hellendoorn Rd SS8 . . . . **164** D2
Helmons La CM2 . . . . **77** A4
Helmore Rd IG11 . . . . **152** F5
Helmores SS15 . . . . **140** F6
Helmsdale SS8 . . . . **163** F5
Helmsdale Cl RM1 . . . . . **113** E3
Helmsdale Rd RM1 . . . . . **113** E3
Helmsley 11 E18 . . . . **132** A8
Helmsley Ho 5 RM3 . . . . **114** E3
Helpeston SS14 . . . . **142** D6
Helston Rd CM1 . . . . **32** E6
Helwys Ct E4 . . . . **109** C4
Hemley Rd RM16 . . . . **174** D7
Hemmells SS15 . . . . **141** B8
Hemmells Pk SS15 . . . . . **119** A1
Hemmings Ct CM9 . . . . . . **58** E8
Hemnal Ho CM16 . . . . **67** E7
Hemnall St CM16 . . . . **67** F8
Hemnall Mews CM16 . . . . **46** A1
Hempstalls SS15 . . . . **141** F5
Hempstead Cl IG9 . . . . . . **110** A8
Hempstead Rd E17 . . . . . **109** D1
Henbane Path RM3 . . . . . **114** D3
Henderson Cl RM11 . . . . **136** B2
Henderson Dr DA1 . . . . . **176** A3
Henderson Gdns
SS12 . . . . **121** E5
Henderson Ho 7
RM10 . . . . **135** A1
Hendon Cl SS12 . . . . **121** D6
Hendon Gdns RM5 . . . . . **113** C4
Hengist Gdns SS11 . . . . . . **99** D1
Henham Cl CM11 . . . . **97** D2
Henham Ct RM5 . . . . **113** C1
Henley Cres SS0 . . . . **147** D4
Henley Ct IG1 . . . . **152** B8
Henley Gdns RM6 . . . . . . **134** E6
Henley Rd IG1 . . . . **152** D8
Henney Ct CM3 . . . . **80** F6
Henniker Gate CM2 . . . . . . **33** A4
Henry De Grey Cl
RM17 . . . . **172** F2
Henry Dr SS9 . . . . **146** B2
Henry Green Prim Sch
RM8 . . . . **134** D2
Henry Moore Prim Sch
The CM17 . . . . **24** D7
Henry Rd CM1 . . . . **32** B4
Henry's Ave IG8 . . . . **109** F5
Henry St 3 RM17 . . . . . . **178** C8
Henry's Wlk IG6 . . . . **111** D3
Henshawe Rd RM8 . . . . . **134** D1
Henson Ave SS8 . . . . **164** E3
Henwood Side IG8 . . . . . **110** F4
Hepburn Cl RM16 . . . . . . **172** D5
Hepworth Ct IG11 . . . . . . **153** A7
Hepworth Gdns IG11 . . . . **153** A7
Hepworth Ho IG8 . . . . . . **110** A7
Heralds Way CM3 . . . . . . **101** E2
Herbage Park Rd CM9 . . . **35** D1
Herbert Gdns RM6 . . . . . **134** D4
Herbert Gr SS1 . . . . **167** B7
Herbert Rd
Canvey Island SS8 . . . . . **164** C4
Hornchurch RM11 . . . . . . **136** F4
Ilford IG3 . . . . **133** E2
Southend-on-S SS3 . . . . **168** C6
Swanscombe DA10 . . . . . **177** F1
Herd La SS17 . . . . **161** C3
Hereford Ct CM2 . . . . **55** A5
Hereford Gdns IG1 . . . . . **132** E4
Hereford Rd E11 . . . . **132** B6
Hereford Wlk SS14 . . . . . **142** F7
Herent Dr IG5 . . . . **132** F8
Hereward Cl EN9 . . . . **65** C7
Hereward Gdns SS11 . . . . **99** D1
Hereward Gn IG10 . . . . . . **89** C8
Hereward Mount CM4 . . . . **75** C1

Hereward Prim Sch
IG10 . . . . **89** C8
Herewood Lincoln Ho
DA11 . . . . **178** D1
Herga Hyll RM16 . . . . **174** B8
Herington Gr CM13 . . . . . **95** A2
Herington House Sch
CM13 . . . . **95** B3
Heriot Ave E4 . . . . **109** A8
Heritage Ctr Mus The★
SS8 . . . . **163** D3
Heritage Quay DA12 . . . . **179** C1
Heritage Way
Latchingdon CM3 . . . . **82** B5
Rochford SS4 . . . . **125** E2
Hermes Dr CM0 . . . . **106** B5
Hermes Way SS3 . . . . . . **168** F8
Hermitage Ave SS7 . . . . . **145** A4
Hermitage Cl SS7 . . . . . . **145** A4
Hermitage Ct 3 E18 . . . . **132** A7
Hermitage Dr SS15 . . . . . **141** C7
Hermitage Rd SS0 . . . . . **166** E8
Hermitage Wlk E18 . . . . . **132** A7
Hermon Hill E11 . . . . **132** A7
Hernen Rd SS8 . . . . **164** C5
Hernshaw CM13 . . . . **117** D3
Heron Ave SS11 . . . . **121** F6
Heron Chase CM13 . . . . . **117** C3
Heron Cl
Buckhurst Hill IG9 . . . . . . **88** A1
Rayleigh SS6 . . . . **123** B2
Sawbridgeworth CM21 . . . . **1** D1
Heron Ct
Chipping Ongar CM5 . . . . . **49** A5
Ilford IG1 . . . . **133** B2
Heron Dale SS14 . . . . **142** D6
Heron Dr SG12 . . . . **8** C3
Heron Flight Ave
RM12 . . . . **155** B5
HERONGATE **117** E3
Herongate
South Benfleet SS7 . . . . . **144** B4
Southend-on-S SS3 . . . . **168** E8
Herongate Rd E12 . . . . . **132** C2
Heron Gdns SS6 . . . . **123** B3
Heron Mead EN3 . . . . **65** A1
Heron Mews IG1 . . . . **133** B2
Herons Ct SS14 . . . . **120** F1
Heronsgate Trad Est
SS14 . . . . **120** F2
Herons La CM5 . . . . **49** D3
Heronswood EN9 . . . . **65** E5
Herons Wood CM20 . . . . . **10** B2
Heronway
Brentwood CM13 . . . . **95** B1
Woodford IG8 . . . . **110** C6
Heron Way
Grays RM20 . . . . **172** B1
Heybridge CM9 . . . . **37** C5
Mayland CM3 . . . . **83** A8
Roydon CM19 . . . . **9** A1
Upminster RM14 . . . . **137** F3
Herringham Gn CM2 . . . . . **33** A4
Herringham Prim Sch
RM16 . . . . **174** B2
Herschell Rd SS9 . . . . . . **146** C1
Hertford Dr SS17 . . . . . . **142** C1
Hertford Rd
Barking IG11 . . . . **152** B5
Canvey Island SS8 . . . . . **163** F3
Hoddesdon EN11 . . . . **21** A7
Ilford IG2 . . . . **133** E5
Hertford Wlk 14 DA17 . . . **169** A1
Hesketh Rd E7 . . . . **132** A1
Hesselyn Dr RM13 . . . . . **155** B5
Hester Ct 5 RM10 . . . . . **154** A4
Hester Ho CM20 . . . . **10** C2
Hester Pl CM0 . . . . **106** C5
Hetton Ho 3 IG10 . . . . . . **88** E4
Hetzand Rd SS8 . . . . **164** F3
Hever Cl SS5 . . . . **124** D6
Hevingham Dr RM6 . . . . . **134** C6
Hewett Rd RM8 . . . . **153** D8
Hewetts Quay IG11 . . . . . **152** C4
Hewins Cl EN9 . . . . **65** C4
Hewitt Ho 2 E4 . . . . **109** D5
Hew Watt Rd RM16 . . . . . **174** A8
HEYBRIDGE
Ingatestone **74** A2
Maldon **37** B6
Heybridge App CM9 . . . . . **36** F5
HEYBRIDGE BASIN **37** D3
Heybridge Ct RM7 . . . . . **135** D5
Heybridge Dr
Ilford IG6 . . . . **133** D8
Redbridge IG6 . . . . **111** D1
Wickford SS12 . . . . **121** D6
Heybridge House Ind Est
CM9 . . . . **37** B4
Heybridge Prim Sch
CM9 . . . . **37** C5
Heybridge Rd CM4 . . . . . . **74** A2
Heybridge St CM9 . . . . . . **37** B5
Heycroft Prim Sch
SS2 . . . . **146** F7
Heycroft Rd
Hockley SS5 . . . . **124** F5
Southend-on-S SS9 . . . . **146** F6
Heycroft Way CM2 . . . . . . **54** C5
Heygate Ave SS1 . . . . . . **167** B7
Heymeads Ct CM9 . . . . . . **37** A5
Heynes Rd RM8 . . . . **153** C8
Heythrop The
Chelmsford CM2 . . . . **32** D4
Ingatestone CM4 . . . . **74** A3
Heywood Ct CM9 . . . . **37** B6
Heywood Way CM9 . . . . . . **37** B6
Hibbard Ho CM14 . . . . . . **116** C6

Hickling Cl SS9 ... 146 B6
Hickling Rd IG1 ... 152 B7
Hickman Ave E4 ... 109 C4
Hickman Rd RM6 ... 134 C4
Hicks Ct
  Dagenham RM10 ... 135 B1
  Grays RM17 ... 173 B1
Hickstars La CM12 ... 119 C7
Hides The CM20 ... 10 D1
Higham Ct [9] IG8 ... 110 A4
Higham Ho E4 ... 109 A4
Higham Rd IG8 ... 110 A4
Highams Chase CM9 ... 39 A8
HIGHAMS PARK ... 109 B3
Highams Park Sch
  E4 ... 109 D4
Highams Park Sta E4 ... 109 D4
Highams Rd SS5 ... 124 F6
Higham Station Ave
  E4 ... 109 B4
Highams The E17 ... 109 C2
Higham View CM16 ... 47 B5
High Ash Cl SS17 ... 175 A2
High Bank
  Basildon SS16 ... 140 F4
  Hullbridge SS5 ... 101 E4
High Barrets SS13 ... 143 A5
HIGH BEACH ... 88 B8
High Beech CE Prim Sch
  IG10 ... 88 A8
High Beeches SS7 ... 144 B3
High Beech Rd IG10 ... 88 B8
Highbourne Ct [2]
  EN11 ... 21 A6
Highbridge Ct [5] EN9 ... 65 B6
Highbridge Ho [6] EN9 ... 65 B6
Highbridge Rd IG11 ... 152 B4
High Bridge Rd CM2 ... 32 C1
Highbridge Ret Pk
  EN9 ... 65 B5
Highbridge St EN9 ... 65 B6
Highbury Ave EN11 ... 21 A8
Highbury Gdns IG3 ... 133 E2
High Chelmer [8] CM1 ... 32 C2
Highclere IG9 ... 110 B8
Highcliff Cres SS4 ... 125 D7
High Cliff Dr SS9 ... 165 F8
Highcliffe Cl SS11 ... 121 F8
Highcliffe Gdns IG4 ... 132 E6
Highcliffe Rd SS11 ... 121 F8
Highcliffe Way SS11 ... 121 F8
Highcliff Rd SS7 ... 163 E8
High Cloister CM11 ... 97 B2
Highcroft Point E17 ... 109 B2
HIGH EASTER ... 6 C2
High Easter Rd CM6 ... 15 C4
High Elms
  Chigwell IG7 ... 111 E6
  Harlow CM18 ... 23 F6
  Upminster RM14 ... 137 E3
  Woodford IG8 ... 110 A5
High Elms Rd SS5 ... 101 E1
Highfield
  Harlow CM18 ... 24 A7
  Hullbridge SS5 ... 101 E3
  Sawbridgeworth CM21 ... 1 E3
Highfield App CM11 ... 119 D8
Highfield Ave SS7 ... 145 C4
Highfield Cl
  Danbury CM3 ... 56 D6
  Romford RM5 ... 113 C4
  Southend-on-S SS0 ... 147 D2
Highfield Cloisters
  SS99 ... 146 C1
Highfield Cres
  Hornchurch RM12 ... 136 F2
  Rayleigh SS6 ... 123 D2
  Southend-on-S SS0 ... 147 D2
Highfield Ct
  Billericay CM11 ... 119 D7
  Wanstead E12 ... 132 C2
Highfield Dr SS0 ... 147 D2
Highfield Gdns
  Grays RM16 ... 173 D5
  Southend-on-S SS0 ... 147 D3
Highfield Gn CM16 ... 67 E8
Highfield Gr SS0 ... 147 D3
Highfield Link RM5 ... 113 D4
Highfield Pl CM16 ... 67 E8
Highfield Rd
  Billericay CM11 ... 119 D7
  Chelmsford CM1 ... 31 E4
  Hornchurch RM12 ... 136 F2
  Romford RM5 ... 113 C4
  Woodford IG8 ... 110 E3
Highfield Rise CM3 ... 83 A3
Highfields Mead CM3 ... 78 B8
Highfields Twrs RM5 ... 113 D5
Highfield Way
  Hornchurch RM12 ... 136 F2
  Southend-on-S SS0 ... 147 D3
High Gables IG10 ... 88 D4
Highgate Gr CM21 ... 1 D2
Highgrove CM15 ... 94 B3
Highgrove Ho [13]
  CM14 ... 116 C8
Highgrove Mews
  RM17 ... 173 C1
Highgrove Rd RM8 ... 153 C8
High House Est CM17 ... 11 F4
High House La RM18 ... 174 D3
High La CM17 ... 12 E6
Highland Ave
  Brentwood CM15 ... 94 D1
  Dagenham RM10 ... 135 C4
  Loughton IG10 ... 88 F3

Highland Ct E18 ... 110 B2
Highland Gr CM11 ... 97 B2
Highland Rd
  Basildon SS17 ... 142 B1
  Lower Nazeing EN9 ... 21 E1
Highlands Ave SS16 ... 142 D4
Highlands Bvd SS9 ... 146 A2
Highlands Cres SS13 ... 143 F6
Highlands Ct SS9 ... 146 B2
Highlands Dr CM9 ... 36 E2
Highlands Gdns IG1 ... 132 F3
Highlands Hill CM3 ... 83 D6
Highlands Prim Sch
  IG1 ... 132 F3
Highlands Rd
  Basildon SS13 ... 143 F6
  Rawreth SS11 ... 101 B2
HIGH LAVER ... 26 B6
High Mdw CM11 ... 97 C2
High Mdws IG7 ... 111 D5
Highmead SS6 ... 123 B2
High Mead
  Chigwell IG7 ... 111 C8
  Hockley SS5 ... 124 E5
Highmead Ct
  Brentwood CM15 ... 94 D1
  Rayleigh SS6 ... 123 C2
High Oaks SS13 ... 141 B3
High Oaks Lo [5] E18 ... 110 A1
HIGH ONGAR ... 49 D3
High Ongar Prim Sch
  CM5 ... 49 C4
High Ongar Rd
  (Chelmsford Rd)
  CM5 ... 49 B5
High Pastures
  Little Baddow CM3 ... 34 D3
  Sheering CM22 ... 12 D8
High Pavement SS14 ... 142 A6
High Rd
  Basildon, Laindon SS16,
    SS15 ... 141 B6
  Basildon, Pitsea SS16 ... 143 A4
  Basildon, Westley Heights
    SS16 ... 141 B2
  Chigwell IG7 ... 111 B7
  Corringham SS17 ... 161 C5
  Dagenham RM6, IG3 ... 134 C4
  Epping CM16 ... 67 D7
  Hockley SS5 ... 124 A5
  Hoddesdon EN10 ... 21 A4
  Horndon on t H SS17 ... 159 F3
  Ilford IG1 ... 133 B2
  Ilford, Seven Kings IG1,
    IG3 ... 133 E2
  Loughton IG10 ... 88 C3
  North Weald Bassett
    CM16 ... 47 B5
  Orsett RM16 ... 174 A8
  Rayleigh SS6 ... 123 C1
  South Benfleet SS7 ... 144 C3
  South Ockendon RM16 ... 172 A5
  Stanford-le-H SS17 ... 160 F1
  Thornwood CM16 ... 46 C4
  Woodford E18 ... 110 A2
High Rd N SS15 ... 119 C1
High Road Buckhurst Hill
  [2] IG9 ... 110 B8
High Road Woodford Gn
  IG8 ... 110 A6
HIGH RODING ... 5 F7
High Silver IG10 ... 88 D5
High St
  Aveley RM15 ... 171 D5
  Billericay CM12 ... 97 A2
  Bradwell on S CM0 ... 42 A2
  Brentwood CM14 ... 116 C8
  Burnham-on-C CM0 ... 106 A4
  Canewdon SS4 ... 104 D2
  Canvey Island SS8 ... 164 C4
  Chelmsford CM1 ... 32 B2
  Chipping Ongar CM5 ... 49 A3
  Epping CM16 ... 67 F8
  Gravesend DA11 ... 179 B1
  Grays RM17 ... 178 A8
  Great Baddow CM2 ... 54 F6
  Great Wakering SS3 ... 150 A4
  Greenhithe DA9 ... 177 B3
  Hadleigh SS7 ... 145 D3
  Harlow CM17 ... 11 C4
  Hatfield Broad Oak CM22 ... 3 F6
  Hoddesdon EN11 ... 21 A5
  Hornchurch RM11,
    RM12 ... 136 D3
  Ilford IG6 ... 133 C8
  Ingatestone CM4 ... 74 B3
  Little Wakering SS3 ... 149 F4
  Maldon CM9 ... 37 A2
  Northfleet RM17 ... 178 C4
  Purfleet RM19 ... 171 A1
  Rayleigh SS6 ... 123 D2
  Redbridge IG6 ... 111 C1
  Romford RM1 ... 135 E6
  Roydon CM19 ... 9 B1
  South Benfleet SS7 ... 144 D1
  Southend-on-S, Leigh-on-S
    SS9 ... 165 D8
  Southend-on-S, Shoeburyness
    SS3 ... 168 F6
  Southend-on-S, Shoeburyness
    SS3 ... 168 G7
  Southend-on-S SS1 ... 167 A8
  Southminster CM0 ... 84 A4
  Stanford-le-H SS17 ... 160 C1
  Stanstead Abbotts SG12 ... 8 C3
  Stock CM4 ... 75 D3
  Swanscombe DA10 ... 177 F2
  Wanstead E11 ... 132 A6

High St continued
  Wickford SS12 ... 121 D7
Highstone Ave E11 ... 132 A5
Highstone Ct [4] E11 ... 132 A5
High Trees DA2 ... 176 B1
Hightrees CM4 ... 75 D2
Highview SS5 ... 101 E4
High View CM0 ... 62 C8
Highview Ave SS16 ... 140 F5
High View Ave RM17 ... 173 C1
Highview Cres CM13 ... 95 C3
Highview Ct [3] IG8 ... 110 A4
High View Ct SS7 ... 144 D2
High View Gdns
  RM17 ... 173 C1
Highview Ho IG9 ... 110 D7
High View Ho RM6 ... 134 E7
High View Par [1] IG4 ... 132 F5
Highview Rd SS7 ... 145 A7
High View Rd E18 ... 109 F1
High View Rise CM11 ... 120 C5
HIGHWOOD ... 52 A4
Highwood IG8 ... 109 F6
Highwood Cl
  Brentwood CM14 ... 94 B2
  Southend-on-S SS9 ... 146 F4
Highwood Cotts CM5 ... 51 E3
Highwood Gdns
  Ilford IG5 ... 133 A7
  Redbridge IG5 ... 132 F7
High Wood Hospl
  CM14 ... 94 C1
Highwood La IG10 ... 89 A3
Highwood Prim Sch
  CM1 ... 52 A4
Highwood Rd
  Edney Common CM1 ... 52 C6
  Roxwell CM1 ... 51 F4
High Wood Rd EN11 ... 8 A1
HIGH WYCH ... 1 B1
High Wych CE Prim Sch
  CM21 ... 1 A1
High Wych La CM21 ... 1 A2
High Wych Rd
  Gilston CM21 ... 10 F7
  High Wych CM21 ... 1 B1
Hilary Cl
  Hornchurch RM12 ... 155 D7
  Rochford SS4 ... 125 E5
Hilary Cres SS6 ... 123 E2
Hilary Dennis Ct E18 ... 132 A7
Hilberry Rd SS8 ... 164 D3
Hilda May Ct RM18 ... 179 C5
Hildaville Dr SS0 ... 147 C2
Hillary Cl
  Chelmsford CM1 ... 32 D4
  Heybridge CM9 ... 37 B5
Hillary Mount CM12 ... 97 A1
Hill Ave SS11 ... 121 F8
Hillboro Ct [1] E18 ... 109 F2
Hillborough Mans
  SS0 ... 147 D3
Hillborough Rd SS0 ... 147 D3
Hill Cl SS7 ... 144 E4
Hillcourt RM11 ... 136 F2
Hill Cres
  Chelmsford CM2 ... 32 D2
  Hornchurch RM11 ... 136 C5
Hillcrest CM3 ... 61 A1
Hillcrest Ave
  Basildon SS16 ... 140 E3
  Grays RM20 ... 177 A8
  Hullbridge SS5 ... 101 E1
Hillcrest Cl SS17 ... 159 F4
Hillcrest Ct RM5 ... 113 C2
Hillcrest Dr DA9 ... 177 A2
Hillcrest Rd
  Chingford E17 ... 109 D1
  Hockley SS5 ... 124 E5
  Hornchurch RM11 ... 136 A4
  Horndon on t H SS17 ... 159 F4
  Loughton IG10 ... 88 D3
  Southend-on-S SS7 ... 167 B8
  South Woodham Ferrers
    CM3 ... 101 C7
  Woodford E18 ... 110 A1
Hill Crest Rd CM5 ... 47 E1
Hillcrest View SS16 ... 142 D3
Hillcrest Way CM16 ... 68 A8
Hillcroft IG10 ... 89 A7
Hill Ct RM1 ... 135 F7
Hilldene Ave RM3 ... 114 D5
Hilldene Cl RM3 ... 114 D5
Hilldene Prim Sch
  RM3 ... 114 C4
Hillfoot Ave RM5 ... 113 C4
Hillfoot Rd RM5 ... 113 C2
Hill Gr RM1 ... 135 E8
Hillgrove Bsns Pk
  EN10 ... 21 C1
Hill Hall* CM16 ... 68 F4
Hillhouse EN9 ... 65 F6
Hillhouse CE Prim Sch
  EN9 ... 65 F6
Hillhouse Cl CM12 ... 97 B4
Hillhouse Dr CM12 ... 97 B4
Hill House Dr RM16 ... 174 C1
Hill House Rd DA2 ... 176 C1
Hillington Gdns IG8 ... 110 D1
Hill La SS5 ... 124 D6
Hillman Cl RM11 ... 136 D8
Hill Rd
  Brentwood CM14 ... 116 A7
  Chelmsford CM2 ... 32 D2
  South Benfleet SS7 ... 144 E4

Hill Rd continued
  Southend-on-S SS2 ... 147 F2
  Theydon Bois CM16 ... 67 C2
Hill Rd S CM2 ... 32 D2
Hill Rise RM14 ... 137 A2
Hillrise Rd RM5 ... 113 C4
Hill's Chace CM14 ... 116 C6
Hillside
  Belvedere DA8 ... 169 C2
  Grays RM17 ... 173 D2
  Harlow CM17 ... 24 C6
Hillside Ave
  Hockley SS5 ... 124 F5
  Woodford IG8 ... 110 C5
Hillside Cl
  Billericay CM11 ... 97 B1
  Woodford IG8 ... 110 C5
Hillside Cres
  Southend-on-S SS9 ... 166 A8
  Stanstead Abbotts SG12 ... 8 B4
Hillside Gr CM2 ... 54 A7
Hillside La SG12 ... 8 A5
Hillside Mews CM2 ... 54 A7
Hillside Rd
  Billericay CM11 ... 97 B1
  Burnham-on-C CM0 ... 106 B5
  Hockley SS5 ... 124 D5
  Rayleigh SS9 ... 146 C8
  South Benfleet SS7 ... 144 C1
  Southend-on-S SS9 ... 165 E8
  Southminster CM0 ... 84 C4
Hillside Wlk CM14 ... 115 F7
Hill's Rd IG9 ... 88 B1
Hill Terr
  Corringham SS17 ... 161 C3
  Woodford IG8 ... 110 E3
Hill The
  Harlow CM17 ... 11 C4
  Northfleet DA11 ... 178 C1
Hill Top IG10 ... 89 A6
Hilltop Ave SS5 ... 101 E1
Hill Top Ave SS7 ... 144 F2
Hilltop Cl SS6 ... 123 C1
Hill Top Cl IG10 ... 89 A6
Hilltop Cotts [9][8] CM16 ... 68 F5
Hill Top Ct IG8 ... 110 F4
Hilltop Jun & Inf Sch
  SS11 ... 122 A8
Hilltop Rd
  Basildon SS15 ... 141 E7
  Grays RM20 ... 177 B8
Hill Top Rise SS16 ... 140 F4
Hill Top View IG8 ... 110 F4
Hill Tree Cl CM21 ... 1 D1
Hill View CM3 ... 56 F1
Hillview Ave RM11 ... 136 D5
Hill View Cl CM0 ... 84 C4
Hillview Cres IG1 ... 132 F5
Hillview Gdns SS17 ... 160 F5
Hillview Rd SS6 ... 123 C3
Hill View Rd CM1 ... 32 C4
Hillway
  Billericay CM11 ... 97 D2
  Southend-on-S SS0 ... 166 A8
Hillway The CM15 ... 95 E8
Hill Way The CM4 ... 73 F1
Hillwood Cl CM13 ... 95 B1
Hillwood Gr
  Brentwood CM13 ... 95 B1
  Wickford SS11 ... 121 E7
Hilly Field CM18 ... 23 F4
Hillyfields IG10 ... 89 A7
Hilly Rd SS15 ... 141 D7
Hilton Rd SS8 ... 164 A5
Hilton Wlk SS8 ... 164 A5
Hilversum Way SS8 ... 164 B5
Hind Cl IG7 ... 111 F5
Hindles Rd SS8 ... 164 D4
Hindmans Way RM9 ... 153 F1
Hind Terr RM20 ... 172 D1
Hinguar Com Prim Sch
  SS3 ... 168 F6
Hinguar St SS3 ... 168 F6
Hintons CM19 ... 23 A4
Hispano Mews EN3 ... 65 A2
Hitchin Cl RM3 ... 114 C6
Hitchman Ho RM5 ... 113 C4
Hither Blakers CM3 ... 101 D8
Hitherfield Rd RM8 ... 134 E2
Hitherwood Cl RM12 ... 155 D8
Hive Cl CM14 ... 116 A8
Hive La DA11 ... 178 B2
Hive The DA11 ... 178 B1
Hobart Cl CM1 ... 31 E5
Hobart Ct IG8 ... 109 E4
Hobart Rd
  Dagenham RM9 ... 153 D8
  Redbridge IG6 ... 111 C1
  Tilbury RM18 ... 179 A1
Hobbiton Hill CM3 ... 101 C6
HOBBS CROSS
  Epping ... 68 D3
  Harlow ... 12 A1
Hobbs Cross Cotts
  CM16 ... 68 D3
Hobbs Cross Rd
  Epping CM16 ... 68 C4
  Harlow CM17 ... 11 F3
Hobbs Mews IG3 ... 133 F2
Hobhouse Rd SS17 ... 160 D4
Hobleythick La SS0 ... 147 C5
Hobtoe Rd CM20 ... 10 A1
HOCKLEY ... 124 D6
Hockley Cl
  Basildon SS14 ... 142 D6
  Bradwell on S CM0 ... 42 C2
Hockley Ct [2] E18 ... 110 A2
Hockley Dr RM2 ... 114 C1

Hockley Gn SS14 ... 142 E6
Hockley La CM0 ... 42 C2
Hockley Mews IG11 ... 152 E2
Hockley Prim Sch
  SS5 ... 124 C6
Hockley Rd
  Basildon SS14 ... 142 D6
  Rayleigh SS6 ... 123 E4
Hockley Rise SS5 ... 124 E5
Hockley Sta SS5 ... 124 E6
Hockley Woods*
  SS5 ... 124 C4
HODDESDON ... 21 C7
Hoddesdon Ind Ctr
  EN11 ... 21 C7
Hoddesdon Rd
  Belvedere DA17 ... 169 A1
  Stanstead Abbotts SG12 ... 8 C3
Hodges Cl RM16 ... 172 D1
Hodgson Ct SS11 ... 122 A5
Hodgson Way SS11 ... 122 B6
Hodings Rd CM20 ... 10 C2
Hodson Pl [1] EN3 ... 65 A1
Hoecroft EN9 ... 21 F1
Hoe La
  Abridge RM4 ... 90 C4
  Great Waltham CM3 ... 18 E6
  Lower Nazeing EN9 ... 22 A2
  Rettendon CM3 ... 100 A6
Hoe Mill Rd CM9 ... 35 E4
Hoe St CM1 ... 30 D4
Hoestock Rd CM21 ... 1 D2
Hoe The CM12 ... 119 B4
Hoffmanns Way CM1 ... 32 B4
Hogarth Ave CM15 ... 116 F7
Hogarth Ct CM1 ... 32 E6
Hogarth Dr SS3 ... 168 G8
Hogarth Prim Sch
  CM15 ... 116 F7
Hogarth Rd
  Dagenham RM8 ... 153 B7
  Grays RM16 ... 173 A5
Hogarth Reach IG10 ... 88 F4
Hogarth Way SS4 ... 125 C6
Hogges Cl [16] EN11 ... 21 A6
Hog Hill Rd RM5 ... 113 A3
Hogwell Chase
  Hullbridge CM3 ... 102 B8
  South Woodham Ferrers
    CM3 ... 80 B1
Holbech Rd SS14 ... 142 F8
Holbek Rd SS8 ... 164 E3
Holbrook Cl
  Billericay CM11 ... 97 D2
  South Woodham Ferrers
    CM3 ... 101 E7
Holbrook Ho SS7 ... 145 E3
Holcombe Rd IG1 ... 133 A4
HOLDBROOK ... 65 A5
Holdbrook Way RM3 ... 114 F1
Holden Cl RM8 ... 134 B1
Holden Gdns
  Basildon SS14 ... 120 F1
  Brentwood CM14 ... 116 D5
Holden Rd SS14 ... 120 F1
Holden Way RM14 ... 137 D4
Holden Wlk SS14 ... 120 F1
Holecroft EN9 ... 65 C9
Hole Haven Cvn Pk
  SS8 ... 163 C1
Holford Rd SS17,
  RM18 ... 174 E4
Holgate SS13 ... 143 C8
Holgate Ct [9] RM1 ... 135 E6
Holgate Gdns RM10 ... 154 A6
Holgate Rd RM10 ... 154 A7
Holkham Ave CM3 ... 101 D5
Holland Ave SS8 ... 163 D5
Holland Cl RM7 ... 135 C6
Holland Ho E4 ... 109 C6
Holland Park Ave IG3 ... 133 F6
Holland Rd
  Southend-on-S SS0 ... 166 D7
  Wallend E6 ... 152 A5
Hollands Wlk SS16 ... 142 D2
Holland Way CM17 ... 11 D1
Holley Gdns CM11 ... 97 B3
Holliday Hill CM2 ... 76 F4
Hollidge Way RM10 ... 154 B5
Hollies RM14 ... 137 B2
Hollies The
  Stanford-le-H SS17 ... 160 D1
  [9] Wanstead E11 ... 132 A6
Hollis Lock CM2 ... 33 A3
Hollis Pl RM17 ... 173 A2
Holloway Cl CM6 ... 15 C7
Holloway Cres CM6 ... 15 C8
Holloway Rd CM9 ... 37 A5
Hollow Cotts RM19 ... 171 A1
Hollowfield Ave
  RM17 ... 173 D2
Hollow La CM1 ... 31 E8
Hollow The IG8 ... 109 F6
Hollybank SS16 ... 140 F4
Hollybush Cl E11 ... 132 A6
Hollybush Hill E11 ... 132 A6
Holly Cl
  Buckhurst Hill IG9 ... 110 D7
  Burnham-on-C CM0 ... 106 B6
Holly Cotts CM16 ... 68 F5
Holly Cres IG8 ... 109 D3
Hollycroft CM2 ... 55 B6
Hollycross Rd SG12 ... 8 B7

Holly Ct
Billericay CM12 . . . . **97** A2
Hockley SS5 . . . . **124** E5
Northfleet DA11 . . . . **178** B1
Holly Dr
Chingford E4 . . . . **87** B2
South Ockendon RM15 . . . **157** D1
Hollyfield CM19 . . . . **23** C5
Hollyford CM11 . . . . **97** C5
Holly Hill Rd DA17 . . . . . . **169** B1
Holly Ho
Brentwood CM15 . . . . **94** D1
Ilford IG3 . . . . **134** A3
Holly Ho Hospl IG9 . . . . . . **110** B8
Hollymead SS17 . . . . **160** E4
Holly Tree Gdns SS6 . . . . **145** B8
Holly Trees Prim Sch
CM14 . . . . **116** B6
Holly Way CM2 . . . . **54** D7
Holly Wlk SS8 . . . . **163** H4
Hollywood Cl CM2 . . . . **54** E6
Hollywood Way IG8 . . . . . **109** D4
Holmans CM3 . . . . **33** E8
Holme Rd RM11 . . . . **137** A3
Holmes Cl SS17 . . . . **159** F3
Holmes Ct
Canvey Island SS8 . . . . . . **164** C4
Chingford E4 . . . . **109** D8
Holmes Mdw CM19 . . . . . . **23** B2
Holme Wlk SS12 . . . . **121** F5
Holmhurst Rd DA17 . . . . . **169** B1
Holmsdale Cl SS0 . . . . **147** C3
Holmswood SS3 . . . . **164** E5
Holmwood Ave CM15 . . . . . **95** A3
Holmwood Rd IG3 . . . . . . **133** E2
Holst Ave SS15 . . . . **141** C8
Holst Cl SS17 . . . . **160** C3
Holstock Rd IG1 . . . . **133** C2
Holsworthy SS3 . . . . **168** D8
Holsworthy Ho RM3 . . . . . **114** D2
Holt Cl IG7 . . . . **111** F5
Holt Farm Inf Sch
SS4 . . . . **125** D3
Holt Farm Jun Sch
SS4 . . . . **125** D3
Holt Farm Way SS4 . . . . . **125** D4
Holton Rd
Canvey Island SS8 . . . . . . **164** F3
Rayleigh SS6 . . . . **124** A4
Holt Rd RM3 . . . . **114** E3
Holt The IG6 . . . . **111** C4
Holt Way IG7 . . . . **111** F5
Holtynge SS7 . . . . **144** C4
Holy Acre CM19 . . . . **9** A1
Holybread La CM3 . . . . **34** C4
Holy Cross RC Prim Sch
Harlow CM18 . . . . **24** A6
South Ockendon RM15 . . . **172** B7
Holy Family RC Prim Sch
SS7 . . . . **144** D5
HOLYFIELD **43** C3
Holyfield Hall Farm★
EN9 . . . . **43** C4
Holyfield Rd EN9 . . . . **43** D2
Holyoak La SS5 . . . . **124** E4
Holyrood Dr SS0 . . . . **147** B2
Holyrood Gdns RM16 . . . . **174** C2
Homebush Rd E4 . . . . **87** B2
Homecherry Ho 6
IG10 . . . . **88** D4
Home Cl CM20 . . . . **23** F8
Homecove Ho SS0 . . . . . . **166** D7
Homecroft Gdns IG10 . . . . **89** B5
Home Farm Cl SS3 . . . . . . **150** B4
Home Farm Ind Pk SG12 . . **8** F5
Home Farm Rd RM18 . . . . **116** E2
Homefield
Southminster CM0 . . . . **84** E5
Waltham Abbey EN9 . . . . . . **66** A7
Homefield Ave IG2 . . . . . . **133** E6
Homefield Cl
Billericay CM11 . . . . **119** D6
Chelmsford CM1 . . . . **31** D5
Epping CM16 . . . . **46** A1
Homefields CM17 . . . . **12** F3
Homefields Ave SS7 . . . . . **144** B5
Home Gdns RM10 . . . . **135** C1
Homeheather Ho 5
IG4 . . . . **132** F6
Homeholly Ho SS11 . . . . . . **99** D2
Homehurst Ho CM15 . . . . . **94** D1
Homelands Gr CM11 . . . . . **98** C4
Homemead 5 DA9 . . . . . . **177** B1
Home Mead
Basildon SS15 . . . . **141** B8
Galleywood CM2 . . . . **54** C2
Harlow CM18 . . . . **23** D6
Writtle CM1 . . . . **31** A1
Homesdale Cl E11 . . . . **132** A6
Homes Of Rest IG1 . . . . . **133** D1
Homestead CM1 . . . . **32** B7
Homestead Ct SS7 . . . . . . **145** D3
Homestead Dr SS16 . . . . . **141** C2
Homestead Gdns SS7 . . . **145** D2
Homestead Rd
Basildon, Bowers Gifford
SS13 . . . . **143** E7
Dagenham RM8 . . . . **134** F2
Hadleigh SS7 . . . . **145** D2
Ramsden Heath SS13 . . . . **120** D8
Homesteads The SG12 . . . . **9** D8
Homestead Way SS7 . . . . **145** D3
Homeway RM3 . . . . **115** B4

Honey Brook EN9 . . . . **65** E6
Honey Cl
Chelmsford CM2 . . . . **54** D6
Dagenham RM10 . . . . **154** B6
Wyatts Green CM15 . . . . . . **72** D4
Honeycombe Lo
DA11 . . . . **178** D1
Honeycroft IG10 . . . . **89** B5
Honey La EN9 . . . . **65** E5
Honeymeade CM21 . . . . **11** C7
Honeypot La
Basildon SS14 . . . . **142** B6
Brentwood CM14 . . . . **116** A8
Stock CM4 . . . . **75** C1
Waltham Abbey EN9 . . . . . **66** C5
Honey Pot La CM3 . . . . **80** D3
Honeypots CM2 . . . . **54** C6
Honeysuckle Cl
Pilgrims Hatch CM15 . . . . . **94** B4
Romford RM3 . . . . **114** C4
Honeysuckle Ct 1
IG11 . . . . **152** B6
Honeysuckle Path 9
CM1 . . . . **32** F6
Honey Tree Ct IG10 . . . . . . **89** B7
Honiley Ave SS12 . . . . **121** E3
Honington Cl SS11 . . . . . . **122** B6
Honiton Rd
Romford RM7 . . . . **135** D5
Southend-on-S SS1 . . . . . **167** C8
Honor Link CM1 . . . . **33** A7
Honor St 7 CM17 . . . . **11** D1
Honywood Bsns Pk
SS14 . . . . **120** F2
Honywood Rd SS14 . . . . . **120** F2
Hood Cl SS12 . . . . **121** E6
Hood Lo E11 . . . . **132** B2
Hood Rd RM13 . . . . **154** F3
Hood Wlk RM7 . . . . **113** B2
HOOK END **72** C4
Hook End La CM15 . . . . . . **72** C5
Hook End Rd CM15 . . . . . . **72** C4
Hook Field CM18 . . . . **23** F6
Hook La RM4 . . . . **91** A3
Hooks Hall Dr RM10 . . . . . **135** C1
Hookstone Way IG8 . . . . . **110** D3
Hooley Dr SS6 . . . . **123** C6
Hoo The CM17 . . . . **11** C5
Hoover Dr SS15 . . . . **140** F6
Hope Ave SS17 . . . . **160** E5
Hope Cl
Ilford RM6 . . . . **134** D7
Mountnessing CM15 . . . . . . **95** E8
2 Woodford IG8 . . . . **110** C4
Hope Rd
Canvey Island SS8 . . . . . . **164** D3
Crays Hill CM11 . . . . **120** C5
South Benfleet SS7 . . . . . **144** D2
Swanscombe DA10 . . . . . . **177** F1
HOPE'S GREEN **144** C2
Hope Terr RM20 . . . . **172** D1
Hopewell Ct RM16 . . . . . . **172** D1
Hop Gardens La CM9 . . . . . **35** F4
Hop Gdns CM5 . . . . **70** A7
Hopkins Cl
Chelmsford CM2 . . . . **33** A3
Romford RM2 . . . . **136** C8
Hopkins Mead CM2 . . . . . . **33** A2
Hopkirk Cl CM3 . . . . **56** F8
Hoppet The CM4 . . . . **74** C4
Hoppett Rd E4 . . . . **109** E8
Hopping Jacks La CM3 . . . **56** F7
Hoppit Rd EN9 . . . . **65** B7
Hoppitt The CM5 . . . . **26** C3
Hopps Ho 4 EN11 . . . . **21** A6
Horace Ave RM7 . . . . **135** D3
Horace Rd
Billericay CM11 . . . . **97** C4
Ilford IG6 . . . . **133** C8
Southend-on-S SS1 . . . . . **167** B7
Horkesley Way SS12 . . . . **121** E6
Horksley Gdns CM13 . . . . . **95** C3
Hornbeam Ave RM14 . . . . **156** A8
Hornbeam Chase
RM15 . . . . **157** D2
Hornbeam Cl
5 Barking IG11 . . . . **153** B2
2 Brentwood CM13 . . . . . **117** B7
Buckhurst Hill IG9 . . . . . . **110** D7
Chelmsford CM2 . . . . **54** A6
Ilford IG1 . . . . **152** D7
Theydon Bois CM16 . . . . . **67** E2
Hornbeam Gr E4 . . . . **109** F7
Hornbeam Ho IG9 . . . . **110** D7
Hornbeam La E4 . . . . **87** E4
Hornbeam Rd
Buckhurst Hill IG10 . . . . . . **110** D7
Theydon Bois CM16 . . . . . **67** D2
Hornbeams SS7 . . . . **144** B8
Hornbeams The CM20 . . . . **10** C2
Hornbeam Way SS15 . . . . **119** D1
Hornby Ave SS0 . . . . **147** D5
Hornby Cl SS0 . . . . **147** D5
HORNCHURCH **136** C2
Hornchurch Cl SS11 . . . . . **122** A6
Hornchurch Ctry Pk★
RM12 . . . . **155** D6
Hornchurch Rd RM11 . . . . **136** B3
Hornchurch Sports Stad
RM14 . . . . **137** A2
Hornchurch Sta
RM12 . . . . **136** D1
Horndon Cl RM5 . . . . **113** C2
Horndon Gn RM5 . . . . **113** C2
Horndon Ind Pk
CM13 . . . . **139** C5

HORNDON ON THE HILL
. . . . **159** E3
Horndon on the Hill CE
Prim Sch SS17 . . . . **159** F4
Horndon Rd
Horndon on t H SS17 . . . **160** A1
Romford RM5 . . . . **113** C2
HORNE ROW **56** D5
Horne Row CM3 . . . . **56** D5
Horner's Cnr SS3 . . . . **149** F4
Hornet Way CM0 . . . . **106** B5
Hornford Way RM7 . . . . . . **135** E4
Horn La IG8 . . . . **110** A3
Hornminster Glen
RM11 . . . . **137** A2
Hornsby La CM3 . . . . **174** A5
Hornsby Sq SS15 . . . . **140** F7
Hornsby Way SS15 . . . . . . **140** F7
Horns Croft IG11 . . . . **152** E5
Hornsland Rd SS8 . . . . . . **164** E3
Horns Rd IG2, IG6 . . . . . . **133** C6
Horsebridge Cl RM9 . . . . . **153** E4
Horsecroft CM5 . . . . **14** D2
Horsecroft Pl CM19 . . . . . . **22** E7
Horsecroft Rd CM19 . . . . . **22** E7
Horse & Groom La
CM2 . . . . **54** A3
Horseman Ct CM15 . . . . . . **71** F2
HORSEMAN SIDE **92** E5
Horseman Side CM14 . . . . . **92** D3
Horseshoe Cl
Billericay CM12 . . . . **97** A5
Waltham Abbey EN9 . . . . . . **66** A5
Horseshoe Cres SS3 . . . . **168** F6
Horseshoe Ct SG12 . . . . **8** D4
Horseshoe Hill EN9 . . . . . . **66** C7
Horseshoe Lawns
SS5 . . . . **101** E4
Horshams CM19 . . . . **23** C8
Horsley Cross SS14 . . . . . **142** B7
Horsley Rd E4 . . . . **109** C8
Hortus Rd E4 . . . . **109** C8
Hospital App CM1 . . . . **19** B3
Hospital Cotts CM14 . . . . . **116** B6
HOSPITAL HILL **111** B3
Hospital Rd SS3 . . . . **168** F6
Houblon Dr CM2 . . . . **54** C2
Houblons Hill
Coopersale CM16 . . . . **46** D1
Epping CM16 . . . . **46** D1
Houchin Dr CM5 . . . . **27** D2
HOUSHAM TYE **12** D2
Hove Cl
Brentwood CM13 . . . . **117** C8
Grays RM17 . . . . **178** A8
Hovefields Ave SS12 . . . . **121** D3
Hovefields Ct SS13 . . . . . **121** D2
Hovefields Cvn Pk
SS13 . . . . **121** C2
Hovefields Dr SS12 . . . . . **121** D3
Hoveton Way IG6 . . . . **111** B3
Howard Bsns Pk EN9 . . . . . **65** D6
Howard Chase SS14 . . . . . **142** A8
Howard Cl
Loughton IG10 . . . . **88** E3
Waltham Abbey EN9 . . . . . . **65** D5
Howard Cres SS13 . . . . . . **143** C5
Howard Ct 12 IG11 . . . . . . **152** D4
Howard Dr CM2 . . . . **33** A2
Howard Lodge Rd
CM14 . . . . **71** C2
Howard Pl SS8 . . . . **164** B2
Howard Rd
Barking IG11 . . . . **152** D4
Dartford RM1 . . . . **176** A1
Grays RM16 . . . . **172** C3
Ilford IG1 . . . . **152** B8
Upminster RM14 . . . . **137** D2
Howards Chase SS0 . . . . . **147** F2
Howards Cl CM3 . . . . **33** E8
Howards Ct SS0 . . . . **166** E8
Howard Way CM20 . . . . **10** F2
Howburgh Ct 7
RM19 . . . . **171** B1
Howe Cl RM7 . . . . **113** A4
HOWEGREEN **80** D8
HOWE GREEN **55** C3
Howe Green Rd CM3 . . . . . . **80** E7
Howell Cl RM6 . . . . **134** D6
Howell Rd SS17 . . . . **160** H6
Howerd Ho 10 CM14 . . . . **116** C6
Howfield Gn EN11 . . . . **8** A1
Howlett Hts SS9 . . . . **146** C7
Howse Rd EN9 . . . . **65** B4
Hows Mead CM16 . . . . **47** D7
Hoylake Gdns RM3 . . . . . . **115** A3
Hoynors CM3 . . . . **57** A7
Hubbard Ct IG10 . . . . **88** E2
Hubbards Chase
RM11 . . . . **137** A6
Hubbards Cl RM11 . . . . . . **137** B6
Hubert Rd
Brentwood CM14 . . . . **116** B7
Rainham RM13 . . . . **154** F3
Hucknall Cl RM3 . . . . **114** F4
Hudson Cres SS9 . . . . **146** E6
Hudson Ct SS9 . . . . **146** E6
Hudson Rd SS9 . . . . **146** D6
Hudsons Cl SS17 . . . . **160** D3
Hudson Way SS8 . . . . **164** A6
Huggens's Coll
(Almshouses) DA11 . . . . **178** B2
Hughes Rd RM16 . . . . **174** A3
Hugh's Twr 4 CM20 . . . . . **10** D1
Hugo Gdns 5 RM13 . . . . . **155** A6
HULLBRIDGE **101** D2
Hullbridge Rd
Rayleigh SS6 . . . . **123** D7

Hullbridge Rd continued
South Woodham Ferrers
CM3 . . . . **101** D6
Hullett's La CM15 . . . . **93** F4
Hull Gn CM17 . . . . **13** D2
Hull Gr CM19 . . . . **23** A3
Hull's La CM2 . . . . **55** E7
Hulse Ave
Barking IG11 . . . . **152** E6
Romford RM7 . . . . **113** B2
Hulton Cl CM3 . . . . **33** E8
Humber Ave RM15 . . . . . . **171** F7
Humber Cl SS6 . . . . **123** C1
Humber Dr RM14 . . . . **137** D5
Humber Rd CM1 . . . . **32** C5
Humber Rd RM18 . . . . **179** B5
Hume Cl RM18 . . . . **179** A4
Humphrey Cl IG5 . . . . **110** F2
Humphrey's Farm La
CM3 . . . . **18** C7
Humphries CM9 . . . . **153** F8
Hungerdown E4 . . . . **87** C1
Hungerford Ho 4
RM3 . . . . **115** A4
HUNSDONBURY **9** C7
Hunsdon Cl RM9 . . . . **153** E6
Hunsdon Rd SG12 . . . . **8** E5
Hunsdon Road Cotts
SG12 . . . . **8** E5
Hunt Ave CM9 . . . . **37** B5
Hunter Ave CM15 . . . . **95** A3
Hunter Ct 11 E11 . . . . **132** A6
Hunter Dr
Hornchurch RM12 . . . . . . **155** C8
Wickford SS12 . . . . **121** E6
Hunters Ave CM12 . . . . . . **119** B7
Hunters Chase
Brentwood CM13 . . . . **96** C2
Chipping Ongar CM5 . . . . . **49** A1
Hunter's Gr RM5 . . . . **113** B5
Hunters Hall Prim Sch
RM10 . . . . **154** B7
Hunters Hall Rd
RM10 . . . . **154** A7
Hunters Rd IG1 . . . . **152** B7
Hunters Sq RM10 . . . . **154** A8
Hunters Way IG1 . . . . **152** B7
Hunters Wlk 4 CM14 . . . . **116** C8
Huntingdon Rd SS1 . . . . . **167** D7
Huntings Farm IG1 . . . . . . **133** E2
Huntings Rd RM10 . . . . . . **154** A6
Huntland Cl RM13 . . . . **170** B8
Huntley Ave DA11 . . . . **178** C1
Hunt's Cl CM1 . . . . **53** B8
Hunt's Dr CM1 . . . . **53** B8
Hunts Hill Cotts
RM14 . . . . **156** C3
Huntsman Rd IG6 . . . . **112** B5
Huntsmans Dr RM14 . . . . . **156** C7
Hunts Mead CM12 . . . . **97** A1
Hurlock Rd CM11 . . . . **97** B2
Hurricane Cl SS11 . . . . . . **122** B5
Hurricane Way
North Weald Bassett
CM16 . . . . **47** A4
Wickford SS11 . . . . **122** A5
Hursley Rd
Chigwell IG7 . . . . **111** F5
Redbridge IG7 . . . . **112** A5
Hurst Ave E4 . . . . **109** A7
Hurstbourne Gdns
IG11 . . . . **152** E6
Hurst Cl E4 . . . . **109** A7
Hurstcombe IG9 . . . . **110** A8
Hurst Ct IG8 . . . . **110** B4
Hurst Ho SS7 . . . . **145** B7
Hurstlands Cl RM11 . . . . . **136** C5
Hurstleigh Gdns IG5 . . . . **111** A4
Hurst Park Ave RM12 . . . . **155** E8
Hurst Rd IG9 . . . . **88** D1
Hurst Way
Chelmsford CM2 . . . . **32** F2
Southend-on-S SS9 . . . . . **146** F4
Hurstwood Ave
Pilgrims Hatch CM15 . . . . . **94** B8
Wanstead E18 . . . . **132** B7
Hurstwood Ct RM14 . . . . . **137** C2
Huskards
Ingatestone CM4 . . . . **74** A5
Upminster RM14 . . . . **137** C2
Hutchins Cl RM12 . . . . **136** E1
Hutchinson Cl RM6 . . . . . . **134** D1
Hutson Terr RM19 . . . . **176** D8
HUTTON **95** E3
Hutton All Saints' CE Prim
Sch CM13 . . . . **95** D3
Hutton Cl IG8 . . . . **110** B4
Hutton Cl CM13 . . . . **95** F2
Hutton Dr CM13 . . . . **95** D2
Hutton Gate CM13 . . . . **95** B3
HUTTON MOUNT **95** B1
Hutton Pl CM13 . . . . **95** B3
Hutton Rd
Brentwood CM15 . . . . **95** A2
Shenfield CM15 . . . . **94** F2
Hutton Village CM13 . . . . . **95** F2
Huxley Dr RM6 . . . . **134** B4
Hyacinth Cl IG11 . . . . **152** B6
Hyacinth Ct 4 CM1 . . . . . . **32** E7
Hycliffe Gdns IG7 . . . . . . **111** C6
HYDE CHASE **57** D4
Hyde Chase
Danbury CM3 . . . . **57** B4
Woodham Mortimer
CM9 . . . . **57** D4
Hyde Cl RM16 . . . . **172** C3

Hyde Gn CM3 . . . . **57** B7
Hyde La CM3 . . . . **57** B6
Hyde Mead RM9 . . . . **43** E8
Hyde Mead Ho EN9 . . . . . . **43** E8
Hyder Rd RM16 . . . . **174** C3
Hyde The SS16 . . . . **141** C4
Hydeway SS7 . . . . **144** F6
Hyde Way SS12 . . . . **121** D6
Hyde Wood La SS4 . . . . . . **125** F7
Hyh Ho E17 . . . . **109** B2
Hyland Cl RM11 . . . . **136** B4
Hyland Gate CM11 . . . . . . **119** D6
Hyland House Sch
E17 . . . . **109** D1
Hylands House Sixth Form
Coll SS9 . . . . **147** A3
Hylands Par CM2 . . . . **54** A6
Hylands Rd E17 . . . . **109** D1
Hylands Sch CM1 . . . . **31** D1
Hylands The SS5 . . . . **124** D5
Hyland Way RM11 . . . . **136** B4
Hyndford Cres DA9 . . . . . . **177** C2
Hyndman Ho 5
RM10 . . . . **135** A1
Hynton Rd RM8 . . . . **134** C2
HYTHE THE **37** B2
Hythe The CM9 . . . . **37** B2

I

Ian Rd CM12 . . . . **96** F4
Ibbetson Path IG10 . . . . **89** B6
Ibrox Ct 4 IG9 . . . . **110** C4
Ibscott Cl RM10 . . . . **154** C6
I Butts Rd SS3 . . . . **150** C1
Iceni Ct SS3 . . . . **88** B1
Icknield Dr IG2 . . . . **133** B6
Ilchester Rd RM8 . . . . **153** C7
ILFORD **133** A2
Ilford Chambers 11
IG1 . . . . **133** B1
Ilford Cty High Sch
IG6 . . . . **111** B1
Ilford Hill IG1 . . . . **133** A1
Ilford Jewish Prim Sch
IG6 . . . . **133** D8
Ilford La IG1 . . . . **152** B7
Ilford Prep Sch IG3 . . . . . . **134** A3
Ilford Ret Pk IG1 . . . . **133** C2
Ilford Sta IG1 . . . . **133** B2
Ilford Trad Est SS14 . . . . **120** E2
Ilford Ursuline High Sch
IG1 . . . . **133** B2
Ilfracombe Ave
Basildon SS13 . . . . **143** D5
Southend-on-S SS1 . . . . . **167** D8
Ilfracombe Cres
RM12 . . . . **155** C8
Ilfracombe Gdns RM6 . . . . **134** B4
Ilfracombe Rd SS2 . . . . . . **148** C1
Ilgars Rd SS11 . . . . **99** E1
Ilmington Dr SS13 . . . . . . **121** A1
Immanuel Sch RM5 . . . . . . **113** D5
Imperial Ave
Mayland CM3 . . . . **60** E1
Southend-on-S SS0 . . . . . **147** C1
Imperial Bsns Pk
DA11 . . . . **178** F1
Imperial Ho 4 SS4 . . . . . . **125** F2
Imperial Lo SS0 . . . . **147** C1
Imperial Pk
Rayleigh SS6 . . . . **123** C6
Southend-on-S SS3 . . . . . **168** E7
Imperial Ret Pk DA11 . . . . **179** A1
Imperial Trad Est
RM13 . . . . **155** C1
Impresa Pk EN11 . . . . **21** C7
Inchbonnie Rd CM3 . . . . . **101** D5
Inchcape Rd CM16 . . . . **68** A5
Ingaestone Bypass
CM15 . . . . **95** C3
INGATESTONE **74** C3
Ingatestone By-Pass
CM4 . . . . **74** B5
Ingatestone & Fryerning
CE Jun Sch CM4 . . . . **74** A3
Ingatestone Hall★
CM4 . . . . **74** C4
Ingatestone Inf Sch
CM4 . . . . **74** B4
Ingatestone Rd
Blackmore CM4 . . . . **72** F7
Edney Common CM4 . . . . . **52** A1
Roxwell CM1 . . . . **51** F2
Stock CM4 . . . . **75** B1
Wanstead E12 . . . . **132** C2
Woodford IG8 . . . . **110** B3
Ingatestone Sta CM4 . . . . . **74** B3
Ingaway SS16 . . . . **141** F5
Ingels Mead CM16 . . . . **45** F2
Ingleby Gdns IG7 . . . . **112** C1
Ingleby Rd
Dagenham RM10 . . . . **154** B6
Grays RM16 . . . . **174** C3
Ilford IG1 . . . . **133** B3
Inglefield Rd SS17 . . . . . . **161** B6
Ingleglen RM11 . . . . **137** A3
Inglehurst Gdns IG4 . . . . **132** F6
Ingleton Ho
4 Ingatestone CM4 . . . . . **74** C4
11 Romford RM3 . . . . . . **114** D4
Inglewood Cl
Hornchurch RM12 . . . . . . **155** D8
Redbridge IG6 . . . . **111** F4
Ingram Cotts CM1 . . . . **51** F4
Ingram Rd RM17 . . . . **173** C2
INGRAVE **117** D5

Ingrave Cl SS12 . . . . .121 E6
Ingrave Ho RM9 . . . . .153 B4
Ingrave Johnstone CE
Prim Sch CM13 . . . . .117 C4
Ingrave Rd
Brentwood CM13,
CM15 . . . . .116 E7
Romford RM1 . . . . .135 E7
Ingrebourne Ct E4 . . . . . . .109 B8
Ingrebourne Gdns
RM14 . . . . .137 D3
Ingrebourne Prim Sch
RM3 . . . . .114 C6
Ingrebourne Rd RM13 . . .155 B1
Ingrebourne Valley★
RM13 . . . . .155 E7
Ingress Gdns DA9 . . . . . .177 D2
Ingress Park Ave DA9 . . .177 C3
Ingreway RM3 . . . . .115 C4
Inkerpole Pl CM2 . . . . .32 F4
Inks Gn E4 . . . . .109 C5
Inmans Row IG6 . . . . .110 A6
Innes Cl SS12 . . . . .121 E5
Innova Way EN3 . . . . .65 A3
Inskip Dr RM11 . . . . .136 E3
Inskip Rd RM8 . . . . .134 D3
Institute Rd CM16 . . . . . . .46 D2
Integrated Support Ctr,
PRU CM18 . . . . .23 F4
International Bsns Pk
SS8 . . . . .163 D3
Inverclyde Gdns RM6 . . .134 D7
Invermay Cl CM15 . . . . . . .94 C1
Inverness Ave SS0 . . . . . .147 D2
Inverness Dr IG6 . . . . . . .111 E4
Invicta Ct CM12 . . . . .96 E3
Invicta Ctr The IG11 . . . . .153 A4
Invicta Rd DA2 . . . . .176 B1
Inworth Wlk SS11 . . . . . .122 A8
Io Ctr IG11 . . . . .152 F1
IO Ctr EN9 . . . . .65 A5
Iona Way SS12 . . . . .121 F6
Ipswich Mews SS16 . . . . .140 F5
Ireton Pl RM17 . . . . .173 C2
Iris Cl
Chelmsford CM1 . . . . . . .32 F5
Pilgrims Hatch CM15 . . . .94 B4
Iris Ct IG11 . . . . .153 B5
Iris Mews SS15 . . . . .141 C5
Iris Path RM3 . . . . .114 C3
Irons Way RM5 . . . . .113 C3
Ironwell La
Hockley SS5 . . . . .125 A3
Rochford SS4 . . . . .125 E2
Irvine Gdns RM15 . . . . . .171 F7
Irvine Pl SS12 . . . . .121 F5
Irvine Way CM12 . . . . .97 A1
Irving Cl SS5 . . . . .124 E5
Irvington Cl SS9 . . . . .146 D4
Irvon Hill Rd SS12 . . . . . .121 C7
Isaac Sq CM2 . . . . .55 B6
Isabel Ct EN11 . . . . .21 B8
Isabella Ho EN8 . . . . .65 A5
Isbell Gdns RM1 . . . . . . .113 E3
Isis Dr RM14 . . . . .137 E5
Island Centre Way EN3 . . .65 A2
Italstyle Bldg The
CM20 . . . . .11 C6
Iver Rd CM15 . . . . .94 B3
Ives Gdns RM1 . . . . .135 F7
Ivinghoe Rd RM8 . . . . . . .153 B7
Ivy Barns La
Ingatestone CM4 . . . . . . .74 A8
Margaretting CM4 . . . . . .52 C1
Ivy Bower Cl DA9 . . . . . . .177 B2
Ivybridge EN10 . . . . .21 A4
IVY CHIMNEYS 67 E7
Ivy Chys Prim Sch
CM16 . . . . .67 F7
Ivy Chys Rd CM16 . . . . . . .67 E7
Ivy Cl DA1 . . . . .176 A1
Ivy Cotts CM0 . . . . .62 A3
Ivy Gate Cl SS11 . . . . . . .121 E8
Ivyhouse Rd RM9 . . . . . . .153 E6
Ivy Lodge La RM3 . . . . . .115 B1
Ivy Rd SS7 . . . . .144 A6
Ivy Terr
Hoddesdon EN11 . . . . . . .21 C8
Ilford IG2 . . . . .133 C5
Ivy Wlk
Canvey Island SS8 . . . . .163 F4
Dagenham RM9 . . . . . . .153 E6

J

Jacaranda Cl CM1 . . . . . . .33 A6
Jack Cook Ho
IG11 . . . . .152 B5
Jack Cornwell St E12 . . . .152 A8
Jackdaw Cl
Billericay CM11 . . . . . . .119 C8
Southend-on-S SS3 . . . . .168 E8
Jack Evans Ct RM15 . . . . .172 A4
Jacklin Gn IG8 . . . . .110 A6
Jacks Cl SS11 . . . . .121 F7
JACK'S HATCH 23 A2
Jack Snipe Ho RM13 . . . .170 A8
Jackson Cl
Greenhithe DA9 . . . . . . .177 A2
Hornchurch RM11 . . . . . .136 F7
Jackson Ct
Dagenham RM10 . . . . . .154 A6
Wanstead E11 . . . . .132 B3
Jackson Pl CM2 . . . . .54 D6
Jackson Rd IG11 . . . . .152 D4
Jacksons Cl CM5 . . . . .49 C4
Jacksons La CM11 . . . . . . .97 C2
Jacksons Mews CM11 . . . .97 C2
Jack Stevens Cl CM17 . . . .24 C6
Jacob Ct EN3 . . . . .65 A2
Jacobs Ave RM3 . . . . .114 E1
Jacobs Cl RM10 . . . . .154 B8
Jacqueline Gdns CM12 . . .97 B5
Jade Cl RM8 . . . . .134 C3
Jade Ho RM13 . . . . .155 A1
Jaffe Rd IG1 . . . . .133 D3
James Alexander Ho
SS5 . . . . .101 D3
James Ave RM8 . . . . .134 F3
James Cl RM2 . . . . .136 A6
James Croft CM2 . . . . .54 B2
James Ct
Chingford E4 . . . . .109 D8
Woodford E18 . . . . . . .110 B1
James Hornsby High Sch
The SS15 . . . . .141 D7
James Lee Sq EN3 . . . . . . .65 A1
James Oglethorpe Prim
Sch The RM14 . . . . .137 F2
James Sq CM11 . . . . .97 E2
James St
Barking IG11 . . . . .152 C5
Epping CM16 . . . . .46 A3
Jane Ct RM1 . . . . .135 F6
Janet Duke Inf Sch
SS15 . . . . .141 D6
Janet Duke Jun Sch
SS15 . . . . .141 D6
Janette Ave SS8 . . . . .163 E3
Janice Mews IG1 . . . . . . .133 B1
Janmead CM13 . . . . .95 B2
Japan Rd RM6 . . . . .134 D5
Jardine Rd SS13 . . . . .143 C8
Jarndyce CM1 . . . . .31 F1
Jarrah Cotts RM19 . . . . . .176 D8
Jarrow Rd RM6 . . . . .134 C5
Jarvis Cl IG11 . . . . .152 E1
Jarvis Field CM3 . . . . .34 D5
Jarvis Rd
Canvey Island SS8 . . . . .164 A6
South Benfleet SS7 . . . . .144 E4
Jarvis Way RM3 . . . . .114 E1
Jasmine Cl
Basildon SS16 . . . . .140 F4
Canvey Island SS8 . . . . .163 F2
Chelmsford CM1 . . . . . . .32 E7
Ilford IG1 . . . . .152 B7
Jasmine Rd RM7 . . . . . . .135 E2
Jason Cl
Brentwood CM14 . . . . . .115 F6
Canvey Island SS8 . . . . .164 B5
Orsett RM16 . . . . .174 E7
Jason Ct CM14 . . . . .115 F6
J Ct CM20 . . . . .10 F1
Jeffcut Rd CM2 . . . . .32 E2
Jefferies Way
SS17 . . . . .160 F3
Jefferson Ave
SS15 . . . . .141 A6
Jefferson Cl IG2 . . . . .133 B6
Jeffery Rd CM2 . . . . .55 A7
Jellicoe Ct E4 . . . . .109 D4
Jena Cl SS3 . . . . .168 E7
Jenkins La IG11 . . . . .152 C2
Jenner Ho
Belvedere DA17 . . . . .169 A3
Romford RM3 . . . . .114 E1
Jenner Mead CM2 . . . . . . .33 A3
Jennerton Dr RM16 . . . . .173 A5
Jennings Pl CM4 . . . . .75 A8
Jenningtree Way
DA17 . . . . .169 C4
Jenny Path RM3 . . . . .114 D3
Jericho Pl CM4 . . . . .72 E8
Jermayns SS15 . . . . .141 E6
Jerningham Ave IG5 . . . . .111 B1
Jerounds CM19 . . . . .23 B6
Jerounds Com Jun & Inf
Sch CM19 . . . . .23 B5
Jersey Cl EN11 . . . . .21 A7
Jersey Gdns SS11 . . . . . .121 D8
Jersey Rd
Ilford IG1 . . . . .152 B8
Maldon CM9 . . . . .37 B1
Rainham RM13 . . . . . . .155 A5
Jervis Ct RM10 . . . . .154 B6
Jesmond Rd
Canvey Island SS8 . . . . .164 B2
Grays RM17 . . . . .173 D5
Jessel Dr IG10 . . . . .89 C7
Jessett Cl DA8 . . . . .169 D2
Jessop Ct EN9 . . . . .65 F5
Jetty Mews SS1 . . . . .167 D7
Jetty Wlk RM17 . . . . .178 A8
Jim Desormeaux Bglws
CM20 . . . . .10 E2
Joan Gdns RM8 . . . . .134 E2
Joan Rd RM8 . . . . .134 E2
Joan Villas RM8 . . . . .133 C4
Jocelyns CM17 . . . . .11 C4
Jodrell Way RM20 . . . . . .171 F1
John Barker Ho IG1 . . . . .133 D2
John Bramston Prim Sch
IG6 . . . . .112 A4
John Burns Dr IG11 . . . . .152 E5
John Chadwick Ho
IG3 . . . . .133 E3
John Childs Way SS6 . . . .123 E2
John Clay Gdns RM16 . . .173 B5
John Cornwell VC Ho
E12 . . . . .152 A8
John Ct EN11 . . . . .8 A1
John Eliot Cl EN9 . . . . .21 E2
John Henry Keene Meml
Homes 32 A4
John Parker Cl RM10 . . . .154 B5
John Perry Prim Sch
RM10 . . . . .154 D6
Johnson Cl
Rochford SS4 . . . . .125 D5
Wickford SS12 . . . . .121 D5
Johnson Ct SS4 . . . . .125 F2
Johnson Rd CM2 . . . . .55 A5
Johnsons Way DA9 . . . . .177 C1
John St
Grays RM17 . . . . .178 C8
Southend-on-S SS3 . . . .168 A6
Johns The CM5 . . . . .49 A4
Johnstone Rd SS1 . . . . . .168 A7
Johnston Rd IG8 . . . . .110 A5
Johnston Way CM9 . . . . . .59 A8
John Warner Sch The
EN11 . . . . .8 B1
John William Cl
RM16 . . . . .172 D1
Jonathans RM11 . . . . . . .136 E3
Jonathon Ho RM17 . . . . .173 D2
Jones Cl SS2 . . . . .147 E3
Jones Cnr SS8 . . . . .164 A3
Jordans Cl RM10 . . . . . . .154 B8
Jordans The SS2 . . . . . . .148 A2
Jordans Way RM13 . . . . .155 D3
Jo Richardson Com Sch
RM9 . . . . .153 D4
Joseph Clarke Sch
E4 . . . . .109 D4
Joseph Ct CM14 . . . . .116 B5
Joseph Lister Lo E11 . . . .132 B3
Joshua Wlk EN8 . . . . .65 A5
Josling Cl RM17 . . . . .177 F8
Joslin Rd RM19 . . . . .171 D1
Joslyn Cl EN3 . . . . .65 A1
Josselin Ct SS13 . . . . . . .121 C2
Josselin Rd SS13 . . . . . . .121 C2
Jotmans Hall Prim Sch
SS7 . . . . .144 B4
Jotmans La
South Benfleet SS7 . . . . .143 F2
South Benfleet SS7 . . . . .144 A3
Journeymans Way
SS2 . . . . .148 A5
Joyce Ct EN9 . . . . .65 D5
Joyce's Chase CM9 . . . . . .39 A8
Joydon Dr RM6 . . . . .134 B5
Joyes Cl RM3 . . . . .114 D6
Joyners Cl RM9 . . . . .153 F8
Joyners Field CM18 . . . . . .23 C4
Jubilee Ave
Broomfield CM1 . . . . . . .19 B2
Chingford E4 . . . . .109 C4
Romford RM7 . . . . .135 C6
Jubilee Cl
Crays Hill CM11 . . . . . . .120 C4
Grays RM20 . . . . .177 B8
Rayleigh SS6 . . . . .123 E2
Jubilee Cotts SS4 . . . . . . .127 D6
Jubilee Dr SS11 . . . . .121 C8
Jubilee Par IG8 . . . . .110 C4
Jubilee Rd
Crays Hill CM11 . . . . . . .120 C4
Grays RM20 . . . . .177 B8
Rayleigh SS6 . . . . .123 E2
Jubilee Rise SS6 . . . . .57 A6
Jubilee Terr
Chelmsford CM1 . . . . . . .32 A4
Woodham Ferrers CM3 . . .79 B4
Jubilee Villas E4 . . . . . . .87 D1
Judge Rd CM2 . . . . .33 B4
Judith Anne Ct RM14 . . . .137 E2
Judith Ave RM5 . . . . .113 B4
Julia Gdns IG11 . . . . .153 D3
Julian Cl CM1 . . . . .19 B1
Julie Ho EN11 . . . . .21 C8
Juliers Cl SS8 . . . . .164 D3
Juliers Rd SS8 . . . . .164 D3
Juliette Way RM15 . . . . . .170 F5
Junction Rd
Basildon SS13 . . . . .143 B4
Brentwood CM14 . . . . . .116 C6
Cold Norton CM3 . . . . . .81 A6
Romford RM1 . . . . .135 F6
Junction Rd E RM6 . . . . . .134 E4
Junction Rd W RM6 . . . . .134 E4
Juniper Cl CM11 . . . . .97 C4
Juniper Ct
Brentwood CM13 . . . . . .116 F7
Ilford IG6 . . . . .134 C5
Juniper Dr
Chelmsford CM2 . . . . . . .54 B6
South Ockendon RM15 . . .157 E2
Juniper Rd
Boreham CM3 . . . . .33 F8
Ilford IG1 . . . . .152 B8
Southend-on-S SS9 . . . . .146 F4
Juniper Way RM3 . . . . . . .114 E2
Jury St DA11 . . . . .179 B1
Jutsums Ave RM7 . . . . . .135 B5
Jutsums Ct RM7 . . . . .135 B5
Jutsums La RM7 . . . . .135 B5

K

Kale Rd SS7 . . . . .144 E4
Kamerwyk Ave SS8 . . . . .164 C4
Kandlewood CM13 . . . . . .95 B2
Karen Cl
Brentwood CM15 . . . . . .94 C2

Karen Cl continued
Rainham RM13 . . . . . . .154 E3
South Benfleet SS7 . . . . .163 E8
Stanford-le-H SS17 . . . . .160 C1
Wickford SS12 . . . . .121 C6
Karen Terr IG2 . . . . .133 D6
Karina Cl IG7 . . . . .111 E5
Katella Trad Est IG11 . . . .152 E2
Katemon Cl SS12 . . . . .8 D4
Katherine Cl SS6 . . . . . . .124 A1
Katherine Gdns IG6 . . . . .111 C3
Katherine Rd SS13 . . . . . .143 E7
KATHERINES 22 F5
Katherines Hatch
CM19 . . . . .23 A6
Katherines Ho CM19 . . . . .23 A6
Katherines Prim Sch
CM19 . . . . .23 A6
Katherine's Way CM19 . . .23 A6
Kathleen Cl SS17 . . . . . . .160 E4
Kathleen Dr SS9 . . . . .146 F2
Kathleen Ferrier Cres
SS15 . . . . .141 D8
Kathryn Ct SS3 . . . . .168 E7
Katonia Ave CM3 . . . . .60 F1
Kavanaghs CM14 . . . . . . .116 B7
Kavanaghs Rd CM14 . . . .116 B7
Kavanaghs Terr CM14 . . .116 B7
Keary Rd DA10 . . . . .177 F1
Keats Ave RM3 . . . . .114 B3
Keats Cl
Chigwell IG7 . . . . .111 C4
Maldon CM9 . . . . .59 A8
Wanstead E11 . . . . .132 B6
Keats Gdns RM18 . . . . . .179 B5
Keats Rd DA17 . . . . .169 C3
Keats Sq CM3 . . . . .101 E6
Keats Way SS12 . . . . .121 C7
Keats Wlk
Brentwood CM13 . . . . . .95 D2
Rayleigh SS6 . . . . .124 A2
Kecksy's CM21 . . . . .1 F4
Keeble Pk CM9 . . . . .58 F8
Keefield CM19 . . . . .23 B3
Keegan Pl SS8 . . . . .164 C4
Keelan Ct IG1 . . . . .133 B1
Keel Cl IG11 . . . . .153 C3
Keelings La CM0 . . . . .85 E8
Keelings Rd CM0 . . . . .85 F8
Keene Way CM2 . . . . .54 B3
Keer Ave SS8 . . . . .164 D2
KEERES GREEN 5 D1
Keighley Mews SS3 . . . . .149 D2
Keighley Rd RM3 . . . . . . .114 E3
Keir Hardie Ho
Belvedere DA17 . . . .169 A3
Grays RM16 . . . . .173 D5
Keir Hardie Way
IG11 . . . . .153 A5
Keith Ave SS11 . . . . .99 D2
Keith Rd IG11 . . . . .152 D3
Keith Way
Hornchurch RM11 . . . . . .136 E4
Southend-on-S SS2 . . . . .147 E3
Kelburn Way RM13 . . . . . .155 A2
Kellington Rd SS8 . . . . . .164 C5
Kelly Ho RM15 . . . . .171 C5
Kelly Rd SS13 . . . . .143 E6
Kelly Way RM6 . . . . .134 E5
Kelsie Way IG6 . . . . .111 E4
Kelso Cl SS6 . . . . .123 C6
Kelso Lo E18 . . . . .110 B1
Kelston Rd IG6 . . . . .111 B1
Kelvedon Cl
Billericay CM11 . . . . .97 C2
Brentwood CM13 . . . . . .95 E3
Chelmsford CM1 . . . . . . .32 A6
Rayleigh SS6 . . . . .123 A3
Kelvedon Gn SS6 . . . . .71 F2
Kelvedon Hall La CM14 . .71 B4
KELVEDON HATCH 71 E2
Kelvedon Hatch Com Prim
Sch CM15 . . . . .71 E2
Kelvedon Hatch Nuclear
Bunker★ CM14 . . . . . . .71 C4
Kelvedon Ho IG9 . . . . .88 E2
Kelvedon Rd CM11 . . . . . .97 C2
Kelvedon Way IG8 . . . . . .110 F4
Kelvedon Wlk RM13 . . . . .154 F4
Kelvin Ho DA17 . . . . . . .169 A3
Kelvin Rd
South Benfleet SS7 . . . . .144 D7
Tilbury RM18 . . . . .179 A5
Kelvinside SS17 . . . . .160 E4
Kembles SS6 . . . . .123 E4
Kemp Ho E6 . . . . .152 A6
Kempley Ct RM17 . . . . . .178 D8
Kemp Rd RM8 . . . . .134 D3
Kempton Ave RM12 . . . . .136 F1
Kempton Cl SS7 . . . . .145 B7
Kempton Rd E6 . . . . .152 A4
Kemsley Cl DA9 . . . . .177 B1
Kendal RM19 . . . . .171 C1
Kendal Ave
Barking IG11 . . . . .152 E4
Epping CM16 . . . . .68 A8
Kendal Cl
Hullbridge SS5 . . . . .101 E1
Rayleigh SS6 . . . . .123 E2
Woodford IG8 . . . . .109 F8
Kendal Croft RM12 . . . . . .155 A7
Kendal Ct
Chingford E4 . . . . .87 C1
Wickford SS12 . . . . .121 A5
Kendale RM16 . . . . .174 B3
Kendal Rd EN9 . . . . .65 C4
Kendal Way SS9 . . . . .146 E7
Kendon Cl E11 . . . . .132 B6

Kenholme SS9 . . . . .146 E4
Kenilworth Ave
Chingford E17 . . . . .109 A1
Romford RM3 . . . . .115 B4
Kenilworth Cl CM12 . . . . . .96 E2
Kenilworth Ct
Chingford E4 . . . . .109 C8
Dartford DA2 . . . . .176 B1
Kenilworth Gdns
Hornchurch RM12 . . . . . .136 D1
Ilford IG3 . . . . .133 F2
Loughton IG10 . . . . .88 F3
Rayleigh SS6 . . . . .123 C3
Southend-on-S SS0,
SS9 . . . . .147 A3
Kenilworth Pl SS15 . . . . .119 E1
Kenley Cl SS11 . . . . .122 B6
Kenley Gdns RM12 . . . . . .136 F2
Kenmar Cl SS6 . . . . .146 A8
Kenmore Cl SS8 . . . . .164 E2
Kennedy Ave SS15 . . . . . .140 F6
Kennedy Cl
Rayleigh SS6 . . . . .146 A8
South Benfleet SS7 . . . . .144 B7
Kennedy Rd IG11 . . . . . . .152 E4
Kennel La CM12,
CM11 . . . . .119 C7
Kennet Cl RM14 . . . . .137 E5
Kennet Gn RM15 . . . . . . .172 B6
Kenneth Ave IG1 . . . . . . .152 B8
Kenneth Chambers Ct
IG8 . . . . .110 E4
Kenneth Gdns SS17 . . . . .160 F5
Kenneth More Rd
IG1 . . . . .133 B1
Kenneth Rd
Basildon SS13 . . . . .143 C7
Dagenham RM6 . . . . . . .134 E4
Thundersley SS7 . . . . . . .144 F5
Kennet Way CM1 . . . . .31 D5
Kenning Rd EN11 . . . . .21 B8
Kennington Ave SS7 . . . . .144 C6
Kenningtons Prim Sch
RM15 . . . . .171 C7
Kennylands Rd IG6 . . . . . .112 A3
Kensington Ct
RM17 . . . . .178 C8
Kensington Dr IG8 . . . . . .110 D1
Kensington Gdns
Billericay CM12 . . . . .97 A4
East Tilbury RM18 . . . . . .175 D2
Redbridge IG1 . . . . .132 F3
Kensington Ho
IG8 . . . . .111 A3
Kensington Rd
Pilgrims Hatch CM15 . . . .94 A3
Romford RM7 . . . . .135 C5
Southend-on-S SS1 . . . . .167 D7
Kensington Way SS5 . . . .124 C6
Kent Ave
Canvey Island SS8 . . . . .164 B5
Dagenham RM9 . . . . . . .154 A1
Southend-on-S SS9 . . . . .146 F5
Kent Cl SS15 . . . . .141 B6
Kent Dr RM12 . . . . .155 D8
Kent Elms Cl SS2 . . . . . . .146 F5
Kent Elms Cnr SS9 . . . . . .146 F5
Kent Green Cl SS5 . . . . . .124 F5
Kent Ho RM7 . . . . .113 A2
Kentish Rd DA17 . . . . . . .169 A3
Kent Kraft Ind Est
DA11 . . . . .178 A2
Kenton Way SS16 . . . . . .140 F5
Kent Rd
Dagenham RM10 . . . . . .154 B7
Grays RM17 . . . . .173 C1
Kents Farm La CM2 . . . . . .76 D3
Kents Hill Inf Sch
SS7 . . . . .144 D4
Kents Hill Jun Sch
SS7 . . . . .144 D4
Kents Hill Rd SS7 . . . . . . .144 D4
Kents Hill Rd N SS7 . . . . .144 D6
Kents La CM16 . . . . .25 D2
Kent View
Aveley RM15 . . . . .171 C4
Rainham RM13 . . . . . . .170 D6
Kent View Ave SS9 . . . . . .166 A8
Kent View Cl SS8 . . . . . . .164 B1
Kent View Gdns IG3 . . . . .133 E2
Kent View Rd SS16 . . . . . .142 F4
Kent Way SS6 . . . . .146 A8
Kentwell Ct SS7 . . . . .144 C3
Kenway
Rainham RM13 . . . . . . .155 D2
Romford RM5 . . . . .113 C1
Southend-on-S SS2 . . . . .148 A2
Kenway Cl RM13 . . . . .155 C2
Kenway Wlk RM13 . . . . . .155 D2
Kenwood Gdns
Ilford IG2 . . . . .133 A6
Wanstead E18 . . . . . .132 B8
Kenwood Rd SS17 . . . . . .161 B4
Keppel Rd RM9 . . . . .153 E8
Kerby Rise CM2 . . . . .32 F2
Kernow Ct RM12 . . . . . . .136 E2
Kerril Croft CM20 . . . . . . .10 A1
Kerry Ave RM15 . . . . .170 F4
Kerry Ct RM14 . . . . .137 F4
Kerry Ct SS11 . . . . .155 C1
Kerry Dr RM14 . . . . .137 F4
Kerry Rd RM16 . . . . .173 D5
Kersbrooke Way
SS17 . . . . .161 B4
Kersey Gdns RM3 . . . . . . .114 F3

Kershaw Cl
Grays RM16 . . . .**172** C2
Hornchurch RM11 . . . .**136** E4
Kershaw Rd RM10 . . . . . .**135** A1
Kershaws Cl SS12 . . . .**121** C6
Kesteven Cl IG6 . . . .**111** F4
Kestrel Cl
Hornchurch RM12 . . . . . .**155** B5
Redbridge IG6 . . . .**112** C6
Kestrel Gr SS6 . . . .**123** B3
Kestrel Ho SS3 . . . .**149** F1
Kestrel Mews CM9 . . . . . .**59** B8
Kestrel Pk CM13 . . . .**95** E4
Kestrel Rd EN9 . . . .**66** A5
Kestrel Wlk CM2 . . . .**54** B5
Keswick Ave
Hornchurch RM11 . . . . . .**136** D3
Hullbridge SS5 . . . .**101** E2
Keswick Cl SS6 . . . .**123** E2
Keswick Gdns
Purfleet RM19 . . . .**176** C8
Redbridge IG4 . . . .**132** E7
Keswick Ho 14 RM3 . . . . .**114** D4
Keswick Rd SS7 . . . .**144** E4
Ketleys CM2 . . . .**54** C3
Kettering Rd RM3 . . . .**114** E3
Kettlebury Way CM5 . . . . .**48** F1
Kevin Cl CM11 . . . .**119** D7
Keyes Cl SS3 . . . .**149** E1
Keyes Rd DA1 . . . .**176** A3
Keynsham Ave IG8 . . . . . .**109** E6
KEYSERS ESTATE **21** B1
Keysers Rd EN10 . . . .**21** B1
Keysland SS7 . . . .**145** B7
Keys The CM13 . . . .**116** C4
Khartoum Pl DA12 . . . . . .**179** C1
Khartoum Rd IG1 . . . .**152** B7
Kibcaps SS16 . . . .**141** F4
Kidd Ho RM9 . . . .**153** F8
Kidman Cl RM2 . . . .**136** C8
Kielder Cl IG6 . . . .**111** F4
Kierbeck Bsns Pk
SS16 . . . .**142** F3
Kilbarry Wlk CM11 . . . . . .**97** D6
Kildare Ho RM3 . . . .**114** E1
Kildowan Rd IG3 . . . .**134** A3
Kilmarnock Gdns
RM8 . . . .**134** C1
Kilmartin Rd IG3 . . . .**134** A2
Kilmartin Way RM12 . . . . .**155** B7
Kilmington Cl CM13 . . . . .**117** B8
Kiln Cotts CM3 . . . .**56** D6
Kilnfield
Chipping Ongar CM5 . . . .**48** F2
Wyatts Green CM15 . . . . .**72** D3
Kiln La CM17 . . . .**24** C7
Kiln Rd
Hadleigh SS7 . . . .**145** B4
North Weald Bassett
CM16 . . . .**47** A4
Kiln Shaw SS16 . . . .**141** E4
Kiln Way RM17 . . . .**172** F1
Kilnwood Ave SS5 . . . .**124** D5
Kiln Wood La RM4 . . . . . .**113** D5
Kilowan Cl SS16 . . . .**140** F4
Kilsby Wlk RM9 . . . .**153** B6
Kilworth Ave
Brentwood CM15 . . . .**95** A3
Southend-on-S SS1 . . . . .**167** B8
Kimberley Ave
Ilford IG2 . . . .**133** E4
Romford RM7 . . . .**135** C5
Kimberley Ct SS7 . . . .**144** E4
Kimberley Rd
Chingford E4 . . . .**87** E1
Little Wakering SS3 . . . . .**149** E6
South Benfleet SS7 . . . . .**144** E4
Kimberley Way E4 . . . .**87** E1
Kimberly Dr SS15 . . . .**119** F2
Kimpton Ave CM15 . . . . . .**94** C2
Kimpton's Cl CM5 . . . .**48** F5
Kinfauns Ave RM11 . . . . .**136** C5
Kinfauns Rd IG3 . . . .**134** B3
Kingaby Gdns RM13 . . . . .**155** A5
King Alfred Rd RM3 . . . . . .**114** F1
King Edmund Sch The
SS4 . . . .**125** E5
King Edward Ave
Burnham-on-C CM0 . . . . .**106** B6
Rainham RM13 . . . .**155** D2
King Edward Ct CM1 . . . . .**32** A3
King Edward Dr
RM16 . . . .**173** E3
King Edward Rd
Basildon SS15 . . . .**141** B8
Brentwood CM14 . . . .**116** C7
Greenhithe DA9 . . . .**177** A2
Romford RM1 . . . .**135** F5
King Edward's Rd
Barking IG11 . . . .**152** D3
South Woodham Ferrers
CM3 . . . .**101** C4
Stanford-le-H SS17 . . . . .**175** D8
King Edward Terr
SS15 . . . .**141** B8
King Edward VI Gram Sch
CM1 . . . .**32** A3
Kingfisher Ave E11 . . . . . .**132** B5
Kingfisher Cl
Brentwood CM13 . . . .**95** A2
Heybridge CM9 . . . .**37** C1
Southend-on-S SS3 . . . . .**168** E8
Stanstead Abbotts SG12 . . . .**8** C3
Kingfisher Cres SS6 . . . . .**123** B3

Kingfisher Dr
Greenhithe DA9 . . . .**177** A1
South Benfleet SS7 . . . . .**144** C2
Kingfisher Hts RM17 . . . . .**173** A1
Kingfisher Lo CM2 . . . .**54** F7
Kingfisher Rd RM14 . . . . .**137** F3
Kingfishers
Basildon SS16 . . . .**142** C4
Ingatestone CM4 . . . .**74** C5
Kingfishers The 1
SS11 . . . .**122** A5
Kingfisher Way CM19 . . . . . .**9** A1
King George Ave IG2 . . . . .**133** D5
King George Cl RM7 . . . . .**135** C8
King George Hospl
IG3 . . . .**134** A6
King George Rd EN9 . . . . .**65** C5
King George's Cl SS6 . . . .**123** D1
King George's Ct SS6 . . . .**123** D1
King George's Pl CM9 . . . . .**37** A2
King George's Rd
CM15 . . . .**94** B3
King George VI Ave
RM18 . . . .**175** B2
King Harold Ct EN9 . . . . . .**65** C6
King Harold Sch EN9 . . . . .**65** E6
King Henrys Cl EN9 . . . . . .**65** C3
King Henry's Dr SS4 . . . . .**147** F7
King Henry's Mews
EN3 . . . .**65** A2
King John Sch The
SS7 . . . .**145** B3
Kingley Cl SS12 . . . .**121** B7
Kingley Dr SS12 . . . .**121** B7
Kings Ave RM6 . . . .**134** F5
King's Ave
Buckhurst Hill IG9 . . . . . .**110** D8
Woodford IG8 . . . .**110** C5
Kingsbridge Cir 6
RM3 . . . .**114** E4
Kingsbridge Cl RM3 . . . . .**114** E4
Kingsbridge Ind Est
IG11 . . . .**152** E2
Kingsbridge Rd
Barking IG11 . . . .**152** D3
Romford RM3 . . . .**114** E4
King's Chase CM14 . . . . . .**116** C7
Kings Cl
Canvey Island SS8 . . . . . .**163** C3
Rayleigh SS6 . . . .**123** E2
Kings Cres SS15 . . . .**119** B1
Kingscroft SS2 . . . .**148** B1
Kings Croft CM0 . . . .**84** D4
Kings Ct
3 Buckhurst Hill IG9 . . . .**110** D8
Burnham-on-C CM0 . . . . .**106** B4
Kingsdale Ct
Swanscombe DA10 . . . . .**177** E1
Waltham Abbey EN9 . . . . .**66** A5
Kingsdale Ind Est The
CM1 . . . .**32** C3
Kingsdon La CM17 . . . .**24** C7
Kingsdown Cl SS13 . . . . . .**143** C6
Kingsdown Sch SS2 . . . . . .**146** F6
Kingsdown Wlk SS8 . . . . .**164** A5
Kings Eight CM14 . . . .**116** C7
Kings Farm
Chingford E17 . . . .**109** B2
Rayleigh SS6 . . . .**123** E5
Kings Farm Mdw CM0 . . . . .**63** E4
Kingsfield EN11 . . . .**21** A8
Kingsford Dr CM2 . . . .**33** B4
Kingsgate Ct SS0 . . . .**166** C8
Kings Gdns
Ilford IG1 . . . .**133** D3
Upminster RM14 . . . .**137** E4
King's Gn IG10 . . . .**88** E6
Kings Gr RM1 . . . .**136** A6
Kingshawes SS7 . . . .**145** B6
Kings Head Ct CM21 . . . .**1** E2
Kings Head Hill E4 . . . .**87** B2
Kings Head Wlk 6
CM2 . . . .**32** C2
King's Hill IG10 . . . .**88** E7
Kingshill Ave RM5 . . . .**113** C5
Kings Keep SS0 . . . .**166** C8
Kingsland CM18 . . . .**23** C6
Kingsleigh Pk Homes
SS7 . . . .**145** B6
Kingsley Ave DA1 . . . .**176** A2
Kingsley Cl RM10 . . . .**154** B8
Kingsley Cres SS7 . . . . . .**145** C8
Kingsley Ct RM2 . . . .**136** B5
Kingsley Gdns
Chingford E4 . . . .**109** A5
Hornchurch RM11 . . . . . .**136** D7
Kingsley Grange 1
E11 . . . .**132** A6
Kingsley La SS7 . . . .**145** B8
Kingsley Mdws SS12 . . . . .**121** C6
Kingsley Mews
Dagenham RM9 . . . .**153** D8
4 Ilford IG1 . . . .**133** B2
Kingsley Rd
Brentwood CM13 . . . .**95** D2
Chingford E17 . . . .**109** C1
Loughton IG10 . . . .**89** D6
Redbridge IG6 . . . .**111** C2
Kingsley Wlk RM16 . . . . . .**174** A2
Kings Lo SS7 . . . .**145** C3
Kings Lynn Dr RM3 . . . . . .**114** D4
Kingsman Dr RM16 . . . . . .**173** B6
Kingsman Rd SS17 . . . . . .**160** B1
Kingsmans Farm Rd
SS5 . . . .**102** A4
Kingsmead
Lower Nazeing EN9,
EN10 . . . .**21** C1

Kingsmead *continued*
Sawbridgeworth CM21 . . . . .**1** E1
Kingsmead Ave RM1 . . . . .**135** F5
Kingsmead Cl CM19 . . . . . .**22** B7
Kingsmead Hill CM19 . . . . .**22** B7
Kingsmead Lo 9 E4 . . . . .**109** C8
Kingsmead Mans 4
RM1 . . . .**135** E5
Kings Meadow Ct EN9 . . . .**66** A5
Kingsmere SS7 . . . .**145** C5
Kings Mews
Chigwell IG7 . . . .**111** C8
Sawbridgeworth CM21 . . . . .**1** E2
Kingsmill Gdns RM9 . . . . .**153** F7
Kingsmill Rd RM9 . . . .**153** F7
KINGSMOOR **23** C3
Kingsmoor Prim Sch
CM18 . . . .**23** C4
Kingsmoor Rd CM19 . . . . .**23** B5
Kings Oak RM7 . . . .**135** A8
King Solomon High Sch
IG6 . . . .**111** D1
Kings Par SS7 . . . .**160** C1
Kings Park Chalet &
Mobile Home Pk
SS8 . . . .**164** E4
Kingspark Ct E18 . . . .**132** A8
Kings Pk SS7 . . . .**144** F5
Kings Pl
Buckhurst Hill IG9 . . . . . .**110** D8
Loughton IG10 . . . .**88** D2
Southminster CM0 . . . . . .**84** D4
Kings Rd
Basildon SS15 . . . .**119** B1
Burnham-on-C CM0 . . . . .**106** B4
Canvey Island SS8 . . . . . .**163** C3
Chelmsford CM1 . . . .**31** F4
Rayleigh SS6 . . . .**123** E2
Southminster CM0 . . . . . .**84** D4
King's Rd
Barking IG11 . . . .**152** C5
Brentwood CM14 . . . .**116** C7
Chingford E4 . . . .**87** D1
Romford RM1 . . . .**136** A6
South Benfleet SS7 . . . . .**144** E2
Southend-on-S SS0 . . . . .**147** B1
Kings Road Prim Sch
CM1 . . . .**31** F4
King St
Gravesend DA12 . . . .**179** B1
High Ongar CM5 . . . .**50** B3
Maldon CM9 . . . .**37** A1
Stanford-le-H SS17 . . . . .**160** C1
Kingsteignton SS3 . . . . . .**168** D8
Kingston Ave
Chelmsford CM2 . . . .**32** E3
Southend-on-S SS3 . . . . .**149** E2
Kingston Chase CM9 . . . . .**36** F5
Kingston Cl RM6 . . . .**134** E8
Kingston Cres CM2 . . . . . .**32** E3
Kingston Ct
Grays RM17 . . . .**173** B3
Northfleet DA11 . . . .**178** B2
Kingston Farm Ind Units
CM17 . . . .**13** C5
Kingston Hill SS16 . . . . . .**141** D2
Kingston Hill Ave
RM6 . . . .**134** E8
Kingston Prim Sch
SS7 . . . .**144** E6
Kingston Rd
Ilford IG1 . . . .**152** C8
Romford RM1 . . . .**135** F8
Kingston Ridge SS16 . . . . .**141** D3
Kingstons Farm CM17 . . . . .**13** D5
Kingston Way SS7 . . . .**144** F6
Kingsview Ct SS0 . . . .**166** C8
Kingsview Ct SS11 . . . .**121** F6
Kingsway
Hullbridge SS5 . . . .**123** D8
Southend-on-S SS0 . . . . .**147** A2
Woodford IG8 . . . .**110** C5
Kings Way
Billericay CM12 . . . .**119** D6
South Woodham Ferrers
CM3 . . . .**79** C1
Kingsway Mews SS0 . . . . .**147** B2
KINGSWOOD **142** A4
Kingswood Chase
SS9 . . . .**146** D3
Kingswood Cl CM11 . . . . . .**97** C2
Kingswood Cres SS6 . . . . .**123** E1
Kingswood Ct
Basildon SS14 . . . .**142** E5
Bradwell on S CM0 . . . . . .**42** B2
Chingford E4 . . . .**109** A5
Kingswood Inf Sch
SS16 . . . .**142** B5
Kingswood Lo
Romford RM2 . . . .**136** A8
Southend-on-S SS9 . . . . .**146** D3
Kingswood Rd
Basildon SS16 . . . .**142** C5
Ilford IG3 . . . .**134** A4
King's Wood Sch
RM3 . . . .**115** A6
King Williams St EN9 . . . . .**65** C4
Kinnaird Way IG8 . . . .**110** F4
Kipling Ave RM18 . . . .**179** C6
Kipling Cl
Brentwood CM14 . . . .**116** B5
Chelmsford CM1 . . . .**32** A5
Kipling Mews SS2 . . . .**148** A2
Kipling Rd DA1 . . . .**176** B2
Kipling Twrs RM3 . . . .**114** B3
Kirby Cl
Loughton IG10 . . . .**88** C2
Redbridge IG6 . . . .**111** E4

Kirby Cl *continued*
Romford RM3 . . . .**115** A5
Kirby Rd SS14 . . . .**142** F6
Kirkham Ave SS16 . . . . . .**159** F7
Kirkham Ho 9 RM3 . . . . .**114** D5
Kirkham Rd SS17 . . . .**159** F8
Kirkham Shaw SS17 . . . . .**159** F8
Kirkland Ave IG5 . . . .**111** A1
Kirklees CM1 . . . .**31** F4
Kirklees Rd RM8 . . . .**153** C7
Kirkmans Rd CM2 . . . .**54** D3
Kirk Mews CM3 . . . .**83** B2
Kirk Pl CM2 . . . .**32** F3
Kirton Cl RM12 . . . .**155** C6
Kitchener Rd
Chingford E17 . . . .**109** B2
Dagenham RM10 . . . .**154** B6
North Fambridge CM3 . . . .**81** A1
Kitkatts Rd SS8 . . . .**164** A3
Kitson Way CM20 . . . .**10** C1
Kittiwake Dr CM9 . . . .**37** C5
Knapton Cl CM1 . . . .**32** D7
Knares The SS16 . . . .**141** F4
Knebworth Ave E17 . . . . . .**109** A2
Knebworth Ho E17 . . . .**109** A2
Knightbridge Wlk
CM12 . . . .**97** A4
Knight Cl RM8 . . . .**134** C2
Knight Ct 1 E4 . . . .**87** C1
Knight Ho IG10 . . . .**89** D5
Knighton Cl
Romford RM7 . . . .**135** D5
Woodford IG8 . . . .**110** B6
Knighton Dr IG8 . . . .**110** B6
Knighton Gn IG9 . . . .**110** B8
Knighton La IG9 . . . .**110** B8
Knighton Rd
Romford RM7 . . . .**135** C5
Wanstead E7 . . . .**132** A1
Knighton Terr 17 E11 . . . . .**132** A6
Knights SS15 . . . .**141** D7
Knightsbridge Gdns 5
RM7 . . . .**135** D6
Knight's Ct
4 Basildon SS14 . . . . . .**142** F8
Sawbridgeworth CM21 . . . . .**1** E2
Knights Manor Way
DA1 . . . .**176** A2
Knights Properties
EN11 . . . .**21** B6
Knight St
Sawbridgeworth CM21 . . . . .**1** E2
South Woodham Ferrers
CM3 . . . .**101** E7
Knights Way IG6 . . . .**111** C4
Knight's Way CM13 . . . . . .**117** A7
Knights Wlk RM4 . . . .**90** B6
Knightswick Ctr SS8 . . . . .**164** C4
Knightswick Rd SS8 . . . . .**164** B4
Knightswood Rd
RM13 . . . .**155** A3
Knivet Cl SS6 . . . .**123** E1
KNOCKHALL **177** C2
Knockhall Com Prim Sch
DA9 . . . .**177** C2
Knockhall Rd DA9 . . . .**177** C2
Knole Cl CM3 . . . .**101** D5
Knollcroft SS3 . . . .**168** D6
Knoll The
Billericay CM12 . . . .**97** B4
Rayleigh SS6 . . . .**123** D2
Knowle Ho EN11 . . . .**21** A5
Knowle The
Basildon SS16 . . . .**142** C4
Hoddesdon EN11 . . . .**21** A5
Knowlton Cotts RM15 . . . .**172** C8
Knox Cl CM9 . . . .**59** A8
Knox Ct SS12 . . . .**121** F5
Kolburg Rd SS8 . . . .**164** D2
Kollum Rd SS8 . . . .**164** F3
Koln Cl SS8 . . . .**163** C3
Komberg Cres SS8 . . . . . .**164** C5
Konnybrook SS7 . . . .**145** A4
Korndyk Ave SS8 . . . .**164** C4
Kursaal Way SS1 . . . .**167** C7
Kyme Rd RM11 . . . .**135** F5
Kynance Cl RM3 . . . .**114** C6
Kynoch Ct SS17 . . . .**160** E1
Kyrkly Ct 11 RM19 . . . . . .**171** B1

L

Laars Ave SS8 . . . .**164** C5
Laburnham Cl RM14 . . . . .**138** A4
Laburnham Ct SS3 . . . . . .**168** F8
Laburnham Gdns
RM14 . . . .**137** F4
Laburnum Ave
Hornchurch RM12 . . . . . .**136** A2
Wickford SS12 . . . .**121** C6
Laburnum Cl
Hockley SS5 . . . .**124** C6
Sheering CM22 . . . .**12** C8
Wickford SS12 . . . .**121** C6
Laburnum Dr
Chelmsford CM2 . . . .**54** C6
Corringham SS17 . . . .**161** B3
Laburnum Gr
Canvey Island SS8 . . . . . .**163** D3
Hockley SS5 . . . .**124** B6
South Ockendon RM15 . . .**157** C1
Laburnum Ho
3 Basildon SS13 . . . . . .**143** B8
3 Dagenham RM10 . . . . .**135** A2
Laburnum Rd
Coopersale CM16 . . . .**46** C2

Laburnum Rd *continued*
Hoddesdon EN11 . . . .**21** B8
Laburnum Way SS6 . . . . . .**123** B6
Laburnum Wlk RM12 . . . . .**155** C8
Labworth Rd SS8 . . . .**164** C2
Lacey Dr RM8 . . . .**134** C1
Ladram Cl SS1 . . . .**168** C8
Ladram Rd SS1 . . . .**168** C8
Ladram Way SS1 . . . .**168** B8
Ladyfields IG10 . . . .**89** C5
Ladyfields Cl IG10 . . . .**89** C5
Ladygate Ctr SS12 . . . .**121** D7
Lady Hamilton Ct SS1 . . . .**168** B8
Lady La CM2 . . . .**54** C8
Lady's Hill CM14 . . . .**70** F1
Ladyshot CM20 . . . .**11** B1
Ladysmith Ave IG2 . . . . . .**133** E4
Ladysmith Way SS15 . . . . .**119** F2
Ladywell La CM2 . . . .**55** B5
Ladywell Prospect
CM21 . . . .**2** A1
Lagonda Ave IG6 . . . .**111** F4
LAINDON **141** B7
Laindon Common Rd
CM12 . . . .**119** A6
Laindon Ctr SS15 . . . .**141** B6
Laindon Link SS15,
SS16 . . . .**141** D5
Laindon Park Prim Sch
SS15 . . . .**141** E8
Laindon Rd CM12 . . . .**119** A8
Laindon Sta SS15 . . . .**141** C5
Laing Cl IG6 . . . .**111** D4
Laird Ave RM16 . . . .**173** D4
Lake Ave
Billericay CM12 . . . .**97** B3
Rainham RM13 . . . .**155** D3
Lake Cl RM8 . . . .**134** D1
Lakedale Ct IG11 . . . .**153** A1
Lake Dr SS7 . . . .**144** F5
Lakefields Cl RM13 . . . . . .**155** D3
Lake Gdns RM10 . . . .**154** A7
Lake House Rd E11 . . . . . .**132** A2
Lakeland Ct IG7 . . . .**112** B6
Lake Meadows Office
Village CM12 . . . .**96** F3
Lakenham Ho SS2 . . . .**147** E5
Lake Rd
Ilford IG6 . . . .**134** D7
Lower Nazeing EN9 . . . . . .**21** E2
Lake Rise
Grays RM20 . . . .**172** A2
Romford RM1 . . . .**135** F8
Lake Rise Trad Est
RM20 . . . .**172** A2
Lakes Cl SG12 . . . .**8** D2
Lakeside
Billericay CM12 . . . .**97** A4
Rainham RM13 . . . .**155** D3
Rayleigh SS6 . . . .**123** D4
Lakeside Ave IG4 . . . .**132** D7
Lakeside Cl IG7 . . . .**111** F6
Lakeside Cres
Brentwood CM14 . . . .**116** D7
Canvey Island SS8 . . . . . .**164** D5
Lakeside Path SS8 . . . . . .**164** A5
Lakeside Ret Pk
RM20 . . . .**172** A2
Lakeside Sh Ctr RM20 . . . .**172** B3
Lakeview SS8 . . . .**164** A5
Lake View SS16 . . . .**140** F4
Lakeview Ct E4 . . . .**109** D4
Lakeview Cvn Pk CM5 . . . . .**26** C3
Lakeview Pk RM3 . . . .**114** C8
Lakin Cl CM2 . . . .**33** A3
Lamb Cl RM18 . . . .**179** C5
Lamberhurst Rd RM8 . . . . .**134** F3
Lambert Ct RM7 . . . .**135** C4
Lambeth Mews SS5 . . . . . .**124** C4
Lambeth Rd
South Benfleet SS7 . . . . .**144** E4
Southend-on-S SS9 . . . . .**146** E6
Lambley Rd RM9 . . . .**153** B6
Lambourn Cl SS3 . . . .**149** E2
LAMBOURNE **90** D5
Lambourne
Canvey Island SS8 . . . . . .**164** A2
East Tilbury RM18 . . . . . .**175** C2
Lambourne Cl IG7 . . . .**112** B7
Lambourne Cres
Basildon SS14 . . . .**142** F5
Chigwell IG7 . . . .**112** B8
Lambourne Ct 5 IG8 . . . . .**110** C3
Lambourne Dr CM13 . . . . . .**95** D3
LAMBOURNE END **90** D1
Lambourne Gdns
5 Barking IG11 . . . .**152** F5
Chingford E4 . . . .**109** A8
Hornchurch RM12 . . . . . .**136** D2
Lambourne Gr CM9 . . . . . .**58** F3
Lambourne Hall Rd
SS4 . . . .**104** F2
Lambourne Mead Cotts
SS4 . . . .**105** A1
Lambourne Prim Sch
RM4 . . . .**90** B6
Lambourne Rd
Barking IG11 . . . .**152** F5
Chigwell IG7 . . . .**111** F7
Ilford IG3 . . . .**133** E2
Lambourne Sq RM4 . . . .**90** C1
Lamb's La N RM13 . . . . . .**155** D2
Lamb's La N RM13 . . . . . .**155** D2
Lamb's La S RM13 . . . . . .**155** C1
Lambs Mdw IG8 . . . .**110** D3
Lamerton Rd IG6 . . . .**111** B1
Lamont Cl 1 SS12 . . . . . .**121** E5
Lamorna Cl E17 . . . .**109** C2

Lampern Cl CM12 . . . . 97 B6
Lampern Cres CM12 . . . . . . 97 C6
Lampern Mews CM12 . . . . . 97 B6
Lampeter Ho **4** RM3 . . . . . 114 E3
Lampetsdowne SS17 . . . . . 161 B3
Lampits EN11 . . . . 21 B6
Lampits Hill SS17 . . . . 161 B4
Lampits Hill Ave
  SS17 . . . . 161 A4
Lampits La SS17 . . . . 161 A4
Lamplighters Cl EN9 . . . . . . 66 A5
Lamson Rd RM13 . . . . 154 F1
Lancaster Ave
  Barking IG11 . . . . 152 E4
  Wanstead E18 . . . . 132 B7
Lancaster Bsns Pk
  SS2 . . . . 147 C7
Lancaster Cl CM15 . . . . 94 A4
Lancaster Cres **3**
  SS1 . . . . 167 B8
Lancaster Dr
  Basildon SS16 . . . . 140 F5
  Hornchurch RM12 . . . . . . 155 C8
  Loughton IG10 . . . . 88 E3
Lancaster Gdns
  Rayleigh SS6 . . . . 146 A8
  Southend-on-S SS1 . . . . . 167 B8
Lancaster Pl IG1 . . . . 152 C8
Lancaster Rd
  Grays RM16 . . . . 172 D2
  North Weald Bassett
    CM16 . . . . 47 A5
  Rayleigh SS6 . . . . 146 A8
Lancaster Sch SS0 . . . . . . 147 C3
Lancelot Rd IG6 . . . . 111 E3
Lancer Way CM12 . . . . 96 F3
Lancing Rd
  Ilford IG2 . . . . 133 D5
  Romford RM3 . . . . 114 E3
Landau Way DA8 . . . . 170 D1
Landermere SS14 . . . . 142 B7
Lander Rd RM17 . . . . 173 D1
Landers Ct CM1 . . . . 31 E5
Landisdale CM3 . . . . 57 A7
Landsburg Rd SS8 . . . . 164 D5
Landscape Rd IG8 . . . . 110 B3
Landseer Ave E12 . . . . 132 A7
Landseer Cl RM11 . . . . 136 B3
Landshill Ct SS0 . . . . 147 C1
Landview Gdns CM5 . . . . . . 49 A1
Landwick Cotts SS3 . . . . . 150 D4
Landwick La CM0 . . . . 85 F7
Lane Ave DA9 . . . . 177 C1
Lane End E17 . . . . 24 E7
Lane Mews E12 . . . . 132 F1
Laneside Ave RM8 . . . . 134 F4
Langdale Cl RM8 . . . . 134 C3
Langdale Ct **10** IG1 . . . . . 133 B1
Langdale Gdns
  Chelmsford CM2 . . . . 54 D8
  Hornchurch RM12 . . . . . . 155 A7
Langdale Ho SS6 . . . . 123 D2
Langdon Conservation
  Ctr★ SS16 . . . . 140 E3
Langdon Cres E6 . . . . 152 A3
LANGDON HILLS 141 C4
Langdon Hills Ctry Pk★
  SS17 . . . . 160 F8
Langdon Mews CM11 . . . . . 97 B3
Langdon Nature Reserve
  (Lincewood)★ SS16 . . . . 141 A3
Langdon Nature Reserve
  (Marks Hill)★ SS16 . . . . 141 C4
Langdon Nature Reserve
  (Willow Park)★
  SS16 . . . . 141 D2
Langdon Rd
  Rayleigh SS6 . . . . 123 B3
  Wallend E6 . . . . 152 A4
Langdon Sch E6 . . . . 152 B4
Langdon Way SS17 . . . . . . 161 B4
Langemore Way CM11 . . . . 97 B3
Langenhoe SS12 . . . . 121 E6
Langfield Cl EN9 . . . . 21 E1
LANGFORD 36 D7
Langford Cres SS7 . . . . . . 144 F6
Langford Gn CM13 . . . . 95 C4
Langford Gr SS13 . . . . 143 C8
Langford Rd
  Heybridge CM9 . . . . 36 F6
  Woodford IG8 . . . . 110 C4
Langfords IG9 . . . . 110 D8
Langham Cres CM12 . . . . . 119 C2
Langham Ct RM11 . . . . 136 C4
Langham Dr
  Ilford RM6 . . . . 134 B5
  Rayleigh SS6 . . . . 123 A3
Langham Ho **3** E11 . . . . 132 B7
Langhorne Rd RM10 . . . . . 154 A4
Langland SS17 . . . . 161 A3
Langley Cl
  Romford RM3 . . . . 114 D3
  Southend-on-S SS9 . . . . 146 B7
Langley Cres
  Dagenham RM9 . . . . 153 D5
  Wanstead E11 . . . . 132 C4
Langley Dr
  Brentwood CM14 . . . . . . 116 A7
  Wanstead E11 . . . . 132 B4
Langley Gdns RM9 . . . . . . 153 D5
Langley Gn EN9 . . . . 21 D1
Langley Mdw IG10 . . . . 89 D7
Langley Pl CM12 . . . . 96 E3
Langleys SS15 . . . . 142 B4
Langport Dr SS0 . . . . 147 B4
Langport Ho **3** RM3 . . . . 114 E3
Langside SS15 . . . . 141 B8
Langston Rd IG10 . . . . 89 D5

Langthorne Cres
  RM17 . . . . 173 C2
Langthornes **1** CM11 . . . 97 B2
Langton Ave
  Chelmsford CM1 . . . . 31 E5
  Wallend E6 . . . . 152 A2
Langtons Jun & Inf Sch
  RM11 . . . . 136 E3
Langton Way RM16 . . . . . . 174 C2
Lanham Pl **7** SS13 . . . . 143 B8
Lanhams SS13 . . . . 143 C8
Lanhams Ct **5** SS13 . . . 143 B8
Lansbury Ave
  Barking IG11 . . . . 153 A5
  Dagenham RM6 . . . . 134 E6
Lansbury Cres DA1 . . . . . . 176 A2
Lansbury Gdns RM18 . . . . 179 A6
Lansdowne Ave SS7 . . . . . 145 F6
Lansdowne Ave SS9 . . . . . 147 A1
Lansdowne Ct
  Hoddesdon EN10 . . . . . . 21 A3
  Redbridge IG5 . . . . 132 E8
Lansdowne Dr SS6 . . . . . . 123 C3
Lansdowne Prim Sch
  RM18 . . . . 178 F5
Lansdowne Rd
  Chingford E4 . . . . 109 A8
  Ilford IG3 . . . . 133 F4
  Wanstead E18 . . . . 132 A8
Lansdowne Sq DA11 . . . . . 178 F1
Lansdown Rd RM18 . . . . . . 179 A5
Lanterns IG10 . . . . 88 F8
Lantern Terr **18** SS1 . . . 167 C7
La Plata Gr CM14 . . . . 116 B7
Lappmark Rd SS8 . . . . 164 D3
Lapwater Cl SS9 . . . . 146 C2
Lapwater Ct SS9 . . . . 146 C2
Lapwing Dr CM9 . . . . 37 C5
Lapwing Ho **8** RM13 . . . 155 A1
Lapwing Rd SS11 . . . . 99 C2
Larch Cl SS15 . . . . 119 C1
Larches The
  Boreham CM3 . . . . 33 E8
  South Benfleet SS7 . . . . 144 C8
Larch Gr CM2 . . . . 54 C6
Larch Wlk CM9 . . . . 37 C6
Larchwood Ave RM5 . . . . . 113 B4
Larchwood Cl
  Romford RM5 . . . . 113 C4
  Southend-on-S SS9 . . . . 146 B6
Larchwood Gdns CM15 . . . . 94 A3
Larchwood Ho **2** IG7 . . . 112 B6
Larchwood Prim Sch
  CM15 . . . . 94 A3
Lark Cl CM14 . . . . 116 B6
Larke Rise SS2 . . . . 147 D5
Larkfield SS17 . . . . 161 B4
Larkfield Cl SS4 . . . . 125 D4
Larkhill Ave SS4 . . . . 104 A2
Lark Hill Rd SS4 . . . . 104 B1
Larkin Cl CM13 . . . . 95 C2
Larks Gr IG11 . . . . 152 E5
Larkrise Prim Sch CM2 . . . 54 E6
Larkshall Bsns Ctr E4 . . . 109 D8
Larkshall Cres E4 . . . . 109 C6
Larkshall Ct
  Chingford E4 . . . . 109 C5
  Romford RM7 . . . . 113 C4
Larkshall Rd E4 . . . . 109 D6
Lark's La
  Broomfield CM3 . . . . 19 A6
  Great Waltham CM3 . . . . 18 F5
Larkspur Cl RM15 . . . . 157 C2
Larkspur Ct **3** CM1 . . . . . 32 F6
Larkswood CM17 . . . . 24 C6
Larkswood Ct E4 . . . . 109 D5
Larkswood Prim Sch
  E4 . . . . 109 B6
Larkswood Rd
  Chingford E4 . . . . 109 B6
  Corringham SS17 . . . . . . 161 B3
Larkswood Wlk **2**
  SS12 . . . . 121 D6
Larsen Dr E4 . . . . 65 D5
Larup Ave SS8 . . . . 164 C4
Larup Gdns SS8 . . . . 164 C4
La Salette RC Prim Sch
  RM13 . . . . 154 F2
Lascelles Cl CM15 . . . . 94 A4
Lascelles Gdns SS4 . . . . . 125 D6
Latchett Rd E18 . . . . 110 B2
Latchetts Shaw SS16 . . . . 142 B4
Latchford Pl IG7 . . . . 112 B6
Latching Ct RM3 . . . . 114 D6
LATCHINGDON 82 A6
Latchingdon CE Prim Sch
  CM3 . . . . 82 B6
Latchingdon Cl SS6 . . . . . 123 A3
Latchingdon Gdns
  IG8 . . . . 110 E4
Latchingdon Rd CM3 . . . . . 81 B5
Latchmore Bank CM22 . . . . 2 B8
Lathcoates Cres CM2 . . . . 54 E8
Lathom Rd E6 . . . . 152 A5
Latimer Dr
  Basildon SS15 . . . . 119 B1
  Hornchurch RM12 . . . . . . 136 D1
LATTON BUSH 24 B5
Latton Bush Bsns Ctr The
  CM18 . . . . 23 F5
Latton Common Rd
  CM18 . . . . 24 B5
Latton Gn CM18 . . . . 23 F4
Latton Green Prim Sch
  CM18 . . . . 23 F4
Latton Hall Cl CM20 . . . . . 11 A1
Latton Ho CM18 . . . . 24 B5

Latton St
  Harlow, Brays Grove CM18,
    CM20 . . . . 24 B7
  Harlow, Potter Street
    CM17 . . . . 24 C5
Launceston Cl RM3 . . . . . . 114 C2
Launder's La RM13 . . . . . . 155 F1
Laundry Cotts RM13 . . . . . 170 D6
Laundry La
  Lower Nazeing EN9 . . . . . 43 E6
  Mountnessing CM15 . . . . 95 D8
Laura Cl E11 . . . . 132 C6
Laurel Ave SS12 . . . . 121 C7
Laurel Cl
  Brentwood CM13 . . . . 95 B4
  Redbridge IG5 . . . . 111 D4
  Southend-on-S SS9 . . . . 165 D8
Laurel Cres RM7 . . . . 135 E3
Laurel Ct
  6 Brentwood CM13 . . . . 95 C3
  Rainham RM13 . . . . 155 C1
Laurel Dr SS15 . . . . 157 D1
Laurel Gdns C4 . . . . 87 B2
Laurel Gr **4** CM2 . . . . 54 A8
Laurel La CM12 . . . . 136 E2
Laurel Mead Ct **8**
  E18 . . . . 110 A2
Laurels The
  8 Belvedere DA17 . . . . 169 A1
  Buckhurst Hill IG9 . . . . . 88 C1
  Rayleigh SS6 . . . . 145 F8
  South Woodham Ferrers
    CM3 . . . . 101 D8
Laurence Croft CM1 . . . . . 31 B1
Laurence Ind Est SS2 . . . 147 B6
Laurie Wlk RM1 . . . . 135 E6
Lauriston Bglws CM9 . . . . 39 C6
Lauriston Pl **1** SS1 . . . . 167 C8
Lavenham Ho E17 . . . . 109 B2
Lavender Ave RM15 . . . . . . 94 B3
Lavender Cl
  Harlow CM20 . . . . 10 C1
  Romford RM3 . . . . 114 D3
  South Ockendon RM15 . . . 157 E1
Lavender Ct **1** CM1 . . . . . 32 F5
Lavender Dr CM0 . . . . 84 C3
Lavender Gr SS0 . . . . 147 D3
Lavender Ho **2** DA1 . . . . 176 A2
Lavender Mews
  Canvey Island SS8 . . . . . 163 F2
  Southend-on-S SS0 . . . . 147 D3
Lavender Pl IG1 . . . . 152 B7
Lavender Way SS12 . . . . . 121 C7
Lavenham Ct CM15 . . . . . . 94 D1
Lavers The SS6 . . . . 123 E3
Lawford Inf Sch CM12 . . . 155 C8
Lawford La
  Chelmsford CM1 . . . . 31 D3
  Writtle CM1 . . . . 31 C1
Lawford Mead Inf Sch
  CM1 . . . . 31 D5
Lawford Mead Jun Sch
  CM1 . . . . 31 D5
Law Ho IG11 . . . . 153 A3
Lawling Ave CM9 . . . . 37 C5
Lawlinge Rd CM3 . . . . 82 B5
Lawn Ave SS2 . . . . 148 B2
Lawn Farm Gr RM6 . . . . . . 134 E7
Lawn Hall Chase CM6 . . . . . 7 D8
Lawn La CM1 . . . . 32 D6
Lawn Prim Sch DA11 . . . . 178 C1
Lawn Rd DA11 . . . . 178 C1
Lawns Cres RM17 . . . . 178 D8
Lawns Ct SS7 . . . . 144 B7
Lawns Pl RM17 . . . . 178 D8
Lawns The
  Brentwood CM14 . . . . . . 116 E5
  Chelmsford CM1 . . . . 32 D5
  Chingford E4 . . . . 109 A5
  East Hanningfield CM3 . . . 78 C4
  South Benfleet SS7 . . . . 144 C7
Lawns Way RM5 . . . . 113 C3
Lawn The CM20 . . . . 11 B3
Lawrence Ave
  Little Ilford E12 . . . . 152 A8
  Sawbridgeworth CM21 . . . 1 E4
  Stanstead Abbotts SG12 . . 8 C4
Lawrence Cres RM10 . . . . . 135 B1
Lawrence Ct **6** IG8 . . . . 110 C4
Lawrence Gdns RM18 . . . . 179 B7
Lawrence Hill E4 . . . . 109 A4
Lawrence Moorings
  CM21 . . . . 1 F2
Lawrence Rd
  Basildon SS13 . . . . 143 F8
  Romford RM2 . . . . 136 B6
Lawrence Trad Est
  RM17 . . . . 177 E8
Lawson Cl IG1 . . . . 152 D7
Lawton Rd IG10 . . . . 89 B6
Laxtons SS17 . . . . 160 D3
Laxtons The SS4 . . . . 125 D5
Layborne Ave RM3 . . . . . . 114 C8
Leach Cl CM2 . . . . 55 B7
Lea Ct **1** E4 . . . . 109 C8
Leadale Ave E4 . . . . 109 A8
Leaden Cl CM6 . . . . 15 D8
LEADEN RODING 15 C8
Leader Ave E12 . . . . 152 A7
Leafy Way CM13 . . . . 95 D1
Lea Hall Bglws CM22 . . . . . 3 B3
Leamington Cl RM3 . . . . . . 115 A4
Leamington Gdns
  IG3 . . . . 133 F2
Leamington Rd
  Hockley SS5 . . . . 124 F7
  Romford RM3 . . . . 115 A5
  Southend-on-S SS1 . . . . 167 C8

Leapingwell Cl CM2 . . . . . 33 A3
Lea Rd
  Grays RM16 . . . . 174 A1
  Hoddesdon EN11 . . . . . . 21 C8
  Holdbrook EN9 . . . . 65 A5
  South Benfleet SS7 . . . . 144 C5
Lea Road Ind Pk EN9 . . . . 65 A5
Leas Cl SS0 . . . . 166 B8
Leas Ct SS0 . . . . 106 C6
Leas Gdns SS0 . . . . 166 B8
Leaside SS7 . . . . 144 C5
Leaside Bsns Ctr EN3 . . . . 87 A7
Leaside Ho **6** EN11 . . . . 21 D8
Leas The
  Burnham-on-C CM0 . . . . 106 C6
  Ingatestone CM4 . . . . . . 74 A2
  Southend-on-S SS0 . . . . 166 C7
  Upminster RM14 . . . . . . 137 D4
Leasway
  Brentwood CM14 . . . . . . 116 D7
  Grays RM16 . . . . 173 C5
  Rayleigh SS6 . . . . 123 C2
  Upminster RM14 . . . . . . 156 C8
  Wickford SS12 . . . . 121 B6
Leasway The SS0 . . . . 166 B8
Leat Cl CM21 . . . . 1 F3
Leathart Cl RM12 . . . . 155 B5
Leatherbottle Hill CM4 . . . 76 A2
Leather La
  Hornchurch RM11 . . . . . . 136 D3
  Southend-on-S SS1 . . . . 167 A8
Lea Valley Rd E4 . . . . 87 A3
Lea Way CM12 . . . . 119 B8
Lechmere App IG8 . . . . . . 110 D1
Lechmere Ave
  Chigwell IG7 . . . . 111 C6
  Woodford IG8 . . . . 110 D1
Leconfield Wlk RM12 . . . . 155 C6
Lectern Mews SS15 . . . . . 141 D6
Lede Rd SS8 . . . . 164 B4
Lee Ave RM6 . . . . 134 E5
Lee Chapel La SS16 . . . . . 141 D3
LEE CHAPEL NORTH 141 E6
Lee Chapel Prim Sch
  SS16 . . . . 141 F4
LEE CHAPEL SOUTH 141 F3
Lee Cl SG12 . . . . 8 C4
Leecon Way SS4 . . . . 125 E3
Lee Ct CM2 . . . . 54 E7
Leeds Rd IG1 . . . . 133 D3
Leeford CM1 . . . . 31 F6
Lee Gardens Ave
  RM11 . . . . 137 A3
Lee Gr IG7 . . . . 111 B8
Leeholm Ho RM15 . . . . . . 171 C4
Lee Lotts SS3 . . . . 150 A4
Lee Rd SS13 . . . . 143 F6
Lees Manor Ct RM11 . . . . 136 F2
Lees The SS6 . . . . 164 A6
Lee Valley Ctry Pk★
  EN10 . . . . 21 B3
Lee Valley Ho EN9 . . . . . . 66 A5
Lee Valley Park Visitor
  Ctr★ EN9 . . . . 43 C3
Lee Valley Park Vst Ctr★
  EN9 . . . . 65 C6
Lee Valley Pk★ EN3 . . . . . 87 A8
Leeview Ct E4 . . . . 87 C1
Leeward Rd CM3 . . . . 101 E5
Leeway The CM3 . . . . 56 F7
Lee Wlk SS16 . . . . 141 E5
Lee Woottens La
  SS16 . . . . 142 A4
Legg St CM1 . . . . 32 B3
Legon Ave RM7 . . . . 135 C3
Legra Ave EN11 . . . . 21 A6
Leicester Ave SS4 . . . . . . 147 F8
Leicester Gdns IG3 . . . . . 133 E4
Leicester Rd
  Tilbury RM18 . . . . 178 F6
  Wanstead E11 . . . . 132 B6
Leige Ave SS4 . . . . 164 A6
Leigham Court Dr
  SS9 . . . . 146 F1
Leighams Rd CM3 . . . . 78 E7
Leigh Ave IG4 . . . . 132 D7
LEIGH BECK 164 F2
Leigh Beck Jun & Inf Schs
  SS8 . . . . 164 E3
Leigh Beck La SS8 . . . . . . 164 F3
Leigh Beck Rd SS8 . . . . . 164 F3
Leighcliff Rd SS9 . . . . 165 F8
Leighcroft Gdns SS9 . . . . 146 D4
Leigh Ct **1** E18 . . . . 110 A1
Leigh Dr RM3 . . . . 114 D6
Leigh Fells SS13 . . . . 143 C6
Leighfields SS7 . . . . 145 B6
Leighfields Ave SS9 . . . . . 146 D6
Leighfields Rd SS9 . . . . . . 146 C6
Leigh Gdns SS9 . . . . 146 C1
Leigh Hall Rd SS9 . . . . . . 146 E1
Leigh Heath Ct SS9 . . . . . 146 A2
Leigh Heritage Ctr★
  SS9 . . . . 165 D8
Leigh Hill SS9 . . . . 165 E8
Leigh Hill Cl SS9 . . . . 165 E8
Leigh Ho SS9 . . . . 165 E8
Leigh Hts SS9 . . . . 145 F3
Leigh Jun & Inf Sch
  SS9 . . . . 146 E1
Leighlands Rd CM3 . . . . . . 101 E7
LEIGH-ON-SEA 146 E1
Leigh-on-Sea Sta
  SS9 . . . . 165 C8
Leigh Park Cl SS9 . . . . . . 146 C1
Leigh Park Ct SS9 . . . . . . 165 D8
Leigh Park Rd SS9 . . . . . . 165 D8

Leigh Rd
  Canvey Island SS8 . . . . . 164 B2
  Southend-on-S SS9 . . . . 146 F1
  Wallend E6 . . . . 152 A6
Leighs Rd CM3 . . . . 19 E6
Leighs Rifleman CM12 . . . 96 F3
Leighton Ave
  Little Ilford E12 . . . . 152 A7
  Southend-on-S SS9 . . . . 146 F1
Leighton Gdns RM18 . . . . 179 B7
Leighton Rd SS7 . . . . 144 C7
Leigh View Dr SS9 . . . . . . 146 F4
Leighville Gr SS9 . . . . 146 D1
Leighwood Ave SS9 . . . . . 146 E5
Leinster Ct IG6 . . . . 112 A4
Leinster Rd SS15 . . . . 141 D6
Leitrim Ave SS3 . . . . 168 C5
Lekoe Rd SS8 . . . . 163 F6
Lena Kennedy Cl E4 . . . . 109 C4
Lenham Way SS13 . . . . . . 143 C6
Lenmore Ave RM17 . . . . . . 173 C3
Lennard Ho RM15 . . . . 171 D5
Lennard Row RM15 . . . . . . 171 D5
Lennox Ave DA11 . . . . 179 A1
Lennox Cl
  Grays RM16 . . . . 172 C2
  Romford RM1 . . . . 135 F5
Lennox Dr SS12 . . . . 121 F5
Lennox Gdns IG1 . . . . 132 F3
Lennox Ho
  7 Belvedere DA17 . . . . 169 A3
  15 Brentwood CM14 . . . 116 C7
Lennox Rd DA11 . . . . 178 F1
Lenthall Ave RM17 . . . . . . 173 A3
Lenthall Rd IG10 . . . . 89 D5
Len Wastel Inf Sch The
  SS13 . . . . 143 A5
Leonard Ave RM7 . . . . 135 D3
Leonard Davis Ho
  CM16 . . . . 47 A4
Leonard Dr SS6 . . . . 123 A4
Leonard Rd
  Basildon SS16 . . . . 142 B2
  Chingford E4 . . . . 109 A4
  Southend-on-S SS0 . . . . 166 D7
Leonard Way CM14 . . . . . . 115 E6
Leon Dr SS16 . . . . 142 D3
Leslie Cl SS9 . . . . 146 D6
Leslie Dr SS9 . . . . 146 D6
Leslie Gdns SS4 . . . . 123 F1
Leslie Newnham Ct **1**
  CM9 . . . . 37 A1
Leslie Pk CM0 . . . . 106 C4
Leslie Rd SS6 . . . . 123 F1
Lesney Gdns SS4 . . . . 125 D3
Lessingham Ave IG5 . . . . 133 A8
Lessington Ave RM7 . . . . . 135 C5
LESSNESS HEATH 169 B1
Lessness Heath Prim Sch
  DA17 . . . . 169 A1
Lessness Pk DA17 . . . . . . 169 A1
Lessness Rd **16** DA17 . . 169 A1
Lester Ho IG8 . . . . 109 D3
Lettons Chase CM3 . . . . . 101 E6
Letzen Rd SS8 . . . . 164 A4
Leveller Row CM12 . . . . . . 96 F3
Leventhorpe Sch The
  CM21 . . . . 1 E4
Lever La SS4 . . . . 125 F1
Lever Sq RM16 . . . . 174 A2
Leverton Inf Sch The
  EN9 . . . . 65 F5
Leverton Jun Sch The
  EN9 . . . . 65 F5
Leverton Way EN9 . . . . . . 65 C6
Leveson Rd RM16 . . . . 174 B3
Levett Gdns IG3 . . . . 152 F8
Levett Rd
  Barking IG11 . . . . 152 E6
  Stanford-le-H SS17 . . . . 160 E2
Levine Gdns IG11 . . . . 153 D3
Lewes Cl RM17 . . . . 178 A8
Lewes Ct SS2 . . . . 148 C3
Lewes Rd
  Romford RM3 . . . . 114 D6
  Southend-on-S SS2 . . . . 148 C3
Lewes Way SS7 . . . . 145 B7
Lewin Pl CM3 . . . . 33 E8
Lewis Ave E17 . . . . 109 A2
Lewis Cl CM15 . . . . 94 F2
Lewisham Ct **9** EN3 . . . . 65 A1
Lewis Ho E4 . . . . 109 A5
Lewis Rd
  Hornchurch RM11 . . . . . . 136 C5
  Swanscombe DA10 . . . . 177 E1
Lewis Way RM10 . . . . 154 B6
Lexden Dr RM6 . . . . 134 B5
Lexdon Ct **1** RM6 . . . . . 134 B5
Lexham Ho **9** IG11 . . . . 152 D4
Lexington Way RM14 . . . . 137 F5
Leybourne Dr CM1 . . . . . . 32 E7
Leyburn Cres RM3 . . . . . . 114 E3
Leyburn Rd RM3 . . . . 114 E3
Leycroft Cl IG10 . . . . 89 A4
Leyland Cl SS1 . . . . 167 B8
Leyland Gdns IG8 . . . . . . 110 C5
Leys Ave RM10 . . . . 154 C5
Leys Cl RM10 . . . . 154 D5
Leysings SS16 . . . . 141 C4
Leys Prim Sch The
  RM10 . . . . 154 C5
Ley St
  Ilford IG1 . . . . 133 B2

Ley St *continued*
Ilford, Newbury Park IG1, IG2 . . . . . 133 D3
Leys The
Basildon SS16 . . . . . 142 C4
Chelmsford CM2 . . . . . 32 F5
Leyswood Dr IG2 . . . . . 133 E6
Liberty Cotts RM4 . . . . . 113 E8
Liberty Ct IG11 . . . . . 153 C3
Liberty II Ctr RM1 . . . . . 135 F6
Liberty The RM1 . . . . . 135 E6
Library Hill CM14 . . . . . 116 D8
Libro Ct E4 . . . . . 109 A6
Lichen Ct IG6 . . . . . 133 B8
Lichfield Cl CM1 . . . . . 31 E4
Lichfield Rd
Dagenham RM8 . . . . . 134 C1
Woodford IG8 . . . . . 109 E6
Lichfields The SS14 . . . . . 142 F7
Lichfield Terr RM14 . . . . . 137 F2
Lifstan Way SS1 . . . . . 167 E7
Lightermans Way DA9 . . . . . 177 C3
Lilac Ave
Canvey Island SS8 . . . . . 164 C4
Wickford SS12 . . . . . 121 C7
Lilac Cl
Chelmsford CM2 . . . . . 54 C6
Pilgrims Hatch CM15 . . . . . 94 B4
Lilac Gdns RM7 . . . . . 135 E3
Lilac Ho 1 DA1 . . . . . 176 A2
Lilac Rd EN11 . . . . . 21 B8
Lilford Rd CM11 . . . . . 97 C4
Lilian Cres CM13 . . . . . 117 C8
Lilian Gdns IG8 . . . . . 110 B2
Lilian Pl SS6 . . . . . 146 A8
Lilian Rd CM0 . . . . . 106 C5
Lillechurch Rd RM8 . . . . . 153 C6
Lilley Cl CM14 . . . . . 115 F6
Lilliard Cl EN11 . . . . . 8 B2
Lilliput Rd RM7 . . . . . 135 D4
Lillyputts Equestrian Ctr RM11 . . . . . 137 A5
Lillyville Wlk SS6 . . . . . 124 A1
Lily Albon Ct RM9 . . . . . 153 F8
Lily Cl CM1 . . . . . 32 F6
Lilystone Cl CM4 . . . . . 75 D1
Lilystone Hall CM4 . . . . . 75 D1
Limberg Rd SS8 . . . . . 163 D4
Limbourne Ave RM8 . . . . . 134 F4
Limbourne Dr CM9 . . . . . 37 D5
Limburg Rd SS8 . . . . . 163 D4
Lime Ave
Brentwood CM13 . . . . . 116 F7
Southend-on-S SS9 . . . . . 146 C2
Upminster RM14 . . . . . 156 A8
Limebrook Way CM9 . . . . . 58 E7
Lime Cl
Buckhurst Hill IG9 . . . . . 110 D8
Romford RM7 . . . . . 135 C7
South Ockendon RM15 . . . . . 157 C2
Lime Ct
Hockley SS5 . . . . . 124 E6
Hornchurch RM11 . . . . . 136 C4
Lime Gr
Doddinghurst CM15 . . . . . 72 D1
Redbridge IG6 . . . . . 111 F4
Lime Lo SS9 . . . . . 146 C2
Lime Pl SS15 . . . . . 119 C1
Lime Rd SS7 . . . . . 144 E4
Limerick Gdns RM14 . . . . . 137 F4
Limes Ave
Chigwell IG7 . . . . . 111 C4
Little Ilford E12 . . . . . 132 F1
Wanstead E11 . . . . . 132 B7
Limes Ct
Brentwood CM15 . . . . . 94 D1
17 Hoddesdon EN11 . . . . . 21 A6
Limes Farm Jun & Inf Sch IG7 . . . . . 111 D5
Limeslade Cl SS17 . . . . . 161 A3
Limes The
Brentwood CM13 . . . . . 116 F7
Galleywood CM2 . . . . . 54 B2
Ingatestone CM4 . . . . . 74 C4
Purfleet RM19 . . . . . 171 A1
Rayleigh SS6 . . . . . 123 F1
Romford RM11 . . . . . 136 D8
Limetree Ave SS7 . . . . . 144 B4
Lime Tree Cl E11 . . . . . 132 C7
Limetree Rd SS8 . . . . . 164 E4
Lime Way CM0 . . . . . 106 A5
Lime Wlk CM2 . . . . . 54 C6
Limewood Ct IG4 . . . . . 132 F6
Lincefield SS16 . . . . . 141 B3
Lincewood Prim Sch
Basildon SS16 . . . . . 141 B3
Basildon SS16 . . . . . 141 C4
Lincoln Ave RM7 . . . . . 135 E3
Lincoln Chase SS2 . . . . . 148 E3
Lincoln Cl RM11 . . . . . 137 A6
Lincoln Ct
2 Ilford IG2 . . . . . 133 C5
Redbridge IG1 . . . . . 132 F4
Lincoln Gdns IG1 . . . . . 132 E4
Lincoln Ho 12 RM3 . . . . . 114 D4
Lincoln Rd
Basildon SS14 . . . . . 142 F7
Rochford SS4 . . . . . 125 C5
Woodford E18 . . . . . 110 A2
Lincolns Field CM16 . . . . . 45 F1
Lincolns La CM14 . . . . . 93 C3
Lincoln Way SS8 . . . . . 163 E4
Linda Gdns CM12 . . . . . 96 E4
Lindal Ct 1 E18 . . . . . 110 A2
Linden Cl
Chelmsford CM2 . . . . . 54 C7
Purfleet RM19 . . . . . 176 C8
Rayleigh SS6 . . . . . 123 F1
South Benfleet SS7 . . . . . 144 C6
Linden Cres IG8 . . . . . 110 B4
Linden Ct
South Benfleet SS7 . . . . . 144 C6
Southend-on-S SS9 . . . . . 147 A2
Linden Leas SS7 . . . . . 144 C6
Linden Rd SS7 . . . . . 144 C6
Linden Rise CM14 . . . . . 116 D5
Lindens EN9 . . . . . 66 C4
Linden St RM7 . . . . . 135 D6
Lindens The
Basildon SS16 . . . . . 141 A5
Loughton IG10 . . . . . 88 F4
Stock CM4 . . . . . 75 F2
Linden Way SS8 . . . . . 163 F4
Linde Rd SS8 . . . . . 164 B4
Lindfield Rd RM3 . . . . . 114 E5
Lindhurst Dr CM11 . . . . . 98 C4
Lindisfarne Ave SS9 . . . . . 147 A2
Lindisfarne Ct
Basildon SS12 . . . . . 122 A5
Maldon CM9 . . . . . 58 E8
Lindisfarne Rd RM8 . . . . . 134 C1
Lindon Rd SS11 . . . . . 99 C3
Lindsell Gn SS14 . . . . . 142 E5
Lindsell La SS14 . . . . . 142 E5
Lindsey Cl CM14 . . . . . 116 A6
Lindsey Ct
Rayleigh SS6 . . . . . 123 A3
14 Wickford SS12 . . . . . 121 E5
Lindsey Rd
Dagenham RM8 . . . . . 134 C1
Great Wakering SS3 . . . . . 150 B4
Lindsey St CM16 . . . . . 46 A2
Lindsey Way RM11 . . . . . 136 C6
Lindum SS1 . . . . . 168 A6
LINFORD 175 A4
Linford Cl CM19 . . . . . 23 C6
Linford Dr SS14 . . . . . 142 F6
Linford End CM19 . . . . . 23 C6
Linford Mews CM9 . . . . . 58 E8
Linford Rd RM16 . . . . . 174 C1
Lingcroft SS16 . . . . . 142 A4
Lingfield Ave RM14 . . . . . 137 A1
Lingfield Dr SS4 . . . . . 126 A3
Lingmere Cl IG7 . . . . . 111 C8
Lingrove Gdns IG9 . . . . . 110 B8
Lingwood Cl CM3 . . . . . 56 E7
Linkdale CM12 . . . . . 119 B8
Link Rd
Canvey Island SS8 . . . . . 163 F4
Dagenham RM9 . . . . . 154 B3
Rayleigh SS6 . . . . . 123 D3
Stanford-le-H SS17 . . . . . 160 D3
Links Ave RM2 . . . . . 114 B1
Links Ct SS1 . . . . . 167 F7
Links Dr CM2 . . . . . 53 F7
Linkside IG7 . . . . . 111 C5
Links Rd IG8 . . . . . 110 A5
Links The CM12 . . . . . 96 E4
Linksway SS9 . . . . . 146 C4
Links Way SS7 . . . . . 145 F3
Linkway
Basildon SS14 . . . . . 142 B6
Dagenham RM8 . . . . . 153 C8
Link Way RM11 . . . . . 136 E3
Linkway Rd CM14 . . . . . 115 F7
Linley Cl RM18 . . . . . 180 D7
Linley Cres RM7 . . . . . 135 C8
Linne Rd SS8 . . . . . 164 C5
Linnet Cl SS3 . . . . . 168 E8
Linnet Dr
Chelmsford CM2 . . . . . 54 B6
South Benfleet SS7 . . . . . 144 C2
Linnet Ho DA9 . . . . . 177 A1
Linnets SS16 . . . . . 142 A3
Linnett Cl E4 . . . . . 109 C6
Linnet Terr IG5 . . . . . 133 A8
Linnet Way RM19 . . . . . 171 B1
Linroping Ave SS8 . . . . . 164 F3
Linsdell Rd IG11 . . . . . 152 C4
Linton Ct RM1 . . . . . 113 E1
Linton Rd
Barking IG11 . . . . . 152 C5
Southend-on-S SS3 . . . . . 168 E6
Lintons Cl EN11 . . . . . 21 B7
Lintons The
1 Barking IG11 . . . . . 152 C5
Chelmsford CM2 . . . . . 55 D6
Linwood CM21 . . . . . 1 E2
Lionel Oxley Ho RM17 . . . . . 178 B8
Lionel Rd SS8 . . . . . 164 B3
Lion Fields SS3 . . . . . 150 B3
Lionfield Terr CM1 . . . . . 32 D3
Lion Hill SS17 . . . . . 161 D3
Lion La CM12 . . . . . 97 A2
Lion & Lamb Ct 7 CM14 . . . . . 116 C8
Liphook Cl RM12 . . . . . 154 F8
Lippits Hill SS16 . . . . . 141 C3
Lippitts Hill IG10 . . . . . 87 F7
Lisa Cl CM12 . . . . . 97 B6
Lisle Pl RM17 . . . . . 173 A3
Lister Ave RM3 . . . . . 114 E1
Lister Rd RM18 . . . . . 179 A5
Lister Tye CM2 . . . . . 54 C7
Liston Way 1 IG8 . . . . . 110 C3
Listowel Rd RM10 . . . . . 135 A1
Litchborough Pk CM3 . . . . . 56 F8
Littell Tweed CM2 . . . . . 33 A3
Little Aston Rd RM3 . . . . . 115 A3
LITTLE BADDOW 34 D4
Little Baddow Rd
Danbury CM3 . . . . . 56 E7
Little Baddow Rd *continued*
Woodham Walter CM9 . . . . . 35 C3
Little Belhus Cl RM15 . . . . . 157 A1
Little Bentley SS14 . . . . . 142 B7
Little Berry La SS16 . . . . . 141 A4
Little Brays CM18 . . . . . 24 A6
Little Brook Hospl DA2 . . . . . 176 C1
Littlebrook Manor Way DA1 . . . . . 176 A2
Little Brook Rd CM19 . . . . . 22 C8
LITTLE BURSTEAD 118 F5
Littlebury Ct
Basildon SS13 . . . . . 143 A8
Kelvedon Hatch CM15 . . . . . 71 F2
Littlebury Gn SS13 . . . . . 143 A8
Little Cattins CM19 . . . . . 22 F4
Little Charlton SS13 . . . . . 143 C6
Little Chittock SS14 . . . . . 142 E6
Littlecroft CM3 . . . . . 101 D6
Little Dodden SS16 . . . . . 141 F4
Little Dorrit CM1 . . . . . 31 E7
Little Dragons IG10 . . . . . 88 D5
LITTLE END 70 E5
Little Fields CM3 . . . . . 57 A7
Little Fretches SS9 . . . . . 146 E4
Little Friday Rd E4 . . . . . 109 E8
Little Garth SS13 . . . . . 143 A5
Little Gaynes Gdns RM14 . . . . . 156 B8
Little Gaynes La RM14 . . . . . 156 B8
Little Gearies IG6 . . . . . 133 B7
Little Gerpins Rd RM14 . . . . . 155 F4
Little & Great Sir Hughes La CM2 . . . . . 55 B2
Little Gregories La CM16 . . . . . 67 D5
Little Grove Field CM19 . . . . . 23 C8
Little Gypps Cl SS8 . . . . . 163 F4
Little Gypps Rd SS8 . . . . . 163 F3
LITTLE HALLINGBURY 2 D8
Little Hallingbury CE Prim Sch CM22 . . . . . 2 C7
Little Hayes Chase
Hullbridge CM3 . . . . . 102 C8
South Woodham Ferrers CM3 . . . . . 80 C1
Little Hays SS9 . . . . . 146 B6
LITTLE HEATH 134 B7
Little Heath
Hatfield Heath CM22 . . . . . 3 A3
Ilford RM6 . . . . . 134 B7
Little Heath Sch RM6 . . . . . 134 B7
Little Hills CM9 . . . . . 36 D8
Little Holt 10 E11 . . . . . 132 A6
Littlehurst La SS15 . . . . . 119 F2
Little Hyde La CM4 . . . . . 74 B6
LITTLE ILFORD 152 A7
Little Kingston SS16 . . . . . 141 D2
LITTLE LAVER 26 F7
Little Laver Rd CM5 . . . . . 26 F7
Little London La CM9 . . . . . 35 D4
Little Lullaway SS15 . . . . . 141 F7
Little Malgraves Ind Est RM14 . . . . . 140 F1
Little Mdw CM1 . . . . . 31 A1
Little Mdws CM9 . . . . . 57 E6
Littlemoor Rd IG1 . . . . . 133 D1
Little Nell CM1 . . . . . 31 E7
Little Norsey Rd CM11 . . . . . 97 C4
Little Oak Mews SS11 . . . . . 121 D7
Little Oaks SS14 . . . . . 142 A6
Little Oxcroft SS15 . . . . . 141 B6
LITTLE OXNEY GREEN 52 E8
LITTLE PARNDON 10 B1
Little Parndon Sch CM20 . . . . . 10 B1
Little Pluckett's Way IG9 . . . . . 88 D1
Little Pound CM15 . . . . . 72 C3
Little Pynchons CM18 . . . . . 24 A5
Little Russets CM13 . . . . . 95 E2
Little Searles SS13 . . . . . 143 B7
Little Spenders SS14 . . . . . 142 D8
Little St EN9 . . . . . 65 C3
Little Stambridge Hall Rd SS4 . . . . . 126 B3
Little Stile CM1 . . . . . 53 A8
Littlethorpe SS16 . . . . . 142 F4
Little Thorpe SS1 . . . . . 149 B1
LITTLE THURROCK 173 D3
Little Thurrock Prim Sch RM17 . . . . . 173 D3
Littleton Ave E4 . . . . . 87 F1
Little Totham Rd CM9 . . . . . 38 D8
LITTLE WAKERING 149 D6
Little Wakering Hall La SS3 . . . . . 150 A4
Little Wakering Rd SS3 . . . . . 149 E6
LITTLE WALTHAM 19 C6
Little Waltham CE Prim Sch CM3 . . . . . 19 B7
Little Waltham Rd CM1 . . . . . 19 D1
LITTLE WARLEY 116 F2
Little Warley Hall La CM13, RM14 . . . . . 138 E6
Little Wheatley Chase SS6 . . . . . 123 A4
Little Wlk CM20 . . . . . 23 D8
Liverymen Wlk 5 DA9 . . . . . 177 C3
Livingstone Cl CM5 . . . . . 49 A2
Livingstone Cotts CM5 . . . . . 49 A2
Livingstone Lo E17 . . . . . 109 A1
Livingstone Terr RM13 . . . . . 154 E4
Llewellyn Cl CM1 . . . . . 32 D3
Lloyd Mews EN3 . . . . . 65 A1
Lloyd Rd RM9 . . . . . 153 F5
Lloyd Wise Cl SS2 . . . . . 148 D3
Lobelia Cl CM1 . . . . . 33 A6
Locarno Ave SS11 . . . . . 99 E2
Locke Cl
Rainham RM13 . . . . . 154 F6
Stanford-le-H SS17 . . . . . 160 C3
Lockhart Lo E4 . . . . . 87 E2
Lock Hill CM9 . . . . . 37 E2
Locks Hill SS4 . . . . . 125 F1
Lockside Marina CM2 . . . . . 32 D1
Locksley Cl SS2 . . . . . 148 F2
Lock View CM21 . . . . . 1 F2
Lockwell Rd RM10 . . . . . 135 A1
Lockwood Pl E4 . . . . . 109 A4
Lockwood Wlk RM1 . . . . . 135 E6
Lockyer Mews EN3 . . . . . 65 B1
Lockyer Rd RM19 . . . . . 176 C8
Lodden Ho 5 RM3 . . . . . 115 A4
Lodge Ave
Dagenham RM8, RM9 . . . . . 153 B7
Great Baddow CM2 . . . . . 54 F7
Romford RM2 . . . . . 136 A7
Lodge Cl
Brentwood CM13 . . . . . 95 E2
Chigwell IG7 . . . . . 112 A7
Rayleigh SS6 . . . . . 123 E1
Thundersley SS7 . . . . . 145 A5
Lodge Cres CM3 . . . . . 33 E7
Lodge Ct RM12 . . . . . 136 E2
Lodge Farm Cl SS9 . . . . . 146 D5
Lodge Hall CM18 . . . . . 23 E4
Lodge Hill IG4 . . . . . 132 E7
Lodge La
Grays RM16, RM17 . . . . . 173 B3
Purleigh CM3 . . . . . 58 C2
Romford RM5 . . . . . 113 A4
Waltham Abbey EN9 . . . . . 65 D4
Lodgelands Cl SS6 . . . . . 123 F1
Lodge Rd
Loughton CM16 . . . . . 67 A5
Maldon CM9 . . . . . 36 F3
Woodham Ferrers CM3 . . . . . 78 F6
Woodham Mortimer CM3, CM9 . . . . . 58 B5
Writtle CM1 . . . . . 53 A8
Lodge The
Epping CM16 . . . . . 46 A1
2 Hornchurch RM11 . . . . . 136 B3
Redbridge IG6 . . . . . 111 E3
Lodge Villas IG8 . . . . . 109 F4
Lodwick SS3 . . . . . 168 C5
Loewen Rd RM16 . . . . . 174 A3
Loftin Way CM2 . . . . . 54 D7
Loftus Rd 5 IG11 . . . . . 152 C6
Logan Ct 3 RM1 . . . . . 135 E6
Logan Link SS12 . . . . . 121 F5
Logan Mews 2 RM1 . . . . . 135 E6
Loman Path RM15 . . . . . 171 F7
Lombard Ave IG3 . . . . . 133 E3
Lombard Ct RM7 . . . . . 135 C7
Lombards Chase CM13 . . . . . 139 D5
Lombards The RM11 . . . . . 136 F4
Lombardy Cl
3 Basildon SS13 . . . . . 143 C6
Redbridge IG6 . . . . . 111 B3
Lombardy Pl CM1 . . . . . 32 B3
London Cruise Terminal RM18 . . . . . 179 A3
London Hill
Chelmsford CM2 . . . . . 53 F2
Galleywood CM2 . . . . . 54 A2
Rayleigh SS6 . . . . . 123 D3
London Mews SS12 . . . . . 121 B7
London Rd
Abridge RM4 . . . . . 90 A6
Aveley RM15 . . . . . 171 A4
Barking IG11 . . . . . 152 C5
Basildon SS13 . . . . . 143 D5
Basildon, Vange SS16 . . . . . 142 D3
Billericay CM12 . . . . . 96 E2
Brentwood CM14 . . . . . 116 A7
Chelmsford CM2 . . . . . 53 E6
Crays Hill CM11, SS12 . . . . . 120 E6
Gravesend DA11 . . . . . 178 E1
Grays RM17, RM20 . . . . . 177 D8
Greenhithe DA9, DA2 . . . . . 177 C2
Hadleigh SS7 . . . . . 145 D3
Harlow CM17 . . . . . 11 C2
Harlow, Latton Bush CM17 . . . . . 24 C4
Maldon CM9 . . . . . 36 D3
Romford RM7 . . . . . 135 B5
Sawbridgeworth CM21 . . . . . 1 E2
South Benfleet SS7 . . . . . 144 D5
Southend-on-S SS9 . . . . . 146 D2
Southend-on-S, Westcliff-on-S SS1 . . . . . 166 F8
Spellbrook CM23 . . . . . 1 F7
Stanford-le-H SS17 . . . . . 160 B1
Stanford Rivers CM5 . . . . . 70 C4
Stapleford Tawney RM4 . . . . . 91 D8
Tilbury RM18 . . . . . 179 B5
Wickford SS11, SS6 . . . . . 122 D5
London Road Purfleet RM19 . . . . . 176 C8
London Road Ret Pk SS0 . . . . . 166 F8
London Road West Thurrock RM20 . . . . . 177 A8
Londons Cl RM14 . . . . . 156 C7
London Southend Airport SS2 . . . . . 147 E7
Longacre CM1 . . . . . 53 E8
Long Acre
Basildon SS14 . . . . . 142 C7
Harlow CM17 . . . . . 11 B4
Longacre Rd E17 . . . . . 109 D2
Longaford Way CM13 . . . . . 95 C1
Long Banks CM18 . . . . . 23 D5
Longborough Cl 2 SS13 . . . . . 121 A1
Longbow SS2 . . . . . 148 E2
Long Brandocks CM1 . . . . . 31 A1
Longbridge Ho 1 RM8 . . . . . 153 B8
Longbridge Rd
Barking IG11 . . . . . 152 E7
Dagenham RM8 . . . . . 153 B8
Long Comm CM9 . . . . . 36 F5
Long Croft Dr EN8 . . . . . 65 A5
Longcroft Rise IG10 . . . . . 89 B4
Longcrofts EN9 . . . . . 65 E5
Long Ct RM19 . . . . . 171 A2
Long Deacon Rd E4 . . . . . 87 E1
Longdon Ct RM1 . . . . . 135 F6
Longfellow Dr CM13 . . . . . 95 C2
Longfellow Rd CM9 . . . . . 37 A1
Longfield
Harlow CM18 . . . . . 24 A6
Loughton IG10 . . . . . 88 D4
Longfield Ave RM11 . . . . . 135 F4
Longfield Cl SS11 . . . . . 122 A7
Longfield Cotts IG10 . . . . . 89 A7
Longfield Rd
Great Baddow CM2 . . . . . 54 E8
South Woodham Ferrers CM3 . . . . . 101 D8
Wickford SS11 . . . . . 122 A7
Long Fields CM5 . . . . . 49 A1
Long Gages SS14 . . . . . 142 B7
Long Gn IG7 . . . . . 111 E5
Long Gr RM3 . . . . . 114 E1
LONG GREEN 44 A6
Longhams Dr CM3 . . . . . 101 D8
Longhayes Ave RM6 . . . . . 134 D7
Longhayes Ct RM6 . . . . . 134 D7
Long Ho CM18 . . . . . 23 F6
Longhouse Rd RM16 . . . . . 174 B3
Long La
Chadwell St M RM16 . . . . . 173 F5
Grays RM16 . . . . . 173 C5
Hullbridge SS5 . . . . . 101 F3
Longland Bridge CM22 . . . . . 12 C8
Longleat Cl CM1 . . . . . 31 F7
Long Ley CM20 . . . . . 23 F8
Longley Mews RM16 . . . . . 173 F4
Long Leys E4 . . . . . 109 C4
Long Lynderswood SS15 . . . . . 141 F6
Longmans SS3 . . . . . 168 G6
Long Mdw
Brentwood CM13 . . . . . 117 C8
Romford RM3 . . . . . 114 C8
Longmead SS13 . . . . . 143 C8
Longmead Ave CM2 . . . . . 54 F8
Longmead Cl CM15 . . . . . 94 E1
Long Meadow Dr SS11 . . . . . 121 E8
Longmeads Cl CM1 . . . . . 31 A1
Longmore Ave CM2 . . . . . 54 E8
Longport Cl IG6 . . . . . 112 A4
Long Rd SS8 . . . . . 164 A3
Longreach Ct IG11 . . . . . 152 D3
Long Reach Rd IG11 . . . . . 152 F1
Long Riding SS14 . . . . . 142 D6
Long Ridings Ave CM13 . . . . . 95 C4
Long Ridings Prim Sch CM13 . . . . . 95 B4
Longrise CM12 . . . . . 119 B8
Longsands SS3 . . . . . 168 D7
Longshaw Prim Sch E4 . . . . . 109 D7
Longshaw Rd E4 . . . . . 109 D7
Longship Way CM9 . . . . . 58 E8
Longshots Cl CM1 . . . . . 19 A1
Long St EN9 . . . . . 66 E7
Longstomps Ave CM2 . . . . . 54 A7
Longtail CM11 . . . . . 97 D5
Longtown Cl RM3 . . . . . 114 C5
Longtown Ct 21 DA2 . . . . . 176 B1
Longtown Rd RM3 . . . . . 114 C5
Longview Way RM5 . . . . . 113 D2
Longwick SS16 . . . . . 141 C4
Long Wlk EN8 . . . . . 43 A1
Long Wood CM18 . . . . . 23 D3
Longwood Cl RM14 . . . . . 156 C7
Longwood Ct RM14 . . . . . 156 C7
Longwood Gdns
Ilford IG5, IG6 . . . . . 133 A8
Redbridge IG5 . . . . . 132 F7
Longwood Par IG6 . . . . . 133 B8
Lonsdale Ave
Brentwood CM13 . . . . . 95 D3
Romford RM7 . . . . . 135 C5
Lonsdale Cres IG2 . . . . . 133 B5
Lonsdale Ct SS2 . . . . . 148 D3
Lonsdale Rd SS2 . . . . . 148 D2
Looe Gdns IG6 . . . . . 133 B8
Loop Rd EN9 . . . . . 65 B7
Lord Ave IG5 . . . . . 132 F8
Lord Gdns IG5 . . . . . 132 F7
Lord Roberts Ave SS9 . . . . . 146 F1
Lords Ct
Basildon SS13 . . . . . 121 B3
Hornchurch RM11 . . . . . 136 B5
Lordship Cl CM13 . . . . . 95 D2
Lordship Rd CM1 . . . . . 31 B3

Lord St EN11 . . . . 21 A6
Lords Way SS13 . . . . 121 B2
Lordswood View CM6 . . . . 15 D7
Lorien Gdns CM3 . . . . 101 C6
Lorne Gdns E11 . . . . 132 C7
Lorne Rd CM14 . . . . 116 C6
Lornes Cl SS2 . . . . 148 D3
Lorraine Cl CM11 . . . . 119 D6
Lorraine Ct
  4 Greenhithe DA9 . . . . . 177 B1
  4 Romford RM1 . . . . . . 135 F6
Lorrimore CM12 . . . . 96 F5
Loten Rd SS7 . . . . 144 B2
Lottem Rd SS8 . . . . 164 D2
Loudoun Ave IG6 . . . . 133 B6
LOUGHTON 88 D3
Loughton Ct EN9 . . . . 66 B6
Loughton La CM16 . . . . . . 67 D2
Loughton Seedbed Ctr
  IG10 . . . . 89 D5
Loughton Sta IG10 . . . . . . 88 E4
Loughton Way IG9 . . . . . . 88 E1
Louisa Ave SS7 . . . . 144 B6
Louis Cl SS6 . . . . 123 A3
Louis Ct **8** RM10 . . . . . . 154 B6
Louis Dr SS6 . . . . 123 A4
Louis Dr E SS6 . . . . 123 B4
Louis Dr W SS6 . . . . 123 A4
Louise Ct **4** E11 . . . . . . 132 B6
Louise Gdns RM13 . . . . . . 154 E2
Louise Graham Ho **5**
  IG11 . . . . 152 D4
Louise Rd SS6 . . . . 123 C4
Louisville Cl SG12 . . . . 8 C4
Louvain Dr CM1 . . . . 32 F7
Louvaine Ave SS12 . . . . . 121 B7
Love La
  Aveley RM15 . . . . 171 C4
  Chigwell IG8 . . . . 110 F4
  Chipping Ongar CM5 . . . 49 A3
  East Tilbury RM18 . . . . 180 C8
  Rayleigh SS6 . . . . 123 C2
Lovelace Ave SS1 . . . . . . 167 D8
Lovelace Gdns
  Barking IG11 . . . . 153 A8
  Southend-on-S SS2 . . . 148 D1
Lovelace Villas SS2 . . . . . 148 D1
Loveland Mans **7**
  IG11 . . . . 152 F5
Lovell Rise SS9 . . . . 147 A6
Lovell Wlk RM12 . . . . 155 A6
Lovens Cl SS8 . . . . 164 C2
Lover's La DA9 . . . . 177 D3
Lovibond Pl **4** CM2 . . . . 32 F4
Lowbrook Rd IG1 . . . . 152 B8
Low Cl DA9 . . . . 177 A2
Lowe Cl IG7 . . . . 112 A5
Lowen Rd RM13 . . . . 154 D3
Lower Alderton Hall La
  IG10 . . . . 89 A4
Lower Anchor St CM2 . . . . 32 A1
Lower Ave SS13 . . . . 143 E8
Lower Bedfords Rd RM1,
  RM3 . . . . 114 A4
LOWER BOBBINGWORTH
  GREEN 48 B7
Lower Broad St RM10 . . . 154 A4
Lower Burnham Rd
  CM3 . . . . 81 C2
Lower Bury La CM16 . . . . . 67 E8
Lower Chase CM3 . . . . 82 F4
Lower Church Hill
  DA9 . . . . 176 E2
Lower Church Rd SS7 . . . 144 B6
Lower Cloister CM11 . . . . . 97 B2
Lower Cres SS17 . . . . 175 A3
Lower Dunton Rd SS17,
  RM14, CM13 . . . . 140 D4
Lower Gn CM2 . . . . 54 C2
LOWER GREEN
  Galleywood 54 C2
  Sandon 55 C6
Lower Lambricks
  SS6 . . . . 123 D4
Lower Mardyke Ave
  RM13 . . . . 154 C3
Lower Mdw CM18 . . . . 23 E4
LOWER NAZEING 21 F1
Lower Noke Cl RM3,
  CM14 . . . . 114 F8
Lower Park Rd
  Belvedere DA17 . . . . . . 169 A2
  Loughton IG10 . . . . 88 C4
  Wickford SS12 . . . . 121 C4
Lower Queen's Rd
  IG9 . . . . 110 D8
Lower Rd
  Belvedere DA17 . . . . . . 169 B3
  Great Amwell SG12 . . . . . 8 A6
  Hockley SS4 . . . . 102 D3
  Hullbridge SS5 . . . . . . 101 E1
  Little Hallingbury CM22 . . 2 C7
  Loughton IG10 . . . . 89 A8
  Mountnessing CM15 . . . 95 D6
  Northfleet DA11 . . . . . . 178 A3
Lower Sheering Rd CM21 . . 2 A3
Lower Southend Rd
  SS11 . . . . 121 D8
Lower St SS15 . . . . 119 E1
Lower Stock Rd CM4 . . . . . 76 C4
Lower Swaines CM16 . . . . 45 F1
Lowe The IG7 . . . . 112 A5
Lowewood Mus★
  EN11 . . . . 21 A5
Lowfield CM21 . . . . 1 E1

Lowfield Ct **14** EN11 . . . . 21 A6
Lowfield La EN11 . . . . 21 A6
Low Hall Cl E4 . . . . 87 B2
Low Hill Rd CM19 . . . . 22 A6
Lowland Gdns RM7 . . . . . 135 B5
Lowlands Rd RM15 . . . . . 171 C5
Lowry Cl
  Erith DA8 . . . . 169 D2
  Southend-on-S SS3 . . . 149 F1
Lowry Rd RM8 . . . . 153 B7
Lowshoe La RM5 . . . . 113 B2
LOW STREET 179 F8
Low Street La
  East Tilbury RM18 . . . . 179 F8
  West Tilbury RM18 . . . . 174 F1
LOXFORD 152 C7
Loxford SS13 . . . . 143 A8
Loxford La IG1 . . . . 152 D7
Loxford Rd IG11 . . . . 152 B8
Loxford Sch of Science &
  Tech IG1 . . . . 152 D7
Loxham Rd E4 . . . . 109 B3
Loxley Ct RM3 . . . . 114 B3
Loyola Prep Sch IG9 . . . . . 88 C1
LOYTER'S GREEN 12 E1
Lubbards Cl SS6 . . . . 123 D5
Lubbins Park Com Prim
  Sch SS8 . . . . 164 C2
Lucam Lo SS4 . . . . 125 F2
Lucas Ave CM2 . . . . 54 C6
Lucas Cres **2** DA9 . . . . 177 C6
Lucas Ct
  Doddinghurst CM15 . . . . 72 C3
  Romford RM2 . . . . 114 D1
  Waltham Abbey EN9 . . . 65 F6
Lucas Rd RM17 . . . . 173 A3
Lucerne Dr SS11 . . . . . . 122 A7
Lucerne Way
  Romford RM3 . . . . 114 D4
  Writtle CM1 . . . . 53 B8
Lucerne Wlk SS11 . . . . . 122 A7
Lucksfield Way CM2 . . . . . 54 F5
Luckyn La SS14 . . . . 141 F8
Lucton Mews IG10 . . . . . . 89 B5
Luctons Ave IG9 . . . . 88 C1
Lucy Gdns RM8 . . . . 134 E1
Lucy Rd SS1 . . . . 167 B7
Ludgate Ho E4 . . . . 87 F5
Ludgores La CM3 . . . . 56 D5
Ludgrove CM3 . . . . 82 A6
Ludham Cl IG6 . . . . 111 C2
Ludlow Ct **3** RM10 . . . . 154 A6
Ludlow Mews SS13 . . . . . 143 B6
Ludlow Pl RM17 . . . . 173 B3
Lugg App E12 . . . . 133 A1
Luker Rd SS1 . . . . 167 A8
Lukin Cres E4 . . . . 109 D7
Lukinstone Cl IG10 . . . . . . 88 E3
Lullington Rd RM9 . . . . . . 153 E5
Lulworth Cl SS17 . . . . . . 175 B8
Lulworth Dr RM5 . . . . . . 113 B5
Lumley Cl SS14 . . . . 142 F5
Luncies Rd SS14 . . . . . . 142 F5
Lundy Cl SS2 . . . . 147 B7
Lupin Cl RM7 . . . . 135 D2
Lupin Cres **3** IG11 . . . . 152 B6
Lupin Dr CM1 . . . . 32 F6
Lupin Mews **1** CM1 . . . . 32 F6
Luppit Cl CM13 . . . . 95 A1
Lushes Cl IG10 . . . . 89 B4
Lushes Rd IG10 . . . . 89 B4
Lutea Cl SS15 . . . . 119 D1
Luthers Cl CM15 . . . . 71 E2
Luton Ho **9** RM3 . . . . . 114 E5
LUXBOROUGH 110 F6
Luxborough La IG7 . . . . . 110 F6
Luxford Pl CM21 . . . . 1 F1
Lych Gate SS15 . . . . 141 C6
Lychgate Ind Est SS6 . . . . 122 E1
Lydford Ct **25** DA2 . . . . 176 B1
Lydford Rd SS0 . . . . 166 E7
Lylt Rd SS8 . . . . 164 A3
Lyme Rd SS2 . . . . 148 C1
Lymington Ave SS9 . . . . . 146 E1
Lymington Rd RM8 . . . . . 134 D3
Lympstone Cl SS0 . . . . . . 147 A5
Lynbrook Cl RM13 . . . . . 154 D3
Lynceley Grange CM16 . . . 46 A2
Lynch The EN11 . . . . 21 B6
Lyndale CM15 . . . . 71 F2
Lyndale Ave SS7 . . . . . . 148 B3
Lyndale Est RM20 . . . . . . 177 B8
Lyndbourne Ct SS7 . . . . . 144 C5
Lyndene SS7 . . . . 144 B6
Lyndhurst Ct **11** E18 . . . 110 A2
Lyndhurst Dr
  Bicknacre CM3 . . . . 56 F1
  Hornchurch RM11 . . . . 136 C4
Lyndhurst Gdns
  Barking IG11 . . . . 152 E6
  Ilford IG2 . . . . 133 D5
Lyndhurst Rd
  Chingford E4 . . . . 109 C3
  Corringham SS17 . . . . . 160 F4
  Rochford SS4 . . . . 103 C1
Lyndhurst Rise IG7 . . . . . 111 A6
Lyndhurst Way CM13 . . . . 95 C2
Lyndon Rd DA17 . . . . 169 A1
Lynford Gdns IG3 . . . . . . 133 F2
Lynfords Ave SS11 . . . . . 100 A3
Lynfords Dr
  Wickford, Runwell
    SS11 . . . . 99 F2
  Wickford SS11 . . . . . . 100 A3
Lynmouth Ave CM2 . . . . . 32 C1
Lynmouth Gdns CM12 . . . . 97 A5
Lynmouth Ho **8** RM3 . . 114 E5
Lynnett Rd RM8 . . . . 134 D2

Lynn Rd IG2 . . . . 133 D4
Lynn View Cl SS7 . . . . . . 144 C5
Lynross Cl RM3 . . . . 114 F1
Lynsted CM19 . . . . 22 A4
Lynstede SS14 . . . . 143 A5
Lynton Ave RM7 . . . . 113 B2
Lynton Cres IG2 . . . . 133 B5
Lynton Ct **6** IG1 . . . . . 133 C2
Lynton Ho **6** IG1 . . . . . 133 C2
Lynton Rd
  Chingford E4 . . . . 109 B5
  Hadleigh SS7 . . . . 145 C3
  Southend-on-S SS1 . . . 167 F6
Lynwood Cl
  Romford RM5 . . . . 113 B4
  Woodford E18 . . . . 110 C2
Lynwood Dr RM5 . . . . . . 113 B3
Lynwood Gn SS6 . . . . . . 146 A8
Lyon Bsns Est IG11 . . . . . 152 E3
Lyon Cl CM2 . . . . 54 B3
Lyon Rd RM1 . . . . 135 F4
Lysander Ct CM16 . . . . . . 47 B5
Lyster Ave CM2 . . . . 55 A7
Lytel Cl IG10 . . . . 89 D6
Lyttel Hall RM17 . . . . . . 173 A3
Lytton Rd
  Chadwell St M RM16 . . . 173 F2
  Grays RM16 . . . . 174 A2
  Romford RM2 . . . . 136 B6
Lyttons Way EN11 . . . . 8 A1

M

Mabey's Wlk CM21 . . . . 1 B1
Mablin Lo IG9 . . . . 88 C1
McAdam Cl E11 . . . . 21 A8
Macarthur Cl DA8 . . . . . . 169 E1
Macarthur Pl **20**
  CM14 . . . . 116 C7
Macaulay Rd E3 . . . . 141 A5
McCalmont Dr SS6 . . . . . 123 C3
Macclesfield Ho **7**
  RM3 . . . . 114 E5
McClintock Pl EN3 . . . . . . 65 B2
McDivitt Wlk SS9 . . . . . . 147 A6
Macdonald Ave
  Dagenham RM10 . . . . . 135 B1
  Hornchurch RM11 . . . . 136 F7
  Southend-on-S SS0 . . . 147 E2
Macdonald Rd E17 . . . . . 109 C1
Macdonald Way
  RM11 . . . . 136 E7
Mace Ct RM17 . . . . 178 E8
Mace Wlk CM1 . . . . 31 F3
McGrail Ct SS8 . . . . 164 F2
Macgregor Dr SS12 . . . . . 121 E5
McIntosh Cl RM1 . . . . . . 135 E8
McIntosh Rd RM1 . . . . . . 135 E8
Macintyres Wlk SS4 . . . . 125 C6
Mackenzie Cl SS12 . . . . . 121 E6
McKenzie Rd EN10 . . . . . . 21 A3
Mackley Dr SS17 . . . . . . 160 F5
Maclaren Way **5**
  SS12 . . . . 121 E5
Maclennan Ave RM13 . . . 155 D2
Macleod Cl RM17 . . . . . . 173 D2
Macmillan Ct **4** CM2 . . . 32 B1
Macmillan Gdns DA1 . . . . 176 A3
Macmurdo Cl SS9 . . . . . . 146 D7
Macmurdo Rd SS9 . . . . . 146 D7
Macon Way RM14 . . . . . . 137 F5
Madden Cl DA10 . . . . 177 E1
Maddox Cl **1** E4 . . . . . . 87 D1
Maddox Rd CM20 . . . . . . 23 C8
Madeira Ave SS9 . . . . . . 146 E2
Madeira Gr IG8 . . . . 110 C4
Madeleine Cl RM6 . . . . . . 134 C5
Madeleine Ct **10** IG7 . . . 111 E5
Madeleines Flats CM19 . . . 23 B7
Madeline Gr IG1 . . . . 152 D7
Madeline Pl CM1 . . . . 31 E6
Madells IG10 . . . . 67 F8
Madford Trade Pk
  DA8 . . . . 169 D1
Madison Ct **3** RM10 . . . 154 B6
Madles La CM4 . . . . 75 F1
Madras Ho IG1 . . . . 152 B8
Madras Rd IG1 . . . . 152 B8
Madrid Ave SS6 . . . . 123 B7
Mafeking Ave IG2 . . . . . . 133 D4
Magazine Rd SS3 . . . . . . 168 E6
Magdalene Gdns E6 . . . . 152 A1
Magdalen Gdns CM13 . . . 95 E3
MAGDALEN LAVER 25 D5
Magenta Cl CM12 . . . . . . 96 E3
Magna Mead SS3 . . . . . . 149 D7
Magnet Point RM20 . . . . 177 C8
Magnet Rd RM20 . . . . . . 177 C8
Magnolia Cl
  Canvey Island SS8 . . . . 164 A2
  Chelmsford CM2 . . . . . . 54 B6
  South Ockendon RM15 . . 157 E1
Magnolia La SS15 . . . . . . 119 C1
Magnolia Lo E4 . . . . 109 B7
Magnolia Pl RM17 . . . . . . 160 E4
Magnolia Rd SS4 . . . . . . 125 B5
Magnolias CM11 . . . . 119 C6
Magnolia Way
  Pilgrims Hatch CM15 . . . 94 B4
  Rochford SS4 . . . . 148 A8
Magnum Rd RM13 . . . . . 155 C1
Magpie La CM13 . . . . 116 E2
Magpies CM16 . . . . 45 A7
Magwitch Cl CM1 . . . . 31 F7
Mahonia Dr SS16 . . . . . . 140 F5
Maida Ave E4 . . . . 87 B2
Maida Rd DA17 . . . . 169 A3
Maida Way E4 . . . . 87 B2
Maidstone Ave RM5 . . . . 113 C1

Maidstone Rd RM17 . . . . 178 A8
Main Dr IG8 . . . . 140 E5
Maine Cres SS6 . . . . 123 B4
Main Rd
  Bicknacre CM3 . . . . 79 A6
  Boreham CM3 . . . . 20 F1
  Broomfield CM1 . . . . 19 B2
  Chelmsford CM2 . . . . . . 55 F7
  Danbury CM3 . . . . 56 A7
  Danbury CM3 . . . . 56 D7
  East Hanningfield CM3 . . 78 B8
  East Hanningfield CM3 . . 78 C5
  Hawkwell SS5 . . . . 124 F4
  Hockley SS5 . . . . 124 D6
  Hullbridge SS5 . . . . . . 101 E4
  Rettendon CM3, SS11 . . 100 B6
  Romford RM1 . . . . 136 A8
  St Lawrence CM0 . . . . . 62 D7
  Thundersley SS7 . . . . . 145 B6
Maitland Pl SS3 . . . . 149 E1
Maitland Rd SS12 . . . . . . 121 E5
Maitlands IG10 . . . . 88 F6
Maizey Ct CM15 . . . . 94 A4
Makepeace Rd E11 . . . . . 132 A7
Makinen Ho IG9 . . . . 88 C1
Malan Sq RM12 . . . . 155 B6
Malby Lo SS0 . . . . 166 C8
Malcolm Way E11 . . . . . . 132 A7
MALDON 37 B3
Maldon Court Sch CM9 . . . 37 F3
Maldon Ct E6 . . . . 152 A4
Maldon District Mus★
  CM9 . . . . 37 B3
Maldon Ho IG9 . . . . 88 C2
Maldon Prim Sch CM9 . . . 37 A2
Maldon Rd
  Bradwell on S CM0 . . . . 42 A1
  Bradwell on S, Mill End
    CM0 . . . . 63 C7
  Bradwell Waterside CM0 . . 41 F1
  Burnham-on-C CM0 . . . 105 E8
  Dagenham RM7 . . . . . . 135 C4
  Danbury, Gay Bowers
    CM3 . . . . 57 B5
  Danbury, Runsell Green
    CM3 . . . . 57 B7
  Goldhanger CM9 . . . . . . 38 E7
  Great Baddow CM2 . . . . 55 C7
  Langford CM9 . . . . 36 D6
  Latchingdon CM3 . . . . . 81 F6
  Maldon CM9 . . . . 59 C6
  Margaretting CM4 . . . . . 75 B8
  Mayland CM3, CM0 . . . . 61 D1
  Southend-on-S SS2 . . . 148 A1
  Woodham Mortimer CM9 . . 57 E1
Maldon Wlk IG8 . . . . 110 C4
Malford Ct E18 . . . . 110 A1
Malford Gr E18 . . . . 110 A1
Malgraves SS13 . . . . 143 B7
Malgraves Pl SS13 . . . . . 143 B7
Malkin Dr CM17 . . . . 24 E7
Mallard Ct RM14 . . . . . . 137 F4
Mallard Ct
  Chingford E4 . . . . 87 D2
  Ilford IG1 . . . . 133 C2
  3 Southend-on-S SS1 . . 167 C8
Mallard Rd CM2 . . . . 54 A5
Mallards
  Mayland CM3 . . . . 83 A8
  Southend-on-S SS3 . . . 149 E1
  Wanstead E11 . . . . 132 A4
Mallards Rd
  Barking IG11 . . . . 153 A1
  Woodford IG8 . . . . 110 B3
Mallards Rise CM17 . . . . . 24 D8
Mallards The SS3 . . . . . . 150 A4
Mallard Way
  Brentwood CM13 . . . . . . 95 B2
  Roydon CM19 . . . . 9 A1
Mallinson Cl RM12 . . . . . 155 C7
Mallion Ct EN9 . . . . 65 F6
Mallories CM20 . . . . 10 F2
Mallory Way CM2 . . . . 97 A1
Mallow Ct RM17 . . . . 178 E8
Mallow Gdns CM12 . . . . . 96 F5
Mallows Gn CM19 . . . . . . 23 A3
Mall The RM11 . . . . 136 B3
Malmesbury Rd E18 . . . . 109 F2
Malmsmead SS8 . . . . . . 168 C8
Malpas Rd
  Dagenham RM9 . . . . . . 153 D6
  Grays RM16 . . . . 174 C3
Malsters Lo **9** EN11 . . . 21 D8
Malta Rd RM18 . . . . 178 F5
Maltese Rd CM1 . . . . 32 A4
Malthouse Pl **6** RM1 . . 135 E6
Malting La RM16 . . . . . . 159 A1
Maltings Chase CM4 . . . . 74 B3
Maltings Dr CM16 . . . . . . 46 A2
Maltings Hill CM5 . . . . . . 26 E3
Maltings Ind Est The
  SG12 . . . . 8 D4
Maltings La CM16 . . . . . . 46 A2
Maltings Rd
  Battlesbridge SS11 . . . . 100 E2
  Great Baddow CM2 . . . . 55 A5
Maltings The
  1 Gravesend DA11 . . . 179 A1
  Romford RM1 . . . . 135 F4
  Southminster CM0 . . . . . 84 E4
Malting Villas Rd SS4 . . . 125 F2
Malvern SS2 . . . . 148 B1
Malvern Ave
  Canvey Island SS8 . . . . 163 D3
  Chingford E4 . . . . 109 D3
Malvern Cl
  Chelmsford CM1 . . . . . . 31 D6
  Rayleigh SS6 . . . . 123 D4

Malvern Dr
  Ilford IG3 . . . . 152 F8
  Woodford IG8 . . . . 110 C6
Malvern Gdns IG10 . . . . . . 88 F3
Malvern Ho DA11 . . . . . . 178 D1
Malvern Rd
  Grays RM17 . . . . 173 E2
  Hockley SS5 . . . . 124 F8
  Hornchurch RM11 . . . . 136 A5
Malvina Cl SS16 . . . . 159 F7
Malwood Dr SS7 . . . . . . 144 B5
Malwood Rd SS7 . . . . . . 144 B5
Malyon Court Cl SS7 . . . . 145 B4
Malyons SS13 . . . . 143 B8
Malyons Cl SS13 . . . . . . 143 B8
Malyons Gn SS13 . . . . . . 143 B8
Malyons La SS5 . . . . 101 D2
Malyons Mews SS13 . . . . 143 B8
Malyons Pl SS13 . . . . . . 143 B8
Malyons The SS7 . . . . . . 145 B4
Manbrough Ave E6 . . . . . 152 A2
Manchester Dr SS9 . . . . . 146 F2
Manchester Way
  RM10 . . . . 154 B8
Mandarin Royal **7**
  RM1 . . . . 135 F5
Mandeville Cl CM17 . . . . . 24 C6
Mandeville Prim Sch
  CM21 . . . . 1 D3
Mandeville Way
  Basildon SS15, SS16 . . 141 B5
  Broomfield CM1 . . . . . . 19 B3
  South Benfleet SS7 . . . 144 C2
Mandeville Wlk CM13 . . . . 95 C2
Manford Cl IG7 . . . . 112 B6
Manford Cross IG7 . . . . . 112 A5
Manford Ct
  Chigwell IG7 . . . . 111 F5
  1 Redbridge IG7 . . . . 112 A5
Manford Prim Sch
  IG7 . . . . 111 F5
Manford Way
  Chigwell IG7 . . . . 111 E5
  Redbridge IG7 . . . . 112 A5
Mangapp Chase CM0 . . . 106 A8
Mangapps Rly Mus★
  CM0 . . . . 106 A8
Manilla Ct **5** RM6 . . . . 134 B5
Manilla Rd SS1 . . . . 167 C7
Mannering Gdns SS0 . . . 147 A3
Manners Cnr SS2 . . . . . . 147 E5
Manners Way SS2 . . . . . 147 E5
Manning Gr SS16 . . . . . . 141 C4
Manning Rd RM10 . . . . . 154 A5
Manning St RM15 . . . . . . 171 C5
Mannin Rd RM6 . . . . 134 B5
Mannock Dr IG10 . . . . . . 89 C7
Mannock Mews E18 . . . . 110 B2
Manns Way SS6 . . . . 123 C5
Manor Ave
  Basildon SS13 . . . . 143 C7
  Hornchurch RM11 . . . . 136 C6
Manor Cl
  Aveley RM15 . . . . 171 C5
  Dagenham RM10 . . . . . 154 D6
  Ramsden Heath CM11 . . 98 C3
  Rayleigh SS6 . . . . 145 D8
  Romford RM1 . . . . 136 A6
Manor Cl S RM15 . . . . . . 171 C5
Manor Cotts RM14 . . . . . 159 A8
Manor Court Lo **13**
  E18 . . . . 110 A2
Manor Cres
  Hornchurch RM11 . . . . 136 C6
  Little Waltham CM3 . . . . 19 B5
Manor Ct
  4 Barking IG11 . . . . . 152 F5
  Chingford E4 . . . . 87 E1
  South Benfleet SS7 . . . 144 D7
  Southend-on-S SS7 . . . 167 C2
  Waltham Abbey EN9 . . . 65 D6
Manor Dr CM2 . . . . 54 F7
Manor Farm Dr E4 . . . . . 109 E7
Manor Hatch CM18 . . . . . 24 A7
Manor Hatch Cl CM18 . . . 24 B7
Manor Ho CM3 . . . . 57 A5
Manor House Gdns **2**
  E11 . . . . 132 B5
Manor Inf Sch IG11 . . . . . 152 F6
Manor Jun Sch IG11 . . . . 152 F6
Manor Prim Sch The
  RM1 . . . . 135 F6
Manor Rd
  Abridge RM4 . . . . 90 E2
  Barking IG11 . . . . 152 F6
  Basildon SS15 . . . . 141 B7
  Chelmsford CM2 . . . . . . 32 C1
  Chigwell IG7 . . . . 111 C5
  Dagenham RM10 . . . . . 154 D6
  Dengie CM0 . . . . 63 D1
  Grays, Little Thurrock
    Marshes RM17 . . . . . . 178 C8
  Grays, West Thurrock
    RM20 . . . . 177 C8
  Harlow CM17 . . . . 11 C5
  High Beach IG10 . . . . . . 88 B8
  Hockley SS5 . . . . 124 C6
  Hoddesdon EN11 . . . . . 21 A7
  Ilford RM6 . . . . 134 D5
  Loughton IG10 . . . . 88 C3
  Maldon CM9 . . . . 36 A4
  Romford RM1 . . . . 136 A6
  South Benfleet SS7 . . . 144 D6
  Southend-on-S SS0 . . . 166 D7

Manor Rd continued
South Woodham Ferrers
CM3 . . . .**101** C8
Stanford-le-H SS17 . . . . . .**160** D1
Swanscombe DA10 . . . . . .**177** D1
Tilbury RM18 . . . .**179** A5
Woodham Walter CM9 . . . . **35** E5
Manor Sq RM8. . . . .**134** C2
Manor The IG8 . . . .**111** A3
Manor Trad Est SS7 . . . .**144** D7
Manorway IG8. . . . .**110** C5
Manor Way
Brentwood CM14. . . . .**116** A7
Chingford E4 . . . .**109** D6
Corringham SS17 . . . .**161** A1
Northfleet RM17 . . . .**178** A3
Rainham RM13 . . . .**154** E1
Swanscombe DA10 . . . . . .**177** E3
Manor Way Bsns Ctr
RM13 . . . .**169** D8
Manorway The
Corringham SS17. . . . .**161** D1
Stanford-le-H SS17 . . . . . .**160** D2
Mansard Cl RM12 . . . .**136** A2
Manse Chase CM9 . . . . . . **37** A1
Mansel Cl SS9 . . . .**146** E6
Mansel Gr E17. . . . .**109** A2
Manser Cl RM13 . . . .**154** E2
Manser Rd RM13. . . . .**154** E3
Mansfield CM21 . . . . **1** A1
Mansfield Gdns
RM12. . . . .**136** D2
Mansfield Hill E4 . . . . **87** B1
Mansfield Rd
Ilford IG1 . . . .**133** A2
Wanstead E11 . . . .**132** B5
Mansfields CM1 . . . . **30** F1
Manstead Gdns
Dagenham RM6 . . . .**134** C4
Rainham RM13 . . . .**170** B7
Mansted Cl CM13 . . . .**140** E5
Mansted Gdns SS4 . . . . . .**125** D5
Manston Rd CM20 . . . . **23** E8
Manston Way RM12 . . . . . .**155** B6
Manton Rd EN3. . . . . **65** A1
MANWOOD GREEN **13** F5
Maple Ave
Heybridge CM9 . . . . **37** C6
Southend-on-S SS9 . . . . . .**165** F8
Upminster RM14 . . . .**156** B8
Maple Cl
Brentwood CM13 . . . .**116** F7
Buckhurst Hill IG9 . . . .**110** D7
Hornchurch RM12 . . . .**136** B1
8 Redbridge IG6 . . . . . .**111** E5
Theydon Bois CM16 . . . . . . **67** D2
Maplecroft La EN9 . . . . . . **21** E2
Maple Ct
7 Dagenham RM8 . . . . .**134** D4
Southend-on-S SS3 . . . . . .**168** F8
Stansted Abbotts SG12 . . . . **8** D3
Mapledene Ave SS5. . . . . .**101** E2
Maple Dr
Chelmsford CM2 . . . . **54** B6
Rayleigh SS6 . . . .**123** C7
South Ockendon RM15 . . . .**157** C1
Mapleford Sweep
SS16 . . . .**142** D4
Maple Gate IG10 . . . . **89** A7
Mapleleaf Cl SS5 . . . .**124** F7
Maple Leaf Cl SG12 . . . . . . **8** D4
Mapleleafe Gdns IG6 . . . .**133** B8
Mapleleaf Gdns SS12 . . . .**121** B6
Maple Lo IG9 . . . . **88** D1
Maple Mead CM12 . . . .**119** C8
Maple Rd RM17 . . . .**178** C8
Maple River Ind Est
CM20 . . . . **11** B6
Maples
Stanford-le-H SS17 . . . . . .**160** E2
Waltham Abbey EN9 . . . . . **66** C4
Maplesfield SS7 . . . .**145** D4
Maple Springs EN9 . . . . . . **66** A7
Maple Sq SS2 . . . .**148** B2
Maple St RM7 . . . .**135** C2
Maplestead SS14 . . . .**142** D8
Maplestead Rd RM9. . . . . .**153** B4
Maples The
Harlow CM19. . . . . **23** B3
4 Wickford SS12 . . . . . .**121** C5
Mapleton Rd E4 . . . .**109** C7
Mapletree La CM4 . . . . **73** E8
Maple Tree La SS16 . . . . . .**140** F5
Maple Way
Burnham-on-C CM0 . . . . . .**106** A6
Canvey Island SS8 . . . . . .**163** E3
Maplin Cl SS7 . . . .**144** C7
Maplin Ct SS3 . . . .**168** G6
Maplin Gdns SS14 . . . .**142** E5
Maplin Mews SS3 . . . .**168** E6
Maplin Way SS1 . . . .**168** C6
Maplin Way N SS1 . . . .**149** C1
Mapperley **3** E11 . . . .**132** A5
Mapperley Dr IG8 . . . .**109** E3
Marchant Cl RM12 . . . .**136** C1
Marconi Gdns CM15 . . . . . **94** C4
Marconi Rd CM1 . . . . **32** B5
Marcos Rd SS8 . . . .**164** D3
Marcus Ave SS1 . . . .**168** B7
Marcus Chase SS1 . . . . . .**168** B7
Marcus Gdns SS1 . . . .**168** B7
MARDEN ASH **49** A1
Marden Ash **7** SS15 . . . .**141** A6

Marden Cl IG7. . . . .**112** B8
Marden Rd **5** RM1 . . . . . .**135** E6
Mardyke Cl RM13 . . . .**154** C3
Mardyke Country Pk★
RM15 . . . .**172** F8
Mardyke Ho RM13 . . . .**154** D3
Mardyke Rd CM20 . . . . **11** A2
Maresby Ho E4 . . . .**109** B8
Margaret Ave
Brentwood CM15. . . . . **95** A3
Chingford E4 . . . . **87** B3
Margaret Bondfield Ave
IG11. . . . .**153** A5
Margaret Cl
Epping CM16 . . . . **45** F2
Romford RM2 . . . .**136** B6
Waltham Abbey EN9 . . . . . **65** D6
Margaret Dr RM11 . . . .**136** F4
Margaret Rd
Epping CM16 . . . . **46** A2
Romford RM2 . . . .**136** B6
MARGARET RODING **15** D5
MARGARETTING **75** A8
Margaretting CE Prim Sch
CM4 . . . . **74** F8
Margaretting Rd
Chelmsford CM2 . . . . **53** F1
Galleywood CM2 . . . . **54** A2
Wanstead E12 . . . .**132** C3
Writtle CM1. . . . . **53** A6
Margaret Way IG4 . . . .**132** E5
Margarite Way SS12 . . . . .**121** B7
Margery Rd RM8 . . . .**134** D1
Margeth Rd CM12. . . . .**119** C3
Margherita Pl EN9 . . . . **66** A5
Margherita Rd EN9 . . . . . . **66** A5
Margraten Ave SS8 . . . . . .**164** D2
Marguerite Dr SS9 . . . .**146** F1
Mariam Gdns RM12 . . . . . .**136** F2
Marian Cl RM16. . . . .**172** E5
Marian Lawson Ct **2**
IG7. . . . .**112** A5
Marie Cl SS17 . . . .**161** A7
Marien Ct E4 . . . .**109** D5
Marigold Cl CM1. . . . . **32** F6
Marigold La CM4 . . . . **75** F1
Marigold Pl CM17. . . . . **11** B4
Marina Ave SS6. . . . .**123** C3
Marina Cl SS2 . . . .**147** E4
Marina Dr DA11. . . . .**178** F1
Marina Gdns RM7. . . . .**135** C6
Marine App SS8 . . . .**164** B2
Marine Ave
Canvey Island SS8. . . . . . .**164** E2
Southend-on-S, Clifftown
SS0 . . . .**166** E7
Southend-on-S SS9 . . . . . .**146** D1
Marine Cl SS9 . . . .**146** A1
Marine Cotts RM13. . . . . . .**170** D6
Marine Ct RM19 . . . .**170** F2
Marine Dr IG11 . . . .**153** B2
Marine Par
Canvey Island SS8. . . . . . .**164** F2
Mayland CM3 . . . . **60** D1
Southend-on-S, Leigh-on-S
SS9 . . . .**146** B1
Southend-on-S SS1 . . . . . .**167** B7
Mariner Rd E12. . . . .**152** A8
Mariners Ct
Great Wakering SS3 . . . . .**150** C3
Greenhithe DA9. . . . .**177** B3
Mariners Way CM9. . . . . . . **59** B8
Marion Cl IG6 . . . .**111** D3
Marionette Stps **7**
SS1. . . . .**167** C7
Marion Gr IG8 . . . .**109** E6
Marisco Cl RM16. . . . .**174** B2
Maritime Ave CM9 . . . . **37** E3
Maritime Cl DA9. . . . .**177** B2
Maritime Gate DA11 . . . . . .**178** E1
Marjorams Ave IG10 . . . . . . **89** A7
Mark Ave E4 . . . . **87** B3
Market Ave SS12. . . . .**121** C8
Market Hill CM9 . . . . **37** A3
Market Hill Ct CM9. . . . . . . **37** A3
Market Ho **2** CM20 . . . . . . **10** D1
Market Link RM1 . . . .**135** E7
Market Pavement **2**
SS14 . . . .**142** A5
Market Pl
Abridge RM4 . . . . **90** B6
Ingatestone CM4. . . . . **74** B4
Maldon CM9. . . . . **36** F2
Romford RM1 . . . .**135** E6
Southend-on-S SS1 . . . . . .**167** A4
Tilbury RM18 . . . .**179** A5
Market Rd
Chelmsford CM1 . . . . **32** B2
Wickford SS12 . . . .**121** C7
Market Sq
Basildon SS14 . . . .**142** A5
6 Chelmsford CM1 . . . . . **32** B2
Rochford SS4 . . . .**125** F2
South Woodham Ferrers
CM3 . . . .**101** E7
Waltham Abbey EN9 . . . . . **65** C6
Market St
Harlow CM17 . . . . **11** C4
Wallend E6. . . . .**152** A3
Markfield Gdns E4. . . . . **87** B2
Mark Hall Cycle Mus &
Gdns★ CM20 . . . . **11** B3
Mark Hall Moors CM20 . . . **11** B3
MARK HALL NORTH **11** A3
Mark Hall Sch CM17 . . . . . **11** C3
MARK HALL SOUTH **11** A1

Markham Ho **1**
RM10. . . . .**135** A1
Markhams SS17 . . . .**160** F3
Markhams Chase
SS15 . . . .**141** D7
Mark La DA12 . . . .**179** E1
Markland Cl CM2 . . . . **54** C3
Markland Dr CM9 . . . . **36** E1
Marklay Dr CM3 . . . .**101** C7
Mark Rd CM0 . . . . **63** F6
Mark's Ave CM5 . . . . **49** A4
Marks Cl
Billericay CM12 . . . . **96** F4
Ingatestone CM4. . . . . **73** F1
Marks Ct SS1 . . . .**167** C7
MARKS GATE **112** E1
Marks Gate Inf Sch
RM6 . . . .**134** E8
Marks Gate Jun Sch
RM6 . . . .**134** E8
Marks Hall CM9 . . . . **15** D3
Marks Hall La CM6. . . . . . . **15** E3
Marks La CM3 . . . . **99** F8
Marks Rd RM7. . . . .**135** D6
Mark Wade Cl E12 . . . .**132** D2
Markwell Wood CM19 . . . . **23** B2
Markyate Rd RM8. . . . .**153** B7
Marlands CM21 . . . . **1** E4
Marlands Rd
Redbridge IG5 . . . .**132** E8
Woodford IG5 . . . .**110** F1
Marlborough Ave CM0 . . . . **63** E3
Marlborough Cl
Grays RM16. . . . .**173** C4
South Benfleet SS7 . . . . . .**144** D7
Upminster RM14 . . . .**137** E3
Marlborough Ct **10**
IG9. . . . .**110** C8
Marlborough Dr IG5 . . . . . .**132** E8
Marlborough Gdns
RM14 . . . .**137** E4
Marlborough Ho
CM14 . . . .**116** B6
Marlborough Pl SS1 . . . . . .**166** F7
Marlborough Rd
2 Chelmsford CM2 . . . . **32** A1
Chingford E4 . . . .**109** B4
Dagenham RM8 . . . .**153** C8
Pilgrims Hatch CM15. . . . . **94** A3
Romford RM7 . . . .**135** B7
Southend-on-S SS1 . . . . . .**167** D8
Wanstead E18 . . . .**132** A8
13 Woodford E18 . . . . . .**110** A1
Marlborough Terr
CM2 . . . . **32** A1
Marlborough Way
CM12 . . . . **97** A5
Marlborough Wlk
SS5 . . . .**124** C6
Marle Gdns EN9 . . . . **65** C7
Marlescroft Way IG10 . . . . . **89** B4
Marlin Cl SS7 . . . .**145** E6
Marlow Ave RM19. . . . .**171** A2
Marlowe Cl
Billericay CM12 . . . . **97** B5
Maldon CM9. . . . . **59** A8
Redbridge IG6 . . . .**111** C2
Marlowe Gdns RM3 . . . . . .**114** C2
Marlowe Ho **12** IG8 . . . . . .**111** A3
Marlow Gdns SS2 . . . .**147** E4
Marlpits Rd CM3, CM9 . . . . **57** C4
Marlyon Rd IG6 . . . .**112** B5
Marmaduke Ave SS6 . . . . .**123** B4
Marmion App E4 . . . .**109** A6
Marmion Ave E4 . . . .**109** A6
Marmion Cl E4 . . . .**109** A6
Marney Cl CM2 . . . . **54** E8
Marney Dr SS14 . . . .**142** F5
Marquis Ct IG11 . . . .**152** E7
Marram Ct RM17. . . . .**178** E8
Mar Rd RM15 . . . .**157** C1
Marriotts CM17 . . . . **11** C5
Marsden Ho **1** RM3. . . . . .**114** F4
Marshall Cl SS9. . . . .**146** A3
Marshalls SS4 . . . .**125** D4
Marshalls Cl SS6. . . . .**123** F2
Marshalls Dr RM1 . . . .**135** E8
Marshalls Park Sch
RM1 . . . .**113** E1
Marshalls Rd RM7 . . . .**135** D7
Marsh Farm Ctry Pk★
CM3 . . . .**101** E5
Marsh Farm Rd CM3 . . . . .**101** D4
Marshfoot Rd RM16,
RM17 . . . .**173** F1
Marshgate Ctr CM19 . . . . . **22** D8
Marsh Green Prim Sch
RM10 . . . .**154** A3
Marsh Green Rd
RM10. . . . .**154** A4
Marsh Hill EN9 . . . . **43** E4
Marsh La
Fobbing SS17 . . . .**161** D5
Harlow CM17. . . . . **11** E5
Mountnessing CM13 . . . . . **96** A7
Stansted Abbotts SG12 . . . . **8** D4
Marsh Rd
Burnham-on-C CM0 . . . . . .**107** B7
Tillingham CM0 . . . . **64** B4
Marsh St
Dartford DA1. . . . .**176** A3
Dartford DA1. . . . .**176** A5
Marsh View Ct SS16. . . . . .**142** E3
Marsh Way RM13 . . . .**169** D8
Marston Ave RM10. . . . . . .**135** A1
Marston Beck CM2. . . . . . . **33** A2
Marston Cl RM10 . . . .**135** A1
Marston Ho RM17. . . . .**178** A8

Marston Rd
Hoddesdon EN11 . . . . **21** B7
Woodford IG5 . . . .**110** E1
Marten Rd E17 . . . .**109** A1
Martham Cl IG6 . . . .**111** B2
Martina Terr **9** IG6. . . . . . .**111** E5
Martin Cl CM11 . . . . **97** B1
Martindale Ave SS15 . . . . .**119** D2
Martin Dr
Dartford DA2. . . . .**176** C1
Rainham RM13 . . . .**155** B1
Martingale SS7 . . . .**145** B5
Martingale Cl CM11 . . . . **97** D5
Martingale Dr CM1. . . . . . . **32** F7
Martingale Rd CM11 . . . . . . **97** D5
Martin Gdns RM8 . . . .**153** D8
Martini Dr EN3 . . . . **65** A2
Martin Rd
Aveley RM15 . . . .**171** D5
Dagenham RM8 . . . .**153** D8
Martins Cl SS17 . . . .**160** D3
Martin's Ct SS2 . . . .**148** A1
Martinsfield Cl IG7 . . . .**111** E6
Martins Mews SS7 . . . .**144** C4
Martinstown Cl RM11 . . . . .**137** A5
Martin Wlk SS5 . . . .**124** F4
Martlesham Cl RM12 . . . . . .**155** C7
Martley Dr IG2 . . . .**133** B6
Martock Ave SS0 . . . .**147** B2
Martyns Gr SS0 . . . .**147** B2
Marvens CM2. . . . . **54** D3
Marwell Cl RM1. . . . .**136** A6
Marylands Ave RM12 . . . . .**124** D7
Mary Macarthur Ho
8 Belvedere DA17 . . . . .**169** A3
11 Dagenham RM10 . . . .**135** A1
Mary Rose Cl RM16 . . . . . .**172** C2
Mary Slessor Ho **14**
DA17 . . . .**169** A3
MASCALLS **115** F5
Mascalls Gdns CM14 . . . . .**115** F6
Mascalls La
Brentwood CM14. . . . .**115** F6
Great Warley CM14. . . . . .**116** A4
Mascalls The CM2 . . . . **54** E8
Mascalls Way CM2 . . . . **54** E8
Masefield Cl CM2 . . . . **32** A1
Masefield Cres RM3. . . . . .**114** C2
Masefield Ct E6 . . . .**152** A3
Masefield Dr RM14. . . . . . .**137** C4
Masefield Gdns E6. . . . . . .**152** A3
Masefield Rd
Dartford DA1. . . . .**176** B2
Grays RM16. . . . .**173** E4
Maldon CM9. . . . . **59** A8
Mashbury **17** C4
Mashbury Rd CM1 . . . . **17** D6
Mashiters Hill RM1 . . . .**113** D2
Mashiters Wlk RM1 . . . .**135** E8
Mason Dr RM3. . . . .**114** E1
Mason Rd IG8 . . . .**109** E6
Mason Way EN9 . . . . **65** F6
Masters Ct **3** RM2 . . . . . .**136** B6
Masthead Cl DA2 . . . .**176** C3
MATCHING **13** B4
Matching Field CM15 . . . . . **71** F2
Matching Gn SS14 . . . .**120** D1
MATCHING GREEN **13** D3
Matching Green CE Prim
Sch CM17 . . . . **13** D2
Matching La
Harlow, Harlow Tye
CM17 . . . . **12** B4
Harlow, Matching CM22 . . . **13** B8
Hatfield Heath CM22 . . . . . . **3** B2
MATCHING TYE **12** E3
Matfield Cl CM1 . . . . **32** D7
Mathart Ct E4 . . . .**109** D4
Mathews Ave E6. . . . .**152** A3
Mathews Mead CM11 . . . . .**120** B5
Mathews Villas CM19 . . . . . **22** E6
Mathieson Ho E4 . . . . **87** E2
Matlock Ct E18 . . . .**109** F2
Matlock Gdns RM12 . . . . . .**136** C1
Matlock Ho **13** RM3 . . . . . .**114** D4
Matlock Rd SS8 . . . .**163** F3
Matson Ct IG8 . . . .**109** E3
Matthews Cl RM3 . . . .**114** F2
Matthews Ct SS12. . . . .**121** D5
Maud Gdns IG11 . . . .**152** F3
Maugham Ct SS12 . . . .**121** D5
Maunder Cl RM16. . . . .**172** D2
Maunds Farm CM18. . . . . . . **23** E4
Maunds Hatch CM18 . . . . . **23** E4
Maurice Ct SS8 . . . .**164** D2
Maurice Ho **5** CM14 . . . . .**116** C6
Maurice Lewis Pl **5**
DA11 . . . .**179** A1
Maurice Rd SS8 . . . .**164** D3
Mavis Gr RM12 . . . .**136** E2
Mawney Cl RM7 . . . .**113** B1
Mawney Rd RM7 . . . .**135** C2
Mawney Sch The
RM7 . . . .**135** D6
Maxey Gdns RM9 . . . .**153** E8
Maxey Rd RM9 . . . .**153** E8
Maximfeldt Rd DA8 . . . .**169** E1
Maxim Rd DA8 . . . .**169** D2
Maxwell Ct IG7 . . . .**112** B7
Maya Angelou Ct E4 . . . . . .**109** C6
Maya Cl SS3 . . . .**168** C4
Mayall Cl EN3 . . . . **65** A1
May Ave SS8 . . . .**164** C3
Maybank Ave
Hornchurch RM12 . . . .**155** C7
Woodford IG8 . . . .**110** B1
Maybank Lo **2** RM12 . . . . .**155** C7
Maybank Rd E18 . . . .**110** C2

Maybells Commercial Est
IG11 . . . .**153** D3
Maybrick Rd RM11 . . . .**136** C5
Maybrook Ct E11 . . . .**132** B2
Maybury Cl IG10 . . . . **89** B5
Maybury Rd IG11 . . . .**153** A3
Maybush Rd RM11 . . . .**136** E4
Maycroft Ave RM17 . . . . . .**173** D1
Maycroft Gdns RM17 . . . . .**173** D1
May Ct RM17 . . . .**178** E8
Maydeb Ct RM6. . . . .**134** F5
Maydells SS13 . . . .**143** B5
Maydells Ct SS13 . . . .**143** B5
Maydene CM3 . . . .**101** D7
Mayer Rd EN9 . . . . **65** B3
Mayesbrook Rd
Barking IG11 . . . .**152** F4
Dagenham IG3, RM8 . . . . .**134** B1
Mayesford Rd RM6 . . . .**134** C4
Mayes La
Chelmsford CM3 . . . . **55** E5
Danbury CM3. . . . . **56** E6
Mayespark Prim Sch
IG3 . . . .**134** A1
Mayfair Ave
Basildon SS13 . . . .**143** C8
Dagenham RM6 . . . .**134** D5
Ilford IG1 . . . .**133** A3
Mayfair Gdns IG8 . . . .**110** A3
Mayfair Ind Area CM3 . . . . **81** F6
Mayfield
Swanscombe DA10 . . . . . .**177** E1
Waltham Abbey EN9 . . . . . **65** D5
Mayfield Ave
Hullbridge SS5. . . . .**101** E2
Southend-on-S SS2 . . . . . .**147** E4
Woodford IG8 . . . .**110** A4
Mayfield Cl CM17 . . . . **11** F7
Mayfield Ct EN9 . . . . **66** A5
Mayfield Ctr CM0 . . . .**106** A5
Mayfield Gdns CM14 . . . . . **94** C1
Mayfield Rd
Belvedere DA17 . . . .**169** C2
Chingford E4 . . . .**109** D8
Dagenham RM8 . . . .**134** C3
Writtle CM1. . . . . **31** A2
Mayfields RM16 . . . .**173** C4
Mayfield Sch RM8 . . . . . .**134** C3
Mayflower Cl
Lower Nazeing EN9 . . . . . . **43** B3
Southend-on-S SS2 . . . . . .**147** B6
South Ockendon RM15 . . . .**157** C1
Mayflower Ct
Canvey Island SS8. . . . . . .**164** D2
Chipping Ongar CM5 . . . . . **49** A4
Harlow CM19. . . . . **23** B4
Mayflower Dr CM9. . . . . **59** A7
Mayflower High Sch
CM12 . . . . **97** C5
Mayflower Ho
2 Barking IG11 . . . .**152** D4
Brentwood CM13. . . . .**116** C4
Mayflower Rd
5 Billericay CM11 . . . . . **97** B2
Grays RM16. . . . .**172** C1
Mayflower Ret Pk
SS14 . . . .**120** D2
Mayflowers SS7 . . . .**144** B7
Mayflower Way CM5 . . . . . . **49** A4
Maygreen Cres RM11 . . . . .**136** A4
Mayhew Cl E4 . . . .**109** A7
Mayhill Lo RM3 . . . .**114** C2
MAYLAND **83** B8
Mayland Ave SS8 . . . .**164** A2
Mayland Cl
Heybridge CM9 . . . . **37** D4
Mayland CM3. . . . . **83** A7
Mayland Gn CM3. . . . . **83** B8
Mayland Hill CM3 . . . . **83** C5
Mayland Mans **4**
IG11. . . . .**152** B5
Mayland Quay CM3 . . . . **60** E1
Maylands Ave RM12. . . . . .**155** B8
MAYLANDSEA **60** F1
Maylandsea Prim Sch
CM3 . . . . **82** F8
Maylands Way RM3 . . . . . .**115** C3
Maylins Dr CM21. . . . . **1** D2
Maynard Ct
2 Holdbrook EN3. . . . . . **65** A1
Waltham Abbey EN9 . . . . . **65** F5
Maynards RM11. . . . .**136** C5
Mayne Crest CM1 . . . . **32** E6
Maypole Cres IG6 . . . .**111** E3
Maypole Dr IG7 . . . .**112** A7
Maypole St CM17 . . . . **11** C1
May Rd E4 . . . .**109** A4
Maystocks E18 . . . .**132** C8
Mayswood Gdns
RM10. . . . .**154** C6
May Terr IG1. . . . .**152** B6
Maytime Prep Sch
E12 . . . .**133** A1
Maytree Cl RM13. . . . .**154** E3
Maytree Wlk SS7 . . . .**144** C6
May Villa RM2 . . . .**114** C1
Mayville Rd IG1 . . . .**152** B7
Maywin Dr RM11 . . . .**136** F3
May Wlk CM2 . . . . **54** C7
Maze The SS9 . . . .**146** D7
Mead Cl
Grays RM16. . . . .**173** B4
Loughton IG10. . . . . **89** D7
Romford RM2 . . . .**114** A1
Mead Cres E4 . . . .**109** C6
Mead Ct EN9 . . . . **65** B5
Meade Cl CM11 . . . . **97** D5
Meade Rd CM11 . . . . **97** D5

Mea–Mis 213

- **Meadgate** SS13 143 C8
- **Meadgate Ave**
  - Great Baddow CM2 54 D8
  - Woodford IG8 110 E5
- **Meadgate Prim Sch** CM2 54 E8
- **Meadgate Rd** EN9 21 C3
- **Meadgate Terr** CM2 54 D8
- **Mead Gr** RM6 134 D8
- **Mead Lo** 3 EN11 21 D8
- **Meadow Cl**
  - 12 Barking IG11 152 F5
  - Chingford E4 87 B1
  - Linford SS17 175 A3
  - Romford RM3 114 C7
  - Thundersley SS7 145 B6
- **Meadow Cross** EN9 65 E5
- **Meadow Ct**
  - Billericay CM11 97 C2
  - Canvey Island SS8 163 F6
  - Harlow CM18 23 E4
  - Wickford SS11 121 E8
- **Meadow Dr**
  - Basildon SS16 160 B8
  - Southend-on-S SS1 167 E7
- **Meadowgate** CM4 75 F2
- **Meadow La** SS11 99 E3
- **Meadowland Rd** SS11 122 A6
- **Meadowlands** RM11 136 E4
- **Meadow Mews** CM3 101 B8
- **Meadow Rd**
  - Barking IG11 153 A5
  - Dagenham RM9 153 F6
  - Epping CM16 45 F2
  - Grays RM16 173 C5
  - Hadleigh SS7 145 E2
  - Hullbridge SS5 101 E2
  - Loughton IG10 88 E4
  - Rettendon CM3 100 C5
  - Romford RM7 135 C3
- **Meadow Rise**
  - Billericay CM11 97 C2
  - Blackmore CM4 72 E8
- **Meadows Cl** CM13 117 C4
- **Meadows Cotts** 1 CM4 74 B3
- **Meadowside**
  - Chelmsford CM2 32 C3
  - Rayleigh SS6 123 D2
  - South Benfleet SS7 144 B3
- **Meadow Side** CM1 32 B3
- **Meadowside Ct** CM3 20 E1
- **Meadowside Rd** RM14 156 C7
- **Meadows The**
  - 3 Chelmsford CM2 32 C2
  - Ingrave CM13 117 C4
  - Sawbridgeworth CM21 2 A2
- **Meadow View**
  - Basildon SS16 140 E4
  - Bicknacre CM3 56 E1
  - Pilgrims Hatch CM15 94 C3
- **Meadow View Wlk** SS8 163 E4
- **Meadow Way**
  - Burnham-on-C CM0 106 A7
  - Chigwell IG7 111 C8
  - Hockley SS5 124 E6
  - Latchingdon CM3 82 A6
  - Sawbridgeworth CM21 2 A1
  - Upminster RM14 137 C1
  - Wickford SS12 121 E3
- **Meadow Way The** CM11 97 C2
- **Meadow Wlk**
  - 5 Chelmsford CM2 32 C2
  - Dagenham RM9 153 F6
  - Wanstead E18 132 A7
- **Mead Park Ind Est** CM20 10 F4
- **Mead Pastures** CM9 35 D3
- **Mead Path** CM2 53 F8
- **Mead Prim Sch** RM3 114 F4
- **Meads Cl** CM4 74 B4
- **Meads Ct** CM15 116 E8
- **Meads La** IG3 133 F4
- **Meads The**
  - Basildon SS16 143 A4
  - Chelmsford CM2 32 A1
  - Ingatestone CM4 74 B4
  - Upminster RM14 137 E2
- **Meadsway** CM13 116 C4
- **Mead The**
  - Basildon SS15 141 B8
  - Hoddesdon EN10 21 B2
- **Meadway**
  - Canvey Island SS8 164 C2
  - Grays RM17 173 D2
  - Hoddesdon EN11 21 A4
  - Ilford IG3 152 E8
  - Maldon CM9 37 B1
  - Rayleigh SS6 123 E1
  - Romford RM2 114 A1
  - South Benfleet SS7 144 C7
  - Woodford IG8 110 C5
- **Meadway Ct** RM8 134 F2
- **Meadway The**
  - Buckhurst Hill IG9 88 D1
  - Loughton IG10 88 F3
  - Southend-on-S SS0 166 B8
- **Mead Wlk** CM5 48 F1
- **Meakins Cl** SS9 147 A7
- **Mearns Pl** 3 CM2 32 F4
- **Meath Rd** IG1 133 C1
- **Medbree Ct** RM16 174 A8
- **Medebridge Rd**
  - Grays RM15, RM16 173 A8
  - South Ockendon RM16 158 A1
- **Medick Ct** RM17 178 E8
- **Medina Rd** RM17 173 D2
- **Medlar Dr** RM15 157 E1
- **Medlar Rd** RM17 178 E8
- **Medlars Mead** CM22 3 F5
- **Medley Way** CM0 62 D7
- **Medoc Cl** SS13 143 C8
- **Medora Rd** RM7 135 D7
- **Meduza Ct** 7 DA12 179 D1
- **Medway** CM0 106 A6
- **Medway Cl**
  - Chelmsford CM1 31 D4
  - Ilford IG1 152 C7
- **Medway Cres** SS9 146 B1
- **Meeson Bglws** CM3 100 C5
- **Meeson Mdws** CM9 58 E8
- **Meeson's La** RM17 172 F1
- **Meesons Mead** SS4 125 E3
- **Meggison Way** SS7 144 C3
- **Meggy Tye** CM2 33 B5
- **Meister Cl** IG1 133 D3
- **Melanie Ct** SS4 125 D6
- **Melba Ct** CM1 31 C1
- **Melba Gdns** RM18 179 B7
- **Melbourne Ave** CM1 31 E5
- **Melbourne Ct**
  - Chelmsford CM1 31 E5
  - Tilbury RM18 178 E6
- **Melbourne Gdns** RM6 134 E6
- **Melbourne Par** CM1 31 E5
- **Melbourne Park Prim Sch** CM1 31 F6
- **Melbourne Quay** 8 DA11 179 B1
- **Melbourne Rd**
  - Ilford IG1 133 B3
  - Tilbury RM18 178 E6
- **Melcombe Rd** SS7 144 C3
- **Meldrum Rd** IG3 134 A2
- **Melford Ave** IG11 152 F6
- **Melford Pl** CM14 94 C1
- **Melford Rd** IG1 133 D2
- **Melksham Cl** RM3 114 F3
- **Melksham Dr** RM3 114 F3
- **Melksham Gdns** RM3 114 F3
- **Melksham Gn** RM3 114 F3
- **Mellish Cl** IG11 152 F4
- **Mellish Gdns** IG8 110 A5
- **Mellish Way** RM11 136 C6
- **Mellor Cl** CM4 74 B4
- **Mellow Mead** SS15 141 B8
- **Mellow Purgess** SS15 141 C6
- **Mellow Purgess Cl** SS15 141 C6
- **Mellow Purgess End** SS15 141 C6
- **Mellows Rd** IG5 132 F8
- **Melstock Ave** RM14 156 C8
- **Melton Gdns** RM1 135 F4
- **Melville Ct**
  - Romford RM3 114 E3
  - Southend-on-S SS1 167 D6
- **Melville Dr** SS12 121 D4
- **Melville Heath** CM3 101 E6
- **Melville Rd**
  - Rainham RM13 155 B1
  - Romford RM5 113 B2
- **Memorial Ave** E12 132 E2
- **Memorial Hts** IG2 133 D5
- **Memory Cl** CM9 59 A7
- **Mendip Cl**
  - Rayleigh SS6 123 D4
  - Wickford SS11 121 E7
- **Mendip Cres** SS0 147 A4
- **Mendip Ho** DA11 178 D1
- **Mendip Rd**
  - Chelmsford CM1 31 D6
  - Hornchurch RM11 136 A4
  - Ilford IG2 133 E6
  - Southend-on-S SS0 147 A4
- **Mendips The** SS9 146 F5
- **Mendoza Cl** RM11 136 E6
- **Menish Way** CM2 33 A3
- **Menthone Pl** RM11 136 D4
- **Mentmore** SS16 141 B4
- **Menzies Ave** SS15 140 F6
- **Meon Cl** CM1 32 C6
- **Meppel Ave** SS8 164 A6
- **Mercer Ave** SS3 150 A4
- **Mercer Rd** CM11 97 D5
- **Mercers** CM19 23 A5
- **Merchant St** CM3 101 E7
- **Mercia Cl** CM2 55 A5
- **Mercury Cl** SS11 121 F8
- **Mercury Ct** 8 RM1 135 F6
- **Mercury Gdns** RM1 135 F6
- **Mercury Pl** CM9 36 F5
- **Merdle Sq** CM1 31 F6
- **Merebridge Rd** RM16 172 F6
- **Meredene** SS14 142 F5
- **Meredith Rd** RM16 174 A2
- **Merefield** CM21 1 E1
- **Meresmans** RM15 171 D7
- **Mereworth Rd** CM3 101 C5
- **Meriadoc Dr** CM3 101 D6
- **Meridan Ho** EN10 21 C2
- **Meriden Cl** IG6 111 C2
- **Meridian Bsns Pk** EN9 65 B4
- **Meridian Ct** RM17 178 B7
- **Meridian Way**
  - Stanstead Abbotts SG12 8 B5
  - Waltham Abbey EN9 65 B4
- **Meridien** RM1 135 F4
- **Meriel Wlk** DA9 177 B3
- **Merilies Cl** SS0 147 B4
- **Merilies Gdns** SS0 147 B3
- **Merino Cl** E11 132 C7
- **Merlin Cl**
  - Grays RM16 172 E3
  - Redbridge IG6 112 C6
  - Romford RM5 113 D4
  - Waltham Abbey EN9 66 A5
- **Merlin Ct** SS8 164 B3
- **Merlin Gdns** RM5 113 D4
- **Merlin Gr** IG6 111 C3
- **Merlin Pl** CM1 31 F5
- **Merlin Rd**
  - Romford RM5 113 D4
  - Wanstead E12 132 D2
- **Merlin Way**
  - North Weald Bassett CM16 47 A6
  - Wickford SS11 99 D1
- **Mermagen Dr** RM13 155 B5
- **Mermaid Way** CM9 59 B8
- **Merriam Cl** E4 109 C5
- **Merricks La** SS16 142 E3
- **Merrielands Cres** RM9 153 F3
- **Merrielands Ret Pk** RM9 153 F3
- **Merring Way** CM19 22 F7
- **Merritt Ho** RM1 135 F4
- **Merrivale** SS7 144 C2
- **Merrivale Ave** IG4 132 D7
- **Merry Fiddlers** RM8 134 F2
- **Merryfield App** SS9 146 E4
- **Merryfields Ave** SS5 124 D7
- **Merryhill Cl** E4 87 B2
- **Merrylands** SS15 141 A7
- **Merrylands Chase** CM13 140 D7
- **Merrylands Prim Sch** SS15 141 A6
- **Merrymeade Chase** CM15 94 D1
- **Mersea Cres** SS12 121 F6
- **Mersea Ho** 4 IG11 152 B6
- **Mersey Ave** RM14 137 D5
- **Mersey Way** CM1 31 C5
- **Merten Rd** RM6 134 E4
- **Merton Ct** IG4 132 E5
- **Merton Pl**
  - Grays RM16 174 A2
  - South Woodham Ferrers CM3 101 F6
- **Merton Rd**
  - Barking IG11 152 F5
  - Hockley SS5 124 A8
  - Ilford IG3 133 F4
  - South Benfleet SS7 144 C4
- **Messant Cl** RM3 114 D1
- **Mess Rd** SS3 168 F5
- **Meteor Rd** SS0 166 D8
- **Meteor Way** CM1 31 F2
- **Metford Cres** EN3 65 A1
- **Methersgate** SS14 142 C7
- **Methuen Rd** DA17 169 B2
- **Metsons La** CM1 51 E2
- **Metz Ave** SS8 164 A4
- **Mews Ct** CM2 32 B1
- **Mews Pl** IG8 110 A6
- **Mews The**
  - Grays RM17 173 C2
  - Harlow CM18 23 E4
  - Hockley SS5 124 C6
  - Redbridge IG4 132 D6
  - Romford RM1 135 E7
  - Sawbridgeworth CM21 1 E3
- **Meyel Ave** SS8 164 C5
- **Meynell Ave** SS8 164 C2
- **Meynell Rd** RM3 114 B3
- **Mey Wlk** SS5 124 C6
- **Mia Ct** CM19 23 B8
- **Micawber Way** CM1 31 D7
- **Michael Gdns** RM11 136 D7
- **Michael's Cotts** SS3 168 D6
- **Midas Bsns Ctr** RM10 154 B8
- **Mid Colne** SS16 142 D4
- **Middle Boy** RM4 90 C6
- **Middle Cloister** 3 CM11 97 B2
- **Middle Crockerford** SS16 142 E4
- **Middlefield Ave** EN11 21 A8
- **Middlefield Cl** EN11 21 A8
- **Middlefield Gdns** IG2 133 B5
- **Middlefield Rd** EN11 21 A8
- **Middle Gn** CM15 72 C2
- **Middleham Ct** 14 DA2 176 B1
- **Middlemead**
  - South Hanningfield CM3 99 C8
  - West Hanningfield CM2 77 C3
- **Middle Mead**
  - Rochford SS4 125 F2
  - Wickford SS11 121 E8
- **Middle Mead Cl** CM2 76 F4
- **Middle Rd**
  - Ingrave CM13 117 C6
  - Waltham Abbey EN9 65 B7
- **Middlesborough Ho** 7 RM3 114 E3
- **Middlesburg** SS8 163 E5
- **Middlesex Ave** SS9 146 F3
- **Middle St** EN9 44 A8
- **Middleton Ave** E4 109 A7
- **Middleton Gdns** IG2 133 B5
- **Middleton Hall La** CM15 116 E8
- **Middleton Rd** CM15 94 F1
- **Middleton Row** CM3 101 E6
- **Midguard Way** CM9 58 F8
- **Midhurst Ave** SS0 147 D4
- **Midhurst Cl** RM12 155 A8
- **Midland Ct** RM1 135 F6
- **Midsummer Mdw** SS3 149 E1
- **Mighell Ave** IG4 132 D6
- **Milbank** CM2 33 B4
- **Milbanke Cl** SS3 149 E1
- **Milbourn Ct** SS4 125 F2
- **Milburn Cres** CM1 31 D1
- **Mildenhall Ho** RM3 115 A5
- **Mildmay Ct** 2 CM2 32 B1
- **Mildmayes** SS16 141 C4
- **Mildmay Ho** CM0 106 B5
- **Mildmay Ind Est** CM0 106 B5
- **Mildmay Jun & Inf Schs** CM2 54 B5
- **Mildmay Rd**
  - Burnham-on-C CM0 106 C5
  - Chelmsford CM2 32 B1
  - Ilford IG1 133 B1
  - Romford RM7 135 C6
- **Mildmays** CM3 56 C7
- **Mildred Cl** DA1 176 A1
- **Mildred Rd** DA8 169 E1
- **Mile Cl** EN9 65 C6
- **Miles Cl** CM19 23 B7
- **Miles Gray Rd** SS14 119 F1
- **Mile Stone Rd** DA2 176 B1
- **Milford Rd** RM16 173 D5
- **Milkwell Gdns** IG8 110 B3
- **Millais Ave** E12 152 A7
- **Millais Pl** RM18 179 B7
- **Millard Terr** RM10 154 A6
- **Millars Cl** CM3 101 E8
- **Millars The** CM1 19 A3
- **Millbank Ave** CM5 48 F2
- **Millbrook**
  - Chigwell IG7 111 D5
  - 1 Wanstead E18 132 A8
  - 6 Woodford E18 110 A1
- **Millbrook Bsns Pk** EN9 22 A1
- **Millbrook Gdns**
  - Dagenham RM6 134 E5
  - Romford RM2 113 E2
- **Mill Cl**
  - Roxwell CM1 30 A5
  - Tillingham CM0 63 E4
- **Mill Cotts**
  - Corringham SS17 161 D4
  - Great Baddow CM2 55 C8
- **Mill Crn** CM19 9 A1
- **Mill Ct** CM20 10 D3
- **MILL END** 63 E8
- **Millennium Wlk** CM14 116 D8
- **Miller Ave** EN3 65 A1
- **Miller Cl** RM5 113 A3
- **Miller Ct** RM2 136 A8
- **Millers Cl** IG7 112 B8
- **Millers Croft** CM2 54 F6
- **Millersdale** CM19 23 B4
- **MILLER'S GREEN** 28 C4
- **Millers Green Rd** CM5 28 B3
- **Millers Ho The** SG12 8 D4
- **Millers La** SG12 8 C4
- **Miller's La** IG7 90 B1
- **Millers Mews** 3 CM4 74 C4
- **Millfield**
  - Burnham-on-C CM0 106 B4
  - High Ongar CM5 49 D3
- **Mill Field** CM17 11 C4
- **Millfield Cl** SS6 123 E3
- **Millfields**
  - Danbury CM3 57 A6
  - Sawbridgeworth CM21 1 F3
  - Writtle CM1 31 A1
- **Mill Gn**
  - Basildon SS13 143 A7
  - Burnham-on-C CM0 106 B4
- **Mill Gr** CM5 49 D4
- **Mill Grange** CM0 106 B7
- **MILL GREEN** 73 F7
- **Mill Green Ct** SS13 143 B7
- **Mill Green Pl** SS13 143 B7
- **Mill Green Rd** CM4 73 F7
- **Mill Hatch** CM20 11 A4
- **Millhaven Cl** RM6 134 B5
- **Millhead Way** SS4 126 B1
- **Mill Hill**
  - Chelmsford CM2 53 F2
  - Purleigh CM3 58 C1
  - Shenfield CM15 94 F2
  - South Benfleet SS7 163 E8
- **Mill Hill Dr** CM12 97 B5
- **Mill Ho**
  - 7 Rochford SS4 125 F2
  - Woodford IG8 109 F5
- **Millhoo Ct** EN9 65 F5
- **Millhouse Inf Sch** SS15 141 C8
- **Millhouse Jun Sch** SS15 141 C8
- **Millhurst Mews** CM17 11 E4
- **Millicent Preston Ho** 4 IG11 152 D4
- **Milligans Chase** CM2 54 B1
- **Mill La**
  - Broomfield CM1 19 C1
  - Corringham SS17 161 C7
  - Dagenham RM6 134 E5
  - Danbury CM3 57 A6
  - Fobbing SS17 161 C6
  - Grays RM16 172 D1
  - Harlow CM17 11 E4
  - Hatfield Heath CM22 2 F3
  - High Ongar CM5 49 D2
  - Hoddesdon EN10 21 A2
  - Horndon on t H SS17 159 F3
  - Ingatestone CM4 74 A6
- **Mill La** *continued*
  - Kelvedon Hatch CM15 71 E2
  - Little Baddow CM3 34 E3
  - Maldon CM9 37 A3
  - Moreton CM5 26 C5
  - Navestock Heath RM4 92 B8
  - Orsett RM16 174 A7
  - Purleigh CM3 58 C1
  - Ramsden Heath CM11 98 B5
  - Rochford SS4 126 B2
  - Sawbridgeworth CM21 1 F3
  - Sewardstone E4 87 B6
  - Stock CM4 75 F2
  - Toot Hill CM5 47 E2
  - Woodford IG8 109 F5
  - Wyatts Green CM15 72 D4
- **Mill Lo** SS3 168 E6
- **Millom Ho** 1 RM3 114 D4
- **Mill Park Ave** RM12 136 E2
- **Mill Race** SG12 8 D4
- **Mill Rd**
  - Aveley RM15 171 C6
  - Billericay CM11 119 D6
  - Burnham-on-C CM0 106 C7
  - Ilford IG1 133 A1
  - Maldon CM9 37 B2
  - Margaret Roding CM1 16 D5
  - Mayland CM3 83 B8
  - Stock CM4 75 F2
  - Tillingham CM0 63 E4
- **Millsmead Way** IG10 88 F7
- **Millson Bank** CM2 33 A4
- **Mill St** CM17 24 F5
- **Mills Way** CM13 95 C1
- **Mill View** RM16 173 E7
- **Mill View Ct** CM1 30 A5
- **Millview Mdws** SS4 125 F1
- **Mill Vue Rd** CM2 32 F2
- **Millwell Cres** IG7 111 D5
- **Milne Ct** 4 E18 110 A2
- **Milner Pl** CM12 96 F5
- **Milner Rd** RM8 134 C2
- **MILTON** 179 D1
- **Milton Ave**
  - Basildon SS16 140 F4
  - Hornchurch RM12 135 F2
  - Southend-on-S SS0 166 E7
- **Milton Cl**
  - Rayleigh SS6 124 A2
  - Southend-on-S SS2 148 A1
- **Milton Cres**
  - Chipping Ongar CM5 48 F5
  - Ilford IG2 133 C5
- **Milton Ct**
  - Dagenham RM6 134 C4
  - Southend-on-S SS0 166 E7
  - Waltham Abbey EN9 65 C5
- **Milton Gdns** RM18 179 B6
- **Milton Hall Cl** SS3 150 A3
- **Milton Hall Prim Sch** SS0 166 E8
- **Milton Pl**
  - Chelmsford CM1 32 A5
  - Gravesend DA12 179 C1
  - Southend-on-S SS1 166 F7
- **Milton Rd**
  - Belvedere DA17 169 A2
  - Brentwood CM14 116 C6
  - Corringham SS17 160 F6
  - Gravesend DA12 179 C1
  - Grays RM17 173 B1
  - Maldon CM9 59 A8
  - Romford RM1 136 A5
  - Southend-on-S SS0 166 E8
  - Swanscombe DA10 177 E1
- **Milton St**
  - Southend-on-S SS2 148 A1
  - Swanscombe DA10 177 D1
  - Waltham Abbey EN9 65 C5
- **Miltsin Ave** SS8 164 C5
- **Milverton Gdns** IG3 133 F2
- **Milwards** CM19 23 B4
- **Milwards Prim Sch** CM19 23 B4
- **Mimosa Cl**
  - Basildon SS16 140 F4
  - Chelmsford CM1 32 F6
  - Pilgrims Hatch CM15 94 B4
  - Romford RM3 114 C3
- **Minchen Rd** CM20 11 A1
- **Minehead Ho** 6 RM3 114 E5
- **Minerva Rd** E4 109 B3
- **MINNOW END** 19 A6
- **Minster Cl** SS6 124 A1
- **Minster Ct** RM11 137 A3
- **Minster Rd** SS15 141 C6
- **Minster Way**
  - Hornchurch RM11 137 A3
  - Maldon CM9 58 E8
- **Minton Hts** SS4 125 C6
- **Minton La** CM17 24 C8
- **Miramar Ave** SS8 163 E3
- **Miramar Way** RM12 155 D7
- **Miranda Ho** 6 DA17 169 A1
- **Mirosa Dr** CM9 37 B1
- **Mirosa Reach** CM9 59 A8
- **Mirravale Ct** 7 IG9 110 C8
- **Mirravale Trad Est** RM6 134 E4
- **Mirror Stps** 1 SS1 167 C7
- **Mistleigh Ct** CM15 94 F2
- **Mistley End** SS16 142 C5
- **Mistley Path** SS16 142 C5
- **Mistley Rd** CM20 11 A2
- **Mistley Side** SS16 142 C5

Mistley Thorn IG1 ...... 133 A4
Mistral Ct E4 .... 109 B7
Mitcham Rd IG3 .... 133 F4
Mitchell Cl
  Erith DA17 .... 169 C3
  Rainham RM13 .... 155 C3
Mitchells Ave SS8 ...... 164 D4
Mitchells Wlk SS8 ...... 164 D4
Mitchell Way CM3 ..... 101 D8
Mitre Bldgs **3** CM20 .... 10 C1
Mitre Ct
  Belvedere DA17 ...... 169 A2
  1 Dagenham RM6 .... 134 B4
  9 Woodford E18 ..... 110 A4
Mitre Ho RM7 .... 135 B7
Mitton Vale CM2 .... 32 F2
Moat Cl
  Doddinghurst CM15..... 72 C3
  Ramsden Heath CM11.... 98 C3
Moat Edge Gdns CM12 .. 97 A4
Moat End SS1 .... 149 B1
Moat Field SS14 .... 142 C8
Moat Ho CM19.......... 22 E7
Moat Lodge Ho **2**
  SS14 .... 142 C7
Moat Rise SS6 .... 123 D1
Moat The CM5 .... 47 F2
Moby Dick RM6 .... 134 F7
Molesworth EN11 .... 8 A2
Mollands SS16......... 142 F4
Mollands Ct RM15 ..... 157 E1
Mollands La CM2....... 55 B6
Mollison Ave EN3 ...... 65 A3
Molrams La CM2....... 55 B6
Molyneaux Ct CM12.... 97 A3
Momples Rd CM20 ..... 11 B1
Monarch Cl
  Rainham RM13 .... 155 A3
  Tilbury RM18 .... 179 B5
Monarch Pl IG9 .... 110 A3
Monarch Rd DA17...... 169 A3
Monarch Way IG2 ..... 133 D5
Monastery Rd SS15 .... 141 C6
Monkchester Cl IG10 ... 89 A8
Monkham's Ave IG8 ... 110 B5
Monkham's Dr IG8.... 110 B5
Monkhams Hall EN9 .. 43 C2
Monkham's La IG8..... 110 B6
Monksbury CM18 ...... 24 A5
Monks Chase CM13 .... 117 C5
Monks Cl EN10 .... 21 A3
Monksford Dr SS5 ..... 101 D1
Monksgrove IG10....... 89 A4
Monks Haven SS17..... 160 E2
Monkside SS14 .... 142 D7
Monks Mead CM3..... 56 F2
Monks Well DA9....... 177 C3
Monk's Well **1** DA9... 177 C3
Monkswick Rd CM20 .. 10 F1
Monks Wlk CM9 .... 40 E8
Monkswood Ave EN9.. 65 D6
Monkswood Gdns
  IG5................. 133 A8
Monkwood Cl RM1..... 136 A6
Monmouth Ave E18 .... 132 B8
Monmouth Mews
  SS16 .... 140 F5
Monmouth Rd RM9 .... 153 F7
Monnow Ave IG1 ...... 171 C6
Monnow Rd RM15 ..... 171 C6
Monoux Cl CM11....... 97 D1
Monoux Gr E17 .... 109 A2
Mons Ave CM11........ 97 D2
Montague Ave SS6 .... 146 B2
Montague Bldgs **2**
  SS1 .... 167 B8
Montague Ct SS0 ..... 166 D8
Montague Ho **13** IG8 .. 111 A3
Montague Pl SS8 ...... 163 E3
Montague Way CM12... 97 A4
Montagu Gdns CM1 .... 32 F7
Montalt Ho IG8 .... 109 F6
Montalt Rd IG8 .... 109 F5
Montbazon Ct CM14.... 94 B1
Monteagle Ave IG11 .. 152 C6
Monteagle Ct IG11..... 152 C5
Monteagle Prim Sch
  RM9 .... 153 B4
Montefiore Ave SS6.... 123 D8
Montfort Ave SS17 ... 161 A3
Montfort Gdns IG6..... 111 C4
Montgomery Ct E4...... 87 D2
Montgomery Inf Sch
  SS7 .... 144 B7
Montgomery Jun Sch
  SS7 .... 144 B7
Montgomery Cl
  Chelmsford CM1 ..... 32 E7
  Grays RM16......... 173 C4
Montgomery Cres
  RM3 .... 114 D5
Montgomery Ct
  2 Dagenham RM10 ... 154 A6
  Southend-on-S SS3 .... 149 E1
Montpelier Cl CM12.... 97 A5
Montpelier Ct **4**
  CM14 .... 116 C7
Montpelier Gdns
  RM6 .... 134 C4
Montpellier Ho IG7 .... 111 C5
Montreal Rd
  Ilford IG1 .... 133 C4
  Tilbury RM18........ 179 A5
Montrose Ave RM2...... 114 C1
Montrose Ave IG8...... 110 A6

Montrose Ho IG2 .... 133 A5
Montrose Rd CM2...... 33 A4
Montsale SS13......... 143 C8
Moons Cl SS4 .... 125 D7
Moorcroft SS4......... 125 D6
Moorcroft Ave SS7..... 145 E6
Moore Ave
  Grays RM20......... 172 E1
  Tilbury RM18........ 179 B5
Moore Cl CM11........ 97 D5
Moore Cres RM9....... 153 B4
Moore Ho RM11 ...... 136 A5
Moore Rd DA10....... 177 E1
Moores Ave SS17 ..... 142 C1
Moorescroft CM15 ..... 71 C2
Moore's Pl CM14...... 116 D8
Moore Twr CM18 ..... 23 F7
Moorfields CM18 ..... 23 C4
Moor Hall La CM3..... 56 E2
Moor Hall Rd CM17.... 12 A4
Moorhen Ave CM0 .... 62 C8
Moorhen Way CM19.... 9 A1
Moor La RM14 .... 137 F4
Moorland Cl RM5 ..... 113 B3
Moorlands Reach CM21 .. 2 A1
Moor Park Cl SS9..... 146 C5
Moor Park Gdns SS9... 146 C5
Mopsies Rd SS14 ..... 142 E6
Moran Ave CM1........ 32 B7
Morant Gdns RM5 .... 113 B5
Morant Rd RM16...... 174 B3
Moray Cl RM1 .... 113 E3
Moray Way RM1 ..... 113 E3
Mordaunt Gdns RM9... 153 E5
Morden Rd RM6...... 134 E4
Mordon Rd IG3 ...... 133 F4
Morecambe Cl RM12... 155 B7
Morecambe Ho **5**
  RM3 .... 114 E5
Moreland Ave SS7..... 144 C7
Moreland Cl
  Great Wakering SS3.. 150 A4
  South Benfleet SS7 ... 144 C6
Moreland Rd SS11..... 99 C2
Morelands Ave RM16... 173 C4
Moreland Way E4...... 109 C7
Moremead EN9........ 65 D6
Mores La CM14 ...... 93 D5
MORETON 26 C2
Moreton Bay Ind Est
  RM2 .... 114 D1
Moreton Bridge CM5... 26 D1
Moreton CE Prim Sch
  CM5 .... 26 C3
Moreton Gates CM5.... 26 C2
Moreton Gdns IG8..... 110 E5
Moreton Rd
  Chipping Ongar CM5... 48 F7
  Fyfield CM5 .... 27 B2
  Moreton CM5........ 48 B8
Moretons
  Basildon SS13 ...... 143 A6
  Galleywood CM2 .... 54 B2
Moretons Ct SS13...... 143 A6
Moretons Mews SS13.. 143 A6
Moretons Pl SS13...... 143 A6
Morgan Cl RM10...... 154 A5
Morgan Cres CM16..... 67 E3
Morgan Terr RM6...... 134 C6
Morgan Way
  Rainham RM13 ...... 155 C2
  Woodford IG8 .... 110 E4
Morland Rd
  Dagenham RM10...... 154 A5
  Ilford IG1 .... 133 B2
Morley Ave E4 .... 109 D3
Morley Gr CM20 ...... 10 C2
Morley Hill SS17...... 160 F5
Morley Link SS17 ..... 160 F5
Morley Rd
  Barking IG11........ 152 D4
  Dagenham RM6...... 134 E6
Morley Sq RM16 ..... 174 A2
Mornington Ave
  Ilford IG1 .... 133 A4
  Rochford SS4....... 126 A2
Mornington Cl IG8..... 110 A6
Mornington Cres
  Canvey Island SS8.... 164 C4
  Hadleigh SS7....... 145 F3
Mornington Ho SS0.... 166 C8
Mornington Rd
  Canvey Island SS8.... 164 C4
  Chingford E4 .... 87 D2
  Loughton IG10....... 89 C6
  Woodford IG8 .... 109 F6
Mornings CM19...... 23 C4
Morpeth Ho **6** RM3.. 114 D4
Morrab Gdns IG3 ..... 133 F1
Morrells SS16 .... 141 F4
Morrin's Chase SS3.... 150 D3
Morrins Ct SS3 ...... 150 D3
Morris Ave CM11..... 97 D1
Morris Ct
  Basildon SS15 ...... 141 B7
  Chingford E4 .... 109 B7
  Holdbrook EN3....... 65 A2
  Waltham Abbey EN9... 65 F5
Morris Gdns DA1..... 176 A2
Morris Ho CM18 ..... 23 C5
Morrison Ave E4...... 109 A4
Morrison Ho RM10.... 173 D4
Morrison Rd IG11..... 153 E3
Morris Rd
  Chelmsford CM2 .... 32 A2
  Dagenham RM8..... 134 F2
  Romford RM3 ...... 114 B3

Mortimer Rd SS6...... 123 E5
Mortlake Rd IG1...... 152 E6
Mosbach Gdns CM13... 117 B8
Moseley St SS2 ...... 148 D1
Moss Bank RM17..... 172 F2
Moss Cl SS16......... 142 E3
Mossdown Cl DA17 ... 169 A2
Moss Dr SS16......... 142 E3
Mossford Ct
  Ilford IG6 .... 133 B8
  Redbridge IG6....... 111 B1
Mossford Gn IG6 ..... 133 C8
Mossford Green Prim Sch
  IG6................ 111 C1
Mossford La IG6 ..... 111 C1
Moss La
  Hornchurch RM11 ... 136 A5
  Romford RM1 ...... 135 F5
Moss Path CM2....... 54 C3
Moss Rd
  Dagenham RM10..... 154 A5
  South Ockendon RM15 . 172 C8
Moss Wlk CM2....... 54 B6
Motehill SS16 .... 141 C4
Motherwell Way
  RM20 .... 172 A1
MOTT'S GREEN 2 D6
Mott St
  High Beach IG10 ..... 88 A8
  Sewardstone IG10..... 87 E8
MOULSHAM 54 A8
Moulsham Chase CM2.. 54 C8
Moulsham Dr CM2 .... 54 B8
Moulsham High Sch
  CM2 .... 54 B7
Moulsham Jun & Inf Schs
  CM2 .... 54 B7
Moulsham St
  Chelmsford CM1 .... 32 B2
  Chelmsford, Moulsham
  CM2 .... 32 B1
Moulsham Thrift CM2.. 54 A8
Moultrie Way RM14 .. 137 E5
Mountain Ash Ave
  SS9 .... 146 B6
Mountain Ash Cl SS9.. 146 B6
Mount Ave
  Brentwood CM13..... 95 B2
  Chingford E4 .... 109 B7
  Hockley SS5........ 124 E7
  Rayleigh SS6 .... 123 C3
  Romford RM3 ...... 115 C4
  Southend-on-S SS0 ... 166 A8
Mountbatten Ct IG9 .. 110 D8
Mountbatten Dr SS3 .. 149 E1
Mountbatten Ho **4**
  RM2 .... 136 C7
Mountbatten Way CM1.. 32 E7
Mount Bovers La SS5 .. 124 E3
Mount Cl
  Rayleigh SS6 .... 123 C2
  Wickford SS11...... 121 E8
Mount Cres
  Brentwood CM14..... 116 D6
  Hockley SS5........ 124 D6
  South Benfleet SS7 .. 144 E4
Mountdale Gdns SS9.. 146 F4
Mount Echo Ave E4.... 87 B1
Mount Echo Dr E4..... 87 B1
MOUNT END 68 F7
Mountfield Cl SS17.... 160 E3
Mountfield Rd E6...... 152 A2
Mountfields SS13..... 143 C4
Mounthill Ave CM2.... 32 D3
Mountier Ct **12** E11... 132 A6
MOUNTNESSING 95 D8
Mountnessing SS7..... 145 D2
Mountnessing CE Prim
  Sch CM15 .... 95 E7
Mountnessing La
  CM15 .... 72 E1
Mountnessing Rd
  Billericay CM12..... 96 E4
  Blackmore CM4..... 72 F6
  Mountnessing CM15,
  CM4 .... 73 A4
Mountney Cl CM4..... 73 F1
Mount Pleasant
  Ilford IG1 .... 152 C7
  Maldon CM9........ 36 F2
Mount Pleasant Ave
  CM13 .... 95 E4
Mount Pleasant Cotts
  CM15 .... 95 A4
Mount Pleasant Rd
  Chigwell IG7....... 111 D6
  Romford RM5 ...... 113 D4
  South Woodham Ferrers
  CM3 .... 101 D7
Mount Rd
  Dagenham RM8..... 134 F3
  Epping CM16....... 68 E6
  South Benfleet SS7 ... 144 F4
  Wickford SS11..... 121 E8
Mounts Rd DA9...... 177 B1
Mount The
  Billericay CM11..... 97 E3
  Brentwood CM14..... 116 C7
  Romford RM3 ...... 114 C7
  Stanford-le-H SS17 ... 160 F3
Mount View
  Billericay CM11..... 97 E2
  Brentwood CM14..... 116 C6
Mountview Cl SS16 ... 142 E3
Mountview Cres CM0... 62 C8
Mount View Rd E4..... 87 D2
Mount Way SS11...... 121 E8
Movers La IG11...... 152 E4

Mowbray Rd CM20 ... 11 A3
Mowbrays Cl RM5..... 113 C1
Mowbrays Rd RM5.... 113 C1
Mowbrey Gdns IG10... 89 C8
Mowden Hall La CM3 .. 35 A8
Muckingford Rd RM18,
  SS17 .... 174 D1
Mucking Hall Cotts
  SS3 .... 149 B8
Mucking Hall Rd SS3.. 149 C8
Mucking Wharf Rd
  SS17 .... 175 C7
Mudlands Ind Est
  RM13 .... 154 F2
Muggeridge Rd RM10.. 154 B8
Muirhead Quay IG11... 152 C3
Muir Pl SS12 .... 121 D5
Muirway SS7 .... 144 B7
Mulberry Cl
  Chingford E4 .... 109 A8
  Romford RM2 ...... 136 C7
Mulberry Ct IG11..... 152 F5
Mulberry Dr RM19 ... 170 F2
Mulberry Gn CM17.... 11 D4
Mulberry Hill CM15... 94 F2
Mulberry Rd SS8..... 163 C3
Mulberrys The SS2.... 148 A3
Mulberry Terr CM17 .. 11 B4
Mulberry Way
  Belvedere DA17 ..... 169 C4
  Chelmsford CM1 .... 32 D4
  Ilford IG6 .... 133 C7
  Woodford E18 ...... 110 B1
Mullberry Gdns SS16.. 141 B5
Mullein Ct RM17..... 178 E8
Mullions The CM12... 96 F3
Multon Lea CM1 ..... 33 A7
MUNDON 59 E2
Mundon Ct SS14 ..... 142 F5
Mundon Gdns IG1 .... 133 D3
Mundon Rd CM9..... 59 D5
Mungo Park Rd RM13 . 155 A6
Munnings Alley CM0... 84 D4
Munsons Dr SS13..... 143 C4
Munsterburg Rd SS8... 164 D5
Munster Ct CM12 .... 96 F5
Murchison Cl CM1 .... 31 E5
Murchison Rd EN11.... 8 B1
Murfitt Way RM14.... 156 A8
Murray Ho SS1 ...... 167 F6
Murray Way SS12 .... 121 D5
Murrell Lock CM2..... 33 A4
Murrels La SS5 ...... 124 A7
Murthering La
  Navestock Heath RM4.. 92 B5
  Stapleford Abbotts RM4 .. 91 F3
Musket Gr SS9 .... 146 B7
Muskham Rd CM20 ... 11 B3
Mus of Power* CM9... 36 D6
Mutton Row CM5 .... 70 C7
Mygrove Cl RM13 .... 155 D3
Mygrove Gdns RM13 .. 155 D3
Mygrove Rd RM13 .... 155 D3
Myine Ct
  Hoddesdon EN11 ..... 8 A1
  Hoddesdon EN11 ..... 21 A8
Myln Mead CM4 ..... 75 F2
Mynards Way CM3 ... 56 C7
Mynchens SS15 ...... 141 E6
Myrtle Gr RM15 ..... 171 C4
Myrtle Rd
  Brentwood CM14..... 116 C6
  Ilford IG1 .... 133 B2
  Romford RM3 ...... 114 C4

N

Nabbott Rd CM1 ..... 31 E2
Nacton Ct RM6...... 134 C6
Nadir Ct SS14 .... 132 A4
Naffenton Rise IG10... 88 D4
Nagle Cl E17 .... 109 D1
Nag's Head La CM14 .. 115 D4
Nairn Ct RM18....... 178 F5
Nairn Ho CM14 ...... 116 C5
Nalla Gdns CM1...... 32 A6
Namur Rd SS14 ..... 164 C5
Nansen Ave SS4 ..... 125 D6
Nantwich Ho **4** RM3.. 114 E5
Napier Ave **9** SS4 ... 167 A8
Napier Cl
  Basildon SS14 ...... 142 D6
  Hornchurch RM11 ... 136 B3
Napier Cres SS12 .... 121 E5
Napier Ct CM1....... 31 E5
Napier Ct W SS1..... 166 F8
Napier Gdns SS7..... 145 C6
Napier Ho RM13 .... 154 F2
Napier Rd
  Rayleigh SS6 .... 123 F3
  Wallend E6......... 152 A4
Narboro Ct RM1 .... 136 A5
Nare Rd RM15 ...... 171 C6
Narvik Cl CM9 ...... 58 E8
Naseby Rd
  Dagenham RM10..... 135 A1
  Woodford IG5 .... 110 F2
Nash Dr CM1 .... 19 A3
Nash Rd RM6....... 134 D7
Natal Rd IG1 .... 152 B8
Natasha Ct RM3..... 114 C3
Nathan Ct RM14 .... 137 E3
Nathan's La CM1..... 52 E5
National Motor Boat
  Mus* SS16.......... 143 B2
Nation Way E4 ...... 87 C1

Naunton Way RM12... 136 D1
Navarre Gdns RM5 ... 113 B5
Navestock Cl
  Chingford E4 .... 109 C7
  Rayleigh SS6 .... 123 A3
Navestock Cres IG8.... 110 C2
Navestock Gdns SS1 .. 148 F1
NAVESTOCK HEATH ... 92 D7
Navestock Ho **2**
  IG11............... 153 B2
NAVESTOCK SIDE 93 C7
Navestock Side CM14 .. 93 C7
Nave The SS15....... 141 D6
Navigation Pl CM9 .... 37 B4
Navigation Rd CM2 ... 32 C2
Nayland Cl SS12 ..... 121 E7
Nayland Ho SS2 ..... 147 E5
NAZEING 22 C1
Nazeingbury Cl EN9... 21 D1
Nazeingbury Par EN9 . 21 D1
Nazeing Comm EN9.... 44 D8
Nazeing Ho IG9....... 88 E2
NAZEING MEAD 21 D3
Nazeing New Rd EN10.. 21 B2
Nazeing Prim Sch EN9 . 43 E8
Nazeing Rd EN9 ..... 21 D1
Nazeing The SS14..... 142 E6
Nazeing Wlk RM13 ... 154 E5
Neal Ct EN9 .... 65 F6
Neale Ct
  Dagenham RM8...... 153 B6
  Hornchurch RM11 ... 136 F2
Neasham Rd RM8..... 153 B7
Neave Cres RM3 ..... 114 D2
Neave Rose Ct RM7 ... 135 C6
Nectar Ct **1** EN11... 21 D8
Needham Cl CM11.... 97 B3
Neil Armstrong Way
  SS9 .... 147 A6
Nelmes Cl RM11...... 136 F6
Nelmes Cres RM11.... 136 F6
Nelmes Ct RM11..... 136 D7
Nelmes Prim Sch
  RM11 .... 136 F7
Nelmes Rd RM11..... 136 E5
Nelmes Way RM11.... 136 E7
Nelson Cl
  Brentwood CM14..... 116 D5
  Rayleigh SS6 .... 123 F4
  Romford RM7 ...... 113 B2
Nelson Cres CM9 ..... 59 B8
Nelson Ct **2** CM0 .... 106 C4
Nelson Dr SS9 ...... 146 F1
Nelson Gdns SS6 ..... 123 F4
Nelson Gr CM1 ...... 31 F3
Nelson Ho
  Greenhithe DA9..... 177 D2
  3 Romford RM3..... 114 E5
Nelson Mews SS1..... 167 A7
Nelson Pl CM3....... 101 E6
Nelson Prim Sch E6 ... 152 A3
Nelson Rd
  Basildon SS14 ...... 142 E6
  Chingford E4 .... 109 B4
  Orsett RM16........ 174 D7
  Rainham RM13 ..... 154 F3
  Rayleigh SS6 .... 123 F4
  Rochford SS4....... 125 D6
  Southend-on-S SS9 ... 147 A2
  South Ockendon RM15 . 157 C3
  Wanstead E11....... 132 B7
Nelson St
  Southend-on-S SS1 ... 167 A7
  Wallend E6......... 152 A4
Nelwyn Ave RM11.... 136 F6
Neon Ct IG6......... 111 C1
Neptune Bsns Pk
  RM19 .... 171 E1
Neptune Cl RM13 .... 154 F3
Neptune Ct
  2 Barking IG11...... 153 B2
  Chelmsford CM1 .... 31 F4
Neptune Wlk DA8..... 169 D2
Nesbit Cl SS12....... 121 C5
Ness Rd SS3......... 168 E6
Nesta Rd IG8 .... 109 F4
Nestuda Way SS2.... 147 B5
Nethan Dr RM15 .... 171 C6
Netherfield SS17 .... 145 A4
Netherfield Ct SG12... 8 D3
Netherfield Gdns
  IG11............... 152 D5
Netherfield La SG12... 8 E3
Nethergate CM13 .... 95 B3
Netherhall Rd CM19... 21 F5
Nether Mayne SS16 ... 142 B3
Netherpark Dr RM2... 113 F1
NETHER PRIORS 142 C6
Nether Priors SS14 ... 142 C6
NETHER STREET 15 A5
Nethewode Ct DA17... 169 B3
Netley Ct IG2........ 133 D6
Netley Rd IG2....... 133 D6
NETTESWELL 10 F1
Netteswellbury Farm
  CM18 .... 23 F7
Netteswell Cross CM20 . 10 E2
Netteswell Orch CM20 . 10 D1
Netteswell Rd CM20... 10 E3
Netteswell Rectory
  CM20 .... 23 E8
Netteswell Twr **5**
  CM20 .... 10 D1
Nevada Rd SS8 ..... 164 C6
Nevell Rd RM16..... 174 B3
NEVENDON 121 D3
Nevendon Grange
  SS12 .... 121 C6

Nevendon Mews
SS13 . . . . 121 A2
Nevendon Rd
Basildon SS13 . . . . 121 A2
Wickford SS12 . . . . 121 B4
Nevendon Trad Est
SS13 . . . . 121 B1
Nevern Cl SS6 . . . . 145 F8
Nevern Rd SS6 . . . . 145 E8
Neville Gdns RM8 . . . . . 134 D1
Neville Rd
Dagenham RM8 . . . . 134 D1
Redbridge IG6 . . . . 111 C2
Neville Shaw SS14 . . . . . 142 B6
Nevill Way IG10 . . . . 88 E3
Nevin Dr E4 . . . . 87 B1
Nevis Cl RM1 . . . . 113 E4
Nevyll Ct SS1 . . . . 168 B8
New Ave SS16 . . . . 141 A4
New Barns Way IG7 . . . . 111 B7
Newberry Side SS15 . . . . 141 C5
New Bowers Way CM1 . . . 32 F6
Newbridge Sch IG3 . . . . 134 B6
Newburgh Rd RM17 . . . . 173 C1
Newbury Cl RM3 . . . . . . 114 D4
Newbury Cotts 4
IG2 . . . . 133 C5
Newbury Ct 7 E11 . . . . . 132 A7
Newbury Gdns
Romford RM3 . . . . 114 D4
Upminster RM14 . . . . . . 136 F1
New Bury Mdw CM22 . . . . .3 F5
NEWBURY PARK 133 D5
Newbury Park Prim Sch
IG2 . . . . 133 D5
Newbury Park Sta
IG2 . . . . 133 D5
Newbury Rd
Chingford E4 . . . . 109 C4
Ilford IG2 . . . . 133 E5
Romford RM3 . . . . 114 D4
Newbury Wlk RM3 . . . . . 114 D5
Newcastle Ave IG6 . . . . . 112 A4
New Century Rd SS15 . . . 141 B6
New Cotts
Basildon SS13 . . . . 143 D5
Rainham RM13 . . . . 170 C7
Rochford SS4 . . . . 127 F5
New Court Bsns Pk
CM18 . . . . 23 C4
Newcourt Rd CM2 . . . . . . 32 D3
New Dukes Way CM2 . . . . 32 F4
Newell Ave SS3 . . . . 168 G8
New England Cl CM3 . . . . 56 F1
New England Cres
SS3 . . . . 150 C2
New England Est
IG11 . . . . 152 C3
New Farm Dr RM4 . . . . . . 90 C6
New Ford Rd EN8 . . . . . . 65 A4
New Forest La IG7 . . . . . 111 A4
New Frontiers Science Pk
CM19 . . . . 22 F6
Newgate St E4 . . . . 109 E7
Newhall SS4 . . . . 125 C6
Newhall Ct EN9 . . . . 65 F6
New Hall Dr RM3 . . . . . . 114 E2
New Hall La CM9 . . . . 59 E4
New Hall Rd SS4 . . . . . . 103 B1
New Hall Sch CM3 . . . . . . 20 A1
New Hall Vineyard★
CM3 . . . . 58 D2
Newham Way E6 . . . . . . 152 A1
New Horizon Bsns Ctr
CM19 . . . . 22 F8
Newhouse Ave
Ilford RM6 . . . . 134 D8
Wickford SS12 . . . . 120 F7
Newhouse La CM16 . . . . . 26 C1
Newington Ave SS2 . . . . 148 E2
Newington Cl SS2 . . . . . 148 F2
Newington Gdns SS2 . . . 148 E2
New Jubilee Ct 1
IG8 . . . . 110 A3
Newlands Cl
Billericay CM12 . . . . 97 B4
Brentwood CM13 . . . . . . 95 D2
Newlands End SS15 . . . . 141 B8
Newlands Rd
Billericay CM12 . . . . 97 B4
Canvey Island SS8 . . . . . 164 D5
Wickford SS12 . . . . 121 D4
Woodford IG8 . . . . 109 F8
Newlands Spring Prim Sch
CM1 . . . . 31 D7
New Lodge Chase CM3 . . . 34 B2
New London Rd CM2 . . . . 32 A1
New Maltings RM11 . . . . 171 D5
Newman Cl RM11 . . . . . 136 E6
Newmans Cl IG10 . . . . . . 89 B6
Newmans Dr CM13 . . . . . 95 C2
NEWMAN'S END 12 F5
Newmans La IG10 . . . . . . 89 B6
Newmarket Ho 2
RM3 . . . . 114 E6
Newmarket Way
RM12 . . . . 155 E8
New Moor Cl CM0 . . . . . . 84 E4
New Moor Cres CM0 . . . . 84 E4
New Nabbotts Way
CM1 . . . . 32 E7
NEWNEY GREEN 30 C2
Newnham Cl IG10 . . . . . . 88 D3
Newnham Gn CM9 . . . . . . 36 E3
Newnham Ho IG10 . . . . . . 88 D3
Newnham Lo 11 DA17 . . 169 A1
Newnham Pl RM16 . . . . . 174 A2
New North Rd IG6 . . . . . 111 E4

New Park Rd
Rochford SS5 . . . . 103 A1
South Benfleet SS7 . . . . 144 C5
Newpiece IG10 . . . . 89 B6
New Place Gdns
RM14 . . . . 137 D2
New Plymouth Ho
RM13 . . . . 154 F2
Newport Ave CM3 . . . . . . 81 B5
Newport Cl CM2 . . . . 55 B6
Newport Ct SS6 . . . . . . 123 B4
Newports CM21 . . . . 1 C1
New Rd
Abridge RM4 . . . . 90 D3
Basildon CM12 . . . . 119 A3
Brentwood CM14 . . . . . . 116 D8
Broomfield CM1 . . . . 19 B1
Burnham-on-C CM0 . . . . 106 C5
Canvey Island SS8 . . . . . 163 E3
Chingford E4 . . . . 109 C6
Dagenham RM9, RM10,
RM13 . . . . 154 C2
Gravesend DA11 . . . . . . 179 B1
Grays RM17 . . . . 178 B8
Great Baddow CM2 . . . . . 55 A6
Great Wakering SS3 . . . . 150 C3
Hadleigh SS7 . . . . 145 D3
Harlow CM17 . . . . 11 D4
Hoddesdon EN10 . . . . . . 21 A4
Ilford IG3 . . . . 133 E2
Ingatestone CM4 . . . . . . 74 C4
Rainham RM13 . . . . 155 B2
Southend-on-S SS9 . . . . 165 D8
Wanstead E12 . . . . 132 E2
New River Ave SG12 . . . . . 8 A4
New River Ct EN11 . . . . . 21 B7
New Row
Paglesham Eastend
SS4 . . . . 128 A5
Sheering CM22 . . . . 12 C8
New Rush Hall Sch The
IG6 . . . . 111 C3
New St
Chelmsford CM1 . . . . 32 B3
Maldon CM9 . . . . 36 F2
Sawbridgeworth CM21 . . . 1 E3
Newstead Ho RM3 . . . . . 114 D6
Newstead Rd SS3 . . . . . 150 B4
Newsum Gdns SS6 . . . . . 123 A3
New Swan Yd DA11 . . . . 179 B1
New Tank Hill Rd RM19,
RM15 . . . . 171 A3
New Tavern Fort★
DA12 . . . . 179 C1
Newteswell Dr EN9 . . . . . 65 D7
NEW THUNDERSLEY
. . . . 144 D7
Newton Cl
Corringham SS17 . . . . . . 161 A4
Hoddesdon EN11 . . . . 8 B2
Newton Dr CM21 . . . . 1 D1
Newton Hall Gdns
SS4 . . . . 125 D6
Newton Ho DA9 . . . . . . 177 D2
Newton Ind Est RM6 . . . 134 D7
Newton Park Rd SS7 . . . 145 B7
Newton Rd
Redbridge IG7 . . . . 112 B5
Tilbury RM18 . . . . 179 A5
Newton's Ct DA2 . . . . . . 176 D3
Newtons Prim Sch
RM13 . . . . 154 D3
New Wanstead E11 . . . . 132 A5
New Waverley Rd
SS15 . . . . 119 E1
NEW WAY 25 C8
New Way La CM17 . . . . . . 12 D1
New Writtle St CM2 . . . . . 32 B1
New Zealand Way
RM13 . . . . 154 F2
Nicholas Cl
South Ockendon
RM15 . . . . 157 C2
Writtle CM1 . . . . 31 B1
Nicholas Ct CM1 . . . . 31 D6
Nicholas Rd RM8 . . . . . . 134 F1
Nicholl Rd
Basildon SS15 . . . . 141 C7
Epping CM16 . . . . 67 F8
Nicholls Field CM18 . . . . 24 B7
Nichols Ct 1 CM2 . . . . . . 32 A1
Nicholson Cres SS7 . . . . 145 C3
Nicholson Ct SS11 . . . . . . 21 B6
Nicholson Gr 15 SS12 . . 121 E5
Nicholson Ho SS1 . . . . . 167 B8
Nicholson Pl CM3 . . . . . . 78 B7
Nicholson Rd SS7 . . . . . 145 B3
Nickleby Rd CM1 . . . . 31 D6
Nicola Mews IG6 . . . . . . 111 B4
Nicolas Wlk RM16 . . . . . 174 B4
Nigel Mews IG1 . . . . . . 152 B8
Nightingale Ave
Chingford E4 . . . . 109 E5
Upminster RM14 . . . . . . 137 F3
Nightingale Cl
Chingford E4 . . . . 109 E4
Rayleigh SS6 . . . . 123 B3
Southend-on-S SS2 . . . . 147 E6
Nightingale Cnr 2
CM9 . . . . 37 A1
Nightingale Cres
RM3 . . . . 114 C1
Nightingale Ct
Grays RM16 . . . . 172 C3
1 Wanstead E11 . . . . 132 B6
Nightingale Gr DA1 . . . . 176 A3
Nightingale La E11 . . . . 132 B6

Nightingale Mews 8
E11 . . . . 132 B6
Nightingale Prim Sch
E18 . . . . 132 C7
Nightingale Rd SS8 . . . . 164 C3
Nightingales
Basildon SS16 . . . . 140 F5
Waltham Abbey EN9 . . . . 65 E5
NINE ASHES 50 C2
Nine Ashes SG12 . . . . 9 D7
Nine Ashes Farm Cotts
CM4 . . . . 50 C2
Nine Ashes Rd
Blackmore CM4 . . . . 50 D1
Stondon Massey CM15 . . . 72 B6
Ninefields EN9 . . . . 65 F6
Nipsells Chase CM3 . . . . . 61 A1
Nita Rd CM14 . . . . 116 C5
Niton Ct SS17 . . . . 175 C8
Niven Cl SS12 . . . . 121 E5
NOAK BRIDGE 119 F1
Noak Bridge Prim Sch
SS15 . . . . 119 F1
Noakes Ave CM2 . . . . 54 E6
NOAK HILL 114 E8
Noak Hill CM12 . . . . 119 C4
Noak Hill Cl CM12 . . . . . 119 B4
Noak Hill Rd
Basildon CM12 . . . . 119 B4
Romford RM3 . . . . 114 D7
Noak Hill Sch RM4 . . . . . 114 E8
Nobel Sq SS13 . . . . 121 C2
Nobel Villas EN9 . . . . 65 D5
NOBLESGREEN 146 F7
Nobles Green Cl SS9 . . . 146 E7
Nobles Green Rd SS9 . . . 146 E7
Noel Sq RM8 . . . . 153 C8
Nonsuch Cl IG6 . . . . 111 B4
Nook The SG12 . . . . 8 A4
Norbury Gdns RM6 . . . . 134 D6
Norbury Rd E4 . . . . 109 A5
Nordenfeldt Rd DA8 . . . . 169 D1
Nordic Lo CM9 . . . . 58 F8
Nordland Rd SS8 . . . . . . 164 D5
Nordmann Pl RM15 . . . . 157 D1
Noredale SS3 . . . . 168 D5
Nore Rd SS9 . . . . 146 F3
Nore View SS16 . . . . . . 140 F4
Norfolk Ave SS9 . . . . . . 146 F3
Norfolk Cl
Basildon SS15 . . . . 141 A6
Canvey Island SS8 . . . . . 164 A5
Dartford DA1 . . . . 176 A1
Maldon CM9 . . . . 36 E1
Norfolk Ct
4 Ilford RM6 . . . . 134 B6
Rochford SS4 . . . . 125 D5
Norfolk Dr CM1 . . . . 32 A7
Norfolk Ho
5 Gravesend DA12 . . . 179 D1
Romford RM7 . . . . 113 A2
Norfolk Pl RM16 . . . . . . 172 C1
Norfolk Rd
Barking IG11 . . . . 152 E5
Dagenham RM10 . . . . . . 154 B7
Gravesend DA12 . . . . . . 179 C1
Ilford IG3 . . . . 133 E4
Maldon CM9 . . . . 36 E1
Romford RM7 . . . . 135 C5
Upminster RM14 . . . . . . 137 A2
Wallend E6 . . . . 152 A4
Norfolk Way SS6 . . . . . . 163 F5
Norham Ct 16 DA2 . . . . 176 B1
Norman Cl
Romford RM5 . . . . 113 B1
Waltham Abbey EN9 . . . . 65 D6
Norman Cres
Brentwood CM13 . . . . . . 117 A7
Rayleigh SS6 . . . . 123 E5
Norman Ct
Ilford IG1 . . . . 133 D4
Woodford IG8 . . . . 110 B5
Normandy Ave CM0 . . . . 106 C5
Normandy Way EN11 . . . . 21 D8
Normanhurst CM13 . . . . . 95 C3
Normanhurst Sch E4 . . . . 87 D2
Norman Pl SS9 . . . . 165 E8
Norman Rd
Belvedere DA17 . . . . . . 169 B3
Hornchurch RM11 . . . . . 136 B4
Ilford IG1 . . . . 152 B7
Normanshire Dr E4 . . . . 109 B6
Normans Rd SS8 . . . . . . 164 D4
Norman Terr SS9 . . . . . 165 E8
Normanton Pk E4 . . . . . 109 E8
Norris La EN11 . . . . 21 A7
Norris Rd EN11 . . . . 21 A6
Norris Rise 4 EN11 . . . . . 21 A7
Norseman Cl 3 IG3 . . . . 134 B3
Norsey Cl CM11 . . . . 97 B3
Norsey Dr CM11 . . . . 97 B3
Norsey Rd CM11 . . . . 97 C4
Norsey View Dr CM12 . . . 97 B6
Norsey Wood Nature
Reserve★ CM11 . . . . . 97 D4
Northallerton Way 15
RM3 . . . . 114 D5
Northampton Gr SS16 . . 140 F4
Northampton Ho 4
RM3 . . . . 114 D6
North Ave
Canvey Island SS8 . . . . . 164 A3
Chelmsford CM1 . . . . . . 31 D5
Southend-on-S SS2 . . . . 148 C2
Northbank Rd E17 . . . . . 109 C1
North Barn EN10 . . . . 21 B1
NORTH BENFLEET 143 F8

North Benfleet Hall Rd
Basildon SS12 . . . . 122 A1
North Benfleet SS12 . . . . 121 F1
North Boundary Rd
E12 . . . . 132 D2
Northbrook Rd IG1 . . . . 133 A2
Northbrooks CM19 . . . . . 23 C7
IG11 . . . . 152 C6
North Circular Rd
Chingford E17 . . . . 109 B2
Ilford IG1, E12 . . . . 133 A1
Wallend E6, E12 . . . . . . 152 A5
Wanstead IG1 . . . . 132 D5
Woodford E18 . . . . 110 C1
North Cl
Dagenham RM10 . . . . . . 154 A4
Redbridge IG7 . . . . 112 A5
North Colne SS16 . . . . . 142 D4
North Cres
Southend-on-S SS2 . . . . 147 D5
Wickford SS12 . . . . 121 D7
North Crescent Prim Sch
SS12 . . . . 121 D7
North Crockerford
SS16 . . . . 142 E4
North Cross Rd IG6 . . . . 133 C7
North Dell 32 E7
North Dene IG7 . . . . 111 D5
Northdown Gdns IG2 . . . 133 E6
Northdown Rd RM11 . . . 136 B4
North Dr
Brentwood CM13 . . . . . . 96 C2
Great Baddow CM2 . . . . . 54 F7
Mayland CM3 . . . . 60 F1
Romford RM2 . . . . 136 C8
NORTHEND 84 E5
Northend CM14 . . . . 116 C5
North End
Buckhurst Hill IG9 . . . . . . 88 C2
Romford RM3 . . . . 114 C8
Southminster CM0 . . . . . 84 E5
Northern Ave SS7 . . . . . 144 C5
Northern Relief Rd
IG11 . . . . 152 C5
Northfalls Rd SS8 . . . . . 164 F3
NORTH FAMBRIDGE 103 A8
North Fambridge Sta
CM3 . . . . 103 B8
Northfield IG10 . . . . 88 D5
Northfield Cl CM11 . . . . . 97 C2
Northfield Cres SS3 . . . . 150 B4
Northfield Gdns RM9 . . . 153 F8
Northfield Path RM9 . . . 153 F8
Northfield Rd
Dagenham RM9 . . . . . . 153 F8
Sawbridgeworth CM21 . . . 1 E4
Northfields RM17 . . . . . 173 D2
NORTHFLEET 178 C2
Northfleet Ind Est
DA10 . . . . 177 F3
Northfleet Sta DA11 . . . 178 B1
North Gate CM20 . . . . . . 10 C1
Northgate Ind Pk
RM5 . . . . 112 F1
North Gr CM18 . . . . 24 A7
North Hill
Horndon on t H SS17 . . . 160 A3
Little Baddow CM3 . . . . . 34 D5
North Hill Bsns Pk
SS17 . . . . 159 F4
North Hill Dr RM3 . . . . . 114 D6
North Hill Gn RM3 . . . . . 114 D6
North Ho CM18 . . . . 23 F6
North Kent Ave DA11 . . . 178 C1
Northlands App SS16 . . . 141 C1
Northlands Cl SS17 . . . . 160 E5
Northlands Farm Chase
SS17 . . . . 160 E7
Northlands Jun & Inf Sch
SS13 . . . . 143 B6
Northlands Pavement 3
SS13 . . . . 143 B5
NORTH OCKENDON 157 B6
Northolme Cl RM16 . . . . 173 C3
Northolt Way RM12 . . . . 155 C7
North Pl
Harlow CM20 . . . . 11 B5
4 Waltham Abbey EN9 . . 65 B6
North Rd
Belvedere DA17 . . . . . . 169 B4
Crays Hill CM11 . . . . . . 120 D5
Dagenham RM6 . . . . . . 134 E6
Havering-atte-B RM4 . . . . 91 F1
Hoddesdon EN11 . . . . . . 21 A7
Ilford IG3 . . . . 133 E2
Purfleet RM19 . . . . 171 C2
Romford RM4 . . . . 113 E7
Southend-on-S SS0 . . . . 147 E1
South Ockendon RM15 . . 157 D4
North Residence IG3 . . . 134 B6
North Road Ave
CM14 . . . . 116 C8
North Service Rd 6
CM14 . . . . 116 C8
NORTH SHOEBURY 149 F1
North Shoebury Rd
SS3 . . . . 149 D1
North St
Barking IG11 . . . . 152 C5
Great Wakering SS3 . . . . 150 B4
Hornchurch RM11 . . . . . 136 D4
Lower Nazeing EN9 . . . . . 21 E1
Maldon CM9 . . . . 37 B2
Rochford SS4 . . . . 125 F2
Romford RM1 . . . . 135 D7
Southend-on-S SS9 . . . . 165 E8
Southminster CM0 . . . . . 84 D4

North St continued
Tillingham CM0 . . . . 63 E4
North Sta★ SS1 . . . . . . 167 A6
NORTH STIFFORD 172 E5
Northumberland Ave
Basildon SS15 . . . . 141 C5
Hornchurch RM11 . . . . . 136 C6
Southend-on-S SS1 . . . . 167 D7
Wanstead E12 . . . . 132 C3
Northumberland Cres
SS1 . . . . 167 D7
Northumberland Ct 1
CM2 . . . . 32 F4
Northumberland Ho 11
IG8 . . . . 111 A3
Northumberland Rd
SS17 . . . . 175 A4
Northview Ave RM18 . . . 179 A6
North View Cvn Site
IG6 . . . . 112 A3
Northview Dr
Southend-on-S SS0 . . . . 147 D2
Woodford IG8 . . . . 110 D1
Northville Dr SS0 . . . . . 147 C4
NORTH WEALD BASSETT
. . . . 47 C5
North Weald Cl
Hornchurch RM12 . . . . . 155 C5
Wickford SS11 . . . . 122 B6
North Weald Sta★
CM16 . . . . 47 B4
Northwick Park Prim Sch
SS8 . . . . 163 E4
Northwick Rd SS8 . . . . . 163 B4
Northwick Ret Pk
SS8 . . . . 163 B4
Northwood RM16 . . . . . 174 B4
Northwood Ave RM12 . . . 155 A8
Northwood Dr 2
DA9 . . . . 177 A1
Northwood Gdns IG5 . . . 133 A7
Norton Ave SS8 . . . . . . 164 E3
Norton Cl
Chingford E4 . . . . 109 A5
Corringham SS17 . . . . . . 161 A3
Norton Ct IG2 . . . . 133 E5
NORTON HEATH 50 D5
Norton Heath Rd CM5 . . . 50 E8
Norton La
High Ongar CM5 . . . . 49 D5
High Ongar, Norton
Mandeville CM4, CM5 . . . 50 C6
NORTON MANDEVILLE
. . . . 49 F6
Norton Pl CM11 . . . . 98 C5
Norton Rd
Chelmsford CM1 . . . . 32 A3
Dagenham RM10 . . . . . . 154 D6
Ingatestone CM4 . . . . . . 74 B4
Norway Wlk RM13 . . . . . 155 C1
Norwich Ave SS2 . . . . . 148 C2
Norwich Cl SS2 . . . . . . 148 C2
Norwich Cres
Ilford RM6 . . . . 134 B6
Rayleigh SS6 . . . . 123 C5
Norwich Ho SS4 . . . . . . 125 D5
Norwich Mews IG3 . . . . 134 A3
Norwich Wlk SS14 . . . . 142 F7
Norwood Ave RM7 . . . . . 135 E4
Norwood Ct DA1 . . . . . . 176 A3
Norwood Dr SS7 . . . . . . 144 E1
NORWOOD END 27 D5
Norwood End
Basildon SS14 . . . . 142 D7
Fyfield CM5 . . . . 27 D5
Nottage Cl SS17 . . . . . . 160 F4
Nottingham Way
SS16 . . . . 140 F5
Nuneaton Rd RM9 . . . . . 153 D6
Nunns Way RM17 . . . . . 173 D2
NUPER'S HATCH 91 E2
Nursery Cl
Ilford RM6 . . . . 134 D5
Rayleigh SS6 . . . . 123 D1
South Ockendon RM15 . . 157 C1
Woodford IG8 . . . . 110 B5
Nursery Fields CM21 . . . . 1 D2
Nursery Gdns SS15 . . . . 141 D8
Nursery La CM3 . . . . 56 F8
Nursery Rd
Chelmsford CM2 . . . . . . 54 B8
Hoddesdon EN11 . . . . 8 B1
Hook End CM15 . . . . 72 D5
Loughton IG10 . . . . 88 D5
Lower Nazeing EN9 . . . . . 21 D2
Stanford-le-H SS17 . . . . 160 E3
Wanstead E12 . . . . 132 E2
Nursery Wlk RM7 . . . . . 135 D5
Nutberry Ave RM16 . . . . 173 B4
Nutberry Cl RM16 . . . . . 173 A4
Nutbowne Rd RM9 . . . . 154 A4
Nutcombe Cres SS4 . . . . 125 D4
Nutfield Gdns IG3 . . . . . 134 A2
Nuthatch Cl CM11 . . . . . 119 C8
Nutter La E11 . . . . 132 C6
Nuxley Rd DA17 . . . . . . 169 A1
Nyall Ct RM2 . . . . 136 D8
Nyssa Cl IG8 . . . . 110 F4
Nyth Cl RM14 . . . . 137 D5

O

Oak Ave
Crays Hill CM11 . . . .**120** C4
Upminster RM14 . . . .**156** B8
Wickford SS11 . . . .**122** C7
Oakbank CM13 . . . .**95** E4
Oak Chase SS12 . . . .**121** A7
Oak Cl
Maldon CM9 . . . .**59** B8
Waltham Abbey EN9 . . . . . .**65** D5
Oak Cnr CM9 . . . .**57** D6
Oak Cotts CM3 . . . .**33** E8
Oak Ct
Chingford E4 . . . .**109** B4
Hadleigh SS7 . . . .**145** E2
South Ockendon RM15 . . . .**157** C3
Oakdale Cl E4 . . . .**109** C5
Oakdale Gdns E4 . . . .**109** C5
Oakdale Inf Sch E18 . . . . . .**110** B1
Oakdale Jun Sch E18 . . . . .**110** B1
Oakdale Rd E18. . . . .**110** B1
Oakdene RM3 . . . .**114** F1
Oak Dene Cl RM11 . . . .**136** B5
Oakdene Rd SS13 . . . .**143** C8
Oakdown Ho IG7 . . . .**111** F5
Oak Dr CM21 . . . .**11** C8
Oak End CM18 . . . .**23** F6
Oaken Grange Dr SS2 . . . .**147** E5
Oak Farm Rd CM9. . . . .**35** E1
Oakfield E4 . . . .**109** B5
Oakfield Cl SS7 . . . .**144** C3
Oakfield Cl SS7 . . . .**144** C3
Oakfield Ho 2 IG1 . . . .**133** B1
Oakfield Lo 9 IG1 . . . .**133** B1
Oakfield Prim Sch
SS12 . . . .**121** E5
Oakfield Rd
Ilford IG1 . . . .**133** B1
Rochford SS4. . . . .**103** A1
South Benfleet SS7 . . . . . .**144** C3
Oakfields
Chigwell IG7 . . . .**111** C5
Loughton IG10. . . . .**89** A4
Oak Glade CM16 . . . .**46** D2
Oak Glen RM11 . . . .**136** E8
Oak Gn CM17 . . . .**97** D1
Oakhall Ct E11. . . . .**132** B5
Oak Hall Rd E11 . . . .**132** B5
Oakham Cl SS16 . . . .**140** F5
Oakham Ct SS9 . . . .**146** E2
Oak Hill IG8 . . . .**109** E3
Oak Hill Cl IG8 . . . .**109** D3
Oak Hill Cres IG8 . . . .**109** E3
Oak Hill Ct IG8 . . . .**109** E3
Oak Hill Gdns IG8. . . . .**109** F2
Oakhill Prim Sch IG8 . . . . .**109** E4
Oak Hill Rd RM4 . . . .**91** E1
Oak Ho SS3 . . . .**168** F8
Oakhurst Cl
Redbridge IG6 . . . .**111** C2
Wickford SS12 . . . .**121** C6
Oakhurst Dr SS12 . . . .**121** C5
Oakhurst Gdns E4 . . . .**87** F1
Oakhurst Rd
Rayleigh SS6 . . . .**145** F8
Southend-on-S SS2 . . . . . .**148** A2
Oak La
Crays Hill CM11 . . . .**120** C3
Woodford IG8 . . . .**109** F6
Oakland Farm Ind Est
CM4 . . . .**97** F6
Oakland Gdns CM13. . . . . . .**95** C4
Oakland Pl IG9 . . . .**110** A8
Oaklands Ave RM1 . . . .**135** F7
Oaklands Cres CM2 . . . .**54** B8
Oaklands Dr
Harlow CM17 . . . .**24** C7
South Ockendon RM15 . . . .**172** C8
Oaklands Inf Sch CM2. . . . .**54** B8
Oaklands Mews SS4 . . . . .**125** C4
Oaklands Park Ave
IG1 . . . .**133** C2
Oaklands Pk CM15 . . . .**95** B1
Oaklands Sch IG10 . . . .**88** D4
Oaklands Way CM3 . . . .**34** E2
Oaklea Ave CM2 . . . .**32** E3
Oakleafe Gdns IG6 . . . .**133** B8
Oakleigh Ave
Hullbridge SS5. . . . .**101** E2
Southend-on-S SS1 . . . . . .**167** D8
Oakleigh Lo IG3 . . . .**134** A1
Oakleigh Park Dr SS9 . . . .**146** E1
Oakleigh Rise CM16. . . . . . .**68** A7
Oakleighs SS7 . . . .**144** C4
Oakley Ave
Barking IG11 . . . .**152** F5
Rayleigh SS6 . . . .**122** F3
Oakley Cl
Chingford E4 . . . .**109** C4
Grays RM20. . . . .**177** C8
Oakley Ct IG10 . . . .**89** A4
Oakley Dr
Billericay CM12 . . . .**96** F5
Romford RM3 . . . .**115** A5
Oak Lo E11 . . . .**132** A4
Oak Lodge Ave IG7 . . . . . .**111** D5
Oak Lodge Tye CM1. . . . . . .**33** A6
Oakmoor Way IG7 . . . .**111** E5
Oak Piece CM16 . . . .**47** C6
Oak Rd
Canvey Island SS8. . . . . . .**164** C3
Crays Hill CM11 . . . .**120** C4

Oak Rd *continued*
Epping CM16 . . . .**45** F1
Grays RM17. . . . .**178** C8
Greenhithe DA9 . . . .**176** E1
Heybridge CM9 . . . .**37** B6
Ramsden Heath CM11 . . . . .**98** D5
Rochford SS4. . . . .**125** E2
Romford RM3 . . . .**114** F2
Oak Rd N SS7. . . . .**145** E2
Oak Rd S SS7. . . . .**145** E2
Oak Rise IG9 . . . .**110** D7
Oaks EN9. . . . .**66** C4
Oaks Ave RM5 . . . .**113** C1
Oaks Gr E4 . . . .**109** E8
Oakside Ct
Redbridge IG6 . . . .**111** D1
Wanstead E11 . . . .**132** A7
Oaks La IG2 . . . .**133** E7
Oaks Park High Sch
IG2. . . . .**133** E6
Oaks Ret Pk CM20 . . . .**10** F3
Oak St RM7. . . . .**135** C6
Oaks The
Billericay CM11 . . . .**119** C6
Chingford IG8 . . . .**109** E3
Dartford DA2. . . . .**176** B1
Oaktree Cl CM13 . . . .**116** F7
Oak Tree Cl IG10 . . . .**89** C8
Oaktree Gdns CM17 . . . .**24** D7
Oaktree Gr IG1 . . . .**152** D7
Oakview Cl SS9. . . . .**146** E3
Oak View Sch IG10. . . . .**89** A6
Oakway RM16 . . . .**173** C5
Oak Wlk
Hockley SS5. . . . .**124** E7
South Benfleet SS7 . . . . . .**144** B8
Southend-on-S SS9 . . . . . .**146** D4
Oakwood EN9 . . . .**65** D5
Oakwood Ave
Brentwood CM13. . . . .**95** E3
Southend-on-S SS9 . . . . . .**146** E5
Oakwood Chase
RM11 . . . .**136** F4
Oakwood Cl
South Benfleet SS7 . . . . . .**144** B5
Woodford IG8 . . . .**110** E4
Oakwood Ct
Althorne CM3. . . . .**83** A3
Chingford E4 . . . .**87** E2
Romford RM2 . . . .**136** C8
Southend-on-S SS9 . . . . . .**146** E5
Oakwood Dr CM12 . . . .**97** C5
Oakwood Est CM20 . . . .**11** B4
Oakwood Gdns IG3 . . . . . .**133** F2
Oakwood Gr SS13. . . . .**143** B6
Oakwood Hill IG10. . . . .**89** B4
Oakwood Hill Ind Est
IG10. . . . .**89** B4
Oakwood Ind Est
DA11. . . . .**178** A2
OakWood Mews 5
CM17 . . . .**11** C4
Oakwood Rd
Corringham SS17. . . . .**161** B3
Rayleigh SS6 . . . .**123** C4
Oakwood Villas SS9. . . . . .**146** C7
Oasis Cl CM1 . . . .**32** F5
Oast Ct 3 SS4 . . . .**125** F2
Oast Way SS4. . . . .**125** F2
Oates Rd RM5 . . . .**113** B5
Oban Ct SS11. . . . .**122** B5
Oban Ho 6 IG11. . . . .**152** D3
Oban Rd SS2 . . . .**148** C1
Occasio Ho CM20 . . . .**23** C8
Ockelford Ave CM1 . . . .**31** F5
Ockendon Rd RM14. . . . . . .**157** B7
Ockendon Sch The
RM15 . . . .**172** A8
Ockendon Sta RM15 . . . . . .**157** B2
Octave Ho CM16 . . . .**67** C3
Odell Cl IG11 . . . .**152** F5
Odeon The IG11 . . . .**152** D5
Odessa Rd SS8 . . . .**164** D3
Odin Lo CM9. . . . .**58** F8
O'Donoghue Ho SS17 . . . . .**160** E2
Ogard Rd EN11 . . . .**21** C8
Ogilvie Ct SS12 . . . .**121** E5
Oglethorpe Rd RM10. . . . . .**135** A1
Okehampton Rd RM3 . . . . .**114** C4
Okehampton Sq RM3. . . . . .**114** C4
Old Barn La CM3 . . . .**77** F2
Old Barns La CM4 . . . .**51** C3
Old Bell La CM3. . . . .**78** B1
Old Brickworks The
RM3 . . . .**115** A3
Oldbury Ave CM2 . . . .**54** E8
Oldbury Cotts SS3. . . . .**149** D3
Oldchurch Gdns RM7 . . . . .**135** D4
Old Church La CM13 . . . .**96** B6
Oldchurch Rd RM7. . . . .**135** E4
Old Church Rd
Basildon SS13 . . . .**143** F5
Chingford E4 . . . .**109** A7
East Hanningfield CM3. . . . .**78** B6
Oldchurch Rise RM7 . . . . . .**135** E4
Old Coastguard Cotts
CM0 . . . .**41** E4
Old College Ct DA17 . . . . . .**169** B1
Old Court Rd CM2. . . . .**32** D3
Old Croft Cl CM1. . . . .**16** D5
Old Crown La CM14 . . . .**93** D7
Old Farm Ct CM12 . . . .**97** A4
Old Farm Yd CM22 . . . .**12** C8
Oldfields CM14 . . . .**116** C6
Old Forge Rd CM4 . . . .**33** E8
Old Forge The SS6 . . . .**123** C3

Old Hall Ct SS3 . . . .**150** A4
Old Hall Rise CM17. . . . .**24** E8
OLD HARLOW **11** D4
Old Heath Rd CM3,
CM0. . . . .**84** A2
Old Highway EN11 . . . .**21** C8
Old Hill Ave SS16 . . . .**160** B8
Oldhouse Croft CM20 . . . . .**10** E2
Old House La
Lower Nazeing EN9 . . . .**43** F8
Roydon CM19. . . . .**22** E6
Old Jenkins Cl SS17. . . . . .**160** B1
Old Leigh Rd SS9 . . . .**147** A1
Old London Rd
Rawreth SS11 . . . .**122** D6
Woodham Walter CM9. . . . .**35** E1
Old Macdonald's
Educational Farm Pk★
CM14 . . . .**92** F1
Old Maltings Ct The 3
EN11 . . . .**21** A6
Old Market Ret Pk 10
SS13 . . . .**143** B5
Old Market Terr 11
CM14 . . . .**116** C8
Old Mead SS2 . . . .**147** A7
Oldmead Ho 13 RM10 . . . . .**154** B6
Old Mill Ct E18 . . . .**132** C8
Old Mill La CM22. . . . .**2** B6
Old Mill Par 2 RM1. . . . . . .**135** E5
Old Mill Pl RM7. . . . .**135** D5
Old Nazeing Rd EN10. . . . . .**21** C1
Old Nevendon Rd
SS13 . . . .**121** B3
Old Oaks EN9. . . . .**65** E7
Old Orch CM18 . . . .**23** D6
Old Rd
Harlow CM17. . . . .**11** D5
Navestock Heath RM4 . . . . .**92** D5
Old Rectory Ct SS2. . . . . . .**148** E1
Old Rectory Rd CM5 . . . .**70** B5
Old Rectory The CM3 . . . . . .**78** B7
Old Savill's Cotts IG7 . . . . .**111** C6
Old School Field CM1 . . . . . .**32** E4
Old School Mdw SS3. . . . . .**149** E4
Old Ship La SS4 . . . .**125** F2
Old Shire La EN9. . . . .**66** A5
Old Southend Rd
Southend-on-S SS1 . . . . . .**167** B7
West Hanningfield CM2. . . . .**77** D8
Old Station Rd IG10 . . . .**88** E4
Old Street Hill CM22 . . . .**3** D5
Old Vicarage Cl CM1. . . . . . .**6** C2
Old Wickford Rd CM3 . . . . .**101** B8
Oldwyk SS16 . . . .**142** E4
Oleastor Ct IG5. . . . .**132** E8
Olive Ave SS9. . . . .**146** A2
Oliver Cl
Brentwood CM15. . . . .**95** A4
Grays RM20. . . . .**177** A7
Rainham RM13 . . . .**154** A4
Olivers RM12 . . . .**136** D2
Olivers Cres SS3 . . . .**150** B4
Oliver Way CM1. . . . .**31** F7
Olive St RM7 . . . .**135** D6
Olivia Dr SS9 . . . .**146** F2
Ollards Ct 1 IG10 . . . .**88** E4
Ollard's Gr IG10 . . . .**88** D5
Olympic Bsns Ctr
SS14 . . . .**120** F2
Olympic Ho 12 IG1 . . . .**133** B1
Omega Ct 1 RM7. . . . .**135** D5
Omnibus Way E17 . . . .**109** A1
One Tree Hill SS16,
SS17 . . . .**141** F1
Ongar Cl RM6 . . . .**134** C6
Ongar Ent Ctr CM5. . . . .**49** A5
Ongar Pl CM14. . . . .**116** D8
Ongar Rd
Abridge RM4. . . . .**90** D7
Brentwood CM15. . . . .**94** B2
Fyfield CM5 . . . .**27** C2
Kelvedon Hatch CM15 . . . . .**71** D4
Margaret Roding CM6 . . . . .**15** D3
Pilgrims Hatch CM15 . . . . . .**94** A3
Stondon Massey CM15 . . . .**71** E8
Writtle CM1. . . . .**30** F1
Ongar Sta★ CM5 . . . .**49** A4
Ongar War Meml Hospl
CM5 . . . .**49** A5
Ongar Way RM13 . . . .**154** E4
Onslow Cl E4 . . . .**109** D8
Onslow Gdns
Chipping Ongar CM5 . . . . . .**49** A4
Wanstead E11 . . . .**132** C8
Opal Mews 2 IG1 . . . .**133** B2
Optima Bsns Pk EN11 . . . . .**21** C7
Orange Gr IG7. . . . .**111** C4
Orange Rd SS8 . . . .**164** D4
Orange Tree Cl CM2 . . . .**54** C6
Orange Tree Hill RM4 . . . . .**113** E6
Orchard Ave
Billericay CM12 . . . .**97** C5
Brentwood CM13. . . . .**116** F7
Downham CM11. . . . .**98** E2
Hockley SS5. . . . .**124** E7
Rainham RM13 . . . .**155** C1
Rayleigh SS6 . . . .**145** C8
Orchard Bglws SS4 . . . . . .**104** F1
Orchard Cl
Billericay CM12 . . . .**96** F4
Chelmsford CM2 . . . .**54** C6
Chingford E4 . . . .**109** A6
Great Wakering SS3 . . . . . .**150** B4
Hockley SS5. . . . .**124** F7

Orchard Cl *continued*
Maldon CM9. . . . .**36** F2
Sheering CM22 . . . .**12** C8
Southminster CM0 . . . .**84** D4
South Ockendon RM15 . . . .**157** C1
Stanstead Abbotts SG12 . . . .**8** C4
Wanstead E11 . . . .**132** B7
Writtle CM1. . . . .**31** B1
Orchard Croft CM20. . . . . . .**11** A2
Orchard Dr
Grays RM17. . . . .**173** A4
Theydon Bois CM16 . . . .**67** E3
Orchard Gdns EN9 . . . .**65** C5
Orchard Gr SS9 . . . .**146** F6
Orchard Ho CM4 . . . .**75** E3
Orchard La
Pilgrims Hatch CM15 . . . . . .**93** F4
Woodford IG8 . . . .**110** C6
Orchard Lea CM21 . . . .**1** C1
Orchard Mead SS9 . . . .**146** E5
Orchard Piece CM4 . . . .**72** F8
Orchard Rd
Belvedere DA17 . . . .**169** A2
Burnham-on-C CM0 . . . . . .**106** C4
Dagenham RM10 . . . .**154** A4
Maldon CM9. . . . .**36** F2
Mayland CM3. . . . .**61** A1
Romford RM7 . . . .**113** B1
South Benfleet SS7 . . . . . .**144** B7
Southminster CM0. . . . .**84** E4
South Ockendon RM15 . . . .**172** C8
Swanscombe DA10 . . . . . .**177** E2
Orchard Side SS9. . . . .**146** F6
Orchard St CM2. . . . .**32** B1
Orchards The
Epping CM16 . . . .**68** A7
Sawbridgeworth CM21 . . . . . .**1** E3
Orchard Terr DA9. . . . .**176** E2
Orchard View CM13 . . . .**140** E5
Orchard Way IG7 . . . .**112** A2
Orchid Cl RM4. . . . .**90** B6
Orchid Pl
Basildon SS15 . . . .**141** D5
South Woodham Ferrers
CM3 . . . .**101** D8
Orchill Dr SS7 . . . .**145** E4
Orchis Gr RM17 . . . .**172** F1
Orchis Way RM3 . . . .**114** F4
Ordnance Rd
Gravesend DA12 . . . .**179** C1
Holdbrook EN3. . . . .**65** A2
Orestes Ct 9 E18 . . . .**132** A8
Oreston Rd RM13 . . . .**155** D2
Orford Cres CM1. . . . .**32** D5
Orford Ct 5 DA2. . . . .**176** B1
Orford Rd E18 . . . .**132** B8
Oriel Gdns IG5 . . . .**132** F8
Oriel Ho 2 RM7 . . . .**135** D5
Orion Ct SS14 . . . .**121** A1
Orkney Gdns SS12 . . . .**121** F5
Orlando Dr SS13 . . . .**121** C1
Ormesby Chine CM3 . . . . . .**101** D5
Ormond Cl RM3. . . . .**114** D1
Ormonde Ave
Rochford SS4. . . . .**125** E3
South Benfleet SS7 . . . . . .**146** A2
Ormonde Ct RM1 . . . .**135** F4
Ormonde Gdns SS9 . . . . . .**146** A2
Ormonde Rise IG9 . . . .**88** C1
Ormond Ho 2 SS4. . . . .**125** F2
Ormonds Cres CM3 . . . .**79** B4
Ormsby Rd SS8 . . . .**163** D3
Orplands Cotts CM0. . . . . . .**41** F1
Orrmo Rd SS8 . . . .**164** F3
ORSETT **146** C5
Orsett Ave SS9 . . . .**146** C5
Orsett CE Prim Sch
RM16 . . . .**174** A8
Orsett End SS14 . . . .**142** F7
ORSETT HEATH **174** A4
Orsett Heath Cres
RM16 . . . .**174** A3
Orsett Hospl RM16 . . . .**174** A8
Orsett Ind Pk RM16 . . . .**174** F8
Orsett Rd
Grays RM17. . . . .**173** B1
Horndon on t H SS17. . . . . .**159** D2
Orsett Terr IG8 . . . .**110** C3
Orton Cl CM4 . . . .**75** A8
Orton Ct RM7 . . . .**135** D6
Orton Ho 2 RM3 . . . .**114** E3
Orwell RM18. . . . .**175** C2
Orwell Cl RM13 . . . .**169** D8
Orwell Ct SS11 . . . .**122** B5
Orwell Lo 2 E18. . . . .**132** A7
Orwell Way CM0 . . . .**106** A6
Osborne Cl RM11 . . . .**136** B5
Osborne Ho 10 IG8. . . . . . .**111** A3
Osborne Hts CM14 . . . .**116** B6
Osborne Rd
Basildon, Barstable
SS16. . . . .**142** C5
Basildon, North Benfleet
SS13. . . . .**143** B8
Buckhurst Hill IG9 . . . .**88** B1
Dagenham RM9. . . . .**153** F7
Hoddesdon EN10. . . . .**21** A4
Hornchurch RM11 . . . .**136** C5
Pilgrims Hatch CM15 . . . . . .**94** B3
Southend-on-S SS0 . . . . . .**147** E1
Osborne Sq RM9. . . . .**153** F8
Osbourne Ave SS5 . . . .**124** C6
Osbourne Ho SS0. . . . .**147** C1
Osbourne Rd DA2. . . . .**176** B1
OSEA ISLAND. **39** B1
Osea Rd CM9 . . . .**38** B3
Osea Way CM1. . . . .**32** F5

Osier Dr SS15. . . . .**119** C1
Osprey Cl
Southend-on-S SS3 . . . . . .**149** E1
Wanstead E11 . . . .**132** A7
Osprey Ct
Brentwood CM14. . . . .**116** B7
Waltham Abbey EN9 . . . . . .**66** A5
Osprey Rd EN9 . . . .**66** A5
Ospreys The SS9. . . . .**146** F1
Osprey Way CM2. . . . .**54** A5
Ostell Cres EN3. . . . .**65** A1
OSTEND **105** F7
Osterley Dr SS16 . . . .**140** F5
Osterley Pl CM3 . . . .**101** D5
Otley App IG2 . . . .**133** B5
Otley Dr IG2. . . . .**133** B5
Ottawa Gdns RM10 . . . . . .**154** D5
Ottawa Rd RM18 . . . .**179** D5
Otterbourne Rd E4. . . . .**109** D7
Ouida Rd SS8. . . . .**164** D3
Oulton Ave SS8 . . . .**163** F5
Oulton Cres IG11 . . . .**152** F7
Oundle Ho 8 RM3. . . . .**114** D6
Our Lady Immaculate RC
Prim Sch CM2. . . . .**32** A1
Our Lady of Lourdes RC
Prim Sch
Southend-on-S SS9 . . . . . .**147** A2
Wanstead E11 . . . .**132** A5
Our Lady of Ransom RC
Prim Sch SS6 . . . .**123** A4
Outing Cl SS1 . . . .**167** C7
Outing's La CM15 . . . .**72** B3
Outwood Common Rd
CM11 . . . .**97** E3
Outwood Farm Cl
CM11 . . . .**97** E3
Outwood Farm Rd
CM11 . . . .**97** E1
Oval Gdns RM17 . . . .**173** C3
Oval Rd N RM10 . . . .**154** B4
Oval Rd S RM10 . . . .**154** B3
Overcliffe DA11. . . . .**179** A1
Overcliff Flats SS0 . . . .**166** D7
Overcliff Rd RM17 . . . .**173** D1
Overmead Dr CM3 . . . .**101** E8
Overstrand Ho RM12 . . . . .**136** B2
Overton Cl SS7 . . . .**144** C5
Overton Ct E11 . . . .**132** A4
Overton Dr
Dagenham RM6 . . . .**134** C4
South Benfleet SS7 . . . . . .**144** C5
Wanstead E11 . . . .**132** B4
Overton Rd SS7. . . . .**144** C6
Overton Way SS7 . . . .**144** B6
Ovington Gdns CM12 . . . . . .**97** A5
Owen Cl RM5 . . . .**113** B4
Owen Gdns IG8 . . . .**110** E4
Owen Waters Ho IG5 . . . . .**111** A2
Owlets Hall Cl RM3 . . . .**136** F8
Owl Pk Cvn Site IG10 . . . . . .**87** F7
Oxcroft Ct SS15. . . . .**141** B6
Oxendon Dr EN11 . . . .**21** A5
Oxford Ave
Grays RM16. . . . .**174** A2
Hornchurch RM11 . . . .**137** A7
Oxford Cl
Basildon SS16 . . . .**140** F5
Romford RM1 . . . .**136** A6
Oxford Ct
Brentwood CM14. . . . .**116** D6
Chelmsford CM2 . . . .**32** E4
Oxford Ho IG6. . . . .**111** C2
Oxford Rd
Canvey Island SS8. . . . . . .**164** D3
Horndon on t H SS17. . . . . .**159** E4
Ilford IG1. . . . .**152** C7
Rochford SS4. . . . .**125** E4
Romford RM3 . . . .**114** F4
Stanford-le-H SS17 . . . . . .**160** B1
Woodford IG8 . . . .**110** D5
Oxley Cl RM2 . . . .**114** C1
Oxley Gdns SS17. . . . .**160** E5
Oxleys Rd EN9 . . . .**66** A7
Oxleys The CM17 . . . .**11** E4
Oxlow La RM10 . . . .**154** A8
Oxney Mead CM1 . . . .**52** F8
Oxted Ho RM3 . . . .**114** F5
Oxwich Ct SS17 . . . .**161** A3
Oyster Catcher Terr
IG5. . . . .**133** A8
Oyster Cotts CM0 . . . .**40** C1
Oyster Ct SS8. . . . .**164** B4
Oyster Pl CM2 . . . .**32** F4
Ozonia Ave SS12. . . . .**121** C5
Ozonia Cl SS12 . . . .**121** B5
Ozonia Way SS12. . . . .**121** C5
Ozonia Wlk 3 SS12 . . . .**121** C5

P

Paarl Rd SS8 . . . .**164** B4
Paceheath Cl RM5 . . . .**113** D4
Pacific Cl DA10 . . . .**177** E2
Pacific Wharf IG11 . . . .**152** B5
Padda Ct SS12. . . . .**121** C7
Paddock Cl
Billericay CM11 . . . .**119** C7
Orsett RM16 . . . .**174** B8
Southend-on-S SS9 . . . . . .**146** E4
Paddock Dr CM1 . . . .**32** E8
Paddock Mead CM18 . . . . . .**23** C3
Paddocks The
High Roding CM6. . . . .**5** E7
Ingatestone CM4 . . . .**74** B3
Orsett RM16 . . . .**174** B8
Rayleigh SS6 . . . .**123** F2

Paddocks The *continued*
Stapleford Abbotts RM4 91 F3
Paddock The
Hoddesdon EN10 21 A3
Stock CM4 75 E3
Padfield Ct 2 RM1 135 F5
Padgets The EN9 65 E5
Padgetts Way SS5 101 D3
PADHAM'S GREEN 96 A7
Padham's Green Rd CM4 96 C8
Padnall Ct RM6 134 D8
Padnall Rd RM6 134 D7
Pageant Cl RM18 179 C6
Page Cl RM9 153 E7
Page Rd SS13 143 F7
Pages La RM3 115 B1
Paget Dr CM12 97 A5
Paget Rd IG1 152 B8
Pagette Way RM17 173 A2
Paglesfield 4 CM13 95 C3
PAGLESHAM CHURCHEND 127 D7
PAGLESHAM EASTEND 128 A5
Paglesham Rd
Paglesham Eastend SS4 128 A5
Rochford SS4 127 C6
Paignton Ave CM1 32 D5
Paignton Cl
Rayleigh SS6 123 D5
Romford RM3 114 D2
Paines Brook Rd RM3 114 F4
Paines Brook Way RM3 114 F4
Painswick Ave SS17 160 F5
Painters Rd IG2, RM6 134 A8
Pakes Way CM16 67 E2
Palace Gdns IG9 88 D1
Palace Gr SS15 141 E8
Palace View Rd E4 109 B5
Palatine Pk SS15 140 F6
Palepit CM3 81 C5
Paley Gdns IG10 89 B6
Palin Ho RM16 173 A5
Palins Way RM16 173 A5
Palladian Cir 4 DA9 177 C3
Pallett Ct EN11 21 B4
Palliser Dr RM13 170 A8
Pall Mall SS9 146 E1
Palm Cl CM2 54 C6
Palmeira Ave SS0 166 D7
Palmeira Mans SS0 166 D7
Palmer Cl SS15 141 D6
Palmer Ct RM1 136 A6
Palmeria Ct SS0 166 D7
Palmer Rd RM8 134 D3
Palmers
Pilgrims Hatch CM15 94 A5
3 Stanford-le-H SS17 160 F3
Palmer's Ave RM17 173 C1
Palmers Coll RM17 173 E2
Palmers Croft CM2 33 A2
Palmers Dr RM17 173 C2
Palmers Gr EN9 21 F1
Palmers Hill CM16 46 A2
Palmerston Ct 3 IG9 110 C8
Palmerstone Rd
Canvey Island SS8 163 D3
Rainham RM13 155 C3
Palmerston Gdns RM20 172 D1
Palmerston Lo CM2 54 F7
Palmerston Rd
Buckhurst Hill IG9 88 C1
Grays RM20 172 D1
Southend-on-S SS0 166 D7
Palm Mews SS15 119 D1
Palm Rd RM7 135 C6
Pamela Ct 5 RM1 135 F6
Pamplins SS15 141 F6
Panadown SS15 141 F6
Pancroft RM4 90 B6
Panfield Mews IG2 133 A5
Panfields SS15 141 A6
Pan La CM3 77 F5
Pantile Ave SS2 148 C3
Pantile Cotts RM14 137 D6
Pantile Ct CM0 84 C4
Pantile Hill CM0 84 C4
Pantiles The CM12 97 A4
Panventon Ct RM18 179 A5
Pan Wlk CM1 31 D5
Papenburg Rd SS8 164 A6
Paprills SS16 141 E5
Parade The
Aveley RM15 171 C4
8 Basildon SS13 143 B5
Brentwood CM14 116 C7
Ilford IG2 133 D5
Romford RM3 115 B4
Romford RM4 113 E7
Swanscombe DA10 177 F2
Paradise Rd
Waltham Abbey EN9 65 C5
Writtle CM1 53 B8
Pargat Dr SS9 146 C7
Pargetters Hyam SS5 124 F6
Parham Dr IG2 133 B6
Paringdon Jun Sch CM18 23 D4
Paringdon Rd CM18, CM19 23 C3
Parish Cl RM11 136 B2
Parish Way 6 SS15 141 C7
Parkanaur Ave SS1 168 B7
Park Ave
Barking IG11 152 C6
Brentwood CM13 95 D1
Canvey Island SS8 164 F2
Chelmsford CM1 31 F4
Grays RM20 177 B8
Harlow CM17 24 C5
Ilford IG1 133 A3
Southend-on-S SS9 146 E6
Upminster RM14 137 E4
Wallend E6 152 A3
Woodford IG8 110 B5
Park Bvd RM2 113 F2
Park Chase SS7 145 E2
Park Cl
North Weald Bassett CM16 47 A4
Wickford SS12 121 C6
Park Cliff Rd DA9 177 C3
Park Cres
Hornchurch RM11 136 A4
Southend-on-S SS0 166 F8
Park Ct
2 Chingford E4 109 C8
Harlow CM20 10 D2
Parkdale CM3 56 C7
Park Dr
Dagenham RM10 135 C1
Hatfield Heath CM22 3 B2
Ingatestone CM4 74 C4
Maldon CM9 37 B1
Romford RM1 135 D7
Upminster RM14 156 C8
Wickford SS12 121 D6
Parkend CM19 22 D8
Park End Rd RM1 135 E7
Parker Ave RM18 179 C6
Parker Ct CM0 41 F4
Parker Rd
Chelmsford CM2 32 C1
Grays RM17 177 F8
Parker's Farm Rd RM16 158 F5
Parkes Rd IG7 111 E5
Park Farm Rd
Hornchurch RM14 155 F7
Upminster RM14 156 A6
Parkfields
Hadleigh SS7 145 C4
Roydon CM19 22 B7
Parkgate SS0 166 F8
Park Gate Rd SS17 161 A7
Park Gdns
Erith DA8 169 D2
Hockley SS5 124 F5
Park Grange IG7 111 D5
Park Hill
Harlow CM17 11 B4
Loughton IG10 88 D4
Parkhill Cl RM12 136 C2
Parkhill Jun & Inf Sch IG5 133 A8
Parkhill Jun Sch IG5 132 F8
Parkhill Rd E4 87 C2
Park Ho SS17 160 F3
Parkhurst Dr SS6 123 C7
Parkhurst Rd
Basildon SS13 143 B5
Little Ilford E12 152 A8
Parkinson Dr CM1 31 F1
Park La
Aveley RM15 171 D5
Aveley RM15 171 D6
Canvey Island SS8 164 F3
Harlow CM20 10 D2
Hornchurch, Elm Park RM12 155 B6
Hornchurch RM11 136 A4
Ilford RM6 134 D5
Ingrave CM13 117 D3
Pleshey CM3 7 F4
Ramsden Heath CM11 98 C3
Southend-on-S, Clifftown SS0 166 F8
Southend-on-S SS1 167 C8
Parkland Ave
Romford RM1 113 F1
Upminster RM14 156 B7
Parkland Cl
Chigwell IG7 111 C7
3 Hoddesdon EN11 8 B1
Parkland Rd IG8 110 B3
Parklands
Billericay CM11 97 B3
Canvey Island SS8 164 A5
Chigwell IG7 111 C7
Coopersale CM16 46 D2
Rochford SS4 125 D3
Waltham Abbey EN9 65 D7
Parklands Ave SS6 123 E2
Parklands Bsns Ctr CM6 15 B7
Parklands Cl IG2 133 C4
Parklands Dr CM1 32 D3
Parklands Inf Sch RM1 135 D8
Parklands Jun & Inf Sch RM1 113 D1
Parklands Jun Sch RM1 135 D8
Parklands Way CM2 54 C2
Parkland Way CM5 48 F1
Park Mdw CM15 72 D1
Parkmead IG10 89 A4
Park Mead CM20 10 B1
Park Mews 6 RM13 155 A6
Parkmill Cl SS17 161 A3
Parkmore Cl IG8 110 A6
Park Rd
Brentwood CM14 116 B8
Burnham-on-C CM0 106 B5
Canvey Island SS8 164 F2
Chelmsford CM1 32 B2
Corringham SS17 161 A2
Grays RM17 173 B1
Hoddesdon EN11 21 A6
Ilford IG1 133 D1
Maldon CM9 36 F2
Pleshey CM3 7 F4
Southend-on-S, Clifftown SS0 166 F8
Southend-on-S SS9 146 B1
Stanford-le-H SS17 160 B1
Swanscombe DA10 177 E1
Thundersley SS7 144 F6
Wanstead E12 132 B2
Park Sch for Girls IG1 133 B3
Parkside
Grays RM16 173 E3
Sheering CM17 12 E3
Park Side
Basildon SS13 143 A7
Billericay CM11 97 C2
Buckhurst Hill IG9 110 B8
Epping CM16 46 B2
Southend-on-S SS0 147 A1
Parkside Ave
Romford RM1 135 D8
Tilbury RM18 179 B5
Parkside Bsns Ctr EN11 21 C8
Parkside Ct 2 E11 132 A5
Parkside Ctr SS2 147 F5
Parkside Ho RM10 135 C1
Parkside Lo DA8 169 C1
Parkside Rd DA17 169 C2
Parkside Terr IG1 152 C7
Park Sq RM4 90 E3
Park St SS0 166 F8
Parks The SS13 121 A2
Parkstone Ave
Hadleigh SS7 145 B4
Hornchurch RM11 136 E5
Wickford SS12 120 F8
Parkstone Dr SS2 147 E4
Park Terr
Greenhithe DA9 177 B2
Southend-on-S SS0 166 F8
Park Vale Ct CM14 94 C1
Park View
Aveley RM15 171 D5
Canvey Island SS8 164 E2
Hoddesdon EN11 21 A5
Park View Cres CM2 54 F5
Parkview Ct IG2 133 E5
Park View Ct
Southend-on-S SS9 146 E6
Wickford SS11 99 C1
Park View Dr SS9 146 B5
Park View Gdns
Grays RM17 173 B1
Redbridge IG4 132 F7
Parkview Ho RM12 136 B2
Park View Ho E4 109 A5
Parkview Mews RM13 170 B8
Park Villas RM6 134 D5
Parkway
Chelmsford CM1 CM2 32 B2
Corringham SS17 161 C4
Harlow CM19 22 E8
Ilford IG3 133 F1
Orsett RM16 174 A8
Rainham RM13 155 A1
Rayleigh SS6 145 F8
Romford RM2 113 F1
Sawbridgeworth CM21 1 F1
Woodford IG8 110 C5
Park Way CM15 94 F1
Parkway Cl SS9 146 F7
Parkway The SS8 164 B2
Parnall Rd CM18 23 D4
Parndon Ho IG10 88 E2
Parndon Mill La CM20 10 B3
Parndon Wood Nature Reserve* CM19 23 D2
Parndon Wood Rd CM18, CM19 23 C3
Parnell Cl RM16 172 C1
Paroma Rd DA17 169 A3
Parr Cl RM16 172 C2
Parrock St 13 DA12 179 B1
Parrotts Field EN11 21 B7
Parry Cl SS17 160 D3
Parsloe Rd CM19 23 B3
Parsloes Ave RM9 153 E7
Parsloes Prim Sch RM9 153 F6
Parsonage Chase CM9 81 D8
Parsonage Cl CM1 19 A1
Parsonage Ct IG10 89 B6
Parsonage Farm Prim Sch RM13 155 C2
Parsonage Field CM15 72 D2
PARSONAGE GREEN 32 A8
Parsonage La
Basildon SS15 141 C6
Little Baddow CM3 34 D2
Margaretting CM4 75 A7
Parsonage Leys CM20 23 F8
Parsonage Rd
Grays RM20 177 C8
Rainham RM13 155 C2
Parsons Cnr SS3 149 D2
Parsons Lawn SS3 149 D1
Parsons Rd SS7 144 D7
Partridge Ave CM1 31 F6
Partridge Ct
Harlow CM18 23 E6
Stanford-le-H SS17 160 D2
Partridge Gn SS13 143 A5
Partridge Rd CM18 23 D5
Parvills EN9 65 D7
Paschal Way CM2 54 F8
Pasfield EN9 65 D6
Paslowes SS16 142 F4
Paslow Hall Cotts CM5 49 F4
PASSINGFORD BRIDGE 91 D8
Passingham Ave CM11 119 C6
Passingham Cl CM11 119 C7
PASSMORES 23 D6
Passmores Sch & Tech Coll CM18 23 D6
Pasteur Dr RM3 114 D1
Paston Cl CM3 79 E1
Pastoral Way CM14 116 B5
Pasture Rd RM9 153 F7
Patching Hall La CM1 32 A6
Paternoster Cl EN9 65 F6
Paternoster Hill EN9 65 F7
Paternoster Row RM4 92 C1
Pathways SS14 142 E5
Patmore Rd EN9 65 E5
Patmore Way RM5 113 B5
Patricia Dr
Corringham SS17 161 C5
Hornchurch RM11 136 E3
Patricia Gdns CM11 119 D7
Patrick Gr EN9 65 B6
Patterdale SS7 144 B7
Patterson Ct DA1 176 A2
Pattiswick Cnr SS14 142 E7
Pattiswick Sq SS14 142 E7
Pattocks SS14 142 E6
Paul Ct RM7 135 C5
Pauline Gdns CM12 96 F4
Paul Robeson Cl E6 152 A2
Pauls Ct SS8 164 A6
Pauls La EN11 21 A6
Paulson Ho 7 IG11 152 B5
Paul's Rd SS15 141 C8
Pavement Mews 1 RM6 134 D4
Pavet Cl RM10 154 B6
Pavilion Cl SS2 148 E1
Pavilion Ct RM9 153 E4
Pavilion Dr SS9 146 F2
Pavilion Rd IG1 132 F4
Pavilions The
Chipping Ongar CM5 49 A4
North Weald Bassett CM16 47 C6
Southend-on-S SS1 166 E7
Pavilion Terr IG2 133 E6
Pavillion Pl CM12 96 F4
Pavitt Mdw CM2 54 C2
Pawle Cl CM2 55 A7
Paxfords SS15 140 F6
Paycocke Cl SS14 120 F2
Paycocke Mews SS14 120 E2
Paycocke Rd SS14 120 F2
Paycock Rd CM19 23 A6
Payne Cl IG11 152 F5
Payne Pl CM3 78 B6
Paynes La EN9 43 C7
Paynters Mead SS16 142 E3
Payzes Gdns IG8 109 F5
Peabody Ct EN3 65 A2
Peach Ave SS5 124 E8
Peach Ct E4 109 A6
Peacock Cl
Dagenham RM8 134 C2
Hornchurch RM11 136 E7
Peacocks CM19 22 F6
Peacock St 7 DA12 179 C1
Peaketon Ave IG4 132 D6
Pea La RM14 157 A6
Pearce Manor CM2 53 F8
Pearcy Cl RM3 114 E3
Pearl Ct 10 EN11 21 A6
Pearlstones Ct RM10 154 A4
Pearmain Cl SS11 99 D1
Pearsons 2 SS17 160 F3
Pearsons Ave SS6 123 B4
Peartree Cl
Doddinghurst CM15 72 D1
Goldhanger CM9 38 E6
Southend-on-S SS2 148 C3
South Ockendon RM15 157 C3
Pear Tree Cl SS15 119 C1
Pear Tree Ct E18 110 B2
Peartree Gdns
Dagenham RM8 153 B8
Romford RM7 113 B1
PEARTREE GREEN 72 D2
Peartree La
Bicknacre CM3 56 F3
Bulphan CM14 139 F1
Doddinghurst CM15 72 D2
Pear Tree Mead CM18 24 A5
Pear Tree Mead Prim Sch CM18 24 A5
Peartrees CM13 117 C4
Pear Trees SS7 144 F4
Peartree Wlk CM12 97 A4
Pease Cl RM12 155 B5
Pease Pl CM3 78 B6
Peas Mead Terr E4 109 C6
Pebmarsh Dr SS12 121 E6
Peck's Hill EN9 21 E2
Pedlars Cl CM3 57 A6
PEDLARS END 26 B2
Pedlars End CM5 26 C2
Pedlars Path CM3 57 A6
Pedley Rd RM8 134 C3
Peel Ave SS3 168 G8
Peel Cl E4 109 B8
Peel Dr IG5 110 E1
Peel Pl IG5 110 E1
Peel Rd
Chelmsford CM2 32 F4
Woodford E18 109 F2
Peel Way RM3 114 F1
Peerage Way RM11 136 F4
Peers Sq CM2 33 A4
Pegasus Ct 5 IG9 110 D8
Pegelm Gdns RM11 136 F4
Peggotty Cl CM1 31 F6
Pegrams Ct CM18 23 C5
Pegrams Rd CM18 23 C5
Peldon Pavement SS14 142 D8
Peldon Rd CM19 23 A6
Pelham Ave IG11 152 F4
Pelham Pl SS17 160 E4
Pelham Rd
Ilford IG1 133 D2
Southend-on-S SS2 148 E1
Wanstead E18 132 B8
Pelly Ct CM16 67 F8
Pemberry Pl SS14 142 D6
Pemberton Ave
Ingatestone CM4 74 B4
Romford RM2 136 B8
Pemberton Ct CM4 74 B4
Pemberton Field SS4 103 B4
Pemberton Gdns RM6 134 E6
Pembrey Way RM12 155 C6
Pembridge Ct 5 SS1 167 C8
Pembroke Ave
Corringham SS17 161 A3
Maldon CM9 36 F1
Pembroke Bsns Ctr SS14 120 E2
Pembroke Cl
Billericay CM12 97 B5
Erith DA8 169 D2
Hornchurch RM11 137 A7
Pembroke Dr RM15 171 C4
Pembroke Gdns RM10 135 B1
Pembroke Ho SS4 147 F7
Pembroke Mews SS13 143 C8
Pembroke Par DA8 169 C1
Pembroke Pl CM1 32 B7
Pembroke Rd
Erith DA8 169 D2
Ilford IG3 133 F4
Pembury Rd SS0 166 C7
Pendine Cl SS17 161 A3
Pendle Cl SS14 121 A1
Pendle Dr SS14 120 F1
Pendlestone SS7 145 C4
Pendower SS6 123 B1
Penerley Rd RM13 170 B8
Penhurst Ave SS2 147 F2
Penhurst Rd IG6 111 B3
Peniel Acad CM15 71 E1
Penistone Wlk RM3 114 C4
Penlow Rd CM18 23 D5
Penn Cl RM16 159 B1
Penn Gdns RM5 113 A3
Pennial Rd SS8 164 A4
Pennine Rd CM1 31 D5
Pennington Cl RM5 113 A4
Penny Cl RM13 155 B2
Penny Ct RM13 155 B2
Pennyfeathers CM5 27 C2
Penny Fields CM14 116 C6
Penny La SS17 160 E4
Pennymead CM20 11 A1
Penny Royal Rd CM3 56 D6
Penny's La CM4 74 F8
Penny Stps 14 SS1 167 C7
Penrhyn Ave E17 109 A2
Penrhyn Cres E17 109 A2
Penrhyn Gr E17 109 A2
Penrith Cres RM13 155 A7
Penrith Rd
Redbridge IG6 111 F4
Romford RM3 115 A4
Penrose Mead CM1 53 B8
Penshurst CM17 11 C3
Penshurst Dr CM3 101 D5
Penson's La
Chipping Ongar CM5 48 D4
Toot Hill CM5 48 B3
Pentire Cl RM14 137 E5
Pentire Rd E17 109 D2
Pentland Ave
Chelmsford CM1 32 A6
Southend-on-S SS3 168 C6
Pentlow Way IG9 88 E2
Pentney Rd 5 E4 87 D1
Pentstemon Dr DA10 177 E2
Penwood Cl CM11 97 D6
Penzance Cl CM1 32 E5
Penzance Gdns RM3 115 A4
Penzance Rd RM3 115 A4
Peony Cl CM15 94 B3
Peony Ct IG8 109 E3
Pepper Alley IG10 88 A8
Pepper Hill SG12 8 A4
PEPPER'S GREEN 16 C2

Pepys Cl
Dartford DA1..............**176** A3
Tilbury RM18..............**179** C6
Pepys Ct
4 Hoddesdon EN11.........**21** D8
Wickford SS12.............**121** C5
Percival Gdns RM6......**134** D5
Percival Ho 3 IG8.......**110** A6
Percival Rd RM11........**136** C5
Percy Cottis Rd SS4....**125** E3
Percy Rd
Ilford IG3................**134** A4
Romford RM7...............**135** C8
Southend-on-S SS9.........**146** D1
Percy St 2 RM17........**178** C8
Peregrine Cl
Basildon SS16.............**142** B4
Southend-on-S SS3.........**149** E1
Peregrine Dr
Chelmsford CM2............**54** A4
South Benfleet SS7........**144** C2
Peregrine Gdns SS6.....**123** B3
Peregrine Rd IG6.......**112** C5
Peregrine Wlk 6
RM12.....................**155** B6
Peregrine Rd EN9.......**66** A5
Perkins Cl DA9.........**176** F2
Perkins Rd IG2.........**133** D6
Perriclose CM1.........**32** D7
Perrin Pl CM2..........**32** A1
Perryfield CM17........**13** C2
Perryfield La CM5......**27** E5
Perryfields Jun & Inf Sch
CM1.....................**32** D6
Perry Gn SS14..........**142** B8
Perry Gr DA1...........**176** A3
Perry Hill
Chelmsford CM1............**32** D3
Lower Nazeing EN9.........**43** F8
Perry Ho RM13..........**154** D3
Perryman Ho IG11.......**152** C4
Perrymans Farm Rd
IG2.....................**133** D6
Perry Rd
Harlow CM18...............**23** C4
South Benfleet SS7........**144** B3
Perry Spring
Basildon SS16.............**142** D5
Harlow CM17...............**24** D6
Perry St CM12..........**97** B5
Perry Way RM15.........**171** C6
Pershore Cl IG2........**133** B6
Perth Ho RM18..........**179** A5
Perth Rd
Barking IG11..............**152** D4
Ilford IG1, IG2...........**133** B4
Perth Terr IG2.........**133** C4
Pertwee Dr
Great Baddow CM2..........**54** F6
South Woodham Ferrers
CM3.....................**101** D7
Petands Ct RM12........**136** D1
Peterborough Ave
RM14.....................**137** F3
Peterborough Gdns
IG1......................**132** E4
Peterborough Way 5
SS14.....................**142** F8
Peter Bradley Ct RM9...**153** F5
Peters Cl RM8..........**134** D3
Peters Ct SS15.........**141** B6
Petersfield CM1........**32** B7
Petersfield Ave RM3....**114** F5
Petersfield Cl RM3.....**115** A4
Peter St CM4...........**97** F8
Peterswood CM18........**23** D4
Peterswood Inf Sch
CM18.....................**23** D4
Petrebrook CM2.........**33** A3
Petre Cl
Ingatestone CM4...........**74** A2
West Horndon CM13.........**139** C5
Petrel Way CM2.........**54** C6
Petresfield Way
CM13.....................**139** C5
Pett Cl RM11...........**136** B2
Petticrow Quays CM0....**106** C3
Pettits Cl RM1.........**113** E1
Pettits La
Doddinghurst CM15........**72** E2
Romford RM1..............**135** F8
Pettits La N RM1.......**113** E2
Pettit's Pl RM10.......**154** A7
Pettit's Rd RM10.......**154** A7
Pettley Gdns RM7.......**135** D6
Petunia Cres CM1.......**32** F6
Petworth Gdns SS2......**148** F2
Petworth Way RM12......**154** F8
Pevensey Ct 10 E18.....**110** A2
Pevensey Gdns SS1......**101** F1
Pevensey Way SS13......**143** B6
Peverel Ho 4 RM10......**135** A2
Peveril Ct 28 DA2......**176** B1
Pewsey Cl E4...........**109** A5
Phelps Rd CM19.........**23** B3
Philan Way RM5.........**113** D4
Philbrick Cres E SS6...**123** C3
Philbrick Cres W SS6...**123** C3
Philip Ave RM7.........**135** D3
Philip Cl
Pilgrims Hatch CM15.......**94** C3
Romford RM7...............**135** D3
Philippa Way RM16......**174** B2

Philip Rd RM13.........**154** E2
Philip Sydney Ct
RM20.....................**172** D1
Philip Sydney Rd
RM20.....................**172** D1
Phillida Rd RM3........**115** A1
Phillips Ho RM16.......**174** A8
Philmead Rd SS7........**144** B2
Philpott Ave SS2.......**148** E2
Phoenix Bldgs 1
RM13.....................**155** B1
Phoenix Ct E4..........**109** B7
Phoenix Gr CM2.........**54** A8
Phoenix Hospl SS0......**147** E2
Phoenix Prim Sch
SS15.....................**141** C6
Phoenix Way SS17.......**145** C7
Picador Ho 6 RM10......**154** B6
Picardy Manorway
DA17.....................**169** B4
Picardy Rd DA17........**169** A2
Picardy St DA17........**169** A3
Picasso Way SS3........**150** A1
Pickering Ave E6.......**152** A2
Pickering Ct 13 DA2....**176** B1
Pickering Rd IG11......**152** C6
Picketts SS8...........**163** D4
Picketts Ave SS9.......**146** E4
Picketts Cl SS9........**146** E4
Pick Hill EN9..........**66** A7
Pickwick Ave CM1.......**31** D6
Pickwick Cl SS15.......**141** D7
Picton Cl SS6..........**123** E1
Picton Gdns SS6........**123** E1
Piercing Hill CM16.....**67** D4
Piercys SS13...........**143** B5
Pier Hill SS1..........**167** A7
Pier Rd
Gravesend DA11...........**178** F1
Greenhithe DA9...........**177** B3
Pierrot Stps 5 SS1.....**167** C7
Pigeon Ct E4...........**109** C4
Piggs Corner Complex
RM17.....................**173** C3
Pigstye Green Rd CM5...**51** A8
Pike La RM14...........**156** F7
Pike Way CM16..........**47** A4
Pilgrims Cl
Billericay CM11..........**97** B2
Pilgrims Hatch CM15......**93** F4
Southend-on-S SS2........**148** E1
Pilgrims Ct DA1........**176** A2
PILGRIMS HATCH.........**94** A4
Pilgrims La RM16.......**172** C5
Pilgrim's La
Pilgrims Hatch, Bentley
CM14....................**93** D5
Pilgrims Hatch CM14......**93** E4
Pilgrims' Rd DA10......**177** E3
Pilgrims View DA9......**177** C1
Pilgrims Way SS7.......**145** F3
Pilgrims Wlk 4 CM11....**97** B2
Pilgrim Way SS15.......**141** C6
Pilkingtons CM17.......**24** D8
Pilot Cl SS11..........**122** A5
Pilots Pl 6 DA2........**179** C1
Pimpernel Way RM3......**114** D4
Pinceybrook Rd CM18....**23** C4
Pincey Mead SS13.......**143** A5
Pindar Rd EN11.........**21** C7
Pine Cl
Canvey Island SS8........**163** E3
Ingatestone CM4..........**74** C4
Southend-on-S SS9........**146** B5
6 Wickford SS12..........**121** C5
Pine Cres CM13.........**95** D5
Pinecroft
Brentwood CM13...........**95** B2
Romford RM2..............**136** C7
Pine Ct RM14...........**156** B8
Pine Dr CM4............**74** C4
Pine Lo SS3............**168** F8
Pine Rd SS7............**145** D2
Pines Rd CM1...........**31** D5
Pines The
Basildon SS15............**119** C1
Grays RM16...............**173** B6
Woodford IG8.............**110** A7
Pine Tree Pl SS4.......**125** E2
Pinetrees SS7..........**145** C3
Pineview Ct E4.........**87** C1
Pine View Manor
CM16....................**46** A1
Pinewood Ave
Rainham RM13.............**155** B1
Southend-on-S SS9........**146** D5
Pinewood Cl
Harlow CM17..............**24** C7
Hullbridge SS5...........**101** E2
Stanford-le-H SS17.......**175** B3
Pinewood Prim Sch
RM5.....................**113** B5
Pinewood Rd RM4........**113** D6
Pinewood Way CM13......**95** D4
Pinfolds RM15..........**171** D7
Pinley Gdns RM9........**153** B4
Pinmill SS14...........**142** B6
PINNACLES..............**23** A8
Pinnacles The RM6......**134** E5
Pinnacles EN9..........**65** E5
Pinners Cl CM0.........**105** F7
Pintail Rd IG8.........**110** B3
Pintails 4 SS13........**143** C6
Pintolls CM3...........**101** D6
Pioneer Ct 4 DA11......**179** A1
Pioneer Sch
Basildon SS14............**142** C7
Basildon SS14............**142** C8

Pipchin Rd CM1.........**31** F6
Piper's Tye CM2........**54** D3
Piper Way IG1..........**133** D3
Pippin Ct SS11.........**121** F8
Pippins Rd CM0.........**106** C6
PIPPS HILL.............**119** F1
Pipps Hill Rd N CM11...**120** B3
Pishiobury Dr CM21.....**11** D8
Pitcairn Cl RM7........**135** A7
Pitmans CM13...........**117** C5
Pitmans Cl SS1.........**167** A8
PITSEA.................**143** B5
Pitsea Hall La SS16....**143** B3
Pitsea Jun Sch SS13....**143** A5
Pitsea Rd SS14.........**143** A5
Pitsea Sta SS13........**143** B4
Pitsea View Rd CM11....**120** D4
Pitseaville Gr SS16....**142** E5
Pitt Chase CM2.........**54** E5
Pittfields SS16........**141** B5
Pittman Cl CM13........**117** C5
Pittman Gdns IG1.......**152** C7
Pittman's Field CM20...**10** F1
Place Cotts CM3........**100** C5
Place Farm La CM15.....**72** A2
Pladda Mews SS12.......**121** F5
Plains The E4..........**87** E2
Plain The CM16.........**46** B3
Plaistow Cl SS17.......**160** D2
Plane Tree Cl
Burnham-on-C CM0.........**106** B6
Chelmsford CM2...........**54** B6
Plantaganet Pl 3 EN9...**65** B6
Plantagenet Gdns
RM6.....................**134** D4
Plantagenet Pl RM6.....**134** D4
Plantation Cl DA9......**176** F1
Plantation Rd CM3......**20** F1
Plashet Cl SS17........**160** D2
Plashet Gdns CM13......**117** A6
Plashets CM22..........**2** D1
Plashetts SS14.........**142** D7
Plas Newydd SS1........**167** E6
Plas Newydd Cl SS1.....**167** E6
Platford Gn RM11.......**136** E7
Platinum Ct RM7........**135** B8
Playfield Ave RM5......**113** C2
Playhouse Sq CM20......**23** C8
Plaza Way SS17.........**167** D8
Pleasant Cl SS1........**167** B7
Pleasant Dr CM12.......**96** E3
Pleasant Mews SS1......**167** B7
Pleasant Rd SS1........**167** B7
Pleasant Terr SS9......**165** E8
Pleasant View DA8......**169** E1
PLESHEY................**7** E2
Pleshey Cl
Southend-on-S SS1........**167** F8
6 Wickford SS12..........**121** E6
Plomer Ave 2 EN11......**8** A1
Plotlands Mus * SS16...**140** E3
Plotters Ct 7 EN11.....**21** D8
Plough Rise RM14.......**137** E4
Plover Gdns RM14.......**137** F3
Plover Ho RM13.........**170** A8
Plovers Barron CM15....**72** D3
Plovers Mead CM15......**72** D3
Plovers The CM0........**62** D7
Plover Wlk CM2.........**54** B5
Plowmans SS6...........**123** E4
Plowman Way RM8........**134** C3
Ployters Rd CM18.......**23** C4
Plumberow SS15.........**141** E6
Plumberow Ave SS5......**124** E7
Plumberow Mount Ave
SS5.....................**124** E8
Plumberow Prim Sch
SS5.....................**124** E7
Plume Ave CM9..........**36** F1
Plume Sch (Lower)
CM9.....................**37** A2
Plume Sch (Upper)
CM9.....................**36** F2
Plumleys SS13..........**143** B7
Plumpton Ave RM12......**136** F1
Plumpton Rd EN11.......**21** C8
Plumptre La CM3........**56** D5
Plumtree Ave CM2.......**54** F6
Plumtree Cl RM10.......**154** C6
Plumtree Mead IG10.....**89** A6
Plymouth Ho 10 IG11....**153** A5
Plymouth Rd
Chelmsford CM1...........**32** E5
Grays RM16...............**172** C2
Plymtree SS1...........**149** C1
Pocklington Cl CM2.....**33** A3
Poets Cnr RM18.........**179** B6
Point Cl SS8...........**164** F3
Point Rd SS8...........**164** F3
Polegate Cotts RM17....**177** E8
Pole Hill Rd E4........**87** C2
Polesworth Rd RM9......**153** D5
Poley Rd SS17..........**160** C1
Pollard Cl IG7.........**112** A5
Pollard Hatch CM19.....**23** B5
Pollards Cl
Loughton IG10............**88** C4
Rochford SS4.............**125** F2
Pollards Ct SS4........**125** E2
Pollard's Gn CM2.......**32** F2
Polstead Cl SS6........**123** A3
Polsteads SS16.........**142** E3
Polsten Mews EN3.......**65** A2
Pomfret Mead SS14......**142** A6
Pompadour Cl CM14......**116** C5
Pond Cl SS5............**101** E3
Pondfield La CM13......**117** A7
Pondfield Rd RM10......**154** B7
Pond La CM22...........**3** A2

Pond Lees Cl RM10......**154** D5
Ponds Rd CM2...........**54** B1
Pond Wlk RM14..........**137** E2
Pontypool Wlk RM3......**114** C4
Poole Ho RM16..........**174** C4
Poole Rd RM11..........**137** A4
Pooles Cl SS3..........**134** A1
Pooles La SS5..........**101** E3
Poolhurst Wlk SS5......**101** E4
Pool's La RM7..........**51** F4
Poors La SS7...........**145** E4
Poors La N SS7.........**146** A5
**Poors' Piece Nature
Trail** * CM3............**34** F1
Popes Cres SS13........**143** B5
Popes Wlk SS6..........**124** A2
Poplar Cl
Blackmore CM4............**72** E8
Chelmsford CM2...........**54** C6
Ingatestone CM4..........**74** A2
South Ockendon RM15......**157** D1
South Woodham Ferrers
CM3....................**101** C8
Poplar Cotts CM17......**24** E5
Poplar Ct
Chingford E4.............**109** B4
Hockley SS5..............**124** E6
Poplar Dr CM13.........**95** C3
Poplar Gr CM0..........**106** B5
Poplar Grove Chase
CM9.....................**37** B8
Poplar Mount DA17......**169** C2
Poplar Rd
Canvey Island SS8........**164** C3
Rayleigh SS6.............**145** F8
Wanstead E12............**132** E2
Poplar Row CM16........**67** E2
Poplars EN9............**66** C4
Poplars Ave SS5........**124** F4
Poplar Shaw EN9........**65** F6
Poplar St RM7..........**135** C7
Poplars The
Abridge RM4..............**90** B6
12 Basildon SS13.........**143** C6
Gravesend DA12...........**179** E1
Poplar Way IG6.........**133** C7
Poppy Cl
Erith DA17...............**169** B3
Pilgrims Hatch CM15......**94** B4
Poppyfield Cl SS9......**146** D6
Poppy Gdns SS15........**141** C5
Poppy Gn CM1...........**33** A6
Porchester Cl RM11.....**136** E5
Porchester Rd CM12.....**97** A5
Porlock Ave SS0........**147** A4
Port Ave RM17..........**177** B1
Portchester Ct SS9.....**146** F1
Porter Cl RM20.........**177** C8
Porters SS13...........**143** C8
Porters Ave RM8........**153** C7
Porters Cl RM14........**94** A1
Porters Grange Prim Sch
SS1.....................**167** B8
PORTERS TOWN...........**148** B1
Portia Ct 12 IG11......**153** A5
Portland Ave SS1.......**167** B8
Portland Cl RM6........**134** E6
Portland Commercial Est
IG11....................**153** C3
Portland Gdns RM6......**134** D6
Portland Pl DA9........**177** C3
Portland Rd DA11.......**178** D1
Portmadoc Ho 2
RM3.....................**114** E6
Portman Dr
Billericay CM12..........**97** B5
Woodford IG8............**110** D1
Portmore Gdns RM5......**113** A5
Portnoi Cl RM1.........**113** D1
Portreath Pl CM1.......**32** A7
Portsea Rd RM18........**179** C6
Portway
Chelmsford CM2...........**33** B4
Rainham RM13.............**155** A4
Poseidon Ct 1 IG11.....**153** B2
Postman's La CM3.......**34** E3
Post Mdw CM11..........**119** D6
Post Office Cotts CM22..**2** C8
Post Office Rd
Chelmsford CM1...........**32** B8
Harlow CM20.............**10** D1
Ingatestone CM4..........**74** B3
Woodham Mortimer CM9.....**57** E6
Postway Mews 1
IG1.....................**133** B1
Potash Rd
Billericay CM11..........**97** D6
Matching Green CM17......**13** D4
Potiphar Pl CM14.......**116** B6
Potteries The EN9......**66** C5
Potters Cl
Danbury CM3..............**57** A6
Loughton IG10............**88** F7
Potters Field CM17.....**24** D6
Potters La CM3.........**78** D2
Potter St CM17.........**24** C6
POTTER STREET..........**24** D6
Potter Street Prim Sch
CM17....................**24** C6
Potters Way SS2........**147** F5
Pottery La CM1.........**32** A1
Potton Dr SS12.........**121** F6
Poulton Cl CM9.........**59** B8
Pound Cl EN9...........**43** E8
Poundfield Rd IG10.....**89** A4
Pound Fields SS1.......**53** B8

Pound La
Basildon, Laindon
SS15....................**141** D8
Basildon, North Benfleet
SS12....................**143** F7
Orsett RM16.............**159** A1
Pound La N SS15........**119** D1
Pound Lane Central
SS15....................**119** D1
Powdermill La EN9......**65** B6
Powdermill Mews 2
EN9.....................**65** B6
Powdermill Way EN9.....**65** B6
Powell Cl SS4..........**125** C1
Powell Gdns RM10.......**154** A8
Powell Rd
Basildon SS15............**141** B7
Buckhurst Hill IG9.......**88** C2
Powle Terr IG1.........**152** D7
Pownsett Terr IG1......**152** C7
Poynder Rd RM18........**179** B6
Poynings Ave SS2.......**148** E2
Poynings Way RM3.......**114** E2
Poyntens SS6...........**123** C1
Poynters La SS3........**150** B2
Pratts Farm La CM3.....**19** D4
Preaching Cross CM4....**97** F6
Precinct The SS17......**160** D1
Premier Ave RM16.......**173** C4
Prentice Cl SS4........**125** F2
Prentice Hall La CM9...**40** B8
Prentice Pl CM17.......**24** C6
Prescott SS16..........**141** C3
Presidents Ct SS15.....**140** F6
Preston Ave E4.........**109** D4
Preston Dr E11.........**132** C4
Preston Gdns
Rayleigh SS6.............**123** D4
Redbridge IG1............**132** E5
Preston Ho 3 RM10......**135** A1
Preston Rd
Romford RM3.............**114** D6
Southend-on-S SS0........**166** D8
Prestwood Cl SS7.......**144** F7
Prestwood Dr
Romford RM5.............**113** C5
Thundersley SS7.........**145** A7
Pretoria Ave SS15......**119** F1
Pretoria Cres E4.......**87** C1
Pretoria Rd
Chingford E4............**87** D1
Ilford IG1..............**152** E3
Romford RM7.............**135** C6
Priestley Ct RM17......**173** C2
Priestley Gdns RM6.....**134** B5
Priests Ave RM1........**113** C1
Priests Field CM13.....**117** C5
Priest's La
Brentwood CM15..........**116** F8
Shenfield CM15..........**94** F1
Primley La CM22........**2** C1
Primrose Ave RM6.......**134** B4
Primrose Cl
Basildon SS16............**141** B4
Canvey Island SS8........**164** A6
Primrose Ct 2 CM14.....**116** C7
Primrose Field CM18....**23** F5
Primrose Glen RM11.....**136** E7
Primrose Hill
Brentwood CM14..........**116** C7
Chelmsford CM1..........**31** F3
Primrose Rd E18........**110** B1
Primrose Wlk
Maldon CM9..............**37** B1
Southminster CM0........**84** C3
Primula Ct SS15........**141** D5
Primula Way CM1........**33** A6
Prince Ave SS2, SS0....**147** C4
Prince Avenue Prim Sch
SS0.....................**147** D5
Prince Charles Ave
RM16....................**159** B1
Prince Cl SS0..........**147** C5
Prince Edward Rd
CM11....................**97** C2
Prince Philip Ave
RM16....................**173** B6
Princes Ave
Corringham SS17.........**161** A2
Mayland CM3.............**83** A8
Southminster CM0........**84** D4
Thundersley SS7.........**144** F6
Woodford IG8............**110** C6
Princes Cl
Basildon SS15............**141** E8
Billericay CM12..........**97** C5
North Weald Bassett
CM16...................**47** C5
Princes Ct
Billericay CM12..........**97** C5
Southend-on-S SS2........**147** E4
Princesfield Rd EN9....**66** B6
Princes Gate CM20......**10** E3
Princes Gate CM0.......**84** D4
Princes Lo SS0.........**166** D7
Princes Mews CM12......**97** C6
Princes Pk RM13........**155** A5
Princes Rd
Buckhurst Hill IG9.......**110** C8
Burnham-on-C CM0........**106** C6
Canvey Island SS8........**163** F3
Chelmsford CM2..........**54** B7
Ilford IG6..............**133** D7
Maldon CM9.............**37** A2
Romford RM1.............**136** A6

Prince's Rd
Navestock Heath CM14,
RM4 . . . . 92 F8
Navestock Side CM14 . . . . . . 93 A7
Princess Alexandra Hospl
CM20 . . . . 10 C1
Princess Ave RM18 . . . . . . 175 C2
Princess Ct SS11 . . . . 122 A8
Princess Gdns SS4 . . . . . . 125 D5
Princess Margaret Rd
RM18 . . . . 180 D7
Princess Par RM10 . . . . . . 154 A3
Princess Rd SS6 . . . . 123 F3
Princes St
Gravesend DA11 . . . . 179 B1
Southend-on-S SS1 . . . . . 166 F8
Princes Way
Brentwood CM13 . . . . 95 A1
Buckhurst Hill IG9 . . . . . . 110 C8
Prince William Ave
SS8 . . . . 163 F6
Printers Way CM20 . . . . 11 A5
Prior Chase RM17 . . . . 172 F2
Prioress Cres DA9 . . . . . . 177 C3
Priories The SS5 . . . . 101 D1
Prior Rd IG1 . . . . 133 C1
Priors SS14 . . . . 142 C6
Priors Ct
Sawbridgeworth CM22 . . . . . 2 A2
Southminster CM0 . . . . 84 E4
Priors E SS14 . . . . 142 C6
Priors Pk RM12 . . . . 136 C1
Prior's Way CM0 . . . . 84 E4
Priory Ave
Chingford E4 . . . . 109 A7
Harlow CM17 . . . . 11 C5
Southend-on-S SS2 . . . . . 147 F3
Priory Chase SS6 . . . . 123 B6
Priory Cl
Chelmsford CM1 . . . . 31 E2
Chingford E4 . . . . 109 A7
Hoddesdon EN11 . . . . 21 A5
Pilgrims Hatch CM15 . . . . . 94 A4
Woodford E18 . . . . 110 A2
Priory Cres SS2 . . . . 147 F4
Priory Ct
Harlow CM18 . . . . 24 B5
[2] Ilford RM6 . . . . 134 B5
Priory Gr RM3 . . . . 114 E6
Priory La CM3 . . . . 56 F1
Priory Mead RM15 . . . . 72 C3
Priory Mews
[1] Hornchurch RM11 . . . . 136 B3
Southend-on-S SS2 . . . . . 148 A3
Priory Park Ind Est
SS2 . . . . 148 A4
Priory Path RM3 . . . . 114 E7
Priory Prim Sch CM3 . . . . 56 F2
Priory Rd
Barking IG11 . . . . 152 D5
Bicknacre CM3 . . . . 56 E1
Loughton IG10 . . . . 88 E5
Romford RM3 . . . . 114 E7
Stanford-le-H SS17 . . . . . 160 E3
Priory Rd SS2 . . . . 147 E3
Priory The
Billericay CM12 . . . . 97 C6
Writtle CM1 . . . . 53 B8
Priory View Rd SS9 . . . . . 146 E5
Priorywood Cres SS9 . . . . 146 E5
Priorywood Dr SS9 . . . . . 146 E5
Pritchett Cl EN3 . . . . 65 A2
Prittlebrook Ind Est
SS2 . . . . 147 F4
PRITTLEWELL 147 C3
Prittlewell CE Jun & Inf
Sch SS2 . . . . 147 F2
Prittlewell Chase
SS0 . . . . 147 D3
Prittlewell Mews SS2 . . . . 147 F2
Prittlewell Priory Mus★
SS2 . . . . 147 F3
Prittlewell Sq SS1 . . . . . . 166 F7
Prittlewell St SS2 . . . . . . 148 A1
Prittlewell Sta SS2 . . . . . 148 A3
Professional Pl [2]
SS11 . . . . 122 A4
Progress Rd SS9 . . . . 146 C6
Promenade CM3 . . . . 60 F1
Promenade The
Burnham-on-C CM0 . . . . . . 106 C4
Southend-on-S SS3 . . . . . 168 C5
Prospect Ave SS17 . . . . . 160 B1
Prospect Bsns Pk
IG10 . . . . 89 D5
Prospect Cl
Belvedere DA17 . . . . 169 A1
Southend-on-S SS1 . . . . . 167 C7
Prospect Pl
[4] Gravesend DA12 . . . . 179 D1
Grays RM17 . . . . 178 B8
Romford RM5 . . . . 113 C1
Prospect Rd
Hornchurch RM11 . . . . . . 136 F8
Woodford IG8 . . . . 110 C5
Prospect Way SS13 . . . . . . 95 E5
Prospero Ho [7] DA17 . . . . 169 A1
Protea Way SS8 . . . . 164 B4
Prout Ind Est SS8 . . . . . . 164 F3
Providence CM0 . . . . 106 C4
Providence Pl RM5 . . . . . . 112 F2
Providence St DA9 . . . . . . 177 A2
Prower Cl CM11 . . . . 97 B1
Prudhoe Ct [15] DA2 . . . . . 176 B1
Prykes Dr CM1 . . . . 32 A2
Pryors Rd CM2 . . . . 54 C2
Puck La SS16 . . . . 142 C5

Puckleside SS16 . . . . 141 C4
Puckridge Cotts IG7 . . . . 111 E7
Pudding La IG7 . . . . 89 F2
Pudsey Hall La SS4 . . . . . 104 A2
Puffin Cl
Barking IG11 . . . . 153 B2
Wickford SS12 . . . . 121 F5
Puffin Pl SS3 . . . . 149 E1
Puffin Terr IG5 . . . . 133 A8
Pugh Pl SS17 . . . . 160 D5
Pulborough Ho [1]
RM3 . . . . 114 E3
Pullman Ct SS11 . . . . 121 D8
Pulpits Cl SS5 . . . . 124 F7
Pulteney Gdns [9] E18 . . . 132 B8
Pulteney Rd E18 . . . . 132 B8
Pump Hill
Great Baddow CM2 . . . . . . 54 F6
Loughton IG10 . . . . 88 F7
Pump La
Chelmsford CM1 . . . . 32 E6
Danbury CM3 . . . . 56 D5
Epping Green CM16 . . . . . . 45 B7
Plesley CM3 . . . . 7 F1
Purleigh CM3 . . . . 58 D1
Pump Mead Cl CM0 . . . . . . 84 D4
Pump St SS17 . . . . 160 A2
Punchard Cres EN3 . . . . . . 65 B1
Purbeck Ct CM2 . . . . 54 E6
Purbeck Rd RM11 . . . . . . 136 A4
Purcell Cl
Basildon SS15 . . . . 141 D8
Stanford-le-H SS17 . . . . . 160 C3
Writtle CM1 . . . . 31 A1
Purcell Way SS17 . . . . . . 160 C3
Purdeys Way SS4 . . . . . . 148 A8
PURFLEET 171 B1
Purfleet By-Pass
RM19 . . . . 171 C1
Purfleet Ind Pk RM15 . . . 170 F4
Purfleet Industrial Access
Rd RM15 . . . . 171 A3
Purfleet Prim Sch
RM19 . . . . 171 A2
Purfleet Rd RM15 . . . . . . 171 B5
Purford Gn CM18 . . . . 24 A7
Purford Green Jun & Inf
Schs CM18 . . . . 24 A6
Purland Cl RM8 . . . . 134 F3
PURLEIGH 58 D1
Purleigh Ave IG8 . . . . 110 E4
Purleigh Cl SS13 . . . . 121 C1
Purleigh Gr CM3 . . . . 81 A5
Purleigh Prim Sch
CM3 . . . . 58 D1
Purleigh Rd SS6 . . . . 123 B3
Purleigh Wash CM9 . . . . . . 59 B2
Purley Cl IG5 . . . . 111 A1
Purley Way SS0 . . . . 147 C5
Purlieu Way CM16 . . . . 67 E4
Putney Gdns RM6 . . . . . . 134 B6
Pye Cnr CM20 . . . . 10 D5
Pyenest Rd CM19 . . . . 23 C6
Pym Pl RM17 . . . . 173 A2
Pyms Rd CM2 . . . . 54 B3
Pynchon Mews CM1 . . . . . 32 D3
Pynchon Paddocks
CM22 . . . . 2 D7
Pyne Gate CM2 . . . . 54 B1
Pynest Green La EN9 . . . . . 66 B2
Pypers Hatch CM20 . . . . . . 23 F8
Pyrgo Priory Sch
RM3 . . . . 115 A6
Pyrles Gn IG10 . . . . 89 B8
Pyrles La IG10 . . . . 89 B7
Pytt Field CM17 . . . . 24 B7

Q

Quadrant Arc RM1 . . . . . . 135 E6
Quadrant The RM19 . . . . . 171 C2
Quaker La EN9 . . . . 65 C5
Quale Rd CM2 . . . . 33 B4
Quantock [6] SS1 . . . . 167 A8
Quarles Cl RM5 . . . . 113 A3
Quarles Park Rd RM6 . . . . 134 B5
Quarry Hill RM17 . . . . . . 173 A1
Quarry Hill Inf Sch
RM17 . . . . 173 B1
Quarry Hill Jun Sch
RM17 . . . . 173 B1
Quarry Mews RM19 . . . . . 171 A2
Quarry Spring CM20 . . . . . 24 A8
Quarter Gate CM3 . . . . . . 101 E5
Quatro Pk SS14 . . . . 120 F2
Quay La DA9 . . . . 177 B3
Quay The CM0 . . . . 106 C4
Quebec Ave [4] SS1 . . . . . 167 B8
Quebec Gdns CM3 . . . . . . 101 D6
Quebec Rd
Ilford IG1 . . . . 133 C4
Tilbury RM18 . . . . 179 C4
Queen Anne's Dr SS0 . . . . 147 C4
Queen Anne's Mews
SS0 . . . . 147 C4
Queen Anns Gr SS5 . . . . . 123 D8
Queenborough Gdns
IG2 . . . . 133 A7
Queenborough Rd
CM0 . . . . 84 D4
Queen Elizabeth Ave
RM18 . . . . 175 B2
Queen Elizabeth Chase
SS4 . . . . 147 F7

Queen Elizabeth Ct
EN9 . . . . 65 C3
Queen Elizabeth Dr
SS17 . . . . 160 F4
Queen Elizabeth II Sq [4]
CM3 . . . . 101 E7
Queen Elizabeth's Hunting
Lo★ E4 . . . . 87 F2
Queen Mary Ave . . . .
RM18 . . . . 175 C2
Queen Mary Cl RM11 . . . . 135 F5
Queen Mary Ct RM18 . . . . 175 C2
Queen Marys Ct EN9 . . . . . 65 C4
Queen Mary Villas [14]
E18 . . . . 110 A2
Queens Ave SS5 . . . . 101 E4
Queen's Ave
Maldon CM9 . . . . 37 A1
Southend-on-S SS9 . . . . . 146 E1
Woodford IG8 . . . . 110 B5
Queensbridge Ind Pk
RM20 . . . . 177 A8
Queensbury IG9 . . . . 88 B1
Queen's Cl CM21 . . . . 1 F4
Queens Ct
Burnham-on-C CM0 . . . . . 106 B4
Southend-on-S, Chalkwell
SS9 . . . . 165 F8
Southend-on-S SS9 . . . . . 146 E1
Queen's Dr SS6 . . . . 65 A5
Queens Gate IG4 . . . . 132 F7
Queensgate Ctr RM17 . . . . 173 A1
Queen's Gate Mews
CM12 . . . . 96 F5
Queens Gdns
Rainham RM13 . . . . 154 D3
Upminster RM14 . . . . 137 F5
Queen's Grove Rd E4 . . . . . 87 D1
Queenside Ct RM7 . . . . . . 135 C7
Queenside Mews
RM12 . . . . 136 E2
Queensland Ave SS4 . . . . 147 F7
Queensland Cres CM1 . . . . 31 E5
Queensland Rd RM18 . . . . 178 F5
Queens Lo SS7 . . . . 145 C3
Queensmere SS7 . . . . 145 B5
Queens Mews [6] IG9 . . . . 110 C8
QUEENS PARK 96 F5
Queens Park Ave CM12 . . . . 97 B5
Queens Park Ct CM12 . . . . 96 F5
Queen's Park Ctry Pk★
CM12 . . . . 97 B6
Queens Park Rd RM3 . . . . 115 A2
Queens Rd
Basildon, Steeple View
SS15 . . . . 119 C1
Crays Hill CM11 . . . . 120 B4
Loughton IG10 . . . . 88 F6
North Weald Bassett
CM16 . . . . 47 B6
Rayleigh SS6 . . . . 123 C4
Southend-on-S, Chalkwell
SS9 . . . . 165 F8
Southend-on-S, Clifftown
SS1 . . . . 166 F8
Queen's Rd
Barking IG11 . . . . 152 C6
Brentwood CM14 . . . . 116 C8
Buckhurst Hill IG9 . . . . . 110 C8
Burnham-on-C CM0 . . . . . 106 C5
Chelmsford CM2 . . . . 32 D2
South Benfleet SS7 . . . . . 144 D2
Queen St
Brentwood CM14 . . . . 116 C5
Chelmsford CM2 . . . . 32 A1
Fyfield CM5 . . . . 27 E2
Gravesend DA12 . . . . 179 B1
Maldon CM9 . . . . 37 A2
Romford RM7 . . . . 135 D5
Southminster CM0 . . . . . . 84 C4
Queenstown Gdns
RM13 . . . . 154 F2
Queensway
Chipping Ongar CM5 . . . . . 48 F5
Southend-on-S SS1 . . . . . 167 B8
Queensway Ho SS8 . . . . . 163 D3
Queensway Lo SS1 . . . . . . 167 B7
Queens Wlk E4 . . . . 87 D1
Queenswood Ave
Brentwood CM13 . . . . 95 D4
Chingford E17 . . . . 109 C2
Queenswood Gdns
E11 . . . . 132 B2
Queenswood Ho
CM14 . . . . 116 D8
Quendon Dr EN9 . . . . 65 D6
Quendon Rd SS14 . . . . . . 142 E8
Quennell Way CM13 . . . . . . 95 D2
Quest End SS6 . . . . 123 D5
Quilp Dr CM1 . . . . 31 F7
Quilters Cl SS14 . . . . 142 D8
Quilters Dr CM12 . . . . 119 A8
Quilters Inf Sch CM12 . . . 97 A1
Quilters Jun Sch CM12 . . . 97 A1
Quilters Straight
SS14 . . . . 142 E8
Quince Tree Cl RM15 . . . . 157 C1
Quinion Cl CM1 . . . . 31 D7
Quorn Gdns SS9 . . . . 146 A1
Quorn The CM4 . . . . 74 A3

R

Rachael Clarke Cl
SS17 . . . . 160 E4
Rachael Ct [1] CM2 . . . . . . 32 E1
Rachel Cl IG6 . . . . 133 D8
Rackenford SS3 . . . . 168 D8
Radbourne Cres E17 . . . . 109 D1
Radford Bsns Ctr CM12 . . 96 F3
Radford Cres CM12 . . . . . . 97 A3
Radford Ct CM12 . . . . 97 B3
Radford Ho CM12 . . . . 97 B3
Radford Way
Barking IG11 . . . . 152 F2
Billericay CM12 . . . . 97 A3
Radley Ave IG3 . . . . 153 A8
Radley Cl IG7 . . . . 111 E6
RADLEY GREEN 51 D8
Radley Green Rd CM4,
CM5 . . . . 51 C7
Radley's La E18 . . . . 110 A1
Radleys Mead RM10 . . . . . 154 B6
Radnor Cres IG4 . . . . 132 F6
Radnor Rd SS4 . . . . 103 C1
Radstock Ho [11] RM3 . . . . 114 D5
Radstocks CM12 . . . . 97 B3
Radwinter Ave SS12 . . . . . 121 D6
Rahn Rd CM16 . . . . 68 A8
Raider Cl RM7 . . . . 113 B2
Railstore The RM2 . . . . . . 136 C8
Railway App SS15 . . . . . . 141 A6
Railway Cotts
Ilford IG6 . . . . 133 D8
Redbridge IG1 . . . . 111 D2
Railway Pl
Belvedere DA17 . . . . 169 A3
[12] Gravesend DA11 . . . . 179 B1
Railway Sq
Brentwood CM14 . . . . 116 C7
Chelmsford CM1 . . . . 32 A3
Railway St
Chelmsford CM1 . . . . 32 A3
Dagenham RM6 . . . . 134 C4
Northfleet DA11 . . . . 178 A2
Railway Terr
Chingford E17 . . . . 109 C2
Southend-on-S SS2 . . . . . 148 A3
Rainbow Ave SS8 . . . . 164 C4
Rainbow La SS17 . . . . 160 F1
Rainbow Mews CM9 . . . . . . 36 F5
Rainbow Rd
Canvey Island SS8 . . . . . 164 C4
Grays RM16 . . . . 172 C2
Sheering CM17 . . . . 12 E3
Raine Gdns [4] IG8 . . . . . 110 A6
RAINHAM 155 A2
Rainham Rd RM13 . . . . . . 154 F4
Rainham Rd N RM10 . . . . . 135 B2
Rainham Rd S RM10 . . . . . 154 C7
Rainham Sta RM13 . . . . . 155 A1
Rainham Trad Est
RM13 . . . . 154 F1
Rainham Village Prim Sch
RM13 . . . . 155 A1
Rainsford Ave CM1 . . . . . . 31 F3
Rainsford La CM1 . . . . 31 F2
Rainsford Rd CM1 . . . . 31 F3
Rainsford Way RM12 . . . . 136 A3
Raleigh Dr SS15 . . . . 141 D5
Ramblers La [5] CM17 . . . . 11 D1
Ramblers Way CM0 . . . . . 106 D4
Ram Gorse CM20 . . . . 10 B2
Rampart St SS3 . . . . 168 G6
Ramparts The SS6 . . . . . . 123 F2
Rampart Terr SS3 . . . . . . 168 G6
Rampton Cl E4 . . . . 109 A7
Ramsay Dr SS16 . . . . 142 E3
Ramsay Gdns RM3 . . . . . . 114 C2
Ramsay Rd E7 . . . . 132 A1
RAMSDEN BELLHOUSE
. . . . 98 B1
Ramsden Dr RM5 . . . . 113 A3
Ramsden Hall Sch
CM11 . . . . 97 F3
RAMSDEN HEATH 98 B4
Ramsden Park Rd
CM11 . . . . 98 D1
Ramsden View Rd
SS12 . . . . 120 F6
Ramsey Chase
Latchingdon CM3 . . . . 82 A6
Wickford SS12 . . . . 121 F6
Ramsey Cl CM9 . . . . 37 D4
Ramsey Ct SS0 . . . . 147 B3
RAMSEY ISLAND 62 B8
Ramsgill App IG2 . . . . 133 F7
Ramsgill Dr IG2 . . . . 133 F7
Rams Gr RM6 . . . . 134 E7
Ramshaw Dr CM2 . . . . 32 F3
Ramuz Dr SS0 . . . . 147 D2
Randall Ct RM13 . . . . 155 B2
Randall Dr
Hornchurch RM12 . . . . . . 155 D8
Orsett RM16 . . . . 174 A8
Randalls Dr CM13 . . . . 95 E3
Randolph Cl
Maldon CM9 . . . . 58 F8
Southend-on-S SS9 . . . . . 146 E3
Randolph Gr RM6 . . . . 134 C6
Rands Rd CM6 . . . . 5 F8
Randulph Terr CM1 . . . . . . 32 D3
Randway SS6 . . . . 123 D1
Ranelagh Gdns
Ilford IG1 . . . . 133 D3
Redbridge IG1 . . . . 132 F3

Pri-Ray | **219**

Ranelagh Gdns continued
Wanstead E11 . . . . 132 C6
Ranelagh Rd E6 . . . . 152 A3
Ranger's Rd
Buckhurst Hill E4, IG9,
IG10 . . . . 88 A2
Chingford E4 . . . . 87 F2
Ransomes Way CM1 . . . . . . 32 B4
Rantree Fold SS16 . . . . . . 141 B4
Ranulf Cl CM17 . . . . 11 C6
Ranworth Ave EN11 . . . . . . 8 B2
Raphael Ave
Romford RM1 . . . . 135 F8
Tilbury RM18 . . . . 179 B7
Raphael Dr
Chelmsford CM1 . . . . 32 F7
Southend-on-S SS3 . . . . . 150 A1
Raphael Ind Sch
RM11 . . . . 136 A5
Raphaels SS15 . . . . 141 E6
Raphaels Ct RM1 . . . . 135 F7
Rapier Cl RM19 . . . . 171 A2
Rat La SS6 . . . . 145 C8
Ratsborough Chase
CM0 . . . . 84 C2
Rat's La IG10 . . . . 66 B1
Rattwick Dr SS8 . . . . 164 F3
Ratty's La EN11 . . . . 21 D6
Ravel Gdns RM15 . . . . 171 C7
Ravel Rd RM15 . . . . 171 D7
Raven Cl CM12 . . . . 96 F4
Raven Cres CM12 . . . . 96 F4
Ravencroft RM16 . . . . 174 B4
Ravendale Way SS3 . . . . . 149 D1
Raven Dr SS7 . . . . 144 C2
Ravenings Par IG3 . . . . . . 134 A3
Raven La CM12 . . . . 96 F4
Ravenoak Way IG7 . . . . . . 111 E5
Raven Rd E18 . . . . 110 C1
Ravensbourne Cres
RM3 . . . . 136 F8
Ravensbourne Dr CM1 . . . 31 E2
Ravensbourne Gdns
IG5 . . . . 111 B2
Ravensbourne Sch
RM3 . . . . 114 D2
Ravenscourt CM15 . . . . 94 D1
Ravenscourt Cl RM12 . . . . 136 E1
Ravenscourt Dr
Basildon SS16 . . . . 142 E5
Hornchurch RM12 . . . . . . 136 E1
Ravenscourt Gr RM12 . . . . 136 E2
Ravens Ct
[6] Gravesend DA12 . . . . 179 D1
Southend-on-S SS1 . . . . . 166 F7
Ravensdale SS16 . . . . 142 A4
Ravensfield SS4 . . . . 142 F6
Ravensfield Cl RM9 . . . . . 153 D8
Ravensmere CM16 . . . . 46 A1
Ravenswood Chase
SS4 . . . . 147 F7
Ravenswood Cl RM5 . . . . . 113 B5
Rawdon Dr EN11 . . . . 21 A5
Rawlings Farm CM3 . . . . . 100 A8
Rawlyn Cl RM16 . . . . 172 C1
RAWRETH 122 E7
Rawreth Gdns SS11 . . . . . 100 E1
Rawreth Ind Est SS6 . . . . 123 B5
Rawreth La SS11 . . . . 123 B6
RAWRETH SHOT 122 C7
Rayburne Ct IG9 . . . . 88 C1
Rayburn Rd RM11 . . . . . . 137 A4
Ray Cl
Canvey Island SS8 . . . . . 164 A2
Southend-on-S SS9 . . . . . 146 B1
Ray Ct IG8 . . . . 110 D4
Raydons Gdns RM9 . . . . . 153 D7
Raydons Rd RM9 . . . . 153 E7
Rayfield CM16 . . . . 46 A2
Ray Gdns IG11 . . . . 153 A3
RAYLEIGH 123 E2
Rayleigh Ave
Rayleigh SS9 . . . . 146 B6
Southend-on-S SS0 . . . . . 147 E1
Rayleigh Cl
Brentwood CM13 . . . . 95 C3
Rayleigh SS9 . . . . 146 B8
Rayleigh Downs Rd
SS6 . . . . 146 B7
Rayleigh Dr SS9 . . . . 146 D3
Rayleigh Ho SS6 . . . . 123 C1
Rayleigh Par [8] CM13 . . . . 95 C3
Rayleigh Prim Sch
SS6 . . . . 123 C2
Rayleigh Rd
Brentwood CM13 . . . . 95 D3
Southend-on-S SS9 . . . . . 146 B6
Stanford-le-H SS17 . . . . . 160 B1
Thundersley SS7 . . . . 145 C6
Woodford IG8 . . . . 110 C3
Rayleigh Sta SS6 . . . . . . 123 C3
Rayley La CM1 . . . . 47 A8
Ray Lodge Prim Sch
IG8 . . . . 110 D4
Ray Lodge Rd IG8 . . . . . . 110 D4
Ray Mead CM3 . . . . 18 F7
Rayment Ave SS8 . . . . 164 D4
Raymond Ave E18 . . . . . . 109 F1
Raymond Gdns IG7 . . . . . . 112 B7
Raymond Rd IG2 . . . . 133 D4
Raymonds Cl CM3 . . . . . . 101 C7
Raymonds Dr SS7 . . . . . . 144 F6
Rayners Ct DA11 . . . . 178 B1
Raynes Ave E11 . . . . 132 C4
Ray Rd RM5 . . . . 113 B5

Rayside SS14 . . . . 142 C5
Ray The CM1 . . . . 32 E5
Ray Wlk SS9 . . . . 146 B1
Reaburn Ct CM1 . . . . 32 E6
Read Cl SS5 . . . . 125 A4
Read Ct EN9 . . . . 66 A6
Reader's Cnr CM2 . . . . 54 E5
Readers Ct CM2 . . . . 54 E6
Reading Cl SS16 . . . . 140 F5
Readings The CM18 . . . . . . 23 F5
Reads Cl IG1 . . . . 133 B1
Rebels La SS3 . . . . 148 F3
Recreation Ave
  Corringham SS17 . . . . 161 C3
  Romford, Harold Wood
    RM3 . . . . 114 F1
  Romford RM7 . . . . 135 C6
  Southend-on-S SS9 . . . . . 146 F2
Recreation Ct SS9 . . . . 146 F2
Recreation Wlk CM11 . . . . . 98 C5
Rectory Ave SS4 . . . . 125 C6
Rectory Chase
  Doddinghurst CM15 . . . . . 72 C2
  Little Warley CM13 . . . . . 138 E7
  Southend-on-S SS2 . . . . . 148 E1
Rectory Cl
  Chingford E4 . . . . 109 A7
  Hadleigh SS7 . . . . 145 E3
  Hunsdonbury SG12 . . . . . 9 D8
  Ingatestone CM4 . . . . . . 74 B4
  Little Waltham CM3 . . . . . 19 C6
  Stock CM4 . . . . 75 D2
Rectory Cres E11 . . . . 132 C5
Rectory Ct
  Basildon SS13 . . . . 143 C7
  Grays RM17 . . . . 178 D8
  Loughton IG10 . . . . 89 A7
  Woodford E18 . . . . 109 F2
Rectory Field CM19 . . . . . . 23 B6
Rectory Garth SS6 . . . . 123 D3
Rectory Gdns
  Basildon SS13 . . . . 143 C6
  Upminster RM14 . . . . . . 137 E2
Rectory Gr
  Southend-on-S SS9 . . . . . 165 D8
  Wickford SS11 . . . . 121 F7
Rectory Ho 7 CM12 . . . . . . 97 B2
Rectory La
  Chelmsford CM1 . . . . 32 B4
  Harlow CM19 . . . . 23 B6
  Ingrave CM13 . . . . 117 E3
  Latchingdon CM3 . . . . . . 82 B3
  Loughton IG10 . . . . 89 B6
  Rettendon SS11 . . . . 100 E6
  Woodham Mortimer CM9 . . 57 F6
Rectory Park Dr SS13 . . . 143 B5
Rectory Rd
  Basildon SS13 . . . . 143 C6
  Dagenham RM10 . . . . . . 154 B5
  Grays RM17 . . . . 173 D2
  Hadleigh SS7 . . . . 145 E3
  Hockley SS5 . . . . 125 B4
  Little Burstead CM12 . . . . 119 A2
  Little Ilford E12 . . . . 152 A7
  North Fambridge CM3 . . . 103 A8
  Orsett RM16 . . . . 174 B8
  Stanford-le-H SS17 . . . . . 160 C1
  West Tilbury RM18 . . . . . 179 D8
  Woodham Walter CM9 . . . 35 D3
  Writtle CM1 . . . . 53 B8
Rectory Terr
  Hockley SS5 . . . . 125 B4
  Stanford-le-H SS17 . . . . . 160 C1
Rectory Wood CM20 . . . . . 10 C1
Redbrick Row CM22 . . . . . . 2 B8
REDBRIDGE 132 C6
Redbridge Coll RM6 . . . . . . 134 B6
Redbridge Ct IG4 . . . . 132 D5
Redbridge Ent Ctr
  IG1 . . . . 133 C2
Redbridge Foyer IG1 . . . . . 133 C2
Redbridge Ho IG4 . . . . 132 D6
Redbridge La E IG4 . . . . . . 132 E6
Redbridge La W E11 . . . . . . 132 C5
Redbridge Mus IG1 . . . . . . 133 B1
Redbridge Prim Sch
  IG4 . . . . 132 E6
Redbridge Sta IG4 . . . . 132 D5
Redbrook Ct SS17 . . . . 175 A3
Redbury Cl RM13 . . . . 155 B1
Redcar Rd RM3 . . . . 114 F5
Redcliff Dr SS9 . . . . 165 F8
Redcliffe Gdns
  Ilford IG1 . . . . 133 A3
  Redbridge IG1 . . . . 133 A3
Redcliffe Rd 8 CM2 . . . . . . 32 A1
Red Cotts CM22 . . . . 12 D8
Redden Court Rd
  RM3 . . . . 136 F8
Redden Court Sch
  RM3 . . . . 136 F8
Reddings La CM0 . . . . 63 C3
Redfern Gdns RM2 . . . . 114 D1
Redgate Cl SS11 . . . . 122 A8
Redgates Pl CM2 . . . . 32 D4
Redgrave Ct 13 CM14 . . . . . 116 C7
Redgrave Rd SS16 . . . . 142 E4
Redgrove Ho CM16 . . . . . . 46 A2
Redhills Rd CM3 . . . . 101 E8
Red Ho The RM3 . . . . 114 D6
Redif Ho RM10 . . . . 154 B8
Redinge The CM11 . . . . 119 D7
Redlie Cl SS17 . . . . 160 D4
Red Lion Cres CM17 . . . . . 24 C6
Red Lion La CM17 . . . . 24 D6

Redmans Ind Est
  RM18 . . . . 180 A8
Redmayne Dr CM2 . . . . 53 F8
Red Oaks Mead CM16 . . . . 67 D2
Redo Ho 2 E12 . . . . 152 A7
Red Rd CM14 . . . . 116 B6
Redricks La CM21 . . . . 11 A6
Redriff Rd RM7 . . . . 113 B1
Redrose La CM4 . . . . 50 E1
Redruth Cl CM1 . . . . 32 E5
Redruth Gdns RM3 . . . . 114 F5
Redruth Rd RM3 . . . . 114 F5
Redruth Wlk RM3 . . . . 114 F5
Redshank Cres CM3 . . . . . . 79 D1
Redshank Dr CM9 . . . . 37 C5
Red Shank Ho RM13 . . . . . . 170 A8
Redstart Mans 8
  E12 . . . . 133 A1
Redstock Rd SS2 . . . . 148 A2
Red Willow CM19 . . . . 22 F5
Redwing Ct RM3 . . . . 114 D3
Redwing Dr CM11 . . . . 119 C8
Redwood Chase
  RM15 . . . . 157 D1
Redwood Cl IG9 . . . . 110 B8
Redwood Ct DA1 . . . . 176 A1
Redwood Dr
  Basildon SS15 . . . . 119 D1
  Writtle CM1 . . . . 30 F1
Redwood Gdns
  Chingford E4 . . . . 87 B3
  Redbridge IG7 . . . . 112 A5
Redwoods The SS8 . . . . . . 163 E3
Reed Ct DA9 . . . . 177 C3
Reede Gdns RM10 . . . . 154 B7
Reede Rd RM10 . . . . 154 B6
Reede Way RM10 . . . . 154 B6
Reedings Jun Sch CM21 . . . 1 E3
Reedings Way CM21 . . . . . . 1 F4
Reed Mans 7 E11 . . . . 132 A5
Reed Pond Wlk
  Basildon SS16 . . . . 141 B4
  Romford RM2 . . . . 113 F1
Reeds Farm CM1 . . . . 30 T3
Reeds Way SS12 . . . . 121 C8
Ree Lane Cotts IG10 . . . . . 89 A7
Reesland Ct E12 . . . . 152 A6
Reeves Cl
  Basildon SS16 . . . . 140 F4
  Stondon Massey CM15 . . . 72 B5
Reeves La CM15 . . . . 22 D5
Reeves Way CM3 . . . . 101 E7
Regal Cl CM2 . . . . 54 D8
Regal Ho IG2 . . . . 133 D5
Regan Cl SS17 . . . . 160 E4
Regarder Rd IG7 . . . . 112 B5
Regarth Ave RM1 . . . . 135 E5
Regatta Ct SS9 . . . . 165 F8
Regency Cl
  Chelmsford CM2 . . . . 32 D3
  Chigwell IG7 . . . . 111 C5
  Rochford SS4 . . . . 125 E2
  Wickford SS11 . . . . 99 D2
Regency Ct
  Brentwood CM14 . . . . 116 C8
  Harlow CM18 . . . . 24 A3
  Heybridge CM9 . . . . 37 A5
  Hockley SS5 . . . . 124 E6
  2 Woodford E18 . . . . 110 A1
Regency Gdns RM11 . . . . . . 136 C4
Regency Gn SS2 . . . . 147 F3
Regency Lo 1 IG9 . . . . 110 D8
Regent Cl
  Grays RM16 . . . . 173 C4
  Rayleigh SS6 . . . . 123 B4
Regent Ct
  Basildon SS15 . . . . 141 E8
  Romford RM2 . . . . 136 B8
Regent Dr CM12 . . . . 96 F5
Regent Gdns IG3 . . . . 134 A5
Regent Rd CM16 . . . . 45 F1
Regents Cl CM0 . . . . 84 D4
Regents Ct
  Burnham-on-C CM0 . . . . . 106 B4
  7 Gravesend DA11 . . . . . . 179 B1
  Southend-on-S SS1 . . . . . 166 F7
Regents Dr IG8 . . . . 111 A3
Regents Pl IG10 . . . . 88 D2
Regent Sq DA17 . . . . 169 B2
Reginald Mews 4
  CM17 . . . . 11 C1
Reginald Rd RM3 . . . . 115 A2
Regina Rd CM1 . . . . 32 C3
Reigate Rd IG3 . . . . 133 F2
Rembrandt Cl
  5 Canvey Island
    SS8 . . . . 164 A3
  Southend-on-S SS3 . . . . . 168 G8
Rembrandt Gr CM1 . . . . 32 E6
Remembrance Ave
  CM0 . . . . 106 B4
Renacres SS16 . . . . 141 F4
Rennie Ct 6 EN3 . . . . 65 A1
Rennie Pl CM2 . . . . 33 B3
Renoir Pl CM1 . . . . 32 F7
Renown Cl RM7 . . . . 113 B2
Renown The SS3 . . . . 168 F8
Renwick Ind Est IG11 . . . . . 153 B3
Renwick Rd IG11 . . . . 153 B2
Repton Ave RM2 . . . . 136 A8
Repton Cl SS13 . . . . 121 A1
Repton Ct SS13 . . . . 121 A1
Repton Ct IG5 . . . . 110 F2
Repton Dr RM2 . . . . 136 A7
Repton Gdns RM2 . . . . 136 A8
Repton Gr
  Southend-on-S SS2 . . . . . 147 A7
  Woodford IG5 . . . . 110 F2

Repulse Cl RM5 . . . . 113 B2
Reservoir Cl DA9 . . . . 177 C1
Rest Cotts SS4 . . . . 104 E1
Retford Cl RM3 . . . . 115 A4
Retford Path RM3 . . . . 115 A4
Retford Rd RM3 . . . . 115 A4
Retingham Way E4 . . . . 109 B8
Retort Cl SS1 . . . . 167 D6
Retreat Cvn Site The
  IG9 . . . . 110 A8
Retreat Rd
  Hockley SS5 . . . . 124 E6
  Southend-on-S SS0 . . . . . 166 E7
Retreat The
  Brentwood CM14 . . . . 94 B1
  Grays RM17 . . . . 178 B8
  Shenfield CM13 . . . . 95 B3
Retreat Way IG7 . . . . 112 B7
RETTENDON 78 B1
Rettendon Cl SS6 . . . . 123 A3
Rettendon Gdns SS11 . . . . . 99 E1
Rettendon Prim Sch
  CM3 . . . . 100 C5
Rettendon Turnpike
  SS11 . . . . 100 C3
Rettendon View SS11 . . . . . 121 F8
Reubens Rd CM13 . . . . 95 B3
Review Lo RM1 . . . . 154 B3
Review Rd RM10 . . . . 154 B4
Rex Par 3 IG8 . . . . 110 C4
Reydon Ave E11 . . . . 132 C5
Reynard Ct CM2 . . . . 54 F6
Reynolds Ave
  Dagenham RM6 . . . . 134 C4
  Little Ilford E12 . . . . 152 A7
Reynolds Ct RM6 . . . . 134 D8
Reynolds Gate CM3 . . . . . . 101 E6
Reynolds Gdns SS4 . . . . . . 125 C5
Reynolds Ho SS2 . . . . 147 F2
Rhapsody Cres CM14 . . . . . 116 B5
Rhoda Rd SS7 . . . . 144 E4
Rhoda Rd N SS7 . . . . 144 E5
RHS Garden Hyde Hall★
  CM3 . . . . 78 E4
Rhum Mews SS12 . . . . 122 A5
Ribble Cl IG8 . . . . 110 C4
Richard Alibon Prim Sch
  RM10 . . . . 154 A7
Richard Blackburn Ho
  RM7 . . . . 135 E2
Richard Burton Ct 5
  IG9 . . . . 110 C8
Richard Fell Ho 8
  E12 . . . . 152 A8
Richards Ave RM7 . . . . 135 C5
Richardson Cl DA9 . . . . 176 F2
Richardson Gdns 17
  RM10 . . . . 154 B6
Richardson Pl CM1 . . . . 31 F4
Riches Rd IG1 . . . . 133 C2
Richmond Ave
  Chingford E4 . . . . 109 D5
  South Benfleet SS7 . . . . . 144 C2
  Southend-on-S, Cambridge
    Town SS3 . . . . 168 D6
  Southend-on-S SS1 . . . . . 167 A7
  Southend-on-S, Westcliff-on-S
    SS0 . . . . 166 E8
Richmond Ave Prim Sch
  SS3 . . . . 168 D6
Richmond Cres E4 . . . . 109 D5
Richmond Ct
  2 Loughton IG10 . . . . 88 D4
  4 Romford RM1 . . . . 135 F5
  Southend-on-S, Chalkwell
    SS9 . . . . 165 F8
  Southend-on-S SS3 . . . . . 168 D6
Richmond Dr
  Rayleigh SS6 . . . . 145 D8
  9 Redbridge IG8 . . . . 111 A3
  Southend-on-S SS0 . . . . . 147 C4
Richmond Pk IG10 . . . . 88 D2
Richmond Rd
  Chelmsford CM2 . . . . 33 A4
  Chingford E4 . . . . 87 D1
  Grays RM17 . . . . 173 C1
  Ilford IG1 . . . . 133 C1
  Romford RM1 . . . . 135 F5
  Wickford SS11 . . . . 99 C2
Richmond St SS2 . . . . 148 B1
Richmond Way E11 . . . . 132 A2
Ricketts Dr CM12 . . . . 96 F3
Rickling SS16 . . . . 142 F4
Riddiford Dr CM1 . . . . 31 F4
Riddings La CM18 . . . . 24 A4
Ridgemount SS7 . . . . 144 E4
Ridges The E4 . . . . 109 A6
Ridge The CM3 . . . . 34 E2
Ridgeway
  Billericay CM12 . . . . 119 A8
  Brentwood CM13 . . . . 95 B1
  Grays RM17 . . . . 173 E2
  Ingatestone CM4 . . . . . . 74 A2
  Maldon CM9 . . . . 59 A8
  Rayleigh SS6 . . . . 123 C1
  Woodford IG8 . . . . 110 C6
Ridge Way SS5 . . . . 101 E4
Ridgeway Gdns
  Redbridge IG4 . . . . 132 E6
  Southend-on-S SS0 . . . . . 166 B8
Ridgeways CM17 . . . . 24 E8
Ridgeway The
  Chingford E4 . . . . 87 C1
  Romford, Harold Wood
    RM3 . . . . 114 F2
  Romford RM2 . . . . 136 A7
  Southend-on-S SS0 . . . . . 166 B8
Ridgewell Ave CM1 . . . . 31 F4

Ridgewell Cl RM10 . . . . . . 154 B4
Ridgewell Gr RM12 . . . . 155 C5
Ridgmont Pl RM11 . . . . 136 D5
Ridgwell Ave RM16 . . . . . . 159 A1
Ridings The
  Canvey Island SS8 . . . . . 164 A5
  Great Baddow CM2 . . . . . 54 D7
  1 Redbridge IG7 . . . . 112 B6
  Rochford SS4 . . . . 125 F1
Ridley Cl
  Barking IG11 . . . . 152 F5
  Romford RM3 . . . . 114 B2
Ridley Cotts CM3 . . . . 80 C3
Ridley Rd
  Basildon SS13 . . . . 121 C1
  Chelmsford CM1 . . . . 32 B8
Riffams Ct SS13 . . . . 143 C8
Riffams Dr SS13 . . . . 143 C8
Riffhams CM13 . . . . 117 B7
Riffhams Chase CM3 . . . . . 34 D2
Riffhams Dr CM2 . . . . 55 A7
Riffhams La
  Danbury CM3 . . . . 56 C8
  Little Baddow CM3 . . . . . 34 C1
Rigby Gdns RM16 . . . . 174 B2
Rigby Mews IG1 . . . . 133 A2
Rigby Pl EN3 . . . . 65 A2
Rignal's La CM2 . . . . 54 D3
Rill Ct 4 IG11 . . . . 152 C5
Ringwood Ave RM12 . . . . . 136 D2
Ringwood Dr SS9 . . . . 146 C7
Ringwood Ho 9 RM3 . . . . . 114 D4
Ripley Rd
  Belvedere DA17 . . . . 169 A2
  Ilford IG3 . . . . 133 F2
Ripley View IG10 . . . . 67 B1
Ripon Gdns IG1 . . . . 132 E4
Ripon Ho 7 RM3 . . . . 114 D4
Ripple Ct 10 IG11 . . . . 152 D4
Ripple Inf Sch IG11 . . . . . . 152 E5
Ripple Jun Sch IG11 . . . . . 152 E4
Ripple Rd
  Barking IG11 . . . . 152 C5
  Barking IG11 . . . . 152 E4
  Dagenham IG11 . . . . 153 D4
Rippleside SS14 . . . . 142 F6
Rippleside Commercial
  Est IG11 . . . . 153 C4
Risdens CM18 . . . . 23 D5
Risebridge Chase
  RM1 . . . . 113 F3
Risebridge Rd RM2 . . . . . . 114 A2
RISE PARK 113 E2
Rise Park Bvd RM1 . . . . . . 113 F2
Rise Park Jun & Inf Sch
  RM1 . . . . 113 D2
Rise Park Par RM1 . . . . 113 E1
Rise Pk SS15 . . . . 141 F6
Rise The
  Buckhurst Hill IG9 . . . . . . 88 D1
  Chingford E4 . . . . 87 E1
  Greenhithe DA9 . . . . 177 A1
  Wanstead E11 . . . . 132 A6
Riseway CM15 . . . . 116 E7
Risings Terr RM11 . . . . 136 F8
Rising The CM11 . . . . 97 D1
Rivendell Vale CM3 . . . . . . 101 C6
Rivenhall
  Thundersley SS7 . . . . 145 B8
  Wickford SS11 . . . . 122 A6
River Ave EN11 . . . . 21 B7
River Blackwater Chalet
  Site CM9 . . . . 37 C3
River Cl
  Holdbrook EN8 . . . . 65 A5
  Rainham RM13 . . . . 170 B8
  Wanstead E11 . . . . 132 C5
River Cotts CM3 . . . . 33 F8
River Ct
  Purfleet RM19 . . . . 170 F2
  Sawbridgeworth CM21 . . . 1 F3
  Wanstead E11 . . . . 132 C5
Riverdale SS9 . . . . 146 D7
Riverdale Cl IG11 . . . . 153 B1
Riverdale Rd DA8 . . . . 169 C1
Riverdene Rd IG1 . . . . 133 B1
River Dr RM14 . . . . 137 D5
Riverfield La CM21★ 1 E3
River Lee Ctry Pk★
  EN9 . . . . 43 B1
Rivermead Gate CM1 . . . . . 32 B4
Rivermead Ind Est
  CM1 . . . . 32 B4
River Meads SG12 . . . . 8 C4
Rivermill CM20 . . . . 10 C2
River Rd
  Barking IG11 . . . . 152 E2
  Barking IG11 . . . . 153 B1
  Brentwood CM14 . . . . 115 F6
  Buckhurst Hill IG9 . . . . . . 88 E1
River Road Bsns Pk
  IG11 . . . . 152 F2
Riversdale Rd RM5 . . . . . . 113 B3
Rivers Hospl (private) The
  CM21 . . . . 1 C1
Riverside CM1 . . . . 32 C3
Riverside Ave EN10 . . . . . . 21 A1
Riverside Cotts
  North Fambridge
    CM3 . . . . 103 A6
  Stanstead Abbotts SG12 . . 8 C4
Riverside Ct
  Chingford E4 . . . . 87 B3
  Harlow CM20 . . . . 11 C6
  Wickford SS11 . . . . 121 D8
Riverside Ho SS11 . . . . 121 D8
Riverside Ind Est
  Barking IG11 . . . . 153 A2

Riverside Ind Est continued
  Rochford SS4 . . . . 125 F1
Riverside Jun & Inf Schs
  SS5 . . . . 101 E4
Riverside Pk CM1 . . . . 32 C3
Riverside Rd CM0 . . . . 106 C4
Riverside Wlk SS12 . . . . . . 121 B8
Riverside Works IG11 . . . . . 152 B5
Riversmead EN11 . . . . 21 A5
Riverton Dr CM0 . . . . 40 B1
Rivertons SS16 . . . . 142 F4
Riverview
  Basildon SS16 . . . . 143 A4
  Dartford DA1 . . . . 176 A3
River View RM16 . . . . 174 A1
River View Cl SS15 . . . . . . 119 C1
Riverview Ct
  Basildon SS16 . . . . 142 E4
  15 Belvedere DA17 . . . . . 169 A1
  Greenhithe DA9 . . . . 176 F1
Riverview Flats 13
  RM19 . . . . 171 B1
Riverview Gdns SS5 . . . . . . 101 C3
Riverview Rd DA9 . . . . 177 A2
River View Rd SS7 . . . . 144 E2
Riverview Terr 1
  RM19 . . . . 171 B1
River View Terr CM3 . . . . . 82 C2
River Way
  Harlow CM20 . . . . 11 B5
  Loughton IG10 . . . . 89 A3
Riviera Dr SS1 . . . . 167 D8
Rivington Ave IG8 . . . . 110 D1
Rivington Ct 5 RM10 . . . . . 154 B6
RJ Mitchell Prim Sch The
  RM12 . . . . 155 B6
  RO24 CM19 . . . . 22 D8
Roach RM18 . . . . 175 C2
Roach Ave SS6 . . . . 123 D1
Roach Vale SS9 . . . . 146 F7
Roach View Bsns Pk
  SS4 . . . . 126 B1
Robert Cl
  4 Barking IG11 . . . . 152 C6
  Billericay CM12 . . . . 96 F2
  Chelmsford CM2 . . . . 32 F4
  Chigwell IG7 . . . . 111 F5
Robert Clack Lower Sch
  RM8 . . . . 134 F2
Robert Clack Upper Sch
  RM8 . . . . 135 A3
Robert Daniels Ct
  CM16 . . . . 67 D2
Robert Drake Prim Sch
  The SS7 . . . . 144 D7
Robert Leonard Ind Est
  SS2 . . . . 147 F5
Roberts Cl RM3 . . . . 114 B2
Roberts Ct CM2 . . . . 54 E7
Roberts Ho RM10 . . . . 154 B5
Robertson Ct RM17 . . . . . . 173 B2
Robertson Dr SS12 . . . . . . 121 C5
Roberts Pl RM10 . . . . 154 A6
Roberts Rd
  Basildon SS15 . . . . 141 B7
  Belvedere DA17 . . . . 169 A4
  Chingford E17 . . . . 109 B2
  North Fambridge CM3 . . . 103 A7
Robert Way SS11 . . . . 121 F6
Robin Cl
  Billericay CM12 . . . . 97 C4
  Romford RM5 . . . . 113 D3
  Stanstead Abbotts SG12 . . 8 C3
Robin Hood Rd CM15 . . . . . 94 C3
Robinia Cl
  Basildon SS15 . . . . 119 D1
  Redbridge IG6 . . . . 111 E4
Robin's La CM16 . . . . 67 C3
Robinson Cl RM12 . . . . 155 B5
Robinson Rd
  Dagenham RM10 . . . . . . 154 A8
  Horndon on t H SS17 . . . . 159 E4
Robinsons Cl CM0 . . . . 84 D3
Robinson Way DA11 . . . . . . 178 A2
Robins The CM15 . . . . 72 D4
Robinsway EN9 . . . . 65 E5
Robin Way CM2 . . . . 54 B5
Robjohns Rd CM1 . . . . 53 E8
Roborough Wlk
  RM12 . . . . 155 C6
Roca Ct E11 . . . . 132 A6
Roche Ave SS4 . . . . 125 E2
Roche Cl SS4 . . . . 125 E2
Rochefort Dr SS4 . . . . 147 F8
Rochehall Way SS4 . . . . . . 148 B8
Rochester Dr SS0 . . . . 147 C4
Rochester Gdns IG1 . . . . . . 132 F4
Rochester Mews SS0 . . . . . 147 C4
Rochester Rd RM12 . . . . . . 155 B5
Rochester Way
  Basildon SS14 . . . . 142 F5
  6 Basildon SS14 . . . . 142 F8
Rocheway SS4 . . . . 126 A2
ROCHFORD 125 E2
Rochford Ave
  Brentwood CM15 . . . . 95 A4
  Ilford RM6 . . . . 134 C6
  Loughton IG10 . . . . 89 C6
  Southend-on-S SS0 . . . . . 147 E1
  Waltham Abbey EN9 . . . . 65 D5
Rochford Cl
  Hornchurch RM12 . . . . . . 155 B6
  Wickford SS11 . . . . 121 F6
Rochford Garden Way
  SS4 . . . . 125 E3
Rochford Gn IG10 . . . . 89 C6
Rochford Hall Cl SS4 . . . . . 125 F1

Roc–Rus 221

Rochford Hall Cotts
SS4 . . . . 125 D1
Rochford Ho EN9 . . . . 65 D6
Rochford Prim Sch
SS4 . . . . 125 E2
Rochford Rd
Canvey Island SS8 . . . . . . 164 D3
Chelmsford CM2 . . . . 32 C1
Southend-on-S SS2 . . . . . 147 E5
Rochford Sta SS4 . . . . . . 125 E1
Rochforte Cl SS4 . . . . . . 125 F2
Rockall SS2 . . . . 147 A7
Rockchase Gdns
RM11 . . . . 136 E5
Rock Gdns RM10 . . . . 154 B7
Rockingham Ave
RM11 . . . . 136 B4
Rocklands Ct RM17 . . . . . 173 C1
Rockleigh Ave SS9 . . . . . 147 A1
Rockleigh Ct CM15 . . . . . 95 A2
Rockwell Rd RM10 . . . . . . 154 B7
Rockwood Gdns IG10 . . . . . 89 C6
Rodbridge Dr SS1 . . . . . . 167 F8
Roden Cl CM17 . . . . 11 F4
Roden St IG1 . . . . 133 A1
Roden Terr CM5 . . . . 15 A1
Roding CM14 . . . . 94 B1
Roding Ave IG8 . . . . 110 E4
Roding Cl
Fyfield CM5 . . . . 27 D2
Great Wakering SS3 . . . . . 150 B4
Roding Dr CM15 . . . . 71 F2
Roding Gdns IG10 . . . . . . 88 E3
Roding Hall RM4 . . . . 90 B6
Roding Hospl (BUPA)
IG4 . . . . 132 D8
Roding La
Buckhurst Hill IG9, IG7 . . . . 88 E1
Chigwell IG7 . . . . 89 A1
Roding La N IG8 . . . . 110 E2
Roding La S IG4 . . . . 132 D7
Roding Leigh CM3 . . . . . . 101 E7
Roding Lo IG1 . . . . 132 D5
Roding Prim Sch
Barking RM8 . . . . 153 C7
Woodford IG8 . . . . 110 E3
Roding Rd IG10 . . . . 88 F3
Rodings Ave SS17 . . . . . . 160 D4
Rodings Ct E4 . . . . 109 D5
Rodings Prim Sch CM6 . . . 15 C8
Rodings The
Southend-on-S SS9 . . . . . . 146 D7
Upminster RM14 . . . . 137 D5
5 Woodford IG8 . . . . 110 C4
Roding Valley High Sch
IG10 . . . . 88 E4
Roding Valley Sta
IG9 . . . . 110 D6
Roding View
Buckhurst Hill IG9 . . . . 88 D1
Chipping Ongar CM5 . . . . . 49 B4
Roding Way
Rainham RM13 . . . . 155 D3
Wickford SS12 . . . . 121 E7
Rodney Cres EN11 . . . . . . 21 A8
Rodney Rd
Chipping Ongar CM5 . . . . . 48 F2
Wanstead E11 . . . . 132 B7
Rodney Way
Chelmsford CM1 . . . . 53 E7
Romford RM7 . . . . 113 B2
Rodwells SS3 . . . . 149 E4
Roebuck Ct E4 . . . . 109 C3
Roebuck Hts IG9 . . . . 88 C2
Roebuck La IG9 . . . . 88 C1
Roebuck Rd IG6 . . . . 112 B4
Roebuck Trad Est
IG6 . . . . 112 B4
Roedean Cl SS2 . . . . 148 F1
Roedean Dr RM1 . . . . 135 E7
Roedean Gdns SS2 . . . . . . 148 F2
Roger Reede's Almshouses RM1 . . . . . . 135 E7
Rogers Gdns RM10 . . . . . . 154 A7
Rogers Ho 9 RM10 . . . . . . 135 A1
Rogers Rd
Dagenham RM10 . . . . 154 A7
Grays RM17 . . . . 173 C2
Roggel Rd SS8 . . . . 164 D2
Rohan Ct SS6 . . . . 101 D6
Rohan Pl 4 IG4 . . . . 132 F6
Rokeby Gdns IG8 . . . . 110 A2
Rokells SS14 . . . . 142 A7
Rokescroft SS13 . . . . 143 A5
Roland La SS8 . . . . 164 B4
Rolands Cl CM1 . . . . 32 B7
Roles Gr RM6 . . . . 134 E7
Rollason Way CM14 . . . . . 116 C7
Rollestons CM1 . . . . 52 F8
Roll Gdns IG2 . . . . 133 A6
Rolls Ct The E4 . . . . 109 C5
Rolls Park Ave E4 . . . . . . 109 B5
Rolls Park Rd E4 . . . . 109 B5
Romagne Cl SS17 . . . . 159 F3
Romainville Way SS8 . . . . . 163 C3
Roman RM18 . . . . 175 C2
Roman Cl
Maldon CM9 . . . . 36 F4
Mountnessing CM15 . . . . . 95 E8
Rainham RM13 . . . . 154 D3
Roman Ct 3 SS11 . . . . . . 122 A5
Roman Ho
3 Chelmsford CM2 . . . . . . 32 B1
Rainham RM13 . . . . 154 D3
Roman Lo IG9 . . . . 88 C1
Roman Mews 7 EN11 . . . . 21 A7
Roman Rd
Ilford IG1 . . . . 152 B6
Roman Rd *continued*
Ingatestone CM4 . . . . 73 F1
Little Waltham CM3 . . . . . . 19 B5
Mountnessing CM15 . . . . . 95 E8
Roman Rise CM21 . . . . . . 1 D2
Romans Farm Chase
CM0 . . . . 106 C7
Romanshurst CM9 . . . . . . 37 A4
Romans Pl CM1 . . . . 31 B1
Roman St 8 EN11 . . . . . . 21 A7
Romans Way CM1 . . . . 31 B1
Roman Vale CM17 . . . . 11 C5
Roman Way
Billericay CM12 . . . . 119 A8
Burnham-on-C CM0 . . . . . 106 B8
Waltham Abbey EN9 . . . . . 65 B4
Romany Stps 17 SS1 . . . . 167 C7
Rom Cres RM7 . . . . 135 F4
Romeland EN9 . . . . 65 C6
ROMFORD 135 D7
Romford Rd
Aveley RM15 . . . . 171 C7
Chipping Ongar CM5 . . . . . 70 F7
Ilford E12 . . . . 133 A1
Redbridge IG6 . . . . 112 C5
Upminster RM15 . . . . 156 C1
Romford Sta RM1 . . . . . . 135 E5
Romney Chase RM11 . . . . . 137 A5
Romney Ho SS4 . . . . 125 F2
Romney Rd CM12 . . . . 96 F1
Romsey Cl
Hockley SS5 . . . . 124 D6
South Benfleet SS7 . . . . . . 144 B5
Stanford-le-H SS17 . . . . . . 160 B1
Romsey Cres SS7 . . . . . . 144 B5
Romsey Dr SS7 . . . . 144 B5
Romsey Gdns RM9 . . . . . . 153 D4
Romsey Rd
Dagenham RM9 . . . . 153 D4
South Benfleet SS7 . . . . . . 144 A5
Romsey Way SS7 . . . . 144 B5
Romside Pl 4 RM7 . . . . . . 135 D7
Rom Valley Way RM7 . . . . 135 E4
Ronald Dr SS6 . . . . 123 A4
Ronald Hill Gr SS9 . . . . . . 146 D1
Ronald Park Ave SS0 . . . . . 147 C2
Ronald Rd RM3 . . . . 115 A2
Roneo Cnr RM12 . . . . 135 F3
Roneo Link RM12 . . . . 135 F3
Ronnie La E12 . . . . 152 A8
Ron Todd Cl RM10 . . . . . . 154 A4
Ronver Lo E4 . . . . 109 E7
Roodegate SS14 . . . . 142 A6
Rook Cl RM13 . . . . 155 A5
Rookery Cl
Rayleigh SS6 . . . . 123 C2
Stanford-le-H SS17 . . . . . . 160 B1
Rookery Cres RM10 . . . . . 154 B5
Rookery Ct RM20 . . . . 177 A8
Rookery Hill SS17 . . . . . . 161 C2
Rookery La CM3 . . . . 80 E1
Rookery Rd CM4 . . . . 50 D3
Rookery The RM20 . . . . . . 177 A8
Rookery View RM17 . . . . . 173 D1
Rookes Cres CM1 . . . . 53 F8
Rookley Ct 15 RM19 . . . . . 171 B1
Rook Lo IG1 . . . . 132 D5
Rookwood Ave IG10 . . . . . 89 C6
Rookwood Cl RM17 . . . . . . 173 B2
Rookwood Gdns E4 . . . . . 109 F8
Rookwood Ho 2
IG11 . . . . 152 D3
Rookyards SS16 . . . . 142 E5
Roosevel Ave SS8 . . . . . . 164 A4
Roosevelt Rd 1 SS15 . . . . 141 A6
Roosevelt Way RM10 . . . . . 154 D6
Roothings The CM9 . . . . . . 37 B5
Roots Hall Ave SS2 . . . . . 147 F2
Roots Hall Dr SS2 . . . . . . 147 E2
Roots Hall (Southend United FC) SS2 . . . . 147 E2
Ropers Ave E4 . . . . 109 C5
Roper's Chase CM1 . . . . . 53 A7
Ropers Yd 12 CM14 . . . . . 116 C8
Rope Wlk CM9 . . . . 37 A1
Rosalind Ct 6 IG11 . . . . . 153 A5
Rosary Ct CM15 . . . . 116 E8
Rosary Gdns SS0 . . . . 147 B4
Rosbach Rd SS8 . . . . 164 D3
Rosberg Rd SS8 . . . . 164 E3
Roscommon Way
SS8 . . . . 163 C4
Rose Acre SS14 . . . . 142 F6
Roseacre Cl RM11 . . . . . . 136 F4
Roseacres CM21 . . . . 1 D3
Rose Ave E18 . . . . 110 B1
Rosebank EN9 . . . . 65 E6
Rose Bank CM14 . . . . 116 D7
Rosebank Ave RM12 . . . . . 155 C7
Rosebay Ave CM12 . . . . . . 96 F5
Roseberry Ave
Basildon SS16 . . . . 141 B4
South Benfleet SS7 . . . . . . 144 C7
Roseberry Cl RM14 . . . . . . 137 F5
Roseberry Ct SS7 . . . . . . 144 C7
Roseberry Gdns
RM14 . . . . 137 F5
Roseberry Wlk SS7 . . . . . 144 C7
Rosebery Rd
Chelmsford CM2 . . . . 54 B8
Grays RM17 . . . . 177 E8
Rosebury Ct CM13 . . . . . . 95 D3
Rosebury Sq 2 IG8 . . . . . . 111 A3
Rose Cl 10 SS12 . . . . 121 E5
Rose Cotts
Harlow CM17 . . . . 24 F5
Willingale CM5 . . . . 28 D3
Rosecroft Cl SS16 . . . . . . 141 A4
Rose & Crown Mews
CM0 . . . . 84 D4
Rose Ct IG1 . . . . 152 B6
Rosedale Dr RM9 . . . . 153 B5
Rosedale Gdns RM9 . . . . . 153 B5
Rosedale Rd
Dagenham RM9 . . . . 153 B5
Grays RM17 . . . . 173 D1
Romford RM1 . . . . 135 C8
Rosedene Gdns IG2 . . . . . 133 A7
Rose Dr CM0 . . . . 84 D3
Rose Glen
Chelmsford CM2 . . . . 54 C7
Romford RM7 . . . . 135 E3
Rosehatch Ave RM6 . . . . . 134 D8
Rose La
Billericay CM12 . . . . 97 A2
Dagenham RM6 . . . . 134 E7
Roselaine SS14 . . . . 142 B7
Roselands Ave EN11 . . . . . 8 A1
Roselawn Fields CM1 . . . . 32 B8
Roseley Cotts CM20 . . . . . 10 B4
Rosemary Ave RM1 . . . . . . 135 F8
Rosemary Cl
1 Harlow CM17 . . . . 11 C4
South Ockendon RM15 . . . . 157 C2
Rosemary Cotts CM3 . . . . . 20 E1
Rosemary Dr IG4 . . . . 132 D6
Rosemary Gdns RM8 . . . . . 134 F3
Rosemary Lo SS2 . . . . 147 F1
Rosemead SS7 . . . . 144 C7
Rosemead Gdns CM13 . . . . 95 D5
Rosemount CM19 . . . . 23 A5
Rosemount Cl IG8 . . . . . . 110 F4
Rose Park Ct IG5 . . . . 110 F1
Rose Rd SS8 . . . . 164 A3
Roserna Rd SS8 . . . . 164 D3
Rose St DA11 . . . . 178 B1
Roses The IG8 . . . . 109 F3
Rose Tree Mews IG8 . . . . . 110 E4
Rosetti Terr 4 RM8 . . . . . 153 B8
Rose Vale EN11 . . . . 21 A6
Rose Valley CM14 . . . . . . 116 D7
Rose Valley Cres
SS17 . . . . 160 E4
Rose Way SS4 . . . . 148 A8
Rosewood Ave RM12 . . . . . 155 A7
Rosewood Cl RM15 . . . . . . 157 E2
Rosewood Ct RM6 . . . . . . 134 C6
Rosewood Ho 8
CM14 . . . . 116 C7
Rosewood La SS3 . . . . 168 F7
Rosher Ho DA11 . . . . 178 F1
ROSHERVILLE 178 E1
Rosherville CE Prim Sch
DA11 . . . . 178 E1
Rosherville Way
DA11 . . . . 178 E1
Rosilian Dr SS5 . . . . 102 C1
Roslings Cl CM1 . . . . 31 D5
Roslyn Gdns RM2 . . . . 113 F1
Rossall Cl RM11 . . . . 136 A5
Ross Ave RM8 . . . . 134 F3
Rossdene Gdns CM6 . . . . . 15 D7
Rossendale CM1 . . . . 31 E1
Rosshill Ind Pk SS2 . . . . . 148 A4
Rossiter Rd SS3 . . . . 168 H8
Rosslyn Ave
Chingford E4 . . . . 109 F8
Dagenham RM8 . . . . 135 A4
Romford RM3 . . . . 114 F1
Rosslyn Cl SS5 . . . . 124 E7
Rosslyn Ct SS17 . . . . 160 C1
Rosslyn Rd
Barking IG11 . . . . 152 D5
Billericay CM12 . . . . 96 F2
Hockley SS5 . . . . 124 E7
Ross Way SS16 . . . . 141 B3
Rothbury Ave RM13 . . . . . 170 B8
Rothbury Ho 5 RM3 . . . . . 114 D4
Rothbury Rd CM1 . . . . 31 D1
Roth Dr CM13 . . . . 117 B8
Rothesay Ave CM2 . . . . . . 54 A8
Rothmans Ave CM2 . . . . . . 54 E6
Rothwell Cl SS9 . . . . 146 C6
Rothwell Gdns RM9 . . . . . . 153 C4
Rothwell Rd RM9 . . . . 153 C4
Rotunda The 1 RM7 . . . . . 135 D6
Rough Hill Farm Cotts
CM3 . . . . 78 C7
Roughtallys CM16 . . . . 46 F4
Roughtons CM2 . . . . 54 C3
Roundacre SS14 . . . . 142 A6
Roundaway Rd IG5 . . . . . . 110 F1
ROUNDBUSH 81 B8
Roundbush Bglws CM9 . . . . 81 C8
ROUNDBUSH GREEN 5 C2
Roundbush Rd CM9 . . . . . . 81 A8
Rounders Ct 12 RM10 . . . . 154 B6
Round Hill Rd SS7 . . . . . . 145 A2
Roundhills EN9 . . . . 65 E4
Roundmead Ave IG10 . . . . . 89 A6
Roundmead Cl IG10 . . . . . 89 A7
Roundwood Ave CM13 . . . . 95 B2
Roundwood Gr CM13 . . . . . 95 B2
Roundwood Lake
CM13 . . . . 95 B2
Rounton Rd EN9 . . . . 65 E6
Rous Chase CM2 . . . . 54 B1
Rous Rd IG9 . . . . 88 E1
Rover Ave IG6 . . . . 111 F4
Rowallen Par RM8 . . . . . . 134 C3
Rowan Cl
Ilford IG1 . . . . 152 D7
Rayleigh SS6 . . . . 123 B6
Rowan Dr CM9 . . . . 37 C5
Rowan Gr RM15 . . . . 171 C6
Rowan Green E CM13 . . . . 116 F7
Rowan Green W
CM13 . . . . 116 F7
Rowan Ho
4 Basildon SS13 . . . . 143 B8
Ilford IG1 . . . . 152 D7
Rowans EN9 . . . . 66 C4
Rowans The
Aveley RM15 . . . . 171 C5
Billericay CM11 . . . . 119 D8
Rayleigh SS9 . . . . 146 B6
Rowans Way
Loughton IG10 . . . . 88 F5
Wickford SS11 . . . . 121 E8
Rowan Way
Canewdon SS4 . . . . 104 E1
Ilford RM6 . . . . 134 C8
South Ockendon RM15 . . . . 157 C1
Rowan Wlk
Hornchurch RM11 . . . . 136 D7
Sawbridgeworth CM21 . . . . . 1 E2
Southend-on-S SS9 . . . . . . 146 D6
Rowden Par E4 . . . . 109 A4
Rowden Park Gdns
E4 . . . . 109 A4
Rowden Rd E4 . . . . 109 B4
Rowdowns Rd RM9 . . . . . . 153 F5
Rowe Gdns IG11 . . . . 153 A3
Rowenhall SS15 . . . . 140 F6
Rowhedge CM13 . . . . 117 B7
Rowhedge Cl SS13 . . . . . . 121 D2
Rowland Cres IG7 . . . . . . 111 E6
Rowlands Rd RM8 . . . . . . 134 F2
Rowlands The SS7 . . . . . . 144 E3
Rowland Wlk RM4 . . . . . . 113 E7
Rowley Mead CM16 . . . . . . 46 C6
Rowley Rd RM16 . . . . 174 A8
Rowney Gdns
Dagenham RM9 . . . . 153 C6
Sawbridgeworth CM21 . . . . 11 C8
Rowney Rd RM9 . . . . 153 B6
Rowney Wood CM21 . . . . . . 1 C1
Rows The 1 CM20 . . . . . . 10 D1
Roxburgh Ave RM14 . . . . . 137 C1
ROXWELL 30 B6
Roxwell Ave CM1 . . . . 31 D3
Roxwell CE Prim Sch
CM1 . . . . 30 A6
Roxwell Cres SS12 . . . . . . 121 E6
Roxwell Gdns CM13 . . . . . 95 C4
Roxwell Ho IG10 . . . . 88 E2
Roxwell Rd
Barking IG11 . . . . 153 A3
Chelmsford CM1 . . . . 31 C4
Roxwell CM1 . . . . 30 E5
Writtle CM1 . . . . 31 A4
Roxwell Way IG8 . . . . 110 C3
Roxy Ave RM6 . . . . 134 C4
Royal Artillery Way
SS2 . . . . 148 F2
Royal Cl
Ilford IG3 . . . . 134 A4
Rochford SS4 . . . . 125 D5
Royal Cres IG2 . . . . 133 D5
Royal Ct
Basildon SS15 . . . . 141 B7
3 Brentwood CM14 . . . . . . 116 C7
Maldon CM9 . . . . 37 A1
Rayleigh SS9 . . . . 146 B8
Southend-on-S SS2 . . . . . . 148 A1
Royal Docks Rd E6 . . . . . . 152 B1
Royal Gunpowder Mills★
EN9 . . . . 65 B7
Royal Jubilee Ct RM2 . . . . 136 A8
Royal Liberty Sch The
RM2 . . . . 136 C8
Royal Mews SS1 . . . . 167 A7
Royal Oak Chase
SS15 . . . . 141 E8
Royal Oak Ct RM8 . . . . . . 134 C2
Royal Oak Dr SS11 . . . . . . 122 A8
Royal Par 16 RM10 . . . . . . 154 B6
Royal Pier Mews 9
DA11 . . . . 179 B1
Royal Pier Rd DA12 . . . . . 179 C1
Royals The SS1 . . . . 167 A7
Royal Terr SS1 . . . . 167 A7
Roycraft Ave IG11 . . . . . . 152 F3
Roycroft Cl E18 . . . . 110 B2
ROYDON 9 B1
Roydon Bridge SS14 . . . . . 142 D8
Roydonbury Ind Est
CM19 . . . . 22 E8
Roydon Cl IG10 . . . . 88 E2
ROYDON HAMLET 22 C4
Roydon Lodge Chalet Est
CM19 . . . . 9 C1
Roydon Mill Leisure Pk
CM19 . . . . 9 A1
Roydon Prim Sch
CM19 . . . . 22 B8
Roydon Rd
Harlow CM19 . . . . 9 E1
Stanstead Abbotts SG12 . . . . 9 E4
Roydon Sta CM19 . . . . 9 B2
Royer Cl SS5 . . . . 125 A4
Roy Gdns IG2 . . . . 133 F6
Royle Cl RM2 . . . . 136 B6
Royston Ave
Basildon SS15 . . . . 119 D1
Chingford E4 . . . . 109 B5
Southend-on-S SS2 . . . . . . 148 B3
Royston Ct IG1 . . . . 132 D5
Royston Gdns IG1 . . . . . . 132 D5
Royston Par IG1 . . . . 132 D5
Royston Rd RM3 . . . . 115 A3
Rubens Cl SS3 . . . . 168 G8
Rubens Gate CM1 . . . . 32 F7
Rubicon Ave SS11 . . . . . . 121 F8
Rubin Pl EN3 . . . . 65 A2
Ruby Ct
5 Rainham RM13 . . . . 155 A1
Southend-on-S SS9 . . . . . . 146 E5
RUDLEY GREEN 58 C2
Rudyard Ct CM14 . . . . 116 B5
Rue De St Lawrence
EN9 . . . . 65 C5
Ruffles Cl SS6 . . . . 123 E3
Rugby Gdns RM9 . . . . 153 C6
Rugby Rd RM9 . . . . 153 C6
Rumbold Rd EN11 . . . . . . 21 C8
Rumbullion Dr CM12 . . . . . 96 F3
Rumford Sh Hall The
RM1 . . . . 135 E7
Rumsey Fields CM3 . . . . . . 56 F7
Rumsey Row CM1 . . . . 31 B1
Runcorn Ho 5 RM3 . . . . . . 114 E4
Rundells CM18 . . . . 24 A4
Rundells Wlk SS14 . . . . . . 142 E7
Rundels Cotts SS7 . . . . . . 145 A6
Rundels The SS7 . . . . 145 A6
Runnel Ct 7 IG11 . . . . 152 C3
Running Mare La CM2 . . . . 54 A3
Running Waters
CM13 . . . . 117 A6
Runnymede Chase
SS7 . . . . 145 A5
Runnymede Ct SS17 . . . . . 160 C1
Runnymede Rd
Canvey Island SS8 . . . . . . 164 B3
Stanford-le-H SS17 . . . . . . 160 C1
Runsell Cl CM3 . . . . 56 F7
RUNSELL GREEN 57 B7
Runsell La CM3 . . . . 56 F8
Runsell View CM3 . . . . 57 A7
RUNWELL 99 E1
Runwell Chase SS11 . . . . . 100 A3
Runwell Gdns SS11 . . . . . . 99 D2
Runwell Hospl SS11 . . . . . 100 A5
Runwell Prim Sch
SS11 . . . . 99 D2
Runwell Rd SS11 . . . . 100 B3
Runwell Terr SS1 . . . . 166 F7
Runwood Rd SS8 . . . . 163 C3
Rupert Rd CM0 . . . . 84 C4
Rural Cl RM11 . . . . 136 B3
Rural Vale DA11 . . . . 178 E1
Rurik Ct CM9 . . . . 58 F8
Rushbottom La SS7 . . . . . . 144 B7
Rush Cl
South Benfleet SS7 . . . . . . 144 B6
Stanstead Abbotts SG12 . . . . 8 C4
Rushcroft Rd E4 . . . . 109 B3
Rush Croft Sports Coll
E4 . . . . 109 B3
Rushdene Ct CM15 . . . . . . 94 C2
Rushdene Rd
Billericay CM12 . . . . 96 F1
Brentwood CM15 . . . . 94 C2
Rushden Gdns
Ilford IG5 . . . . 133 A8
Redbridge IG5 . . . . 111 A1
Rushdon Cl
Grays RM17 . . . . 173 A3
Romford RM1 . . . . 136 A6
Rushdon Ct RM1 . . . . 136 A6
Rush Dr EN9 . . . . 65 C3
Rushes La CM0 . . . . 63 A1
Rushes Mead CM18 . . . . . . 23 E6
Rushfield CM21 . . . . 1 E2
Rush Green Gdns
RM7 . . . . 135 C3
Rush Green Inf Sch
RM7 . . . . 135 D3
Rush Green Jun Sch
RM7 . . . . 135 D3
Rush Green Rd RM7 . . . . . 135 D3
Rushley SS13 . . . . 121 D1
Rushley Cl
Grays RM16 . . . . 173 D5
Great Wakering SS3 . . . . . 150 A4
Rushleydale CM1 . . . . 32 E5
Rushmere Ave RM14 . . . . . 137 C1
Rusholme Ave RM10 . . . . . 135 A1
Rushton Gr CM17 . . . . 24 E8
Ruskin Ave
Southend-on-S SS2 . . . . . . 148 B2
Upminster RM14 . . . . 137 C4
Waltham Abbey EN9 . . . . . . 65 E5
Ruskin Dene CM12 . . . . . . 97 A3
Ruskin Gdns RM3 . . . . 114 B3
Ruskin Gr DA1 . . . . 176 A2
Ruskin Path 2 SS12 . . . . . 121 D5
Ruskin Rd
Belvedere DA17 . . . . 169 A2
Chelmsford CM2 . . . . 32 E2
Grays RM16 . . . . 174 A2
Stanford-le-H SS17 . . . . . . 160 C1
Ruskoi Rd SS8 . . . . 163 F5
Rusper Rd RM9 . . . . 153 C6
Russell Cl
Basildon SS15 . . . . 141 B6
Brentwood CM15 . . . . 94 B2
Russell Ct SS11 . . . . 121 F7
Russell Gdns
Chelmsford CM2 . . . . 54 A4
Ilford IG1 . . . . 133 D4
Wickford SS11 . . . . 121 F7
Russell Gr SS4 . . . . 126 A2
RUSSELL GREEN 20 D6
Russell Lo 5 E4 . . . . 109 C8
Russell Quay DA11 . . . . . . 179 A1
Russell Rd
Buckhurst Hill IG9 . . . . 88 C1

Russell Rd *continued*
Gravesend DA12 . . . . **179** D1
Grays RM17 . . . . **173** A2
North Fambridge CM3 . . . . **81** B1
Tilbury RM18 . . . . **178** F5
Tilbury RM18 . . . . **178** F6
Russell Way CM1 . . . . . . **53** E7
Russell Wilson Ct
RM3 . . . . **115** A2
Russet Cl SS17 . . . . **160** D3
Russet Ho RM17 . . . . . . **178** C7
Russets CM2 . . . . **54** D3
Russets Cl E4 . . . . **109** D6
Russets The SS4 . . . . . . **125** D5
Russetts
Basildon SS16 . . . . **141** A5
Hornchurch RM11 . . . . . **136** E7
Russet Way
Burnham-on-C CM0 . . . . **106** C6
Hockley SS5 . . . . **124** F4
Rustic Cl RM14 . . . . **137** E3
Rutherford Cl
Billericay CM12 . . . . **97** A5
Southend-on-S SS9 . . . . **146** C6
Rutherfords CM1 . . . . . . **19** B1
Ruthven Cl SS12 . . . . . . **121** D6
Ruthven Rd SS15 . . . . . **141** A6
Rutland App RM11 . . . . . **137** A6
Rutland Ave SS1 . . . . . . **167** E7
Rutland Cl SS15 . . . . . . **141** A6
Rutland Dr
Hornchurch RM11 . . . . . **137** A6
Rayleigh SS6 . . . . **123** C7
Rutland Gate DA17 . . . . . **169** B1
Rutland Gdns
Dagenham RM8 . . . . . . **153** C7
Rochford SS4 . . . . **125** C5
Rutland Ho RM7 . . . . . . **113** A1
Rutland Rd
Chelmsford CM1 . . . . . . **32** A7
Ilford IG1 . . . . **133** B1
North Fambridge CM3 . . . **103** A7
Wanstead E11 . . . . **132** B6
Rutley Cl RM14 . . . . **114** D1
Ryan Ct RM7 . . . . **135** C5
Rydal Cl
Hullbridge SS5 . . . . **101** D3
Rayleigh SS6 . . . . **123** E2
Rydal Dr CM9 . . . . **59** B8
Ryde Cl SS9 . . . . **146** B5
Ryde Dr SS17 . . . . **175** C8
Ryder Gdns RM13 . . . . . **154** F6
Ryder Way SS13 . . . . . . **121** D2
Ryde The SS9 . . . . **146** B5
Rye Cl RM12 . . . . **155** C7
Ryecroft CM19 . . . . **23** B8
Ryecroft Ave IG5 . . . . . . **111** B1
Ryedene SS16 . . . . **142** F3
Ryedene Cl SS16 . . . . . . **142** E3
Ryedene Com Prim Sch
SS16 . . . . **142** F3
Ryedene Pl SS16 . . . . . . **142** F3
Ryefeld Cl EN11 . . . .**8** B2
Rye Field The CM3 . . . . . . **34** D3
RYE HILL **23** E1
Rye Hill Rd CM18 . . . . . . **23** E2
Rye House Gatehouse *★*
EN11 . . . . **21** D8
Rye House Sta EN11 . . . . **21** C8
Rye Mead SS16 . . . . **141** C4
Rye Mead Cotts EN11 . . . **21** C8
RYE PARK **21** B7
Rye Park Ind Est EN11 . . . **21** D7
Rye Rd EN11 . . . . **21** C8
Ryes La CM22 . . . .**3** B7
Rye Wlk CM4 . . . . **74** A2
Rykhill RM16 . . . . **174** B3
Rylands Rd SS2 . . . . **148** D2
Ryle The CM1 . . . . **53** A8
Rysley CM3 . . . . **34** D4

S

Sabina Rd RM16 . . . . **174** C2
SABINE'S GREEN **92** F6
Sabines Rd RM4 . . . . **92** E6
Sable Way SS15 . . . . **140** F7
Sachfield Dr RM16 . . . . . **172** E3
Sackville Cl CM1 . . . . **31** E3
Sackville Cres RM3 . . . . . **114** E2
Sackville Gdns IG1 . . . . . **132** F3
Sackville Rd SS4 . . . . . . **148** E1
Sacred Heart of Mary
Girls' Sch RM14 . . . . . . **137** B2
Sacred Heart RC Prim Sch
SS1 . . . . **167** C8
Saddle Rise CM1 . . . . **32** E8
Saddleworth Rd RM3 . . . . **114** C4
Saddleworth Sq RM3 . . . . **114** C4
Sadlers SS7 . . . . **144** B6
Sadlers Cl CM11 . . . . **97** D5
Sadlers Mead CM18 . . . . . **24** A7
Saffory Cl SS9 . . . . **146** C7
Saffron Cl
Horndon on t H SS17 . . . **160** A3
West Horndon CM13 . . . . **139** D5
Saffron Croft CM9 . . . . . . **36** E2
Saffron Ct SS15 . . . . **140** F6
Saffron Dr SS14 . . . . **142** D7
Saffron Gdns SS17 . . . . . **159** F1
Saffron Rd
Grays RM16 . . . . **172** C2
Romford RM5 . . . . **113** D1
Saffron Wlk CM11 . . . . . . **97** B2
Sage Mews SS17 . . . . . . **160** E3

St Agnes Dr SS8 . . . . **163** D4
St Agnes Rd CM12 . . . . . **119** C3
St Aidans Ct 4 IG11 . . . . **153** B3
St Aidan's RC Prim Sch
IG1 . . . . **133** D3
St Albans Ave RM14 . . . . **137** E2
St Alban's Ave E6 . . . . . . **152** A2
St Alban's Cres IG8 . . . . . **110** A2
St Albans RC Prim Sch
CM20 . . . . **10** F2
St Alban's RC Prim Sch
RM12 . . . . **155** B5
St Albans Rd IG3 . . . . . . **133** F4
St Alban's Rd
Coopersale CM16 . . . . . . **46** D2
Woodford IG8 . . . . **110** A3
St Andrews Ave
Hornchurch RM12 . . . . . **155** A8
Rainham RM12 . . . . **154** F7
St Andrews CE Prim Sch
CM16 . . . . **47** C6
St Andrew's CE Prim Sch
SG12 . . . .**8** D4
St Andrews Cl
Canvey Island SS8 . . . . . **163** D4
North Weald Bassett
CM16 . . . . **47** D7
St Andrews Ct 15
DA11 . . . . **179** B1
St Andrews Dr CM11 . . . . . **97** B3
St Andrew's Ho CM20 . . . . **10** F2
St Andrews La 2
SS15 . . . . **141** C7
St Andrew's Mdw
CM18 . . . . **23** F7
St Andrews Pl CM15 . . . . **116** F8
St Andrews Rd
Boreham CM3 . . . . **20** F1
Romford RM7 . . . . **135** D5
Southend-on-S SS3 . . . . **168** D6
St Andrew's Rd
Redbridge IG1 . . . . **132** F4
Rochford SS4 . . . . **125** E2
Tilbury RM18 . . . . **178** E5
St Anne Line RC Jun & Inf
Schs SS15 . . . . **141** F6
St Annes RM16 . . . . **173** A4
St Annes Cl RM16 . . . . . **173** B5
St Annes Ct CM1 . . . . **32** C3
St Anne's Pk EN10 . . . . . . **21** A4
St Annes Rd SS8 . . . . . . **164** E3
St Anne's Rd CM15 . . . . . **95** C8
St Anne's Sch CM2 . . . . . . **32** A1
St Annes Terr 6 IG6 . . . . **111** E5
St Ann's IG11 . . . . **152** C4
St Anns Cl 3 SS15 . . . . . **141** C7
St Ann's Rd
2 Barking IG11 . . . . . . **152** C4
Southend-on-S SS2 . . . . **148** A1
St Anselm's RC Prim Sch
DA1 . . . . **176** A2
St Anthony's Ave IG8 . . . . **110** C3
St Anthony's Dr CM2 . . . . . **54** C7
St Antony's RC Prim Sch
IG8 . . . . **110** A6
St Aubyn's Sch IG8 . . . . . **109** F3
St Audrey's SS1 . . . . **168** B7
St Augustine Rd
RM16 . . . . **174** B2
St Augustine's Ave
SS1 . . . . **168** B7
St Augustine's RC Prim
Sch
Hoddesdon EN11 . . . . . . **21** B6
Ilford IG2 . . . . **133** B6
St Awdry's Rd IG11 . . . . . **152** D5
St Barnabas Rd IG8 . . . . **110** C3
St Bede's RC Prim Sch
RM6 . . . . **134** C6
St Benet's Rd SS2 . . . . . **147** F3
St Bernard's High Sch &
Art Coll SS0 . . . . **166** E8
St Catharine's Rd EN10 . . . **21** A4
St Catherine's Hoddesdon
CE Prim Sch EN11 . . . . **21** B6
St Catherine's Rd
Chelmsford CM1 . . . . . . **31** E2
Chingford E4 . . . . **109** A8
St Cecilia Rd RM16 . . . . . **174** B2
St Cedd's CE Prim Sch
CM0 . . . . **42** B2
St Cedds Ct RM16 . . . . . **173** B5
St Cedd's Sch CM1 . . . . . . **32** A4
St Chads Cl 4 SS15 . . . . **141** C7
St Chad's Gdns RM6 . . . . **134** E4
St Chad's Rd
Dagenham RM6 . . . . . . **134** E4
Tilbury RM16, RM18 . . . . **179** A7
St Charles Dr SS11 . . . . . **121** E7
St Charles Rd CM14 . . . . . **94** B1
St Christopher Sch The
SS9 . . . . **146** F4
St Christophers Cl
SS8 . . . . **163** D4
St Clair Cl IG5 . . . . **110** F1
St Clare Mdw SS4 . . . . . . **125** F3
St Clement's Ave
Grays RM20 . . . . **177** B8
Southend-on-S SS9 . . . . **146** E2
St Clements Cl SS5 . . . . . **125** A4
St Clement's Cl SS7 . . . . **144** D5
St Clement's Cres
SS7 . . . . **144** D5
St Clements Ct
3 Grays RM17 . . . . **177** F8
Purfleet RM19 . . . . **171** A2
Waltham Abbey EN9 . . . . **65** C6

St Clement's Ct SS9 . . . . **165** D8
St Clements Ct SS9 . . . . . **165** D8
St Clements Rd DA9 . . . . **177** C3
St Clement's Rd
Grays RM20 . . . . **177** C7
South Benfleet SS7 . . . . **144** D5
St Clement's Way
RM20 . . . . **176** F8
St Cleres Cres SS11 . . . . **121** F7
St Clere's Sch SS17 . . . . . **175** C8
St Cleres Way CM3 . . . . . **56** D7
St Cross Ct EN11 . . . . **21** A4
St Cross RC Prim Sch
EN11 . . . . **21** A4
St Cuthberts Rd EN11 . . . . .**8** C1
St Davids Ct
Basildon SS16 . . . . **142** E3
5 Wanstead E11 . . . . . **132** B6
St David's Ct RM1 . . . . . . **135** F4
St David's Dr SS9 . . . . . . **146** A3
St David's Rd SS16 . . . . . **141** B4
St Davids Terr SS9 . . . . . **146** A3
St David's Way SS11 . . . . **121** E7
St Davids Wlk SS8 . . . . . **163** D4
St Dionis Rd E12 . . . . **132** E1
St Dunstan's Rd SG12 . . . . .**9** D8
St Edith's Ct CM12 . . . . . . **97** A1
St Ediths La CM12 . . . . . . **97** A1
St Edmund's Cl SS2 . . . . **148** C3
St Edmunds Rd DA1 . . . . **176** A3
St Edmund's Rd IG1 . . . . **132** F5
St Edmund's Way
CM17 . . . . **11** C4
St Edward's CE Comp Sch
RM7 . . . . **135** A5
St Edward's CE Prim Sch
RM1 . . . . **135** E8
St Edwards Way RM1,
RM7 . . . . **135** D6
St Egberts Way E4 . . . . . . **87** C1
SS Peter & Paul's Prim
Sch IG3 . . . . **133** D1
St Erkenwald Mews
IG11 . . . . **152** D4
St Erkenwald Rd
IG11 . . . . **152** D4
St Erkenwalds Ct SS1 . . . **167** C8
St Ethelburga Rd RM3 . . . **115** A1
St Fabian's Dr CM1 . . . . . . **31** E4
St Fidelis' Rd DA8 . . . . . . **169** D1
St Francis Ct SS2 . . . . . . **148** C1
St Francis RC Prim Sch
CM9 . . . . **36** F3
St Francis' Rd DA8 . . . . . **169** D2
St Francis Way
Grays RM16 . . . . **174** C3
Ilford IG1 . . . . **152** D8
St Gabriel's Cl E11 . . . . . **132** B3
St Gabriels SS13 . . . . . . **143** B5
St George's Ave
Grays RM17 . . . . **173** C2
Hornchurch RM11 . . . . . **136** F4
St Georges Cl
Heybridge Basin CM9 . . . **37** E3
Hook End CM15 . . . . **72** B4
St Georges Ct
Brentwood CM13 . . . . . . **95** C2
Romford RM7 . . . . **135** C7
St George's Ct CM14 . . . . **94** B2
St George's Ctr DA11 . . . . **179** B1
St George's Hospl
RM12 . . . . **155** D7
St George's La SS3 . . . . . **168** F6
St George's Park Ave
SS0 . . . . **147** B2
St George's RC Prim Sch
SS3 . . . . **168** E8
St Georges Rd RM9 . . . . . **153** E8
St George's Rd IG1 . . . . . **132** F4
St Georges Wlk
Canvey Island SS8 . . . . . **163** D4
South Benfleet SS7 . . . . **144** B6
St Giles Ave RM10 . . . . . **154** B5
St Giles Cl
Dagenham RM10 . . . . . . **154** B5
Maldon CM9 . . . . **36** E2
Orsett RM16 . . . . **174** A8
St Giles Cres CM9 . . . . . . **36** E2
St Gregorys Ho CM1 . . . . . **68** A8
St Guiberts Rd SS8 . . . . . **163** E5
St Helens Ct RM13 . . . . . **155** A1
St Helen's Ct CM16 . . . . . **46** A1
St Helen's RC Inf Sch
CM14 . . . . **116** D8
St Helen's RC Prim Sch
SS0 . . . . **166** F8
St Helen's Rd
Redbridge IG1 . . . . **132** F5
Southend-on-S SS0 . . . . **166** E8
St Helens Wlk CM12 . . . . . **96** F4
St Hildas Sch SS0 . . . . . **147** C1
St Ives Cl RM3 . . . . **114** F3
St Ivians Dr RM2 . . . . . . **136** A8
St James Ave SS1 . . . . . . **168** B7
St James' Ave CM5 . . . . . **49** A1
St James Ave E SS17 . . . . **160** E3
St James Ave W SS17 . . . **160** E3
St James CE Prim Sch
CM18 . . . . **23** D4
St James Cl
Canvey Island SS8 . . . . . **163** D4
Southend-on-S SS0 . . . . **147** A3

St James Ctr CM20 . . . . . **11** A4
St James Gate IG9 . . . . . . **88** B1
St James Gdns
Ilford RM6 . . . . **134** B7
Southend-on-S SS0 . . . . **147** A3
St Jame's Ho 9 RM1 . . . **135** F6
St James La DA9 . . . . . . **176** E1
St James Mews CM12 . . . . **97** A2
St James Pk CM1 . . . . **31** D4
St James Rd SS16 . . . . . **142** D5
St James's Ave DA11 . . . . **179** A1
St James's Rd
Brentwood CM14 . . . . . **116** C7
Gravesend DA11 . . . . . . **179** A1
St James's St DA11 . . . . . **179** A1
St James's Wlk SS4 . . . . **124** C6
St John Fisher RC Jun Sch
IG10 . . . . **89** C7
St John Payne RC Comp
Sch CM1 . . . . **31** F6
St John's Ave
Brentwood CM14 . . . . . **116** D6
Chelmsford CM2 . . . . . . **54** B8
Harlow CM17 . . . . **11** C4
St John's CE Prim Sch
IG9 . . . . **88** B1
St John's CE Sch CM16 . . . **45** E1
St Johns Cl
1 Basildon SS15 . . . . . **141** C7
Great Wakering SS3 . . . . **150** B3
St John's Cl RM13 . . . . . **155** A5
St Johns Cres SS8 . . . . . **163** D3
St Johns Ct
Erith DA8 . . . . **169** D1
Mayland CM3 . . . . **83** A8
Southend-on-S SS1 . . . . **166** F7
St John's Ct IG9 . . . . **88** B1
St John's Danbury CE
Prim Sch CM3 . . . . **56** E7
St John's Dr SS6 . . . . . . **122** F4
St John's Gn CM1 . . . . **31** B1
St John's Hospl CM2 . . . . . **53** F6
St John's Lo IG10 . . . . **88** F7
St John's La SG12 . . . .**8** A6
St Johns Mews SS17 . . . . **160** F4
St Johns Pl CM11 . . . . **98** B4
St Johns RC Sch IG8 . . . . **111** A5
St Johns Rd
Grays RM16 . . . . **174** B1
Ilford IG2 . . . . **133** E4
Romford RM5 . . . . **113** C5
St John's Rd
Barking IG11 . . . . **152** E4
Billericay CM11 . . . . **97** B3
Chelmsford CM2 . . . . . . **54** B8
Chingford E4 . . . . **109** B6
Chingford, Highams Park
E17 . . . . **109** C1
Epping CM16 . . . . **45** F1
Erith DA8 . . . . **169** D1
Great Wakering SS3 . . . . **150** B3
Hadleigh SS7 . . . . **145** C3
Loughton IG10 . . . . **88** F7
Southend-on-S SS0 . . . . **166** E8
Writtle CM1 . . . . **31** B1
St John's Sch CM12 . . . . . **97** B3
St John's Way SS17 . . . . . **160** F4
St Johns Wlk CM17 . . . . . . **11** C4
St John The Baptist CE
Prim Sch CM13 . . . .**8** A5
St Joseph's Convent Sch
E11 . . . . **132** A5
St Joseph's Ct E4 . . . . **87** D2
St Josephs RC Prim Sch
IG11 . . . . **152** C4
St Joseph's RC Prim Sch
Canvey Island SS8 . . . . . **164** B4
Dagenham RM9 . . . . . . **153** F8
South Woodham Ferrers
CM3 . . . . **101** E7
Stanford-le-H SS17 . . . . **160** D2
Upminster RM14 . . . . . . **137** D2
St Joseph The Worker RC
Prim Sch CM13 . . . . **95** C3
St Judes Ct IG8 . . . . **110** E3
St Katherine's CE Prim
Sch SS8 . . . . **164** A5
St Katherines Ct SS8 . . . . **163** E3
St Kathryns Pl RM14 . . . . **137** C2
St Kilda's Rd CM15 . . . . . . **94** C2
ST LAWRENCE **62** B8
St Lawrence Ct SS9 . . . . **146** E6
St Lawrence Dr
Steeple CM0 . . . . **62** B8
St Lawrence CM0 . . . . . . **40** B1
St Lawrence Gdns
Blackmore CM4 . . . . **72** E8
Southend-on-S SS9 . . . . **146** E6
St Lawrence Hill CM0 . . . . **62** E5
St Lawrence Rd
Tillingham CM0 . . . . **63** D5
Upminster RM14 . . . . . . **137** C2
St Leonard's Ave E4 . . . . . **109** C4
St Leonards Cl RM17 . . . . **177** F8
St Leonards Gdns
IG1 . . . . **152** C7
St Leonards Rd EN9 . . . . . **43** D6
St Leonard's Rd SS1 . . . . **167** B7
St Leonards Way
RM11 . . . . **136** B2
St Luke's Ave IG1 . . . . . . **152** B7
St Lukes Cl
8 Basildon SS15 . . . . . **141** C6
Canvey Island SS8 . . . . . **163** D4
St Luke's Path 1 IG1 . . . . **152** B7
St Lukes Pl SS4 . . . . **125** E2
St Luke's RC Prim Sch
CM19 . . . . **23** C6

St Luke's Rd SS2 . . . . . . **148** C2
ST MARGARETS **8** A4
St Margarets IG11 . . . . . . **152** D4
St Margaret's Ave
SS17 . . . . **175** C8
St Margarets CE Prim Sch
IG11 . . . . **152** C5
St Margaret's CE Prim Sch
SS13 . . . . **143** D3
St Margaret's Hospl
CM16 . . . . **46** B2
St Margaret's Rd
Chelmsford CM2 . . . . . . **32** E3
Hoddesdon SG12 . . . .**8** B2
Wanstead E12 . . . . **132** C2
St Margaret's Sta SG12 . . . .**8** C4
St Mark's Ave DA11 . . . . . **178** F1
St Mark's Field SS4 . . . . . **125** F2
St Marks Pl RM10 . . . . . . **154** B6
St Marks Rd SS8 . . . . . . **163** D4
St Mark's Rd SS7 . . . . . . **145** C3
St Mark's West Essex RC
Sch CM18 . . . . **23** E7
St Martins Cl
South Benfleet SS7 . . . . **144** B7
White Roothing or White
Roding CM6 . . . . **14** C7
St Martin's Cl SS6 . . . . . . **145** C8
St Martin's Mews CM5 . . . **49** A2
St Martin's Rd EN11 . . . . . **21** C6
St Martin's Sch CM13 . . . . **95** C1
St Martins Sq SS14 . . . . . **142** A6
St Marys IG11 . . . . **152** D4
St Mary's Ave
Billericay CM12 . . . . **97** A2
Brentwood CM15 . . . . . . **95** A4
Wanstead E11 . . . . **132** B4
St Mary's Bglws CM1 . . . . . .**6** B2
St Mary's Cath *★* CM1 . . . **32** B2
St Mary's CE Prim Sch
Burnham-on-C CM0 . . . . **106** C6
Hatfield Broad Oak CM22 . . . .**3** F6
Shenfield CM15 . . . . **94** F3
Woodham Ferrers CM3 . . . **79** B4
St Marys Cl
South Benfleet SS7 . . . . **144** D1
Southend-on-S SS3 . . . . **149** D1
St Mary's Cl
Grays RM17 . . . . **178** D3
Great Baddow CM2 . . . . . **54** F3
St Mary's Cres SS13 . . . . **143** C7
St Mary's Ct CM9 . . . . **37** B2
St Mary's Ct SS2 . . . . **147** F2
St Mary's Dr SS7 . . . . . . **144** C1
St Mary's Hare Park Sch
RM2 . . . . **136** C8
St Mary's Ho 6 CM0 . . . . **106** C4
St Mary's La
Maldon CM9 . . . . **37** B2
Upminster RM14 . . . . . . **138** D3
West Horndon CM13 . . . . **139** B4
St Mary's Lo E11 . . . . **132** B5
St Mary's Mead CM1 . . . . . **19** A1
St Mary's Path SS13 . . . . **143** C7
St Mary's Prittlewell CE
Prim Sch SS2 . . . . **147** F1
St Mary's RC Prim Sch
Chingford E4 . . . . **87** D1
Hornchurch RM12 . . . . . **136** A3
Tilbury RM18 . . . . **178** F5
St Marys Rd
Ilford IG1 . . . . **133** D2
Wickford SS12 . . . . **121** B5
St Mary's Rd
Burnham-on-C CM0 . . . . **106** B6
Grays RM16 . . . . **174** B2
Greenhithe DA9 . . . . . . **176** E2
South Benfleet SS7 . . . . **163** E8
Southend-on-S SS2 . . . . **147** F2
St Marys Way IG7 . . . . . . **111** A5
St Matthew's CI RM13 . . . **155** A5
St Michaels CE Prep Sch
SS9 . . . . **146** C1
St Michaels Cl
Aveley RM15 . . . . **171** C6
Harlow CM20 . . . . **10** E1
Latchingdon CM3 . . . . . . **82** A5
St Michael's Dr CM1 . . . . . **30** A5
St Michael's Mews
CM6 . . . . **15** C7
St Michaels Rd
Canvey Island SS8 . . . . . **163** D4
Grays RM16 . . . . **174** B1
St Michael's Rd
Chelmsford CM2 . . . . . . **54** B8
Hadleigh SS7 . . . . **145** F6
Hoddesdon EN10 . . . . . . **21** C2
St Michaels Wlk CM2 . . . . **54** C2
St Mildreds Rd CM2 . . . . . **54** B8
St Nazaire Rd CM1 . . . . . . **31** E6
St Neot's Rd RM3 . . . . . . **114** F4
St Nicholas Ave
RM12 . . . . **136** A1
St Nicholas CE Prim Sch
CM0 . . . . **63** E4
St Nicholas CE Sch
SS6 . . . . **123** B5
St Nicholas Cl E4 . . . . . . **109** C4
St Nicholas Gn 1
CM17 . . . . **11** D1
St Nicholas Gr CM13 . . . . **117** C5
St Nicholas La SS15 . . . . **141** D7
St Nicholas Pl IG10 . . . . . . **89** A5
St Nicholas Rd CM0 . . . . . **63** E4
St Nicholas Sch
Harlow CM17 . . . . **11** F3
Southend-on-S SS2 . . . . **148** E2

St Olave's Rd E6 . . . . 152 A4
St Omar Cl SS12 . . . . 121 E6
St Patrick's Ct E3 . . . . . . 109 E3
St Patrick's Pl RM16 . . . . 174 C2
St Patrick's RC Prim Sch
  RM7 . . . . 113 B2
St Paul's Ct RM15 . . . . . . 171 C6
St Paul's Ct SS0 . . . . 166 E8
St Pauls Gdns CM12 . . . . . 97 A4
St Paul's Pl RM15 . . . . . . 171 C6
St Pauls Rd
  Barking IG11 . . . . 152 C4
  Canvey Island SS8 . . . . . 163 D4
St Pauls Way EN9 . . . . 65 D6
St Peter's Ave
  Chipping Ongar CM5 . . . . 49 A5
  Maldon CM9 . . . . 36 F2
St Peters CE Prim Sch
  CM2 . . . . 76 F4
St Peter's CE Prim Sch
  CM14 . . . . 115 E8
St Peter's Chapel★
  CM0 . . . . 182 A5
St Peters Cl
  Goldhanger CM9 . . . . 38 E6
  Ilford IG2 . . . . 133 F7
St Peter's Ct SS3 . . . . 168 G7
St Peter's Ct CM0 . . . . 63 E8
St Peters Field CM0 . . . . . 106 A7
St Peter's High Sch
  CM0 . . . . 106 B6
St Peter's Hospl CM9 . . . . 36 F2
St Peter's Pavement
  SS14 . . . . 120 F1
St Peters RC Prim Sch
  CM11 . . . . 119 E6
St Peter's RC Prim Sch
  Dagenham RM9 . . . . 153 F4
  Romford RM1 . . . . 135 E8
St Peters Rd
  Canvey Island SS8 . . . . . 163 D4
  Grays RM16 . . . . 174 B2
  Hockley SS5 . . . . 124 B7
St Peter's Rd
  Brentwood CM14 . . . . . . 116 B6
  Chelmsford CM1 . . . . 31 E2
St Peter's Terr SS12 . . . . . 121 C7
St Peters Wlk CM12 . . . . . . 96 F4
St Philip's Priory Sch
  CM2 . . . . 54 A8
St Pius X RC Prim Sch
  CM1 . . . . 31 F6
St Raphaels Pl CM14 . . . . 116 B5
St Ronans Cres IG8 . . . . . 110 A3
St Stephens Cres
  CM13 . . . . 117 A6
St Stephens Ct CM3 . . . . . . 83 A8
St Stephens Rd CM3 . . . . . . 81 A4
St Swithins Cotts 55 C3
Saint's Wlk RM16 . . . . . . 174 C2
St Teresa RC Prim Sch
  The RM8 . . . . 153 C8
St Teresas's SS14 . . . . . . 142 F5
St Teresa's RC Prim Sch
  Basildon SS14 . . . . 142 F6
  Rochford SS4 . . . . 125 E3
St Teresa Wlk RM16 . . . . . 174 B3
St Theresa Ct E4 . . . . 87 D2
St Thomas' Ct CM14 . . . . . 116 D8
St Thomas Gdns IG1 . . . . . 152 C6
St Thomas More High Sch
  for Boys SS0 . . . . 147 A3
St Thomas of Canterbury
  CE Inf Sch CM15 . . . . 94 D2
St Thomas of Canterbury
  CE Jun Sch CM15 . . . . . . 94 D2
St Thomas of Canterbury
  RC Prim Sch RM17 . . . . . 173 B2
St Thomas Rd
  Belvedere DA17 . . . . 169 C4
  Brentwood CM14 . . . . . . 116 D8
  Rochford SS4 . . . . 103 B4
St Thomas's Cl EN9 . . . . . . 66 B6
St Thomas's Pl ▨
  RM17 . . . . 178 C8
St Thomas's Row CM0 . . . . 42 B2
St Ursula's RC Jun & Inf
  Schs RM3 . . . . 114 B4
St Vincents Ave A1 . . . . . . 176 A2
ST VINCENT'S HAMLET
  . . . . 93 B1
St Vincent's RC Prim Sch
  RM8 . . . . 134 C2
St Vincents Rd
  Chelmsford CM2 . . . . 54 B8
  Dartford DA1 . . . . 176 A1
St Vincent's Rd SS0 . . . . . 166 E7
St Winifred's Cl IG7 . . . . . 111 C5
Sairard Cl SS9 . . . . 146 D7
Sairard Gdns SS9 . . . . 146 D7
Sakins Croft CM18 . . . . 23 F5
Saladin Dr RM19 . . . . 171 A2
Salamons Way RM13 . . . . 169 F2
Salcombe Dr RM6 . . . . 134 F5
Salcombe Pk IG10 . . . . 88 D4
Salcott Cres SS12 . . . . . . 121 F6
Salcott Mews SS12 . . . . . 121 F6
Salem Wlk SS6 . . . . 123 B4
Salerno Way CM1 . . . . 31 E6
Salesbury Dr CM11 . . . . . . 97 D2
Salforal Cl CM3 . . . . 78 B1
Saling Gn SS15 . . . . 119 F2
Salisbury Ave
  Barking IG11 . . . . 152 E6
  Southend-on-S SS0 . . . . 147 E1
  Stanford-le-H SS17 . . . . 160 D1
Salisbury Cl
  Rayleigh SS6 . . . . 123 C5

Salisbury Cl continued
  Upminster RM14 . . . . . . 137 F2
Salisbury Ct SS9 . . . . 146 D2
Salisbury Gdns ▨
  IG9 . . . . 110 D8
Salisbury Hall Gdns
  E4 . . . . 109 A4
Salisbury Rd
  Chingford E4 . . . . 109 A7
  Dagenham RM10 . . . . . . 154 B6
  Grays RM17 . . . . 173 C1
  Hoddesdon EN11 . . . . 21 C8
  Ilford IG3 . . . . 133 E2
  Romford RM2 . . . . 136 B6
  Southend-on-S SS9 . . . . 146 D2
Salix Rd RM15 . . . . 178 E8
Sally Murray Cl E12 . . . . . 152 A8
Salmond's Gr CM13 . . . . . 117 C5
Salmon Par CM1 . . . . 32 B3
Salmon Rd DA17 . . . . 169 A1
Saltash Rd IG6 . . . . 111 D3
Saltcoats CM3 . . . . 101 D8
Saltcoats Pk & Compass
  Gdns★ CM3 . . . . 101 F7
Saltcote Maltings CM9 . . 37 E4
Saltern Ct ▨ IG11 . . . . . . 153 B2
Salter Pl CM2 . . . . 32 F2
Saltford Cl DA8 . . . . 169 E1
Saltings The
  Greenhithe DA9 . . . . . . 177 C3
  Hadleigh SS7 . . . . 145 D3
Salt's Gn CM1 . . . . 16 D2
Salway Cl IG8 . . . . 110 A3
Samantha Mews RM4 . . . 113 E7
Samian Cl CM9 . . . . 36 F5
Samphire Ct RM17 . . . . . . 178 E8
Samson Ct ▨ DA17 . . . . . 169 A2
Samson Ho SS15 . . . . 119 B1
Samuel Manor CM2 . . . . . . 32 F3
Samuel Rd SS16 . . . . 141 B4
Samuel's Cnr SS3 . . . . 150 D3
Samuels Dr SS1 . . . . 168 B8
Sanctuary Gdn SS17 . . . . 160 E2
Sanctuary Rd SS9 . . . . . . 146 A3
Sandbanks SS7 . . . . 145 D2
Sandcliff Rd DA8 . . . . 169 D1
Sanderling Gdns CM9 . . . 37 C5
Sanderlings SS7 . . . . 144 C3
Sanderling Way DA9 . . . . 177 A1
Sanders Draper Sch &
  Specialist Science Coll
  The RM12 . . . . 155 D8
Sanderson Cl CM13 . . . . . 139 C5
Sanderson Ct SS7 . . . . . . 144 C5
Sanders Rd SS8 . . . . 164 A6
Sandford Ave IG10 . . . . . . 89 C6
Sandford Mill Rd
  Chelmsford CM2 . . . . 32 F2
  Chelmsford CM2 . . . . 33 B2
  Great Baddow CM2 . . . . . 55 C8
Sandford Rd CM2 . . . . 32 E3
Sandgate Cl RM7 . . . . 135 D2
Sandhill Rd SS9 . . . . 146 C8
Sandhurst SS8 . . . . 163 C3
Sandhurst Cl SS9 . . . . 146 F4
Sandhurst Cres SS9 . . . . . 146 F4
Sandhurst Dr IG3 . . . . 152 F8
Sandhurst Rd RM18 . . . . . 179 C5
Sand Island Ctr CM0 . . . . 106 A5
Sandleigh Rd SS9 . . . . 147 A1
SANDON 55 D6
Sandon Brook Pl CM2 . . . 55 E8
Sandon Cl
  Basildon SS14 . . . . 142 F5
  Rochford SS4 . . . . 125 D3
Sandon Ct
  Basildon SS14 . . . . 142 F5
  Ilford IG3 . . . . 134 A1
SANDON GREEN 55 C6
Sandon Hall Bridleway
  CM2 . . . . 55 D4
Sandon Pl CM5 . . . . 49 A1
Sandon Rd SS14 . . . . 142 F5
Sandon Sch The CM2 . . . 55 B6
Sandown Ave
  Dagenham RM10 . . . . . . 154 C6
  Hornchurch RM12 . . . . . 136 D2
  Southend-on-S SS0 . . . . 147 B2
Sandown Cl SS11 . . . . 122 A7
Sandown Ct RM10 . . . . . . 154 C6
Sandown Rd
  Orsett RM16 . . . . 174 E7
  Thundersley SS7 . . . . . . 145 B7
  Wickford SS11 . . . . 122 A7
Sandpiper Cl
  Greenhithe DA9 . . . . . . 177 A1
  Heybridge CM9 . . . . 37 C5
  Southend-on-S SS3 . . . . 168 E8
Sandpipers SS3 . . . . 168 G6
Sandpiper Terr IG5 . . . . . . 133 B8
Sandpiper Wlk CM0 . . . . . 54 C6
Sandpit La
  Burnham-on-C CM0 . . . . 106 C5
  Pilgrims Hatch CM14 . . . 93 F2
Sandpit Rd SS3 . . . . 168 H8
Sandringham Ave
  Harlow CM19 . . . . 22 E8
  Hockley SS5 . . . . 124 D6
Sandringham Cl
  Ilford IG6 . . . . 133 C8
  Stanford-le-H SS17 . . . . 160 E3
Sandringham Ct SS7 . . . . 145 E2
Sandringham Gdns
  IG6 . . . . 133 C8
Sandringham Lo ▨
  EN11 . . . . 21 A6
Sandringham Pl CM2 . . . . 32 C2

Sandringham Rd
  Barking IG11 . . . . 152 F6
  Basildon SS15 . . . . 141 E8
  Pilgrims Hatch CM15 . . . 94 B3
  Southend-on-S SS1 . . . . 167 D7
Sands Way IG8 . . . . 110 F4
Sandyhill Rd IG1 . . . . 152 B8
Sandy La
  Aveley RM15 . . . . 171 A6
  Grays, Chadwell St M
  RM16 . . . . 174 C1
  Grays, West Thurrock
  RM20 . . . . 177 B8
Sangster Ct SS6 . . . . 123 F2
San Juan Dr RM16 . . . . . . 172 C2
San Luis Dr RM16 . . . . . . 172 C2
San Marcos Dr RM16 . . . . 172 C2
San Remo Mans SS0 . . . . 166 E4
San Remo Par SS0 . . . . . . 166 E7
San Remo Rd SS8 . . . . 164 D3
Sans Souci SS9 . . . . 165 D8
Santiago Way RM16 . . . . . 172 D1
Sappers CM21 . . . . 1 F2
Sapphire Cl RM8 . . . . 134 C3
Sapphire Ct SS1 . . . . 167 D6
Sapphire Rd ▨ RM13 . . . . 155 B3
Sara Cres DA9 . . . . 177 B3
Sarbir Ind Pk CM17 . . . . . 11 C5
Sark Gr SS12 . . . . 121 F5
Sarre Ave RM16 . . . . 155 C6
Sassoon Way ▨ CM9 . . . . . 37 A1
Satanita Rd SS0 . . . . 166 D8
Saunders Cl IG1 . . . . 133 D3
Saunton Rd RM12 . . . . 136 A2
Savannah Hts SS9 . . . . . . 147 A1
Savernake Rd CM1 . . . . . . 31 E1
Savill Ct IG8 . . . . 109 F4
Saville Rd RM6 . . . . 134 F4
Savill Row IG8 . . . . 109 F4
Savoy Cl SS16 . . . . 141 A5
Savoy Wood CM19 . . . . . . 23 B2
SAWBRIDGEWORTH 1 C3
Sawbridgeworth Rd
  Hatfield Heath CM22 . . . . 2 D3
  Little Hallingbury CM22 . . 2 B6
Sawbridgeworth Sta
  CM21 . . . . 2 A3
Sawkins Ave CM2 . . . . 54 D6
Sawkins Cl CM2 . . . . 54 D6
Sawkins Gdns CM2 . . . . . . 54 D6
Sawney Brook CM1 . . . . . . 31 A1
Sawston Ct ▨ RM19 . . . . . 171 B1
Sawyer's Chase RM4 . . . . . 90 B6
Sawyer Cl CM15 . . . . 94 F3
Sawyers Gr CM15 . . . . 94 D1
Sawyers Hall Coll of
  Science & Tech
  CM15 . . . . 94 C2
Sawyer's Hall La CM15 . . . 94 D1
Saxham Rd IG11 . . . . 152 E3
Saxlingham Rd E4 . . . . . . 109 D7
Saxon Cl
  Brentwood CM13 . . . . . 117 A7
  Rayleigh SS6 . . . . 123 C5
  Romford RM3 . . . . 114 F1
  Wickford SS11 . . . . 99 E1
Saxon Ct
  Maldon CM9 . . . . 37 A3
  South Benfleet SS7 . . . . 144 C5
Saxon Gdns SS3 . . . . 168 D7
Saxon Ho RM14 . . . . 138 D4
Saxon Pl SS4 . . . . 125 F2
Saxon Rd IG1 . . . . 152 B7
Saxonville SS7 . . . . 144 B4
Saxon Way
  Chelmsford CM1 . . . . 32 B7
  Maldon CM9 . . . . 37 B1
  South Benfleet SS7 . . . . 144 C2
  Waltham Abbey EN9 . . . . 65 C6
Sayer Cl DA9 . . . . 177 A2
Sayers SS7 . . . . 145 A7
Sayesbury Ave CM21 . . . . . 1 E3
Sayesbury Rd CM21 . . . . . . 1 E2
Sayes Gdns CM21 . . . . 1 F2
Saywell Brook CM2 . . . . . . 33 A2
Scalby Rd CM0 . . . . 84 A3
Scaldhurst SS13 . . . . 143 C8
Scarborough Dr SS9 . . . . 146 E2
Scarborough Rd CM0 . . . . 84 A3
Scargill Jun & Inf Sch
  RM13 . . . . 155 A6
Scarles Croft CM3 . . . . 78 C7
Scarletts SS14 . . . . 142 C8
Scholars Ct ▨ RM2 . . . . . 136 B6
Scholars Ho ▨ E4 . . . . 87 D1
Scholars Rd E4 . . . . 87 D1
Scholars Way ▨ RM2 . . . . 136 B6
School Bglws CM1 . . . . 30 A5
Schoolfield Rd RM20 . . . . 177 A8
School Green La CM16 . . . 47 C6
Schoolhouse Gdns
  IG10 . . . . 89 B5
School La
  Abbess Roding CM5 . . . . 14 F3
  Basildon SS16 . . . . 122 A4
  Beauchamp Roding CM5 . 28 A7
  Broomfield CM1 . . . . 19 B1
  Chelmsford CM1 . . . . 31 F8
  Chigwell IG7 . . . . 111 F6
  Harlow CM20 . . . . 10 E2
  High Easter CM1 . . . . 6 B3
  Ingrave CM13 . . . . 117 C4
  Orsett RM16 . . . . 174 A8
  South Benfleet SS7 . . . . 163 D8
  Stock CM4 . . . . 75 D2
  Tilgate Green CM5 . . . . . 25 D6
School Rd
  Billericay CM12 . . . . 119 A8

School Rd continued
  Dagenham RM10 . . . . . . 154 B4
  Downham CM11 . . . . 98 F5
  Kelvedon Hatch CM15 . . . 71 F2
  Margaret Roding CM1 . . . 16 C5
  Stanford Rivers CM5 . . . . 70 B7
School View Rd CM1 . . . . . 31 F3
School Villas CM6 . . . . 5 E7
School Way
  Dagenham RM8 . . . . 134 C1
  Southend-on-S SS9 . . . . 146 F3
Schooner Cl IG11 . . . . 153 B2
Schooner Ct DA2 . . . . 176 C3
Schooner Ho DA8 . . . . 169 E1
Scilla Ct RM17 . . . . 178 D8
Scimitar Park Ind Est
  SS13 . . . . 121 D2
Scimitar Pk SS13 . . . . 121 D2
Scimitar Pk CM19 . . . . 9 F1
Scoter Cl IG8 . . . . 110 B3
Scotland Rd IG9 . . . . 88 C1
Scotney Wlk RM12 . . . . . . 155 D7
SCOT'S GREEN 31 E8
Scott Ave SG12 . . . . 8 B4
Scott Ho
  Grays RM16 . . . . 172 C1
  Romford RM11 . . . . 136 A5
  Southend-on-S SS9 . . . . 147 A7
Scott Rd RM16 . . . . 174 A2
Scotts Cl RM12 . . . . 155 C7
Scotts Hall Cotts SS4 . . . 126 D8
Scotts Hall Rd SS4 . . . . . . 126 D7
Scotts Hill CM0 . . . . 84 B4
Scotts Prim Sch
  RM12 . . . . 155 C7
Scotts Wlk
  Chelmsford CM1 . . . . 31 D5
  Rayleigh SS6 . . . . 124 A2
Scraley Rd CM9 . . . . 37 E6
Scratton Rd
  Southend-on-S SS1 . . . . 166 F7
  Stanford-le-H SS17 . . . . 160 D2
Scrattons Terr IG11 . . . . . 153 D4
Scrub La SS7 . . . . 145 F3
Scrub Rise CM12 . . . . 118 F8
Scurvy Hall La CM3 . . . . . . 19 B8
Scylla Cl CM9 . . . . 37 C6
Seaborough Rd RM16 . . . 174 C3
Seabrink SS9 . . . . 166 A8
Seabrooke Rise RM17 . . . 178 B8
Seabrook Gdns
  Boreham CM3 . . . . 20 F1
  Romford RM7 . . . . 135 A4
Seabrook Rd
  Dagenham RM8 . . . . 134 D1
  Great Baddow CM2 . . . . . 55 A6
Seaburn Cl RM13 . . . . 154 E3
Sea-End Cvn Site
  CM0 . . . . 106 D3
Seaforth Ave SS2 . . . . 148 C2
Seaforth Cl RM1 . . . . 113 E2
Seaforth Ct EN11 . . . . 21 B4
Seaforth Gdns IG8 . . . . . . 110 C5
Seaforth Gr SS2 . . . . 148 D2
Seaforth Rd SS0 . . . . 166 D7
Seagry Rd E11 . . . . 132 B4
Seagull Cl IG11 . . . . 153 A2
Seally Rd RM17 . . . . 173 A1
Seamans La CM4 . . . . 76 C2
Seamer Rd CM0 . . . . 84 A3
Seamore Ave SS7 . . . . 144 C7
Seamore Ct SS7 . . . . 144 C6
Seamore Wlk SS7 . . . . 144 C7
Sea Reach SS9 . . . . 165 E8
Seaton Ave IG3 . . . . 152 F7
Seaview Ave SS16 . . . . . . 142 D3
Seaview Dr SS3 . . . . 150 C3
Seaview Rd
  Canvey Island SS8 . . . . . 164 E2
  Southend-on-S, Leigh-on-S
  SS9 . . . . 165 E8
  Southend-on-S, Shoeburyness
  SS9 . . . . 168 E6
Seaview Terr SS7 . . . . 145 D1
Sea Watch SS1 . . . . 167 B7
Seaway
  Canvey Island SS8 . . . . . 164 B2
  Southend-on-S SS1 . . . . 167 B7
  St Lawrence CM0 . . . . . . 62 C8
Seax Ct SS15 . . . . 140 F7
Seax Way SS15 . . . . 140 F7
Sebastian Ave SS15 . . . . . 95 A3
Sebastian Ct ▨ IG11 . . . . 152 F5
Sebert Cl CM11 . . . . 119 D7
Second Ave
  Basildon SS16 . . . . 140 E4
  Billericay CM12 . . . . 118 F7
  Canvey Island SS8 . . . . . 163 E4
  Chelmsford CM1 . . . . 32 B5
  Dagenham RM10 . . . . . . 154 B3
  Grays RM20 . . . . 177 A8
  Harlow CM18, CM20 . . . . 23 F8
  Hook End CM15 . . . . 72 C5
  Hullbridge SS5 . . . . 101 F1
  Ilford RM6 . . . . 134 C6
  Southend-on-S SS0 . . . . 166 B7
  Stanford-le-H SS17 . . . . 160 D3
  Thundersley SS7 . . . . . . 145 A6
  Wickford SS11 . . . . 122 A6
Seddon Ct ▨ RM7 . . . . . . 135 D7

Seddons Wlk SS5 . . . . 124 E6
Sedge Ct RM17 . . . . 178 E7
Sedgefield Cl RM3 . . . . . . 114 F6
Sedgefield Cres RM3 . . . . 114 F6
Sedge Gn EN9 . . . . 21 E3
Sedgemoor SS3 . . . . 149 D1
Sedgemoor Dr RM10 . . . . 154 A8
Sedley Rise IG10 . . . . 88 F7
Seedbed Ctr SS3 . . . . 168 F7
Seedbed Ctr The
  RM7 . . . . 135 E4
Seeleys CM17 . . . . 11 C4
Seetha Ho IG1 . . . . 133 D2
Sejant Ho RM17 . . . . 178 B8
Selborne Ave E12 . . . . 152 A8
Selborne Rd IG1 . . . . 133 A2
Selbourne Rd
  Hockley SS5 . . . . 124 E6
  South Benfleet SS7 . . . . 144 D6
  Southend-on-S SS2 . . . . 148 C3
Seldon Cl SS0 . . . . 147 B3
Selinas La RM8 . . . . 134 F4
Selsdon Cl RM5 . . . . 113 C2
Selsdon Rd E11 . . . . 132 A4
Selwood Rd CM14 . . . . . . 115 F7
Selworthy Cl
  Billericay CM11 . . . . 119 C7
  Wanstead E11 . . . . 132 A6
Selwyn Ave
  Chingford E4 . . . . 109 C4
  Ilford IG3 . . . . 133 F5
Selwyn Prim Sch E4 . . . . 109 C4
Selwyn Rd
  Southend-on-S SS2 . . . . 148 C2
  Tilbury RM18 . . . . 178 F5
Semper Rd RM16 . . . . 174 C4
Semples SS17 . . . . 160 F2
Serena Ct RM12 . . . . 136 C2
Sergeants Green La
  EN9 . . . . 66 C6
Service Industry Bays
  CM20 . . . . 10 F2
Seton Gdns RM9 . . . . 153 C5
Settle Rd RM3 . . . . 115 A6
Seven Acres SS11 . . . . . . 121 F8
Seven Arches Rd
  CM14 . . . . 116 E7
Seven Ash Gn CM1 . . . . . . 32 C5
SEVEN KINGS 133 F3
Seven Kings High Sch
  IG1 . . . . 133 D4
Seven Kings Rd IG3 . . . . . 133 F3
Seven Kings Sta IG3 . . . . 133 E3
Sevenoaks Cl RM3 . . . . . . 114 C6
Seventh Ave
  Canvey Island SS8 . . . . . 163 E4
  Chelmsford CM1 . . . . 32 B6
Seven Ways Par IG2 . . . . 133 A6
Severn RM18 . . . . 175 B3
Severn Ave RM2 . . . . 136 B8
Severn Dr RM14 . . . . 137 D5
Severn Rd RM15 . . . . 171 C7
Severns Field CM16 . . . . . 46 A2
Sewards End SS12 . . . . . . 121 E6
SEWARDSTONE 87 C8
SEWARDSTONEBURY 87 E4
Sewardstone Gdns E4 . . . 87 B4
Sewardstone Rd
  Chingford E4 . . . . 87 B5
  Sewardstone E4, EN9 . . . 65 D3
  Waltham Abbey EN9 . . . . 65 C5
Sewardstone St EN9 . . . . . 65 C5
Sewell Cl RM16 . . . . 172 C1
Sewell Harris Cl CM20 . . . 10 F1
Sexton CM13 . . . . 154 C4
Sexton Rd RM18 . . . . 178 F6
Seymer Rd RM1 . . . . 135 D8
Seymour Cl
  Basildon SS15 . . . . 141 D6
  Loughton IG10 . . . . 88 E3
Seymour Ct E4 . . . . 109 F8
Seymour Gdns IG1 . . . . . . 132 F3
Seymour Mews CM21 . . . . 11 E7
Seymour Pl RM11 . . . . . . 136 D4
Seymour Rd
  Chingford E4 . . . . 87 B1
  Hadleigh SS7 . . . . 145 F3
  Southend-on-S SS0 . . . . 147 C1
  Tilbury RM18 . . . . 178 F6
Seymours
  Harlow CM19 . . . . 22 F5
  Harlow CM19 . . . . 23 A5
Seymour's IG10 . . . . 89 A8
Seymour St CM2 . . . . 32 A4
Shafter Rd RM10 . . . . 154 C6
Shaftesbury IG10 . . . . 88 D6
Shaftesbury Ave SS1 . . . . 167 E6
Shaftesbury Ct RM6 . . . . . 134 C4
Shaftesbury La DA1 . . . . . 176 B3
Shaftesbury Rd
  Chingford E4 . . . . 87 D1
  Epping CM16 . . . . 45 F2
  Romford RM1 . . . . 135 F7
Shaftesburys The
  IG11 . . . . 152 C3
Shaftsbury Ct SS13 . . . . . 143 B7
Shakespeare Ave
  Basildon SS16 . . . . 141 A5
  Billericay CM11 . . . . 97 D2
  Rayleigh SS6 . . . . 124 A2
  Southend-on-S SS0 . . . . 147 E2
  Tilbury RM18 . . . . 179 B6
Shakespeare Ct EN11 . . . . 8 A2
Shakespeare Dr
  Maldon CM9 . . . . 59 A8

Shakespeare Dr *continued*
  Southend-on-S SS0 .....147 E2
Shakespeare Rd
  Dartford DA1.........176 B3
  [8] Romford RM1......135 F5
Shakespeare Sq IG6 ...111 C4
Shakeston Cl CM1 .....53 B8
Shalford [4] IG8......110 C4
Shalford Lo CM1......32 B8
Shalford Rd CM11......97 D2
Shanklin Ave CM12 .....97 A2
Shanklin Cl SS0......147 B2
Shannon Ave SS6.....123 D1
Shannon Cl SS9......146 E4
Shannon Way
  Aveley RM15.........171 C6
  Canvey Island SS8....163 D3
Shardelow Ave CM1...33 A8
Sharlands Cl SS11....121 F8
Sharnbrook SS3.......149 D2
Sharpecroft CM19.....23 C8
Sharpington Cl CM2...54 C3
Shaw Ave IG11........153 E3
Shawbridge CM19......23 C5
Shaw Cl
  Hornchurch RM11.....136 B3
  Wickford SS12........121 D5
Shaw Cres
  Brentwood CM13......95 D5
  Tilbury RM18.........179 C6
Shaw Gdns IG11......153 E3
Shaw Prim Sch RM15...172 B7
Shaw The CM22.......3 A3
Shearers Way CM3.....20 F1
Shearwater Cl IG11...153 A2
Sheepcotes CM2......33 B5
Sheepcotes La
  Little Waltham CM3...19 C7
  Southminster CM0....84 E7
Sheepcotes Rd RM6...134 E7
SHEERING...........12 D8
Sheering CE Prim Sch
  CM22..............12 D8
Sheering Ct SS6......123 A3
Sheering Dr CM17.....11 E4
Sheering Lower Rd
  CM21..............2 A2
Sheering Mill La CM21..1 F2
Sheering Rd CM17.....11 F4
Sheerwater Cl CM0...106 B5
Sheffield Dr RM3.....115 A5
Sheffield Gdns RM3...115 A5
Sheila Cl RM5........113 B3
Sheila Rd RM5........113 B3
Sheilings The RM11...136 F6
Sheldon Ave IG5......111 B1
Sheldon Cl
  Corringham SS17.....161 B4
  Harlow CM17.........24 E8
Sheldon Ct CM13......95 B3
Sheldon Ho E4........109 C4
Sheldon Rd
  Canvey Island SS8....164 E3
  Dagenham RM9.......153 E5
Sheldrick Link CM2...33 B4
Shelford Cl RM16.....174 A8
Shellbeach Rd SS8....164 D2
SHELLEY............48 F5
Shelley Ave RM12.....135 F2
Shelley Cl
  Chipping Ongar CM5...48 F5
  Maldon CM9..........59 A8
Shelley Ct
  Waltham Abbey EN9...65 F6
  [8] Wanstead E11.....132 A4
Shelley Gr IG10.......88 F5
Shelley Pl
  Rayleigh SS6.........123 A3
  Tilbury RM18.........179 B6
Shelley Prim Sch CM5..48 F5
Shelley Rd
  Brentwood CM13......95 D2
  Chelmsford CM2......32 D2
Shelley Sq SS2.......148 B2
SHELLOW BOWELLS....28 F4
Shellow Rd CM5......28 D4
Shelly Ave SS16......141 A5
Shelsley Dr SS16.....141 C3
SHENFIELD...........94 E2
Shenfield Cres CM15..116 E7
Shenfield Ct CM18....23 C5
Shenfield Gdns CM13..95 B3
Shenfield Gn CM15....95 A2
Shenfield High Sch
  CM15..............95 A4
Shenfield Pl CM15....94 E2
Shenfield Rd
  Brentwood CM15......94 E1
  Woodford IG8........110 B3
Shenfield Sta CM15...95 A2
Shenley Rd DA1......176 A1
Shen Place Almshouses
  CM15..............94 D1
Shenstone Gdns
  Ilford IG2...........133 F6
  Romford RM3........114 C2
Shenval Ho CM20.....11 A4
Shenval Ind Est CM20..11 A4
Shepard Cl SS9.......147 A6
Shepeshall SS16......141 E5
Shephards Ct SS5.....124 E5
Shepherds Cl
  Hadleigh SS7........145 E4
  Ilford RM6..........134 D7

Shepherds Hill RM3...115 B1
Shepherds Wlk SS7...145 E4
Shepley Mews EN3....65 A2
Sheppard Dr CM2.....33 A4
Sheppards CM19......22 F5
Sheppey Gdns RM9...153 C5
Sheppey Rd RM9......153 C5
Sherards Ho CM19....23 B6
Sherards Orch CM19...23 B6
Sherborne Gdns RM5..113 A5
Sherborne Rd CM1....32 D5
Sherbourne Cl SS2....147 E6
Sherbourne Dr SS13...121 A1
Sherbourne Gdns
  SS2...............147 E6
Sheredan Rd E4......109 E5
Shere Rd IG2.........133 A6
Sherfield Rd RM17....178 B8
Sheridan Ave SS7....145 B3
Sheridan Cl
  Rayleigh SS6.........123 F2
  Romford RM3........114 C3
Sheridan Ct DA1......176 A3
Sheridan Mews [3]
  E11...............132 B5
Sheridan Rd DA17....169 A2
Sheringham Ave
  Little Ilford E12......152 A7
  Romford RM7........135 C5
Sheringham Cl SS17...160 E3
Sheringham Dr IG11...153 A7
Sheriton Sq SS6......123 D4
Sherman Gdns RM6...134 C5
Shernbroke Rd EN9...65 F5
Shernwood Ho [1]
  E18...............132 A7
Sherry Mews IG11....152 D5
Sherry Way SS7......145 E6
Sherwood Ave E18....132 B8
Sherwood Cl SS16....141 A4
Sherwood Cres SS7...145 E4
Sherwood Dr CM1.....31 D1
Sherwood Gdns IG11..152 D5
Sherwood Ho CM18...23 F6
Sherwood Rd IG6.....133 D7
Sherwood Way SS2...148 E2
Shevon Way CM14....115 F6
Shillibeer Wlk IG7....111 F7
Shillingstone SS3.....149 D1
Shingle Ct EN9.......66 A6
Ship Cotts CM2.......76 B6
Ship La RM15.........171 E4
Ship Rd
  Burnham-on-C CM0...106 C4
  West Hanningfield CM2..76 C5
Shipton Cl RM8.......134 D1
Shipwrights Cl SS7....145 B2
Shipwrights Dr SS7...145 B3
Shire Cl
  Billericay CM11.......97 C8
  Chelmsford CM1......32 F7
Shirley Ct
  Ilford IG2...........133 D6
  Loughton IG10.......88 F7
Shirley Gdns
  Barking IG11.........152 E6
  Basildon SS13.......143 C8
  Hornchurch RM12....136 C2
Shirley Lo SS9.......146 E5
Shirley Rd SS3.......146 E5
Shoebury Ave SS3....168 F7
Shoebury Common Rd
  SS3...............168 C5
SHOEBURYNESS.......168 C5
Shoeburyness High Sch
  SS3...............168 D7
Shoeburyness Sta
  SS3...............168 F7
Shoebury Rd
  Great Wakering SS3...150 C3
  Southend-on-S SS1...149 B1
Shoe La SS0..........147 D1
Shonks Mill Rd RM4...70 C1
Shooters Dr EN9......21 E1
Shopland Hall Rd
  SS4...............148 D6
Shopland Rd SS4.....148 C7
Shop Row SS4.......128 A5
Shorefield SS7.......144 B3
Shorefield Gdns SS0..166 F7
Shorefield Rd SS0....166 D7
Shore Point IG9......110 B8
Shore Rd CM0........106 C4
Shore The DA11......178 C2
Short Acre SS14......142 C6
Shortcroft CM15......71 F2
Shortcrofts Rd RM9...153 F6
Shorter Ave CM15....94 F2
Short La CM11........98 C4
Shortlands SS14......142 B6
Shortlands Ave CM5...48 F5
Short Rd
  Canvey Island SS8....164 B4
  Hadleigh SS7........145 D2
Short St SS2.........148 A1
Shorwell Ct [18] RM19..171 B1
SHOTGATE...........122 B6
Shrewsbury Cl SS16..140 F5
Shrewsbury Dr SS7...144 D7
Shropshire Cl CM2....54 F5
Shrubberies The
  Chigwell IG7.........111 C5
  Ilford IG2...........133 F6
  Woodford E18........110 A1
  Writtle CM1.........52 F8
Shrubbery Cl SS15...141 D8

Shrubbery The
  Upminster RM14......137 C1
  [7] Wanstead E11.....132 B6
Shrublands Cl
  Chelmsford CM2......32 C2
  Chigwell IG7.........111 C4
Sibley Row EN9.......22 E2
Siddons Cl SS17......175 A3
Sidings The IG10......88 B3
Sidmouth Ave SS0....147 D5
Sidmouth Rd CM1.....32 E6
Sidney Elson Way E6..152 A3
Sidney Pl CM1........33 A7
Sidney Rd
  Theydon Bois CM16...67 D3
  Wanstead E7.........132 A1
Sidwell Ave SS7......144 E1
Sidwell Chase SS7....144 E1
Sidwell La SS7.......144 E1
Sidwell Pk SS7.......144 E1
Sierra Dr RM10.......154 B3
Silchester Cnr SS3....149 A3
Silva Island Way SS12..121 F5
Silver Birch Ave CM16..46 E4
Silver Birches CM13...95 A1
Silver Birch Lo SS4...125 E2
Silver Birch Mews
  IG6...............111 C4
Silverdale
  Rayleigh SS6.........145 E8
  Stanford-le-H SS17...160 D4
  Thundersley SS7.....144 F7
Silverdale Ave
  Ilford IG3...........133 F6
  Southend-on-S SS0...147 E2
Silverdale Dr RM12...155 B7
Silverdale E SS17.....160 D4
Silverdale Par IG3....133 F6
Silverdale Rd E4......109 D4
Silver La CM5.........29 A2
Silverlink St SS8......163 F5
Silverlocke Rd RM17..178 D8
Silvermead [7] E18....110 A2
Silvermere SS16......141 A5
Silvermere Ave RM5..113 B4
Silverpoint Marine
  SS8...............165 A3
Silver Rd CM0........106 C4
Silvers IG9...........88 C1
Silversea Dr SS0......147 B2
Silver Spring Cl DA8..169 B1
Silver St
  Abridge RM4.........90 B6
  Maldon CM9.........36 F3
  Waltham Abbey EN9...65 C6
Silverthorn Cl SS4....125 D4
Silverthorne SS8......163 F3
Silverthorn Gdns E4...109 A8
Silvertown Ave SS17..160 D2
Silvertree Cl SS5.....124 B6
Silver Way
  Romford RM7........135 B8
  [1] Wickford SS11....121 C8
Silverwood Cl
  Grays RM16.........173 A6
  Harlow EN9.........22 E3
Silvester Way CM2....33 B4
Simmonds La CM9....59 A1
Simmonds Way CM3...56 F8
Simmons Dr RM8.....134 C1
Simmons La E4.......109 D8
Simmons Pl RM16....173 A5
Simon Campion Ct
  CM16..............46 A1
Simplicity La [6] CM17..11 D1
Simpson Rd RM13....154 F6
Sims Cl RM1.........135 F7
Sinclair Rd E4........109 A5
Sinclair Wlk SS12....121 D5
Singleton Cl RM12....154 F8
Singleton Rd RM9....153 F7
Sippetts Ct IG1.......133 D3
Sirdar Rd SS6........145 D8
Sir Francis Way CM14..116 B8
Sir George Monoux Sixth
  Form Coll E17.......109 B1
Sir Walter Raleigh Dr
  SS6...............123 C4
Sir W Petre Almshouses
  CM4..............74 B3
Sisley Rd IG11........152 F4
Siviter Way RM10....154 B5
Sixpenny Ct [6] IG11..152 C6
Sixth Ave
  Canvey Island SS8....163 E4
  Chelmsford CM1......32 B6
  Thundersley SS7.....145 A5
Skarnings Ct EN9.....66 A6
Skeale's Ct CM12.....136 C1
Skelter Stps [9] SS1...167 C7
Skerry Rise CM1......32 B7
Skinner's La CM2.....54 B3
Skipper Ct [6] IG11...152 C4
Skippers Cl [4] DA9...177 B2
Skipsey Ave E6.......152 A1
Skreens Ct CM1......31 D4
Skylark Cl CM11......97 C1
Skylark Wlk CM2.....54 B5
Sky Peals Rd IG8.....109 D3
Slacksbury Hatch
  CM19..............23 B8
Slade End CM16......67 F3
Slade's La CM2.......54 A3
Slades The SS16......142 E3
Slaney Rd RM1......135 E6
Sleepers Farm Rd
  RM16..............174 B4

Slewins Cl RM11......136 C6
Slewins La RM11.....136 C6
Slipe La EN10.........43 A7
Sloane Mews SS12....96 F5
Sloan Ho RM10......154 B5
Slough La CM3........57 D3
Slough Rd
  Danbury CM3........57 C3
  High Easter CM1......6 B2
Smallgains Ave SS8...164 E4
Small Gains La CM4...97 E8
Smallholdings SS2....147 D6
Smarden Cl DA17....169 A1
Smart Cl RM3........114 B2
Smart's La IG10......88 E5
Smartt Ave SS8......164 A4
Smeaton Cl EN9......65 E7
Smeaton Rd
  Chigwell IG8.........110 F5
  Holbrook EN3........65 A2
Smither's Chase SS2..148 B5
Smithers Dr CM2.....55 A6
Smiths Ave CM3......83 A8
Smiths Ct CM16......46 C6
Smith St SS3.........168 F6
Smithy The CM21.....1 E1
Smollett Pl SS12.....121 D4
Smugglers Wlk [3]
  DA9...............177 B2
Smyatts Cl CM0......84 D3
Smythe Cl CM11......97 D5
Smythe Rd CM11.....97 D5
Smythe Row CM3....80 C4
Snakes Hill CM14.....93 C6
Snakes La SS2........147 A6
Snakes La E IG8......110 C4
Snakes La W IG8.....110 B4
SNARESBROOK......132 A7
Snaresbrook Hall [12]
  E18...............132 A8
Snaresbrook Prim Sch
  E18...............132 A7
Snaresbrook Sta E11..132 A6
Snelling Gr CM2......54 F6
Snoreham Gdns CM3..82 B5
Snowden Hill DA11...178 A2
Snowdon Ct [5] RM2..136 C7
Snowdonia Cl SS13...143 C8
Snowdrop Cl CM1.....32 E7
Snowdrop Path RM3..114 D3
Soames Mead CM15..72 A6
Soane St SS13.......121 B1
Softwater La SS7.....145 E3
Solar Ct RM12........136 C2
Solid La CM15........93 F8
Solway RM18.........175 C3
Somerby Cl RM3......114 E4
Somerby Rd IG11.....152 D5
Somercotes SS15.....141 C5
Somercotes Ct SS15..141 C5
Somerdean [2] SS13..143 C6
Somersby Gdns IG4...132 F6
Somerset Ave
  Rochford SS4.........125 E3
  Southend-on-S SS0...147 B4
Somerset Cl IG8......110 A2
Somerset Cres SS0...147 B4
Somerset Ct [9] IG9..110 C8
Somerset Gdns
  Basildon SS13.......143 B6
  Hornchurch RM11....137 A3
Somerset Pl CM1.....32 A7
Somerset Rd
  Basildon SS15.......141 B6
  Holbrook EN3........65 A1
  Linford SS17.........175 A4
Somers Heath Prim Sch
  RM15..............172 A6
Somerton Ave SS5....147 B5
Somerville Gdns SS9..165 F8
Somerville Rd RM6...134 C6
Somnes Ave SS8......163 E6
Sonning Way SS3....149 D1
Sonters Down CM3...100 C5
Soper Mews [6] EN3..65 A1
Soper Sq [2] CM17....11 C1
Sopwith Cres SS11...122 B5
Sorrel Ct RM17.......178 D8
Sorrell Cl
  Goldhanger CM9.....38 E7
  Little Waltham CM3...19 B6
Sorrells The SS17.....160 F3
Sorrels The SS7......144 D7
Sorrel Wlk RM1......135 F8
Southall Ho [4] RM3..114 E4
Southall Way CM14...115 F6
South Ave
  Basildon SS16.......160 B7
  Chingford E4........87 C2
  Hullbridge SS5.......101 E1
  Southend-on-S SS2...148 C1
South Beech Ave
  SS12..............121 D7
SOUTH BENFLEET....144 E3
South Benfleet
Foundation Prim Sch
  SS7...............144 D2
South Block CM21....1 F2
South Boundary Rd
  E12...............132 F1
Southbourne Gdns
  Ilford IG1...........152 C7
  Southend-on-S SS0...147 B4
Southbourne Gr
  Hockley SS5.........125 A6

Southbourne Gr *continued*
  Southend-on-S SS0...147 B3
  Wickford SS12.......121 A8
Southbrook CM21.....1 E1
Southbury Cl RM12...155 D7
Southbury Ct [8] RM1..135 E5
South Charlton Mead La
  EN11..............21 D5
SOUTHCHURCH......167 E8
Southchurch Ave
  Southend-on-S,
  Shoeburyness SS3...168 G7
  Southend-on-S SS1...167 B8
Southchurch Bvd SS2..148 F1
Southchurch Hall Cl
  SS1...............167 C8
Southchurch Hall Mus★
  SS1...............167 C8
Southchurch Rd SS1..167 C8
South Cl RM10.......154 A4
Southcliff SS7........144 C4
South Colne SS16....142 D4
Southcote Cres SS14..142 F8
Southcote Row [2]
  SS14..............142 F8
Southcote Sq SS14...142 F8
South Cres SS2......147 D5
South Crockerford
  SS16..............142 E4
South Cross IG6.....133 C6
Southdale IG7........111 D6
Southdown Cres IG2..133 E6
Southdown Rd RM11..136 B4
South Dr
  Brentwood CM13.....116 D6
  Romford RM2........136 C3
  Wanstead E12.......132 E1
South East Essex Coll of
Arts & Tech
  Southend-on-S SS1...166 F8
  Southend-on-S SS2...147 F1
South East Essex Sixth
  Form Coll SS7.......145 A5
Southend Arterial Rd
  Basildon SS12, SS6,
  SS7...............122 B2
  Basildon, Steeple View CM12,
  SS15..............119 D1
  Great Warley CM13,
  RM14..............138 C6
  Rayleigh SS6........145 E8
  Romford RM2........114 D1
  Upminster RM14,
  RM11..............137 D7
  West Horndon CM13..139 D7
Southend Central Sta
  SS1...............167 A8
Southend East
(Southchurch Village)Sta
  SS1...............167 C8
Southend High Sch for
  Boys SS0...........147 D3
Southend High Sch for
  Girls SS2...........148 F1
Southend Ho SS17...160 E3
SOUTHEND-ON-S.....166 E6
Southend-on-Sea Central
Mus & Planetarium★
  SS2...............148 A1
Southend-on-Sea Sea Life
  Ctr★ SS1...........167 C6
Southend-on-Sea
(Victoria) Sta SS2...148 A1
Southend Pier Mus★
  SS1...............167 B7
Southend Pier Rlwy★
  SS1...............167 B5
Southend Rd
  Billericay CM11......119 D7
  Grays RM17.........173 C2
  Great Baddow CM2...55 B4
  Great Wakering SS3..149 C3
  Hockley SS5.........124 E5
  Howe Green CM2....55 D2
  Rochford SS4........147 F7
  Stanford-le-H SS17...160 E4
  Wallend E6..........152 A6
  Wickford SS11.......122 B7
  Woodford IG8.......110 D1
  Woodham Mortimer
  CM9..............57 C5
South End Rd RM12,
  RM13.............155 B8
Southend Rd (North
Circular Rd) E17,
  E18...............109 F1
Souther Cross CM1...16 E5
Souther Cross Cotts
  CM1..............16 D5
Souther Cross Rd CM1..16 D5
Southern Dr
  Loughton IG10.......88 F3
  South Woodham Ferrers
  CM3..............101 C7
Southernhay
  Basildon SS14.......142 B5
  Basildon SS14.......142 B6
  Loughton IG10.......88 D4
  Southend-on-S SS9...146 E5
Southern Lo CM19...23 C5
Southern Terr [2] EN11..8 E1
Southern Way
  Harlow CM18........23 D5
  Romford RM7........135 D5
Southey Cl CM9......37 C4
Southey Wlk RM18...179 B6
Southfalls Rd SS8....164 F3

SOUTH FAMBRIDGE 103 B4
Southfield Chase
  CM12 .... 118 E1
Southfield Cl SS7 ..... 145 E5
Southfield Dr SS7 ..... 145 E5
Southfield Rd EN11 .... 21 A7
SOUTHFIELDS
  Basildon 140 F7
  Chadwell St Mary 174 D7
Southfield Way CM0 .... 84 C4
Southfleet Rd DA10 .... 177 F1
South Gate
  Harlow CM20 .... 23 D8
  Purfleet RM19 .... 171 C2
Southgate Ho 1
  SS14 .... 142 A6
Southgate Mews SS3 ... 150 B3
South Gate Rd E12 ..... 132 E1
SOUTH GREEN 119 D7
South Green Jun & Inf
  Schs CM11 .... 119 C7
South Gunnels 1
  SS14 .... 142 B6
South Hall Dr RM13 .... 170 B8
SOUTH HANNINGFIELD
  .... 99 C8
South Hanningfield Rd
  CM3, SS11, CM11 ...... 99 C8
South Hanningfield Way
  SS11 .... 99 D3
South Hill
  Basildon SS16, SS17 .. 160 A7
  Horndon on t H SS17 .. 160 A3
South Hill Cl CM3 ..... 56 D6
South Hill Cres SS17 .. 160 A3
SOUTH HORNCHURCH
  .... 154 F3
South House Chase
  CM9 .... 59 C7
South Kent Ave DA11 ... 178 C1
Southlands Chase CM2 .. 55 E2
Southlands Rd CM11 .... 120 E6
Southland Terr 3
  RM19 .... 171 B1
South Mayne SS14 ...... 143 A5
South Mews SS2 .... 148 C1
SOUTHMINSTER 84 E4
Southminster CE Prim Sch
  CM0 .... 84 D4
Southminster Rd
  Althorne SS4 .... 83 C4
  Asheldham CM0 .... 85 A7
  Burnham-on-C CM0 ..... 106 B8
  St Lawrence CM0 ...... 62 F3
Southminster Sta CM0 .... 84 E4
SOUTH OCKENDON 172 C7
South Ordnance Rd
  EN3 .... 65 A2
South Par
  Canvey Island SS8 .... 164 E2
  South Ockendon RM15 .. 172 C8
South Park Bsns Ctr
  IG3 .... 133 E2
South Park Cres IG1 ... 133 E1
South Park Dr
  Barking IG11 .... 152 E8
  Ilford IG3 .... 133 E1
South Park Prim Sch
  IG1 .... 133 E1
South Park Rd IG1 ..... 133 D1
South Park Terr IG1 ... 133 E1
South Park Villas IG3 . 152 E8
South Pl
  Harlow CM20 .... 11 A4
  Waltham Abbey EN9 .... 65 C6
South Point SS0 .... 147 C4
South Primrose Hill
  CM1 .... 31 F3
South Rd
  Basildon, Vange SS17 . 142 C1
  Crays Hill CM11 ...... 120 D5
  Dagenham RM6 .... 134 E5
  Harlow CM20 .... 11 A4
  Ilford RM6 .... 134 C6
  South Ockendon RM15 .. 172 C8
South Residence IG3 ... 134 B6
South Ridge CM11 ...... 97 C3
South Riding SS14 ..... 142 E6
Southsea Ave SS9 ...... 146 D1
Southsea Ho 13 RM3 .... 114 D5
South St
  Bradwell on S CM0 .... 42 A2
  Brentwood CM14 .... 116 C8
  Great Waltham CM3 .... 18 E7
  Rainham RM13 .... 154 D3
  Rochford SS4 .... 125 F1
  Romford RM1 .... 135 E6
  Romford RM1 .... 135 F5
  Stanstead Abbotts SG12 8 C4
  Tillingham CM0 .... 63 E3
South Sta★ SS1 .... 167 B3
SOUTH STIFFORD 172 E1
South View RM14 .... 174 B8
Southview Ave RM18 .... 179 A6
Southview Cl CM3 ...... 101 D8
South View Cl SS6 ..... 145 F8
South View Cres IG2 ... 133 B5
Southview Dr
  Southend-on-S SS0 .... 147 C2
  Wanstead E18 .... 132 B8
South View Dr RM14 .... 137 B1
Southview Hts RM20 .... 177 C8
Southview Rd
  Basildon SS16 .... 142 E5
  Danbury CM3 .... 56 D6
  Hockley SS5 .... 124 F7
South View Rd
  Grays RM20 .... 177 C8

South View Rd *continued*
  Loughton IG10 .... 88 F3
  Rettendon CM3 .... 100 C5
  South Benfleet SS7 ... 144 C3
Southview Terr CM3 .... 56 D6
Southwalters SS8 ...... 163 F4
Southwark Path SS14 ... 142 F7
South Wash Rd SS15 .... 119 E1
Southway SS16 .... 141 D2
South Way RM19 .... 171 E3
SOUTH WEALD 115 E8
South Weald Dr EN9 .... 65 D6
South Weald Rd
  CM14 .... 116 A7
Southwell Cl RM16 ..... 172 C1
Southwell Link SS15 ... 141 D5
Southwell Rd SS7 ...... 144 E4
Southwick Gdns SS8 .... 163 F3
Southwick Rd SS8 ...... 163 F3
South Wlk SS14 .... 142 B5
Southwold Cres SS7 .... 144 C5
Southwold Dr IG11 ..... 153 A7
Southwood Chase
  CM3 .... 57 A4
Southwood Ct
  Basildon SS14 .... 142 D8
  Billericay CM11 ...... 119 C7
South Woodford Sta
  E18 .... 110 B1
Southwood Gdns
  Ilford IG2 .... 133 B7
  Rayleigh SS9 .... 146 B8
SOUTH WOODHAM
FERRERS 101 E8
South Woodham Ferrers
  Sta CM3 .... 101 E8
Southwood Prim Sch
  RM9 .... 153 E8
Sovereign Cl SS4 ...... 125 E2
Sovereign Ct
  7 Brentwood CM14 .... 116 C7
  Harlow CM19 .... 23 B3
  Southend-on-S, Leigh-on-S
    SS9 .... 146 E2
  Southend-on-S, Shoeburyness
    SS3 .... 168 E7
  Southend-on-S, Southchurch
    SS1 .... 167 E6
Sovereign Hts 5 SS4 ... 125 F2
Sovereign Mews SS0 .... 166 E8
Sovereign Pk SS14 ..... 120 E1
Sovereign Rd IG11 ..... 153 C2
Sowerberry Cl CM1 ..... 31 F7
Sowrey Ave RM13 .... 155 A6
Spa Cl SS1 .... 124 E6
Spa Ct SS5 .... 124 E6
Spa Dr CM0 .... 40 B1
Spains Hall Pl SS16 ... 142 C5
Spains Hall Rd CM5 .... 28 E2
Spalding Ave CM1 ...... 31 E5
Spalding Ct CM1 .... 32 A3
Spalding Way CM2 ...... 54 F8
Spalt Cl CM13 .... 117 B8
Spanbeek Rd SS8 .... 164 B5
Spanbrook IG7 .... 111 B7
Spa Rd SS5 .... 124 E6
Spareleaze Hill IG10 .. 88 F5
Sparkbridge 8 SS15 ... 141 A6
Sparks Ct RM8 .... 134 D2
Spar La CM3 .... 58 C3
Sparrow Ct E4 .... 109 C4
Sparrow Gn RM10 .... 135 B1
Sparrows Cl CM1 .... 52 A5
Sparrows Herne SS14 ... 142 B4
Sparrow's La
  Hatfield Heath CM22 .. 3 F1
  White Roothing or White
    Roding CM17, CM22 .. 13 C6
Sparsholt Rd IG11 ..... 152 E4
Spearpoint Gdns IG2 ... 133 F7
Spectrum Twr 1 RM1 ... 133 C2
Speedwell Ct RM17 ..... 178 E7
SPELLBROOK 1 F8
Spellbrook Cl SS12 .... 121 F6
Spellbrook La E CM22 .. 1 F8
Spellbrook La W CM23 .. 1 E7
Spellbrook Prim Sch
  CM23 .... 1 F7
Spells Cl CM0 .... 84 D4
Spencer Cl
  Billericay CM12 ...... 96 F5
  Epping CM16 .... 46 B2
  Maldon CM9 .... 59 A8
  Woodford IG8 .... 110 C5
Spencer Ct
  Hornchurch RM12 ...... 136 A1
  South Woodham Ferrers
    CM3 .... 101 E7
Spencer Gdns SS4 ...... 125 E5
Spencer Ho SS0 .... 147 A1
Spencer Rd
  Chingford E17 .... 109 C1
  Ilford IG3 .... 133 F3
  Rainham RM13 .... 154 D3
  South Benfleet SS7 ... 144 D6
Spencers SS5 .... 124 F4
Spencers Croft CM18 ... 24 B6
Spencers Ct SS12 ...... 121 C7
Spencer Wlk RM18 ...... 179 B6
Spenders Cl SS14 ...... 142 D8
Spenlow Dr CM1 .... 31 D7
Spenser Cres RM14 ..... 137 C4
Speyside Wlk 2 SS12 .. 121 E5
Spey Way RM1 .... 113 E3
Spillbutters CM15 ..... 72 B3
Spilsby Rd RM3 .... 114 E3
Spindle Beams SS4 ..... 125 F1

Spindles RM18 .... 179 A7
Spingate RM12 .... 155 D7
Spinnaker Cl IG11 ..... 153 E2
Spinnaker Dr CM9 ...... 37 E3
Spinnakers The SS7 .... 144 B4
Spinnaker The CM3 ..... 101 E5
Spinney Cl
  Rainham RM13 .... 154 E3
  Wickford SS11 .... 121 F7
Spinney Ct CM21 .... 1 E2
Spinney Gdns RM9 ...... 153 E7
Spinney Jun & Inf Schs
  CM20 .... 11 A1
Spinneys The
  Hockley SS5 .... 124 D5
  Rayleigh SS6 .... 124 A1
  Southend-on-S SS9 .... 146 F7
Spinney The
  Billericay CM12 ...... 97 B4
  Brentwood CM13 .... 95 C3
  Chipping Ongar CM5 ... 48 F1
  1 Harlow CM20 .... 11 A1
  Loughton IG10 .... 89 B5
  Orsett RM16 .... 159 A1
Spinneywood SS15 ...... 141 A8
Spinning Wheel Mead
  CM18 .... 24 A5
Spire Green Ctr CM19 .. 22 E7
Spire Rd SS15 .... 141 C7
Spires The
  Brentwood CM14 .... 116 D8
  Great Baddow CM2 ..... 54 F6
SPITALBROOK 21 B4
Spital La CM14 .... 115 F6
Spital Rd
  Maldon CM9 .... 36 F2
  Maldon CM9 .... 58 D7
Sporehams La
  Danbury CM3 .... 56 C4
  Howe Green CM2, CM3 .. 55 F4
Sporhams SS16 .... 141 F4
Spots Wlk CM2 .... 54 D3
Spratt Hall Rd E11 .... 132 A5
Spread Eagle Pl 2
  CM4 .... 74 C4
Spriggs Ct CM16 .... 46 A2
Spriggs Ct SS4 .... 51 A2
Spriggs Oak CM16 ...... 46 A2
Springbank Ave
  RM12 .... 155 C7
Springbok Ho CM2 ...... 54 F5
Spring Cl
  Dagenham RM8 .... 134 D3
  Little Baddow CM3 .... 34 D5
Spring Ct
  Southend-on-S SS0 .... 147 D2
  10 Wanstead E18 ..... 132 B8
Spring Elms La CM3 .... 34 F3
Springfarm Cl RM13 .... 155 D2
SPRINGFIELD 32 E6
Springfield
  Brentwood CM15 .... 94 C1
  Epping CM16 .... 67 F7
  Hadleigh SS7 .... 145 B4
Springfield Ave CM13 .. 95 E2
Springfield Basin CM2 . 32 C2
Springfield Cl CM5 .... 48 F5
Springfield Cotts CM9 . 37 B5
Springfield Ct
  2 Ilford IG1 .... 152 B7
  Rayleigh SS6 .... 123 A4
  Upminster RM14 .... 137 B1
Springfield Dr
  Ilford IG2 .... 133 C5
  Southend-on-S SS0 .... 147 D3
Springfield Gdns
  Upminster RM14 .... 137 C1
  Woodford IG8 .... 110 C3
Springfield Gn CM1 .... 32 E4
Springfield Ind Est
  CM0 .... 106 A5
Springfield Lyons App
  CM2 .... 33 A5
Springfield Nursery Est
  CM0 .... 106 A6
Springfield Park Ave
  CM2 .... 32 E2
Springfield Park Hill
  CM2 .... 32 D2
Springfield Park La
  CM2 .... 32 E2
Springfield Park Par
  CM2 .... 32 D2
Springfield Park Rd
  CM2 .... 32 E2
Springfield Pl CM1 .... 32 E5
Springfield Rd
  Billericay CM12 ...... 97 B5
  Burnham-on-C CM0 ..... 106 A6
  Canvey Island SS8 .... 164 F3
  Chelmsford CM1 .... 32 E4
  Chingford E4 .... 87 E2
  Grays RM16 .... 173 E4
  Wickford SS11 .... 121 F8
Springfields
  Basildon SS16 .... 142 F4
  Waltham Abbey EN9 .... 65 E5
Spring Gardens Ind Est
  RM7 .... 135 C5
Spring Gdns
  Hornchurch RM12 ...... 155 B8
  Rayleigh SS6 .... 123 C2
  Romford RM7 .... 135 C5
  Woodford IG8 .... 110 C3
Spring Gr IG10 .... 88 D3
Springhall Ct CM21 .... 1 E2
Springhall La CM21 .... 1 E1
Springhall Rd CM21 .... 1 E2

Springhead Rd DA11 .... 178 D1
Spring Hills CM20 ..... 10 B1
Spring Hills Twr CM20 . 10 A1
Springhouse La SS17 ... 161 A2
Springhouse Rd SS17 ... 160 F4
Spring La CM9 .... 37 B4
Springleigh Pl SS0 .... 147 D2
Spring Mews CM21 ...... 1 E2
Spring Pl 2 IG1 .... 152 C3
Spring Pond Cl CM2 .... 54 E8
Spring Pond Mdw
  CM15 .... 72 C4
Springpond Rd RM9 ..... 153 E7
Spring Rise CM2 .... 54 C2
Spring Vale DA9 .... 177 C1
Springwater Cl SS9 .... 146 C7
Springwater Gr SS9 .... 146 C7
Springwater Rd SS9 .... 146 C8
Springwell Ct SG12 .... 8 C3
Springwood Way
  RM1 .... 136 A6
Spruce Cl SS15 .... 119 C1
Spruce Hill CM18 ...... 23 E3
Spruce Hills Rd E17 ... 109 C1
Sprundel Ave SS8 ...... 164 D2
Spur Cl RM4 .... 90 B6
Spurgate CM13 .... 95 B1
Spurgeon Cl 11 RM17 .. 178 C8
Spurling Rd RM9 .... 153 F6
Spurling Wks EN11 .... 21 C7
Spur Rd IG11 .... 152 C2
Spurway Par 2 IG2 .... 132 F6
Squadrons App RM12 .... 155 D6
Square St 3 CM17 ..... 11 C1
Square The
  10 Brentwood CM14 ... 116 C8
  Heybridge CM9 .... 37 A5
  Horndon on t H SS17 .. 159 F3
  Ilford IG1 .... 133 A4
  Sawbridgeworth CM21 .. 1 E2
  Stock CM4 .... 75 E2
  Tillingham CM0 .... 63 E4
  Woodford IG8 .... 110 A5
Squires Ct EN11 .... 21 A5
Squire St CM3 .... 101 E7
Squires The RM7 .... 135 B5
Squirrells Ct CM1 ..... 31 F5
Squirrels SS16 .... 141 B3
Squirrel's Chase
  RM16 .... 174 A4
Squirrels Ct RM2 ...... 136 C7
Squirrel's Heath Ave
  RM2 .... 136 B8
Squirrels Heath Inf Sch
  RM2 .... 136 B6
Squirrels Heath Jun Sch
  RM2 .... 136 B6
Squirrels Heath La RM11,
  RM2 .... 136 D7
Squirrels Heath Rd
  RM3 .... 114 F1
Squirrel's La IG9 ..... 110 D7
Stablecroft CM1 .... 32 E8
Stable Mews SS2 .... 147 F2
Stables The
  Buckhurst Hill IG9 ... 88 C2
  Sawbridgeworth CM21 .. 2 B3
Stacey Dr SS16 .... 141 C2
Stacey's Mount CM11 ... 120 C5
Stackfield CM20 .... 11 A3
Staddles CM22 .... 2 B8
Stadium Rd SS2 .... 148 A1
Stadium Trad Est
  SS7 .... 145 C7
Stadium Way
  Harlow CM19 .... 9 F1
  Thundersley SS7 ...... 145 C7
Staffa Cl SS12 .... 121 F5
Stafford Ave RM11 ..... 136 D8
Stafford Cl
  Grays RM16 .... 172 C2
  Greenhithe DA9 .... 176 F2
  Linford SS17 .... 175 A3
  Southend-on-S SS9 .... 147 A6
Stafford Ct EN10 ...... 21 A3
Stafford Dr EN10 ...... 21 A3
Stafford Gn SS16 ...... 140 F4
Stafford Ho EN10 ...... 21 A3
Stafford Ind Est
  RM11 .... 136 D8
Staffords CM17 .... 11 E4
Stafford Wlk SS8 ...... 164 A5
Stagden Cross SS14 .... 142 F5
Stagden Cross Villas
  CM1 .... 6 E2
Staggart Gn IG7 .... 111 F4
Stag Hts IG9 .... 110 B8
Stag La IG9 .... 110 B8
Staines Rd IG1 .... 152 D8
Stainforth Rd IG2 ..... 133 D5
Stairs Rd SS3 .... 150 F4
Stalham Way IG6 .... 111 B2
Stambridge Prim Sch
  SS4 .... 126 C2
Stambridge Rd SS4 ..... 126 C2
Stamford Gdns RM9 ..... 153 C5
Stamford Rd RM9 .... 153 C5
Stammers Ct CM0 .... 84 D4
Standard Rd DA17 ...... 169 A1
Standen Ave
  Hornchurch RM12 ...... 136 E1
  South Woodham Ferrers
    CM3 .... 101 D4
Standfield Gdns
  RM10 .... 154 A6
Standfield Rd RM10 .... 154 A7
Standingford CM19 ..... 23 B3
Stanetta Ct 3 RM6 .... 134 B4

Staneway SS16 .... 141 D3
Stanfield Rd SS2 ...... 148 A1
Stanfields Ct CM20 .... 10 E1
Stanford Cl
  Romford RM7 .... 135 B5
  Woodford IG8 .... 110 E5
Stanford Ct EN9 .... 66 A6
Stanford Gdns RM15 .... 171 E5
Stanford Hall 1 SS17 . 160 F3
Stanford Ho
  3 Barking IG11 ...... 153 B3
  East Tilbury RM18 .... 175 B2
STANFORD-LE-H 160 E1
Stanford-Le-Hope By-
Pass
  Basildon SS16, SS17 .. 142 B1
  Orsett RM16 .... 174 D8
  Stanford-le-H SS17 ... 160 D4
Stanford-le-Hope Prim
  Sch SS17 .... 160 D1
Stanford-le-Hope Sta
  SS17 .... 160 C1
Stanford Marshes Nature
  Reserve★ SS17 ...... 175 E7
Stanford Rd
  Canvey Island SS8 .... 164 A3
  Grays RM16 .... 173 E4
  Orsett SS17, RM16 .... 174 E8
  Stanford-le-H SS17 ... 160 B1
STANFORD RIVERS 70 C6
Stanford Rivers Rd
  CM5 .... 71 A8
Stanhope Gdns
  1 Dagenham RM8 ...... 134 F1
  Redbridge IG1 .... 132 F3
Stanhope Rd
  Dagenham RM8 .... 134 F1
  Rainham RM13 .... 155 A3
  Swanscombe DA10 ..... 177 F1
Stanier Cl SS1 .... 167 C8
Stanley Ave
  Barking IG11 .... 152 F3
  Dagenham RM8 .... 134 F3
  Romford RM2 .... 136 A7
Stanley Cl
  Greenhithe DA9 .... 176 E2
  Hornchurch RM12 ...... 136 C2
  Romford RM2 .... 136 A7
Stanley Pl CM5 .... 49 A2
Stanley Rd
  Bulphan RM14 .... 158 F8
  Canvey Island SS8 .... 164 D4
  Chingford E4 .... 87 D1
  Grays RM17 .... 178 B8
  Hornchurch RM12 ...... 136 D2
  Ilford IG1 .... 133 D2
  Rochford SS4 .... 125 C2
  South Benfleet SS7 ... 144 D6
  Southend-on-S SS1 .... 167 B7
  Swanscombe DA10 ..... 177 F1
  Woodford E18 .... 109 F2
Stanley Rd N RM13 ..... 154 E4
Stanley Rd S RM13 ..... 154 F3
Stanley Rise CM2 ...... 32 F3
Stanley Terr CM12 ..... 97 A1
Stanmore Rd
  Belvedere DA17 .... 169 C2
  Wickford SS11 .... 122 B6
Stanmore Way IG10 ..... 89 A8
Stannetts SS15 .... 141 B8
Stansfield Ct SS7 ..... 144 B7
Stansfield Rd SS7 ..... 144 B7
Stansgate Rd
  Dagenham RM10 .... 135 A1
  Steeple CM0 .... 61 F5
STANSTEAD ABBOTTS 8 E4
Stanstead Dr EN11 ..... 21 B8
Stanstead Rd
  Hoddesdon EN11 .... 8 B1
  Wanstead E11 .... 132 B6
Stansted Cl
  Billericay CM11 ...... 97 D2
  Chelmsford CM1 .... 31 E1
  Hornchurch RM12 ...... 155 B6
Stanton Ct 4 RM10 .... 154 A6
Stanton Gate RM7 ...... 135 D6
Stantons CM20 .... 10 B1
Stanway Cl 2 IG7 ..... 111 E5
Stanway Rd
  South Benfleet SS7 ... 144 C5
  Waltham Abbey EN9 .... 66 A6
Stanwyck Dr IG7 .... 111 C5
Stanwyck Gdns RM3 ..... 114 B5
STAPLEFORD ABBOTTS
  .... 91 C3
Stapleford Abbotts Prim
  Sch RM4 .... 91 C4
Stapleford Ave IG2 .... 133 E6
Stapleford Cl
  Chelmsford CM2 .... 32 A1
  Chingford E4 .... 109 C7
Stapleford End SS11 ... 122 B5
Stapleford Gdns RM5 ... 113 A4
Stapleford Rd RM4 ..... 91 B5
STAPLEFORD TAWNEY
  .... 69 C2
Stapleford Way IG11 ... 153 B2
Staplegrove SS3 .... 168 D8
Staples Rd IG10 .... 88 E6
Staples Road Jun & Inf
  Sch IG10 .... 88 E6
Stapleton Cres RM13 ... 155 A6
Staple Tye CM18 .... 23 D5
Staple Tye Sh Mews
  CM18 .... 23 C5

Stapley Rd DA17 . . . . **169** A1
Starboard Ave DA9 . . . . . **177** B1
Starboard View CM3 . . . . **101** E6
Star Bsns Ctr RM13 . . . . **169** D8
Starch House La IG6 . . . **111** D1
Star La
  Epping CM16 . . . . **46** A1
  Great Wakering SS3 . . . . **149** E3
  Ingatestone CM4 . . . . . . **74** C4
Star Lane Ind Est SS3 . . . **149** E3
Starling Cl
  Buckhurst Hill IG9 . . . . **88** A1
  Thundersley SS7 . . . . **145** B7
Starmans Cl RM9 . . . . . . **153** E4
State Mans IG6 . . . . **111** C1
State Par IG6 . . . . **111** C1
Station App
  Basildon, Laindon
    SS15 . . . . **141** C5
  Basildon, Pitsea SS16 . . **143** B4
  Buckhurst Hill IG9 . . . . . **110** D6
  Burnham-on-C CM0 . . . . **106** B5
  Canvey Island SS8 . . . . . **163** F6
  Grays RM17 . . . . **178** A8
  Harlow CM20 . . . . **11** C5
  Hockley SS5 . . . . **124** E6
  North Fambridge CM3 . . **103** B8
  Southend-on-S, Prittlewell
    SS2 . . . . **147** F2
  Southend-on-S SS1 . . . . **167** A8
  South Woodham Ferrers
    CM3 . . . . **101** C8
  Theydon Bois CM16 . . . . . **67** E3
  Upminster RM14 . . . . . . **137** C2
  Wanstead E11 . . . . **132** A6
  Wickford SS11 . . . . **121** D8
  Woodford IG8 . . . . **110** B4
  2 Woodford, Snaresbrook
    E18 . . . . **110** B1
Station Ave
  Rayleigh SS6 . . . . **123** C3
  Southend-on-S SS2 . . . . **148** A3
  Wickford SS11 . . . . **121** D8
Station Cres
  Cold Norton CM3 . . . . **80** F5
  Rayleigh SS6 . . . . **123** D3
Station Ct
  Chipping Ongar CM5 . . . . **49** A3
  Wickford SS11 . . . . **121** D8
Station Est **1** E18 . . . . . **110** B1
Station Gate SS15 . . . . . **141** C5
Station Ind Est CM0 . . . . **106** B5
Station La
  Basildon SS13 . . . . **143** B5
  Hornchurch RM12 . . . . . **136** D2
  Ingatestone CM4 . . . . **74** B3
Station Par
  Barking IG11 . . . . **152** C5
  Dagenham RM10 . . . . . . **154** A6
  Hornchurch RM12 . . . . . **155** B8
  3 Romford RM1 . . . . . **135** E5
  2 Wanstead E11 . . . . **132** A6
  Woodford IG9 . . . . **110** D6
Station Pas E18 . . . . . . **110** B1
Station Rd
  Althorne CM3 . . . . **82** F1
  Belvedere DA17 . . . . . . **169** A3
  Billericay CM12 . . . . **96** F2
  Burnham-on-C CM0 . . . . **106** B5
  Canvey Island SS8 . . . . . **164** E2
  Chigwell IG7 . . . . **111** B7
  Chingford E4 . . . . **87** D1
  Cold Norton CM3 . . . . **81** A5
  East Tilbury RM18 . . . . . **180** B7
  Epping CM16 . . . . **68** A8
  Greenhithe DA9 . . . . **177** A2
  Greenhithe DA9 . . . . **177** A3
  Harlow CM17 . . . . **11** C4
  Hockley SS5 . . . . **124** E6
  Hoddesdon EN10 . . . . . . **21** A3
  Holdbrook EN9 . . . . **65** A5
  Ilford, Barkingside IG6 . . **133** D8
  Ilford IG1 . . . . **133** B1
  Loughton IG10 . . . . **88** E4
  Maldon CM9 . . . . **37** A3
  Northfleet DA11 . . . . . . **178** B1
  North Weald Bassett
    CM16 . . . . **47** B4
  Rayleigh SS6 . . . . **123** C3
  Romford, Chadwell Heath RM6,
    RM8 . . . . **134** D4
  Romford, Harold Wood
    RM3 . . . . **114** F2
  Romford RM2 . . . . **136** C7
  Sawbridgeworth CM21 . . . **1** F3
  South Benfleet SS7 . . . . **163** D8
  Southend-on-S, Eastwood
    SS9 . . . . **146** E3
  Southend-on-S, Leigh-on-S
    SS9 . . . . **146** E1
  Southend-on-S, Thorpe Bay
    SS1 . . . . **168** B8
  Southend-on-S, Westcliff-on-S
    SS0 . . . . **166** D7
  Southminster CM0 . . . . . . **84** E4
  Stanstead Abbotts SG12 . . **8** C4
  Upminster RM14 . . . . . . **137** C2
  West Horndon CM13 . . . **139** D5
  Wickford SS11 . . . . **99** C2
Station Rd N DA17 . . . . **169** B3
Station Sq RM2 . . . . . . **136** B7
Station Way
  Basildon SS14, SS16 . . . . **142** A5
  Buckhurst Hill IG9 . . . . . **110** D6
Staveley Rd **4** E11 . . . . **132** A6

Staverton Rd RM11 . . . . **136** D5
Stays La CM5 . . . . **29** A3
Steadman Ho **4**
  RM10 . . . . **135** A1
Steamer Terr **2** CM1 . . . . **32** A3
Stebbings SS16 . . . . **141** C4
Stebbings Ct **5** CM0 . . . **106** C4
Stebbing Way IG11 . . . . **153** A3
Steed Cl RM11 . . . . **136** B2
Steeds Way IG10 . . . . **88** E6
Steele Ave DA9 . . . . **177** A2
Steen Cl CM4 . . . . **74** B4
STEEPLE **61** E3
Steeple Cl
  Heybridge CM9 . . . . **37** D5
  Rochford SS4 . . . . **125** D3
Steeplefield SS9 . . . . . . **146** E6
Steeple Gate SS7 . . . . . **145** E2
Steeplehall SS13 . . . . . . **143** A5
Steeple Hts SS7 . . . . . . **144** B6
Steeple Mdws CM0 . . . . . **84** B4
Steeple Rd
  Latchingdon CM3 . . . . **82** D7
  Steeple CM0 . . . . **62** C4
  Steeple CM0 . . . . **84** B7
STEEPLE VIEW **119** B1
Steeple View RM17 . . . . **173** A1
Steeple Way CM15 . . . . . **72** B2
Steerforth Cl CM1 . . . . . . **31** D7
Steli Ave SS8 . . . . **163** F5
Stella Maris Cl SS8 . . . . **164** F3
Sten Cl EN3 . . . . **65** A2
Stenning Ave SS17 . . . . **175** B2
Stephen Ave RM13 . . . . **155** A6
Stephens Cl RM3 . . . . . **114** C5
Stephens Cres SS17 . . . **159** F3
Stephenson Ave
  RM18 . . . . **179** A6
Stephenson Cl
  Hoddesdon EN11 . . . . . . **21** C6
  Hoddesdon EN11 . . . . . . **21** D6
Stephenson Rd
  North Fambridge
    CM3 . . . . **103** A8
  Southend-on-S SS9 . . . . **146** C6
Sterling Ind Est RM10 . . **154** B8
Stern Cl IG11 . . . . **153** C3
Sterry Cres RM10 . . . . . **154** A7
Sterry Gdns RM10 . . . . . **154** A6
Sterry Ho RM13 . . . . . . **155** B2
Sterry Rd
  Barking IG11 . . . . **152** F4
  Dagenham RM10 . . . . . . **154** A7
Stevanne Ct **1** DA17 . . . **169** A1
Stevenage Rd E6 . . . . . . **152** A6
Stevens Cl SS8 . . . . **164** D4
Stevenson Way SS12 . . **121** C5
Stevens Rd RM8 . . . . . . **134** C1
Stevens Way IG7 . . . . . . **111** E6
STEWARDS **23** E3
Stewards Cl CM16 . . . . . . **68** A6
Stewards Elm Farm La
  SS4 . . . . **126** D4
STEWARD'S GREEN **68** B7
Stewards Green Rd
  CM16 . . . . **68** B6
Stewards Sch CM18 . . . . . **23** D4
Stewart Ave RM14 . . . . . **137** B1
Stewart Pl SS12 . . . . . . **121** F5
Stewart Rainbird Ho **1**
  E12 . . . . **152** A7
Stewart Rd CM2 . . . . **54** A6
Steyning Ave SS2 . . . . . **148** E1
Stickland Rd DA17 . . . . . **169** A2
Stifford Clays Inf Sch
  RM16 . . . . **173** B6
Stifford Clays Jun Sch
  RM16 . . . . **173** B5
Stifford Clays Rd
  Grays RM16 . . . . **173** B6
  Orsett RM16 . . . . **173** B7
Stifford Hill RM16 . . . . . **172** C5
Stifford Prim Sch
  RM17 . . . . **172** F1
Stifford Rd
  Aveley RM15 . . . . **171** E5
  South Ockendon RM15 . . **172** B6
Stile Croft CM18 . . . . **24** A6
Stile La SS6 . . . . **123** D2
Stilemans SS11 . . . . **121** D8
Stiles Cl DA8 . . . . **169** B1
Stiles The **37** E3
Stillwells SS4 . . . . **126** A2
Stirling Ave SS9 . . . . **146** B2
Stirling Cl
  Rainham RM13 . . . . **155** B2
  Rayleigh SS6 . . . . **123** B5
Stirling Pl SS13 . . . . . . **143** B8
Stirrup Cl CM1 . . . . **32** E7
Stivvy's Rd CM9 . . . . **35** C3
STOCK **75** F3
Stock CE Prim Sch
  CM4 . . . . **75** D3
Stock Chase CM9 . . . . . . **37** B5
Stock Cl SS2 . . . . **147** F4
Stockdale Rd RM8 . . . . . **134** F2
Stocker Gdns RM9 . . . . . **153** C5
Stockfield Gr EN11 . . . . . **21** B8
Stock Ind Pk SS2 . . . . . . **148** A4
Stock La CM4 . . . . **74** D3
Stockland Rd RM7 . . . . . **135** D5
Stock Park Ct SS9 . . . . . **146** E6
Stock Rd
  Billericay CM12 . . . . **97** C5
  Galleywood CM2 . . . . **54** B2
  Southend-on-S SS2 . . . . **147** F4

Stock Rd continued
  Stock CM4 . . . . **75** D1
  Stock CM4 . . . . **76** B6
Stocksfield CM15 . . . . . . **71** F2
Stocks La CM15 . . . . **71** F1
Stock Terr CM9 . . . . **37** B5
Stockwell Cl CM11 . . . . . **119** D7
Stockwood SS7 . . . . **145** B7
Stoke Ave IG6 . . . . **112** A4
Stokefelde SS13 . . . . . . **143** B7
Stoke Rd RM13 . . . . **155** D2
Stokesay **11** DA2 . . . . . . **176** B1
Stokes Cotts IG6 . . . . . . **111** C2
Stokes Ct SS2 . . . . **148** E2
Stonard Rd RM8 . . . . . . **153** B8
Stonards Hill
  Epping CM16 . . . . **68** C8
  Loughton IG10 . . . . **88** F4
STONDON MASSEY **72** A6
Stondon Rd CM5 . . . . **49** B1
STONE **176** F2
STONEBRIDGE **149** A6
Stonebridge Rd DA11 . . **178** B2
STONE CASTLE **177** A1
Stone Castle Dr DA9 . . . **177** A1
Stonechat Rd CM11 . . . . **119** C8
Stone Cl RM8 . . . . **134** F2
Stone Cross **3** CM20 . . . . **10** D1
Stone Crossing Halt
  DA9 . . . . **176** F2
Stone Ct DA8 . . . . **169** F1
Stonegate CM4 . . . . **74** C3
Stonehall Way IG1 . . . . . **132** E5
Stonehall Bsns Pk
  CM17 . . . . **13** B5
Stonehill Cl SS9 . . . . **146** F4
Stonehill Ct E4 . . . . **87** B2
Stonehill Rd
  Roxwell CM1 . . . . **29** F3
  Southend-on-S SS9 . . . . **146** F5
Stone Ho RM12 . . . . **136** D1
Stonehouse Cnr
  RM19 . . . . **176** E8
Stoneleigh CM21 . . . . **1** D3
Stoneleigh Ct IG5 . . . . . **132** E8
Stoneleigh Dr EN11 . . . . . **8** B1
Stoneleigh Rd IG5 . . . . . **132** F8
Stoneleighs SS7 . . . . . . **144** F6
Stonely Cres DA9 . . . . . **177** C3
Stoneness Rd RM20 . . . **177** C2
Stone Place Rd DA9 . . . . **176** E2
Stone St DA11 . . . . **179** B1
Stonewood Rd DA8 . . . . **169** E1
Stoney Bridge Dr EN9 . . . **66** A5
Stoneycroft Rd IG8 . . . . . **110** E4
Stone Yd **2** CM14 . . . . . . **116** C8
STONEYHILLS **106** C8
Stoney Hills
  Burnham-on-C CM0 . . . . **106** C8
  Ramsden Heath CM11 . . . **98** B5
Stony La CM5 . . . . **48** C8
Stony Path IG10 . . . . **88** F8
Stonyshotts EN9 . . . . **65** E6
Stony Wood CM18 . . . . . . **23** E7
Storas Ct **9** RM19 . . . . . **171** B1
Stormonts Way SS16 . . . **141** D2
Storms Way CM2 . . . . **33** B2
Stornoway Rd SS2 . . . . . **148** D1
Storr Gdns CM13 . . . . **95** D4
Stortford Rd
  Hatfield Heath CM22 . . . . . **2** E4
  Hoddesdon EN11 . . . . . . **21** C7
  Leaden Roding CM6 . . . . **15** B7
Stort Mill CM20 . . . . **11** B6
Stour Cl SS3 . . . . **168** E6
Stour Rd
  Dagenham RM10 . . . . . . **135** A2
  Grays RM16 . . . . **174** A1
Stour Way RM14 . . . . . . **137** E5
Stowe Ct SS0 . . . . **147** E1
Stowe Pl SS2 . . . . **148** C2
Stowe's La CM0 . . . . **63** D4
Stowe Villas SS2 . . . . . . **167** C8
STOW MARIES **80** C4
Stow Rd CM3 . . . . **80** D5
Stow The CM20 . . . . **10** F2
Stow Villas CM3 . . . . **80** C4
Stradbroke Dr IG7 . . . . . **111** B4
Stradbroke Gr
  Buckhurst Hill IG9 . . . . . . **88** D1
  Ilford IG5 . . . . **133** A8
  Redbridge IG5 . . . . **132** F8
  Woodford IG5 . . . . **110** E1
Stradbroke Pk IG7 . . . . . **111** B4
Strafford Ave IG5 . . . . . . **111** A1
Straight Rd RM3 . . . . **114** C3
Straits The EN9 . . . . **65** B7
Strangman Ave SS7 . . . . **145** B4
Strasbourg Rd SS8 . . . . **164** D5
Stratford Cl
  Barking IG11 . . . . **153** A5
  Dagenham RM10 . . . . . . **154** C5
Stratford Gdns SS17 . . . **160** D3
Stratford Ho
  Rayleigh SS6 . . . . **123** D2
  6 Romford RM3 . . . . . **114** D4
Strathfield Gdns
  IG11 . . . . **152** D6
Strathmore RM18 . . . . . . **175** C2
Strathmore Gdns
  RM12 . . . . **135** F3
Strathmore Rd CM3 . . . . **103** B8
Stratton Dr IG11 . . . . **152** F6
Stratton Ho SS1 . . . . . . **166** F7
Stratton Rd RM3 . . . . . . **115** A5
Stratton Wlk RM3 . . . . . **115** A5
Street The
  Galleywood CM2 . . . . **54** B2

Street The continued
  High Ongar CM5 . . . . **49** D4
  High Roding CM6 . . . . **5** E7
  Latchingdon CM3 . . . . . . **82** A5
  Little Waltham CM3 . . . . . **19** B6
  Mashbury CM1 . . . . **17** B8
  Pleshey CM3 . . . . **7** F2
  Purleigh CM3, CM9 . . . . . **58** F1
  Roxwell CM1 . . . . **30** B6
  Sheering CM22 . . . . **12** C8
  Steeple CM0 . . . . **61** F2
  Stow Maries CM3 . . . . **80** C4
  Willingale CM5 . . . . **28** D3
  Woodham Ferrers CM3 . . . **79** B4
  Woodham Walter CM9 . . . **35** D2
Stroma Ave SS8 . . . . . . **163** F6
Stroma Gdns SS3 . . . . . **168** D6
Stromburg Rd SS8 . . . . . **163** F5
Stromness Pl **6** SS2 . . . . **167** C8
Stromness Rd SS2 . . . . . **148** C1
Strood Ave RM7 . . . . **135** D3
STROUD GREEN **125** B2
Stroud Ho **12** RM3 . . . . . **114** D5
Strouds Cl RM6 . . . . **134** B6
Struan Ave SS17 . . . . . . **160** E5
Struan Ho **15** E11 . . . . . **132** A6
Stuart Cl
  Canvey Island SS8 . . . . . **164** B4
  Great Baddow CM2 . . . . . **55** B6
  Great Wakering SS3 . . . . **149** F4
  Pilgrims Hatch CM15 . . . . **94** B4
  Southend-on-S SS2 . . . . **148** A2
Stuart Ct E4 . . . . **109** F8
Stuart Ho EN9 . . . . **65** F6
Stuart Rd
  Barking IG11 . . . . **152** F4
  Gravesend DA11 . . . . . . **179** A1
  Grays RM17 . . . . **173** B1
  Southend-on-S SS2 . . . . **148** B2
Stuarts RM11 . . . . **136** E3
Stuart St SS2 . . . . **148** A3
Stuart Way CM11 . . . . **97** E1
Stubbers La RM14 . . . . . **156** E5
Stubbs Mews **5** RM8 . . . **153** B8
Stublands SS13 . . . . **142** F6
Studland Ave SS12 . . . . **120** F8
Studley Ave E4 . . . . **109** D3
Studley Ct IG4 . . . . **132** D5
Studley Dr IG4 . . . . **132** D5
Studley Rd RM9 . . . . **153** D5
Stump La CM1 . . . . **32** D4
Sturge Ave E17 . . . . **109** B1
Sturrocks SS16 . . . . **142** E3
Sudbrook Cl SS12 . . . . . **121** D6
Sudbury Cl SS5 . . . . **124** F4
Sudbury Ct **1** RM6 . . . . . **134** B6
Sudbury Rd
  Barking IG11 . . . . **152** F7
  Canvey Island SS8 . . . . . **163** F5
  Downham CM11 . . . . **99** A5
Sudburys Farm Rd
  CM12 . . . . **118** C6
Sudeley Gdns SS15 . . . . **124** D6
Sudicamps Ct EN9 . . . . . **66** A6
Suffield Rd E4 . . . . **109** B6
Suffolk Ave SS9 . . . . **146** F3
Suffolk Cres CM9 . . . . . . **36** E1
Suffolk Ct
  Ilford IG3 . . . . **133** E5
  2 Ilford, Little Heath
    RM6 . . . . **134** C5
  Rochford SS4 . . . . **125** D3
Suffolk Dr
  Basildon SS15 . . . . **141** B6
  Chelmsford CM2 . . . . **33** A4
Suffolk Ho RM7 . . . . **113** A2
Suffolk Rd
  Barking IG11 . . . . **152** D5
  Dagenham RM10 . . . . . . **154** C7
  Gravesend DA12 . . . . . . **179** D1
  Ilford IG3 . . . . **133** E5
  Maldon CM9 . . . . **36** E1
Suffolk Way
  Canvey Island SS8 . . . . . **163** E4
  Hornchurch RM11 . . . . . **137** A7
Suffolk Wlk SS8 . . . . **163** E4
Sugden Ave SS12 . . . . . **121** A7
Sugden Way IG11 . . . . . **152** F3
Sullivan Br RM18 . . . . . . **179** A6
Sullivan Way SS16 . . . . **141** A5
Sultan Rd E11 . . . . **132** B7
Summercourt Rd SS0 . . **166** E8
Summerdale
  Althorne CM3 . . . . **83** A3
  Billericay CM12 . . . . **97** A2
Summerfield Ho RM9 . . . **153** D8
Summerfield Rd IG10 . . . **88** D3
Summerfields CM4 . . . . . **74** C3
Summerhill CM3 . . . . **83** A3
Summerlands SS3 . . . . . **163** F5
Summerwood Cl SS7 . . . **145** C3
Summit Dr IG8 . . . . **110** D1
Summit The IG10 . . . . **88** F8
SUMNERS **23** A4
Sumners Farm Cl
  CM19 . . . . **23** A3
Sumpners Link SS15 . . . **140** E6
Sumpters Way SS2 . . . . **147** F5
Sunbury Ct SS3 . . . . **149** E2
Sunbury Way CM9 . . . . . **58** F8
Sunderland Way E12 . . . **132** D2
Sundew Ct RM17 . . . . . . **178** D8
Sundridge Cl DA1 . . . . . **176** A1
Sunflower Cl **5** CM1 . . . . **32** F6
Sunflower Way RM3 . . . . **114** D2
SUNKEN MARSH **164** D5
Sunnedon SS16 . . . . **142** D5
Sunningdale SS8 . . . . . . **164** C4

Sunningdale Ave
  Barking IG11 . . . . **152** D5
  Rainham RM13 . . . . **155** B1
  Southend-on-S SS9 . . . . **147** A1
Sunningdale Ct SS1 . . . . **167** A8
Sunningdale Rd
  Althorne CM3 . . . . **82** E2
  Chelmsford CM1 . . . . **31** E4
  Rainham RM13 . . . . **155** A5
Sunninghill Gdns IG2 . . . **133** F6
Sunnings La RM14 . . . . . **156** D5
Sunnybank Cl SS9 . . . . . **146** F6
Sunny Croft CM18 . . . . . . **23** F5
Sunnycroft Gdns
  RM14 . . . . **137** F4
Sunnydene Ave E4 . . . . . **109** D5
Sunnydene Cl RM3 . . . . . **114** F3
Sunnyfield Gdns SS5 . . . **124** B6
Sunnymead Flats **10**
  CM0 . . . . **106** C4
SUNNYMEDE **97** D1
Sunnymede IG7 . . . . **112** B7
Sunnymede Cl SS7 . . . . . **145** A6
Sunnymede Dr IG6 . . . . . **133** B7
Sunnymede Inf Sch
  CM11 . . . . **97** D1
Sunnymede Jun Sch
  CM11 . . . . **97** D1
Sunny Mews RM5 . . . . . . **113** C3
Sunny Rd SS5 . . . . **124** E5
Sunnyside
  Basildon SS16 . . . . **140** F4
  Lower Nazeing EN9 . . . . . **21** F1
Sunnyside Dr E4 . . . . **87** C2
Sunnyside Gdns
  RM14 . . . . **137** C1
Sunnyside Rd
  Epping CM16 . . . . **67** F7
  Ilford IG1 . . . . **133** D1
Sunny Way CM0 . . . . **62** C8
Sunnyway Cotts CM3 . . . . **56** E3
Sun Ray Ave CM13 . . . . . . **95** E3
Sunray Ho SS0 . . . . **166** D8
Sun Rd DA10 . . . . **177** F1
Sunrise Ave
  Chelmsford CM1 . . . . **32** A5
  Hornchurch RM12 . . . . . **136** C1
Sunrise Lo RM12 . . . . . . **136** C1
Sunset Ave
  Chingford E4 . . . . **87** B4
  Woodford IG8 . . . . **109** F6
Sunset Ct **4** IG8 . . . . . . **110** C3
Sunset Dr RM3 . . . . **114** B5
Sunset Mews RM5 . . . . . **113** C4
Sunshine Cl SS5 . . . . . . **101** E3
Sun St
  Billericay CM12 . . . . **97** A1
  Sawbridgeworth CM21 . . . **1** F1
  Waltham Abbey EN9 . . . . . **65** C6
Surbiton Ave SS1 . . . . . **167** D8
Surbiton Rd SS2 . . . . . . **148** D1
Surig Rd SS8 . . . . **164** A4
Surman Cres CM13 . . . . . **95** C2
Surmans Cl RM9 . . . . . . **153** C4
Surman Terr RM1 . . . . . . **136** A6
Surrey Ave SS9 . . . . **146** F3
Surrey Dr RM11 . . . . **137** A7
Surrey Ho RM7 . . . . **113** A2
Surrey Rd
  Barking IG11 . . . . **152** E5
  Dagenham RM10 . . . . . . **154** B7
Surrey Way SS15 . . . . . . **141** B6
Surridge Cl RM13 . . . . . **155** C2
Susan Cl RM7 . . . . **135** C8
Susan Fielder Cotts **3**
  SS8 . . . . **164** A3
Susan Lawrence Ho **4**
  E12 . . . . **152** A8
Sussex Ave RM3 . . . . . . **114** F3
Sussex Cl
  Basildon SS15 . . . . **141** B6
  Boreham CM3 . . . . **33** F8
  Canvey Island SS8 . . . . . **164** A5
  Hoddesdon EN11 . . . . . . **21** A7
  Redbridge IG4 . . . . **132** F6
Sussex Ct CM12 . . . . **97** B6
Sussex Ho RM7 . . . . **113** A2
Sussex Rd
  Brentwood CM14 . . . . . . **116** B6
  Wallend E6 . . . . **152** A4
Sussex Terr **2** RM19 . . . . **171** B1
Sussex Way
  Billericay CM12 . . . . **97** B6
  Canvey Island SS8 . . . . . **164** A5
Sutcliffe Cl SS12 . . . . . . **121** D6
Sutherland Bvd SS9 . . . . **146** B2
Sutherland Cl DA9 . . . . . **176** D2
Sutherland Ho
  Chelmsford CM1 . . . . **32** A4
  5 Redbridge IG8 . . . . **111** A3
Sutherland Pl SS12 . . . . **121** D5
Sutherland Rd DA17 . . . . **169** A3
Sutton Acres CM22 . . . . . **2** D7
Sutton Cl IG10 . . . . **88** D2
Sutton Court Dr SS4 . . . . **147** F7
Sutton Ct SS2 . . . . **148** C2
Sutton Ford Cotts
  SS4 . . . . **148** B8
Sutton Gdns IG11 . . . . . **152** E3
Sutton Gn IG11 . . . . **152** E4
Sutton Mead CM2 . . . . . . **33** A4
Sutton Rd
  Barking IG11 . . . . **152** E4
  Rochford SS4, SS4 . . . . . **148** B6
  Southend-on-S SS2 . . . . **148** B2
SUTTONS **168** H8
Suttons Ave RM12 . . . . . **136** D1

Suttons Bsns Pk
RM13 . . . . .154 E2
Suttons Gdns RM12 . . . .136 D1
Suttons La RM12 . . . . . .155 D7
Suttons Prim Sch
RM12 . . . . .155 D8
Suttons Rd SS3 . . . . . . .168 H8
Swaffham Ct **1** RM6 . . .134 C5
Swaines Ind Est SS4 . . . .125 D3
Swale Cl RM15. . . . . . . .171 C7
Swale Rd SS7 . . . . .145 B5
Swallow Cl
Grays RM16. . . . . .172 C2
Greenhithe DA9. . . . . . .176 F2
Rayleigh SS6 . . . . .123 B3
Swallowcliffe SS3 . . . . .149 D1
Swallow Ct
9 Brentwood CM14 . . . . .116 C7
Chingford IG8 . . . . .109 D3
Ilford IG2 . . . . .133 C6
Swallow Dale SS16 . . . .142 C4
Swallow Dr SS7. . . . . . .144 C2
Swallow Path CM2 . . . . . .54 B5
Swallow Rd SS11 . . . . . . .99 C2
Swallows CM17 . . . . .11 C4
SWALLOWS CROSS 73 A2
Swallows The CM11 . . . .119 C8
Swallow Wlk **5** RM12 . .155 B6
Swanage Rd
Chingford E4 . . . . .109 C3
Southend-on-S SS2 . . . .148 B1
Swanbourne Dr
RM12 . . . . .155 D8
Swan Cl SS15 . . . . .141 E6
Swan Ct
Maldon CM9. . . . . .37 B4
South Benfleet SS7 . . . .144 B5
Wickford SS11 . . . . . . .121 D8
Swan La
Kelvedon Hatch CM15 . . . .71 E2
Loughton IG10. . . . . .88 C2
Stock CM4 . . . . .75 C5
Wickford SS11 . . . . .99 D1
Swan Mead SS16 . . . . . .142 D4
Swan Paddock **5**
CM14 . . . . .116 C8
Swan & Pike Rd EN3 . . . .65 A1
SWANSCOMBE 177 D1
Swanscombe Bsns Ctr
DA10 . . . . .177 E2
Swanscombe Cross
DA10 . . . . .177 D2
Swanscombe St DA10 . .177 F1
Swanscombe Sta
DA10 . . . . .177 F2
Swans Green Cl SS7 . . . .145 A6
Swanshope IG10. . . . . . . .89 B7
Swans Pasture CM1. . . . . .32 C6
Swanstead SS16 . . . . . .142 E4
Swan Way CM19 . . . . .9 A1
Swan Wlk
Kelvedon Hatch CM15 . . . .71 E2
Romford RM1 . . . . .135 E6
Swatchways SS1 . . . . . .167 D6
Sweet Briar Ave SS7 . . . .144 D2
Sweet Briar Dr SS15 . . . .119 D1
Sweetbriar Lo SS3 . . . . .163 E4
Sweet Chestnut Mews
CM12 . . . . .97 A2
Sweyne Ave
Hockley SS5. . . . . .125 A4
Southend-on-S SS2 . . . .147 F1
Sweyne Cl SS6. . . . . . . .123 B4
Sweyne Ct SS2 . . . . . . .147 F1
Sweyne Park Sch The
SS6 . . . . .123 C4
Sweyne Rd DA10 . . . . . .177 C1
Sweyns CM17. . . . . .24 C6
Swift Cl
Stanstead Abbotts SG12 . . .8 C3
Upminster RM14 . . . . . .137 E3
Swift Ho **8** E18. . . . . . .132 B8
Swiftsure Rd RM16. . . . .172 C2
Swinborne Ct SS13 . . . .121 B2
Swinborne Rd SS13 . . . .121 C1
Swinburne Gdns
RM18 . . . . .179 B6
Swindon Cl
Ilford IG3 . . . . .133 B3
Romford RM3 . . . . .114 F5
Swindon Gdns RM3 . . . .114 F5
Swindon La RM3. . . . . . .114 F5
Swingboat Terr **3**
SS1 . . . . .167 C7
Swiss Ave CM1 . . . . .32 A4
Sycamore Ave RM14 . . . .156 A8
Sycamore Cl
Canvey Island SS8. . . . .163 F3
Loughton IG10. . . . . .89 B7
Rayleigh SS6 . . . . .123 B6
Tilbury RM18. . . . . .179 A5
Sycamore Ct
Erith DA8. . . . . .169 D1
Romford RM12. . . . . . . .135 F3
Southend-on-S SS3 . . . .168 F7
Wickford SS11 . . . . . . .121 D8
Sycamore Dr SS9 . . . . . . .94 C1
Sycamore Field CM19 . . . .23 A5
Sycamore Gr
Romford RM2 . . . . .114 A1
Southend-on-S SS2 . . . .148 B2
Sycamore Ho
7 Buckhurst Hill IG9 . . . .110 D8
Southend-on-S SS3 . . . .168 F7
Wickford SS11 . . . . . . .121 E7
Sycamore Mews DA8. . . .169 D1
Sycamore Rd CM9 . . . . . .37 C6
Sycamores EN9. . . . . . . .66 C4

Sycamores The
Aveley RM15 . . . . .171 D5
14 Basildon SS13 . . . . . .143 C6
Sycamore Way
Canewdon SS4. . . . . . . .104 D1
Chelmsford CM2 . . . . . . .54 C6
South Ockendon RM15 . .157 D1
Sycamore Wlk IG6. . . . . .133 C8
Sydenham Cl RM1 . . . . . .135 F7
Sydervelt Rd SS8 . . . . . .164 A4
Sydner Cl CM2. . . . . .55 A5
Sydney Rd
Redbridge IG6 . . . . .111 C1
South Benfleet SS7 . . . .144 C4
Southend-on-S SS9 . . . .146 B2
Tilbury RM18. . . . . .179 A5
Wanstead E11 . . . . .132 B5
Woodford IG8 . . . . .110 A6
Sydney Russell Sch The
RM9 . . . . .153 D7
Sykes Mead SS6 . . . . . . .123 D1
Sylvan Ave
Dagenham RM6 . . . . . . .134 F5
Hornchurch RM11 . . . . .136 F5
Sylvan Cl
Basildon SS15 . . . . .141 B6
Canvey Island SS8. . . . .164 B4
Chelmsford CM2 . . . . . . .54 B6
Grays RM16. . . . . .172 E3
Sylvan Ct SS15 . . . . . . .140 F7
Sylvan Mews DA9. . . . . .177 B3
Sylvan Rd
Ilford IG1 . . . . .133 C2
Wanstead E11 . . . . .132 A6
Sylvan Tryst CM12 . . . . . .97 B4
Sylvan Way
Basildon SS15 . . . . .140 F7
Chigwell IG7 . . . . .112 B7
Dagenham RM8 . . . . . . .134 B1
Southend-on-S SS9 . . . .146 A4
Sylvester Gdns IG6 . . . . .112 B5
Sylvesters IG7 . . . . .22 F6
Sylvia Ave CM13 . . . . . . .117 C8
Sylvia Pankhurst Ho **10**
RM10 . . . . .135 A1
Symons Ave SS9 . . . . . . .146 E2
Syracuse Ave RM13 . . . .155 E2
Syringa Ct RM17 . . . . . . .178 D8

T

Tabora Ave SS8. . . . . . . .163 F5
Tabors Ave CM2 . . . . .54 F8
Tabors Ct CM15. . . . . . . .94 F2
Tabor's Hill CM2. . . . . . . .54 F7
Tabrum's La SS11. . . . . .101 A6
Tabrums The CM3 . . . . . . .79 C1
Tabrums Way RM14. . . . .137 E4
Tadlows Cl RM14 . . . . . .156 B7
Tadworth Par RM12. . . . .155 B8
Taffrail Gdns CM3 . . . . . .101 E5
Tailors Cl SS2 . . . . .147 F5
Tait Mews CM9 . . . . .37 A2
Taits SS17. . . . . .160 F2
Takeley Cl
Romford RM5 . . . . .113 D1
Waltham Abbey EN9 . . . .65 D6
Takely End SS16 . . . . . . .142 A5
Takely Ride SS16 . . . . . .142 A5
Talbot Ave SS6 . . . . .123 C3
Talbot Gdns IG3 . . . . . . .134 A2
Talbot Rd
Dagenham RM9 . . . . . . .153 F5
Wallend E6. . . . . .152 A3
Talbrook CM14 . . . . .115 F7
Talgarth Ho **1** RM3 . . . .114 E4
Talisman Cl **2** IG3. . . . .134 B3
Talisman Wlk CM11 . . . . .97 D6
Tallis Cl SS17. . . . . .160 C3
Tallis Ct RM2 . . . . .136 C8
Tallis Rd SS15 . . . . .141 D8
Tallis Way CM14 . . . . . . .116 B5
Tallon Rd CM13. . . . . .95 E4
Tallow Cl RM9 . . . . .153 E6
Tallow Gate CM3 . . . . . . .101 E6
Tall Trees CM RM11 . . . .136 E5
Tally-Ho Dr CM13. . . . . . .96 C1
Talus Cl RM19 . . . . .171 D2
Tama Cotts RM14 . . . . . .137 F2
Tamar Cl RM14 . . . . .137 E5
Tamar Dr RM15 . . . . . . .171 C7
Tamarisk SS7. . . . . .144 C4
Tamarisk Rd RM15 . . . . .157 C1
Tamar Rise CM1 . . . . .32 C6
Tamar Sq IG8 . . . . .110 B4
Tamworth Ave IG8 . . . . . .109 E4
Tanfield Dr CM12 . . . . . . .97 A2
Tanfield Tye Cotts
CM2 . . . . .76 E7
Tangent Link RM3 . . . . .114 D2
Tangham Wlk SS14 . . . . .142 C7
Tangmere Cl SS11 . . . . .122 B6
Tangmere Cres RM12 . . .155 B6
Tan House La
Navestock Heath CM14 . . .92 F3
Navestock Side CM14 . . . .93 A6
Tankerville Dr SS9. . . . . .146 D3
Tank Hill Rd
Purfleet RM15 . . . . .171 A3
Purfleet RM19 . . . . .171 A3
Tank La RM19 . . . . .171 B2
Tanners La IG6 . . . . .133 C8
Tanner St IG11 . . . . .152 C6
Tanners Way
Hunsdonbury SG12 . . . . . .9 D8
South Woodham Ferrers
CM3 . . . . .101 C8

Tannery Cl RM10. . . . . . .135 B1
Tanswell Ave SS13 . . . . .143 B6
Tanswell Cl SS13 . . . . . .143 B6
Tanswell Ct SS13 . . . . . .143 B7
Tansy Cl RM3 . . . . .114 E4
Tantelen Rd SS8 . . . . . . .163 F5
Tantony Gr RM6 . . . . . . .134 D8
Tanys Cl CM20. . . . . .10 F3
Tany's Dell CM20 . . . . . . .11 A3
Tany's Dell Com Prim Sch
CM20. . . . . .11 A3
Tapley Rd CM20 . . . . .31 F7
Taranto Rd SS8 . . . . . . .164 D3
Tarlings CM20 . . . . .10 F3
Tarnworth Rd RM3. . . . . .115 A4
TARPOTS 144 C4
Tarragon Ct IG1, IG3 . . . .133 E2
Tasker Ho **3** IG11 . . . . .152 D3
Tasker Rd RM16. . . . . . .174 B3
Tasman Cl SS17. . . . . . .160 F4
Tasman Ct SS8. . . . . . . .164 A1
Tasman Ct RM1 . . . . .31 E5
Tasmania Ho RM18. . . . .179 A6
Tatsfield Ave EN9. . . . . . .43 E8
Tatsford Villas EN9 . . . . .21 C1
Tattenham Rd SS15 . . . .141 B7
Tattersall Gdns SS9 . . . .146 A1
Tattersall Way CM1 . . . . .31 A2
Tattershall Ct **19** DA2 . .176 B1
Tatton St **6** CM17 . . . . .11 C1
Taunton Cl IG6 . . . . .111 F4
Taunton Dr SS0 . . . . . . .147 B4
Taunton Rd RM3 . . . . . . .114 F5
Taunton Rd
Chelmsford CM1 . . . . . . .32 E5
Northfleet DA11. . . . . . .178 A2
Romford RM3 . . . . .114 C6
Tavenners Green Cl
SS12 . . . . .121 E6
TAVERNERS GREEN 4 C8
Taverners Way
Chingford E4 . . . . .87 E1
Hoddesdon EN11. . . . . . .21 A6
Tavistock Cl RM3 . . . . . .114 D2
Tavistock Gdns IG3 . . . . .152 E8
Tavistock Ho **1** IG8. . . .111 A3
Tavistock Rd
Basildon SS15 . . . . .141 C8
Chelmsford CM1 . . . . . . .32 E5
Wanstead E18 . . . . .132 A8
Tawney Comm CM16. . . . .69 B7
Tawney La RM4. . . . . .69 D4
Tawneys Rd RM18 . . . . . .23 F6
Tawny Ave RM14. . . . . . .156 B7
Tawny Ave CM1 . . . . .31 E5
Taylor Cl RM5 . . . . .113 A3
Taylor Gdns RM3 . . . . . .114 C8
Taylors IG7 . . . . .90 A3
Taylors Ave EN11 . . . . . . .21 A5
Tayside Wlk **6** SS12 . . .121 E5
Tay Way RM1 . . . . .113 F2
Teagles SS15 . . . . .141 E6
Teakcroft Ctr RM13 . . . . .169 D7
Teal Ave SS8. . . . . .83 A8
Teal Ct CM3 . . . . .83 A8
Teale Ho **5** EN11 . . . . . .21 D8
Teazle Mead CM16. . . . . .46 B6
Ted Hennem Ho
RM10 . . . . .135 B1
Tees Cl RM14 . . . . .137 D5
Tees Dr RM3 . . . . .114 D7
Tees Rd CM1 . . . . .32 C6
Teignrace SS3. . . . . .168 D8
Teignmouth Dr SS6. . . . .123 D5
Telegraph Mews
Ilford, Goodmayes
IG3 . . . . .134 A3
Ilford, Seven Kings IG3. .133 F3
Telese Ave SS8 . . . . . . .164 D3
Telford Ho **2** DA17 . . . .169 A3
Telford Pl CM1 . . . . .32 D4
Telham Rd E6 . . . . .152 A3
Tempest Mead CM16 . . . .47 B4
Tempest Way RM13 . . . . .155 A6
Templar Ct RM7 . . . . . . .135 B7
Templar Ho RM13. . . . . .154 D7
Temple Ave RM8. . . . . . .135 A3
Temple Bank CM20 . . . . .11 B5
Temple Cl
Basildon SS15 . . . . .141 C7
Billericay CM12 . . . . .96 F5
Hadleigh SS7 . . . . .145 F3
Temple Ct SS2. . . . . . . .148 C3
Temple Farm Ind Est
CM2 . . . . .76 B6
Temple Farm Trad Est
CM2 . . . . .76 C6
TEMPLE FIELDS 11 A4
Templefields Ent Ctr
CM20 . . . . .11 A3
Temple Gate Cotts
SS2 . . . . .148 B5
Temple Gdns RM8 . . . . . .134 D1
Temple Hall Ct E4 . . . . . .109 D8
TEMPLE HILL 176 A2
Temple Hill Com Prim Sch
DA1. . . . . .176 A2
Temple Mead CM19 . . . . . .9 B1
Templer Ave E4 . . . . .109 B6
Temple Sutton Prim Sch
SS2 . . . . .148 C3
Templeton Ave E4 . . . . . .109 B6
Temple Way
Maldon CM9. . . . . .36 F5
Rayleigh SS6 . . . . .123 B5
Templewood Rd SS7 . . . .145 D3

Temple Wood Est CM2 . . .76 B6
Templewood Rd SS7 . . . .145 D3
Tempton Ave SS8 . . . . . .164 E4
Tempus Ct E18 . . . . .110 A2
Ten Acre App CM9 . . . . . .36 F5
Tenby Ct RM6 . . . . .134 C5
Tenby Rd RM6 . . . . .134 E5
Tendring Ave SS6. . . . . . .123 A3
Tendring Ct CM13. . . . . . .95 D4
Tendring Mews CM18 . . . .23 E7
Tendring Rd CM18 . . . . . .23 E6
Tendring Way RM6 . . . . .134 C6
Tenney Ho RM17. . . . . . .178 C7
Tennyson Ave
Grays RM17. . . . . .173 C3
Southend-on-S SS2 . . . .148 B2
Waltham Abbey EN9 . . . .65 E5
Wanstead E11 . . . . .132 A4
Tennyson Cl SS15 . . . . .146 A2
Tennyson Dr **9** SS13 . .143 B5
Tennyson Ho CM16 . . . . .68 A3
Tennyson Rd
Brentwood CM13. . . . . . .95 D2
Chelmsford CM1 . . . . . . .31 F5
Dartford DA1. . . . . .176 A2
Maldon CM9. . . . . .59 A8
Romford RM3 . . . . .114 C3
Tennyson Way RM12 . . . .135 F2
Tennyson Wlk RM18 . . . .179 B5
Tensing Gdns CM12 . . . . .97 A1
Tenterden Rd RM8. . . . . .134 F2
Tenterfield Rd CM9 . . . . . .37 A2
Tenterfields SS13 . . . . . .121 C1
Teramo Rd SS8 . . . . . . .164 D3
Tercel Path IG7 . . . . .112 B6
Terence Webster Rd
SS12 . . . . .121 E6
Terling SS16. . . . . .142 B5
Terling Rd RM8. . . . . . . .135 A2
Terlings Pk CM20 . . . . . . .10 D4
Terlings The CM14 . . . . .116 A7
Terminal Cl SS13 . . . . . .168 F7
Terminus Dr SS16 . . . . . .143 B4
Terminus St CM20 . . . . . .10 D1
Terms Ave SS8 . . . . .164 A5
Tern Cl CM3 . . . . .83 A8
Tern Ct CM14 . . . . .115 F6
Tern Gdns RM14 . . . . . . .137 E3
Terni Rd SS8 . . . . .164 D3
Tern Way CM14 . . . . . . .115 E6
Terrace St DA12 . . . . . . .179 B1
Terraces The SS3 . . . . . .168 F6
Terrace The
Chingford E4 . . . . .109 E7
2 Gravesend DA12 . . . .179 C1
Rayleigh SS6 . . . . .123 C7
Southend-on-S, Chalkwell
SS9 . . . . .165 E8
1 Woodford IG8 . . . . . .110 A4
Terrace Wlk RM9 . . . . . .153 E7
Terr The SS7 . . . . .163 D8
Teviot Ave RM15. . . . . . .171 C7
Tewkesbury Cl IG10 . . . . .88 E3
Tewkes Rd SS8 . . . . .164 D5
Thackeray Ave RM18 . . . .179 B6
Thackeray Dr RM6 . . . . .134 B4
Thackeray Row **1**
SS12 . . . . .121 C5
Thalmassing Cl CM13 . . .117 B8
Thames Ave
Chelmsford CM1 . . . . . . .31 D4
Dagenham RM9 . . . . . . .154 C2
Thames Cl
Corringham SS17. . . . . .161 E5
Rainham RM13 . . . . . . .170 B7
Rayleigh SS6 . . . . .123 C1
Southend-on-S SS9 . . . .146 B1
Thames Cres SS17 . . . . .161 C4
Thames Ct SS8. . . . . . . .164 A3
Thames Dr
Grays RM16. . . . . .174 A1
Southend-on-S SS9 . . . .146 A1
Thames Gate DA1. . . . . .176 A2
Thamesgate Sh Ctr **19**
DA11. . . . . .179 B1
Thames Gateway Pk
RM9 . . . . .153 F2
Thames Haven Rd
SS17 . . . . .161 B2
Thameshill Ave RM5 . . . .113 C1
Thameside Cres **6**
SS8 . . . . .164 A3
Thameside Inf Sch
RM17 . . . . .178 C8
Thameside Jun Sch
RM17 . . . . .178 C8
Thames Ind Pk RM18. . . .175 B1
Thames Rd
Barking IG11. . . . . .153 A2
Canvey Island SS8. . . . .163 F3
Grays RM17. . . . . .178 B7
Thamesview DA9. . . . . . .177 C2
Thames View
Basildon SS16 . . . . .141 C1
Grays RM16. . . . . .174 A1
2 Ilford IG1 . . . . .133 C2
Thames View Bsns Ctr
RM13 . . . . .169 E8
Thamesview Ct SS7 . . . . .145 F2
Thames View Inf Sch
IG11 . . . . .153 A3
Thames View Jun Sch
IG11 . . . . .152 F3
Thames View Lo IG11 . . .152 F2
Thames Way
Burnham-on-C CM0 . . . .106 A6
Gravesend DA11 . . . . . .179 A1
Northfleet DA11. . . . . . .178 B1

Sut-Tho 227

Thamley RM19. . . . . . . .171 A2
Thanet Grange SS0 . . . . .147 C5
Thatchers Cl IG10 . . . . . . .89 C7
Thatchers Croft CM3 . . . .81 F6
Thatches Gr RM6 . . . . . .134 E7
Thaxted Bold CM13 . . . . .95 D4
Thaxted Gn CM13 . . . . . .95 C4
Thaxted Ho RM10 . . . . . .154 B8
Thaxted Lo **3** E18 . . . . .132 B8
Thaxted Rd IG9. . . . . .88 C2
Thaxted Way RM13 . . . . .65 D6
Thaxted Wlk RM13 . . . . .154 C5
Thear Cl SS0 . . . . .147 C4
Thele Ave SG12. . . . . .8 D4
Thele Est SG12 . . . . .8 A3
Theleway Cl EN11. . . . . . .8 B1
Thelma Ave SS8 . . . . . . .164 A4
Theobalds Ave RM17 . . . .173 C1
Theobalds Cl SS9 . . . . . .146 C1
Theobalds Rd SS9 . . . . .146 C1
Thetford Ct CM1 . . . . .31 E1
Thetford Gdns RM9 . . . . .153 E6
Thetford Pl SS15. . . . . . .119 D1
Thetford Rd RM9 . . . . . .153 D5
THEYDON BOIS 67 D3
Theydon Bois Prim Sch
CM16 . . . . .67 E3
Theydon Bois Sta
CM16 . . . . .67 F3
Theydon Bold CM13 . . . . .95 D4
Theydon Bower CM16 . . . .68 A8
Theydon Cres SS14 . . . . .120 F1
Theydon Ct EN9 . . . . . . .66 A3
THEYDON GARNON 68 C3
Theydon Gdns RM13 . . . .154 F5
Theydon Gr
Epping CM16 . . . . .46 A1
Woodford IG8 . . . . .110 A1
THEYDON MOUNT 69 A3
Theydon Park Rd
CM16 . . . . .67 E1
Theydon Pl CM16 . . . . . . .67 E8
Theydon Rd CM16. . . . . . .67 D6
Thicket Gr RM9 . . . . .153 C6
Thielen Rd SS8 . . . . .164 A4
Thieves' Cnr CM1 . . . . . . .31 A4
Third Ave
Basildon SS16 . . . . .140 E3
Canvey Island SS8 . . . . .163 E4
Chelmsford CM1 . . . . . . .32 B5
Dagenham RM10 . . . . . .154 B3
Grays RM20. . . . . .177 A8
Harlow CM18, CM19 . . . .23 C7
Ilford RM6. . . . . .134 C5
Stanford-le-H SS17 . . . .160 E4
Thundersley SS7 . . . . . .145 A6
Wickford SS11 . . . . . . .122 A6
Third Wlk SS8 . . . . .163 E4
Thirlmere Rd SS7. . . . . . .144 C7
Thirslet Dr CM9. . . . . .37 C4
Thisselt Rd SS8 . . . . . . .164 B4
Thistle Cl SS15 . . . . .119 F1
Thistledene Ave RM5 . . . .113 B5
Thistledown Cl SS14 . . . .142 C6
Thistle Mead IG10 . . . . . .89 A6
Thistley Cl
Goldhanger CM9 . . . . . . .38 E6
Southend-on-S SS9 . . . .146 F4
Thoby La CM15 . . . . .73 C1
Thomas Arnold Prim Sch
RM9 . . . . .153 F5
Thomas Bata Ave
RM18 . . . . .175 B2
Thomas Cr
Brentwood CM15. . . . . .116 E7
Chelmsford CM2 . . . . . . .32 F3
Thomas Dr SS8 . . . . . . .163 E5
Thomas England Ho **3**
RM7 . . . . .135 D5
Thomasin Rd SS13 . . . . .121 C2
Thomas Rd SS13 . . . . . .143 E7
Thomas Sims Ct
RM12 . . . . .155 B7
Thomas Willingale Sch
IG10 . . . . .89 C6
Thompson Ave SS8 . . . . .164 F3
Thompson Cl IG1. . . . . . .133 C2
Thompson Rd RM9. . . . . .134 F1
Thorington Ave SS7. . . . .145 D6
Thorington Rd SS6. . . . . .124 A1
Thorin's Gate CM3 . . . . .101 C6
Thorley Rd RM16 . . . . . .173 A5
Thornborough Ave
CM3 . . . . .101 F7
Thornbridge SS7 . . . . . . .144 B4
Thornbrook CM16 . . . . . . .46 D6
Thornbury Cl EN11. . . . . .8 B2
Thornbury Ho **3**
RM3 . . . . .114 D5
Thornbush SS15 . . . . . . .141 E6
Thorncroft RM11 . . . . . . .136 B5
Thorndale SS7. . . . . .145 B7
Thorndales CM14 . . . . . .116 D6
Thorndon App CM13 . . . .117 D3
Thorndon Ave CM13 . . . .139 C6
Thorndon Countryside
Ctr★ CM13 . . . . .116 F3
Thorndon Ct CM13. . . . . .116 E4
Thorndon Ctry Pk★
Ingrave CM13 . . . . .117 D1
Little Warley CM13 . . . . .116 F3
Thorndon Gate CM13. . . .117 B4
Thorndon Hall CM13 . . . .117 B4

Thorndon Lo CM13....... 117 C4
Thorndon Park Cl
SS9 .... 146 C5
Thorndon Park Cres
SS9 .... 146 B5
Thorndon Park Dr
SS9 .... 146 C5
Thorney Bay Rd SS8 .... 164 A2
Thorneycroft Dr EN3 .... 65 A2
Thornford Gdns SS2 .... 147 F5
Thornhill
North Weald Bassett
CM16 .... 47 C5
Purleigh CM3 .... 58 D1
Southend-on-S SS9 .... 146 B4
Thornhill Gdns IG11 .... 152 E5
Thorn La RM13 .... 155 D3
Thornridge CM14 .... 94 B1
Thorns The CM15 ...... 93 E8
Thornton Ho 8 E11 ..... 132 A5
Thornton Pl CM4 .... 75 E2
Thornton Rd
Belvedere DA17 .... 169 B2
Ilford IG1 .... 152 B8
Thorntons CM13 ...... 117 D4
Thorntons Farm Ave
RM7 .... 135 D2
Thornton Way SS15 .... 141 A6
THORNWOOD 46 C7
Thornwood Cl E18 ..... 110 B1
Thornwood Ct SS9 .... 146 D6
Thornwood Ho IG9 ..... 88 E2
Thornwood Rd CM16 ... 46 B3
Thorogood Way
RM13 .... 154 E4
Thorold Rd IG1 .... 133 C3
Thorolds SS16 .... 142 E3
THORPE BAY 168 B7
Thorpe Bay Sta SS1 ... 168 B8
Thorpe Bold CM13 ..... 95 D4
Thorpe Cl
Hockley SS5 .... 124 F4
Wickford SS12 .... 121 F6
Thorpedale Gdns IG1,
IG6 .... 133 B7
Thorpedene Ave SS5 ... 101 C2
Thorpedene Gdns
SS3 .... 168 D6
Thorpedene Inf Sch
SS3 .... 168 C7
Thorpedene Jun Sch
SS3 .... 168 C7
Thorpe Espl SS1 ...... 168 B6
Thorpe Gdns SS5 ..... 124 F4
Thorpe Greenways Inf Sch
SS1 .... 167 E7
Thorpe Greenways Jun
Sch SS1 .... 167 E7
Thorpe Hall Ave SS1 ... 168 A7
Thorpe Hall Cl SS1 .... 168 A8
Thorpe Hall Prim Sch
E17 .... 109 C2
Thorpe Hall Rd E17 ... 109 C2
Thorpe Hall Sch SS1 ... 149 A2
Thorpe Lo
Romford RM11......... 136 D5
Southend-on-S SS1 .... 167 D6
Thorpe Rd
Barking IG11......... 152 D5
Chingford E17 .... 109 C1
Hockley SS5 .... 124 F3
Hockley SS5 .... 124 F4
Wanstead E7 .... 132 A1
Thorp Leas SS8 ...... 164 B2
Thorrington Bold
CM13 .... 95 D4
Thorrington Cross
SS14 .... 142 C6
Thors Oak SS17 ...... 160 E2
Thrapston Ho 10 RM3 .. 114 E5
Threadneedle St 2
CM1 .... 32 B2
Three Horseshoes Rd
CM19 .... 23 B6
Three Mile Hill CM4 ... 53 C2
Threshelford SS16 .... 141 F4
THRESHERS BUSH ... 25 B7
Thrift Gn CM13 .... 117 A7
Thrifts Mead CM16 .... 67 E2
Thrift Wood CM3 ..... 56 F1
Thriftwood Sch CM2 ... 54 B3
Throwley Cl SS13 .... 143 C5
Thunderer Rd RM9 ... 153 E1
THUNDERSLEY 144 E6
Thundersley Church Rd
SS7 .... 144 D5
Thundersley Gr SS7 ... 144 F5
Thundersley Park Rd
SS7 .... 144 E3
Thundersley Prim Sch
SS7 .... 145 A6
Thurgood Rd EN11 .... 21 A8
Thurlby Cl IG8 .... 110 F5
Thurlby Ho IG8 ...... 110 F5
Thurlestone Ave IG3 .. 152 F8
Thurloe Gdns RM1 ... 135 F5
Thurloe Wlk RM17 ... 173 A3
Thurlow Cl E4 .... 109 B4
Thurlow Ct 5 E11 .... 132 A6
Thurlow Dr SS1....... 167 F8
Thurlow Gdns IG6 .... 111 D4
Thurlstone SS7 ...... 145 C5

Thurrock & Basildon Coll
(Nethermayne Campus)
SS16 .... 141 F4
Thurrock & Basildon Coll
(Woodview Campus)
RM16 .... 173 F2
Thurrock Bsns Ctr
RM20 .... 176 F8
Thurrock Com Hospl
RM16 .... 173 C5
Thurrock Commercial Ctr
RM15 .... 170 F4
Thurrock Commercial Pk
RM15 .... 170 F5
Thurrock Ent Ctr
RM17 .... 178 A8
Thurrock Local History
Mus* RM17 .... 173 B1
Thurrock Park Way
RM18 .... 178 D7
Thurso Ct RM3........ 115 B4
Thurstans CM19 ...... 23 C3
Thurston Ave SS2 .... 148 E1
Thynne Rd CM11 ..... 97 C2
Tickenhall Dr CM17 ... 24 D7
Tickfield Ave SS2 .... 147 F2
Tideway
Maldon CM9 .... 59 B8
Southend-on-S SS1 .... 167 D6
Tidworth Ave SS11 .... 99 E2
Tidy's La CM16 .... 46 B2
Tighfield Wlk CM3 .... 101 C5
Tilburg Rd SS8 ...... 164 A4
TILBURY 179 B4
Tilbury Fort* RM18 ... 179 C3
Tilbury Manor Inf Sch
RM18 .... 179 B7
Tilbury Manor Jun Sch
RM18 .... 179 B7
Tilbury Mead CM18 ... 24 A6
Tilbury Rd CM13 ..... 139 E5
Tilbury Town Sta
RM18 .... 178 F5
Tilegate Ho CM18 .... 23 F6
Tilegate Rd
Harlow CM18.......... 23 F6
Tilgate Green CM5 .... 25 D5
TILGATE GREEN 25 E6
Tilia Ct RM11 .... 136 D4
TILLINGHAM 63 F4
Tillingham Bold CM13 . 95 D4
Tillingham Ct EN9 .... 66 A6
Tillingham Gn 6
SS15 .... 141 A6
Tillingham Hall CM0 .. 63 E4
Tillingham Rd
Southminster CM0 .... 84 F6
Tillingham CM0 .... 63 B2
Tillingham Way SS6 .. 123 A3
Tillotson Rd IG1 ..... 133 A4
Tillwicks Rd CM18 .... 24 A6
Tilney Ct IG9 .... 110 A8
Tilney Dr IG9 .... 110 A8
Tilney Rd
Buckhurst Hill IG9 .... 110 B8
Dagenham RM9 .... 153 F6
Tilney Turn SS16..... 142 E6
Timber Ct RM17 ..... 178 A8
Timberdene Ave IG6 .. 111 C2
Timberlog Cl SS14 ... 142 E6
Timberlog La SS14,
SS16 .... 142 E6
Timbermans View
SS16 .... 142 F4
Timber Wharf Cotts
SS11 .... 100 E2
Time Sq SS14 .... 142 A5
Timsons La CM2 ..... 32 E4
Tindall Ct RM3....... 114 F1
Tindall Mews RM12 .. 136 C1
Tindal Sq 3 CM1 .... 32 B2
Tindal St CM1 ...... 32 B2
Tine Rd
Chigwell IG7......... 111 E5
Chigwell IG7 .... 111 F5
Tinker's La SS4 ..... 125 F1
Tinkler Side SS14 ... 142 B6
Tinnocks La CM0 .... 40 B1
Tintagel Ct RM11 .... 137 A3
Tintagel Way CM9 ... 58 E8
Tintern Ave SS0 ..... 147 C2
Tintern Mews SS0 ... 147 C1
Tiplers Bridge CM11 . 98 B5
Tippersfield SS7 .... 144 E4
Tipps Cross CM15 ... 72 B5
Tipps Cross La CM15 . 72 B4
Tips Cross Mead CM15 72 B4
Tiptree Cl
Chingford E4.......... 109 C7
Hornchurch RM11 .... 137 A3
Southend-on-S SS9 ... 146 F4
Tiptree Cres
Ilford IG5............ 133 A8
Redbridge IG5 .... 111 A1
Tiptree Ct CM13 .... 95 D4
Tiptree Gr SS12 .... 121 D7
Tiree Chase SS12 ... 121 F5
Titan Rd RM17 ...... 173 A1
Tithe Barn Agricultural &
Folk Mus The*
RM14 .... 137 D4
Titihelands CM19 .... 23 A5
Tithe The SS12 ..... 121 B6
Titley Cl E4......... 109 A5
Tiverton Ave IG5 .... 133 A8
Tiverton Gr RM3 .... 115 A5
Tobruk Rd E1 ...... 31 F6
Toddbrook CM19 .... 23 B7

Todd Cl RM13 .... 155 D1
Toft Ave RM17 ...... 173 D2
Tofts Chase CM3 .... 34 E5
Tolbut Ct 5 RM1 .... 135 F5
Tolcairn Ct 2 DA17 .. 169 A1
Toledo Cl SS1 ...... 167 B8
Toledo Rd SS1 ...... 167 B8
TOLLESBURY 40 E8
Tollesbury Cl 1 SS12 . 121 E6
Tollesbury Ct CM13 .. 95 D4
Tollesbury Gdns IG6 . 133 D8
Tollgate SS7 .... 145 C6
Tollgate Rd DA2 .... 176 D1
Tolworth Gdns RM6 . 134 D6
Tolworth Par RM6 ... 134 E6
Tomkins Cl SS17 .... 160 C3
Tomkyns La
Romford RM14......... 115 D1
Upminster RM14 ..... 137 D7
Tomlinson Ho 19
CM14 .... 116 C7
Tomlins Orch IG11 ... 152 C4
Tomlyns Cl CM13 .... 95 E3
Tom Mann Cl IG11 ... 152 E4
Tomswood Ct IG6 .... 111 C2
Tomswood Hill IG6 ... 111 C3
Tomswood Rd IG7 ... 111 A4
Tom Tit La CM9..... 57 C7
Tonbridge Rd
Hockley SS5.......... 124 F8
Romford RM3 .... 114 D3
Tongres Rd SS8 .... 164 A4
Took Dr CM3 .... 101 C6
TOOT HILL 47 F2
Toot Hill Rd CM5..... 47 F1
Topaz Ct 3 RM13 ... 155 A1
Top House Rise E4... 87 C2
Toplands Ave RM15 .. 171 C5
Toppesfield Ave SS12 121 C5
Top Rd CM9 .... 35 D2
Tora Ct 12 IG9 ..... 110 C8
Torbitt Way IG2 .... 133 F6
Tor Bryan CM4 ..... 74 B2
Torfell 5 E18 ...... 109 F1
Torney Ct SS16 ..... 140 F4
Toronto Rd
Ilford IG1............ 133 C3
Tilbury RM18......... 179 A6
Torquay Cl SS6 .... 123 D5
Torquay Dr SS9..... 146 E1
Torquay Gdns IG4 ... 132 D7
Torquay Rd CM1 .... 32 D5
Torrance Cl RM11 ... 136 C3
Torrell's Hall Cotts
CM5 .... 28 E5
Torridge RM18....... 175 C2
Torrington SS3 ..... 168 D8
Torrington Cl CM1 ... 32 E5
Torrington Dr IG10 .. 89 C5
Torrington Gdns IG10 89 C5
Torrington Rd
Dagenham RM8........ 134 F3
Wanstead E18 .... 132 A8
Torsi Rd SS8 ...... 164 D3
Torvill Ct 17 CM14 .. 116 C7
Totman Cl SS6...... 145 D8
Totman Cres SS6 ... 145 D8
Totnes Wlk CM1 .... 32 E6
Toucan Cl SS3 ..... 149 E1
Toucan Way SS16.... 142 A3
Tovey Ave EN11 .... 21 A8
Tovey Cl EN9 ...... 43 E8
Tower Ave
Basildon SS15........ 141 C7
Chelmsford CM1 ..... 31 F4
Tower Cl
North Weald Bassett
CM16 .... 47 D7
Redbridge IG6 .... 111 B4
Tower Court Mews
SS0 .... 166 E7
Tower Ct
Brentwood CM14...... 116 C8
Chipping Ongar CM5 .. 49 A2
Southend-on-S SS0 ... 166 E7
Tower Ctr 1 EN11 ... 21 A6
Towerfield Cl SS3 ... 168 E7
Towerfield Rd SS3 ... 168 E7
Tower Hill CM14 .... 116 C8
Tower Ho RM13...... 95 D2
Tower Hts 10 EN11 .. 21 A7
TOWER PARK 101 E4
Tower Rd
Belvedere DA17....... 169 C2
Epping CM16 .... 45 F1
Writtle CM1 .... 30 F1
Tower Side SS5..... 101 E4
Towers Inf Sch RM11.. 136 C4
Towers Jun Sch
RM11 .... 136 C4
Towers Rd
Grays RM17.......... 173 C1
Heybridge CM9 ...... 37 C5
Town Croft CM1 .... 32 A5
Towneley Cotts RM4 . 91 E1
Townend Rd SS4.... 125 F2
Townfields SS2 ..... 148 A2
Townfield St CM1.... 32 B3
Townfield Wlk SS3... 149 D4
Towngate Bsns Pk
IG11 .... 153 A2
Town Mead Rd EN9 .. 65 C5
TOWN PARK 10 E7
Town Pier Sq DA11 .. 179 B1
Town Quay IG11..... 152 B4
Town Quay Wharf
IG11 .... 152 B4
Townsend CM2 ..... 33 B5

Town Sq SS14 ...... 142 A6
Tracyes Rd CM18 ... 24 B6
Traddles Ct CM1 ... 31 F6
Trade City RM3 .... 114 D2
Trafalgar Bsns Ctr
IG11 .... 152 F1
Trafalgar Ct 6 SS14 . 142 A4
Trafalgar Ho IG11 ... 153 B2
Trafalgar Pl E11 .... 132 A7
Trafalgar Rd
Rainham RM13........ 154 F3
Southend-on-S SS3 .. 168 D7
Trafalgar Way CM12 . 97 B5
Trafford Cl IG6 ..... 111 F4
Tramway Ho DA8 ... 169 E1
Tranquil Rise DA8 ... 169 E1
Trap's Hill IG10..... 88 F5
Trasa Ct 9 RM17 ... 178 C8
Travers Way SS13 ... 143 A6
Trayford Ct 8 RM19 . 171 B1
Treacle Mine Rdbt
RM16 .... 172 F4
Trebble Rd DA10 ... 177 E1
Treebeard Copse
CM3 .... 101 C6
Treeby Ct EN3 ..... 65 A2
Treecot Dr SS9 ..... 147 A4
Treelawn Dr SS9 ... 146 F4
Treelawn Gdns SS9 . 146 F4
Tree Top Mews RM10 154 D6
Tree Tops
Brentwood CM15...... 94 C1
1 Woodford IG8 .... 110 A6
Treetops Sch RM17 .. 173 B2
Treetops View IG10 . 88 D2
Trefgarne Rd RM10 . 135 A2
Trefoil Ho RM17 .... 178 B7
Tregaron Ho 3 RM3 . 114 D4
Trehearn Rd IG6..... 111 B3
Trelawn CM3 ...... 33 E8
Trelawney Pl RM16 . 172 C3
Trelawney Rd IG6 ... 111 D3
Trenance Gdns IG3 . 134 A1
Trenchard Cres CM1 . 32 D8
Trenchard Lo CM1 .. 32 D7
Trenders Ave SS6... 123 B7
Trenham Ave SS13.. 143 D7
Trent RM18 .... 175 C2
Trent Ave SS6 ..... 137 D5
Trentbridge Cl IG6.. 111 F4
Trent Cl
Burnham-on-C CM0 ... 106 A6
Wickford SS12 ...... 121 D6
Trent Ct E11 ...... 132 A6
Trent Rd
Buckhurst Hill IG9 .... 88 B1
Chelmsford CM1 ..... 31 B5
Trescoe Gdns RM5 . 113 C5
Tresco Gdns IG3.... 134 A2
Tresco Way SS12 ... 121 F5
Tresham Rd IG11 ... 152 F5
Treswell Rd RM9..... 153 E4
Trevera Ct EN11 ... 21 A7
Trevor Cl CM12 .... 118 F7
Trevor Rd IG8 ..... 110 A3
Trevose Rd E17 .... 109 D2
Trewithen Ct SS6 ... 146 A8
Triangle Garage CM9 37 B5
Triangle The
Barking IG11......... 152 C6
Basildon SS16 ...... 141 B4
Trianon Ct 10 SS13 . 143 C6
Trident Ind Est EN11 . 21 C7
Trienna Ct CM3 .... 117 B7
Trillo Ct IG1 ...... 133 E4
Trimble Ct CM4 .... 74 B4
Trimley Cl SS14 .... 142 C7
Trindehay SS15 .... 141 E5
Trinder Way SS12 ... 121 B6
Tring Cl
Ilford IG2............ 133 D6
Romford RM3 .... 114 F6
Tring Gdns RM3 .... 114 F6
Tring Gn RM3...... 114 F6
Tring Wlk RM3 .... 114 E6
Trinidad Gdns RM10 154 D5
Trinity Ave SS0 ..... 166 E7
Trinity Cl
Basildon SS15........ 141 C6
Billericay CM11 ..... 119 C6
Chelmsford CM2 ..... 32 D3
Rayleigh SS6 .... 123 E1
Trinity Ct 8 E4...... 109 C8
Trinity Gdns 11 E18 . 132 B8
Trinity Ho RM17 .... 178 B7
Trinity Lo SS2 ..... 148 D1
Trinity RC High Sch
(Lower) IG8......... 110 A6
Trinity RC High Sch
(Upper) IG8......... 110 A6
Trinity RC High Sch
(Upper Sch) IG8...... 109 F6
Trinity Rd
Billericay CM11....... 119 C6
Chelmsford CM2 ..... 32 D2
Ilford IG6............ 133 C8
Rayleigh SS6 .... 123 E1
Southend-on-S SS2 .. 148 D1
Trinity Road Prim Sch
CM2 .... 32 D2
Trinity Row 6 CM3 . 101 E7
Trinity St Mary's CE Prim
Sch CM3 .... 101 E7
Trinity Sch
Belvedere DA17....... 169 C2
Dagenham RM10 ..... 154 A8
Trinity Sq SS3 ..... 101 E7
Trinity Terr IG9..... 88 B2

Trinity Wood Rd SS5 . 125 A8
Tripat Cl SS17 ..... 161 D4
Tripton Rd CM18 ... 23 E7
Triton Ct IG9 ...... 110 A8
Triton Lo DA8 ..... 169 E1
Triton Way SS7 .... 145 B6
Triumph Cl RM16 ... 172 C2
Triumph Ho IG11 ... 153 A2
Trivett Cl DA9 ..... 177 A2
Trojan Terr CM21 ... 1 E3
Troopers Dr RM3 ... 114 D6
Tropical Wings World of
Wildlife* CM3....... 101 A8
Trotter's Gap SG12.. 8 E4
Trotters Rd IG7 .... 111 D4
Trotwood IG7 ...... 111 D4
Trotwood
Brentwood CM15...... 94 E1
Chelmsford CM1 ..... 31 E7
Troubridge Cl CM3.. 101 F7
Trowbridge Rd RM3. 114 E4
Trueloves La CM4.... 73 E2
Truman Ct 2 SS15 . 141 A6
Trumpeter Ct CM12 . 96 F3
Trunnions The SS4.. 125 F1
Truro Cres SS6 .... 123 C5
Truro Gdns IG1 .... 132 E4
Truro Wlk RM3 .... 114 C4
Trusses Rd
Bradwell on S CM0 ... 42 A3
Bradwell Waterside CM0... 41 F3
Trustons Gdns RM11 . 136 A4
Trust The RM12 .... 136 F2
Tryfan Cl IG4....... 132 D6
Tuck Rd RM13 ..... 155 A1
Tudor Ave
Romford RM2......... 136 A8
Stanford-le-H SS17 ... 160 E4
Tudor Cl
Brentwood CM15...... 95 A3
Chigwell IG7 .... 111 A6
Hunsdonbury SG12 .. 9 D8
Ingatestone CM4..... 74 A2
Rayleigh SS6 .... 123 F2
Southend-on-S SS9 .. 146 C2
Thundersley SS7 .... 144 F5
Woodford IG8 .... 110 B5
Tudor Court Prim Sch
RM16 .... 172 F4
Tudor Cres IG6 .... 111 C4
Tudor Ct
Basildon SS15........ 119 F2
Romford RM3 .... 115 B4
Sawbridgeworth CM21... 1 E3
Tudor Dr RM2 ..... 136 A7
Tudor Gdns
Romford RM2......... 136 A7
Southend-on-S, Cambridge
Town SS3 .... 168 D6
Southend-on-S SS9 .. 146 D3
Upminster RM14 ..... 137 C1
Tudor Mews
Romford RM1......... 135 F6
Southend-on-S SS9 .. 146 C8
Tudor Par RM6 .... 134 C4
Tudor Pl
Buckhurst Hill IG9 .... 110 E8
Mayland CM3 .... 83 A8
Tudor Rd
Barking IG11......... 152 F5
Canvey Island SS8.... 163 D3
Chingford E4 .... 109 B4
Southend-on-S, Noblesgreen
SS9 .... 146 C7
Southend-on-S SS0 .. 147 E2
Tudor Way
Hockley SS5.......... 124 F4
Waltham Abbey EN9 . 65 D6
Wickford SS12 ...... 121 B7
Tudor Wlk SS12 .... 121 A7
Tufter Rd IG7 ...... 111 F5
Tufton Rd E4 ...... 109 A6
Tugby Pl CM1 ..... 31 E6
Tulip Cl
Chelmsford CM1...... 32 E7
Pilgrims Hatch CM15 . 94 B4
Romford RM3 .... 114 D4
Tulip Gdns
Chingford E4......... 109 D7
Ilford IG1 .... 152 B6
Tumbler Rd CM18 .. 24 B7
Tunbridge Rd SS2 .. 147 F2
Tunfield Rd EN11 ... 8 B1
Tunnel Cotts RM20.. 177 A8
Tunnel Est RM20.... 171 F2
Tunnmeade CM20.... 11 A1
Tunstall Ave IG6.... 112 A4
Tunstall Cl SS13 ... 143 C5
Tupman Cl CM1..... 31 D6
Turkey Oaks CM1 .. 32 D3
Turnage Rd RM8 ... 134 E3
Turner Cl
Basildon SS15........ 141 D5
Southend-on-S SS3 .. 168 F8
Turner Rd RM12 ... 135 F2
Turners Cl CM5 .... 48 F2
Turners Ct RM4 .... 90 B6
Turnors CM20 ..... 23 C8
Turnpike La RM18 .. 174 D1
Turold Rd SS17 .... 160 E4
Turp Ave RM16 .... 173 C4
Turpin Ave RM5 ... 113 B4
Turpin Cl EN3 ..... 65 A2
Turpin's La IG8 .... 110 F5
Turpins The SS14 .. 142 C7
Turret Ct CM5 ..... 49 A2
Tusser Ct CM2 .... 54 D8
Tutors Way CM3 ... 101 E7

Tuttlebee La IG9 . . . . 110 A8
Tuttleby Cotts RM4 . . . . . 90 E2
Twain Terr **2** SS12 . . . . 121 C5
Tweed RM18 . . . . 175 C2
Tweed Glen RM1 . . . . . . 113 D3
Tweed Gn RM1 . . . . 113 D3
Tweed Way RM1 . . . . . . 113 D3
Twelve Acre Ho **5**
  E12 . . . . 133 A1
Twentyman Cl IG8 . . . . . 110 A5
Twine Cl IG11 . . . . 153 B2
Twin Oaks CM2 . . . . 33 A4
Twinstead SS12 . . . . 121 F6
Twitten La CM2 . . . . 54 B2
Twitty Fee CM3 . . . . 57 A8
Two Tree Island Nature
  Reserve★ SS9 . . . . 165 B7
Twyford Ave SS3 . . . . . . 150 A4
Twyford Rd IG1 . . . . 152 C7
Twyzel Rd SS8 . . . . 164 C5
Tyburns The CM13 . . . . . 117 D8
Tycehurst Hill IG10 . . . . . 88 F5
TYE COMMON 118 F8
Tye Common Rd
  CM12 . . . . 118 E7
TYE GREEN 23 E6
Tye Green Village
  CM18 . . . . 23 F5
Tyelands CM12 . . . . 118 F8
Tye The CM3 . . . . 78 C7
Tyle Gn RM11 . . . . 136 F7
Tylehurst Gdns IG1 . . . . . 152 C7
Tyler Ave SS15 . . . . 141 C6
Tylers Ave
  Billericay CM12 . . . . 97 C5
  Southend-on-S SS1 . . . . 167 A8
Tylers Cl
  Chelmsford CM2 . . . . . . 54 B6
  Loughton IG10 . . . . 88 E2
Tylers Cres RM12 . . . . . . 155 C7
Tylers Ct **9** CM14 . . . . . 116 C6
TYLERSCROSS 22 E3
Tylers St **9** 22 D3
Tylers Rd CM19 . . . . 22 D3
TYLER'S GREEN 47 D7
Tylers Ride CM3 . . . . . . 101 E7
Tyler Way CM14 . . . . . . 94 B1
Tylewood SS7 . . . . 145 C3
Tilney Ave SS4 . . . . 125 E3
Tilney Cl IG7 . . . . 111 F6
Tilney Croft CM19 . . . . . . 23 B6
Tyms Way SS6 . . . . 123 E4
Tyndale Cl SS5 . . . . 101 D3
Tyndale Ho SS5 . . . . 101 D3
Tyndales La CM3 . . . . . . 57 B5
Tyne RM18 . . . . 175 C2
Tyne Cl RM14 . . . . 137 D5
Tyne Gdns RM15 . . . . . . 171 C4
Tyne Way CM1 . . . . 31 D5
Tyrell Rise CM14 . . . . . . 116 C5
Tyrells SS5 . . . . 124 D5
Tyrells Cl
  Chelmsford CM2 . . . . . . 32 E4
  Upminster RM14 . . . . . . 137 B2
Tyrells The SS17 . . . . . . 161 A2
Tyrells Way CM2 . . . . . . 54 F7
Tyrone Cl CM11 . . . . 119 C6
Tyrone Rd
  Billericay CM11 . . . . . . 119 C6
  Southend-on-S SS1 . . . . 168 A7
Tyrrel Dr SS1 . . . . 167 B8
Tyrrell Ct **6** SS13 . . . . . 143 C6
Tyrrell Rd SS7 . . . . 144 B2
Tyrrells Hall Cl RM17 . . . 178 D8
Tyrrells Mews CM11 . . . . 119 D6
Tyrrells Rd CM11 . . . . . . 119 D6
Tyrrells Sch The CM1 . . . 32 E5
Tysea Cl CM18 . . . . 23 F5
Tysea Hill RM4 . . . . 91 F2
Tysea Rd CM18 . . . . 23 F5
Tyssen Mead CM3 . . . . . 33 E8
Tyssen Pl RM15 . . . . 157 C2
Tythe Barn Way CM3 . . . 101 C8
Tythe Cl CM1 . . . . 32 E8

U

Udall Gdns RM5 . . . . 113 A4
Ullswater Cl **9** E18 . . . . 110 A1
Ullswater Rd SS7 . . . . . . 144 E7
Ullswater Way RM12 . . . . 155 A7
Ulster Ave SS3 . . . . 168 D6
ULTING 35 C6
Ulting Hall Rd CM9 . . . . . 35 E7
Ulting La CM9 . . . . 35 E6
Ulting Rd CM9 . . . . 35 C8
Ulting Way SS11 . . . . . . 122 A8
Ulverston Rd CM19 . . . . . 176 C8
Ulverston Ho **1** RM3 . . . 114 E4
Ulverston Rd
  Chingford E17 . . . . 109 D1
  Rochford SS4 . . . . 103 C1
Una Rd SS13 . . . . 143 F6
Undercliff Gdns SS9 . . . . 165 F8
Underhill Rd SS7 . . . . . . 144 E3
Underwood Rd
  Chingford E4 . . . . 109 B5
  Woodford IG8 . . . . 110 D3
Underwood Sq SS9 . . . . . 146 C2
Unicorn Wlk DA9 . . . . . . 176 F2
Union La SS4 . . . . 125 C2
Units D1–D2 CM21 . . . . 1 F2
Univ of East London
  RM8 . . . . 153 A8
Univ of Essex (Southend
  Campus) SS1 . . . . 167 A8
Unwin Pl SS1 . . . . 75 C2
Uphall Prim Sch IG1 . . . . 152 B7

Uphall Rd IG1 . . . . 152 B7
Uphavering Ho RM12 . . . 136 C2
Upland Cl CM12 . . . . 96 F4
Upland Court Rd RM3 . . . 114 F1
Upland Dr CM12 . . . . . . 96 F4
Upland Rd
  Billericay CM12 . . . . 96 F4
  Southend-on-S SS9 . . . . 166 A8
  Thornwood CM16 . . . . . 45 F6
Uplands Cl
  Hockley SS5 . . . . 124 F5
  South Benfleet SS7 . . . . 144 B3
Uplands Dr CM1 . . . . 32 D7
Uplands Park Ct SS6 . . . . 123 E3
Uplands Park Rd SS6 . . . 123 D3
Uplands Rd
  Brentwood CM14 . . . . . 116 E6
  Hockley SS5 . . . . 124 F5
  Ilford RM6 . . . . 134 D8
  South Benfleet SS7 . . . . 144 B3
  Woodford IG8 . . . . 110 E3
Uplands The IG10 . . . . . . 88 F6
UPMINSTER 137 C2
Upminster Bridge Sta
  RM12 . . . . 136 F2
Upminster Inf Sch
  RM14 . . . . 137 C2
Upminster Jun Sch
  RM14 . . . . 137 C2
Upminster Mill★
  RM14 . . . . 137 B2
Upminster Rd RM11 . . . . 136 F2
Upminster Rd N
  RM13 . . . . 155 D2
Upminster Rd S RM13 . . . 155 B1
Upminster Sta RM14 . . . . 137 C2
Upminster Trad Pk
  RM14 . . . . 138 D4
Upney Cl RM12 . . . . 155 D7
Upney Ct **2** IG11 . . . . . 152 F5
Upney La IG11 . . . . 152 F5
Upney Sta IG11 . . . . 152 F5
Uppark Dr IG2 . . . . 133 C5
Upper Abbey Rd
  DA17 . . . . 169 A2
Upper Ave SS13 . . . . 143 E8
Upper Brentwood Rd
  RM2 . . . . 136 C8
Upper Bridge Rd CM2 . . . 32 A1
Upper Chase
  Althorne CM3 . . . . 82 F3
  2 Chelmsford CM2 . . . 54 A8
Upper Church Hill
  DA9 . . . . 176 E2
Upper Cornsland
  CM14 . . . . 116 D7
Upper Holly Hill Rd
  DA17 . . . . 169 B1
Upper Hook CM18 . . . . . 23 F6
Upper Lambricks SS6 . . . 123 E4
Upper Market Rd **3**
  SS12 . . . . 121 C8
Upper Marsh La EN11 . . . 21 A5
Upper Mayne SS14,
  SS15 . . . . 141 F7
Upper Mealines CM18 . . . 24 A5
Upper Moors CM3 . . . . . 18 F7
Upper Park Rd
  Belvedere DA17 . . . . . . 169 B2
  Wickford SS12 . . . . 121 D4
Upper Pk
  Harlow CM20 . . . . 10 B1
  Loughton IG10 . . . . 88 D4
Upper Rainham Rd
  Hornchurch RM12 . . . . . 135 F2
  Rainham RM12 . . . . 154 F8
Upper Roman Rd CM2 . . . 32 B1
Upper Ryle CM14 . . . . . . 94 B2
Upper Sheridan Rd **3**
  DA17 . . . . 169 A2
Upper Stonyfield CM19 . . 23 B8
Upper Swaines CM16 . . . 45 F1
UPSHIRE 66 D7
Upshire Mews EN9 . . . . . 66 A6
Upshire Prim Foundation
  Sch EN9 . . . . 66 B6
Upshire Rd EN9 . . . . 66 A6
Upton Cl SS17 . . . . 160 D2
Upton Ho **5** RM3 . . . . . 114 D5
Upway SS13 . . . . 123 D3
Upway The SS14 . . . . . . 142 C8
Upwood Ct RM1 . . . . 135 F7
Urban Ave RM12 . . . . . . 136 C1
Urmond Rd SS8 . . . . 164 A4
Urswick Gdns RM9 . . . . . 153 E5
Urswick Rd RM9 . . . . . . 153 E5
Usk Rd RM15 . . . . 171 D7
Uttons Ave SS9 . . . . 165 D8
Uvedale Rd RM10 . . . . . . 135 A1
Uxbridge Cl SS11 . . . . . . 121 F6

V

Vaagen Rd SS8 . . . . 164 B4
Vadsoe Rd SS8 . . . . 164 B5
Valance Ave E4 . . . . 87 F1
Valance Way SS16 . . . . . 141 C4
Vale Ave SS2 . . . . 148 A2
Valebrook IG1 . . . . 133 A2
Vale Cl CM15 . . . . 93 F4
Vale Ct CM4 . . . . 97 D6
Vale End CM2 . . . . 54 C3
Valence Ave RM8 . . . . . . 134 E4
Valence Cir RM8 . . . . 134 D1
Valence House Mus★
  RM8 . . . . 134 E2
Valence Inf Sch RM8 . . . 134 D2

Valence Jun Sch
  RM8 . . . . 134 D2
Valence Wood Rd
  RM8 . . . . 134 E1
Valentines
  Stock CM4 . . . . 75 F2
  6 Wickford SS12 . . . . 121 D6
Valentines High Sch
  (Upper) IG2 . . . . 133 A5
Valentines Rd IG1 . . . . . . 133 B3
Valentines Way RM7 . . . . 135 E2
Valentine The IG2 . . . . . 133 A5
Valerie Ho SS9 . . . . 146 E2
Vale The
  Basildon SS16 . . . . 142 D3
  Brentwood CM14 . . . . . 94 C1
  Stock CM4 . . . . 97 D7
  Woodford IG8 . . . . 110 A3
Valiant Cl RM7 . . . . 113 B1
Valkyrie Rd SS0 . . . . 166 D8
Vallance Ct SS2 . . . . 148 E3
Valletta Cl CM1 . . . . 32 A3
Valley Bridge CM1 . . . . . 32 B6
Valley Cl
  Loughton IG10 . . . . 88 F3
  Waltham Abbey EN9 . . . 65 C7
Valley Ct IG8 . . . . 110 B3
Valley Gdns DA9 . . . . . . 177 B1
Valley Hill IG10 . . . . 88 E3
Valley Lo IG10 . . . . 88 F3
Valley Rd
  Billericay CM11 . . . . 97 C2
  Erith DA8 . . . . 169 D2
Valley Side E4 . . . . 87 A1
Valley Side Par E4 . . . . . 109 A8
Valley View DA9 . . . . 177 B1
Valmar Ave SS17 . . . . . . 160 B1
Vanbilt Ave SS6 . . . . 123 C8
Vanderwalt Ave SS8 . . . . 164 D3
Van Dieman's La CM2 . . . 54 C8
Van Dieman's Rd CM2 . . . 54 C8
Van Diemens Pass
  SS8 . . . . 164 F3
Vanessa Cl DA17 . . . . . . 169 A1
VANGE 142 E4
Vange Corner Dr
  SS16 . . . . 142 B1
Vange Hill Ct SS16 . . . . . 142 E3
Vange Hill Dr SS16 . . . . . 142 E4
Vange Park Rd SS16 . . . . 142 B1
Vange Prim Sch SS17 . . . 142 D2
Vange Riverview Ctr
  SS16 . . . . 142 F4
Vanguard Cl RM7 . . . . . . 113 B1
Vanguards The SS3 . . . . 168 F7
Vanguard Way SS3 . . . . . 168 F7
Vanryne Ho IG10 . . . . . . 88 E6
Vantorts Cl CM21 . . . . . 1 E2
Vantorts Rd CM21 . . . . . 1 E2
Varden Cl CM1 . . . . 31 F6
Vardon Dr SS9 . . . . 146 B3
Vaughan Ave
  Hornchurch RM12 . . . . . 155 E8
  Southend-on-S SS2 . . . . 148 E1
Vaughan Cl SS4 . . . . 125 E5
Vaughan Gdns
  Ilford IG1 . . . . 133 A4
  Redbridge IG1 . . . . 132 F4
Vaughan Williams Rd
  SS1 . . . . 141 C8
Vaughan Williams Way
  CM14 . . . . 116 B6
Vaulx Rd SS8 . . . . 164 B4
Velizy Ave CM20 . . . . . . 10 D1
Vellacotts CM1 . . . . 32 B7
Venables Cl
  Canvey Island SS8 . . . . 164 C4
  Dagenham RM10 . . . . . 154 B8
Venette Ct RM13 . . . . . . 170 B8
Venlo Rd SS8 . . . . 164 B5
Venmead Ct **7** DA17 . . . 169 A2
Venta Way SS8 . . . . 59 B8
Ventnor Gdns IG11 . . . . . 152 E6
Ventnor Mans IG11 . . . . . 152 E6
Veny Cres RM12 . . . . . . 155 D7
Vera Rd CM11 . . . . 99 A2
Verbena Cl RM15 . . . . . . 172 C7
Verderers Rd IG7 . . . . . . 112 A6
Vere Rd IG10 . . . . 89 C5
Vermeer Cres SS3 . . . . . 168 G8
Vermeer Ride CM1 . . . . . 32 F7
Vermont Cl SS13 . . . . . . 143 C8
Verney Gdns RM9 . . . . . 153 E8
Verney Rd RM9 . . . . 153 E8
Vernon Ave
  Rayleigh SS6 . . . . 123 B4
  Woodford IG8 . . . . 110 B3
Vernon Cnr CM4 . . . . 75 D2
Vernon Cres CM13 . . . . . 117 A7
Vernon Ct SS9 . . . . 146 C5
Vernon Rd
  Ilford IG3 . . . . 133 F3
  North Fambridge CM3 . . 81 A1
  Romford RM5 . . . . 113 C5
  Southend-on-S SS9 . . . . 146 C1
  Swanscombe DA10 . . . . 177 F1
Vernons Wlk **4** SS13 . . . 121 A1
Veronica Cl CM11 . . . . . 114 C3
Veronique Gdns IG6 . . . . 133 C6
Verons Wlk **10** SS14 . . . 142 F8
Vert Ho RM17 . . . . 178 C7
Vestry Cl SS15 . . . . 141 C7
Vexil Cl RM19 . . . . 171 D2
Veysey Gdns RM10 . . . . . 135 A1
Viaduct The E18 . . . . 110 B1
Viaduct Rd CM1 . . . . 32 A2
Viborg Gdns CM9 . . . . . . 58 E8
Vica Cotts CM3 . . . . 34 D5

Vicarage Cl
  Basildon SS15 . . . . 141 C6
  Brentwood CM14 . . . . . 115 E6
  Canvey Island SS8 . . . . 163 D3
  Roxwell CM1 . . . . 30 B5
Vicarage Ct
  8 Billericay CM12 . . . . 97 B2
  Southminster CM0 . . . . . 84 D3
  Waltham Abbey EN9 . . . 66 A5
  Woodford IG8 . . . . 110 E3
Vicarage Dr
  Barking IG11 . . . . 152 C5
  Northfleet DA11 . . . . . . 178 C1
Vicarage Field Sh Ctr The
  IG11 . . . . 152 C5
Vicarage Hill SS7 . . . . . . 144 E2
Vicarage Hts SS7 . . . . . . 144 E1
Vicarage La
  Chigwell IG7 . . . . 111 D7
  Great Baddow CM2 . . . . 54 F5
  Ilford IG1 . . . . 133 D3
  Mundon CM9 . . . . 59 E2
  North Weald Bassett
    CM16 . . . . 47 B7
  North Weald Bassett, Tyler's
    Green CM16 . . . . 47 D7
  Tillingham CM0 . . . . . . 63 E4
  Wallend E6 . . . . 152 A2
Vicarage Mdw CM0 . . . . 84 D3
Vicarage Mews CM2 . . . . 54 F6
Vicarage Rd
  Chelmsford CM2 . . . . . . 54 B8
  Coopersale CM16 . . . . . 46 C2
  Dagenham RM10 . . . . . 154 B5
  Hornchurch RM12 . . . . . 136 A3
  Pleshey CM3 . . . . 7 E2
  Roxwell CM1 . . . . 30 D5
  Woodford IG8 . . . . 110 E3
Vicarage Sq RM17 . . . . . 178 A8
Vicarage Wood CM20 . . . 11 A1
Vicar's Wlk RM8 . . . . 134 B1
Viceroy Ct
  Horndon on t H SS17 . . . 159 F3
  Southend-on-S SS0 . . . . 166 B7
Vickers Rd
  Erith DA8 . . . . 169 D1
  Southend-on-S SS2 . . . . 147 D6
Victor App RM12 . . . . . . 136 D3
Victor Ave SS13 . . . . 143 D6
Victor Cl RM12 . . . . 136 D3
Victor Ct
  Hornchurch RM12 . . . . . 136 D3
  Rainham RM13 . . . . 154 D3
Victor Dr SS9 . . . . 165 F8
Victor Gdns
  Hockley SS5 . . . . 124 F5
  Hornchurch RM12 . . . . . 136 D3
Victoria Ave
  Basildon SS16 . . . . 141 C3
  Grays RM16 . . . . 173 C4
  Rayleigh SS6 . . . . 123 B4
  Romford RM5 . . . . 113 B4
  Southend-on-S SS2 . . . . 147 F2
  Wickford SS12 . . . . 121 C5
Victoria Bsns Pk SS2 . . . 148 A2
Victoria Cl
  Basildon SS15 . . . . 141 B7
  Grays RM16 . . . . 173 C4
Victoria Cotts
  Heybridge CM9 . . . . 37 A5
  Ilford IG6 . . . . 133 C6
Victoria Cres
  Basildon SS15 . . . . 141 B8
  Chelmsford CM1 . . . . . . 32 A3
  Wickford SS12 . . . . 121 B7
Victoria Ct
  1 Brentwood CM14 . . . 116 C6
  Harlow CM20 . . . . 10 E1
  Romford RM1 . . . . 136 A6
  1 Southend-on-S SS2 . . 147 F1
  Southend-on-S, Westcliff-S
    SS0 . . . . 166 E7
  1 Wanstead E18 . . . . . 132 B8
  Wickford SS11 . . . . 122 A5
Victoria Dr
  Great Wakering SS3 . . . 150 C2
  Southend-on-S SS9 . . . . 146 E1
Victoria Ho
  2 Romford, Ardleigh Green
    RM2 . . . . 136 C7
  1 Romford RM1 . . . . . 135 F5
Victoria Lanes Sh Ctr
  SS1 . . . . 167 A7
Victoria Plaza **4** SS1 . . . 167 A8
Victoria Plaza Sh Ctr **1**
  SS1 . . . . 167 A8
Victoria Rd
  Barking IG11 . . . . 152 B6
  Basildon, Laindon SS15 . 141 A4
  Basildon, Vange SS16 . . 142 D2
  Brentwood CM14 . . . . . 116 C6
  Buckhurst Hill IG9 . . . . . 110 D8
  Bulphan RM14 . . . . 158 F8
  Chelmsford CM1 . . . . . . 32 B3
  Chingford E4 . . . . 87 C1
  Chingford, Highams Park
    E17 . . . . 109 C1
  Cold Norton CM3 . . . . . 80 F6
  Dagenham RM10 . . . . . 154 C7
  Horndon on t H SS17 . . . 159 F3
  Maldon CM9 . . . . 37 A2
  Rayleigh SS6 . . . . 123 E3
  Romford RM1 . . . . 135 F5
  Southend-on-S, Chalkwell
    SS9 . . . . 165 D5
  Southend-on-S SS1 . . . . 167 D7
  South Woodham Ferrers
    CM3 . . . . 101 D6

Victoria Rd continued
  Stanford-le-H SS17 . . . . 160 C2
  Waltham Abbey EN9 . . . 65 C5
  Wanstead E18 . . . . 132 B8
  Writtle CM1 . . . . 30 F1
Victoria Rd S CM1 . . . . . 32 B2
Victoria's Way RM15 . . . . 172 C8
Victor Mew Cl SS12 . . . . 121 D5
Victor's Cres CM13 . . . . . 117 B8
Victor Wlk RM12 . . . . . . 136 D3
Victory Cl
  Grays RM16 . . . . 172 D2
  Wickford SS11 . . . . 122 A5
Victory Ct **4** IG11 . . . . . 153 B2
Victory La SS4 . . . . 125 D6
Victory Lo DA8 . . . . 169 E1
Victory Rd
  Rainham RM13 . . . . 155 A3
  Wanstead E11 . . . . 132 B7
Victory Way
  Dartford DA2 . . . . 176 C3
  Romford RM7 . . . . 113 B1
Vienna Cl IG5 . . . . 110 D1
View Cl IG7 . . . . 111 D5
Viewpoint RM17 . . . . 178 A8
Vigerons Way RM16 . . . . 174 B2
Vignoles Rd RM7 . . . . . . 135 A4
Vi & John Rubens Ho
  IG2 . . . . 133 A5
Viking Bsns Ctr RM7 . . . . 135 C4
Viking Cl SS3 . . . . 168 C7
Viking Rd CM9 . . . . 36 E1
Vikings Way SS8 . . . . . . 163 D3
Viking Way
  Belvedere DA8 . . . . 169 C3
  Pilgrims Hatch CM15 . . . 94 B3
  Rainham RM13 . . . . 155 A1
  Wickford SS11 . . . . 99 E2
Village Arc The **2** E4 . . . 87 D1
Village Cl
  Chingford E4 . . . . 109 C5
  Hoddesdon EN11 . . . . . 21 D8
Village Dr SS8 . . . . 163 E3
Village Gate CM2 . . . . . . 33 A2
Village Gn SS4 . . . . 104 D1
Village Hall Cl SS8 . . . . . 163 D3
Village Home The
  IG6 . . . . 133 C8
Village Hts IG8 . . . . 109 F5
Village Inf Sch RM10 . . . . 154 A5
Village Sq CM2 . . . . 33 A3
Village Way IG6 . . . . 133 C8
Villa Rd SS7 . . . . 144 C4
Villiers Pl CM3 . . . . 33 E8
Villiers Way SS7 . . . . 144 F5
Vincent Ave SS17 . . . . . 159 F3
Vincent Cl
  Corringham SS17 . . . . . 161 B2
  Redbridge IG6 . . . . 111 C4
  Southend-on-S SS3 . . . . 168 E7
Vincent Ct CM14 . . . . . . 116 B8
Vincent La CM3 . . . . 101 E6
Vincent Mews SS3 . . . . . 168 E7
Vincent Rd
  Chingford E4 . . . . 109 D4
  Dagenham RM9 . . . . . . 153 E5
  Rainham RM13 . . . . 155 C1
  Rochford SS4 . . . . 103 B1
Vincent Way CM12 . . . . . 97 A5
Vine Cl SS14 . . . . 142 E6
Vine Ct **10** DA11 . . . . . 179 B1
Vine Gdns IG1 . . . . 152 C7
Vine Gr CM20 . . . . 10 E5
Vineries Ct RM9 . . . . 153 F6
Vine St RM7 . . . . 135 C7
Vine Way CM14 . . . . 94 C1
Vineyards The CM2 . . . . . 54 F7
Vintage Mews E4 . . . . . . 109 A6
Vintners The SS2 . . . . . . 147 F5
Viola Cl
  Basildon SS15 . . . . 141 C5
  South Ockendon RM15 . . 157 C2
Violet Cl CM1 . . . . 32 E7
Violet Rd E18 . . . . 110 B1
Virginia Cl
  Romford RM5 . . . . 113 C3
  South Benfleet SS7 . . . . 144 B7
Virginia Gdns IG6 . . . . . 111 D1
Virley Cl CM9 . . . . 37 D4
Vista Dr IG4 . . . . 132 D6
Vista Rd SS11 . . . . 121 F7
Vista The E4 . . . . 87 D2
Voluntary Pl E11 . . . . . . 132 A5
Volwycke Ave CM9 . . . . . 58 F8
Voorburg Rd SS8 . . . . . . 164 D4
Vowler Rd SS16 . . . . 141 B4
Voysey Gdns SS13 . . . . . 121 B1

W

Waalwyk Dr SS8 . . . . . . 164 C4
Waarden Rd SS8 . . . . . . 164 B4
Waarem Ave SS8 . . . . . . 164 B4
Wadeville Ave RM6 . . . . . 134 F4
Wadeville Cl DA17 . . . . . 169 A1
Wadham Ave E17 . . . . . . 109 B3
Wadham Cl CM4 . . . . . . 74 B4
Wadham Park Ave
  SS5 . . . . 102 A1
Wadham Rd E17 . . . . . . 109 B2
Wadhurst Ct E6 . . . . 152 A3
Wagon Mead CM22 . . . . 3 A3
Wagstaff Gdns RM9 . . . . 153 C5
Wagtail Dr CM9 . . . . 37 C5

Waikato Lo IG9 88 C1
Wainfleet Ave RM5 113 C1
Wainwright Ave CM13 95 D3
Wake Arms Rdbt IG10 66 F3
Wakefield Ave CM12 97 A2
Wakefield Gdns IG1 132 E5
Wakefield Rd DA9 177 C2
Wakelin Chase CM4 74 A3
Wakerfield Cl RM11 136 F6
Wakering Ave SS3 168 G7
Wakering Rd
 Barking IG11 152 C5
 Great Wakering SS3 150 B1
 Southend-on-S SS1, SS3 149 A2
Wakescolne SS11 122 A6
Walace Ct EN3 65 A2
Walbrook 10 E18 132 A8
Waldeck Rd DA1 176 A1
Waldegrave SS16 142 B4
Waldegrave Ct
 11 Barking IG11 152 D4
 Upminster RM14 137 B3
Waldegrave Gdns RM14 137 B2
Waldegrave Rd RM8 134 C2
Walden Ave RM13 154 D3
Walden Rd RM11 136 D5
Walden Way
 Hornchurch RM11 136 D5
 Redbridge IG6 111 E3
Waldon RM18 175 C3
Waldringfield SS14 142 B7
Walford Pl CM2 32 F2
Walfords Cl CM17 11 C3
Walfrey Gdns RM9 153 E5
Walker Ave CM5 27 D2
Walker Dr SS9 146 A2
Walkers Cl CM1 32 D7
Walkers Sq SS17 160 D1
Walkey Way SS3 168 H7
Walk The
 Billericay CM12 97 A1
 Hornchurch RM11 136 F2
 Hullbridge SS5 101 D3
Walkways SS8 163 F5
Wallace Binder Cl CM9 36 F1
Wallace Cl SS5 101 D3
Wallace Cres CM2 54 D8
Wallace Dr SS12 121 E5
Wallace Gdns DA10 177 E1
Wallace Rd RM17 173 A2
Wallace's La CM3 20 F4
Wallace St SS3 168 F7
Wallace Way RM1 113 D2
Wallasea Gdns CM1 32 F5
WALLASEA ISLAND 105 F2
Wall Chase CM6 7 F7
WALLEND 152 A4
Wall End Ct E6 152 A4
Wall End Rd E6 152 A5
Wallenger Ave RM2 136 B8
Wallers Cl
 Dagenham RM9 153 E4
 Woodford IG8 110 F4
Waller's Hoppet IG10 88 F7
Wallers Way EN11 8 B1
Wallflower Ct 11 CM1 32 F6
Wallingford Ho 2 RM3 114 E4
Wallington Rd IG3 133 F4
Wallis Ave SS2 147 F2
Wallis Cl RM11 136 B3
Wallis Ct EN9 65 B4
Wallis Pk DA11 178 B2
Wall Rd SS8 164 F3
WALL'S GREEN 29 B2
Walmer Cl
 Chingford E4 109 B8
 Romford RM7 113 B1
Walnut Cl
 Basildon SS15 119 C1
 Ilford IG6 133 C7
Walnut Cotts CM21 1 E3
Walnut Ct SS5 124 E7
Walnut Gr
 Harlow CM20 10 B1
 Hornchurch RM12 136 D3
Walnut Tree Ave CM21 1 E4
Walnut Tree Cl EN11 21 A6
Walnut Tree Cotts CM3 18 E5
Walnut Tree Cres CM21 1 E3
Walnut Tree Rd
 Dagenham RM8 134 E2
 Erith DA8 169 E1
Walnut Way IG9 110 D7
Walpole Cl RM17 173 C2
Walpole Rd E18 109 F2
Walpole Wlk SS6 124 A2
Walsham Ent Ctr RM17 173 C1
Walsingham Cl 7 SS15 141 C7
Walsingham Ho E4 87 D2
Walsingham Rd SS2 148 B2
Walsingham Way CM12 97 B5
Walter Hurford Par 5 E12 152 A8
Walter Mead Cl CM5 49 A4
Walters Cl
 Galleywood CM2 54 C3
 Southend-on-S SS9 146 E6
WALTHAM ABBEY 65 D7
Waltham Abbey★ EN9 65 C6
Waltham Cl 1 CM13 95 C3
Waltham Cres SS2 148 B3
Waltham Ct E17 109 C2
Waltham Forest Coll E17 109 B1
Waltham Glen CM2 54 C7
Waltham Holy Cross Inf Sch EN9 65 D6
Waltham Holy Cross Jun Sch EN9 65 D6
Waltham Park Way E17 109 A3
Waltham Pk E17 109 A2
Waltham Rd
 Lower Nazeing EN9 44 A6
 Rayleigh SS6 123 B3
 Woodford IG8 110 E4
Walthams SS13 143 B7
Walthams Pl SS13 143 B7
Walthamstow Acad E17 109 A2
Walthamstow Ave E4 109 A3
Walthamstow Ave (North Circular Rd) E4 109 A3
Walthamstow Bsns Ctr E17 109 C1
Waltham Way E4 87 A1
Walton Ct
 Basildon SS15 141 C8
 Hoddesdon EN11 21 C8
Walton Gdns
 Brentwood CM13 95 C4
 Waltham Abbey EN9 65 B6
Walton Hall Farm Mus★ SS17 175 B5
Walton Hall La CM3 58 B1
Walton Rd
 Hoddesdon EN11 21 C8
 Little Ilford E12 152 A8
 Romford RM5 112 F3
 Southend-on-S SS1 167 F6
Walton's Hall Rd SS17 175 B5
Wambrook SS3 149 D1
Wambrook Cl CM13 95 C1
Wamburg Rd SS8 164 E4
Wanderer Dr IG11 153 C2
Wangey Rd RM6 134 D4
Wannock Gdns IG6 111 B3
Wansfell Coll CM16 67 D4
Wansfell Gdns SS1 167 F8
Wansford Cl CM14 115 F7
Wansford Rd IG8 110 C2
WANSTEAD 132 C5
Wanstead Church Sch E11 132 A6
Wanstead High Sch E11 132 C5
Wanstead Hospl E11 132 B7
Wanstead Hts 8 E11 132 A6
Wanstead La IG1 132 E5
Wanstead Park Ave E12 132 D2
Wanstead Park Rd
 Ilford IG1 133 A2
 Redbridge IG1 132 E3
Wanstead Pl E11 132 A6
Wanstead Sta E11 132 B5
Wantage Ho 10 RM3 114 D4
Wantfield Cotts CM4 74 F8
Wantz Chase CM9 37 A2
Wantz Cnr CM2 76 E5
Wantz Haven CM9 37 A2
Wantz La RM13 155 B1
Wantz Rd
 Dagenham RM10 154 B7
 Maldon CM9 37 A2
 Margaretting CM4 75 A8
Warboys Cres E4 109 C5
Warburtons SS17 161 A2
Warburton Terr E17 109 B1
Ward Ave RM17 173 B2
Ward Cl SS15 141 D5
Warden Ave RM5 113 C5
Ward Gdns RM3 114 E1
Ward Hatch CM20 11 A3
Wardle Way CM1 31 E7
Wardona Ct
 Northfleet DA11 178 B2
 Swanscombe DA10 177 F1
Wardour Ct 9 DA2 176 B1
Ward Path CM2 33 B4
Wards Rd IG2 133 D4
Waremead Rd IG2 133 B6
Ware Rd EN11 8 A1
Warescot Cl CM15 94 B2
Warescot Rd CM15 94 B2
Wares Rd
 Margaret Roding CM1 16 E5
 Mashbury CM1 17 A4
WARLEY 116 D5
Warley Ave RM8 134 F4
Warley Gap CM13 116 C3
Warley Hall La RM14 138 F4
Warley Hill CM13, CM14 116 C5
Warley Hill Bsns Pk The CM13 116 C4
Warley Hospl CM14 116 B5
Warley Mount CM14 116 C6
Warley Prim Sch CM14 116 C5
Warley Rd
 Great Warley CM13 116 B3
 Redbridge IG5 111 A2
 Romford CM13 115 E1
 Woodford IG8 110 B3
Warley St CM13, RM14 138 C5
Warleywoods Cres CM14 116 B6
Warlow Cl EN3 65 A2
Warminster Ho RM3 114 F5
Warner Cl CM11 97 D1
Warners Bridge Chase SS4 147 F6
Warners Cl IG8 110 A5
Warners Gdns SS4 147 E6
Warren Chase SS7 145 A4
Warren Cl
 Broomfield CM1 19 B3
 Rayleigh SS6 145 C8
 Stanford-le-H SS17 160 D1
Warren Comp Sch The RM6 134 F6
Warren Ct IG7 111 D6
Warren Dr
 Basildon SS14 142 E6
 Hornchurch RM12 136 B1
 Wickford SS11 122 A8
Warren Dr The E11 132 C4
Warren Farm Cotts RM6 134 F7
Warren Field CM16 68 A7
Warren Hastings Ct DA11 178 F1
Warren Hill IG10 88 C4
Warren Hts
 Grays RM16 172 E2
 Loughton IG10 88 C4
Warren Jun Sch RM6 134 F6
Warren La
 Doddinghurst CM15 94 A8
 Grays RM16 172 D2
Warren Pond Rd E4 87 F2
Warren Prim Sch RM16 172 C3
Warren Rd
 Chingford E4 109 C8
 Ilford IG6 133 D6
 Southend-on-S SS9 146 A3
 South Hanningfield CM3 99 D7
 Wanstead E11 132 C4
Warren Terr
 Grays RM16 172 D4
 Ilford RM6 134 D7
Warren The CM12 96 E4
Warriner Ave RM12 136 D2
Warrington Gdns RM11 136 D5
Warrington Rd RM8 134 E2
Warrington Sq
 Billericay CM12 96 F3
 Dagenham RM8 134 D2
Warrior Ho 7 SS1 167 A8
Warrior Sq
 Little Ilford E12 152 A8
 Southend-on-S SS1 167 A8
Warrior Sq E SS1 167 A8
Warrior Sq N SS1 167 A8
Warrior Square Rd SS3 168 F5
Warwick Cl
 Canvey Island SS8 164 A5
 Hornchurch RM11 136 F7
 Maldon CM9 37 A1
 Rayleigh SS6 123 F1
 South Benfleet SS7 144 D7
Warwick Cres CM9 37 A1
Warwick Ct
 Brentwood CM13 117 B7
 Burnham-on-C CM0 106 B4
Warwick Dr
 Maldon CM9 37 A1
 Rochford SS4 147 F7
Warwick Gdns
 Ilford IG1 133 B3
 Rayleigh SS6 123 F1
 Romford RM2 136 C8
Warwick Gn SS6 124 A1
Warwick La RM13, RM14 156 B3
Warwick Par CM3 101 D8
Warwick Pl
 Basildon SS16 140 F4
 Northfleet DA11 178 B2
 Pilgrims Hatch CM14 93 C5
Warwick Rd
 Chingford E4 109 A5
 Rainham RM13 155 D2
 Rayleigh SS6 123 F1
 Rayleigh SS6 146 B8
 Southend-on-S SS1 167 F6
 Wanstead E11 132 B6
Warwick Sq CM1 31 F4
Washington Ave SS15 141 A6
Washington Cl CM9 36 E1
Washington Ct CM9 36 E1
Washington Rd
 Maldon CM9 36 F1
 2 Woodford E18 109 F1
Wash La CM9 38 B7
Wash Rd
 Basildon SS15 119 E2
 Brentwood CM13 95 E4
Watchfield La SS6 123 C1
Watchouse Rd CM2 54 C3
Waterbeach Rd RM9 153 C6
Waterdene SS8 163 F5
Waterfall 20 SS1 167 C7
Waterfalls The SS16 141 B3
Waterfield Cl DA17 169 A3
Waterford Rd SS3 168 D5
Waterfront Wlk SS14 120 B1
Watergardens The IG8 110 A5
Waterglade Ind Pk RM20 176 F8
Waterhale SS1 149 A1
Waterhall Ave E4 109 E6
Waterhouse La CM1 31 F1
Waterhouse Moor CM18 23 F7
Waterhouse St CM1 31 F1
Water La
 Harlow CM19 23 A5
 Ilford IG3 133 F1
 Purfleet RM19 171 A2
 Roydon CM19 22 E4
Water Lane Prim Sch CM19 23 A4
Waterloo Gdns RM7 135 E5
Waterloo La CM1 32 C2
Waterloo Rd
 Brentwood CM14 94 C1
 Redbridge IG6 111 C1
 Romford RM7 135 E5
 Southend-on-S SS3 168 D7
Watermans RM1 135 F6
Watermans Way
 Greenhithe DA9 177 B3
 North Weald Bassett CM16 47 A4
Watermark Ct 4 RM6 134 B5
Water Mdws
 Basildon SS13 143 A4
 Linford SS17 175 A3
Waters Edge SS0 166 D7
Waters Edge Ct DA8 169 F1
Waters Gdns RM10 154 A7
Waterside SS1 167 D6
Waterside Cl
 Barking IG11 153 A8
 Romford RM3 115 A3
Waterside Ind Est EN11 21 D5
Waterside Mead SS8 163 F6
Waterside Pl CM22 2 A2
Waterside Rd
 Bradwell Waterside CM0 41 F3
 Paglesham Eastend SS4 128 A5
Waters Mead SS1 168 A6
Watersmeet CM19 23 B4
Waterson Rd RM16 174 C2
Waterson Vale CM2 54 C8
Waters Villas CM22 4 A6
Waterville Dr SS16 143 A4
Waterways Bsns Ctr 11 EN3 65 A1
Waterworks La SS17 161 D5
Watery La
 Battlesbridge SS11 101 C1
 Matching Green CM17 26 D8
Wates Way CM15 94 D1
Watford Ho RM3 114 F5
Watkin Mews EN3 65 A2
Watkins Cl SS13 121 D1
Watkins Way SS3 149 F1
Watlington Rd
 Harlow CM17 11 D4
 South Benfleet SS7 144 B2
Watson Ave E6 152 A5
Watson Cl
 Grays RM20 177 A6
 Southend-on-S SS3 168 D7
Watson Ct 18 CM14 116 C7
Watson Gdns RM3 114 D1
Watsons Lo 9 RM10 154 B6
WATTON'S GREEN 92 B3
Watts Cres RM19 171 C2
Watt's La SS4 125 F1
Wat Tyler Ctry Pk★ SS16 143 B2
Wat Tyler Way SS16 162 B8
Wavell Cl CM1 32 D8
Waveney Dr CM1 32 C6
Waverley Bridge Ct CM9 37 B5
Waverley Cl E18 110 C1
Waverley Cres
 Romford RM3 114 C3
 Wickford SS11 99 C3
Waverley Gdns
 Barking IG11 152 E3
 Grays RM16 173 A4
 Ilford IG6 111 C1
 Redbridge IG6 111 C1
Waverley Rd
 Basildon SS15 119 E1
 Rainham RM13 155 B2
 South Benfleet SS7 144 C6
 Woodford E18 110 C2
Wavertree Rd
 South Benfleet SS7 144 B4
 Woodford E18 110 A1
Waxwell Rd SS5 101 E2
Waycross Rd RM14 137 E5
Wayfarer Gdns CM0 106 A5
Wayfaring Gn RM17 172 F1
Waylands Ct IG1 152 D8
Wayletts
 Basildon SS15 141 A8
 Southend-on-S SS9 146 B6
Waymans RM15 171 D7
Wayre St CM17 11 C4
Wayre The CM17 11 C4
Wayside CM3 56 E8
Wayside Ave RM12 136 D2
Wayside Cl RM1 135 F8
Wayside Commercial Est IG11 153 A3
Wayside Gdns RM10 154 A7
Wayside Mews IG2 133 A6
Weald Bridge Rd CM16 25 E2
Weald Cl CM14 116 A7
Weald Ctry Pk★ CM14 93 E2
Weald Ctry Pk Visitor Ctr★ CM14 93 D1
Wealden Ho CM15 94 B3
Weald Hall La CM16 46 E6
Weald Hall Lane Ind Est CM16 46 C6
Weald Park Way CM14 115 F7
Weald Pl CM14 116 C8
Weald Rd
 South Weald CM14 93 C1
 South Weald CM14 93 F1
Weald The SS8 163 E4
Weald Way RM7 135 B5
Weale Rd E4 109 D7
Wear Dr CM1 32 D6
Weare Gifford SS3 168 C8
Weaverdale SS3 149 E1
Weavers SS16 143 A4
Weavers Cl 2 CM11 97 B2
Weavers Ho 5 E11 132 A5
Webb Cl CM2 33 B3
Webber Ho 6 IG11 152 B5
Webb Ho 2 RM10 135 A1
Webbscroft Rd RM10 154 B8
Webley Ct EN3 65 A2
Webster Cl
 Hornchurch RM12 136 D1
 Waltham Abbey EN9 66 A6
Webster Ct SS6 123 D2
Webster Pl CM4 75 E2
Webster Rd SS17 160 E2
Websters Way SS6 123 D2
Wedderburn Rd IG11 152 E4
Wedds Way SS3 150 B4
Wedgewood Cl CM16 46 A1
Wedgewood Dr CM17 24 E7
Wedgwood Ct SS4 125 D6
Wedgwood Way SS4 125 C6
Wedhey CM19 23 C8
Wedlake Cl RM11 136 E3
Wedmore Ave IG5 111 A2
Wednesbury Gdns RM3 114 F3
Wednesbury Gn RM3 114 F3
Wednesbury Rd RM3 114 F3
Weelkes Cl SS17 160 C3
Weel Rd SS8 164 D2
Weight Rd CM2 32 C2
Weind The CM16 67 E3
WEIR 145 C8
Weirbrook SS7 145 B8
Weir Farm Rd SS6 145 C8
Weir Gdns SS6 123 C1
Weir Pond Rd SS4 125 F2
Weir Wynd CM12 97 B1
Welbeck Cl SS5 124 F5
Welbeck Dr SS16 141 A4
Welbeck Rd SS8 164 B3
Welbeck Rise SS16 141 A4
Welch Cl SS2 148 E2
Welland RM18 175 C2
Welland Ave CM1 31 C5
Welland Rd CM0 106 A6
Well Cottage Cl E11 132 C4
Weller Gr CM1 31 E7
Wellesley CM19 23 A3
Wellesley Hospl SS2 148 C3
Wellesley Rd
 Brentwood CM14 94 C1
 Ilford IG1 133 B3
 Wanstead E11 132 A6
Well Field CM1 31 A1
Wellfields IG10 89 A6
Wellingborough Ho RM3 114 F5
Wellingbury SS7 144 C5
Welling Rd RM16 174 D7
Wellington Ave
 Chingford E4 109 B8
 Hullbridge SS5 123 D8
 Southend-on-S SS0 147 B1
Wellington Cl
 Chelmsford CM1 31 D5
 Dagenham RM10 154 C5
Wellington Ct RM16 173 B5
Wellington Dr RM10 154 C5
Wellington Hill IG10 66 B1
Wellington Ho RM2 136 C7
Wellingtonia Ave RM4 113 E7
Wellington Mews CM12 97 A5
Wellington Pas 7 E11 132 A6
Wellington Pl CM14 116 C5
Wellington Prim Sch E4 109 B8
Wellington Rd
 Hockley SS5 102 F1
 Maldon CM9 36 F2
 North Weald Bassett CM16 47 A4
 Rayleigh SS6 123 F4
 Tilbury RM18 179 A5
 Wanstead E11 132 A6
Wellingtons The CM0 84 D3
Well La
 Danbury CM3 56 C7
 Galleywood CM2 54 B2
 Harlow CM19 10 A1

Well La continued
Harlow CM20...........23 A8
Pilgrims Hatch CM15.....93 F6
South Ockendon RM16...172 E5
Stock CM4..............75 E1
Wellmead IG3..........134 A4
Well Mead CM12........119 C7
Wellmeads CM2........54 B8
Wells Ave SS2.........147 D6
Wells Ct
Chelmsford CM1........32 D5
6 Romford RM1.......135 E5
Wellsfield SS6.........123 E4
Wells Gdns
7 Basildon SS14......142 F8
Dagenham RM10.......154 B7
Rainham RM13........154 F6
Redbridge IG1........132 E4
Wells Ho 4 IG11.....153 A5
Wells Park Sch IG7....111 F6
Wells Prim Sch IG8....110 A6
Well's St 3 CM1.......32 A3
Wellstead Gdns SS0...147 B3
Wellstead Rd E6.......152 A3
Wellstye Gn SS14.....142 E8
Well Terr.............37 B5
Wellwood Rd IG3......134 A4
Welton Way SS4........126 A1
Wembley Ave CM3......83 A8
Wendene SS16.........142 F4
Wendon Cl SS4........125 C4
Wendover Ct SS17.....160 D1
Wendover Gdns
CM13...............117 B7
Wendover Way RM12...155 C2
Wenham Dr SS0.......147 C2
Wenham Gdns CM13....95 C3
Wenlocks La CM4......72 E6
WENNINGTON..........170 E6
Wennington Rd RM13...170 C7
Wensley Ave IG8......110 A3
Wensley Cl RM5.......113 A5
Wensleydale Ave IG5...110 E1
Wensley Rd SS7.......145 B5
Wentworth Ct 5 E4...109 D5
Wentworth Ho 6
IG8................111 A3
Wentworth Mdws CM9...36 F2
Wentworth Pl RM16....173 D3
Wentworth Prim Sch
CM9...............36 F1
Wentworth Rd SS2.....148 B3
Wentworth Way
RM13..............155 B2
Werneth Hall Rd
Ilford IG5...........133 A8
Redbridge IG5........132 F8
Wesley Ct SS1........167 B8
Wesley Gdns CM12.....96 F5
Wesley Rd SS1........167 B7
Wessem Rd SS8.......164 B5
Wessex Cl IG3........133 E5
Wessley Cl CM0.......63 E4
Westall Rd IG10.......89 C6
West Ave
Althorne CM3.........82 E2
Basildon SS16........140 E4
Chelmsford CM1.......31 F5
Hullbridge SS5.......101 C3
Mayland CM3.........60 E1
West Bank IG11.......152 B4
West Beech Ave SS11...121 E7
West Beech Cl SS11...121 E7
West Beech Mews
SS12..............121 D7
West Belvedere CM3...56 F7
Westborough Prim Sch
The SS0............147 E2
Westborough Rd SS0...147 D2
Westbourne Cl
Hadleigh SS7........145 D5
Hockley SS5.........125 A7
Westbourne Ct SS0...147 B2
Westbourne Dr CM14...115 F6
Westbourne Gdns
CM12..............97 B5
Westbourne Gr
Chelmsford CM2......54 D7
Southend-on-S SS0...147 B3
West Bowers Rd CM9...35 C4
Westbury SS4.........125 D4
Westbury Ct
3 Barking IG11......152 D4
1 Buckhurst Hill IG9..110 C8
Westbury Dr CM14....116 C8
Westbury Ho SS2.....148 C2
Westbury La IG9......110 C8
Westbury Rd
Barking IG11.........152 D4
Brentwood CM14......116 C8
Buckhurst Hill IG9....88 C1
Ilford IG1...........133 A2
Redbridge IG1.......133 A2
Southend-on-S SS2...148 C2
Westbury Rise CM17...24 D7
Westbury Terr RM14...137 E2
West Chase
Maldon CM9..........36 F3
Mundon CM9.........59 E1
West Cl
Hoddesdon EN11......21 A8
Rainham RM13.......155 B1
Westcliff Ave SS0......166 E4
Westcliff Dr SS0......146 D1
Westcliff Gdns SS8....164 E2
Westcliff High Sch for
Boys SS0............147 A3

Westcliff High Sch for
Girls SS0............147 A3
WESTCLIFF-ON-SEA
..................166 D8
Westcliff Par SS0......166 E7
Westcliff Park Dr
SS0...............147 D2
Westcliff Prep Day Sch
SS0...............166 C8
Westcliff Sta SS0.....166 D8
West Cloister CM11....97 B2
West Cres SS6........163 F4
West Crescent Rd 1
DA12..............179 C1
West Croft CM11......97 B1
Westcroft Ct EN10....21 A4
West Ct CM21.........1 E3
West Dene Dr RM3....114 D5
Westerdale CM1.......32 D7
Westerings
Bicknacre CM3........56 F2
Purleigh CM3........58 D1
Westerings Prim Sch The
SS5...............124 E4
Westerings The
Great Baddow CM2...54 F5
Hockley SS5.........124 E5
Westerland Ave SS4...164 D3
Western Approaches
SS2...............147 A7
Western Ave
Brentwood CM14......94 C8
Dagenham RM10......154 D6
Epping CM16.........67 F7
Romford RM2.........114 C1
Western Cross Cl
DA9...............177 C1
Western Ct 10 RM1...135 E6
Western Espl
Canvey Island SS8....164 B1
Southend-on-S SS0,
SS1...............166 E7
Western Gdns 3
CM14..............116 C8
Western Mews CM12...97 A2
Western Rd
Billericay CM12.......97 A2
Brentwood CM14......116 C8
Burnham-on-C CM0...106 C4
Hadleigh SS7........145 E6
Lower Nazeing EN9....21 E1
Rayleigh SS6.........123 B1
Romford RM1........135 F6
Southend-on-S SS9...146 B1
Western Terr 1 EN11...8 B1
Western View CM12....96 F1
Westernville Gdns
IG2...............133 C4
Westfield
Basildon SS15.......141 A8
Harlow CM16.........23 E7
Loughton IG10........88 C4
Westfield Ave CM1....32 A4
Westfield Bglws CM9...59 E1
Westfield Cl
Rayleigh SS6.........123 B5
Wickford SS11.......121 F8
Westfield Gdns RM6...134 C5
Westfield Park Dr
IG8................110 E4
Westfield Rd
Dagenham RM9.......153 F8
3 Hoddesdon EN11...21 A7
Westfleet Trad Est
SS11..............121 F6
Westgate
Basildon SS14.......142 A6
Southend-on-S SS3...168 E6
West Gate
1 Harlow CM20......10 C1
Harlow CM20........23 C8
Westgate Ho 6 SS4...125 F2
Westgate Pk SS14....142 A6
West Gn SS7.........144 B5
West Gr IG8..........110 C5
WEST HANNINGFIELD
..................77 B4
West Hanningfield Rd
Great Baddow CM2...55 A3
West Hanningfield CM2..76 E7
West Hatch High Sch
IG7...............110 F5
West Hayes CM22.....3 A3
West Ho IG11.........152 B6
West Hook SS16.......140 F4
WEST HORNDON.......139 C5
West Horndon Prim Sch
CM13..............139 D6
West Horndon Sta
CM13..............139 C5
West House Est CM0...84 D4
West Kent Ave DA11...178 C1
Westlake Ave SS13....143 E6
Westland Ave RM11...136 E3
Westlands Com Prim Sch
CM1...............31 E4
Westland View RM16...173 A5
West Lawn CM2.......54 C2
Westleigh Ave SS9....146 D1
Westleigh
Southend-on-S SS9...146 D1
16 Wanstead E11.....132 A6
West Leigh Jun & Inf Schs
SS9...............146 D2
West Ley CM0.........106 C5
WESTLEY HEIGHTS....141 D2
Westley Rd SS16......141 C2
West Lo RM17........173 B2

Westlyn Cl RM13......155 C1
West Malling Way
RM12..............155 C7
Westman Rd SS8......164 E3
Westmarch CM3.......101 C6
West Mayne SS15.....140 E6
Westmayne Ind Pk
SS15..............140 E6
Westmede
Basildon SS16........141 C5
Chigwell IG7.........111 C4
West Mill DA11.......178 F1
Westminster Ct 4
E11...............132 B5
Westminster Dr
Hockley SS5.........124 D6
Southend-on-S SS0...147 B2
Westminster Gdns
Barking IG11.........152 E3
Chingford E4.........87 E1
Redbridge IG6.......111 D1
Westminster Mans
SS0...............147 B2
Westmoreland Ave
RM11..............136 C6
Westmorland Cl E12...132 D2
Weston Ave RM20.....171 F1
Weston Cl CM13......95 C2
Westone Mans 6
IG11..............152 F5
Weston Gn RM9.......153 F8
Weston Rd
Dagenham RM9.......153 E8
Southend-on-S SS1...167 A7
West Park Ave CM12...97 A3
West Park Cl RM6.....134 E6
West Park Cres CM12...97 A2
West Park Dr CM12....97 A2
West Park Hill CM14...116 A7
West Pl CM20.........11 A3
West Point Pl SS8.....163 C3
Westray Wlk SS12....122 A5
West Rd
Dagenham RM6.......134 E5
Harlow CM20........11 A4
Romford RM7........135 D4
Sawbridgeworth CM21..1 C3
Southend-on-S, Cambridge
Town SS3..........168 D6
Southend-on-S SS0...147 L1
South Ockendon RM15..157 B2
West Ridge CM12.....119 A8
Westrow Dr IG11......153 A7
Westrow Gdns IG3....133 F1
Westside Apartments 7
E12...............133 A1
Westside Bsns Ctr
CM19..............22 F7
West Sq
2 Harlow CM20......10 C1
Maldon CM9.........36 F3
West St
Erith DA8...........169 E1
Gravesend DA11......179 B1
Grays RM17.........178 A8
Rochford SS4.......125 E2
Southend-on-S, Chalkwell
SS9...............165 E8
Southend-on-S SS0,
SS2...............147 E2
West Station Ind Est
CM9...............36 E1
West Station Rd CM9...36 E1
West Thorpe SS16.....142 B6
WEST THURROCK......177 D8
West Thurrock Prim Sch
RM20..............177 A8
West Thurrock Way
Grays RM20.........172 B2
Purfleet RM20.......171 F2
WEST TILBURY.......179 E8
West View
Ilford RM6..........134 C6
Loughton IG10.......88 F6
West View Cl RM13....155 C2
Westview Dr RM13....110 D1
West View Dr SS6.....123 B1
Westward Ho SS1.....166 F7
Westward Rd E4......109 A5
Westwater SS7.......144 B4
Westway
Chelmsford CM1......53 E8
South Woodham Ferrers
CM3..............101 C7
West Way CM14......116 A7
West Wlk CM20.......23 C8
Westwood Ave CM14...116 A6
West Wood Cl SS7....145 C4
Westwood Gdns SS7...145 D5
Westwood Lo SS7....145 C5
Westwood Prim Sch
SS7...............145 D4
Westwood Rd
Canvey Island SS8....164 B3
Ilford IG3...........134 A4
Wetherland SS16.....141 F5
Wetherly Cl E17......11 F4
Wethersfield Cl SS6...123 A3
Wethersfield Way
SS11..............122 B5
Weybourne Cl SS2....148 B3
Weybourne Gdns SS2...148 B3
Weybridge Wlk SS3...149 E1
Weylond Rd RM8......134 F1
Weymarks SS15......141 D7
Weymouth Dr RM20...172 D1
Weymouth Rd CM1....32 E6

Whadden Chase CM4...74 A3
Whalebone Ave RM6...134 F5
Whalebone Gr RM6....134 F5
Whalebone La N RM6...134 E8
Whalebone La S RM6,
RM8..............134 F4
Wharf Cl SS17........160 D1
Wharf Ho DA8........169 E1
Wharf Rd
Brentwood CM14......116 C7
Chelmsford CM2......32 C2
Fobbing SS17........161 D3
Gravesend DA12......179 E1
Grays RM17.........177 F8
Heybridge Basin CM9...37 F4
Hoddesdon EN10......43 A7
Stanford-le-H SS17...175 E7
Wharf Rd S RM17.....177 F8
Wharfside CM3.......169 F1
Wharley Hook CM18...24 A5
Wharncliffe Ho 3
DA9...............177 B1
Wharton Dr CM1......33 A7
Wheatear Pl CM11....97 C1
Wheatfields
3 Brentwood CM14...116 C6
Harlow CM17........11 D6
Rochford SS4........126 D4
Wheatfield Way
Basildon SS16........141 A4
Chelmsford CM1......31 F3
Wheatley Cl
Greenhithe DA9......177 A2
Hornchurch RM11....136 D6
Rochford SS4........125 D4
Sawbridgeworth CM21..1 C1
Wheatley Mans 8
IG11..............153 A5
Wheatley Rd SS17....161 B4
Wheatsheaf Rd RM1...135 F5
Wheatstone Rd DA8...169 D1
Wheeler Cl IG8.......110 F5
Wheelers CM16.......46 A2
Wheelers Cl EN9......21 F1
Wheelers Cross IG11...152 D3
Wheelers Farm Gdns
CM16..............47 B5
Wheeler's Hill CM3....19 D6
Wheelers La
Fobbing SS17........161 D4
Pilgrims Hatch CM14...93 B6
Wheel Farm Dr RM10...135 C1
Wheelwrights The
SS2...............148 A5
Whernside Ave SS8...164 C5
Whieldon Grange
CM17..............24 E7
Whinhams Way CM12...96 F3
Whist Ave SS11.......99 F1
Whistler Mews 1
RM8..............153 B7
Whistler Rise SS3.....168 G8
Whitakers Way IG10...88 F8
Whitbread Pl 11
CM14..............116 C7
Whitby Ave CM13.....117 D4
Whitby Cl DA9........177 A2
Whitby Rd CM0.......84 B2
Whitchurch Rd RM3...114 E6
Whitcroft SS15.......141 C3
Whitebarn La RM10...154 A4
Whitebeam Cl CM2....53 F7
Whitebeam Dr RM15...157 C2
White Bridge Jun & Inf
Schs The IG10......88 F2
White Elm Rd CM3....57 A2
Whitefield Ct CM3....83 A8
Whitefield Schs E17...109 D1
Whitefriars Cres SS0...166 C8
Whitegate Rd SS1....167 A8
White Gdns RM10.....154 A6
White Gates RM12....136 C3
White Hall RM4.......90 B6
Whitehall Cl
Chigwell IG7.........112 A7
Lower Nazeing EN9...21 E1
Whitehall Cotts SG12...9 D8
Whitehall Est CM19....22 E7
Whitehall Gdns E4....87 E1
Whitehall La
Corringham SS17.....161 C6
Grays RM17.........173 C1
Woodford IG9........110 A8
Whitehall Lo IG8.....110 A8
Whitehall Prim Sch
E4................109 E8
Whitehall Rd
Chingford E4........109 E8
Grays RM17.........173 C2
Woodford IG8........110 A7
White Hall Rd SS3....150 B4
White Hart Cotts CM2...33 A6
White Hart La
Brentwood CM14......116 C8
Chelmsford CM1......32 F8
Hockley SS5.........124 F5
Romford RM7........113 A1
White Hart Yd DA11...179 B1
Whitehead Cl CM1....53 B8
Whitehills Rd IG10....89 A6
White Horse La CM9...36 F2
White Ho The IG3.....134 A3
White House Chase 1
SS6..............123 E1
White House Ct 3
SS6..............123 E1

Whitehouse Mdws
SS9...............147 A6
Whitehouse Mews 2
SS6..............123 E1
Whitehouse Rd
Southend-on-S SS9...147 A6
South Woodham Ferrers
CM3..............101 D8
Whitelands CM15......72 C4
Whitelands Cl SS11...99 E1
Whitelands Way RM3...114 D2
White Lyons Rd CM14...116 C7
White Mead CM1......19 B2
White Post Field CM21...1 C2
White Rd SS8.........163 C3
WHITE ROOTHING OR
WHITE RODING......14 C8
Whites Ave IG2.......133 E5
Whitesbridge La CM4...53 D1
Whites Cl DA9........177 C1
White's Hill CM4......75 F1
Whiteshott SS16......142 A4
Whitesmith Dr CM12...96 E3
Whitethorn Gdns
Chelmsford CM2......54 C7
Hornchurch RM11....136 C5
White Tree Ct CM3....101 B6
Whitewaits CM20.....10 E1
Whiteways
Billericay CM12.......97 E3
Canvey Island SS8....164 D2
Southend-on-S SS9...146 F6
Whitfield Ct IG1......132 F4
Whitfield Link CM2....54 D7
Whitfields SS17.......160 F2
Whiting Ave IG11.....152 B5
Whitings The IG2.....133 E6
Whitley Ct EN11......21 B8
Whitley Rd EN11......21 B8
Whitmore Ave
Grays RM16.........173 B6
Romford RM3.........114 C1
Whitmore Cl RM16....174 E7
Whitmore Cres CM2...33 B4
Whitmore Ct SS14....142 E8
Whitmore Jun & Inf Sch
SS14..............120 E1
Whitmore Way SS14...142 D8
Whitney Ave IG4......132 D7
Whittingham Ave SS2...148 E2
Whittingstall Rd EN11...21 C8
Whittington Rd CM13...95 D4
Whitwell Ct SS17......175 C8
Whitworth Cres EN3...65 A2
Whybrews SS17.......160 F2
Whybridge Cl RM13...154 F4
Whybridge Inf Sch
RM13..............155 A4
Whybridge Jun Sch
RM13..............154 F4
Whytewaters SS16....142 F4
Whyverne Cl CM1......32 E6
Wick Beech Ave SS11...121 E7
Wick Chase SS2......148 F1
Wick Cres SS12.......121 E5
Wick Dr
Wickford, Nevendon
SS12..............121 E5
Wickford SS12.......121 D7
Wickets Way IG6......111 F4
Wick Farm Rd CM0....62 C8
Wickfield Ash CM1....31 D6
WICKFORD..........121 A5
Wickford Ave SS13...143 B5
Wickford Bsns Pk 6
SS11..............122 A5
Wickford CE Inf Sch
SS11..............121 B8
Wickford Cl RM3.....114 F5
Wickford Ct 9 SS13...143 A6
Wickford Dr RM3.....114 F5
Wickford Hall SS11...121 F8
Wickford Inf Sch The
SS12..............121 C7
Wickford Jun Sch
SS12..............121 C8
Wickford Mews 7
SS13..............143 A6
Wickford Pl 8 SS13...143 A6
Wickford Rd
Southend-on-S SS0...166 E7
South Woodham Ferrers
CM3..............101 B8
Wickford Sta SS12...121 C8
Wick Glen CM12......96 F4
Wickham Bsns Pk
SS14..............120 F2
Wickham Cres CM1...31 F6
Wickham Pl SS16.....142 C5
Wickham Rd
Chingford E4........109 C3
Grays RM16.........174 C4
Wickham's Chase CM3...57 C2
Wickhay SS15........141 F5
Wickhay Cotts CM3...34 D5
Wick La SS11.........121 E7
Wicklands Rd SG12....9 D8
Wicklow Ave CM1.....31 D6
Wicklow Wlk SS3.....168 C3
Wickmead Cl SS2.....148 E2
Wick Place Farm
RM14..............159 A8
Wick Rd CM0.........106 D4
Widbrook CM15.......72 C3

232 Wid–Woo

Wid Cl CM13 ... 95 D4
Widecombe Cl RM3 ... 114 D2
Widecombe Gdns IG4 ... 132 E7
WIDFORD ... 53 E6
Widford Chase CM2 ... 53 F7
Widford Cl CM2 ... 53 F7
Widford Gr CM2 ... 53 F7
Widford Ind Est CM1 ... 53 E8
Widford Lodge Sch CM2 ... 53 F7
Widford Park Pl CM2 ... 53 F7
Widford Rd CM2 ... 53 F7
Widgeons SS13 ... 143 C6
Wid Terr CM15 ... 72 C3
Widworthy Hayes CM13 ... 95 B1
Wiggins La CM12 ... 118 E6
Wiggin's La CM12 ... 118 E7
Wiggins View CM2 ... 33 B4
Wigham Ho IG11 ... 152 C5
Wigley Bush La CM14 ... 115 E7
Wigram Rd E11 ... 132 C5
Wigton Rd RM3 ... 114 E6
Wigton Way RM3 ... 114 E6
Wilde Cl RM18 ... 179 C5
Wilfred Ave RM13 ... 170 A8
Wilfred St 13 DA11 ... 179 B1
Wilkes Rd CM13 ... 95 D4
Wilkin Ct SS9 ... 146 D2
Wilkinson Cl DA1 ... 176 A3
Wilkinson Drop SS7 ... 145 E2
Wilkinsons Mead CM2 ... 33 A4
Willetts Mews EN11 ... 21 A7
William Ash Cl RM9 ... 153 B6
William Bellamy Inf Sch RM10 ... 135 A2
William Bellamy Jun Sch RM10 ... 135 A2
William Cl RM5 ... 113 D2
William Ct
4 Belvedere DA17 ... 169 A2
Ilford IG6 ... 133 D7
William de Ferrers Sch CM3 ... 101 E7
William Edwards Sch & Sports Coll RM16 ... 173 B6
William Ford CE Jun Sch RM10 ... 154 A5
William Hunter Way CM14 ... 116 C8
William Martin CE Jun & Inf Schs CM18 ... 23 F6
William Pike Ho 4 RM7 ... 135 D5
William Rd SS13 ... 143 F6
William Read Prim Sch SS8 ... 163 F3
Williams Gn SS5 ... 101 E3
William Smith Ho 10 DA17 ... 169 A3
Williamsons Way SS17 ... 160 F5
Williams Rd CM1 ... 19 B1
William St
Barking IG11 ... 152 C5
Grays RM17 ... 178 C8
William Tansley Smith Ho RM12 ... 136 F2
William Torbitt Prim Sch IG2 ... 133 F6
WILLINGALE ... 28 D3
Willingale Ave SS6 ... 123 A3
Willingale Cl
Brentwood CM13 ... 95 E3
Loughton IG10 ... 89 C7
Woodford IG8 ... 110 C4
Willingale Ct CM16 ... 67 E3
Willingale Rd
Fyfield CM5 ... 27 F2
Loughton IG10 ... 89 D7
Willingale CM4, CM5 ... 50 E6
Willingales The 9 SS15 ... 141 A6
Willingale Way SS1 ... 149 A1
Willinghall Cl EN9 ... 65 D7
Willis Ho 2 E12 ... 133 A1
Willis Rd DA8 ... 169 D2
Willmott Rd SS2 ... 147 D6
Willoughby Dr
Chelmsford CM2 ... 32 F2
Rainham RM13 ... 154 E5
Willowbank CM2 ... 54 B3
Willowbrook Prim Sch CM13 ... 95 D3
Willow Cl
Brentwood CM13 ... 95 B3
Broomfield CM1 ... 19 B1
Buckhurst Hill IG9 ... 110 D7
Burnham-on-C CM0 ... 106 B6
Canvey Island SS8 ... 163 F3
Doddinghurst CM15 ... 72 D1
Hockley SS5 ... 124 F6
Hornchurch RM12 ... 136 B1
Rayleigh SS6 ... 123 D4
Southend-on-S SS9 ... 146 F6
Willow Cotts CM3 ... 79 A6
Willow Ct
8 Dagenham RM8 ... 134 D4
Ilford IG1 ... 152 C7
Willowdale Ctr SS12 ... 121 D8
Willowdene CM15 ... 93 F4
Willowdene Ct CM14 ... 116 C6
Willow Dr SS6 ... 123 C4
Willowfield
Basildon SS15 ... 119 C1
Harlow CM18 ... 23 D6
Willow Gn CM4 ... 74 B4
Willow Gr CM3 ... 79 A1
Willowherb Wlk RM3 ... 114 C3
Willowhill SS17 ... 160 E5
Willow Ho 1 SS13 ... 143 B8
Willow Lo
South Benfleet SS7 ... 144 F6
Southend-on-S SS3 ... 168 F8
Willowmead IG7 ... 112 A7
Willow Mead CM21 ... 1 E2
Willowmeade CM11 ... 98 C5
Willow Par RM14 ... 137 E3
Willow Path EN9 ... 65 E5
Willow Pk CM4 ... 74 D4
Willow Pl CM17 ... 25 A4
Willow Rd RM6 ... 134 E5
Willows Prim Sch SS14 ... 142 C8
Willow St
Chingford E4 ... 87 D2
Romford RM7 ... 135 C7
Willows The
13 Basildon SS13 ... 143 C6
Billericay CM11 ... 119 D7
Boreham CM3 ... 33 F8
Chelmsford CM1 ... 32 A2
Grays RM17 ... 178 E8
1 Loughton IG10 ... 88 D4
South Benfleet SS7 ... 144 B4
Southend-on-S SS1 ... 149 A1
Wallend E12 ... 152 A5
Willow Tree Cl RM4 ... 90 B6
Willow Way RM3 ... 115 B4
Willow Wlk
Canewdon SS4 ... 104 D1
Hadleigh SS7 ... 145 D3
Heybridge CM9 ... 37 C6
Hockley SS5 ... 124 F6
Upminster RM14 ... 137 E3
Will Perrin Ct RM13 ... 155 A4
Wills Hill SS17 ... 160 D3
Wilmington Gdns IG11 ... 152 E5
Wilmot Gn CM13 ... 116 C4
Wilmot Ho CM13 ... 116 C4
Wilmslowe SS8 ... 164 E5
Wilmslow Ho 3 RM3 ... 114 E6
Wilnett Ct 4 RM6 ... 134 B4
Wilnett Villas 5 RM6 ... 134 B4
Wilrich Ave SS8 ... 164 D3
Wilshire Ave CM2 ... 32 F3
Wilsman Rd RM15 ... 157 C3
Wilsner SS13 ... 143 C7
Wilson Cl SS17 ... 175 C8
Wilson Ct SS12 ... 121 C6
Wilson Rd
Redbridge IG1 ... 132 F4
Southend-on-S SS1 ... 166 F7
Wilson's Cnr CM14, CM15 ... 116 D8
Wilson's Ct CM9 ... 37 B2
Wilthorne Gdns RM10 ... 154 B5
Wilton Ct 7 IG8 ... 110 A4
Wilton Dr RM5 ... 113 D3
Wiltshire Ave RM11 ... 136 F7
Wiltshire Ct IG1 ... 152 C6
Wimarc Cres SS6 ... 123 B4
Wimbish Ct SS13 ... 143 B6
Wimbish End SS13 ... 143 B6
Wimbish Mews SS13 ... 143 B6
Wimborne Cl
Buckhurst Hill IG9 ... 110 C8
Sawbridgeworth CM21 ... 1 D2
Wimborne Rd SS2 ... 148 B1
Wimbourne SS15 ... 141 A7
Wimhurst Cl SS5 ... 124 E7
Winbrook Cl SS6 ... 145 E8
Winbrook Rd SS6 ... 145 E8
Wincanton Gdns
Ilford IG6 ... 133 B8
Redbridge IG6 ... 111 B1
Wincanton Rd RM3 ... 114 D7
Winchcombe Cl SS9 ... 146 E3
Winchelsea Dr CM2 ... 54 E7
Winchester Ave RM14 ... 137 F2
Winchester Cl
Southend-on-S SS9 ... 146 F7
8 Waltham Abbey EN9 ... 65 B6
Winchester Ct 9 DA17 ... 169 A1
Winchester Dr SS6 ... 123 B6
Winchester Gdns SS15 ... 119 C1
Winchester Ho 5 IG11 ... 153 A5
Winchester Rd
Chingford E4 ... 109 C3
Ilford IG1 ... 133 D1
Winckford Cl CM3 ... 19 B6
Wincoat Cl SS7 ... 144 C3
Wincoat Dr SS7 ... 144 C3
Windermere Ave
Hornchurch RM12 ... 155 A8
Hullbridge SS5 ... 101 D2
Windermere Gdns IG4 ... 132 E6
Windermere Rd
South Benfleet SS7 ... 144 E7
Southend-on-S SS1 ... 167 C8
Wind Hill CM5 ... 26 A4
Winding Way RM8 ... 134 C1
Windley Tye CM1 ... 31 E3
Windmill Ct
Upminster RM14 ... 137 A2
Waltham Abbey EN9 ... 65 E5
Windmill Fields CM17 ... 11 F4
Windmill Hts CM12 ... 119 B8
Windmill Mdws CM6 ... 5 C2
Windmill St DA12 ... 179 B1
Windmills The CM1 ... 19 B3
Windmill Stps 6 SS1 ... 167 C7
Windmill Way CM15 ... 71 E2
Windrush Ct DA8 ... 169 E1
Windrush Dr CM1 ... 32 C6
Windsor Ave
Corringham SS17 ... 161 A4
Grays RM16 ... 173 B4
Windsor Cl
Canvey Island SS8 ... 164 B3
Southend-on-S SS9 ... 146 E3
Windsor Gdns
Hadleigh SS7 ... 145 C4
Hockley SS5 ... 125 B4
Wickford SS11 ... 99 D1
Windsor Mews SS6 ... 123 C1
Windsor Rd
Basildon SS13, CM11 ... 143 E8
Chingford E4 ... 109 B6
Dagenham RM8 ... 134 E1
Hornchurch RM11 ... 136 C4
Ilford IG1 ... 152 C8
Pilgrims Hatch CM15 ... 94 B3
Ramsden Heath CM11 ... 98 D4
Southend-on-S SS0 ... 147 E1
Wanstead E11 ... 132 A2
Windsors The IG9 ... 110 E8
Windsor Trad Est CM11 ... 98 D4
Windsor Way
Chelmsford CM1 ... 31 E1
Rayleigh SS6 ... 123 E1
Windsor Wood EN9 ... 65 E6
Windward Way CM3 ... 101 F6
Windy Hill CM13 ... 95 C1
Winfields SS13 ... 143 C7
Winford Dr EN10 ... 21 A1
Wingate Rd IG1 ... 152 B7
Wingfield RM17 ... 172 F1
Wingfield Cl CM13 ... 117 A7
Wingfield Dr RM16 ... 174 A8
Wingfield Gdns RM14 ... 137 F5
Wingletye La RM11 ... 137 A5
Wingrave Cres CM14 ... 115 E6
Wingrave Ct CM14 ... 115 E6
Wingrove Ct CM1 ... 32 A6
Wingrove Dr 6 RM19 ... 171 B1
Wingrove Ho E4 ... 87 B2
Wingway CM14 ... 94 C1
Winifred Ave RM12 ... 155 E8
Winifred Rd
Basildon SS13 ... 143 B6
Dagenham RM8 ... 134 E3
Erith DA8 ... 169 E1
Winmill Rd RM8 ... 134 F1
Winn Bridge Cl IG8 ... 110 D2
Winningales Ct IG5 ... 132 E8
Winnowers Ct 1 SS4 ... 125 F1
Winns Ave E17 ... 109 A1
Winns Terr E17 ... 109 A1
Winsbeach E17 ... 109 D1
Winsford Gdns SS0 ... 147 A4
Winsford Way CM2 ... 33 C6
Winslow Gr E4 ... 109 E8
Winstanley Way SS14 ... 142 A8
Winstead Gdns RM10 ... 154 C7
Winston Cl
Greenhithe DA9 ... 176 F1
Romford RM7 ... 135 B7
Winston Way IG1 ... 133 B1
Winstree SS13 ... 143 B8
Winstree Rd CM0 ... 106 B5
Winterbourne Rd RM8 ... 134 C2
Winter Folly SS15 ... 141 E5
WINTER GARDENS ... 163 E6
Winter Gardens Jun & Inf Schs SS8 ... 164 A5
Winter Gardens Path SS8 ... 163 E7
Winterscroft Rd 5 EN11 ... 21 A7
Winter's Ct E4 ... 109 B7
Winters Way EN9 ... 66 A6
Winterswyk Ave SS8 ... 164 E3
Winton Ave
Southend-on-S SS0 ... 166 E7
Wickford SS12 ... 121 A8
Winton Lo SS0 ... 147 C1
Wiscombe Hill SS16 ... 141 C3
Wisdons Cl RM10 ... 135 B3
Wisemans Gdns CM21 ... 1 C1
Wissants CM19 ... 23 C4
Wistaria Cl CM15 ... 94 B4
Wisteria Cl IG1 ... 152 B7
Wisteria Lo 7 CM1 ... 32 F6
Witchards SS16 ... 142 B5
Witham Cl IG10 ... 88 E3
Witham Gdns CM13 ... 139 D5
Witham Rd
Dagenham RM10 ... 154 A7
Langford CM9 ... 36 D7
Romford RM2 ... 136 B6
Witherings The RM11 ... 136 F6
Withy Mead E4 ... 109 D7
Withypool SS3 ... 149 D1
Withywindle The CM3 ... 101 C6
Witney Rd CM0 ... 106 C4
Wittem Rd SS8 ... 164 B5
Wittenham Way E4 ... 109 D7
Witterings The SS8 ... 164 A5
Wittering Wlk RM12 ... 155 C6
Wivenhoe Rd IG11 ... 153 B3
Wix Rd RM9 ... 153 D4
Woburn Ave
Hornchurch RM12 ... 155 A8
Theydon Bois CM16 ... 67 E2
Woburn Ct
Chelmsford CM2 ... 32 A1
Hornchurch RM12 ... 155 A8
8 Woodford E18 ... 110 A1
Woburn Ho CM16 ... 67 E2
Woburn Pl CM12 ... 96 F5
Wodehouse Rd DA1 ... 176 A3
Wokindon Rd RM16 ... 174 B3
Wollaston Cres SS13 ... 121 D2
Wollaston Way SS13 ... 121 D2
Wolmers Hey CM3 ... 18 F7
Wolseley Rd
Chelmsford CM2 ... 32 A1
Romford RM7 ... 135 D4
Wolsey Ave E6 ... 152 A2
Wolsey Gdns IG6 ... 111 C4
Wolverton Ho 1 RM3 ... 114 E5
Wonston Rd CM0 ... 84 C4
Wood Ave
Hockley SS5 ... 124 E8
Purfleet RM19 ... 171 C2
Woodberry Cl
Canvey Island SS8 ... 164 A6
Southend-on-S SS9 ... 146 C5
Woodberry Down CM16 ... 46 A3
Woodberry Rd SS11 ... 122 A6
Woodberry Way E4 ... 87 C2
Woodbine Cl CM19 ... 23 C6
Woodbine Close Pk EN9 ... 66 C4
Woodbine Pl E11 ... 132 A5
Woodbridge Cl RM3 ... 114 D6
Woodbridge Ct IG8 ... 110 E3
Woodbridge High Sch IG8 ... 110 B3
Woodbridge La RM3 ... 114 D6
Woodbridge Rd IG11 ... 152 F7
Woodbrook Cres CM12 ... 96 F3
Woodbrooke Way SS17 ... 161 B4
Woodbrook Gdns EN9 ... 65 E6
Woodburn Cl SS7 ... 145 B4
Woodbury Cl E11 ... 132 B7
Woodbury Hill IG10 ... 88 E7
Wood Cnr CM9 ... 36 B2
Woodcote App SS7 ... 144 B7
Woodcote Ave RM12 ... 155 A8
Woodcote Cres 7 SS13 ... 143 C6
Woodcote Mews IG10 ... 88 D2
Woodcote Rd
Southend-on-S SS9 ... 147 A2
Wanstead E11 ... 132 A4
Woodcotes SS3 ... 149 E1
Woodcote Way SS7 ... 144 B7
Woodcroft CM18 ... 23 D6
Woodcroft Ave SG12 ... 8 E4
Woodcroft Cl SS7 ... 145 C4
Woodcutters CM0 ... 106 B8
Woodcutters Ave
Grays RM16 ... 173 C4
Southend-on-S SS9 ... 146 D5
Woodcutters Cl RM11 ... 136 D7
Wood Dale CM2 ... 54 E6
Woodedge Cl E4 ... 87 F1
WOODEND ... 14 D1
Wood End SS5 ... 124 D5
Woodend Cl SS7 ... 145 C4
Woodend Rd E17 ... 109 C1
Wood Farm Cl SS9 ... 146 D4
Woodfield 5 SS12 ... 121 D6
Woodfield Cotts
Heybridge CM9 ... 37 C6
Ingatestone CM4 ... 74 D5
Woodfield Dr RM2 ... 136 A7
Woodfield Gdns SS9 ... 165 F8
Woodfield Park Dr SS9 ... 147 A1
Woodfield Rd
Hadleigh SS7 ... 146 A3
Southend-on-S SS9 ... 166 A8
Woodfield Terr CM16 ... 46 C6
Woodfield Way RM12 ... 136 D3
Woodfines The RM11 ... 136 D5
WOODFORD ... 110 D5
Woodford Ave
Ilford IG2 ... 133 A6
Redbridge IG4 ... 132 F5
WOODFORD BRIDGE ... 110 E3
Woodford Bridge Rd IG4 ... 132 E7
Woodford Ct EN9 ... 66 A6
Woodford Cty High Sch for Girls IG8 ... 109 F4
WOODFORD GREEN ... 110 B3
Woodford Green Prep Sch IG8 ... 110 A4
Woodford Green Prim Sch IG8 ... 110 A5
Woodford Ho 5 E18 ... 132 A7
Woodford New Rd
Chingford E17 ... 109 E1
Woodford IG8, E17 ... 109 F3
Woodford Rd E18 ... 132 A8
Woodford Sta IG8 ... 110 B4
Woodford Trad Est
Redbridge IG8 ... 132 D8
Woodford IG8 ... 110 D1
WOODFORD WELLS ... 110 B7
Wood Gn SS13 ... 121 B1
Woodgrange Cl SS1 ... 167 E8
Woodgrange Ct EN11 ... 21 A5
Woodgrange Dr SS1 ... 167 E7
WOOD GREEN ... 66 C5
Woodgreen Rd EN9 ... 66 C5
Woodhall Cres RM11 ... 136 F3
Woodhall Hill CM1 ... 18 C2
Woodhall Par CM1 ... 32 A7
Woodhall Rd CM1 ... 32 A7
Woodham Ct 2 CM3 ... 101 E7
WOODHAM FERRERS ... 79 B4
Woodham Halt CM3 ... 101 C8
Woodham Ley Prim Sch SS7 ... 144 B6
WOODHAM MORTIMER ... 57 F6
Woodham Mortimer Rd CM9 ... 57 E8
Woodham Park Dr SS7 ... 144 C2
Woodham Rd
Battlesbridge SS11 ... 100 E4
South Benfleet SS7 ... 144 B2
South Woodham Ferrers CM3 ... 101 F8
Stow Maries CM3 ... 80 B3
WOODHAM WALTER ... 35 E2
Woodham Walter CE Prim Sch CM9 ... 35 D3
Woodham Way SG12 ... 8 C4
Woodhaven Gdns IG6 ... 133 C7
Woodhays 1 SS13 ... 143 C6
WOODHILL ... 56 B5
Woodhill CM18 ... 23 E5
Woodhill Common Rd CM3 ... 56 B5
Woodhill Rd
Chelmsford CM2 ... 55 E6
Danbury CM3 ... 56 B6
Woodhouse La CM3 ... 19 A4
Woodhurst Rd SS8 ... 163 E3
Wooding Gr CM19 ... 23 B8
Wood La
Dagenham RM8, RM9, RM10 ... 134 F1
Heybridge CM9 ... 37 A5
Hockley SS5 ... 124 E8
Hornchurch RM12 ... 155 A7
Mundon CM9 ... 59 E1
Willingale CM5 ... 28 F3
Woodford IG8 ... 109 F5
Woodland Ave
Brentwood CM13 ... 95 D4
Little Ilford E12 ... 132 F1
Wanstead E12 ... 132 E1
Woodland Cl
Brentwood CM13 ... 95 C4
Ingatestone CM4 ... 74 C4
South Benfleet SS7 ... 146 A3
Woodford IG8 ... 110 B7
Woodland Ct 13 E11 ... 132 A6
Woodland Gr CM16 ... 68 A7
Woodland Park Chase CM3 ... 83 A7
Woodland Rd
Chelmsford CM1 ... 32 A4
Chingford E4 ... 87 C1
Loughton IG10 ... 88 E6
Woodlands
Althorne CM3 ... 83 A3
Broomfield CM1 ... 19 A4
Epping CM16 ... 68 A8
Great Waltham CM1 ... 18 F4
Woodlands Ave
Dagenham RM6 ... 134 E4
Hornchurch RM11 ... 136 E6
Rayleigh SS6 ... 145 E8
Wanstead E11 ... 132 B3
Woodlands Cl
Basildon SS16 ... 142 F4
Grays RM16 ... 173 E3
Hockley SS5 ... 124 D5
Hoddesdon EN11 ... 21 A5
Rayleigh SS6 ... 145 D8
Woodlands Dr
Basildon SS17 ... 142 C1
Hoddesdon EN11 ... 21 A4
Woodlands Inf Sch IG1 ... 152 D7
Woodlands Jun Sch IG1 ... 152 D7
Woodlands Par SS5 ... 124 D5
Woodlands Pk SS9 ... 146 A3
Woodlands Rd
Hockley SS5 ... 124 D5
Ilford IG1 ... 133 C1
Romford, Harold Wood RM3 ... 115 A2
Romford RM1 ... 135 F8
Wickford SS12 ... 121 D7
Woodlands Sch
Basildon SS16 ... 142 A4
Chelmsford CM1 ... 31 F6
Great Warley CM13 ... 138 D7
Woodlands The SS3 ... 168 F8
Woodland Way
Chipping Ongar CM5 ... 48 F1
Greenhithe DA9 ... 177 A3
Theydon Bois CM16 ... 67 E4
Woodford IG8 ... 110 B7
Woodleigh 3 E18 ... 110 A2
Woodleigh Ave SS9 ... 146 D3
Woodleys CM20 ... 11 A1
Woodley Wlk SS3 ... 149 E2
Woodlow SS7 ... 145 B6
Woodmanhurst Rd SS17 ... 160 F5
Woodman La E4 ... 87 E4

Woodman Path IG6...... 111 E4
Woodman Rd
 Brentwood CM14....116 D5
 Redbridge IG7........111 F5
Wood Meads CM16..... 46 B2
Woodmill Mews EN11.... 21 B8
Woodpond Ave SS5......124 E5
Wood Rd CM9........... 37 B6
Woodredon Cl CM19 .... 22 B7
Woodredon Farm La
 CM16................. 66 D4
Woodridden Hill EN9,
 CM16................. 66 E3
Woodroffe Cl CM2...... 33 A3
Woodrose Lo 6 CM1... 32 F6
Woodrush Way RM6....134 D7
Woodshire Rd RM10 ....135 B1
Woodside
 Buckhurst Hill IG9......110 C8
 Little Baddow CM3 ...... 34 F1
 Mundon CM9............ 59 E2
 Southend-on-S SS9 .....146 B5
 Southminster CM0....... 84 C4
 Thornwood CM16....... 46 D5
Woodside Ave SS7......144 C8
Woodside Chase SS5 ...124 E4
Woodside Cl
 Brentwood CM13........ 95 D4
 Rainham RM13 ....155 C1
 Southend-on-S SS9 .....146 B6
Woodside Cotts
 Edney Common CM1.... 52 C5
 Ingatestone CM4........ 73 F7
 Mundon CM9............ 59 E2
Woodside Ct
 Southend-on-S SS9 .....146 B5
 Wanstead E12..........132 C3
Woodside Gdns E4......109 B4
Woodside Gn CM22 .... 3 A8
Woodside Ind Est
 CM16................. 46 D5
Woodside Prim Sch
 RM16................173 F3
Woodside Rd
 Hockley, South Fambridge
 SS5................102 F1
 Hockley SS5............124 B5
 Woodford IG8 ....110 A6
Woodside Sch DA17 ....169 B2
Woodside View SS7....144 D8
Wood St
 Chelmsford CM2........ 54 A7
 Grays RM17............178 C8
Woods The SS7........145 F3
Woodstock Ave RM3....115 B4
Woodstock Cres
 Basildon SS15 ....140 F6
 Hockley SS5............124 D6
Woodstock Gdns
 Basildon SS15 ....140 F6
 Ilford IG3............134 A2
Woodstock Pl CM2...... 54 F5
Woodstock Rd E17......109 D1
Woodview SS16 ....140 E4

Wood View RM16,
 RM17................173 E2
Woodview Ave E4......109 C6
Woodville Cl SS4......125 D3
Woodville Gdns IG6 ....133 B7
Woodville Prim Sch The
 CM3................. 79 D1
Woodville Rd
 Canvey Island SS8......164 D3
 Woodford E18..........110 B1
Woodward Cl RM17.....173 B2
Woodward Gdns RM9 ...153 C5
Woodward Hts RM17....173 B2
Woodward Rd RM9 .....153 C5
Woodwards CM19.......23 C6
Woodward Terr DA9 ....176 E1
Woodway CM13........ 95 A1
Woodyards
 Bradwell on S CM0...... 42 A3
 Bradwell Waterside CM0.. 41 F3
Woodyard The CM16.... 46 C3
Wool CM3.............7 F2
Woolards Way CM3.....101 D7
Woolden Ho E4........ 87 E2
Woolf Wlk RM18........179 C5
Woolhampton Way
 IG7................112 B7
Woolifers Ave SS17 ....161 B3
Woollard St EN9........ 65 C5
Woollard Way CM4...... 72 E8
Woolmer Gn SS15 ......141 E7
Woolmonger's La CM4... 72 A8
Woolpack SS3 ....168 D7
Woolshotts Rd SS12 ....120 F7
Woolwich Ct 10 EN3 ... 65 A1
Woolwich Manor Way
 E6................152 A1
Woolwich Rd DA17.....169 A1
Wootton Cl RM11 ......136 D6
Worcester Ave RM14....137 F2
Worcester Cl
 Basildon SS16 ....140 F5
 Greenhithe DA9.........177 B3
 Mayland CM3........... 61 A1
 Stanford-le-H SS17 .....160 D3
Worcester Cres IG8.....110 C6
Worcester Ct CM2...... 55 A5
Worcester Dr SS6.......123 F1
Worcester Gdns IG1 ....132 E4
Worcester Rd CM0......106 C6
Wordsworth Ave
 Maldon CM9............ 59 A8
 Woodford E18..........109
 F1Wordsworth Cl
 Romford RM3 ....114 C2
 Southend-on-S SS2 .....148 B2
 Tilbury RM18...........179 C5
Wordsworth Ct CM1 ... 32 A5
Wordsworth Way
 DA1................176 A3
Workhouse La CM3..... 79 B2
Wormley Ct EN9........ 66 A6
Wormyngford Ct EN9... 66 A6
Worrin Cl CM15........ 94 F1

Worrin Rd CM15........ 94 F1
Worthing Cl RM17......177 E8
Worthing Rd SS15......141 B6
Wouldham Rd RM17....177 E8
Wrackhall Ct SS8......164 E2
Wrangley Ct EN9....... 66 A6
Wray Ave IG5..........133 A8
Wray Cl RM11..........136 D4
Wraysbury Dr SS15.....119 D1
Wren Ave SS9..........146 D7
Wren Cl
 Billericay CM11......... 97 C1
 South Benfleet SS7......144 B6
 Southend-on-S SS9 .....146 D7
Wren Dr EN9........... 66 A5
Wren Gdns
 Dagenham RM9.........153 D7
 Hornchurch RM12.......135 F3
Wren Pl CM14..........116 D7
Wren Rd RM9..........153 D7
Wrens The CM19....... 23 B8
Wren Terr
 Ilford IG5.............133 A8
 Loughton IG10.......... 89 B8
Wren Wlk RM18........179 B7
Wrexham Rd
 Basildon SS15 ....141 B5
 Romford RM3...........114 D7
Wright Cl DA10........177 D1
Wright Mead CM2...... 33 B4
Wrightsbridge Rd
 Brentwood CM14........ 92 F1
 South Weald CM14...... 93 A1
Wrights Cl RM10.......154 B8
Wrights Ct
 Brentwood CM13........ 95 D3
 Harlow CM17........... 24 C6
WRIGHT'S GREEN 2 D7
Wrights Green La CM22 ... 2 D7
Wrights La CM15........ 72 D3
Wrigley Cl E4..........109 D5
Wrington Ho RM3.......114 F5
WRITTLE 31 A2
Writtle Coll CM1........ 31 B3
Writtle Coll (Cow
 Watering Campus)
 CM1................. 30 E2
Writtle Jun & Inf Schs
 CM1................. 53 A8
Writtle Park Cotts CM1... 52 B4
Writtle Rd
 Chelmsford CM1........ 53 E8
 Margaretting CM4....... 52 F2
Writtle Wlk
 Basildon SS14 ....142 E7
 Rainham RM13 ....154 E4
Wroths Path IG10....... 88 F8
Wroxall Ct 14 RM19 ....171 B1
Wroxall Rd RM9 ....153 C6
Wroxham Cl SS9........146 B6
Wroxham Way IG6......111 B2
Wr Twr Rd CM14.......116 C5
Wr Twr Site CM5....... 14 B2
Wyatts Dr SS1.........167 F8

WYATTS GREEN 72 D4
Wyatts Green La CM15 ... 72 D3
Wyatt's Green Rd
 CM15................. 72 E2
Wyburn Rd SS7........145 E6
Wyburns Ave SS6......145 E8
Wyburns Ave E SS6 ....145 E8
Wyburns Prim Sch
 SS6.................145 F8
Wych Elm CM20....... 10 C1
Wych Elm Rd RM11.....137 A4
Wych Elm Rd RM11.....137 A5
Wychford Dr CM21...... 1 C1
Wych Mews SS15 ......119 D1
Wychwood Gdns
 Ilford IG5.............133 A7
 Redbridge IG5..........132 F7
Wycke Hill CM9........ 58 D8
Wycke Hill Bsns Pk
 CM9................. 58 E8
Wycke La CM9......... 40 E8
Wycombe Ave SS7......144 B6
Wycombe Rd IG2.......132 F6
Wyemead Cres E4......109 E8
Wyfields IG5...........111 B2
Wyhill Wlk RM10.......154 C6
Wykeham Ave
 Dagenham RM9.........153 C6
 Hornchurch RM11.......136 D5
Wykeham Gn RM9......153 C6
Wykeham Prim Sch
 RM12................136 A3
Wykeham Rd CM1...... 31 B1
Wykes Gn SS14........142 D7
Wyldwood Cl CM17 .... 11 C6
Wymark Cl RM13.......155 A3
Wynndale Rd E18.......110 B2
Wynters SS16..........142 B4
Wyse's Rd
 Edney Common CM1.... 52 A6
 Roxwell CM1.......... 51 F7
Wythams SS13.........143 C7
Wythefield SS13........143
 A6Wythenshawe Rd
 RM10................135 A1
Wyvern Ho RM17.......178 B8

Y

Yale Way RM12........155 A8
Yamburg Rd SS8........164 D3
Yantlet SS9............146 E2
Yardeley SS15 ....141 E6
Yardley Bsns Pk SS14 ...141 F8
Yardley Cl E4.......... 87 B4
Yardley La E4.......... 87 B4
Yardley Prim Sch E4.... 87 C3
Yarnacott SS3 ....168 D8
Yarnton Way DA17.....169 A3
Yarwood Rd CM2...... 32 E2
Yeldham Lock CM2..... 33 A2
Yellowpine Way IG7....112 B6
Yelverton Cl RM3.......114 D2

Yeoman Way IG6.......111 C4
Yeovil Chase SS0 ....147 B4
Yeovil Cl SS2...........148 D2
Yevele Way RM11.......136 E4
Yew Cl
 Basildon SS15 ....119 D1
 Buckhurst Hill IG9.......110 D8
Yewlands
 Hoddesdon EN11........ 21 A5
 Sawbridgeworth CM21 ... 1 E1
Yewlands Dr EN11...... 21 A5
Yew Tree Cl CM13 ...... 95 B3
Yew Tree Gdns
 Chelmsford CM2 .... 54 C6
 Dagenham RM6.........134 E6
 4 Romford RM7........135 D6
Yew Wlk EN11........ 21 A5
Yonge Cl CM3.......... 20 E1
York Ave SS17.........161 A4
York Cl
 Rayleigh SS6...........146 A8
 Shenfield CM15......... 94 F2
York Cres IG10......... 88 E6
Yorkes SS18........... 23 F5
York Hill IG10......... 88 E6
York Ho
 Chingford E4...........109 A6
 1 Ilford IG1...........133 B2
 Loughton IG10......... 89 D5
York Mews IG1.........133 A1
York Pl IG1............133 A2
York Rd
 Billericay CM12......... 97 A5
 Burnham-on-C CM0......106 C4
 Chelmsford CM2........ 54 A8
 Chingford E4...........109 A6
 Horndon on t H SS17....159 F4
 Ilford IG1.............133 A1
 North Weald Bassett
 CM16................. 47 A4
 Rainham RM13 ....154 D5
 Rayleigh SS1...........146 A8
 Rochford SS4...........125 C7
 Shenfield CM15......... 94 F2
 Southend-on-S SS1 .....167 B7
York Rise SS6..........146 A8
Young Cl SS9...........147 A7
Youngs Rd IG2.........133 D6
Yoxford Ct 6 RM6.....134 B6
Yoxley App IG2.........133 C5
Yoxley Dr IG2..........133 C5

Z

Zandi Rd SS8..........164 D2
Zealand Dr SS8.........164 E3
Zelham Dr SS8.........164 F3
Zenith SS14 ....120 E2
Zider Pass SS8 ....164 F3

Addresses

Name and Address	Telephone	Page	Grid reference

Name and Address	Telephone	Page	Grid reference

Addresses

Name and Address	Telephone	Page	Grid reference

Any feature in this atlas can be given a unique reference to help you find the same feature on other Ordnance Survey maps of the area, or to help someone else locate you if they do not have a Street Atlas.

The grid squares in this atlas match the Ordnance Survey National Grid and are at 500 metre intervals. The small figures at the bottom and sides of every other grid line are the National Grid kilometre values (**00** to **99** km) and are repeated across the country every 100 km (see left).

To give a unique National Grid reference you need to locate where in the country you are. The country is divided into 100 km squares with each square given a unique two-letter reference. Use the administrative map to determine in which 100 km square a particular page of this atlas falls.

The bold letters and numbers between each grid line (**A** to **F**, **1** to **8**) are for use within a specific Street Atlas only, and when used with the page number, are a convenient way of referencing these grid squares.

Example   The railway bridge over DARLEY GREEN RD in grid square B1

Step 1: Identify the two-letter reference, in this example the page is in **SP**

Step 2: Identify the 1 km square in which the railway bridge falls. Use the figures in the southwest corner of this square: Eastings **17**, Northings **74**. This gives a unique reference: **SP 17 74**, accurate to 1 km.

Step 3: To give a more precise reference accurate to 100 m you need to estimate how many tenths along and how many tenths up this 1 km square the feature is (to help with this the 1 km square is divided into four 500 m squares). This makes the bridge about **8** tenths along and about **1** tenth up from the southwest corner.

This gives a unique reference: **SP 178 741**, accurate to 100 m.

Eastings (read from left to right along the bottom) come before Northings (read from bottom to top). If you have trouble remembering say to yourself "Along the hall, THEN up the stairs"!

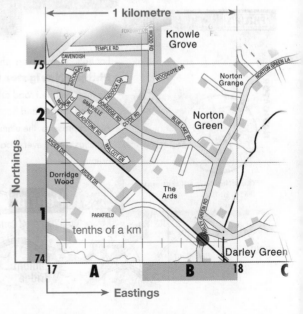

PHILIP'S MAPS

the Gold Standard for drivers

◆ **Philip's street atlases cover every county in England, Wales, Northern Ireland and much of Scotland**

- ◆ Every named street is shown, including alleys, lanes and walkways
- ◆ Thousands of additional features marked: stations, public buildings, car parks, places of interest
- ◆ Route-planning maps to get you close to your destination
- ◆ Postcodes on the maps and in the index
- ◆ Widely used by the emergency services, transport companies and local authorities

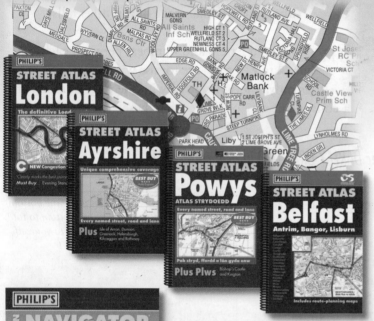

PHILIP'S STREET ATLAS **London**
The definitive Lond...
'Clearly marks the best journ...
Must Buy ... Evening Stanc...

PHILIP'S STREET ATLAS **Ayrshire**
Unique comprehensive coverage
BEST BUY
Every named street, road and lan...
Plus Isle of Arran, Dunoon, Greenock, Helensburgh, Kilcreggan and Rothesay

PHILIP'S STREET ATLAS **Powys**
ATLAS STRYDOEDD
Every named street, road and lane
BEST BUY
Pob stryd, ffordd a lôn gyda new
Plus Plws Bishop's Castle and Kington

PHILIP'S STREET ATLAS **Belfast**
Antrim, Bangor, Lisburn
Includes route-planning maps

PHILIP'S NAVIGATOR **Britain**
New speed 30 camera sites, now with speed limits
Major roads named as well as numbered
Thousands of farms, houses, tracks and footpaths
'The ultimate in UK mapping'
The Sunday Times

For national mapping, choose
Philip's Navigator Britain
the most detailed road atlas available of England, Wales and Scotland. Hailed by Auto Express as 'the ultimate road atlas', the atlas shows every road and lane in Britain.

Street atlases currently available

England

Bedfordshire and Luton	Surrey
Berkshire	East Sussex
Birmingham and West Midlands	West Sussex
Bristol and Bath	Tyne and Wear
Buckinghamshire and Milton Keynes	Warwickshire and Coventry
Cambridgeshire and Peterborough	Wiltshire and Swindon
Cheshire	Worcestershire
Cornwall	East Yorkshire Northern Lincolnshire
Cumbria	North Yorkshire
Derbyshire	South Yorkshire
Devon	West Yorkshire
Dorset	
County Durham and Teesside	**Wales**
Essex	Anglesey, Conwy and Gwynedd
North Essex	Cardiff, Swansea and The Valleys
South Essex	Carmarthenshire, Pembrokeshire and Swansea
Gloucestershire and Bristol	Ceredigion and South Gwynedd
Hampshire	
North Hampshire	Denbighshire, Flintshire, Wrexham
South Hampshire	Herefordshire Monmouthshire
Herefordshire Monmouthshire	Powys
Hertfordshire	
Isle of Wight	**Scotland**
Kent	Aberdeenshire
East Kent	Ayrshire
West Kent	Dumfries and Galloway
Lancashire	Edinburgh and East Central Scotland
Leicestershire and Rutland	Fife and Tayside
Lincolnshire	Glasgow and West Central Scotland
Liverpool and Merseyside	Inverness and Moray
London	Lanarkshire
Greater Manchester	Scottish Borders
Norfolk	
Northamptonshire	**Northern Ireland**
Northumberland	County Antrim and County Londonderry
Nottinghamshire	County Armagh and County Down
Oxfordshire	
Shropshire	Belfast
Somerset	County Tyrone and County Fermanagh
Staffordshire	
Suffolk	

How to order

Philip's maps and atlases are available from bookshops, motorway services and petrol stations. You can order direct from the publisher by phoning **0207 531 8473** or online at **www.philips-maps.co.uk**
For bulk orders only, e-mail philips@philips-maps.co.uk